ENCOUNTERING CULTURES

Reading and Writing in a Changing World

EDITED BY

RICHARD HOLETON
Stanford University

A BLAIR PRESS BOOK

PRENTICE HALL, ENGLEWOOD CLIFFS, NJ 07632

Encountering cultures : reading and writing in a changing world /
  edited by Richard Holeton.
      p.   cm.
  "A Blair Press book."
  Includes bibliographical references and index.
  ISBN 0-13-276379-6. -- ISBN 0-13-276387-7 (instructor's ed.)
    1. College readers.   2. English language--Rhetoric.   3. Readers-
-Intercultural communication.   4. Intercultural communication-
-Problems, exercises, etc.   I. Holeton, Richard
PE1417.E46   1992
808'.0427--dc20   91-30960
                                                                 CIP

Editorial/production supervision: Sally Thompson Steele
Interior design: Sally Thompson Steele
Cover design: Bruce Kenselaar
Prepress buyer: Herb Klein
Manufacturing buyer: Patrice Fraccio
Cover photo: Peter Ellermann; handcoloring by Blue Dog Design,
  Palo Alto, California

Acknowledgments appear on pages 636–639, which constitute
a continuation of the copyright page.

Blair Press
The Statler Building
20 Park Plaza, Suite 1113
Boston, MA 02116-4399

 © 1992 by Richard Holeton

Printed in the United States of America

10 9 8 7 6 5 4 3 2 1

ISBN 0-13-276379-6

Prentice-Hall International (UK) Limited, *London*
Prentice-Hall of Australia Pty. Limited, *Sydney*
Prentice-Hall Canada Inc., *Toronto*
Prentice-Hall Hispanoamericana, S.A., *Mexico*
Prentice-Hall of India Private Limited, *New Delhi*
Prentice-Hall of Japan, Inc., *Tokyo*
Simon & Schuster Asia Pte. Ltd., *Singapore*
Editora Prentice-Hall do Brasil, Ltda., *Rio de Janeiro*

FOR VERONICA

PREFACE

Encountering Cultures is a composition reader that addresses issues of cultural interaction both at home and abroad. My premise is that the increasing cultural diversity in the United States can be best understood in a global context; my goal is to engage students in critical reading and writing by encouraging them to articulate, test, and enlarge their perspective on cultural differences and similarities. I take a broad view of "culture" in this book, using the metaphor of travel to emphasize interactions across cultural boundaries based not only on race, ethnicity, and national origin, but also on language communities, regional subcultures, class, gender, and sexual orientation.

Selections

I have chosen the sixty-three full-length selections for their excellence of expression and their wide range of difficulty, viewpoints, aims, audiences, and styles. An abundance of analytical, argumentative, and documented academic essays offers intellectual frameworks that can be applied to the other selections—of oral history, personal experience, journalism, and fiction—making *Encountering Cultures* both reflexive and largely self-contained.

All of the main selections were written by contemporary Americans or by people who now live in the United States. In one sense, then, *Encountering Cultures* is about "Us"—Americans—encountering one another at home and encountering "Them" abroad. Exactly who constitutes Us and Them, however, is one of the ongoing debates in this book; reflecting the "changing world" of the subtitle, more than half of the authors are women and nearly half are people of color.

This diversity extends to the fifty-one Brief Encounters, short selections that open each chapter, introduce major themes, and place these themes in a broader historical or international context. I have also chosen the Brief Encounters for their high interest level and their usefulness—based on extensive classroom experience—as the stimulus for discussion, as the basis for exercises, and as models of writing strategies and techniques.

Eleven complete, contemporary short stories, one self-contained novel excerpt, and seven fictional Brief Encounters give *Encountering Cultures* a strong literary component. These stories, many anthologized in a composition reader for the first time, dramatize the major themes of the book movingly and powerfully.

Organization

The selections are grouped into six chapters:

1. The Writer in a Changing World: Encountering Language and Culture
2. The Writer as Traveler: Discovering American Places and People
3. The Writer as Traveler: Discovering Foreign Places and People
4. The Critical Journey: Encountering Diversity at Home
5. The Critical Journey: Encountering Cultures Abroad
6. The Imaginary Traveler: A Stranger Comes to Town

Chapter 1 addresses some of the current pressures on the English language, introduces the idea of writing as a social and political act, and suggests connections among self-discovery, writing, language, and culture.

Chapters 2 through 5 alternate between domestic and global perspectives on cultural interactions. Chapter 2 establishes a range of American experiences, emphasizing places and people, that can be used to explore domestic diversity more critically in Chapter 4. Similarly, Chapter 3 offers a variety of American experiences abroad as a basis for exploring international cultures more critically in Chapter 5.

Chapter 6 groups together all the fiction in the book, allowing instructors maximum flexibility in integrating short stories with earlier chapters or choosing to teach a separate literary unit.

This organization reflects the order that many composition courses follow—from reading and writing that grows out of personal experience ("The Writer as Traveler") to more analytical, argumentative, and academic discourse ("The Critical Journey")—and allows students to try to develop their own critical perspectives before reading those of the "experts." Except for the distinction between fiction and nonfiction, however, I do not draw these lines rigorously or rigidly in any chapter. On the contrary, I have placed some personal writing with a strong argumentative edge early in the book and have included, in Chapters 4 and 5, analytical and scholarly pieces that express a personal voice. And in the questions concluding each chapter, I suggest many connections among readings throughout the book, so that instructors can easily proceed in any order they wish.

Apparatus

I have carefully designed the editorial apparatus, based on my classroom experience with the readings, to be as useful as possible without being obtrusive.

A general **introduction** gives students an overview of the book, its broad concerns, and its organization.

Brief **chapter introductions** indicate why each chapter's readings have been grouped together, explain their place in the overall logic of the book, suggest a few of their major common themes, and offer background information for additional context. I try not to direct students how to interpret any individual selection.

The **headnotes** (actually, footnotes) accompanying each selection are brief, objective, and nondirective. They give the essential context of the reading (where and when it appeared originally), locate the author in time and place, and list selected publications. In an anthology with pluralistic intentions, I believe it is especially important not to position writers relative to one another with glowing adjectives, recitations of awards, or other value judgments.

About thirty **questions,** most of them classroom-tested, appear at the end of each chapter, in three groups:

1. *Reading and Writing about [the subject of the chapter]* includes questions about individual selections and students' own experiences. These questions emphasize critical thinking by asking students to make connections between their experience and their reading and between the readings themselves; they emphasize the interdependence of form and content by integrating questions about technique with questions about substance and purpose. They may be variously appropriate for discussion, exercises, essay assignments, or collaborative work, in or out of class. Those questions which in my experience lend themselves particularly well to a certain approach—such as small-group or partner work—will specify that approach.

2. *Making Further Connections* reaches out, with questions similar to those in the first group, to other chapters in the book. These questions may refer to short stories from Chapter 6 or Brief Encounters from any chapter, but, to avoid redundancy, they refer to main selections only from previous chapters. Instructors using the book nonsequentially need only refer to each group of *Making Further Connections* questions to find useful connections that run in both directions; thus, any chapter can act as the hub of these spokes.

3. *Exploring New Sources* makes suggestions for research papers and projects. Some of these ask students to gather their own primary materials and to integrate them with academic sources. Other questions—reflecting the influence of my colleagues at Stanford and elsewhere who are integrating public service and "real writing" projects into their composition courses—encourage students to get involved in the local community and to make proposals to real-world audiences.

A **rhetorical index** organizes the readings according to writing strategies. I treat the traditional strategies as complementary and as subordinate to the writer's purpose rather than as mutually exclusive; each selection, therefore, may exemplify several strategies at once.

A thorough **Instructor's Manual,** bound separately, includes overviews of all the readings; suggested responses to the end-of-chapter questions; additional questions; recommendations for related selections; and other classroom-tested suggestions. Rhetorical strategies are listed with each main selection and for all selections (including the Brief Encounters) in an alphabetical index.

Acknowledgments

I am grateful to all those who have helped me and encouraged me with this project. I especially want to thank the following:

At Blair Press—Nancy Perry, Publisher, for her top-notch collaboration from start to finish in making this a better book; Leslie Arndt, for her good-humored, professional handling of countless details; Virginia Biggar, for carrying out the daunting task of obtaining permissions; and Sally Steele, in association with Blair Press, for her inspired text design and quality production.

At home—Roni, Rachel, and Miranda, for continually compromising their time and space to make it all possible.

At Stanford—Charles Fifer, Professor Emeritus and former Director of the Freshman English Program, for his support during a difficult year and for his past support in developing the courses from which this book grew; Ann Watters, Acting Director of the program, for her initial encouragement; Rava Eleasari, for her classroom testing of new materials; and my other fellow Freshman English instructors, for helping me become a better teacher. Special thanks to Marjorie Ford of Stanford and Jon Ford of Alameda College, for their referrals and mentoring in the world of textbook authoring.

At Cañada Community College—John Friesen, Gerry Messner, Jack Swenson, and their colleagues in composition, for giving me the chance in this profession.

At both Stanford and Cañada—my students, present and past, for teaching me about these readings.

Here and there—Stan Goldberg and Kim Nabi, friends and fellow travelers, for inspiring my interest in encountering cultures; and Nancy Brown, for her help in expressing this interest by selecting and handcoloring the cover photograph.

Finally, at colleges and universities around the country—Nancy K. Barry, Luther College; Susan E. Carlisle, Harvard University; Kitty Chen Dean, Nassau Community College; Georgia Rhoades, University of Louisville; Melita Schaum, University of Michigan—Dearborn; Judith Ortiz Shushan, Cabrillo College; and Linda Woodson, University of Texas—San Antonio, for offering candid criticism and helpful suggestions at various stages of the project.

—Richard Holeton

CONTENTS

> My experience as a writer coming from a culture of colonialism, a culture of
> Black people riven from each other, . . . is similar to the experience of other
> writers whose origins are in countries defined by colonialism.

> Studies have proven that the use of ethnic dialects decreases power in the mar-
> ketplace. "I be" is acceptable on the corner, but not with the boss.

> My parents thought that by mastering the English language, I would be able to
> attain the Chinese American dream: a college education, a good-paying job, a
> house in the suburbs, a Chinese husband and children.

I was sheltered from growing up, on those army posts. You had to go through a sentry gate to get in. I lived on this little protected island in the middle of America.

The history books were always lying. My dad would correct the history like Pancho Villa and the Alamo, and say, "This is a bunch of lies. These gringos are telling you a bunch of lies."

I grew like a wild weed and soaked up all the opportunities. . . . Amidst a family of blue-eyed blonds, though, I stood out like a sore thumb.

Residents on the edge of Green Swamp, Florida, had been reporting to the police that they had seen a Wild Man. When they stepped toward him, he made strange noises as in a foreign language and ran back into the saw grass.

Impermanence haunts the city, with its mushroom industries—the aircraft perpetually becoming obsolete, the oil which must one day be exhausted, the movies which fill America's theatres for six months and are forgotten.

The majority of San Franciscans could still ignore the growing gay population in their midst in part because the city—in spite of the endless views of self afforded by its hills—was still decentralized, its residential neighborhoods a series of ethnic villages.

He looked up and down the Flushing Avenue platform, at the old lady and the Muslim and the running water and the vandalized signs. "Rule one is—don't ride the subway if you don't have to."

I suspect that my original motive for coming here was to "lose myself" in new and unpopulated territory. Instead of producing the numbness I thought I wanted, life on the sheep ranch woke me up.

The idea of praising God in a tent was confusing, to say the least. . . . Would God the Father allow His only Son to mix with this crowd of cotton pickers and maids, washerwomen and handymen?

America's honorary fifty-second state had received much more, of course, from its former rulers than star-spangled love songs and hand-me-down jeans. The commercial area of Manila, Makati, looked . . . like some textbook upper-middle-class California suburban tract.

The visitor slowly realized he was being flirted with, and that therefore this woman was middle-class. In Venezuela, only the negligible middle class *flirts.*

Black-and-white police cars cruise in pairs, each with the barrel of a rifle extruding from an open window. Roadblocks materialize at random, soldiers fanning out from trucks and taking positions, fingers always on triggers.

A sea of chadori, the long terrible veil, the full length of it, like a dress descending to the floor, ancient, powerful, annihilating us.

[The] blurring of cultural styles occurs in everyday life in the United States to a greater extent than anyone can imagine and is probably more prevalent than the sensational conflict between people of different backgrounds that is played up and often encouraged by the media.

In fact there had come to exist in South Florida two parallel cultures, separate but not exactly equal, a key distinction being that only one of the two, the Cuban, exhibited even a remote interest in the activities of the other.

Under this system of colorism—the system which prevailed in my childhood in Jamaica, and which has carried over to the present—rarely will dark and light people co-mingle.

The Saudis could gradually phase in the right of women to drive. First they'd let women drive but Saudi men would be allowed to tell woman-driver jokes. Then, after a decent interval, the men would have to give up the woman-driver jokes.

Arabs characteristically believe that many if not most things in life are controlled, ultimately, by fate rather than by humans, that everyone loves children, that wisdom increases with age, and that the inherent personalities of men and women are vastly different.

The Westerner is drawn to the tradition of the Easterner, and almost covets his knowledge of suffering, but what attracts the Easterner to the West is exactly the opposite—his future, and his freedom from all hardship.

More often than not the ways of a people are praised by that same people while looked upon with suspicion or disapproval by the others, and often in both cases with surprisingly little understanding of what those ways really are and mean.

Teachers find it hard to believe that the average American speaks for only 10 to 11 minutes a day and that more than 65 percent of the social meaning of a typical two-person exchange is carried by nonverbal cues.

Analysts no longer seek out harmony and consensus to the exclusion of differrence and inconsistency. For social analysis, cultural borderlands have moved from a marginal to a central place.

CHAPTER 6   THE IMAGINARY TRAVELER: A STRANGER COMES TO TOWN 500

ARTURO ISLAS THANKSGIVING BORDER CROSSING   512

Sancho . . . looked at Josie very hard and said, "I do not ever want to hear you use that word in my presence again. About anybody. We are not aliens. We are American citizens of Mexican heritage."

FRANK CHIN RAILROAD STANDARD TIME   521

Cartoons were our nursery rhymes. Summers inside those neon-and-stucco downtown hole-in-the-wall Market Street Frisco movie houses blowing three solid hours of full-color seven-minute cartoons was school, was rows and rows of Chinamans learning English in a hurry from Daffy Duck.

BHARATI MUKHERJEE TAMURLANE   527

We knew where to hide, Mohan and I. . . . We could hear the Mounties up in the kitchen, and we didn't know how Gupta would handle himself. Sometimes they'll let one of us off, if he can turn in three or four.

LOUISE ERDRICH AMERICAN HORSE   533

They were out there all right, Albertine saw them. Two officers and that social worker woman. Vicki Koob. There had been no whistle, no dream, no voice to warn her that they were coming.

DAVID LEAVITT TERRITORY 544

In four hours, Wayne, his lover of ten months and the only person he has ever imagined he could spend his life with, will be in this house, where no lover of his has ever set foot.

VALERIE MATSUMOTO TWO DESERTS   562

She was groping for the language to make him understand, to make him leave her in peace, but he was bent on not understanding, not seeing, not leaving until he got what he wanted.

GRACE PALEY THE LONG-DISTANCE RUNNER   571

She said, Get in and shut that door tight. She took a hard pinching hold on my upper arm. Then she bolted the door herself. Them hustlers after you. They make me pink. Hide this white lady now, Donald.

INTRODUCTION

In the 1990s, few people in the United States would deny that what happens in, say, Kansas or Rhode Island can be shaped by events in a Kansas-size country in Africa or a Rhode Island–size country in the Middle East—even if many Americans could not locate Uganda or (until recently) Kuwait on a world map.

Global economic interdependence—exemplified by the relationship between political events in the Persian Gulf and the price of gasoline at the corner pump—is one feature of our changing world on the verge of the twenty-first century. Other features include lightning-speed communication and media coverage, ecological pressures from overpopulation and industry, great gaps between wealthy nations and poor ones, regional tensions based on ethnic or religious divisions, movements for freedom and political self-determination, the threat posed by weapons of mass destruction, and large migrations of people fleeing lost dreams or seeking new opportunities.

This book asks you to think about this changing world in conjunction with the increasing cultural diversity of the United States. As Ishmael Reed writes in Chapter 4, "The world is here"; indeed, "The world has been arriving at these shores for at least ten thousand years from Europe, Africa, and Asia."

The newest Americans—the immigrants and refugees coming in record numbers over the past two decades from Central America, Asia, the Caribbean, and other places—have made the rest of the world's problems visible in the United States now more than at any other time in recent history. In addition, other minority groups with deeper roots in the United States—African Americans and Mexican Americans—are growing faster than the white-Anglo majority. In the fastest-growing states such as Texas and Florida, many cities and counties no longer have any single ethnic majority. In California, whites already make up less than half the population of Los Angeles, San Francisco, San Jose, and Oakland, and by the year 2003 they are expected to lose their majority status statewide.[1]

While experts predict that ethnic diversity in the United States will continue to increase dramatically, political and economic power has been much slower to shift. California, for example, is quickly becoming one of the most culturally diverse and complex societies in history, but whites still held 37 of the state's 45 congressional seats and 104 of 120 seats in the state legislature in 1991.[2] And nationwide, compared with Anglos, much higher proportions of blacks, Mexican Americans, and other ethnic groups live in poverty.

Change and resistance to change are the constants of human history. How will you cope with the new world you are inheriting? You can choose, with Anglo-Indian novelist Salman Rushdie (Chapter 1), to celebrate "the transformation that comes of new and unexpected combinations of human beings, cultures, ideas, politics, movies, songs." You might share with the narrator of Grace Paley's short story "The Long-Distance Runner" (Chapter 6) a "wide geographical love of mankind," but still—like Joan Didion in El Salvador, Kate Millett in Iran, and other overseas travelers in Chapter 3—"be attacked by local fears." Or perhaps you, like migrant worker Maria Moreno in Chapter 4, are still "waiting and hoping" for a better life in the United States.

In *Encountering Cultures* you will find a range of perspectives on cultural diversity in the United States and the global context from which it grows. The authors of the main selections are all Americans or people who have come to live in the United States; reflecting their "changing world," nearly half are people of color and more than half are women. You will see that they differ widely in their experiences, attitudes, opinions, and styles of writing; you will also discover attitudes and styles shared by people of different cultural backgrounds.

Culture, according to anthropologist Renato Rosaldo in Chapter 5, "refers broadly to the forms through which people make sense of their lives, rather than more narrowly to the opera or art museums." These forms include everything from the dialect or language people speak to the way they eat their food, build their homes, educate their children, treat strangers, define gender roles, tell stories, or

---

[1] Carol Ness, "The Un-whitening of California," *San Francisco Examiner*, April 14, 1991, p. A-1.

[2] Edward Blakely, professor of economic development planning, University of California, Berkeley, speaking at the Stanford Centennial Symposium on Ethnicity, Equity, and the Environment, Stanford University, April 12, 1991.

write essays. But since people within the same group also differ individually in all these ways, just where do you draw the boundaries between groups? That depends, of course, on who you ask. If you ask the authors of the selections in *Encountering Cultures,* you will get answers based not only on race or ethnicity or national origin, but also on rural, urban, suburban, or regional differences and on language communities, economic class, educational status, gender, and sexual orientation.

This book uses as an organizing principle the metaphor of travel or the journey to emphasize people's interactions across these cultural boundaries:

Chapter 1, "The Writer in a Changing World: Encountering Language and Culture," explores the connections between self-exploration and writing, culture, and language.

Chapter 2, "The Writer as Traveler: Discovering American Places and People," considers how Americans relate to their local community, the place they grew up, or less familiar places or people close to home.

Chapter 3, "The Writer as Traveler: Discovering Foreign Places and People," takes Americans overseas, focusing on meetings with strangers or unfamiliar customs.

Chapter 4, "The Critical Journey: Encountering Diversity at Home," returns to the United States with a more analytical, critical look at cultural differences and similarities.

Chapter 5, "The Critical Journey: Encountering Cultures Abroad," takes a similarly analytical look at international cross-cultural encounters, adding the perspectives of social critics and social scientists.

Chapter 6, "The Imaginary Traveler: A Stranger Comes to Town," dramatizes both domestic and international cultural encounters in short stories, exploring in contemporary fiction many of the themes raised earlier in the book.

Each chapter begins with a brief introduction highlighting some of its major themes, to help you put the readings into a larger perspective. Concluding each chapter are three groups of questions that ask you to think critically about the readings by (1) reflecting on your own experience in conjunction with what you've read, (2) making connections among the readings, and (3) considering various ways to learn more about the subjects that most interest you. At the back of the book, a rhetorical index organizes the readings according to common writing strategies; you may find this index useful when you're asked to write certain kinds of essays, such as a description, comparison, or analysis.

As the reader, you are the most important "traveler" who encounters cultures in *Encountering Cultures.* Just as an ideal traveler does not simply listen to canned lectures from a tour guide but goes out and experiences the culture firsthand, the ideal reader of this book will not be a passive receiver of knowledge but will actively and critically engage the readings. And if, as anthropologist Rosaldo writes, "all human conduct is culturally mediated," you will also ask yourself to what extent the personal and cultural baggage that you carry colors your view of the journey.

The importance of this journey cannot be overemphasized for those who see the United States—with its cultural diversity, its gap between rich and poor, its deep-seated racial divisions, its economic opportunities and egalitarian ideals—as a microcosm of the world's worst problems and best hopes. This country is often called an experiment. If history proves that people have not yet learned to deal constructively with their differences as well as their similarities, then you can make no better use of your reading and writing than helping to make this experiment succeed.

1
==

THE WRITER IN A CHANGING WORLD: ENCOUNTERING LANGUAGE AND CULTURE

These are exciting and challenging times to be speaking and writing in the English language. As June Jordan points out in this chapter, more than 330 million people in five countries speak English as a native language. Even more people learn English as a second or additional language, contributing to an estimated total of more than 700 million speakers worldwide. According to Richard Bailey, however, because of higher birth rates in Third World countries, "English is diminishing proportionately" in the 1990s rather than becoming the universal language that some people predicted.

The increasing diversity of North American speakers is a powerful influence on standard American English. California—which, along with Texas and Florida, leads the United States in both population growth and ethnic diversity—reported that the majority of its entering kindergarten class of 1990–1991 does not speak English as a native language. By the time this class graduates from high school in 2003, some have predicted that Spanish will be spoken as commonly as English in this country.[1] Although that prediction is controversial, experts agree that the 1990s will bring, legally and illegally, record numbers of immigrants to the United States—the largest influx since the beginning of the century. The vast majority of these new residents are coming from Asia and Central and South America.

All of us, including the majority for whom English remains the first and usually only language, are feeling these influences on our culture as well as our language. This chapter asks you to think about

---

[1] Thomas Weyr, *Hispanic USA, Breaking the Melting Pot* (New York: Harper and Row, 1988), cited by Marilyn P. Davis in *Mexican Voices/American Dreams: An Oral History of Mexican Immigration to the United States* (New York: Henry Holt and Company, 1990), p. xii.

1

the connections between language, writing, and culture—your language, your writing, and your culture—in these changing times. What is "correct" English, and who determines this? What is good writing, and how does this relate to your ethnic, racial, or cultural identity? To what extent is the way you view the world determined by the language or languages you speak? How is writing used to reinforce the values of the majority culture or for specific political purposes? How important are cultural and political values in your own writing?

In the Brief Encounters that follow, Beryl Markham, Patricia Hampl, and Glen Jackson suggest that the journey of self-discovery mapped out by these questions should begin in our own memory, deeply rooted in the geography of our childhood, and Kurt Vonnegut links individual writing style to the particular place where we grew up. Claude Lévi-Strauss traces writing to its origins in neolithic times, arguing that historically the main function of literacy has been "the enslavement of other human beings," and June Jordan asserts that standard English in the United States remains, indeed, "White English." On the other hand, the widespread multilingualism predicted for the future by Richard Bailey "can be an unqualified good," according to Jane Miller, and Gloria Anzaldúa and Salman Rushdie both find, in the very tensions caused by diversity, the heart of their own writing process and creativity.

The chapter's main selections explore many of these issues in greater depth:

- Michelle Cliff takes us on her personal "journey into speech"—from the speechlessness she felt as a native Jamaican first writing in the academic world, to the freedom she now feels to "[tear] into the indoctrination of the colonizer."

- Rachel Jones, by contrast, sees standard English and the educational opportunities it affords as the only logical means for her fellow black Americans to escape economic disadvantage.

- Kit Yuen Quan relates her hurtful experiences with "language blocks" as a working-class Asian American woman, reconnecting as an adult with the Chinese language of her childhood.

- Michael Ventura argues provocatively that for all students, not just ethnic minorities, "the university is where language goes to die."

- Rose del Castillo Guilbault, in reminding Anglos of the original Hispanic sense of the word *macho*, asks us to think about "a deeper cultural misunderstanding beyond mere word definitions."

- Charles Berlitz traces the sometimes surprising origins of some other cross-cultural expressions: those highly charged national and racial slurs such as *gringo, spik, kike,* and *Chink.*
- Haig Bosmajian catalogues the dehumanizing stereotypes that have been used to portray Native Americans throughout U.S. history, asking us to consider how such language has contributed to their social and economic oppression.
- Amy Tan takes aim at the stereotyping, based on misinterpreted language differences, of Chinese people and Chinese Americans as "discreet and modest."
- Peter Farb explains how linguists view such cross-cultural misunderstandings in terms of the different categories that determine the meaning of words in different languages, which is what makes translation so difficult.
- Robin Lakoff offers another perspective from linguistics on the way our language is used to reinforce social norms or devalue groups of people—in this case, women.

BRIEF ENCOUNTERS

A Hundred Places to Start

BERYL MARKHAM

How is it possible to bring order out of memory? I should like to begin at the beginning, patiently, like a weaver at his loom. I should like to say, "This is the place to start; there can be no other."

But there are a hundred places to start for there are a hundred names—Mwanza, Serengetti, Nungwe, Molo, Nakuru. There are easily a hundred names, and I can begin best by choosing one of them—not because it is first nor of any importance in a wildly adventurous sense, but because here it happens to be, turned uppermost in my logbook. After all, I am no weaver. Weavers create. This is remembrance—revisitation; and names are keys that open corridors no longer fresh in the mind, but nonetheless familiar in the heart.

—FROM *WEST WITH THE NIGHT*, 1942

Memoir as Travel Writing

PATRICIA HAMPL

No one owns the past, though typically the first act of new political regimes, whether of the left or the right, is to attempt to rewrite history, to grab the past and make it over so the end comes out right. So their power looks inevitable.

No one owns the past, but it is a grave error (another age would have said a grave sin) not to inhabit memory. Sometimes I think it is all we really have. But that may be a trifle melodramatic. At any rate, memory possesses authority for the fearful self in a world where it is necessary to have authority in order to Question Authority.

There may be no more pressing intellectual need in our culture than for people to become sophisticated about the function of memory. The political implications of the loss of memory are obvious. The authority of memory is a personal confirmation of selfhood. To write one's life is to live it twice, and the second living is both spiritual and historical, for a memoir reaches deep within the personality as it seeks its narrative form and also grasps the life-of-the-times as no political treatise can.

4

Our most ancient metaphor says life is a journey. Memoir is travel writing, then, notes taken along the way, telling how things looked and what thoughts occurred. But I cannot think of the memoirist as a tourist. This is the traveler who goes on foot, living the journey, taking on mountains, enduring deserts, marveling at the lush green places. Moving through it all faithfully, not so much a survivor with a harrowing tale to tell as a pilgrim, seeking, wondering.

—FROM "MEMORY AND IMAGINATION," IN *THE DOLPHIN READER*, 1985

The Process as Journey

GLENN F. JACKSON

. . . You should think of the written product as part of a continuing journey. Each product is simply a piece of the long journey we have broken off usually for convenience's sake. In other words, each product is simply a part of the one poetical journey we are continually making and writing. But because we have to stop from time to time, we arbitrarily break off or separate parts of the journey and label them as products.

It might be more helpful for us to think of the products or pieces as rest stops along the way. This could lessen the emphasis we give to the separate products. We would be better off concentrating our efforts on making the journey. . . .

My ability to make the journey, to create my own myths comes from my awareness of place as geography. Even in my consciousness, but particularly in my imagination, I am never far away from my place. I know the land intimately where I grew up. I believe I could draw you a map of my place that would take you to any place you want to go within a fifty-mile radius.

This little piece of land is the source of my imagination.

—FROM "THE PROCESS AS JOURNEY," IN *CREATIVITY AND THE WRITING PROCESS*, 1982

Sound like Yourself

KURT VONNEGUT

The writing style which is most natural for you is bound to echo the speech you heard when a child. English was the novelist Joseph Conrad's third language, and much that seems piquant in his use of English was no doubt colored by his first language, which was Polish. And lucky indeed is the writer who has grown up in Ireland, for the English spoken there is so amusing and musical. I myself grew up in Indianapolis, where common speech sounds like a band saw cutting galvanized tin, and employs a vocabulary as unornamental as a monkey wrench.

In some of the more remote hollows of Appalachia, children still grow up hearing songs and locutions of Elizabethan times. Yes, and many Americans grow up hearing a language other than English, or an English dialect a majority of Americans cannot understand.

All these varieties of speech are beautiful, just as the varieties of butterflies are beautiful. No matter what your first language, you should treasure it all your life. If it happens not to be standard English, and if it shows itself when you write standard English, the result is usually delightful, like a very pretty girl with one eye that is green and one that is blue.

I myself find that I trust my own writing most, and others seem to trust it most, too, when I sound most like a person from Indianapolis, which is what I am. What alternatives do I have?

—FROM "HOW TO WRITE WITH STYLE," 1982

The Primary Function of Writing

CLAUDE LÉVI-STRAUSS

. . . Between the invention of writing and the birth of modern science, the western world has lived through some five thousand years, during which time the sum of its knowledge has rather gone up and down than known a steady increase. It has often been remarked that there was no great difference between the life of a Greek or Roman citizen and that of a member of the well-to-do European classes in the eighteenth century. In the neolithic age, humanity made immense strides forward without any help from writing; and writing did not save the civilizations of the western world from long periods of stagnation. Doubtless the scientific expansion of the nineteenth and twentieth centuries could hardly have occurred, had writing not existed. But this condition, however necessary, cannot in itself explain that expansion.

If we want to correlate the appearance of writing with certain other characteristics of civilization, we must look elsewhere. The one phenomenon which has invariably accompanied it is the formation of cities and empires: the integration into a political system, that is to say, of a considerable number of individuals, and the distribution of those individuals into a hierarchy of castes and classes. Such is, at any rate, the type of development which we find, from Egypt right across to China, at the moment when writing makes its debuts; it seems to favor rather the exploitation than the enlightenment of mankind. This exploitation made it possible to assemble workpeople by the thousand and set them tasks that taxed them to the limits of their strength: to this, surely, we must attribute the beginnings of architecture as we know it. If my hypothesis is correct, the primary function of writing, as a means of communication, is to facilitate the enslavement of other human beings.

—FROM "A WRITING LESSON," *TRISTES TROPIQUES*, 1955

English in the Next Decade

RICHARD W. BAILEY

I invite readers to reflect on three political and cultural developments that will shape the use of English in the next decade.

The first is the remarkable rise in multilingualism. (More people than ever before, both numerically and proportionately, now routinely use two or more languages.) As Peter Strevens has pointed out, those who command only one language are at a distinct disadvantage, especially those monolinguals (including English-speaking monolinguals) who seek consent and commerce from language communities richer or more powerful than their own.[1]

A second trend will have even greater impact: far from approaching the status of a universal language, English is diminishing proportionately as explosive birthrates shift the balance of the world's population toward other language communities. No doubt English is the most frequently chosen *additional* language, and it is likely to continue to enjoy that popularity. But even the major centers of the anglophone world (Britain, Canada, the United States, and Australia) are becoming more and more diverse in languages and language varieties. These demographic facts have implications for the future of English and for the kinds of languages we will use in the future.

A third issue that merits our present consideration derives from research in second-language instruction: the attitude of those acquiring a new language is the most influential of the variables that pre-

---

[1] See Peter Strevens, "Language Teaching Contributes to and Is Influenced by the Spread of Languages," in *Language Spread and Language Policy: Issues, Implications, and Case Studies*, ed. Peter H. Lowenberg (Washington, D.C., 1988), pp. 320–330.

dict the rate and success of learning—more important than aptitude, age, or teaching method.

—FROM "ENGLISH AT ITS TWILIGHT," IN *THE STATE OF THE LANGUAGE*, 1990

Standard English and White English

JUNE JORDAN

What we casually call "English" less and less defers to England and its "gentlemen." "English" is no longer a specific matter of geography or an element of class privilege; more than thirty-three countries use this tool as a means of "intranational communication." Countries as disparate as Zimbabwe and Malaysia, or Israel and Uganda, use it as their non-native currency of convenience. Obviously, this tool, this "English," cannot function inside thirty-three discrete societies on the basis of rules and values absolutely determined somewhere else, in a thirty-fourth other country, for example.

In addition to that staggering congeries of non-native users of English, there are five countries, or 333,746,000 people, for whom this thing called "English" serves as a native tongue. Approximately 10% of these native speakers of "English" are Afro-American citizens of the U.S.A. I cite these numbers and varieties of human beings dependent on "English" in order, quickly, to suggest how strange and how tenuous is any concept of "Standard English." Obviously, numerous forms of English now operate inside a natural, an uncontrollable, continuum of development. I would suppose "the standard" for English in Malaysia is not the same as "the standard" in Zimbabwe. I know that standard forms of English for Black people in this country do not copy those of whites. And, in fact, the structural differences between these two kinds of English have intensified, becoming more Black, or less white, despite the expected homogenizing effects of television and other mass media.

Nonetheless, white standards of English persist, supreme and unquestioned, in these United States. Despite our multilingual population, and despite the deepening Black and white cleavage within that conglomerate, white standards control our official and popular judgements of verbal proficiency and correct, or incorrect, language skills, including speech. In contrast to India, where at least fourteen languages coexist as legitimate Indian languages, in contrast to Nicaragua, where all citizens are legally entitled to formal school instruction in their regional or tribal languages, compulsory education

in America compels accommodation to exclusively white forms of "English." White English, in America, is "Standard English."
—FROM "NOBODY MEAN MORE TO ME THAN YOU AND THE FUTURE LIFE OF WILLIE JORDAN," *ON CALL*, 1984

Bilingual Advantages

JANE MILLER

Where a child grows up speaking more than one language or dialect, and those languages or dialects have equivalent status in his own and in other people's eyes, and where the connections between those languages and their differences are made explicit, multilingualism can be an unqualified good. Mr. Orme's pupil, Andreas, is in that rare position. He still visits Cyprus. English people know about Greek, even hear it spoken on their holidays. Andreas speaks Greek for most of the time at home, but other members of his family speak English too; and he is not aware of making conscious decisions about which language to speak to whom, about what or where. He could read and write in Greek before he arrived in England, and he learned English in a school where it was assumed, rightly, that he was competent linguistically even if he didn't know English, and where they have come to rely on and to admire his success. He was lucky too to embark on the second of his languages before he was too old to do so easily and to learn it principally through using it with children of his own age. As an example of bilingual advantages he is ideal, though hardly typical.

It is a characteristic irony that while the learning of languages can be an expensive business, nearly all those people in the world who grow up bilingual do so because their mother tongue or dialect has associations with poverty which make it likely to be thought inappropriate for education and some kinds of employment.
—FROM "HOW DO YOU SPELL *GUJARATI*, SIR?" IN *THE STATE OF THE LANGUAGE*, 1980

Writing Blocks and Cultural Shifts

GLORIA ANZALDÚA

Blocks (*Coatlicue* states) are related to my cultural identity. The painful periods of confusion that I suffer from are symptomatic of a larger creative process: cultural shifts. The stress of living with cultural ambiguity both compels me to write and blocks me. It isn't until I'm almost at the end of the blocked state that I remember and recognize it for what it is. As soon as this happens, the piercing light of awareness melts the block and I accept the deep and the darkness and I hear one of my voices saying, "I am tired of fighting. I surrender. I give up, let go, let the walls fall. On this night of the hearing of faults, *Tlazolteotl, diosa de la cara negra*,[1] let fall the cockroaches that live in my hair, the rats that nestle in my skull. Gouge out my lame eyes, rout my demon from its nocturnal cave. Set torch to the tiger that stalks me. Loosen the dead faces gnawing at my cheekbones. I am tired of resisting. I surrender. I give up, let go, let the walls fall."

And in descending to the depths I realize that down is up, and I rise up from and into the deep. And once again I recognize that the internal tension of oppositions can propel (if it doesn't tear apart) the mestiza writer out of the *metate*[2] where she is being ground with corn and water, eject her out as *nahual,* an agent of transformation, able to modify and shape primordial energy and therefore able to change herself and others into turkey, coyote, tree, or human.

—FROM "*TLILLI, TLAPALLI:* THE PATH OF THE RED AND BLACK INK," *BORDERLANDS/ LA FRONTERA: THE NEW MESTIZA,* 1987

The Satanic Verses: A Migrant's-Eye View

SALMAN RUSHDIE

. . . If *The Satanic Verses*[1] is anything, it is a migrant's-eye view of the world. It is written from the very experience of uprooting, disjuncture and metamorphosis (slow or rapid, painful or pleasurable) that is the migrant condition, and from which, I believe, can be derived a metaphor for all humanity.

Standing at the center of the novel is a group of characters, most of whom are British Muslims, or not-particularly-religious persons of Muslim background, struggling with just the sort of great problems that have arisen to surround the book, problems of hybridization and ghettoization, of reconciling the old and the new. Those who oppose the novel most vociferously today are of the opinion that in-

---

[1] *diosa de la cara negra:* goddess of the black face. (Ed.)

[2] *metate:* the stone on which corn is traditionally ground. (Ed.)

[1] Rushdie's 1988 novel, which angered many Muslims, was banned in eleven Islamic countries and resulted in a long-standing death-threat by the late Ayatollah Khomeini of Iran and his followers. (Ed.)

termingling with a different culture will inevitably weaken and ruin their own. I am of the opposite opinion. *The Satanic Verses* celebrates hybridity, impurity, intermingling, the transformation that comes of new and unexpected combinations of human beings, cultures, ideas, politics, movies, songs. It rejoices in mongrelization and fears the absolutism of the Pure. Mélange, hotch-potch, a bit of this and a bit of that is *how newness enters the world.* It is the great possibility that mass migration gives the world, and I have tried to embrace it. *The Satanic Verses* is for change-by-fusion, change-by-conjoining. It is a love-song to our mongrel selves.

Throughout human history, the apostles of purity, those who have claimed to possess a total explanation, have wrought havoc among mere mixed-up human beings. Like many millions of people, I am a bastard child of history. Perhaps we all are, black and brown and white, leaking into one another, as a character of mine once said, *like flavors when you cook.*

—from "In Good Faith: A Pen against the Sword," in *Newsweek*, 1990

A Journey into Speech

MICHELLE CLIFF

The first piece of writing I produced, beyond a dissertation on intel- 1
lectual game-playing in the Italian Renaissance, was entitled "Notes
on Speechlessness," published in *Sinister Wisdom*, no. 5. In it I talked
about my identification with Victor, the wild boy of Aveyron, who,
after his rescue from the forest and wildness by a well-meaning doctor of Enlightenment Europe, became "civilized," but never came to
speech. I felt, with Victor, that my wildness had been tamed—that
which I had been taught was my wildness.

My dissertation was produced at the Warburg Institute, Univer- 2
sity of London, and was responsible for giving me an intellectual belief in myself that I had not had before, while at the same time distancing me from who I am, almost rendering me speechless about
who I am. At least I believed in the young woman who wrote the
dissertation—still, I wondered who she was and where she had
come from.

I could speak fluently, but I could not reveal. I immersed myself 3
in the social circles and academies of Siena, Florence, Urbino, as
well as Venice, creating a place for myself there, and describing this
ideal world in eloquent linear prose.

When I began, finally, partly through participation in the femi- 4
nist movement, to approach myself as a subject, my writing was
jagged, nonlinear, almost shorthand. The "Notes on Speechlessness" were indeed notes, written in snatches on a nine-to-five job. I
did not choose the note form consciously; a combination of things
drew me to it. An urgency for one thing. I also felt incompetent to
construct an essay in which I would describe the intimacies, fears,
and lies I wrote of in "Speechlessness." I felt my thoughts, things I
had held within for a lifetime, traversed so wide a terrain, had so
many stops and starts, apparent non sequiturs, that an essay—with
its cold-blooded dependence on logical construction, which I had
mastered practically against my will—could not work. My subject

Michelle Cliff (1946–   ), born in Kingston, Jamaica, and now living in California, is the author of the poetry collection *Claiming an
Identity They Taught Me to Despise* (1980) and the novel *Abeng* (1984).
"A Journey into Speech" is from *The Land of Look Behind* (1985), a
collection of prose and poetry.

could not respond to that form, which would have contradicted the idea of speechlessness. This tender approach to myself within the confines and interruptions of a forty-hour-a-week job and against a history of forced fluency was the beginning of a journey into speech.

To describe this journey further, I must begin at the very begin- 5 ning, with origins, and the significance of these origins. How they have made me the writer I am.

I originate in the Caribbean, specifically on the island of Jamaica, 6 and although I have lived in the United States and in England, I travel as a Jamaican. It is Jamaica that forms my writing for the most part, and which has formed for the most part, myself. Even though I often feel what Derek Walcott expresses in his poem "The Schooner *Flight*": "I had no nation now but the imagination." It is a complicated business.

Jamaica is a place halfway between Africa and England, to put it 7 simply, although historically one culture (guess which one) has been esteemed and the other denigrated (both are understatements)—at least among those who control the culture and politics of the island—the Afro-Saxons. As a child among these people, indeed of these people, as one of them, I received the message of anglocentrism, of white supremacy, and I internalized it. As a writer, as a human being, I have had to accept that reality and deal with its effect on me, as well as finding what has been lost to me from the darker side, and what may be hidden, to be dredged from memory and dream. And it *is* there to be dredged. As my writing delved longer and deeper into this part of myself, I began to dream and imagine. I was able to clearly envision Nanny, the leader of a group of guerilla fighters known as the Windward Maroons, as she is described: an old Black woman naked except for a necklace made from the teeth of white men. I began to love her.

It is a long way from the court of Urbino to Nanny the Coroman- 8 tyn warrior. (Coromantyn, or Coromantee, was used by the British in Jamaica to describe slaves from the Gold Coast of Africa, especially slaves who spoke Akan.)

One of the effects of assimilation, indoctrination, passing into 9 the anglocentrism of British West Indian culture is that you believe absolutely in the hegemony of the King's English and in the form in which it is meant to be expressed. Or else your writing is not literature; it is folklore, and folklore can never be art. Read some poetry by West Indian writers—some, not all—and you will see what I mean. You have to dissect stanza after extraordinarily anglican stanza for Afro-Caribbean truth; you may never find the latter. But this has been our education. The anglican ideal—Milton, Wordsworth, Keats—was held before us with an assurance that we were unable, and would never be enabled, to compose a work of similar correctness. No reggae spoken here.

To write as a complete Caribbean woman, or man for that mat- 10
ter, demands of us retracing the African part of ourselves, reclaim-
ing as our own, and as our subject, a history sunk under the sea, or
scattered as potash in the canefields, or gone to bush, or trapped in
a class system notable for its rigidity and absolute dependence on
color stratification. On a past bleached from our minds. It means
finding the art forms of these of our ancestors and speaking in the
patois forbidden us. It means realizing our knowledge will always be
wanting. It means also, I think, mixing in the forms taught us by the
oppressor, undermining his language and co-opting his style, and
turning it to our purpose. In my current work-in-progress, a novel, I
alternate the King's English with *patois,* not only to show the class
background of characters, but to show how Jamaicans operate
within a split consciousness. It would be as dishonest to write the
novel entirely in *patois* as to write entirely in the King's English. Neither is the novel a linear construction; its subject is the political up-
heavals of the past twenty years. Therefore, I have mixed time and
incident and space and character and also form to try to mirror the
historical turbulence.

For another example, I wrote a long poem, actually half-poem, 11
half-prose, in which I imagine the visit of Botha of South Africa to
the heads of western Europe in the summer of 1984. I wrote this as a
parody of Gilbert and Sullivan because their work epitomizes salient
aspects of the British Empire which remain vibrant. And because as
a child I was sick to death of hearing "I am the very model of a modern major general." I enjoyed writing this, playing with rhyme and
language—it was like spitting into their cultural soup.

We are a fragmented people. My experience as a writer coming 12
from a culture of colonialism, a culture of Black people riven from
each other, my struggle to get wholeness from fragmentation while
working within fragmentation, producing work which may find its
strength in its depiction of fragmentation, through form as well as
content, is similar to the experience of other writers whose origins
are in countries defined by colonialism.

Ama Ata Aidoo, the Ghanaian writer, in her extraordinary book, 13
Our Sister Killjoy or Reflections from a Black-Eyed Squint (NOK Publishers, Lagos and New York, 1979), plots this fragmentation, and
shows how both the demand and solace of the so-called mother
country can claim us, while we long for our homeland and are
shamed for it and ourselves at the same time. The form Aidoo uses
to depict this dilemma of colonial peoples—part prose, fictional and
epistolary, part poetry—illustrates the fragmentation of the heroine

and grasps the fury of the heroine, living in Europe but drawn back to Ghana, knowing she can never be European. She will only be a been-to; that is, one who has been to the mother country. *Our Sister Killjoy* affected me directly, not just because like Aidoo's heroine I was a been-to. I was especially drawn by the way in which Aidoo expresses rage against colonialism—crystallized for her by the white man she calls the "Christian Doctor" throughout, excising Black African hearts to salvage white South African lives. In her expression of the rage she feels her prose breaks apart sharply into a staccato poetry—direct, short, brilliantly bitter—as if measured prose would disintegrate under her fury.

I wanted that kind of directness in my writing, as I came into 14 closer contact with my rage, and a realization that rage could fuel and shape my work. As a light-skinned colonial girlchild, both in Jamaica and in the Jamaican milieu of my family abroad, rage was the last thing expected of me.

After reading Aidoo I knew I wanted to tell exactly how things 15 were, what had been done, to us and by us, without muddying the issue with conventional beauty, avoiding becoming trapped in the grace of language for its own sake, which is always seductive.

In *Claiming an Identity They Taught Me to Despise*, a piece pub- 16 lished before I read Aidoo, halfway between poetry and prose, as I am halfway between Africa and England, patriot and expatriate, white and Black, I felt my use of language and imagery had sometimes masked what I wanted to convey. It seemed sometimes that the reader was able to ignore what I was saying while admiring the way in which it was said.

And yet, *Claiming* is an honest self-portrait of who I was at the 17 time. Someone who was unable, for the most part, to recapture the native language of Jamaica, and who relied on the King's English and European allusions, but who wrote from a feminist consciousness and a rapidly evolving consciousness of colonialism, and a knowledge of self-hatred. Someone who also dreamed in Latin—as I did and as I recorded in the title section, included here. *Claiming*'s strengths, I think, are in the more intimate, private places of the piece, which I constructed much as the "Notes on Speechlessness" are constructed. Shorthand—almost—as memory and dream emerge; fast, at once keen, at once incomplete. I was also, in those sections, laboring under the ancient taboos of the assimilated: don't tell outsiders anything real about yourself. Don't reveal *our* secrets to *them*. Don't make us seem foolish, or oppressed. Write it quickly before someone catches you. Before you catch yourself.

After reading *Our Sister Killjoy*, something was set loose in me, I 18 directed rage outward rather than inward, and I was able to write a piece called "If I Could Write This in Fire I Would Write This in Fire." In it I let myself go, any thought of approval for my words vanished; I strung together myth, dream, historical detail, observation, as I had done before, but I added native language, tore into the indoctrination of the colonizer, surprised myself with the violence of my words.

   That piece of writing led to other pieces in which I try to depict 19 personal fragmentation and describe political reality, according to the peculiar lens of the colonized.

What's Wrong with Black English

RACHEL L. JONES

William Labov, a noted linguist, once said about the use of black English, "It is the goal of most black Americans to acquire full control of the standard language without giving up their own culture." He also suggested that there are certain advantages to having two ways to express one's feelings. I wonder if the good doctor might also consider the goals of those black Americans who have full control of standard English but who are every now and then troubled by that colorful, grammar-to-the-winds patois that is black English. Case in point—me. 1

I'm a 21-year-old black born to a family that would probably be considered lower-middle class—which in my mind is a polite way of describing a condition only slightly better than poverty. Let's just say we rarely if ever did the winter-vacation thing in the Caribbean. I've often had to defend my humble beginnings to a most unlikely group of people for an even less likely reason. Because of the way I talk, some of my black peers look at me sideways and ask, "Why do you talk like you're white?" 2

The first time it happened to me I was nine years old. Cornered in the school bathroom by the class bully and her sidekick, I was offered the opportunity to swallow a few of my teeth unless I satisfactorily explained why I always got good grades, why I talked "proper" or "white." I had no ready answer for her, save the fact that my mother had from the time I was old enough to talk stressed the importance of reading and learning, or that L. Frank Baum and Ray Bradbury were my closest companions. I read all my older brothers' and sisters' literature textbooks more faithfully than they did, and even lightweights like the Bobbsey Twins and Trixie Belden were allowed into my bookish inner circle. I don't remember exactly what I told those girls, but I somehow talked my way out of a beating. 3

Rachel L. Jones (1961–   ), from Chicago, is the author of journalism and opinion pieces and currently does investigative reporting for *The Chicago Reporter*. "What's Wrong with Black English" appeared as a guest editorial in *Newsweek* (1982) when Jones was a sophomore at Southern Illinois University.

I was reminded once again of my "white pipes" problem while   4
apartment hunting in Evanston, Illinois, last winter. I doggedly
made out lists of available places and called all around. I would immediately be invited over—and immediately turned down. The
thinly concealed looks of shock when the front door opened clued
me in, along with the flustered instances of "just getting off the
phone with the girl who was ahead of you and she wants the
rooms." When I finally found a place to live, my roommate stirred
up old memories when she remarked a few months later, "You
know, I was surprised when I first saw you. You sounded white
over the phone." Tell me another one, sister.

I should've asked her a question I've wanted an answer to for   5
years: how does one "talk white"? The silly side of me pictures a
rabid white foam spewing forth when I speak. I don't use Valley
Girl jargon, so that's not what's meant in my case. Actually, I've
pretty much deduced what people mean when they say that to me,
and the implications are really frightening.

It means that I'm articulate and well-versed. It means that I can   6
talk as freely about John Steinbeck as I can about Rick James. It
means that "ain't" and "he be" are not staples of my vocabulary and
are only used around family and friends. (It is almost Jekyll and
Hyde-ish the way I can slip out of academic abstractions into a long,
lean, double-negative-filled dialogue, but I've come to terms with
that aspect of my personality.) As a child, I found it hard to believe
that's what people meant by "talking proper"; that would've meant
that good grades and standard English were equated with white
skin, and that went against everything I'd ever been taught. Running into the same type of mentality as an adult has confirmed the
depressing reality that for many blacks, standard English is not only
unfamiliar, it is socially unacceptable.

James Baldwin once defended black English by saying it had   7
added "vitality to the language," and even went so far as to label it a
language in its own right, saying, "Language [i.e., black English] is
a political instrument" and a "vivid and crucial key to identity." But
did Malcolm X urge blacks to take power in this country "any way
y'all can"? Did Martin Luther King Jr. say to blacks, "I has been to
the mountaintop, and I done seed the Promised Land"? Toni Morrison, Alice Walker and James Baldwin did not achieve their elo-
quence, grace and stature by using only black English in their writing. Andrew Young, Tom Bradley and Barbara Jordan did not
acquire political power by saying, "Y'all crazy if you ain't gon vote
for me." They all have full command of standard English, and I
don't think that knowledge takes away from their blackness or commitment to black people.

I know from experience that it's important for black people, 8 stripped of culture and heritage, to have something they can point to and say, "This is ours, *we* can comprehend it, *we* alone can speak it with a soulful flourish." I'd be lying if I said that the rhythms of my people caught up in "some serious rap" don't sound natural and right to me sometimes. But how heartwarming is it for those same brothers when they hit the pavement searching for employment? Studies have proven that the use of ethnic dialects decreases power in the marketplace. "I be" is acceptable on the corner, but not with the boss.

Am I letting capitalistic, European-oriented thinking fog the is- 9 sue? Am I selling out blacks to an ideal of assimilating, being as much like white as possible? I have not formed a personal political ideology, but I do know this: it hurts me to hear black children use black English, knowing that they will be at yet another disadvantage in an educational system already full of stumbling blocks. It hurts me to sit in lecture halls and hear fellow black students complain that the professor "be tripping dem out using big words dey can't understand." And what hurts most is to be stripped of my own blackness simply because I know my way around the English language.

I would have to disagree with Labov in one respect. My goal is 10 not so much to acquire full control of both standard and black English, but to one day see more black people less dependent on a dialect that excludes them from full participation in the world we live in. I don't think I talk white, I think I talk right.

The Girl Who Wouldn't Sing

KIT YUEN QUAN

It was really hard deciding how to talk about language because I had 1
to go through my blocks with language. I stumble upon these blocks
whenever I have to write, speak in public or voice my opinions in a
group of native English speakers with academic backgrounds. All of
a sudden as I scramble for words, I freeze and am unable to think
clearly. Minutes pass as I struggle to retrieve my thoughts until I
finally manage to say something. But it never comes close to expressing what I mean. I think it's because I'm afraid to show who I
really am. I cannot bear the thought of the humiliation and ridicule.
And I dread having to use a language that has often betrayed my
meaning. Saying what I need to say using my own words usually
threatens the status quo.

People assume that I don't have a language problem because I 2
can speak English, even when I ask them to take into account that
English is my second language. This is the usual reaction I have gotten while working in the feminist movement. It's true that my language problems are different from those of a recent immigrant who
cannot work outside of Chinatown because she or he doesn't speak
enough English. Unlike my parents, I don't speak with a heavy accent. After twenty years of living in this country, watching American television and going through its school system, I have acquired
adequate English skills to function fairly well. I can pass as long as I
don't have to write anything or say what I really think around those
whom I see as being more educated and articulate than I am. I can
spend the rest of my life avoiding jobs that require extensive reading
and writing skills. I can join the segment of the population that
reads only out of necessity rather than for information, appreciation
or enlightenment.

It's difficult for people to accept that I believe I have a literacy 3
problem because they do not understand the nature of my blocks
with language. Learning anything new terrifies me, especially if it
involves words or writing. I get this overwhelming fear, this heart-

Kit Yuen Quan (1961–   ), born in Hong Kong, is on the staff of a
publishing house in San Francisco and works on literacy issues.
"The Girl Who Wouldn't Sing" is from *Making Face, Making Soul/Ha-
ciendo Caras: Creative and Critical Perspectives by Women of Color*, edited by Gloria Anzaldúa (1990).

stopping panic that I won't understand it. I won't know how to do it. My body tenses up and I forget to breathe if there is a word in a sentence that I don't know or several sentences in a paragraph containing unfamiliar words. My confidence dwindles and I start to feel the ground falling from under me. In my frustration I feel like crying, running out or smashing something, but that would give me away, expose my defect. So I tune out or nod my head as if there is nothing wrong. I've had to cover it up in order to survive, get jobs, pass classes and at times to work and live with people who do not care to understand my reality.

Living with this fear leaves me exhausted. I feel backed against a   4
wall of self-doubt, pushed into a corner, defeated, unable to stretch or take advantage of opportunities. Beyond just being able to read and write well enough to get by, I need to be able to learn, understand, communicate, to articulate my thoughts and feelings, and participate fully without feeling ashamed of who I am and where I come from.

When I first arrived in San Francisco from Hong Kong at age   5
seven and a half, the only English I knew was the alphabet and a few simple words: cat, dog, table, chair. I sat in classrooms for two to three years without understanding what was being said, and cried while the girl next to me filled in my spelling book for me. In music class when other kids volunteered to go up in front of the class to play musical instruments, I'd never raise my hand. I wouldn't sing. The teacher probably wondered why there were always three Chinese girls in one row who wouldn't sing. In art class, I was so traumatized that I couldn't be creative. While other kids moved about freely in school, seeming to flow from one activity to the next, I was disoriented, out of step, feeling hopelessly behind. I went into a "survivor mode" and couldn't participate in activities.

I remember one incident in particular in the fourth grade during   6
a kickball game. I had just missed the ball when Kevin, the class jock, came running across the yard and kicked me in the butt. Had I been able to speak English, I might have screamed my head off or called for the teacher, but I just stood there trying to numb out the pain, feeling everyone's eyes on me. I wasn't sure it wasn't all part of the game.

At home I spoke the sam yup dialect of Cantonese with my par-   7
ents, who were completely unaware of the severity of my problems at school. In their eyes I was very lucky to be going to school in America. My father had had only a high school education before he had to start working. And we children would not have had any chance to go to college had we stayed in Hong Kong. We had flown over the Pacific Ocean three times between the time I was seven and

a half and eight and a half because they were so torn about leaving their home to resettle in a foreign country and culture. At the dinner table after a day of toiling at their jobs and struggling with English, they aired their frustrations about the racism and discrimination they were feeling everywhere: at their jobs, on the bus, at the super-market. Although they didn't feel very hopeful about their own lives, they were comforted by the fact that my brother and I were getting a good education. Both my parents had made incredible sacrifices for my education. Life would be easier for us, with more opportunities and options, because we would know the language. We would be able to talk back or fight back if need be. All we had to do was study hard and apply ourselves. So every day after school I would load my bag full of textbooks and walk up two hills to where we lived the first few years after we landed here. I remember open-ing each book and reading out loud a paragraph or two, skipping over words I didn't know until I gave up in frustration.

My parents thought that by mastering the English language, I   8 would be able to attain the Chinese American dream: a college edu-cation, a good-paying job, a house in the suburbs, a Chinese hus-band and children. They felt intimidated and powerless in American society and so clung tightly to me to fulfill their hopes and dreams. When I objected to these expectations using my limited Chinese, I received endless lectures. I felt smothered by their traditional values of how a Chinese girl should behave and this was reason enough not to learn more Chinese. Gradually language came to represent our two or more opposing sets of values. If I asserted my individual-ity, wanted to go out with my friends, had opinions of my own, or disagreed with their plans for me, I was accused of becoming too smart for my own good now that I had grown wings. *"Cheun neuih,* stupid girl. Don't think you're better than your parents just because you know more English. You don't know anything! We've eaten more salt than you've eaten rice." Everything I heard in Chinese was a dictate. It was always one more thing I wasn't supposed to do or be, one more way I wasn't supposed to think. At school I felt stupid for not knowing the language. At home I was under attack for my rebellious views. The situation became intolerable after I came out to my parents as a lesbian.

When I ran away from home at sixteen, I sought refuge in the   9 women's community working part-time at a feminist bookstore. I felt like I had no family, no home, no identity or culture I could claim. In between hiding from my parents and crashing at various women's houses, I hung out in the Mission playing pool with other young dykes, got high, or took to the streets when I felt like I was going to explode. Sometimes at night I found myself sitting at the counter of some greasy spoon Chinese restaurant longing for a home-cooked meal. I was lonely for someone to talk to who could understand how I felt, but I didn't even have the words to communicate what I felt.

At the bookstore, I was discovering a whole other world: 10 women, dykes, feminists, authors, political activists, artists—people who read and talked about what they were reading. As exciting as it all was, I didn't understand what people were talking about. What was political theory? What was literary criticism? Words flew over my head like planes over a runway. In order to communicate with other feminists, most of whom were white or middle class or both, educated, and at least ten years older than me, I had to learn feminist rhetoric.

Given my uprooted and transplanted state, I have a difficult 11 time explaining to other people how I feel about language. Usually they don't understand or will even dispute what I'm saying. A lot of times I'll think it's because I don't have the right words, I haven't read enough books, or I don't know the language. That's how I felt all the time while working at a feminist bookstore. It wasn't only white, educated people who didn't understand how I felt. Women of color or Third World women who had class privilege and came from literary backgrounds thought the problem was more my age and my lack of political development. I often felt beaten down by these kinds of attitudes while still thinking that my not being understood was the result of my inability to communicate rather than an unreceptive environment.

Even though feminist rhetoric does give me words to describe 12 how I'm being oppressed, it still reflects the same racist, classist standards of the dominant society and of colleges and universities. I get frustrated because I constantly feel I'm being put down for what I'm saying or how I talk. For example, in a collective meeting with other women, I spoke about how I felt as a working class person and why I felt different from them. I told them they felt "middle class" to me because of the way they behaved and because of the values they had, that their "political vision" didn't include people with my experience and concerns. I tried to say all of this using feminist rhetoric, but when I used the term "working class," someone would argue. "You can't use that term. . . ." Because they were educated they thought they owned the language and so could say, "You can't use 'middle class,' you can't use 'working class,' because nowadays everybody is working class and it's just a matter of whether you're poor or comfortable." They did not listen to the point I was trying to make. They didn't care that I was sitting there in the circle stumbling along, struggling to explain how I felt oppressed by them and the structure and policies of the organization. Instead of listening to why I felt that way, they invalidated me for the way I used language and excluded me by defending themselves and their positions and claiming that my issues and feelings were "personal" and that I should just get over them.

Another example of my feeling excluded is when people in a   13 room make all sorts of literary allusions. They make me feel like I should have read those books. They throw around metaphors that leave me feeling lost and confused. I don't get to throw in my metaphors. Instead of acknowledging our different backgrounds and trying to include me in the discussion, they choose to ignore my feelings of isolation. I find that among feminists, white and colored, especially those who pride themselves on being progressive political activists with credentials, there's an assumption that if a person just read more, studied more, she would find the right words, the right way to use them, and even the right thoughts. A lot of times my language and the language of other working class, non-academic people become the target of scrutiny and criticism when others don't want to hear what we have to say. They convince themselves we're using the wrong words: "What definition are you using?" "What do you mean by that?" And then we get into debate about what was meant, we get lost in semantics and then we really don't know what we're saying.

Why should I try to use all of these different words when I'm   14 being manipulated and suppressed by those whose rhetoric is more developed, whether it's feminist, academic, or leftist?

Those of us who feel invisible or misunderstood when we try to   15 name what is oppressing us within supposedly feminist or progessive groups need to realize that our language is legitimate and valid. It comes from our families, our cultures, our class backgrounds, our experiences of different and conflicting realities. And we don't need to read another book to justify it. If I want to say *I'm working class*, I should be able to *say* I'm working class without having to read or quote Marx. But just saying that I'm working class never gives me enough of the understanding that I want. Because our experiences and feelings are far too complex to be capsulized in abstractions like "oppression," "sexism," "racism," etc., there is no right combination of these terms which can express why we feel oppressed.

I knew that I needed to go some place where some of my experi-   16 ences with language would be mirrored. Through the Refugee Women's Program in the Tenderloin district of San Francisco, I started to tutor two Cambodian refugee girls. The Buth family had been in the U.S. for one and a half years. They lived, twelve people to a room, in an apartment building on Eddy Street half a block from the porno theaters. I went to their home one evening a week and on Sundays took the girls to the children's library. The doorbells in the building were out of order, so visitors had to wait to be let in by someone on their way out. Often I stood on their doorsteps watching the street life. The fragrant smell of jasmine rice wafting from the windows of the apartment building mixed with the smell of booze and piss on the street. Newspapers, candy wrappers and all kinds of garbage swept up by the wind colored the sidewalks. Cars honked and sped past while Asian, Black and white kids played up and down the street. Mothers carrying their babies weaved through loose gatherings of drunk men and prostitutes near the corner store. Around me I heard a medley of languages: Vietnamese, Chinese, Cambodian, English, Black English, Laotian.

Sometimes, I arrived to find Yan and Eng sitting on the steps be- 17 hind the security gate waiting to let me in. Some days they wore their school clothes, while on other days they were barefooted and wore their traditional sarongs. As we climbed the stairs up to their apartment, we inhaled fish sauce and curry and rice. Six-year-old Eng would chatter and giggle but Yan was quieter and more reserved. Although she was only eight years old, I couldn't help but feel like I was in the company of a serious adult. I immediately identified with her. I noticed how, whenever I gave them something to do, they didn't want to do it on their own. For example, they often got excited when I brought them books, but they wouldn't want to read by themselves. They became quiet and withdrawn when I asked them questions. Their answer was always a timid "I don't know," and they never asked a question or made a request. So I read with them. We did everything together. I didn't want them to feel like they were supposed to automatically know what to do, because I remembered how badly that used to make me feel.

Play time was the best part of our time together. All the little 18 kids joined in and sometimes even their older brothers. Everybody was so excited that they forgot they were learning English. As we played jigsaw sentences and word concentration and chickens and whales, I became a little kid again, except this time I wasn't alone and unhappy. When they made Mother's Day cards, I made a Mother's Day card. When they drew pictures of our field trip to the beach, I sketched pictures of us at the beach. When we made origami frogs and jumped them all over the floor, I went home and made dinosaurs, kangaroos, spiders, crabs and lobsters. Week after week, I added to my repertoire until I could feel that little kid who used to sit like the piece of unmolded clay in front of her in art class turn into a wide-eyed origami enthusiast.

As we studied and played in the middle of the room surrounded 19 by the rest of the family who were sleeping, nursing, doing home-work, playing cards, talking, laughing or crying, Yan would fre-quently interrupt our lesson to answer her mother. Sometimes it was a long conversation, but I didn't mind because English was their second language. They spoke only Cambodian with their fam-ily. If they laughed at something on television, it was usually at the picture and not at the dialogue. English was used for schoolwork and to talk to me. They did not try to express their thoughts and feelings in English. When they spoke to each other, they were not alone or isolated. Whether they were living in a refugee camp in the Philippines or in Thailand or in a one-room apartment on Eddy Street, they were connected to each other through their language and their culture. They had survived war, losing family members, their country and their home, but in speaking their language, they were able to love and comfort each other. Sitting there on the bam-boo mat next to the little girls, Eng and her younger sister Oeun, lis-tening to their sweet little voices talking and singing, I understood for the first time what it was like to be a child with a voice and it made me remember my first love, the Chinese language.

While searching for an address, I came across a postcard of the 20 San Francisco–Oakland Bay Bridge. I immediately recognized it as the postcard I had sent to my schoolmate in Hong Kong when I first got here. On the back was my eight-and-a-half-year-old handwrit-ing.

In English it says: 21

> Dear Kam Yee, I received your letter. You asked if I've been to school yet. Yes, I've already found a school. My family has decided to stay in America. My living surroundings are very nice. Please don't worry about me. I'm sorry it has taken so long for me to re-turn your letter. Okay lets talk some more next time. Please give my regards to your parents and your family. I wish you happiness. Signed: Your classmate, Yuen Kit, August 30th.

The card, stamped "Return to Sender," is postmarked 1970. Al- 22 though I have sketchy memories of my early school days in Hong Kong, I still remember the day when Kam Yee and I found each other. The bell rang signaling the end of class. Sitting up straight in our chairs, we had recited "Goodbye, teacher" in a chorus. While the others were rushing out the door to their next class, I rose from my desk and slowly put away my books. Over my left shoulder I saw Kam Yee watching me. We smiled at each other as I walked over to her desk. I had finally made a friend. Soon after that my family left Hong Kong and I wrote my last Chinese letter.

All the time that I was feeling stupid and overwhelmed by lan- 23 guage, could I have been having the Chinese blues? By the time I was seven, I was reading the Chinese newspaper. I remember because there were a lot of reports of raped and mutilated women's bodies found in plastic bags on the side of quiet roads. It was a thrill when my father would send me to the newsstand on the corner to get his newspaper. Passing street vendors peddling sweets and fruit, I would run as quickly as I could. From a block away I could smell the stinky odor of *dauh fuh fa*, my favorite snack of slippery, warm, soft tofu in sweet syrup.

Up until a year ago, I could only recognize some of the Chinese 24 characters on store signs, restaurant menus and Chinese newspapers on Stockton and Powell Streets, but I always felt a tingle of excitement whenever I recognized a word or knew its sound, like oil sizzling in a wok just waiting for something to fry.

On Saturdays I sit with my Chinese language teacher on one of 25 the stone benches lining the overpass where the financial district meets Chinatown and links Portsmouth Square to the Holiday Inn Hotel. We have been meeting once a week for me to practice speaking, reading and writing Chinese using whatever material we can find. Sometimes I read a bilingual Chinese American weekly newspaper called the *East West Journal*, other times Chinese folk tales for young readers from the Chinatown Children's Library, or bilingual brochures describing free services offered by non-profit Chinatown community agencies, and sometimes even Chinese translations of Pacific Bell Telephone inserts. I look forward to these sessions where I reach inward to recover all those lost sounds that once were the roots of my childhood imagination. This exercise in trying to use my eight-year-old vocabulary to verbalize my thoughts as an adult is as scary as it is exhilarating. At one time Chinese was poetry to me. Words, their sounds and their rhythms, conjured up images that pulled me in and gave me a physical sense of their meanings. The Chinese characters that I wrote and practiced were pictographs of water, grass, birds, fire, heart and mouth. With my calligraphy brush made of pig's hair, I made the rain fall and the wind blow.

Now, speaking Chinese with my father is the closest I have felt 26 to coming home. In a thin but sage-like voice, he reflects on a lifetime of hard work and broken dreams and we slowly reconnect as father and daughter. As we sit across the kitchen table from one another, his old and tattered Chinese dictionary by his side, he tells me of the loving relationship he had with his mother, who encouraged him in his interest in writing and the movies. Although our immigrant experiences are generations apart and have been impacted differently by American culture, in his words I see the core of who I am. I cannot express my feelings fully in either Chinese or English or make him understand my choices. Though I am still grappling with accepting the enormous love behind the sacrifices he has made to give me a better life, I realize that with my ability to move in two different worlds I am the fruit of his labor.

For 85 cents, I can have unlimited refills of tea and a *gai mei baau*   27 at The Sweet Fragrance Cafe on Broadway across from the World Theatre. After the first bite, the coconut sugar and butter ooze down my palm. Behind the pastry counter, my favorite clerk is consolidating trays of walnut cupcakes. Pointing to some round fried bread covered with sesame seeds, she urges the customer with "Four for a dollar, very fresh!"

Whole families from grandparents to babies sleeping soundly on   28 mothers' backs come here for porridge, pastries and coffee. Mothers stroll in to get sweets for little ones waiting at home. Old women carrying their own mugs from home come in to chat with their buddies. Workers wearing aprons smeared with pig's blood or fresh fish scales drop in for a bite during their break. Chinese husbands sit for hours complaining and gossiping not unlike the old women in the park.

A waitress brings bowls of beef stew noodles and pork liver por-   29 ridge. Smokers snub out their cigarettes as they pick up their chopsticks. The man across from me is counting sons and daughters on the fingers of his left hand: one son, another son, my wife, one daughter. He must have family in China waiting to immigrate.

The regulars congregate at the back tables, shouting opinions   30 from one end of the long table to the other. The Chinese are notorious for their loud conversations at close range that can easily be mistaken for arguments and fights until someone breaks into laughter or gives his companion a friendly punch. Here the drama of life is always unfolding in all different dialects. I may not understand a lot of it, but the chuckling, the hand gestures, the raising of voices in protest and in accusation, and the laughter all flow like music, like a Cantonese opera.

Twenty years seems like a long time, but it has taken all twenty   31 years for me to understand my language blocks and to find ways to help myself learn. I have had to create my own literacy program. I had to recognize that the school system failed to meet my needs as an immigrant and that this society and its institutions doesn't reflect or validate my experiences. I have to let myself grieve over the loss of my native language and all the years wasted in classrooms staring into space or dozing off when I was feeling depressed and hopeless. My various activities now help to remind me that my relationship with language is more complex than just speaking enough English to get by. In creative activity and in anything that requires words,

I'm still eight years old. Sometimes I open a book and I still feel I can't read. It may take days or weeks for me to work up the nerve to open that book again. But I do open it and it gets a little easier each time that I work through the fear. As long as there are bakeries in Chinatown and as long as I have 85 cents, I know I have a way back to myself.

Talkin' American 2

MICHAEL VENTURA

Flannery O'Connor[1] wrote American with the cut and grace of a   1
master. She said this once about the sort of language encouraged on
our campuses: "Everywhere I go I'm asked if I think the university
stifles writers. My opinion is that they don't stifle enough of them."

The university is where language goes to die—and where young   2
people, expecting to be taught, ingest corruption as education. For it
is corrupt to analyze art with words that intimidate people less mon-
eyed or lucky than you; it's a way of keeping them out of the gal-
leries and museums, a way of keeping culture all to yourself and
your kind. And it is corrupt to teach literature (which would not exist except for passion) in terms that deny or mock passion; what's really
being taught is that all behavior beyond the repartee of a faculty dinner party is ridiculous or unclean. And finally, it is corrupt to express theories about the psyche or society in words that conceal the
consequences of your thought—words beyond reach of those who
must bear the burden of whatever bright ideas will excuse the next
excesses of power.

This corruption hides in plain sight, in something as obvious   3
and as overlooked as vocabulary. There's a jargon to be learned for
every study now—usually a multisyllable mishmash guaranteed to
drain the life out of any sentence and strain the attention of any listener. But it doesn't take a lot of syllables to be pernicious. Literature students, for instance, no longer delve into novels and poems,
they study "texts." Same stuff, but with very different assumptions
about it. See, the word "poem" still holds just enough residue of intensity that one approaches it as something at least strange, something with secrets to tell. And presences as disturbing as Dostoevski's[2] follow the word "novel" into your mind. But "text" is

---

[1] American novelist and short story writer (1925–1964). (Ed.)
[2] Feodor Dostoevski (1821–1881), Russian novelist. (Ed.)

Michael Ventura (1945–   ), born in the South Bronx, New York
City, and now living in Arizona, is the author of *The Mollyhawk Poems* (1977), the essay collection *Shadow Dancing in the U.S.A.* (1985),
and the novel *Night Time Losing Time* (1989). "Talkin' American 2"
first appeared in the *L.A. Weekly* (1990).

barren, a cold word, clinical and belittling. The intent in calling, say, *As I Lay Dying*[3] a "text" is to make the book passive, short out its charge, control it before it gets *to* you. Don't let Faulkner's spirit take over the classroom—that would show up the prof. Such language allows professors to appear more important, more in command, than mere texts and the fragile, driven people who compose them.

How different this is from what Rilke[4] says: "Works of art are of [4] an infinite loneliness and with nothing so little to be reached as with criticism. Only love can grasp and hold and be just toward them." But what does Rilke know? He didn't have anything better to do with his life than make up texts.

If the student senses that to parrot these technical vocabularies [5] would do violence to something within, and senses this so strongly that he or she can't or won't learn the stuff—that student fails. Consider: what may well be a victory of the student's heart over a chilly system is framed instead as a lack, and the student is lessened in the eyes of the world. All of which works nicely to weed out the spirited: not only won't they get the credentials that carry such weight in our society, but they'll be looked down on and their confidence will have been shaken, so it's less likely they'll be a threat. As for those who stay in the university system, spirited or not, their jargons make them separate. They can talk only to each other. They can't go most places and discuss their knowledge and be understood. There grows a wall of language between these "educated" people and the rest of society. They've been ghettoized, trapped by the very terms in which they've been trained to think. It's a good way to keep knowledgeable people from causing trouble.

Crueler yet, most of these students are diving deep into debt for [6] the privilege of having their minds crippled. They're going to have to behave, and behave very well, as soon as they get out of college, to handle this debt. Then they *really* won't be a threat. They've been had, coming and going. And did I say their minds are crippled? Does "crippled" seem too strong a word? Make no mistake: hobble someone's language and they'll never be what they might have been. At least, not without putting in hard time to undo the damage—an effort most don't attempt, because most don't know they've been hurt. Not consciously, anyway. They *think* they've been educated. It says so on the diploma. The diminishment they feel, the sense of being littler inside than they once were—what could *that* possibly have to do with their education? It must be their own fault.

---

[3] 1930 novel by American author William Faulkner (1897–1962). (Ed.)
[4] Rainer Maria Rilke (1875–1926), German-Austrian poet. (Ed.)

Or their parents'. Or God's. And, thinking like this, they feel yet *more* diminished, more ineffectual.

That's some racket. Whether it was intended or whether, as they say in the South, it "jes grew," it's vicious: teach a bunch of innocents just enough to run your technological society, but teach them in such a way that they'll feel lousy about themselves and cut off from the rest of their people. And yes, there are *some* inspiring teachers, *some* inspired students; there are always a few tough and canny enough to break the bounds. But once we spoke a united language up and down the culture, and now we don't; fragmentation has been instituted in our mouths, it is a social disaster, and it happened in the very places that are supposed to protect against such things. (Interesting that this insidious usage didn't exist or hadn't dug in during the student wildness of the '60s. Universities have become more passive the deeper such vocabularies have taken hold.)   7

And what about the professors? They must really believe they're instructing, not enslaving. Yet, whatever the field, most can't see beyond the medium of the jargons that pay their rent. You can only think as flexibly as your language. So they, too, are trapped inside the matrix of their words, a style learned when they were as impressionable as their students. Their very vocabulary walls them off from the freshness they need.   8

These are the brutal prices paid for giving up the common tongue, for concocting specialized speech that people must pay to learn. Understand it's not that the American language won't carry the weight of our time. It's still Shakespeare's child. Or grandchild. True, it speaks in mostly one- and two-syllable words, but so did he. ("To be or not to be, that is the question.") The enormous vocabulary our American language has picked up from all over the world— and its flair for turning verbs and adjectives into nouns, and nouns, adjectives and even names into verbs—make it a language where, as Robert Bly[5] says, "hairy words sit down next to shiny words, scholarly words next to groovy words," with an agility that can handle just about anything. (Bly adds, defending big words too, "Language is the greatest gift of our ancestors, and we need to keep words like 'transfiguration' as well as 'bread' and 'yeast.'") So these new synthesized jargons on sale at your nearby campus don't exist because they're needed *as language;* rather, they exist because it profits people to control and sell syntax that befuddles and discourages anyone outside the managing class.   9

But some don't befuddle easy: 10

---

[5] American poet (1926–   ). (Ed.)

> I have the wall against my back . . .
> I can't run nor fly nor hide so I ATTACK!

That's Earl the Poet, in a rap video on MTV. The great thing is 11
that language doesn't need the campuses of the middle class to keep
it alive, nor can it be destroyed by their evasions. The liveliest American speech is rising back up from the street, as always. Writing
about rap in 1984, I said, "While the media and the government
have written off [urban blacks] as functional illiterates, they themselves have developed rapping . . . an incredible, instinctual fight to
preserve the integrity of [their] language," and hence the vitality of
their minds. Rap had been the major medium in black neighborhoods for a while by then, but in 1984 you still couldn't see it on TV,
hear it on the radio or buy it at chain record stores. All that's
changed. Rap is everywhere now, and the reason was summed up
well by a member of the group N.W.A: "You can turn on some rap
music and hear everything that's goin' on."

We hunger for vivid language with an almost physical need to 12
"hear everything that's goin' on," to speak and be spoken to with
words that beat like hearts. Our need can be messed with, but the
words it draws forth can't be crushed. In an age when a new management class with vast resources is trying to impose a stupefying
lingo so we can't question its management—a young man like Ver-
non Reid, of the group Living Colour, breaks through and describes
how the 20th century *feels* with more accuracy than any poet, sociologist, scientist, critic or novelist. And he does it in seven words that
anyone can understand, and millions hear: "Everything is possible,
but nothing is real."

That's 1990. While the sense that everything is possible sparks 13
energy, the feeling that nothing is real weakens and sabotages that
energy. Stating both in one line of forceful music gives strength to
what might be possible and helps break through the unreality.
When the song is over we're in a different place.

No one can overestimate how valuable it is that someone said 14
this to and for everyone. People hear it and a hardness in them un-
knots. "Ah, that's right, that's how these crazy days make *me* feel.
What will I do with that feeling, now that these words help me
touch it?" the psyche wonders deep below the level of thought. And
some change starts to happen, way down, juiced by the clarity of
the line. A rebellion rises, questions our confusion, begins to pierce
it: the knowledge that some things *are* real and it's our job to search
them out, name them all over again if we have to, share the names,
make the stand. That's what vivid language makes possible. You
can't do the work until you do the words.

Americanization Is Tough on "Macho"

ROSE DEL CASTILLO GUILBAULT

What is *macho*? That depends which side of the border you come 1
from.

Although it's not unusual for words and expressions to lose 2
their subtlety in translation, the negative connotations of *macho* in
this country are troublesome to Hispanics.

Take the newspaper descriptions of alleged mass murderer
Ramon Salcido. That an insensitive, insanely jealous, hard-drinking,
violent Latin male is referred to as *macho* makes Hispanics cringe.

"Es muy macho," the women in my family nod approvingly, de- 4
scribing a man they respect. But in the United States, when women
say, "He's so macho," it's with disdain.

The Hispanic *macho* is manly, responsible, hardworking, a man 5
in charge, a patriarch. A man who expresses strength through silence. What the Yiddish language would call a *mensch*.

The American *macho* is a chauvinist, a brute, uncouth, selfish, 6
loud, abrasive, capable of inflicting pain, and sexually promiscuous.

Quintessential *macho* models in this country are Sylvester Stallone,
Arnold Schwarzenegger and Charles Bronson. In their movies, they
exude toughness, independence, masculinity. But a closer look reveals their machismo is really violence masquerading as courage,
sullenness disguised as silence and irresponsibility camouflaged as
independence.

If the Hispanic ideal of *macho* were translated to American screen 8
roles, they might be Jimmy Stewart, Sean Connery and Laurence
Olivier.

In Spanish, *macho* ennobles Latin males. In English it devalues 9
them. This pattern seems consistent with the conflicts ethnic minority males experience in this country. Typically the cultural traits

---

Rose del Castillo Guilbault (1952–   ), born in Ciudad Obregon
in Sonora, Mexico, is director of editorials and public affairs for a
San Francisco television station and a syndicated writer for Pacific
News Service. "Americanization is Tough on 'Macho'" is from her
regular column for *This World* (1989), a weekly magazine of the *San
Francisco Chronicle*.

other societies value don't translate as desirable characteristics in America.

I watched my own father struggle with these cultural ambiguities. He worked on a farm for twenty years. He laid down miles of irrigation pipe, carefully plowed long, neat rows in fields, hacked away at recalcitrant weeds and drove tractors through whirlpools of dust. He stoically worked twenty-hour days during harvest season, accepting the long hours as part of agricultural work. When the boss complained or upbraided him for minor mistakes, he kept quiet, even when it was obvious the boss had erred. 10

He handled the most menial tasks with pride. At home he was a good provider, helped out my mother's family in Mexico without complaint, and was indulgent with me. Arguments between my mother and him generally had to do with money, or with his stubborn reluctance to share his troubles. He tried to work them out in his own silence. He didn't want to trouble my mother—a course that backfired, because the imagined is always worse than the reality. 11

Americans regarded my father as decidedly un-*macho*. His character was interpreted as nonassertive, his loyalty non-ambition, and his quietness, ignorance. I once overheard the boss's son blame him for plowing crooked rows in a field. My father merely smiled at the lie, knowing the boy had done it, but didn't refute it, confident his good work was well known. But the boss instead ridiculed him for being "stupid" and letting a kid get away with a lie. Seeing my embarrassment, my father dismissed the incident, saying "They're the dumb ones. Imagine, me fighting with a kid." 12

I tried not to look at him with American eyes because sometimes the reflection hurt. 13

Listening to my aunts' clucks of approval, my vision focused on the qualities America overlooked. "He's such a hard worker. So serious, so responsible." My aunts would secretly compliment my mother. The unspoken comparison was that he was not like some of their husbands, who drank and womanized. My uncles represented the darker side of *macho*. 14

In a patriarchal society, few challenge their roles. If men drink, it's because it's the manly thing to do. If they gamble, it's because it's how men relax. And if they fool around, well, it's because a man simply can't hold back so much man! My aunts didn't exactly meekly sit back, but they put up with these transgressions because Mexican society dictated this was their lot in life. 15

In the United States, I believe it was the feminist movement of the early '70s that changed *macho*'s meaning. Perhaps my generation 16 of Latin women was in part responsible. I recall Chicanas complaining about the chauvinistic nature of Latin men and the notion they wanted their women barefoot, pregnant and in the kitchen. The generalization that Latin men embodied chauvinistic traits led to this interesting twist of semantics. Suddenly a word that represented something positive in one culture became a negative prototype in another.

The problem with the use of *macho* today is that it's become an 17 accepted stereotype of the Latin male. And like all stereotypes, it distorts truth.

The impact of language in our society is undeniable. And the 18 misuse of *macho* hints at a deeper cultural misunderstanding that extends beyond mere word definitions.

The Etymology of the International Insult

CHARLES F. BERLITZ

"What is a kike?" Disraeli once asked a small group of fellow politi- 1
cians. Then, as his audience shifted nervously, Queen Victoria's
great Jewish Prime Minister supplied the answer himself. "A kike,"
he observed, "is a Jewish gentleman who has just left the room."

The word kike is thought to have derived from the ending -ki or 2
-ky found in many names borne by the Jews of Eastern Europe. Or,
as Leo Rosten suggests, it may come from *kikel*, Yiddish for a circle,
the preferred mark for name signing by Jewish immigrants who
could not write. This was used instead of an X, which resembles a
cross. Kikel was not originally pejorative, but has become so
through use.

Yid, another word for Jew, has a distinguished historic origin, 3
coming from the German *Jude* (through the Russian *zhid*). *Jude* itself
derives from the tribe of Judah, a most honorable and ancient appel-
lation. The vulgar and opprobrious word "Sheeny" for Jew is a real
inversion, as it derives from *shaine* (Yiddish) or *schön* (German),
meaning "beautiful." How could beautiful be an insult? The answer
is that it all depends on the manner, tone or facial expression or
sneer (as our own Vice President[1] has trenchantly observed) with
which something is said. The opprobrious Mexican word for an
American—*gringo*, for example, is essentially simply a sound echo of
a song the American troops used to sing when the Americans were
invading Mexico—"Green Grow the Lilacs." Therefore the Mexicans
began to call the Americans something equivalent to "los green-
grows" which became Hispanized to *gringo*. But from this innocent
beginning to the unfriendly emphasis with which many Mexicans

---

[1]Spiro Agnew, Vice President to Richard Nixon. (Ed.)

Charles F. Berlitz (1914–   ), born in New York City, is a linguist,
the author of more than one hundred language-teaching books,
and the grandson of the founder of the Berlitz School. Since 1967,
Mr. Berlitz has not been connected with the Berlitz schools in any
way. "The Etymology of the International Insult" was originally
published in *Penthouse* magazine (1970).

say *gringo* today there is a world of difference—almost a call to arms, with unforgettable memories of past real or fancied wrongs, including "lost" Texas and California.

The pejorative American word for Mexicans, Puerto Ricans,   4
Cubans and other Spanish-speaking nationals is simply *spik*, excerpted from the useful expression "No esspick Englitch." Italians, whether in America or abroad, have been given other more picturesque appellations. *Wop*, an all-time pejorative favorite, is curiously not insulting at all by origin, as it means, in Neapolitan dialect, "handsome," "strong" or "good looking." Among the young Italian immigrants some of the stronger and more active—sometimes to the point of combat—were called *guappi*, from which the first syllable, "wop," attained an "immediate insult" status for all Italians.

"Guinea" comes from the days of the slave trade and is derived   5
from the African word for West Africa. This "guinea" is the same word as the British unit of 21 shillings, somehow connected with African gold profits as well as New Guinea, which resembled Africa to its discoverers. Dark or swarthy Italians and sometimes Portuguese were called *Guineas* and this apparently spread to Italians of light complexion as well.

One of the epithets for Negroes has a curious and tragic historic   6
origin, the memory of which is still haunting us. The word is *"coons."* It comes from *baracoes* (the *o* gives a nasal *n* sound in Portuguese), and refers to the slave pens or barracks *("baracoons")* in which the victims of the slave trade were kept while awaiting transshipment. Their descendants, in their present emphasizing of the term "black" over "Negro," may be in the process of upgrading the very word "black," so often used pejoratively, as in "blackhearted," "black day," "black arts," "black hand," etc. Even some African languages uses "black" in a negative sense. In Hausa "to have a black stomach" means to be angry or unhappy.

The sub-Sahara African peoples, incidentally, do not think that   7
they are black (which they are not, anyway). They consider themselves a healthy and attractive "people color," while whites to them look rather unhealthy and somewhat frightening. In any case, the efforts of African Americans to dignify the word "black" may eventually represent a semantic as well as a socio-racial triumph.

A common type of national insult is that of referring to nationali-   8
ties by their food habits. Thus "Frogs" for the French and "Krauts" for the Germans are easily understandable, reflecting on the French addiction to *cuisses de grenouilles* (literally "thighs of frogs") and that of the Germans for various kinds of cabbage, hot or cold. The French call the Italians *"les macaronis"* while the German insult word

for Italians is *Katzenfresser* (Cat-eaters), an unjust accusation considering the hordes of cats among the Roman ruins fed by individual
cat lovers—unless they are fattening them up? The insult word for
an English person is "limey," referring to the limes distributed to
seafaring Englishmen as an antiscurvy precaution in the days of sailing ships and long periods at sea.

At least one of these food descriptive appellations has attained a   9
permanent status in English. The word "Eskimo" is not an Eskimo
word at all but an Algonquin word unit meaning "eaters-of-flesh."
The Eskimos naturally do not call themselves this in their own language but, with simple directness, use the word *Inuit*—"the men" or
"the people."

Why is it an insult to call Chinese "Chinks"? Chink is most prob-   10
ably a contraction of the first syllables of *Chung-Kuo-Ren*—"Middle
Country Person." In Chinese there is no special word for China, as
the Chinese, being racially somewhat snobbish themselves (although *not* effete, according to recent reports), have for thousands
of years considered their land to be the center or middle of the
world. The key character for China is therefore the word *chung* or
"middle" which, added to *kuo*, becomes "middle country" or
"middle kingdom"—the complete Chinese expression for "China"
being *Chung Hwa Min Kuo* ("Middle Flowery People's Country"). No
matter how inoffensive the origin of "Chink" is, however, it is no
longer advisable for everyday or anyday use now.

Jap, an insulting diminutive that figured in the . . . [1968] na-   11
tional U.S. election (though its use in the expression "fat Jap" was
apparently meant to have an endearing quality by our Vice President) is a simple contraction of "Japan," which derives from the Chinese word for "sun." In fact the words "Jap" and "Nip" both mean
the same thing. "Jap" comes from Chinese and "Nip" from Japanese
in the following fashion: *Jihpen* means "sun origin" in Chinese,
while *Ni-hon* (Nippon) gives a like meaning in Japanese, both indicating that Japan was where the sun rose. Europeans were first in
contact with China, and so originally chose the Chinese name for
Japan instead of the Japanese one.

The Chinese "insult" words for whites are based on the observa-   12
tions that they are too white and therefore look like ghosts or devils,
fan kuei (ocean ghosts), or that their features are too sharp instead of
being pleasantly flat, and that they have enormous noses, hence *ta-
bee-tsu* (great-nosed ones). Differences in facial physiognomy have
been fully reciprocated by whites in referring to Asians as "Slants"
or "Slopes."

Greeks in ancient times had an insult word for foreigners too,   13
but one based on the sound of their language. This word is still with

us, though its original meaning has changed. The ancient Greeks divided the world into Greeks and "Barbarians"—the latter word coming from a description of the ridiculous language the stranger was speaking. To the Greeks it sounded like the "baa-baa" of a sheep—hence "Barbarians!"

The black peoples of South Africa are not today referred to as 14 Negro or Black but as Bantu—not in itself an insult but having somewhat the same effect when you are the lowest man on the totem pole. But the word means simply "the men," *ntu* signifying "man" and *ba* being the plural prefix. This may have come from an early encounter with explorers or missionaries when Central or South Africans on being asked by whites who they were may have replied simply "men"—with the implied though probably unspoken follow-up questions, "And who are you?"

This basic and ancient idea that one's group are the only peo- 15 ple—at least the only friendly or nondangerous ones—is found among many tribes throughout the world. The Navajo Indians call themselves *Dine*—"the people"—and qualify other tribes generally as "the enemy." Therefore an Indian tribe to the north would simply be called "the northern enemy," one to the east "the eastern enemy," etc., and that would be the *only* name used for them. These ancient customs, sanctified by time, of considering people who differ in color, customs, physical characteristics and habits—and by enlargement all strangers—as potential enemies is something mankind can no longer afford, even linguistically. Will man ever be able to rise above using insult as a weapon? It may not be possible to love your neighbor, but by understanding him one may be able eventually to tolerate him. Meanwhile, if you stop calling him names, he too may eventually learn to dislike *you* less.

The Language of Indian Derision

HAIG A. BOSMAJIAN

Few white Americans of the past few centuries were as understanding as Benjamin Franklin when he said of the Indians in 1784: "Savages we call them because their manners differ from ours, which we think the perfection of civility, they think the same of theirs. . . . Our laborious manner of life, compared with theirs, they esteem slavish and base; and the learning on which we value ourselves, they regard as frivolous and useless."[1]

Still fewer whites ever recognized what Thomas Jefferson saw in the Indians: "I am safe in affirming that the proofs of genius given by the Indians of North America place them on a level with whites in the same uncultivated state. The North of Europe furnishes subjects enough for comparison with them, and for a proof of their equality, I have seen some thousands myself, and conversed much with them, and have found in them a masculine, sound understanding. . . . I believe the Indian to be body and mind equal to the white man."[2]

Had these images, these definitions prevailed, the oppression of Indians would have been much more difficult to justify. It was much more defensible to rob them of their lands, to deny them ordinary human rights and privileges by defining them as the Pueblo Indians were by the New Mexico Supreme Court in 1869: "They were wandering savages, given to murder, robbery, and theft, living on the game of the mountains, the forest, and the plains, unaccustomed to the cultivation of the soil, and unwilling to follow the pursuits of civilized man. Providence made this world for the use of the man who had the energy and industry to pull off his coat, and roll up his sleeves, and go to work on the land, cut down the trees, grub up the brush and briars, and stay there on it and work it for the support of himself and family, and a kind and thoughtful Providence did not charge man a single cent for the whole world made for mankind and intended for their benefit. Did the Indians ever purchase the land,

---

Haig A. Bosmajian (1928–   ), born in Fresno, California, is professor of speech at the University of Washington. He is the author of *This Great Argument: The Rights of Women* (1972), *Justice Douglas and Freedom of Speech* (1980), and other books about communication and rhetoric. "The Language of Indian Derision" is from *The Language of Oppression* (1974).

41

or pay anyone a single cent for it? Have they any deed or patent on it, or has it been devised to them by anyone as their exclusive inheritance?

"Land was intended and designed by Providence for the use of   4
mankind, and the game that it produced was intended for those too lazy and indolent to cultivate the soil . . . The idea that a handful of wild, half-naked, thieving, plundering, murdering savages should be dignified with the sovereign attributes of nations, enter into solemn treaties, and claim a country five hundred miles wide by one thousand miles long as theirs in fee simple, because they hunted buffalo and antelope over it, might do for beautiful reading in Cooper's novels or Longfellow's *Hiawatha*, but is unsuited to the intelligence and justice of this age, or the natural rights of mankind."[3]

As Peter Farb declared in the December 16, 1971, issue of *The*   5
New York Review: "Cannibalism, torture, scalping, mutilation, adultery, incest, sodomy, rape, filth, drunkenness—such a catalogue of accusations against a people is an indication not so much of their depravity as that their land is up for grabs."[4]

The land-grabbing, the "de-civilization," the dehumanization   6
and redefinition of the "American Indian" began with the arrival of Columbus in the New World. The various and diverse peoples of the "Americas," even though the differences between them were as great as between Italians and Irish or Finns and Portuguese, were all dubbed "Indians," and then "American Indians." Having redefined the inhabitants, the invaders then proceeded to enslave, torture, and kill them, justifying this by labeling the Indians as "savages" and "barbarians."

Plundering and killing of the Indians in the West Indies out-   7
raged the Spanish Dominican missionary, Bartolome de las Casas, who provided the following account of the conquest of the Arawaks and Caribs in his *Brief Relation of the Destruction of the Indies:* "They [the Spaniards] came with their Horsemen well armed with Sword and Launce, making most cruel havocks and slaughters. . . . Overrunning Cities and Villages, where they spared no sex nor age; neither would their cruelty pity Women with childe, whose bellies they would rip up, taking the Infant to hew it in pieces. . . . The children they would take by the feet and dash their innocent heads against the rocks, and when they were fallen into the water, with a strange and cruel derision they would call to them to swim. . . . They erected certain Gallowses . . . upon every one of which they would hang thirteen persons, blasphemously affirming that they did it in honor of our Redeemer and his Apostles, and then putting fire under them, they burnt the poor wretches alive. Those whom their

pity did think to spare, they would send away with their hands cut off, and so hanging by the skin."[5]

After the arrival of the Spaniards "whole Arawak villages disap-   8
peared through slavery, disease, and warfare, as well as by flight into the mountains. As a result the native population of Haiti, for example, declined from an estimated 200,000 in 1492 to a mere 29,000 only twenty-two years later."[6]

The ideas of white supremacy which the Europeans brought   9
with them affected the redefinition of the Indians. In his book *The Indian Heritage in America*, Alvin M. Josephy, Jr. observes that "in the early years of the sixteenth century educated whites, steeped in the theological teaching of Europe, argued learnedly about whether or not Indians were humans with souls, whether they, too, derived from Adam and Eve (and were therefore sinful like the rest of mankind), or whether they were a previously subhuman species."[7] Uncivilized and satanic as the Indians may have been, according to the European invaders, they could be saved; but if they could not be saved then they would be destroyed.

As Roy H. Pearce has pointed out, "convinced thus of his divine   10
right to Indian lands, the Puritan discovered in the Indians . . . evidence of a Satanic opposition to the very principle of divinity,"[8] although, somehow, the Indian "also was a man who had to be brought to the civilized responsibilities of Christian manhood, a wild man to be improved along with wild lands, a creature who had to be made into a Puritan if he was to be saved. Save him, and you saved one of Satan's victims. Destroy him, and you destroyed one of Satan's partisans."[9] Indians who resisted Puritan intrusions of their lands were "heathens" who could be justifiably killed if they refused to give up their lands to the white invaders: "When the Pequots resisted the migration of settlers into the Connecticut Valley in 1637, a party of Puritans surrounded the Pequot village and set fire to it. . . . Cotton Mather was grateful to the Lord that 'on this day we have sent six hundred heathen souls to hell.'"[10]

The Europeans, having defined themselves as culturally supe-   11
rior to the inhabitants they found in the New World, proceeded to their "manifest destiny" through massive killing of the "savages." The "sense of superiority over the Indians which was fostered by the religious ideology they carried to the new land," L. L. Knowles and K. Prewitt tell us in *Institutional Racism in America*, "found its expression in the self-proclaimed mission to civilize and Christianize— a mission which was to find its ultimate expression in ideas of a 'manifest destiny' and a 'white man's burden.'"[11] But the Christianizing and "civilizing" process did not succeed and "thus began

an extended process of genocide, giving rise to such aphorisms as 'The only good Indian is a dead Indian.'. . . Since Indians were capable of reaching only the state of 'savage,' they should not be allowed to impede the forward (westward, to be exact) progress of white civilization. The Church quickly acquiesced in this redefinition of the situation."[12]

If the Indians were not defined as outright "savages" or "barbarians," they were labeled "natives," and as Arnold Toynbee has shrewdly observed in *A Study of History*, "when we Westerners call people 'Natives' we implicitly take the cultural colour out of our preceptions of them. We see them as trees walking, or as wild animals infesting the country in which we happen to come across them. In fact, we see them as part of the local flora and fauna, and not as men of like passions with ourselves; and, seeing them thus as something infra-human, we feel entitled to treat them as though they did not possess ordinary human rights."[13] Once the Indians were labeled "natives," their domestication or extermination became, ostensibly, permissible. [12]

At the nation's Constitutional Convention in 1787 it had to be decided which inhabitants of the total population in the newly formed United States should be counted in determining how many representatives each state would have in Congress. The decision was that "representatives and direct taxes shall be apportioned among the several states . . . according to their respective numbers, which shall be determined by adding to the whole number of free persons, including those bound to service for a term of ten years, and excluding Indians not taxed, three fifths of all other persons." The enslaved black came out three fifths of a person and the Indian was treated as a nonentity. [13]

When the Indians had been defined as "savages" with no future, the final result, as Pearce states, "was an image of the Indian out of society and out of history." Once the Indians were successfully defined as governmental nonentities, no more justification was needed to drive them off their lands and to force them into migration and eventual death. During the nineteenth century, even "civilized Indians" found themselves being systematically deprived of life and property. The Five Civilized Tribes (Choctaws, Chicasaws, Creeks, Cherokees, and Seminoles) took on many of the characteristics of the whites' civilization: "Many of them raised stock, tilled large farms, built European style homes, and even owned Negro slaves like their white neighbors. They dressed like white men, learned the whites' methods, skills, and art, started small industries, and became Christians."[14] [14]

They were still Indians, however, and in the 1820s and 1830s the 15
United States Government forced the Five Civilized Tribes from
their lands and homes and sent them "to new homes west of the
Mississippi River to present-day Oklahoma, which was then
thought to be uninhabitable by white men. Their emigrations were
cruel and bitter trials."[15] Fifteen thousand Cherokees who had become "civilized" and "Christianized" and who resisted the white's
demands that they move west were systematically decimated by the
United States Army: "Squads of soldiers descended upon isolated
Cherokee farms and at bayonet point marched the families off to
what today would be known as concentration camps. Torn from
their homes with all the dispatch and efficiency the Nazis displayed
under similar circumstances, the families had no time to prepare for
the arduous trip ahead of them. No way existed for the Cherokee
family to sell its property and possessions and the local Whites fell
upon the lands, looting, burning, and finally taking possession."[16]

In a speech he delivered in 1846, Senator Thomas Hart Benton of 16
Missouri spoke to the United States Senate about the inferiority of
the Indians and the superiority of the white race. He gave the Indians a choice: become "civilized" or face extinction. But as indicated
above, the Indians' adoption of the whites' civilization was no guarantee against suppression, cruelty, and extinction. Senator Benton
expressed his preference for the white "civilization" over the Indians' "savagery": "The Red race has disappeared from the Atlantic
Coast: the tribes that resisted civilization, met extinction. For my
part, I cannot murmur at which seems to be the effect of divine
law. . . . Civilization, or extinction, has been the fate of all people
who have found themselves in the track of the advancing Whites,
and civilization, always the preference of the Whites, has been
pressed as an object, while extinction has followed as a consequence
of resistance. The Black and Red Races have often felt their amelio-
rating influence."[17]

During debate on peace with the Indians, Senator Abraham 17
Howard declared on July 17, 1867 that the Indian could not be
"civilized" or "Christianized": "The Indians are a roving race. You
will find it utterly impossible by any course of education or teaching
or preaching, or by whatever means you may see fit to employ, to
reconcile the wild Indians such as these tribes are to the business of
agriculture or to the habits of civilized life. That experiment has been
going on for the last two hundred years and more. It commenced
with the very discovery of this country, and good men, philan-
thropists, Christians, missionaries of every denomination, have had
the subject very much at heart, and have expended millions of dol-

lars from the days that Elliot first commenced the attempt in Massachusetts down to the present time; and what is the present result of all these humane and philanthropic efforts to civilize and Christianize the Indian? Sir, the net result of the whole is hardly worth speaking about. From some fatality or other, no matter what, it is perfectly apparent that the North American Indian cannot be civilized, cannot be Christianized."[18]

Senator Howard went on to turn his attention to the necessity of [18] the Indian to "yield before the advance of the white man": "He cannot throw himself across the path of progress. It is the very nature of things that barbarism, which is but another name for feebleness and dependence, must yield before the firm tread of the white man, carrying forward, as he always will, the flag and the institutions of civilization."[19]

Senator Howard's portrayal of the Indian as a "barbarian" who [19] could never be "civilized" was attacked by Senator Edward Morrill in the Senate debate: "Sir, there are civilized Indians in this country. Does the Senator know that? There are many civilized Indians. In spite of the merciless and faithless policy of this Government there are civilized Indians, and there are many of them, and there are enough to repel this assumption of the honorable Senator and to vindicate their race to a place in the scale of humanity, and show that they are the children of a common father; that they belong to human kind, that they are susceptible to its emotions, that they may be influenced by the considerations which influence other human beings. The history of American civilization shows no such thing as the honorable Senator supposes, and I am sorry that the utterance has come from him."[20]

Later in the debate, Senator Morrill spoke of the spirit in which [20] Indians were absorbed into white communities: "Is the spirit of the border eminently kind to the Indian? Not a bit of it. The sentiment is, 'he is a savage; he is a barbarian; a bounty on his head; is his presence compatible with our rights?' That is the spirit of the border. Nobody will deny that. And that spirit is to absorb him! I have already said what that means; it means extinction. Absorption is the Indian's scalp for a bounty."[21]

In response to Morrill's criticisms of the whites' treatment of the [21] Indians, Senator Howard retorted: "Sir, it is not necessary for me to vindicate the character and policy of the Government of the United States against so serious an imputation as this; and I will content myself simply saying that, according to my reading of the history of our relations with the Indians, there are very few cases in which the United States have been in the wrong."[22] Having defined the Indians as he did, Senator Howard's attempts to justify the whites' treatment of the Indians was greatly simplified.

In 1879, with the addition of the Fourteenth Amendment to the Constitution, it was decided that "all persons born or naturalized in the United States, and subject to the jurisdiction thereof, are citizens of the United States and of the State wherein they reside." 22

But the Fourteenth Amendment was subsequently held not to apply to the Indians. The question came to the United States Supreme Court in 1884 in *Elk v. Wilkins,* [23] a case involving an Indian who had moved off the reservation, severed tribal ties and completely surrendered himself to the jurisdiction of the United States and of his resident state, where he attempted to register to vote and was refused. The Court decided against John Elk, contending that the Fourteenth Amendment had not made him a citizen. In its decision the Court affirmed that the Fourteenth Amendment applied to the freed slaves, "but Indians not taxed are still excluded from the count, for the reason that they are not citizens. Their absolute exclusion from the basis of representation, in which all other persons are now included, is wholly inconsistent with their being considered citizens." [24] The Court placed the "privilege" of defining citizenship rights of Indians in the hands of the national government; it was the government which was to decide whether the Indians had advanced far enough into the white civilization to warrant citizenship. Even the Indians who had left their tribes to take up the ways of the whites, who left their "barbaric" state to become "civilized," could in no way be defined as citizens. 23

In *Elk v. Wilkins* the Court cited Judge Deady of Oregon, who stated in *United States v. Osborne* that "an Indian cannot make himself a citizen of the United States without the consent and cooperation of the government. The fact that he has abandoned his nomadic life or tribal relations, and adopted the habits and manners of civilized people, may be a good reason why he should be made a citizen of the United States, but does not of itself make him one." [25] By some strange white logic, the blacks taken from their tribal homes in Africa to be placed in slavery in the United States came to be defined as citizens of this country, while the original inhabitants, the Indians, were to remain defined as inferior and uncivilized nomads in their own land. 24

In an effort to "civilize" the Indians, the Government established schools for the "savages," and one aspect of the education received by the children was an attempt to teach the Indians to pay homage to their oppressor. In 1901 the United States Superintendent of Indian Schools prepared "A Course of Study for Indian Schools" 25 which was printed by the Government Printing Office and distributed to "Agents, Superintendents, and Teachers of Schools." It was the author's hope that this course of study would lead the Indians to "better morals, a more patriotic and Christian citizenship and ability for self-support."[26] While most of the publication dealt with subjects such as agriculture, baking, basketry, gardening, and harness making, a chapter was devoted to the study of history. While recognizing the need for the teacher to relate to the Indians something about their heritage, the chapter also suggested that the teacher instruct the youths in the history of the United States; the course of study recommended that the Indians should know about United States history "to be good, patriotic citizens":

"They should learn a few important dates, such as that of the discovery of America, settlement of Virginia, Declaration of Independence, etc. [26]

"Describe historical events, as the discovery of America and the landing of the Pilgrims. [27]

"See that the event turns on the person, showing examples of patriotism, valor, self-sacrifice, heroism. . . . [28]

"The names of our greatest men, such as Washington, Franklin, and Lincoln, should also be learned and something about the character and work of each."[27] [29]

The chapter suggested that the teacher also adapt "stories appropriate to Thanksgiving, Christmas, New Year's Day, Arbor Day, etc. Enlarge upon national holidays; history of our flag; patriotism; loyalty to a cause; one's institution; one's country."[28] [30]

The teacher was told that "patriotic songs must be taught in every school, and every child should be familiar with the words as well as the music of our inspiring national songs."[29] Further, "in every school the salute to the flag must be taught and where the climate will permit, this exercise must be engaged in out of doors, by the whole school, morning and evening; and where the climate is too severe, it can be done in the classroom daily and at the evening hour."[30] This practice of demanding that the oppressed honor and pay homage to the oppressor was itself part of the dehumanizing process. [31]

By some strange reasoning, "the important date" of the settlement of Virginia was considered something which would contribute to the "patriotism" of the Indians, although in Virginia the white invaders had referred to the Indians as "beasts," "savages," "miscreants," and "barbarians." In Virginia in 1622, after the Indians had killed approximately three hundred fifty English invaders, the English took revenge by burning the crops of the Indians, putting the torch to their homes, and driving them from their villages. In [32]

1623 Indians who approached the Virginians with the intent to sue for peace were shot. To teach Indian youths to see the white Virginia "colonists" as examples of "patriotism, valor, self-sacrifice, and heroism," to teach these students to regard the very people who had suppressed and killed their ancestors as exemplary was a travesty of education.

The travesty and humiliation were compounded by requiring 33 the Indian children to learn the words of "our inspiring national songs." The significance to the Indian of one of these songs has been observed by Vine Deloria, Jr., in *Custer Died for Your Sins: An Indian Manifesto:* "One day at a conference we were singing 'My Country 'Tis of Thee' and we came across the part that goes: 'Land where our fathers died, Land of the Pilgrims' pride. . . .' Some of us broke out laughing when we realized that our fathers undoubtedly died trying to keep those Pilgrims from stealing our land. In fact, many of our fathers died because the Pilgrims killed them as witches. We didn't feel much kinship with those Pilgrims, regardless of who they did in."[31]

Not only were Indian youths to be taught to show delight in the 34 discovery of America and the settlement of Virginia and to learn the words of "our inspiring national songs," they were also to be taught the salute to the flag of the United States at a time when Indian citizenship was not guaranteed, when Indian suffrage was denied in various states, when "liberty and justice for all" simply did not apply to Indians. The children were in effect forced to salute the flag under which their conquerors and oppressors had marched. One might as well have forced the blacks in this country to salute the Confederate flag or the Jews in Germany to salute the Nazi swastika flag. If an oppressed group of people can be forced, without their actively rebelling, to pledge allegiance to the flag of their masters, the humiliation and subjugation are outwardly manifested for all to see.

One of the rituals some Indians were subjected to when they 35 sought to become citizens required they give up their "Indian names" and take on "white ones." The ritual clearly compelled the Indian to deny his or her previous identity through the renaming and redefining process. For male Indians the procedure was as follows:

"For men: (Read name)—(White name). What was your Indian 36 name? (Gives name).—(Indian name.) I hand you a bow and an arrow. Take this bow and shoot the arrow. (He shoots.)

"—(Indian name.) You have shot your last arrow. That means 37 that you are no longer to live the life of an Indian. You are from this day forward to live the life of the white man. . . ."[32]

The male Indian then was asked to place his hands on a plow to 38 symbolize the choice to "live the life of the white man—and the white man lives by work." Then he was given a purse: "(White name.) I give you a purse. This purse will always say to you that the money you gain from your labor must be wisely kept." Then an American flag was placed in his hands and he was told: "This is the only flag you have ever had or ever will have. . . ." The ritual was similar for the female Indian, except that she had placed into her hands a work bag and a purse. In taking these items she had "chosen the life of the white woman—and the white woman loves her home."[33] A ritualistic effort requiring one to deny one's identity, to give up one's control over his or her self, could hardly have been more complete.

While the state and church as institutions have defined the Indian into subjugation, there has been in operation the use of a suppressive language by society at large which has perpetuated the dehumanization of the Indian. Commonly used words and phrases relegate the Indian to an inferior, infantile status: "The only good Indian is a dead Indian"; "Give it back to the Indians"; "drunken Indians"; "dumb Indians"; "Redskins"; "Indian giver." Writings and speeches include references to the "Indian problem" in the same manner that references have been made by whites to "the Negro problem" and by the Nazis to "the Jewish problem." There was no "Jewish problem" in Germany until the Nazis linguistically created the myth; there was no "Negro problem" until white Americans created the myth; similarly, the "Indian problem" has been created in such a way that the oppressed, not the oppressor, evolve as "the problem." 39

As the list of negative "racial characteristics" of the "Indian race" grew over the years, the redefinition of the individual Indian became easier and easier. He or she was trapped by the racial definitions, stereotypes, and myths. No matter how intelligent, how "civilized" the Indian became, he or she was still an Indian. Even the one who managed to become a citizen (prior to 1924) could not discard his or her 'Indian-ness' sufficiently to participate fully in white society. The law's language was used to reinforce the redefinition of the oppressed into nonpersons and this language of suppression, as law, became governmentally institutionalized, and in effect legitimatized. In 1831, the United States Supreme Court defined the Indians "in a state of pupilage. Their relation to the United States resembles that of a ward to his guardian."[34] 40

In 1832 the Alabama Supreme Court labeled the Indians "beasts," "savages," and "wildmen," definitions which in turn were used to "prove" that the Indians were not entitled to "rank in the family of independent nations," that the Indians' lands could be ap- 41 propriated by the whites since "the right of the agriculturists was paramount to that of the hunter tribes."[35]

Alabama's high court asked: "Were the natives of this vast continent, at the period of the advent of the first Europeans, in the possession and enjoyment of those attributes of sovereignty, to entitle them to rank in the family of independent governments?"[36] The court answered its question by declaring in part: "The fairest quarter of the globe is roamed over by the wildman, who has no permanent abiding place, but moves from camp to camp, as the pursuit of game may lead him. He knows not the value of any of the comforts of civilized life. As well might a treaty, on terms of equality, be attempted with the beast of the same forest that he inhabits."[37]

In 1857, at the same time he was denying human rights to the black slaves in the United States, Chief Justice Taney of the United States Supreme Court declared in his *Dred Scott* opinion: "Congress might . . . have authorized the naturalization of Indians, because they were aliens and foreigners. But, in their then untutored and savage state, no one would have thought of admitting them as citizens in a civilized community. . . . No one supposed then that any Indian would ask for, or was capable of enjoying, the privileges of an American citizen, and the word white was not used with any particular reference to them."[38]

One of the most blatant examples of the use of the racial characteristic argument is evident in an 1897 Minnesota Supreme Court decision dealing with the indictment of one Edward Wise for selling intoxicating liquors to an Indian who had severed all his relations with his tribe and had through the provision of the "Land in Severality Act" of February 8, 1887, become a citizen of the United States. Wise was indicted for violating a statute which provided that "whosoever sells . . . any spiritous liquors or wines to any Indian in this state shall on conviction thereof be punished. . . ."

In finding against Wise, the Minnesota Supreme Court emphasized the weakness of the "Indian race" and the fact that as a race Indians were not as "civilized" as the whites: ". . . in view of the nature and manifest purpose of this statute and the well-known conditions which induce its enactment, there is no warrant for limiting it by excluding from its operation sales of intoxicating liquors to any person of Indian blood, even although he may have become a citizen of the United States, by compliance with the act of congress. The statute is a police regulation. It was enacted in view of the well-known social condition, habits, and tendencies of Indians as a race. While there are doubtless notable individual exceptions to the rule, yet it is a well-known fact that Indians as a race are not as highly civilized as the whites; that they are less subject to moral restraint, more liable to acquire an inordinate appetite for intoxicating liquors, and also more liable to be dangerous to themselves and others when intoxicated."[39]

The Minnesota statute, said the court, applied to and included 46 "all Indians as a race, without reference to their political status. . . . The difference in condition between Indians as a race and the white race constituted a sufficient basis of classification."[40] Under the court's reasoning, the individual Indian could not control his or her identity. Like it or not, the individual Indian was defined by the court's language, by the "well-known fact" that "Indians as a race are not as highly civilized as whites," that Indians are "less subject to moral restraint." Like it or not, the individual Indian was identified in terms of "characteristics" of the "Indians as a race," whether he or she had those characteristics or not, whether he or she was a citizen of the United States or not.

Twenty years later Minnesota denied voting rights to Indians on 47 the basis of their not being "civilized." In *In re Liquor Election in Beltrami County*,[41] the state's Supreme Court, denying voting rights to the Minnesota Indians involved in that 1917 case, noted their "uncivilized" status. The court's language was in keeping with the spirit of the Minnesota Constitution which stipulated that every male person of the age of twenty-one years and older belonging to one of the following three classes was entitled to vote if he had resided in the state and election district the specified time: (1) citizens of the United States who have been such for a period of three months next preceding any election; (2) persons of mixed Indian blood, who have adopted customs and habits of civilization; (3) persons of Indian blood who have adopted the language, customs, and habits of civilization.

The inhumanity of the racist language in *In re Liquor Election in* 48 *Beltrami County* was complemented by the sexism in the decision: "It is true that a mixed-blood Indian is a citizen if his father was. . . . And no doubt more mixed bloods spring from a white father and an Indian or mixed-blood mother than from a white mother and an Indian or mixed-blood father. But it is also probably true that very many of the mixed bloods of a white father are not the issue of lawful wedlock. An illegitimate child takes the status of the mother. . . . It is also well known that many of the white men who assumed relations with Indian women were not citizens. The citizenship of mixed and full bloods residing upon this reservation seems to us so extremely doubtful that we think contestant made a prima facie case of non-citizenship as to all of the sixty-eight who voted. . . ."[42]

Minnesota's Supreme Court then turned its attention to whether 49 the Indians in question were qualified to vote under the second provision cited above. It decided that the mixed-bloods did not fall into the second category: "It is not to be denied that these mixed-bloods have adopted the habits and customs of civilization to a certain extent. With the assistance of the federal government and the schools maintained by it these Indians have advanced considerable on the road to civilization. They, however, still cling to some of the customs and habits of their race, and are governed in their relation with each other by their peculiar tribal rules and practices."[43]

Asserting that the framers of the Constitution did not intend to grant the right of suffrage to persons who were under no obligation to obey the laws enacted as a result of such grant, the court said: "No one should participate in the making of laws which he need not obey. As truly said by contestant: 'The tribal Indian contributes nothing to the state. His property is not subject to taxation, or to the process of its courts. He bears none of the burdens of civilization and performs none of the duties of the citizens."[44] The court concluded by stating that the right of suffrage in Minnesota was "held out as an inducement to the Indians to sever their tribal relations and adopt in all respects the habits and customs of civilization."[45]

How was an Indian to demonstrate that he or she had taken on "the habits and customs of civilization"? How was a person of mixed blood to demonstrate that he or she was living "a civilized life"? In a case involving the segregated schools in Sitka, Alaska, the court dealt with a statute which said in part: "That the schools specified and provided for in this act shall be devoted to the education of white children and children of mixed blood who lead a civilized life. The education of the Eskimos and Indians in the district of Alaska shall remain under the direction and control of the Secretary of the Interior. . . ." The court explained, "a clear distinction is here made between the school for the native—i.e., the Eskimo and the Indian, whether civilized or otherwise—and the school for the white child, or the child with the white man's blood in its veins, though it be mixed with that of another race. But of the child of mixed blood there is made the further requirement, to wit, that he shall live in a civilized life."[46]

In deciding that two of the children, ages seven and eight, had been legitimately prohibited from attending the whites' school, the court pointed to the "fact" that the children came from a family which was not "civilized": "Walton [stepfather of the youths] owns a house in the native village, lying on the outskirts of the town of Sitka. The children live there with their mother and stepfather. Their associates and playmates are presumably the native children who live in the Indian village. So far as these plaintiffs are concerned, there is nothing to indicate any difference between them and the other children of the Sitka native village, except the testimony of Walton and others as to Walton's business. Walton conducts a store on the edge of the town of Sitka, in which he manufactures and sells Indian curios, and for which he pays the business license tax by the laws of Alaska. . . . He and his family have adopted the white man's style of dress. All who testified concerning Walton himself speak of him as an industrious, law-abiding, intelligent native. He seems, so far as business matters are concerned, to have endeavored to conduct his business according to civilized methods, even to the installation of an expensive cash register in his store. He speaks, reads, and writes the English language."[47]

But conducting business, manufacturing curios, paying the busi-   53 ness license tax, adopting the whites' style of dress, being industrious, law-abiding, and intelligent "native," speaking, reading and writing English—characteristics and qualities many whites themselves did not possess—were not enough to make the Walton family "civilized."

The court went on to ask: "What is the manner of their life?   54 What are their domestic habits? Who are their associates and intimates? These matters do not appear. True, the Waltons are members of the Presbyterian Church; but many natives, for whom the claim of civilization would not be made, are members of churches of the various denominations which are striving to better the conditions of this country. . . . The burden of establishing that the plaintiffs live the civilized life is upon them, and I fail to find in the testimony evidence of a condition that inclines me to the opinion that the . . . children have that requisite."[48] Having thus defined the "native" family and children the court justified the segregation of the children and ordered them out of the whites' school.

In determining the "civilized" status of another family whose   55 child was also prohibited from attending the white school the court took into consideration the following:

"It appears that his [plaintiff's] wife is a good housekeeper, so   56 far as their means, and station in life will allow her to be; that the pots and kettles and frying pans are not left upon the floor, after the native fashion, but are hung up, and that curtains drape the windows of their house. This indicates progress; but does it satisfy the test? It is urged that Allard and his wife have been entertained by white men of culture and refinement; but that cannot be considered as a criterion of civilization . . . it is an evidence of the kindliness and of the interest and effort of the hosts in behalf of a people among and for whom they have labored long and assiduously, not an evidence of the civilization of the guests. . . . Those who from choice make their homes among an uncivilized or semi-civilized peo-

ple and find there their sole social enjoyments and personal pleasures and associations cannot, in my opinion, be classed with those
who live a civilized life."[49] As in the Walton case, the court found
the Allard children and family "uncivilized" and denied the children
access to the Sitka school established for "the education of white
children and children of mixed blood who lead a civilized life."

In 1944 five states prohibited intermarriages between Indians
and whites: Arizona, Nevada, North Carolina, South Carolina, and
Virginia. The Supreme Court of Arizona upheld a lower court holding that the marriage between a descendant of an Indian and a
member of the Caucasian race was illegal and void. Arizona's miscegenation statute read: "The marriage of persons of Caucasian blood,
or their descendants, with Negroes, Hindus, Mongolians, members
of the Malay race, or Indians, and their descendants, shall be null
and void." In describing the two persons involved in the marriage
considered in *State v. Pass,* the court stated:

"The evidence is undisputed that defendant's mother was the
child of an English father and Piute Indian woman and that his father was a Mexican, so he was a descendant of three races, to wit,
Caucasian, Indian and Mexican.

"Ruby Contreras Pass testified that her father was a Spaniard
and her mother half-French and half-Mexican. And to the question,
'Do you have any Indian blood in you?' she answered, 'Not that I
know of.' Thus she is a descendant of two races, to wit, Spanish and
French."[50]

The absurdity of Arizona's miscegenation statute was not
missed by the court even though it held the statute constitutional:
"It makes a marriage of a person of Caucasian blood and his descendants to one of Indian blood and his descendants null and void. Under it a descendant of mixed blood such as defendant cannot marry
a Caucasian or a part Caucasian, for the reason that he is part Indian. He cannot marry an Indian or a part Indian because he is part
Caucasian. For the same reason a descendant of mixed Negro and
Caucasian blood may not contract marriage with a Negro or a part
Negro, etc. We think the language used by the lawmakers went far
beyond what was intended. In trying to prevent the white race from
interbreeding with Indians, Negroes, Mongolians, etc., it has made
it unlawful for a person with 99% Indian blood and 1% Caucasian
blood to marry an Indian, or a person with 99% Caucasian blood
and 1% Indian blood to marry a Caucasian. We mention this and the
absurd situations it creates believing and hoping that the legislature
will correct it by naming the percentage of Indian and other tabooed
blood that will invalidate a marriage. The miscegenation statutes of
the different states do fix the degree or percentage of blood in a Ne-

gro, an Indian, etc. preventing marriage alliances with Caucasians."[51]

In 1944, two years after the above Arizona Supreme Court decision, the Circuit Court of Appeals, Tenth Circuit, decided in Oklahoma that the marriage of Stella Sands, "a full-blooded Creek Indian," to William Stevens who was of African descent was a "nullity" since under Oklahoma law as "a full-blooded Creek Indian" she was classified as white, and Oklahoma law prohibited marriages between whites and persons of African descent. In deciding the marriage a "nullity," the Circuit Court cited Article XXIII, Section 11, of the Oklahoma Constitution which provided that "where-ever in the constitution and laws of the state the word or words 'colored' or 'colored race,' 'negro' or 'negro race,' are used it or they shall be construed to mean and apply to all persons of African descent, and that the term 'white race' shall include all other persons."[52] The effect of the inconsistencies of white legislators and judges was that a person was defined "white" in one state and not "white" in another.   61

Arizona, the state with the largest Indian population, until 1948 did not allow Indians the right to vote. Article 7 of the state's Constitution concerning the qualifications of voters placed the Indians in the same category as traitors and felons, the same category as persons not of sound mind and the insane. Article 7 provided in part: "No person under guardianship, *non compos mentis* or insane shall be qualified to vote in any election or shall any person convicted of treason or felony, be qualified to vote at any election unless restored to civil rights."   62

In 1928 the Arizona Supreme Court decided in *Porter v. Hall*[53] that Arizona Indians did not have the right to vote since they were within the specific provisions of Article 7 denying suffrage to "persons under guardianship." The court held that "so long as the federal government insists that, notwithstanding their citizenship, their responsibility under our law differs from that of the ordinary citizen, and that they are, or may be, regulated by that government, by virtue of its guardianship, in any manner different from that which may be used in the regulation of white citizens, they are, within the meaning of our constitutional provision, 'persons under guardianship,' and not entitled to vote."[54]   63

In defining the Indians of Arizona as it did in *Porter v. Hall*, the Arizona Supreme Court denied suffrage rights to the Indians even though four years earlier, on June 2, 1924, all non-citizen Indians born within the territorial limits of the United States were declared citizens thereof by an Act of Congress. After devoting a paragraph to defining "insanity" and *"non compos mentis,"* the court followed   64 with a definition and discussion of "persons under guardianship," the category into which the Indians were placed:

"Broadly speaking, persons under guardianship may be defined 65 as those, who, because of some peculiarity of status, defect of age, understanding, or self-control, are considered incapable of managing their own affairs, and who therefore have some other person lawfully invested with the power and charged with the duty of taking care of their persons or managing their property, or both. It will be seen from the foregoing definitions that there is one common quality found in each: The person falling within any one of the classes is to some extent and for some reason considered by the law as incapable of managing his own affairs as a normal person, and needing some special care from the state."[55]

In 1948, however, the *Porter* decision was overruled in the case 66 of *Harrison v. Laveen*,[56] thus allowing Indians in Arizona the right to vote. In the 1948 decision, the Supreme Court of Arizona stated that the designation of "persons under guardianship" as it appeared in Article 7 did not apply to Indians. As to the argument that the Indians generally fell into that group of people "incapable of managing their own affairs," the court said in 1948 that "to ascribe to all Indians residing on reservations the quality of being 'incapable of handling their own affairs in an ordinary manner' would be a grave injustice, for amongst them are educated persons as fully capable of handling their affairs as their white neighbors."[57]

At long last, four-and-a-half centuries after Columbus 67 "discovered" America, almost all the descendants of the original occupants of this land were allowed by the descendants of the invaders to participate through the vote, in affecting some control (however small) over their destiny in their own land. Almost all of the "red natives" of the land finally were recognized legally as beings as fully capable of handling their affairs as "their white neighbors." Almost all.

As late as the middle of the 1950s Indians were still battling for 68 the right to vote. In 1956, the Utah Supreme Court, in *Allen v. Merrell*,[58] denied the vote to reservation Indians in Utah, arguing, among other things, that low literacy and lack of civic involvement and responsibilities were Indian characteristics which disqualified them from having voting rights in Utah. The Utah court listed the Indians' "deficiencies":

"It is not subject to dispute that Indians living on reservations 69 are extremely limited in their contact with state government and its units and for this reason also, have much less interest in or concern with it than do other citizens. It is a matter of common knowledge that all except a minimal percentage of reservation Indians live, not in communities, but in individual dwellings or hogans remotely isolated from others and from contact with the outside world. Though such a state is certainly not without its favorable aspects, they have practically no access to newspapers, telephones, radio or television; a very high percentage of them are illiterate; and they do not speak English but in their dealings with others and even in their tribal courts, use only their native Indian languages."[59]

But how to reconcile the fact that Utah had no literacy requirement for voters with the argument that, since the Indians were illiterate they could not be allowed to vote? The Utah Supreme Court added the following footnote to its "observation" about the high percentage of the Indians being illiterate: "Utah has no literacy requirement. This observation relates only to their present general character of life."[60] After pointing out the Indians' lack of civic involvement, the court stated that "it is thus plain to be seen that in a county where the Indian population would amount to a substantial proportion of the citizenry, or may even outnumber the other inhabitants, allowing them to vote might place substantial control of the county government and expenditures of its funds in a group of citizens who, as a class, had extremely limited interest in its function and very little responsibility in providing the financial support thereof."[61] In effect the same legal system which made it virtually impossible for Indians to practice "civic involvement" ruled that Indians could not vote because of their lack of "civic involvement." The same system which kept the Indians isolated ruled that Indians could not vote because they lived in communities and dwellings "isolated from others and from contact with the outside world."

The definitions and stereotypes of the Indians developed over the past three centuries found their way into the history books. The linguistic dehumanization of Indians in history texts and the effects of these portrayals on Indian children have been noted by Alvin Josephy, Jr., Mary Gloyne Byler and others.

Josephy, observing that "many historians termed them [Indians] dirty, lazy, brutish, unproductive, and on the level with wild beasts,"[62] has called attention to the effects of such definitions: "There are now some 750,000 Indians and Eskimos in the United States, and many of their children are attending schools and colleges where they are subjected to the use of insulting books. Their high dropout rates, self-hatred, a suicide rate far in excess of the national average, and their lack of motivation can be traced in great part to the feelings of disgrace and humiliation they suffer from their continual confrontation with stereotype thinking about them."[63]

In her study of the image of American Indians projected by non-Indian writers, Mary Gloyne Byler observes that "it has been well established by sociologists and psychologists that the effect on children of negative stereotypes and derogatory images is to engender and perpetuate undemocratic and unhealthy attitudes that will plague our society for years to come."[64]

Once one has been categorized through the language of oppression, one loses most of the power to determine one's future and control over one's identity and destiny. As a writer observes in *Our Brother's Keeper: The Indian in White America*, "ultimately, self-realization requires the power to shape one's future, to control one's destiny, to choose from a variety of alternatives. The Indian has no such power, no control and no choice."[65] Once the Indians had been successfully defined by the Europeans and their descendants as "heathens," "beasts," "savages," "barbarians," "wildmen," "uncivilized," "in a state of pupilage," their power to define themselves and their destinies passed from their own hands to the hands of their oppressors.

References

1. Cited in Jack Forbes (ed.), *The Indian in America's Past* (Englewood Cliffs, New Jersey: Prentice-Hall, 1964), p. 19.
2. *Ibid.*
3. *United States v. Lucero*, 1 N.M. 422 (1869).
4. Peter Farb, "Indian Corn," *New York Review*, 17 (December 16, 1971), p. 36.
5. Alvin M. Josephy, Jr., *The Indian Heritage of America* (New York: Bantam Books, 1969), p. 286.
6. Peter Farb, *Man's Rise to Civilization as Shown by the Indians of North America from Primeval Times to the Coming of the Industrial State* (New York: E. P. Dutton and Company, 1968) p. xx.
7. Josephy, p. 4.
8. Roy H. Pearce, *The Savages of America* (Baltimore: The Johns Hopkins Press, 1965), p. 21.
9. *Ibid.*, pp. 21–22.
10. Farb, *Man's Rise to Civilization*, p. 247.
11. Louis L. Knowles and Kenneth Prewitt, (eds.), *Institutional Racism in America* (Englewood Cliffs, New Jersey: Prentice-Hall, 1969), p. 7.
12. *Ibid.*
13. Arnold Toynbee, *A Study of History* (London: Oxford University Press, 1935), I, p. 152. For further discussion of the connotation of "natives," see Volume II of *A Study of History*, pp. 574–580.
14. Josephy, p. 107.
15. *Ibid.*, p. 108.
16. Farb, *Man's Rise to Civilization*, p. 253.
17. U. S., *Congressional Globe*, 29th Cong., 1st Sess., 1846, 15, p. 918.
18. U. S., *Congressional Globe*, 40th Cong., 1st Sess., 1867, 38, p. 684.
19. *Ibid.*
20. *Ibid.*, p. 685.
21. *Ibid.*, p. 686.
22. *Ibid.*, p. 712.
23. *Elk v. Wilkins*, 112 U. S. 94 (1884).
24. *Ibid.*, p. 102.
25. *Ibid.*, p. 109.
26. Estelle Reel, *Course of Study for the Indian Schools* (Washington, D. C.: Government Printing Office, 1901), p. 6.

27. *Ibid.*, p. 145.

28. *Ibid.*, p. 146.

29. *Ibid.*, p. 109.

30. *Ibid.*, p. 111.

31. Vine Deloria, Jr., *Custer Died for Your Sins: An Indian Manifesto* (New York: Avon Books, 1970), p. 10.

32. Vine Deloria, Jr. (ed.), *Of Utmost Good Faith* (San Francisco: Straight Arrow Books, 1971), p. 93.

33. *Ibid.*

34. *The Cherokee Nation v. The State of Georgia*, 30 U. S. 1, 16 (1831).

35. *Caldwell v. State of Alabama*, 1 Stew. & Potter (Ala.) 327, 335 (1832).

36. *Ibid.*, p. 333.

37. *Ibid.*, p. 334.

38. *Dred Scott v. Sanford*, 61 U. S. 1, 23 (1857).

39. *State v. Wise*, 72 N.W. 843, 844 (1897).

40. *Ibid.*, p. 844.

41. *In re Liquor Election in Beltrami County*, 163 N.W. 988 (1917).

42. *Ibid.*, p. 989.

43. *Ibid.*

44. *Ibid.*

45. *Ibid.*, p. 990.

46. *Davis v. Sitka School Board*, 3 Alaska 481, 484 (1908).

47. *Ibid.*, pp. 490–491.

48. *Ibid.*, p. 491.

49. *Ibid.*, p. 494.

50. *State v. Pass*, 121 p. 2d 882 (1942).

51. *Ibid.*, p. 884.

52. *Stevens v. United States*, 146 F. 2d 120, 123 (1944).

53. *Porter v. Hall*, 271 p. 411 (1928).

54. *Ibid.*, p. 419.

55. *Ibid.*, p. 416.

56. *Harrison v. Laveen*, 196 p. 2d 456 (1948).

57. *Ibid.*, p. 463.

58. *Allen v. Merrell*, 305 p. 2d 490 (1956).

59. *Ibid.*, p. 494.

60. *Ibid.*

61. *Ibid.*, p. 495.

62. Alvin M. Josephy, Jr., "Indians in History," *Atlantic Monthly*, 225 (June 1970), p. 68.

63. *Ibid.*, p. 71.

64. Mary Gloyne Byler, "The Image of American Indians Projected by Non-Indian Writers," *Library Journal*, 99 (February 15, 1974), p. 549.

65. Edgar S. Cahn (ed.), *Our Brother's Keeper: The Indian in White America* (Washington, D. C.: New Community Press, 1969), p. 123.

The Language of Discretion

AMY TAN

At a recent family dinner in San Francisco, my mother whispered to 1
me: "Sau-sau [Brother's Wife] pretends too hard to be polite! Why
bother? In the end, she always takes everything."

My mother thinks like a *waixiao*, an expatriate, temporarily away 2
from China since 1949, no longer patient with ritual courtesies. As if
to prove her point, she reached across the table to offer my elderly
aunt from Beijing the last scallop from the Happy Family seafood
dish.

Sau-sau scowled. *"B'yao, zhen b'yao!"* (I don't want it, really I 3
don't!) she cried, patting her plump stomach.

"Take it! Take it!" scolded my mother in Chinese. 4

"Full, I'm already full," Sau-sau protested weakly, eyeing the 5
beloved scallop.

"Ai!" exclaimed my mother, completely exasperated. "Nobody 6
else wants it. If you don't take it, it will only rot!"

At this point, Sau-sau sighed, acting as if she were doing my 7
mother a big favor by taking the wretched scrap off her hands.

My mother turned to her brother, a high-ranking communist 8
official who was visiting her in California for the first time: "In
America a Chinese person could starve to death. If you say you
don't want it, they won't ask you again forever."

My uncle nodded and said he understood fully: Americans take 9
things quickly because they have no time to be polite.

I thought about this misunderstanding again—of social contexts fail- 10
ing in translation—when a friend sent me an article from the *New
York Times Magazine* (24 April 1988). The article, on changes in New
York's Chinatown, made passing reference to the inherent ambivalence of the Chinese language.

Chinese people are so "discreet and modest," the article stated, 11
there aren't even words for "yes" and "no."

That's not true, I thought, although I can see why an outsider 12
might think that. I continued reading.

Amy Tan (1952–   ), from San Francisco, is the author of the
novels *The Joy Luck Club* (1989) and *The Kitchen God's Wife*. "The
Language of Discretion" is from *The State of the Language*, edited by
Christopher Ricks and Leonard Michaels (1990).

If one is Chinese, the article went on to say, "One compromises, 13 one doesn't hazard a loss of face by an overemphatic response."

My throat seized. Why do people keep saying these things? As 14 if we truly were those little dolls sold in Chinatown tourist shops, heads bobbing up and down in complacent agreement to anything said!

I worry about the effect of one-dimensional statements on the 15 unwary and guileless. When they read about this so-called vocabulary deficit, do they also conclude that Chinese people evolved into a mild-mannered lot because the language only allowed them to hobble forth with minced words?

Something enormous is always lost in translation. Something insidious seeps into the gaps, especially when amateur linguists continue to compare, one-for-one, language differences and then put forth notions wide open to misinterpretation: that Chinese people have no direct linguistic means to make decisions, assert or deny, affirm or negate, just say no to drug dealers, or behave properly on the witness stand when told, "Please answer yes or no."

Yet one can argue, with the help of renowned linguists, that the 17 Chinese are indeed up a creek without "yes" and "no." Take any number of variations on the old language-and-reality theory stated years ago by Edward Sapir: "Human beings . . . are very much at the mercy of the particular language which has become the medium for their society. . . . The fact of the matter is that the 'real world' is to a large extent built up on the language habits of the group."[1]

This notion was further bolstered by the famous Sapir-Whorf 18 hypothesis, which roughly states that one's perception of the world and how one functions in it depends a great deal on the language used. As Sapir, Whorf, and new carriers of the banner would have us believe, language shapes our thinking, channels us along certain patterns embedded in words, syntactic structures, and intonation patterns. Language has become the peg and the shelf that enables us to sort out and categorize the world. In English, we see "cats" and "dogs"; what if the language had also specified *glatz*, meaning "animals that leave fur on the sofa," and *glotz*, meaning "animals that leave fur and drool on the sofa"? How would language, the enabler, have changed our perceptions with slight vocabulary variations?

And if this were the case—of language being the master of destined thought—think of the opportunities lost from failure to evolve 19 two little words, *yes* and *no*, the simplest of opposites! Ghenghis

---

[1] Edward Sapir, *Selected Writings*, ed. D. G. Mandelbaum (Berkeley and Los Angeles, 1949).

Khan could have been sent back to Mongolia. Opium wars might have been averted. The Cultural Revolution could have been sidestepped.

There are still many, from serious linguists to pop psychology 20 cultists, who view language and reality as inextricably tied, one being the consequence of the other. We have traversed the range from the Sapir-Whorf hypothesis to est and neurolinguistic programming, which tell us "you are what you say."

I too have been intrigued by the theories. I can summarize, al- 21 beit badly, ages-old empirical evidence: of Eskimos and their infinite ways to say "snow," their ability to *see* the differences in snowflake configurations, thanks to the richness of their vocabulary, while non-Eskimo speakers like myself founder in "snow," "more snow," and "lots more where that came from."

I too have experienced dramatic cognitive awakenings via the 22 word. Once I added "mauve" to my vocabulary I began to see it everywhere. When I learned how to pronounce *prix fixe,* I ate French food at prices better than the easier-to-say *à la carte* choices.

But just how seriously are we supposed to take this? 23

Sapir said something else about language and reality. It is the 24 part that often gets left behind in the dot-dot-dots of quotes: ". . . No two languages are ever sufficiently similar to be considered as representing the same social reality. The worlds in which different societies live are distinct worlds, not merely the same world with different labels attached."

When I first read this, I thought, Here at last is validity for the 25 dilemmas I felt growing up in a bicultural, bilingual family! As any child of immigrant parents knows, there's a special kind of double bind attached to knowing two languages. My parents, for example, spoke to me in both Chinese and English; I spoke back to them in English.

"Amy-ah!" they'd call to me. 26

"What?" I'd mumble back. 27

"Do not question us when we call," they scolded me in Chinese. 28 "It is not respectful."

"What do you mean?" 29

"Ai! Didn't we just tell you not to question?" 30

To this day, I wonder which parts of my behavior were shaped 31 by Chinese, which by English. I am tempted to think, for example, that if I am of two minds on some matter it is due to the richness of my linguistic experiences, not to any personal tendencies toward wishy-washiness. But which mind says what?

Was it perhaps patience—developed through years of decipher- 32 ing my mother's fractured English—that had me listening politely while a woman announced over the phone that I had won one of five valuable prizes? Was it respect—pounded in by the Chinese imperative to accept convoluted explanations—that had me agreeing that I might find it worthwhile to drive seventy-five miles to view a time-share resort? Could I have been at a loss for words when asked, "Wouldn't you like to win a Hawaiian cruise or perhaps a fabulous Star of India designed exclusively by Carter and Van Arpels?"

And when this same woman called back a week later, this time 33 complaining that I had missed my appointment, obviously it was my type A language that kicked into gear and interrupted her. Certainly, my blunt denial—"Frankly I'm not interested"—was as American as apple pie. And when she said, "But it's in Morgan Hill," and I shouted, "Read my lips. I don't care if it's Timbuktu," you can be sure I said it with the precise intonation expressing both cynicism and disgust.

It's dangerous business, this sorting out of language and behav- 34 ior. Which one is English? Which is Chinese? The categories manifest themselves: passive and aggressive, tentative and assertive, indirect and direct. And I realize they are just variations of the same theme: that Chinese people are discreet and modest.

Reject them all! 35

If my reaction is overly strident, it is because I cannot come 36 across as too emphatic. I grew up listening to the same lines over and over again, like so many rote expressions repeated in an English phrasebook. And I too almost came to believe them.

Yet if I consider my upbringing more carefully, I find there was 37 nothing discreet about the Chinese language I grew up with. My parents made everything abundantly clear. Nothing wishy-washy in their demands, no compromises accepted: "Of course you will become a famous neurosurgeon," they told me. "And yes, a concert pianist on the side."

In fact, now that I remember, it seems that the more emphatic 38 outbursts always spilled over into Chinese: "Not that way! You must wash rice so not a single grain spills out."

I do not believe that my parents—both immigrants from main- 39 land China—are an exception to the modest-and-discreet rule. I have only to look at the number of Chinese engineering students skewing minority ratios at Berkeley, MIT, and Yale. Certainly they were not raised by passive mothers and fathers who said, "It is up to you, my daughter. Writer, welfare recipient, masseuse, or molecular engineer—you decide."

And my American mind says, See, those engineering students 40 weren't able to say no to their parents' demands. But then my Chinese mind remembers: Ah, but those parents all wanted their sons and daughters to be *pre-med*.

Having listened to both Chinese and English, I also tend to be   41 suspicious of any comparisons between the two languages. Typically, one language—that of the person doing the comparing—is often used as the standard, the benchmark for a logical form of expression. And so the language being compared is always in danger of being judged deficient or superfluous, simplistic or unnecessarily complex, melodious or cacophonous. English speakers point out that Chinese is extremely difficult because it relies on variations in tone barely discernible to the human ear. By the same token, Chinese speakers tell me English is extremely difficult because it is inconsistent, a language of too many broken rules, of Mickey Mice and Donald Ducks.

Even more dangerous to my mind is the temptation to compare   42 both language and behavior *in translation*. To listen to my mother speak English, one might think she has no concept of past or future tense, that she doesn't see the difference between singular and plural, that she is gender blind because she calls my husband "she." If one were not careful, one might also generalize that, based on the way my mother talks, all Chinese people take a circumlocutory route to get to the point. It is, in fact, my mother's idiosyncratic behavior to ramble a bit.

Sapir was right about differences between two languages and their   43 realities. I can illustrate why word-for-word translation is not enough to translate meaning and intent. I once received a letter from China which I read to non-Chinese speaking friends. The letter, originally written in Chinese, had been translated by my brother-in-law in Beijing. One portion described the time when my uncle at age ten discovered his widowed mother (my grandmother) had remarried—as a number three concubine, the ultimate disgrace for an honorable family. The translated version of my uncle's letter read in part:

> In 1925, I met my mother in Shanghai. When she came to me, I didn't have greeting to her as if seeing nothing. She pull me to a corner secretly and asked me why didn't have greeting to her. I couldn't control myself and cried, "Ma! Why did you leave us? People told me: one day you ate a beancake yourself. Your sister-in-law found it and sweared at you, called your names. So . . . is it true?" She clasped my hand and answered immediately, "It's not true, don't say what like this." After this time, there was a few chance to meet her.

"What!" cried my friends. "Was eating a beancake so terrible?"   44

Of course not. The beancake was simply a euphemism; a ten-   45
year-old boy did not dare question his mother on something as
shocking as concubinage. Eating a beancake was his equivalent for
committing this selfish act, something inconsiderate of all family
members, hence, my grandmother's despairing response to what
seemed like a ludicrous charge of gluttony. And sure enough, she
was banished from the family, and my uncle saw her only a few
times before her death.

While the above may fuel people's argument that Chinese is in-   46
deed a language of extreme discretion, it does not mean that Chinese people speak in secrets and riddles. The contexts are fully understood. It is only to those on the *outside* that the language seems
cryptic, the behavior inscrutable.

I am, evidently, one of the outsiders. My nephew in Shanghai,   47
who recently started taking English lessons, has been writing me letters in English. I had told him I was a fiction writer, and so in one
letter he wrote, "Congratulate to you on your writing. Perhaps one
day I should like to read it." I took it in the same vein as "Perhaps
one day we can get together for lunch." I sent back a cheery note. A
month went by and another letter arrived from Shanghai. "Last one
perhaps I hadn't writing distinctly," he said. "In the future, you'll
send a copy of your works for me."

I try to explain to my English-speaking friends that Chinese lan-   48
guage use is more *strategic* in manner, whereas English tends to be
more direct; an American business executive may say, "Let's make a
deal," and the Chinese manager may reply, "Is your son interested
in learning about your widget business?" Each to his or her own
purpose, each with his or her own linguistic path. But I hesitate to
add more to the pile of generalizations, because no matter how
many examples I provide and explain, I fear that it appears defensive and only reinforces the image: that Chinese people are "discreet
and modest"—and it takes an American to explain what they really
mean.

Why am I complaining? The description seems harmless enough (af-   49
ter all, the *New York Times Magazine* writer did not say "slippery and
evasive"). It is precisely the bland, easy acceptability of the phrase
that worries me.

I worry that the dominant society may see Chinese people from   50
a limited—and limiting—perspective. I worry that seemingly benign
stereotypes may be part of the reason there are few Chinese in top
management positions, in mainstream political roles. I worry about

the power of language: that if one says anything enough times—in *any* language—it might become true.

Could this be why Chinese friends of my parents' generation are   51
willing to accept the generalization?

"Why are you complaining?" one of them said to me. "If people   52
think we are modest and polite, let them think that. Wouldn't
Americans be pleased to admit they are thought of as polite?"

And I do believe anyone would take the description as a compli-   53
ment—at first. But after a while, it annoys, as if the only things that
people heard one say were phatic remarks: "I'm so pleased to meet
you. I've heard many wonderful things about you. For me? You
shouldn't have!"

These remarks are not representative of new ideas, honest emo-   54
tions, or considered thought. They are what is said from the polite
distance of social contexts: of greetings, farewells, wedding thank-
you notes, convenient excuses, and the like.

It makes me wonder though. How many anthropologists, how   55
many sociologists, how many travel journalists have documented
so-called "natural interactions" in foreign lands, all observed with
spiral notebook in hand? How many other cases are there of the
long-lost primitive tribe, people who turned out to be sophisticated
enough to put on the stone-age show that ethnologists had come to
see?

And how many tourists fresh off the bus have wandered into   56
Chinatown expecting the self-effacing shopkeeper to admit under
duress that the goods are not worth the price asked? I have witnessed it.

"I don't know," the tourist said to the shopkeeper, a Cantonese   57
woman in her fifties. "It doesn't look genuine to me. I'll give you
three dollars."

"You don't like my price, go somewhere else," said the shop-   58
keeper.

"You are not a nice person," cried the shocked tourist, "not a   59
nice person at all!"

"Who say I have to be nice," snapped the shopkeeper.   60

"So how does one say 'yes' and 'no' in Chinese?" ask my friends a   61
bit warily.

And here I do agree in part with the *New York Times Magazine* ar-   62
ticle. There is no one word for "yes" or "no"—but not out of necessity to be discreet. If anything, I would say the Chinese equivalent
of answering "yes" or "no" is dis*crete,* that is, specific to what is
asked.

Ask a Chinese person if he or she has eaten, and he or she 63
might say *chrle* (eaten already) or perhaps *meiyou* (have not).

Ask, "So you had insurance at the time of the accident?" and the 64
response would be *dwei* (correct) or *meiyou* (did not have).

Ask, "Have you stopped beating your wife?" and the answer 65
refers directly to the proposition being asserted or denied: stopped
already, still have not, never beat, have no wife.

What could be clearer?   66

As for those who are still wondering how to translate the language 67
of discretion, I offer this personal example.

My aunt and uncle were about to return to Beijing after a three- 68
month visit to the United States. On their last night I announced I
wanted to take them out to dinner.

"Are you hungry?" I asked in Chinese.   69

"Not hungry," said my uncle promptly, the same response he 70
once gave me ten minutes before he suffered a low-blood-sugar attack.

"Not too hungry," said my aunt. "Perhaps you're hungry?"   71

"A little," I admitted.   72

"We can eat, we can eat," they both consented.   73

"What kind of food?" I asked.   74

"Oh, doesn't matter. Anything will do. Nothing fancy, just 75
some simple food is fine."

"Do you like Japanese food? We haven't had that yet," I sug- 76
gested.

They looked at each other.   77

"We can eat it," said my uncle bravely, this survivor of the Long 78
March.

"We have eaten it before," added my aunt. "Raw fish."   79

"Oh, you don't like it?" I said. "Don't be polite. We can go 80
somewhere else."

"We are not being polite. We can eat it," my aunt insisted.   81

So I drove them to Japantown and we walked past several 82
restaurants featuring colorful plastic displays of sushi.

"Not this one, not this one either," I continued to say, as if 83
searching for a Japanese restaurant similar to the last. "Here it is," I
finally said, turning into a restaurant famous for its Chinese fish
dishes from Shandong.

"Oh, Chinese food!" cried my aunt, obviously relieved.   84

My uncle patted my arm. "You think Chinese."   85

"It's your last night here in America," I said. "So don't be polite. 86
Act like an American."

And that night we ate a banquet.   87

How to Talk about the World

PETER FARB

If human beings paid attention to all the sights, sounds, and smells   1
that besiege them, their ability to codify and recall information
would be swamped. Instead, they simplify the information by
grouping it into broad verbal categories. For example, human eyes
have the extraordinary power to discriminate some ten million colors, but the English language reduces these to no more than four
thousand color words, of which only eleven basic terms are commonly used. That is why a driver stops at all traffic lights whose
color he categorizes as *red*, even though the lights vary slightly from
one to another in their hues of redness. Categorization allows people to respond to their environment in a way that has great survival
value. If they hear a high-pitched sound, they do not enumerate the
long list of possible causes of such sounds: a human cry of fear, a
scream for help, a policeman's whistle, and so on. Instead they become alert because they have categorized high-pitched sounds as in-
dicators of possible danger.

Words, therefore, are more than simply labels for specific ob-   2
jects; they are also parts of sets of related principles. To a very
young child, the word *chair* may at first refer only to his highchair.
Soon afterward, he learns that the four-legged object on which his
parents sit at mealtimes is also called a *chair*. So is the thing with
only three legs, referred to by his parents as a *broken chair*, and so is
the upholstered piece of furniture in the living room. These objects
form a category, *chair*, which is set apart from all other categories by
a unique combination of features. A *chair* must possess a seat, legs,
and back; it may also, but not necessarily, have arms; it must accommodate only one person. An object that possesses these features
with but a single exception—it accommodates three people—does
not belong to the category *chair* but rather to the category *couch*, and
that category in turn is described by a set of unique features.

Peter Farb (1929–1980), from Amherst, Massachusetts, was the author of *Man's Rise to Civilization as Shown by the Indians of North
America from Primeval Times to the Coming of the Industrial State*
(1968), *Humankind* (1978), and other books about science and social
science. "How to Talk about the World" is from *Word Play: What
Happens When People Talk* (1974).

Furthermore, Americans think of *chairs* and *couches* as being re-   3
lated to each other because they both belong to a category known in
English as *household furniture*. But such a relationship between the
category *chair* and the category *couch* is entirely arbitrary on the part
of English and some other speech communities. Nothing in the external world decrees that a language must place these two categories
together. In some African speech communities, for example, the category *chair* would most likely be thought of in relation to the category *spear*, since both are emblems of a ruler's authority.

The analysis of words by their categories for the purpose of de-   4
termining what they mean to speakers of a particular language—
that is, what the native speaker, and not some visiting linguist, feels
are the distinguishing features or components of that word—is
known as "componential analysis" or "formal semantic analysis."
The aim, in brief, is to determine the components or features that
native speakers use to distinguish similar terms from one another so
that more exact meanings can be achieved.

Anyone who visits an exotic culture quickly learns that the peo-   5
ple are linguistically deaf to categories he considers obvious, yet
they are extraordinarily perceptive in talking about things he has no
easy way to describe. An English-speaking anthropologist studying
the Koyas of India, for example, soon discovers that their language
does not distinguish between dew, fog, and snow. When questioned about these natural phenomena, the Koyas can find a way to
describe them, but normally their language attaches no significance
to making such distinctions and provides no highly codable words
for the purpose. On the other hand, a Koya has the linguistic resources to speak easily about seven different kinds of bamboo—
resources that the visiting anthropologist utterly lacks in his own
language. More important than the significance, or the lack of it,
that a language places on objects and ideas is the way that language
categorizes the information it does find significant. A *pig*, for example, can be categorized in several ways: a mammal with cloven hoofs
and bristly hairs and adapted for digging with its snout; a mold in
which metal is cast; a British sixpence coin. The Koyas categorize the
pig in none of these ways; they simply place it in the category of animals that are edible. Their neighbors, Muslims, think of it in a different way by placing it in the category of defiled animals.

Everyone, whether he realizes it or not, classifies the items he   6
finds in his environment. Most speakers of English recognize a category that they call *livestock*, which is made up of other categories
known as *cattle, horses, sheep,* and *swine* of different ages and sexes.
An English speaker who is knowledgeable about farm life categorizes a barnyardful of these animals in a way that establishes rela-

tionships based on distinguishing features. For example, he feels that a *cow* and a *mare*, even though they belong to different species, are somehow in a relationship to each other. And of course they are, because they both belong to the category of Female Animal under the general category of Livestock. The speaker of English unconsciously groups certain animals into various sub-categories that exclude other animals:

Livestock

	Cattle	**Horses**	**Sheep**	**Swine**
Female	cow	mare	ewe	sow
Intact Male	bull	stallion	ram	boar
Castrated Male	steer	gelding	wether	barrow
Immature	heifer	colt/filly	lamb	shoat/gilt
Newborn	calf	foal	yeanling	piglet

A table such as this shows that speakers of English are intuitively aware of certain contrasts. They regard a *bull* and a *steer* as different—which they are, because one belongs to a category of Intact Males and the other to a category of Castrated Males. In addition to discriminations made on the basis of livestock's sex, speakers of English also contrast mature and immature animals. A *foal* is a newborn horse and a *stallion* is a mature male horse.

The conceptual labels by which English-speaking peoples talk 7 about barnyard animals can now be understood. The animal is defined by the point at which two distinctive features intersect: sex (male, female, or castrated) and maturity (mature, immature, or newborn). A *stallion* belongs to a category of horse that is both intact male and mature; a *filly* belongs to a category of horse that is both female and immature. Nothing in external reality dictates that barnyard animals should be talked about in this way; it is strictly a convention of English and some other languages.

In contrast, imagine that an Amazonian Indian is brought to the 8 United States so that linguists can intensively study his language. When the Indian returns to his native forests, his friends and relatives listen in disbelief as he tells about all the fantastic things he saw. He summarizes his impressions of America in terms of the familiar categories his language has accustomed him to. He relates that at first he was bewildered by the strange animals he saw on an American farm because each animal not only looked different but also seemed to represent a unique concept to the natives of the North American tribe. But after considerable observation of the curious folkways of these peculiar people, at last he understood American barnyard animals. He figured out that some animals are good for work and that some are good for food. Using these two components—rather than the Americans' features of sex and maturity—his classification of livestock is considerably different. He categorized *stallion, mare,* and *gelding* as belonging to both the Inedible and Work (Riding) categories. The *bull* also belonged to the Inedible category but it was used for a different kind of Work as a draught animal. He further placed a large number of animals—*cow, ewe, lamb, sow,* and so on—in the category of Edible but Useless for Work. Since his method of categorizing the barnyard failed to take into account the breeding process, which depends upon the categories of sex and maturity, he no doubt found it inexplicable that some animals—*ram, colt, boar,* and so on—were raised even though they could not be eaten or used for work.

To an American, the Amazonian Indian's classification of barnyard animals appears quite foolish, yet it is no more foolish than the American's system of classification by the features of sex and maturity. Speakers of each language have the right to recognize whatever features they care to. And they have a similar right to then organize these features according to the rules of their own speech communities. No one system is better than another in making sense out of the world in terms that can be talked about; the systems are simply different. A speaker of English who defines a *stallion* as a mature, male horse is no wiser than the Amazonian who claims it is inedible and used for riding. Both the speaker of English and the speaker of the Amazonian language have brought order out of the multitudes of things in the environment—and, in the process, both have shown something about how their languages and their minds work.

All speech communities similarly recognize categories of kinship by which they give verbal labels to their relatives. And the simpler the culture, the more apt it is to emphasize kinship categories—because people in simple cultures must rely upon their kinsmen for protection and cooperation in the absence of the political and economic institutions typical of more complex societies. Americans unconsciously assume that their way of categorizing relatives is standard because it has been familiar to them since birth. But the American system no doubt furnished endless amusement to the hypothetical Amazonian visitor to the United States. He must have thought that Americans were joking, or possibly were simpleminded, when he heard them use the word *uncle* to refer both to their father's brother and to their mother's brother.

Most people think that all kinship systems are approximately the same because they deal with obvious differences between males and females, between siblings, and between generations. That may be true of most European languages, but kinship categories in other parts of the world usually are more complicated. Even the categories used by most Americans are not quite so simple as they might appear. The American system possesses, first of all, a category of basic kinship terms—*father, mother, brother, sister, son,* and *daughter*—that refers to the people usually regarded as the "closest" relatives. These labels can be used with the modifiers *-in-law* and *step-* to produce such combinations as *mother-in-law* and *stepdaughter.*

A second category consists of *grandfather, grandmother, grandson,* 12 *granddaughter, uncle, aunt, nephew,* and *niece,* all of which can be used with the modifiers *grand-* or *great-.* The kin belonging to this second category are felt to be slightly more remote than those in the first category. And such a feeling is indeed true in fact: A *niece* is one degree more remote than a *daughter* in genealogical distance; *grandparents* are one generation more remote than *parents.* And the use of a modifying *great-* or *grand-* removes these kin an additional degree.

All kinsmen who are more distant are described in the English 13 language by the basic term *cousin.* It is the only kin term that can be used with such modifiers as *first, second, third* (and, in some American dialects, *once removed, twice removed, three times removed*) to refer to the most remote relatives. No precise boundary exists in English at which people consider relatives too distant to be given labels, but in most cases the division takes place at about *second* or *third cousin.* (The Famous Relative Exception, though, allows the relationship to a distinguished person to be traced no matter how distant he or she may be. Witness the several million people in the United States who are said to be F.F.V.s—First Families of Virginia—who claim descent from Pocahontas and John Rolfe.)

In addition to these categories, English distinguishes between 14 consanguineal kinsmen (blood relatives) and affinal kinsmen (in-laws), although this distinction is weaker than it is in many other languages. *Uncle,* for example, usually refers to a blood relative, the brother of one's father or mother, and often to the man who marries one's blood aunt. But a man who becomes an uncle because of one's marriage to his niece is usually referred to as *my wife's uncle.* No such ambiguity exists, though, in regard to the affinal relations of the basic kin: *father, mother, brother, sister, son, daughter.* If these relatives are kin by marriage, then they are all obligatory *-in-law.*

A peculiarity of the English categories for relatives is that they 15 are permanent. Once kin, always kin; divorce, remarriage, or death does not dissolve the bond. A man still refers to his divorced wife as *my ex-wife* and to her mother as *my former mother-in-law.* After the death of one's blood uncle, his wife is usually still called *aunt*—even though she never was a consanguineal relative, her bond of affinal relationship was dissolved at the death of the blood uncle, and she may even have remarried into another family altogether.

Clearly, the English-speaking system of naming kin is more 16 complex than it appears at first thought. English makes three basic contrasts: sex (*brother/sister*), generation (*father/grandfather*), and genealogical distance (*uncle/nephew*). Then it makes two additional distinctions in regard to consanguinity (that is, blood relative versus in-law) and the precise generational location of someone who becomes kin by marriage (such as *daughter-in-law* or *father-in-law*).

People who speak non-European languages usually talk about 17 their relatives in quite different fashion. For one thing, they often place much farther out the boundary at which kinship ends. Some American Indian speakers, for example, know the precise kinship label for every person in their community, no matter how distant the relationship and whether the relationship is real or imagined. Secondly, some languages lump several American categories into a single category—as in Hawaiian, which uses the same word to refer to both "father" and "father's brother." Thirdly, many languages split a single American category into several categories, such as making a distinction between the kinds of cousins that are known as the "mother's brother's child" and the "mother's sister's child."

Speakers of Jinghpaw, a language of northern Burma, are inter- 18 ested in making much different distinctions about relatives than speakers of English make. The Jinghpaw language offers eighteen basic terms for kin, not one of which can be translated into an equivalent English word. For example, the Jinghpaw word *nu* refers not only to the person called *mother* in English but also to any female relative, such as a maternal aunt, who belongs to the mother's family and is in her approximate age group. *Hpu* can be one's older brother and also the older son of the father's brother; *nau* might be a younger brother, a sister, or even a child of the father's brother. English often seems preoccupied with giving labels to differences between the sexes and to generational–genealogical relationships, but Jinghpaw kinship is concerned with the social order. Jinghpaw's vocabulary emphasizes who belongs to a family unit, who has an obligation to help whom, who can marry. The Jinghpaw system seems very strange to speakers of English, but of course to the Jinghpaws it functions very well in their kind of culture. They would no doubt consider it trivial that an aged American male bothers to make a distinction between his *grandson* and his *grandnephew*, since both of them would be equally obliged to help the old man.

Categorization is related to the problem of what is generally 19 called the "meaning" of words and sentences—a problem that has proved so troublesome that many linguists, until very recently, have chosen to ignore it altogether. One difficulty is that linguists have been unable to agree on the "meaning" of "meaning," and another is that they have been suspicious of any elusive concept that often resists analysis. Not only linguists but philosophers and logicians (like Lewis Carroll) have been plagued by the problem of meaning, as is seen in this exchange from *Through the Looking-Glass:*

> "When *I* use a word," Humpty Dumpty said, in rather a scornful tone, "it means just what I choose it to mean—neither more nor less."
>
> "The question is," said Alice, "whether you *can* make words mean so many different things."
>
> "The question is," said Humpty Dumpty, "which is to be master—that's all."

Despite what most people believe, dictionaries do not give the "meanings" of words, nor do they define words in terms of components or features recognized by the speech community, in the way that this chapter has dealt with livestock and relatives. Rather, dictionaries present "meanings" by offering a selection of synonymous words and phrases—which are themselves listed in the dictionary. The dictionary thus is a closed system in which someone interested in the meaning of a word can go around and around and end up exactly where he started, simply because words are defined in terms of other words, and these, in turn, are defined in terms of still other words. Most dictionaries, for example, define *beauty* in terms of *pleasing quality; pleasing* is then defined in terms of *agreeable;* consult *agreeable* and it is found to "mean" *pleasing.* A person can energetically explore a dictionary and still be left with other words, not with "meanings." [20]

The scholarly dictionaries do a somewhat better job of supplying meaning when they present the full derivational roots of a word— the tracing of its lineage, for example, back through Middle English, Old French, and Latin—for words, like human beings, are sometimes better understood when the reader knows the company they keep. That is why some dictionaries, like the *Oxford English Dictionary,* also give numerous examples of usage to breathe life into words. *Unplumbed,* standing isolated in the dictionary columns, sounds like a rather unpleasant word evocative of plumbing or of an architect's plumb. But the word comes alive in the context of Matthew Arnold's haunting line from his poem "Isolation"—"The unplumb'd, salt, estranging sea." The "meaning" of a word in the dictionary, therefore, is not the meaning at all. It serves merely as a reminder to a speaker who already knows his language, has grown [21] up in a speech community that uses the word, and who employs the hints in the dictionary to make a guess at the meaning.

The dictionary emphasizes the trivial matters of language at the 22 expense of what is truly important. The precise spelling of a word is relatively trivial because, no matter how the word is spelled, it nevertheless remains only an approximation of the spoken word. A *machine chose the chords* is a correctly spelled English sentence, but what is written as *ch* is spoken with the three different sounds heard in the words *sheen, catch,* and *kiss.* A further flaw in all dictionaries is that they give a distorted view of a language because they are organized alphabetically. This kind of organization emphasizes the prefixes, which come at the beginning of words, rather than the suffixes, which come at the end. Yet, in English and in many other languages, suffixes as a whole have more effect on words than do prefixes. Finally, an adequate dictionary usually takes at least a decade to prepare (the *Oxford English Dictionary* required about fifty years), and by the time it has been completed it is the dictionary of a changed language, simply because the meanings of words do not stay the same from year to year.

Most people assume that a text in one language can be accu- 23 rately translated into another language, so long as the translator uses a good bilingual dictionary. But that is not so, because words that are familiar in one language may have no equivalent usage in another. The word *home,* for example, has special meaning for English speakers, particularly those who live in the British Isles. To an Englishman, a *home* is more than the physical structure in which he resides; it is his castle, no matter how humble, the place of his origins, fondly remembered, as well as his present environment of happy family relationships. *This is my home* says the Englishman, and he thereby points not only to a structure but also to a way of life. The same feeling, though, cannot be expressed even in a language whose history is as closely intertwined with English as is French. The closest a Frenchman can come is *Voilà ma maison* or *Voilà mon logis*—words equivalent to the English *house* but certainly not to the English *home.*

Mark Twain humorously demonstrated the problems of transla- 24 tion when he published the results of his experiment with French. He printed the original version of his well-known story "The Celebrated Jumping Frog of Calaveras County," followed by a Frenchman's translation of it, and then a literal translation from the French back into English. Here are a few sentences from each version:

> *Twain's Original Version:* "Well, there was a feller here once by the name of Jim Smiley, in the winter of '49—or maybe it was the spring of '50—I don't recollect exactly, somehow though what

makes me think it was one or the other is because I remember the big flume wasn't finished when he first come to the camp."

French Version: "Il y avait une fois ici un individu connu sous le nomme de Jim Smiley: c'était dans l'hiver de 49, peut-être bien au printemps de 50, je ne me rappelle pas exactement. Ce qui me fait croire que c'était l'un ou l'autre, c'est que je me souviens que le grand bief n'était pas achevé lorsqu'il arriva au camp pour le première fois."

Literal Retranslation into English: "It there was one time here an individual known under the name of Jim Smiley; it was in the winter of '49, possibly well at the spring of '50, I no me recollect exactly. That which makes me to believe that it was one or the other, it is that I shall remember that the grand flume was no achieved when he arrives at the camp for the first time."

Such anecdotes about failures in translation do not get at the heart of the problem, because they concern only isolated words and not the resistance of an entire language system to translation. For example, all languages have obligatory categories of grammar that may be lacking in other languages. Russian—like many languages but not like English—has an obligatory category for gender which demands that a noun, and often a pronoun, specify whether it is masculine, feminine, or neuter. Another obligatory category, similarly lacking in English, makes a verb state whether or not an action has been completed. Therefore, a Russian finds it impossible to translate accurately the English sentence *I hired a worker* without having much more information. He would have to know whether the *I* who was speaking was a man or a woman, whether the action of *hired* had a completive or noncompletive aspect ("already hired" as opposed to "was in the process of hiring"), and whether the *worker* was a man or a woman. 25

Or imagine the difficulty of translating into English a Chinese story in which a character identified as a *piaomei* appears. The obligatory categories to which this word belongs require that it tell whether it refers to a male or a female, whether the character is older or younger than the speaker, and whether the character belongs to the family of the speaker's father or mother. *Piaomei* therefore can be translated into English only by the unwieldy statement "a female cousin on my mother's side and younger than myself." Of course, the translator might simply establish these facts about the character the first time she appears and thereafter render the word as "cousin," but that would ignore the significance in Chinese culture of the repetition of these obligatory categories. 26

The Russian and Chinese examples illustrate the basic problem in any translation. No matter how skilled the translator is, he cannot 27 rip language out of the speech community that uses it. Translation obviously is not a simple two-way street between two languages. Rather, it is a busy intersection at which at least five thoroughfares meet—the two languages with all their eccentricities, the cultures of the two speech communities, and the speech situation in which the statement was uttered.

Many linguists who have worked with completely unrelated 28 tongues bear testimony to just how intractable language can be. Each language represents a system of conceptual patterns that have evolved over a long period of time, and each language has developed its own categories with its own style of expressing them. Therefore, an inner resistance often makes translation impossible, even for an anthropological linguist who is not only fluent in the exotic language but also knowledgeable about the total culture.

Portions of the Bible have been translated into some two thou- 29 sand languages around the world—and in every case the process of translation involved the loss of information originally in the Bible, the addition of new information, or the distortion of information. Eugene A. Nida, who has made a study of attempts to translate the Bible, states the problem directly: "The basic principles of translation mean that no translation in a receptor language can be the exact equivalent of the model in the source language." As an example of loss, see what sometimes happens to the rhetorical device often used in the Bible of repeating words for emphasis, as in "Truly, truly, I say to you." This device cannot be used in a number of languages of the Philippines. In these languages, repetition is a device of de-emphasis, so that "truly, truly" would really mean something like "perhaps."

More commonly, additions must be made to the original Bible 30 text because of obligatory categories in the language it is being translated into. Very early in the Gospel According to St. Matthew we are told that Jesus visited Capernaum, but we are not told whether this was his first trip or whether he had visited the place previously. In many languages, though, a speaker is forced to distinguish between actions which occur for the first time and those which have occurred previously. The translator is offered no other choice, and so he must guess at information which is not given in the Gospel. Another example: Considerable ambiguity exists in the New Testament as to Jesus' status as a rabbi; his followers recognized his role as a teacher, others in Palestine were skeptical, and still others actively disputed that role. We cannot always be certain about the exact opinion of each person in the New Testament who addresses Jesus—yet some languages, such as Javanese and others in eastern Asia, oblige the translator to be certain, because these languages demand the use of different levels of speech and honorifics.

And in case after case, statements in the Bible must be distorted, 31 occasionally beyond recognition. (The penalty for failing to distort can sometimes be severe. When the Biblical expression "heap coals of fire on one's head"—which, of course, means making a person feel very ashamed by being good to him—was literally translated into some languages of the Congo, the speakers there interpreted the statement as an excellent new method of torture.) It is impossible to translate without distortion Jesus' statement "Get thee behind me, Satan" into the Quechua language of Peru, for the simple reason that this language conceptualizes the orientation of experience differently than most other languages. A Quechua speaker thinks of the future as being "behind oneself" and the past as being "ahead of one." He very logically states that past events can be seen in the mind since they already happened, and therefore they must be in front of his eyes. But since he cannot "see" into the future, these events must therefore be out of sight or "behind" him.

Even though Quechua and English speakers orient themselves 32 differently in regard to what is behind and what is in front, the thoughts of one language can still be expressed in the other language—if we are willing to admit a certain number of distortions, circumlocutions, and awkward grammatical constructions. But no way whatever exists to capture an unrelated language's style, as is demonstrated by a comparison between English and Yokuts, an American Indian language spoken in California. English, like other languages, occasionally makes changes in words for no apparent grammatical reason and for no advantages in improved meaning; an example is the consonant change from *invade* to *invasion*. But Yokuts is unremitting in its attention to such formalities, and it does so without bestowing any other benefit upon its speakers than the esthetic pleasure that such changes in style entail. The Yokuts language does many other things that are strange to speakers of English. It does them not to convey subtle meanings but to achieve what Yokuts speakers regard as elegant speech—and these stylistic features are completely untranslatable into English.

Yokuts style emphasizes symmetry and consistency at the ex- 33 pense of variety and richness of metaphor, two characteristics of English. A speaker of English has many ways of expressing *walk*, for example; he can say *stroll, saunter, tread, plod, amble, peregrinate, trudge, shuffle, step along, stamp, lurch, waddle,* and so on. English style regards variety in its verbs as a virtue, and Miss Fidditch works laboriously to extirpate repetition of the same words in a sentence.

A Yokuts speaker is confused by the variety of English, and he lacks in his own verbs any equivalent way to express the delicate nuances characteristic of each of the English synonyms for *walk*. To a Yokuts, the verb stem that means "walk" is sufficient, and he will repeat it in sentence after sentence. He is also likely to deplore the reckless way in which English separates words from their literal meanings and uses them figuratively, as in a *"sharp" tongue, "foot" of the mountain,* or *a family "tree."* Yokuts is stubbornly literal; a "tree" is a woody plant that grows out of the ground, not a family lineage. The Yokuts language makes it extremely difficult for its speakers to use the vivid imagery, poetic metaphors, and word play so characteristic of English. Yokuts not only fails to cut any capers; it could not even express this cliché.

Yokuts and English clearly exist in different domains of style. To a speaker of English, Yokuts appears monotonous, drab, colorless, lacking in vitality. In contrast to English's spirited and varied structures, Yokuts sentences are brief, almost cryptic, and they progress from one thought to another with what seems like the sterility of a telegram. On his part, a Yokuts speaker would undoubtedly have a low estimation of English because it lacks the restraint and consistency that he is proud to have attained in his own language. His sentences are all consistently of about the same length, and he finds English erratic and arbitrary as it makes some sentences so short that they are abrupt and other sentences so long that they are tedious. He would undoubtedly consider the most beautiful sentences in the English language to be freaks because of their feverish piling up of subordinate clauses, their qualifiers, their tricks of using words that mean one thing to express a metaphor about something completely different. Inevitably, he must conclude that English lacks the quiet dignity, balance, and restraint of Yokuts. And no doubt he must also conclude that he could never translate English into Yokuts.

Sources

An excellent source for more information about how languages categorize phenomena is Tyler (1969), which reprints several papers I list below. Other important studies, which I could not discuss because of space limitations, are: Witherspoon (1971) and Kluckhohn (1960) on Navaho categories; Pospisil (1965) for Papuan laws of inheritance; Lounsbury (1965) and Wallace and Atkins (1960) on kinship; Frake (1961) for an interesting analysis of the way a Philippines tribe categorizes disease; Haugen (1957) for categories of Icelandic navigation. An irreverent view of many such studies is Burling (1964). Ways to categorize livestock was inspired by Lamb (1964), whose discussion I have enlarged upon.

My description of the American kinship system is abridged from Goodenough (1965); a somewhat different system is Romney and D'Andrade (1964). See also a critique by Schneider, reprinted along with the Goodenough paper in Tyler (1969). A fuller discussion of Jinghpaw is in Leach (1966).

The quotation is from Carroll (1960), p. 269. An intriguing essay on *Alice in Wonderland* in relation to language is by Warren Shibles in his *Wittgenstein, Language & Philosphy* (Dubuque, Iowa: Kendall/Hunt Publishing, 1969). A brief, but excellent, summary of some specific flaws readers will find in dictionaries is in Bolinger (1968), pp. 286–292. The Mark Twain translations are from *The Complete Humorcus Sketches and Tales of Mark Twain*, edited by Charles Neider (Doubleday, 1961), pp. 261–276. My Russian examples were inspired by Jakobson (1959). The Nida quotation and examples of Biblical translation problems are from his (1959). Material on the Yokuts language is from Gayton and Newman (1940). Important papers about many aspects of translation can be found in Brower (1959).

References

Bolinger, Dwight. 1968. *Aspects of Language*. Harcourt Brace Jovanovich.

Brower, R. A., editor. 1959. *On Translation*. Harvard University Press.

Burling, Robbins. 1964. "Cognition and Componential Analysis: God's Truth or Hocus-Pocus?" *American Anthropologist*, vol. 66, pp. 20–28. (See also further discussions of this paper in the same publication, vol. 66, pp. 116–121.)

Carroll, Lewis. 1960. *The Annotated Alice*, edited by Martin Gardner. Clarkson Potter.

Frake, Charles O. 1961. "The Diagnosis of Disease among the Subanum of Mindanao." *American Anthropologist*, vol. 63, pp. 113–132.

Gayton, Ann H., and Newman, Stanley S. 1940. *Yokuts and Western Mono Myths*. University of California Publications, Anthropological Records, vol. 5.

Goodenough, Ward H. 1965. "Yankee Kinship Terminology: A Problem in Componential Analysis." In Hammel (1965), pp. 259–287.

Hammel, E. A., editor. 1965. *Formal Semantic Analysis*. American Anthropological Association Special Publication, vol. 67.

Haugen, Einar. 1957. "The Semantics of Icelandic Orientation." *Word*, vol. 13, pp. 447–459.

Jakobsen, Roman. 1959. "On Linguistic Aspects of Translation." In Brower (1959), pp. 232–239.

Kluckhohn, Clyde. 1960. "Navaho Categories." In *Culture and History*, edited by Stanley A. Diamond (1960), pp. 65–98. Columbia University Press.

Lamb, Sydney. 1964. "The Sememic Approach to Structural Semantics." In Romney and D'Andrade (1964), pp. 57–78.

Leach, Edmund. 1966. *Rethinking Anthropology*. Humanities Press.

Lounsbury, F. G. 1965. "Another View of the Trobriand Kinship Categories." American Anthropological Association Special Publication, vol. 67, pp. 142–186.

Pospisil, Leopold. 1965. "A Formal Analysis of Substantive Law: Kapauku Papuan Laws of Inheritance." American Anthropological Association Special Publication, vol. 67, pp. 166–185.

Romney, A. K. and D'Andrade, R. G., editors. 1964. *Transcultural Studies in Cognition*. American Anthropological Association Special Publication, vol. 66.

Schneider, David M. 1965. "American Kin Terms and Terms for Kinsmen." In Hammel (1965), pp. 288–308.

Tyler, Stephen A., editor. 1969. *Cognitive Anthropology*. Holt, Rinehart & Winston.

Wallace, A. F. C., and Atkins, John. 1960. "The Meaning of Kinship Terms." *American Anthropologist*, vol. 62, pp. 58–80.

Witherspoon, Gary. 1971. "Navajo Categories of Objects at Rest." *American Anthropologist*, vol. 73, pp. 110–127.

Talking like a Lady

ROBIN LAKOFF

"Women's language" shows up in all levels of the grammer of En- 1
glish. We find differences in the choice and frequency of lexical
items; in the situations in which certain syntactic rules are performed; in intonational and other supersegmental patterns. As an
example of lexical differences, imagine a man and a woman both
looking at the same wall, painted a pinkish shade of purple. The
woman may say (1):

(1) The wall is mauve,

with no one consequently forming any special impression of her as a
result of the words alone; but if the man should say (1), one might
well conclude he was imitating a woman sarcastically or was a homosexual or an interior decorator. Women, then, make far more precise discriminations in naming colors than do men; words like *beige,
ecru, aquamarine, lavender,* and so on are unremarkable in a woman's
active vocabulary, but absent from that of most men. I have seen a
man helpless with suppressed laughter at a discussion between two
other people as to whether a book jacket was to be described as
"lavender" or "mauve." Men find such discussion amusing because
they consider such a question trivial, irrelevant to the real world.

We might ask why fine discrimination of color is relevant for 2
women, but not for men. A clue is contained in the way many men
in our society view other "unworldly" topics, such as high culture
and the Church, as outside the world of men's work, relegated to
women and men whose masculinity is not unquestionable. Men
tend to relegate to women things that are not of concern to them, or
do not involve their egos. Among these are problems of fine color
discrimination. We might rephrase this point by saying that since
women are not expected to make decisions on important matters,
such as what kind of job to hold, they are relegated the noncrucial

Robin Lakoff (1942–   ), from Brooklyn, New York, is professor
of linguistics at the University of California, Berkeley, and coauthor
of *Face Value: The Politics of Beauty* (1984) and *When Talk Is Not Cheap:
Or, How to Find the Right Therapist When You Don't Know Where to Begin* (1985). "Talking like a Lady" is from her study *Language and
Woman's Place* (1975).

decisions as a sop. Deciding whether to name a color "lavender" or "mauve" is one such sop.

If it is agreed that this lexical disparity reflects a social inequity 3 in the position of women, one may ask how to remedy it. Obviously, no one could seriously recommend legislating against the use of the terms "mauve" and "lavender" by women, or forcing men to learn to use them. All we can do is give women the opportunity to participate in the real decisions of life.

Aside from specific lexical items like color names, we find differ- 4 ences between the speech of women and that of men in the use of particles that grammarians often describe as "meaningless." There may be no referent for them, but they are far from meaningless: they define the social context of an utterance, indicate the relationship the speaker feels between himself and his addressee, between himself and what he is talking about.

As an experiment, one might present native speakers of stan- 5 dard American English with pairs of sentences, identical syntactically and in terms of referential lexical items, and differing merely in the choice of "meaningless" particle, and ask them which was spoken by a man, which a woman. Consider:

(2) (a) Oh dear, you've put the peanut butter in the refrigerator again.
    (b) Shit, you've put the peanut butter in the refrigerator again.

It is safe to predict that people would classify the first sentence 6 as part of "women's language," the second as "men's language." It is true that many self-respecting women are becoming able to use sentences like (2)(b) publicly without flinching, but this is a relatively recent development, and while perhaps the majority of Middle America might condone the use of (b) for men, they would still disapprove of its use by women. (It is of interest, by the way, to note that men's language is increasingly being used by women, but women's language is not being adopted by men, apart from those who reject the American masculine image [for example, homosexuals]. This is analogous to the fact that men's jobs are being sought by women, but few men are rushing to become housewives or secretaries. The language of the favored group, the group that holds the power, along with its nonlinguistic behavior, is generally adopted by the other group, not vice versa. In any event, it is a truism to state that the "stronger" expletives are reserved for men, and the "weaker" ones for women.)

Now we may ask what we mean by "stronger" and "weaker" 7 expletives. (If these particles were indeed meaningless, none would be stronger than any other.) The difference between using "shit" (or "damn," or one of many others) as opposed to "oh dear," or "goodness," or "oh fudge" lies in how forcefully one says how one feels—perhaps, one might say, choice of particle is a function of how strongly one allows oneself to feel about something, so that the strength of an emotion conveyed in a sentence corresponds to the strength of the particle. Hence in a really serious situation, the use of "trivializing" (that is, "women's") particles constitutes a joke, or at any rate, is highly inappropriate. (In conformity with current linguistic practice, throughout this work an asterisk (*) will be used to mark a sentence that is inappropriate in some sense, either because it is syntactically deviant or used in the wrong social context.)

(3) (a) *Oh fudge, my hair is on fire.
    (b) *Dear me, did he kidnap the baby?

As children, women are encouraged to be "little ladies." Little   8
ladies don't scream as vociferously as little boys, and they are chastised more severely for throwing tantrums or showing temper: "high spirits" are expected and therefore tolerated in little boys; docility and resignation are the corresponding traits expected of little girls. Now, we tend to excuse a show of temper by a man where we would not excuse an identical tirade from a woman: women are allowed to fuss and complain, but only a man can bellow in rage. It is sometimes claimed that there is a biological basis for this behavior difference, though I don't believe conclusive evidence exists that the early differences in behavior that have been observed are not the results of very different treatment of babies of the two sexes from the beginning; but surely the use of different particles by men and women is a learned trait, merely mirroring nonlinguistic differences again, and again pointing out an inequity that exists between the treatment of men, and society's expectations of them, and the treatment of women. Allowing men stronger means of expression than are open to women further reinforces men's position of strength in the real world: for surely we listen with more attention the more strongly and forcefully someone expresses opinions, and a speaker unable—for whatever reason—to be forceful in stating his views is much less likely to be taken seriously. Ability to use strong particles like "shit" and "hell" is, of course, only incidental to the inequity that exists rather than its cause. But once again, apparently accidental linguistic usage suggests that women are denied equality partially for linguistic reasons, and that an examination of language points up precisely an area in which inequity exists. Further, if someone is allowed to show emotions, and consequently does, oth-

ers may well be able to view him as a real individual in his own right, as they could not if he never showed emotion. Here again, then, the behavior a woman learns as "correct" prevents her from being taken seriously as an individual, and further is considered "correct" and necessary for a woman precisely because society does *not* consider her seriously as an individual.

Similar sorts of disparities exist elsewhere in the vocabulary.   9 There is, for instance, a group of adjectives which have, besides their specific and literal meanings, another use, that of indicating the speaker's approbation or admiration for something. Some of these adjectives are neutral as to sex of speaker: either men or women may use them. But another set seems, in its figurative use, to be largely confined to women's speech. Representative lists of both types are below:

neutral	women only
great	adorable
terrific	charming
cool	sweet
neat	lovely
	divine

As with the color words and swear words already discussed, for   10 a man to stray into the "women's" column is apt to be damaging to his reputation, though here a woman may freely use the neutral words. But it should not be inferred from this that a woman's use of the "women's" words is without its risks. Where a woman has a choice between the neutral words and the women's words, as a man has not, she may be suggesting very different things about her own personality and her view of the subject matter by her choice of words of the first set or words of the second.

(4) (a) What a terrific idea!
    (b) What a divine idea!

It seems to me that (a) might be used under any appropriate conditions by a female speaker. But (b) is more restricted. Probably it is used appropriately (even by the sort of speaker for whom it was normal) only in case the speaker feels the idea referred to be essentially frivolous, trivial, or unimportant to the world at large—only an amusement for the speaker herself. Consider, then, a woman advertising executive at an advertising conference. However feminine an advertising executive she is, she is much more likely to express her approval with (4)(a) than with (b), which might cause raised eyebrows, and the reaction: "That's what we get for putting a woman in charge of this company."

On the other hand, suppose a friend suggests to the same 11
woman that she should dye her French poodles to match her
cigarette lighter. In this case, the suggestion really concerns only
her, and the impression she will make on people. In this case, she
may use (b), from the "woman's language." So the choice is not really free: words restricted to "women's language" suggest that concepts to which they are applied are not relevant to the real world of
(male) influence and power.

One may ask whether there really are no analogous terms that 12
are available to men—terms that denote approval of the trivial, the
personal; that express approbation in terms of one's own personal
emotional reaction, rather than by gauging the likely general reaction. There does in fact seem to be one such word: it is the hippie invention "groovy," which seems to have most of the connotations
that separate "lovely" and "divine" from "great" and "terrific" ex-
cepting only that it does not mark the speaker as feminine or effeminate.

(5) (a) What a terrific steel mill!
    (b) *What a lovely steel mill! (male speaking)
    (c) What a groovy steel mill!

I think it is significant that this word was introduced by the hippies,
and, when used seriously rather than sarcastically, used principally
by people who have accepted the hippies' values. Principal among
these is the denial of the Protestant work ethic: to a hippie, something can be worth thinking about even if it isn't influential in the
power structure, or moneymaking. Hippies are separated from the
activities of the real world just as women are—though in the former
case it is due to a decision on their parts, while this is not uncontro-
versially true in the case of women. For both these groups, it is possible to express approval of things in a personal way—though one
does so at the risk of losing one's credibility with members of the
power structure. It is also true, according to some speakers, that
upper-class British men may use the words listed in the "women's"
column, as well as the specific color words and others we have categorized as specifically feminine, without raising doubts as to their
masculinity among other speakers of the same dialect. (This is not
true for lower-class Britons, however.) The reason may be that commitment to the work ethic need not necessarily be displayed: one
may be or appear to be a gentleman of leisure, interested in various
pursuits, but not involved in mundane (business or political) affairs,
in such a culture, without incurring disgrace. This is rather
analogous to the position of a woman in American middle-class society, so we should not be surprised if these special lexical items are

usable by both groups. This fact points indeed to a more general conclusion. These words aren't, basically, "feminine"; rather, they signal "uninvolved," or "out of power." Any group in a society to which these labels are applicable may presumably use these words; they are often considered "feminine," "unmasculine," because women are the "uninvolved," "out-of-power" group par excellence.

Another group that has, ostensibly at least, taken itself out of 13 the search for power and money is that of academic men. They are frequently viewed by other groups as analogous in some ways to women—they don't really work, they are supported in their frivolous pursuits by others, what they do doesn't really count in the real world, and so on. The suburban home finds its counterpart in the ivory tower: one is supposedly shielded from harsh realities in both. Therefore it is not too surprising that many academic men (especially those who emulate British norms) may violate many of these sacrosanct rules I have just laid down: they often use "women's language." Among themselves, this does not occasion ridicule. But to a truck driver, a professor saying, "What a lovely hat!" is undoubtedly laughable, all the more so as it reinforces his stereotype of professors as effete snobs.

When we leave the lexicon and venture into syntax, we find that 14 syntactically too women's speech is peculiar. To my knowledge, there is no syntactic rule in English that only women may use. But there is at least one rule that a woman will use in more conversational situations than a man. (This fact indicates, of course, that the applicability of syntactic rules is governed partly by social context— the positions in society of the speaker and addressee, with respect to each other, and the impression one seeks to make on the other.) This is the rule of tag-question formation.[1]

---

[1] Within the lexicon itself, there seems to be a parallel phenomenon to tag-question usage, which I refrain from discussing in the body of the text because the facts are controversial and I do not understand them fully. The intensive *so,* used where purists would insist upon an absolute superlative, heavily stressed, seems more characteristic of women's language than of men's, though it is found in the latter, particularly in the speech of male academics. Consider, for instance, the following sentences:

(a) I feel *so* unhappy!
(b) That movie made me *so* sick!

Men seem to have the least difficulty using this construction when the sentence is unemotional, or nonsubjective—without reference to the speaker himself:

(c) That sunset is *so* beautiful!
(d) Fred is *so* dumb!

Substituting an equative like *so* for absolute superlatives (like *very, really, utterly*) seems to be a way of backing out of committing oneself strongly to an opinion, rather like tag questions (cf. discussion below, in the text). One might hedge in this way with perfect right in making aesthetic judgments, as in (c), or intellectual judgments, as in (d). But it is somewhat odd to hedge in describing one's own mental or emotional state: who, after all, is qualified to contradict one on this? To hedge in this situation is to seek to avoid making any strong statement: a characteristic, as we have noted already and shall note further, of women's speech.

A tag, in its usage as well as its syntactic shape (in English) is 15 midway between an outright statement and a yes-no question: it is less assertive than the former, but more confident than the latter. Therefore it is usable under certain contextual situations: not those in which a statement would be appropriate, nor those in which a yes-no question is generally used, but in situations intermediate between these.

One makes a statement when one has confidence in his knowl- 16 edge and is pretty certain that his statement will be believed; one asks a question when one lacks knowledge on some point and has reason to believe that this gap can and will be remedied by an answer by the addressee. A tag question, being intermediate between these, is used when the speaker is stating a claim, but lacks full confidence in the truth of that claim. So if I say

(6) Is John here?

I will probably not be surprised if my respondent answers "no"; but if I say

(7) John is here, isn't he?

instead, chances are I am already biased in favor of a positive answer, wanting only confirmation by the addressee. I still want a response from him, as I do with a yes-no question; but I have enough knowledge (or think I have) to predict that response, much as with a declarative statement. A tag question, then, might be thought of as a declarative statement without the assumption that the statement is to be believed by the addressee: one has an out, as with a question. A tag gives the addressee leeway, not forcing him to go along with the views of the speaker.

There are situations in which a tag is legitimate, in fact the only 17 legitimate sentence form. So, for example, if I have seen something only indistinctly, and have reason to believe my addressee had a better view, I can say:

(8) I had my glasses off. He was out at third, wasn't he?

Sometimes we find a tag question used in cases in which the 18 speaker knows as well as the addressee what the answer must be, and doesn't need confirmation. One such situation is when the speaker is making "small talk," trying to elicit conversation from the addressee:

(9) Sure is hot here, isn't it?

In discussing p. sonal feelings or opinions, only the speaker 19
normally has any way of knowing the correct answer. Strictly speaking, questioning one's own opinions is futile. Sentences like (10) are
usually ridiculous.

(10) *I have a headache, don't I?

But similar cases do, apparently, exist, in which it is the speaker's
opinions, rather than perceptions, for which corroboration is
sought, as in (11):

(11) The way prices are rising is horrendous, isn't it?

While there are of course other possible interpretations of a sen- 20
tence like this, one possibility is that the speaker has a particular answer in mind—"yes" or "no"—but is reluctant to state it baldly. It is
my impression, though I do not have precise statistical evidence,
that this sort of tag question is much more apt to be used by women
than by men. If this is indeed true, why is it true?

These sentence types provide a means whereby a speaker can 21
avoid committing himself, and thereby avoid coming into conflict
with the addressee. The problem is that, by so doing, a speaker may
also give the impression of not being really sure of himself, of looking to the addressee for confirmation, even of having no views of his
own. This last criticism is, of course, one often leveled at women.
One wonders how much of it reflects a use of language that has
been imposed on women from their earliest years.

Related to this special use of a syntactic rule is a widespread dif- 22
ference perceptible in women's intonational patterns.[2] There is a peculiar sentence intonation pattern, found in English as far as I know
only among women, which has the form of a declarative answer to a
question, and is used as such, but has the rising inflection typical of
a yes-no question, as well as being especially hesitant. The effect is
as though one were seeking confirmation, though at the same time
the speaker may be the only one who has the requisite information.

(12) (a) When will dinner be ready?
     (b) Oh . . . around six o'clock . . . ?

---

[2] For analogues outside of English to these uses of tag questions and special intonation patterns, cf. my discussion of Japanese particles in "Language in Context," *Language*, 48 (1972), pp.
907–927. It is to be expected that similar cases will be found in many other languages as well. See,
for example, M. R. Haas's very interesting discussion of differences between men's and women's
speech mostly involving lexical dissimilarities in many languages, in D. Hymes, ed., *Language in
Culture and Society* (New York: Harper & Row, 1964).

It is as though (b) were saying, "Six o'clock, if that's OK with you, if you agree." (a) is put in the position of having to provide confirmation, and (b) sounds unsure. Here we find unwillingness to assert an opinion carried to an extreme. One likely consequence is that these sorts of speech patterns are taken to reflect something real about character and play a part in not taking a woman seriously or trusting her with any real responsibilities, since "she can't make up her mind" and "isn't sure of herself." And here again we see that people form judgments about other people on the basis of superficial linguistic behavior that may have nothing to do with inner character, but has been imposed upon the speaker, on pain of worse punishment than not being taken seriously.

Such features are probably part of the general fact that women's 23 speech sounds much more "polite" than men's. One aspect of politeness is as we have just described: leaving a decision open, not imposing your mind, or views, or claims on anyone else. Thus a tag question is a kind of polite statement, in that it does not force agreement or belief on the addressee. A request may be in the same sense a polite command, in that it does not overtly require obedience, but rather suggests something be done as a favor to the speaker. An overt order (as in an imperative) expresses the (often impolite) assumption of the speaker's superior position to the addressee, carrying with it the right to enforce compliance, whereas with a request the decision on the face of it is left up to the addressee. (The same is true of suggestions: here, the implication is not that the addressee is in danger if he does not comply—merely that he will be glad if he does. Once again, the decision is up to the addressee, and a suggestion therefore is politer than an order.) The more particles in a sentence that reinforce the notion that it is a request, rather than an order, the politer the result. The sentences of (13) illustrate these points: (a) is a direct order, (b) and (c) simple requests, and (d) and (e) compound requests.[3]

    (13) (a) Close the door.
           (b) Please close the door.
           (c) Will you close the door?
           (d) Will you please close the door?
           (e) Won't you close the door?

Let me first explain why (e) has been classified as a compound 24 request. (A sentence like *Won't you please close the door* would then count as a doubly compound request.) A sentence like (13)(c) is close

---

[3] For more detailed discussion of these problems, see Lakoff, "Language in Context."

in sense to "Are you willing to close the door?" According to the normal rules of polite conversation, to agree that you are willing is to agree to do the thing asked of you. Hence this apparent inquiry functions as a request, leaving the decision up to the willingness of the addressee. Phrasing it as a positive question makes the (implicit) assumption that a "yes" answer will be forthcoming. Sentence (13)(d) is more polite than (b) or (c) because it combines them: *please* indicating that to concede will be to do something for the speaker, and *will you*, as noted, suggesting that the addressee has the final decision. If, now, the question is phrased with a negative, as in (13)(e), the speaker seems to suggest the stronger likelihood of a negative response from the addressee. Since the assumption is then that the addressee is that much freer to refuse, (13)(e) acts as a more polite request than (13)(c) or (d); (c) and (d) put the burden of refusal on the addressee, as (e) does not.

Given these facts, one can see the connection between tag ques- 25
tions and tag orders and other requests. In all these cases, the speaker is not committed as with a simple declarative or affirmative. And the more one compounds a request, the more characteristic it is of women's speech, the less of men's. A sentence that begins *Won't you please* (without special emphasis on *please*) seems to me at least to have a distinctly unmasculine sound. Little girls are indeed taught to talk like little ladies, in that their speech is in many ways more polite than that of boys or men, and the reason for this is that polite-ness involves an absence of a strong statement, and women's speech is devised to prevent the expression of strong statements.

READING AND WRITING
ABOUT LANGUAGE AND CULTURE

1. Discuss your previous experiences in writing or English classes. Which classes, assignments, or teachers have been most helpful for improving your writing, and which have been least helpful? To what extent do you think learning to write well is mostly a matter of:

    a. pleasing different teachers;
    b. pleasing an audience other than your teacher;
    c. pleasing yourself;
    d. fulfilling some objective, independent standards for good writing?

    Based on their Brief Encounters, how might Claude Lévi-Strauss or June Jordan answer this question differently than Glenn Jackson, Kurt Vonnegut, or Gloria Anzaldúa?

2. List the qualities you associate with the kind of writing you are usually expected to do for school. What other qualities of academic language are stated or implied by Michelle Cliff, Kit Yuen Quan, and Michael Ventura? Compare the different ways each of these authors criticizes academic writing or language. How would you describe or classify their own writing in each case? For what audience does each seem to be writing?

3. Rachel Jones offers a different view of "talking proper." How can you use her argument to reply to Cliff or Ventura? Test your attitudes and experiences with standard English or academic writing against those of Jones, Cliff, and Ventura.

4. What larger purpose do you think Rose del Castillo Guilbault intends in comparing the American and Hispanic definitions of *macho*? Who is she primarily addressing? Besides offering an extended definition, what other writing strategies or techniques does she use to accomplish her purpose?

5. Discuss or write about a personal experience in which one of the racial or ethnic slurs discussed by Charles Berlitz was used against you, by you, or around you. What happened? How did you feel? If you were upset by this usage, did you confront the offender? Why, or why not? Does Berlitz's explanation of the origin of this term change your feelings about the incident in any way?

6. Which evidence of the long history of abuse against Native Americans catalogued by Haig Bosmajian do you find most persua-

sive, especially regarding the use of language as a tool of oppression? Do you agree that the way whites have treated Indians in this country is comparable to the way they have treated blacks, or to the way the Nazis treated Jews in Germany during the 1930s and 1940s, as Bosmajian implies in paragraph 34? Defend your answer.

7. Analyze Amy Tan's essay as a test of the "Sapir-Whorf hypothesis," which she paraphrases in paragraph 18. In determining Tan's final position on this linguistic controversy, weigh the evidence she presents both for and against Sapir-Whorf. If you are bilingual or multilingual, test the hypothesis with your own experience: to what extent do you think differently in different languages? Try writing a dialogue, as Tan does, to demonstrate cultural differences and similarities.

8. Peter Farb writes, regarding the problems of translation, that "the thoughts of one language can still be expressed in the other language—if we are willing to admit a certain number of distortions, circumlocutions, and awkward grammatical constructions" (paragraph 32). Apply this idea to Guilbault's or Tan's essay. What distortions, circumlocutions, or awkward constructions do you detect, and to what extent do they prevent communication? How does Farb's "componential" or "formal semantic analysis" (paragraph 4)—determining the categories that give words in any language their meaning—help you understand Guilbault's grappling with the word *macho*, or Tan's explanation of how to say "yes" and "no" in Chinese?

9. The ways Robin Lakoff says language is used to oppress women appear to be more subtle than the ways Bosmajian shows Indians to have been dehumanized by official government and legal definitions. Explain the differences between the lexical, syntactical, and intonational levels of language that Lakoff discusses. With members of your class or small group, have the "incorrect" gender read aloud some of Lakoff's sample sentences (that is, have men read the "women's language" and women read the "men's language"), and discuss the results. How much do you think things have changed since Lakoff wrote her book (1975)? Update Lakoff's essay by providing more recent examples of gender-specific language from your experience.

10. Analyze how one or more of the women authors in this chapter other than Lakoff—such as Cliff, Quan, or Guilbault—is affected by her gender in her encounter with language and culture.

11. One of the larger themes running through this chapter is the way language and writing may be used for political purposes, whether to oppress groups of people or to liberate individuals from such oppression. Think about the political roles writing has played in your life, then write an essay addressing this theme that draws upon several of the chapter's selections.

12. Cliff, Berlitz, and Tan begin their essays with anecdotes or narratives. Reread these openings, then reread the beginnings of other essays in this chapter and identify several different opening strategies. Do the different strategies seem appropriate for each essay? How do you judge this appropriateness? Which openings do you find most effective? Why?

13. A sense of cultural ambiguity as it relates to language is addressed by many of this chapter's authors, including Jordan, Miller, Anzaldúa, Rushdie, Cliff, Jones, Quan, Ventura, Guilbault, Bosmajian, Tan, and Farb. Identify any conflicts you have felt about an aspect of your own cultural identity—such as your regional identity, social or economic class, religious background, or ethnic or racial identity—and consider how these conflicts have surfaced in language, written or spoken, by you or by others. Tell a brief story or anecdote that illustrates the complexity of your feelings, then explain the meaning of this incident for you. Address this explanation to someone not of your ethnic or cultural background.

MAKING FURTHER CONNECTIONS

1. In this chapter, several authors confront their sense of cultural ambiguity more or less directly. Read the Brief Encounters for Chapter 2 or 4, and look for evidence of a similar feeling of cultural dislocation, perhaps expressed more subtly, on the part of either the authors or the people they write about.

2. For the Brief Encounters of Chapter 2, 3, or 6, find selections in which language—the language of the characters or the author—plays a crucial part in the interaction or is especially revealing of the local culture.

3. To what extent is the father character, Sancho, "macho"—according to either the Americanized or the Hispanic definitions offered by Guilbault—in the excerpt from Arturo Islas's novel, "Thanksgiving Border Crossing," in Chapter 6?

4. Use the selections by Jordan, Cliff, and Jones as a backdrop to discuss the role that Black English plays in Grace Paley's story, "The Long-Distance Runner," in Chapter 6. How would the story be different if the speeches by black characters were rendered in standard English? How skillful is Paley at capturing inner-city black speech?

5. Use Lakoff's analysis of "women's language" to study the way language is used by men or women in the story by Islas, Paley, Frank Chin ("Railroad Standard Time"), David Leavitt ("Territory"), Valerie Matsumoto ("Two Deserts"), or Joanna Russ ("When It Changed") in Chapter 6. Find an angle that reveals Lakoff's essay, the story, or both in a new light. For example, to what extent does the way the gay men talk in Leavitt's "Territory" contradict the stereotypes about homosexual language described by Lakoff?

6. Many of the writers in Chapter 1—including Lévi-Strauss, Bailey, Jordan, and Miller in the Brief Encounters, and Berlitz, Bosmajian, Farb, and Lakoff in the main selections—are social scientists and/or college professors. In Paul Bowles's story, "A Distant Episode," in Chapter 6, what is the significance of the Professor's occupation as an academic and, in particular, as a linguist? How does Bowles seem to feel about Western social science? What evidence do you find of the importance Bowles attaches to language as a key to human identity?

EXPLORING NEW SOURCES

1. Investigate more thoroughly one of the three trends for the upcoming decade outlined in the Brief Encounter by Bailey: the worldwide rise in multilingualism, the diminishing proportion of English-speakers, or the changing attitudes of those learning English as a second language. Find and read Bailey's essay, and use his references as a starting point for your research.

2. Find another word or term—like Guilbault's *macho*—that is used differently by the majority of American speakers than by the speakers of the language or dialect it comes from. Conduct library research on the origins and history of the term, then design and administer a questionnaire for your fellow students on how they use it. Report your results. What conclusions do you draw?

3. Research the etymology of another insulting slang term not discussed by Berlitz. Instead of a racial or ethnic slur, consider terms applied to members of other social groups, such as gays, the disabled, wealthy people, or working class people. You might find out, for example, why Quan—who identifies herself as a lesbian—uses the word *dyke*, which historically has been considered offensive.

4. Recreate the debate surrounding one of the "English-only" laws adopted during the 1980s in eleven states. How well has the particular law you're investigating worked in practice? Use your research to argue your own position on this controversial issue.

5. Find the most recent studies you can on bilingual education efforts in the United States, narrowing your research to a particular group, such as Mexican Americans or Vietnamese Americans. Which programs or approaches have addressed this group's particular educational difficulties most effectively?

6. If your school has an English as a Second Language or English for Foreign Students program, research and write about it. Interview teachers, administrators, and students, and ask them for suggestions about books and journal articles to help you put the program in a larger perspective. How successful is the program? On what current theories is it based? Could particular changes, theoretical or practical, improve the program? Address your paper to the administrator, department, or committee that oversees the program.

7. Use Farb's references to research in more depth one of the speech communities he discusses, such as the Navajo or another Native American tribe; update his sources with studies from the 1980s.

8. Review Lakoff's method for studying "women's language" in terms of lexical, syntactic, and intonational differences, then duplicate this method in studying the way some other group uses language. This group might be one you're familiar with—for example, fellow workers at your job or people from the region where you grew up. What patterns do you detect? Can you find evidence for such patterns in professional linguistic studies?

2

THE WRITER AS TRAVELER: DISCOVERING AMERICAN PLACES AND PEOPLE

The journey of self-exploration—the search for personal and cultural identity—must begin close to home, with our relationships to local places and people. The places might be the town where we grew up or new places we've passed through or moved to; the people might be the families and neighbors of our childhood or the strangers we've met on the road. As Patricia Hampl suggests in Chapter 1, when we write about where we've been—about the past—we are doing a kind of "travel writing." Travel, in Chapter 2, includes the trip across country, the trip across town or around the block, and the homecoming trip, as well as the journey back into memory.

Whether leaving or returning home, Americans are on the move in this chapter. You should ask of these domestic travelers not how far they've gone or how exotic their destination is, but how attuned their powers of observation are. How well do they capture the sights, sounds, smells, tastes, and feel of their piece of the American mosaic, and how does their piece help you understand yours in a new or different way? To what extent do they penetrate the surfaces they observe, revealing the human motivations behind the everyday commotion and demonstrating what's special or extraordinary about ordinary places and people?

It might help to distinguish travelers from tourists, who are more focused on the surfaces of things, the postcard destinations, the souvenirs and trinkets. In probing their experiences, travelers may need to look within themselves at the same time they look without; in learning to trust their feelings and judgments, travelers may need to explore their particular immigrant or ethnic heritage as well. On the other hand, in distancing themselves to achieve greater critical objectivity, travelers may begin to resemble social scientists in the way they observe and report people's behavior, pose hypotheses, and draw conclusions about the local culture.

This tension between subjectivity and objectivity in our reading and writing is an ongoing theme in this book. How much of what we see is colored by who we are? The various versions of American culture offered in Chapter 2 reflect the diversity of the authors represented here. Their styles and techniques range widely, too: this chapter includes oral histories, a personal letter, journalistic writing, memoir writing, and literary essays.

The Brief Encounters span the United States both geographically and historically. Adam Nicolson describes a Hopi Indian village that is said to be the oldest continuously inhabited place in the United States, and John Heckewelder encounters some eighteenth-century Ohio Indians. Kate Simon and Nikki Giovanni recreate their childhood neighborhoods in, respectively, the Bronx of the 1920s and Knoxville of the 1960s. Joan Didion calls Las Vegas "the most extreme and allegorical of American settlements," and Trevor Fishlock follows some modern whiskered pioneers preparing to journey to the "Last Frontier" of Alaska. Malgorzata Niezabitowska, a Pole who traveled across the United States, offers a taste of small-town hospitality—and immigrant variety—in Nebraska. Ernesto Galarza describes the "kaleidoscope of colors and languages and customs" of the Sacramento, California, *barrio* of his youth, while Jamaica Kincaid tells what it feels like to be a newcomer in New York City.

This geographical and authorial diversity increases in Chapter 2's main selections:

- Studs Terkel's oral history of "Ann Banks" portrays a "very American" woman who grew up in several different places, observed her neighbors like "a little ten-year-old anthropologist," and rebelled against an overprotective environment.

- Juan Cadena, in another oral history, traces prejudices against Mexican Americans from the history textbooks of his Texas school days to his adult work with migrant workers in Michigan and Iowa.

- Siu Wai Anderson's letter to her infant daughter explores the feelings of an Asian American mother who was raised by Anglo parents and who is still searching for her Chinese identity.

- Maxine Hong Kingston reports on a strange incident in a small Florida town where authorities hunt down a mysterious, foreign "Wild Man" who lives in the swamp.

- Christopher Isherwood has the "worst possible" first impres-

sions of Los Angeles, although the Englishman eventually settled in Hollywood and became a U.S. citizen.

- Frances FitzGerald describes the colorful craziness of Gay Freedom Day in San Francisco, capturing gay pride and cultural exuberance at what may have been its peak, before the discovery
  and spread of AIDS.
- Paul Theroux, accompanied by two transit policemen, describes
  the homeless "skells" and other characters who populate New
  York City's subways.
- Gretel Ehrlich explores a more expansive, traditional sense of
  place and space in Wyoming, where the animals outnumber the
  people and the "Western Code" prevails.
- Maya Angelou tempers her childhood impressionability with her
  adult skepticism in writing about an American cultural original—the big-time, big-tent revival meeting.
- N. Scott Momaday explores his Kiowa Indian heritage en route
  to visit the grave of his grandmother, Aho, who "belonged to
  the last culture to evolve in North America."

BRIEF ENCOUNTERS

Walpi Village, Arizona

ADAM NICHOLSON

We drove up on to the first mesa in the Hopi Reservation. After the Pueblo Revolt in 1680, the Hopi took their villages up on to the defensible mesas and there they are today. Notices warned visitors not to behave badly. Our guidebook told us not to go into people's houses without knocking and not to pick at the jewelry that the Hopi might be wearing nor to ask how much they would sell it for, as this would be rude. God knows what white people must have done here in the past. The village of Walpi is built on the end of a finger of rock, cliffed on either side and with long, protective views to north and south across the grasslands. It has a stronger sense of place and permanence than any white settlement in America. It is the only village I have seen where the houses touch each other. They are packed together like boxes in a warehouse, with a dusty lane leading in and out between them. The twin tree-poles of ladders stuck out through the roofs of the hidden kivas. Olivia said she hated doing this to a place, hated looking in on somewhere that had its arms tightly bound around its chest in a sense of privacy and difference that is almost absent in white America.

—FROM *TWO ROADS TO DODGE CITY*, 1987

Indians on the Muskingum River, Ohio

JOHN GOTTLIEB ERNESTUS HECKEWELDER

Some traveling Indians having in the year 1777, put their horses over night to pasture in my little meadow, at Gnadenhutten on the Muskingum, I called on them in the morning to learn why they had done so. I endeavored to make them sensible of the injury they had done me, especially as I intended to mow the meadow in a day or two. Having finished my complaint, one of them replied: "My friend, it seems you lay claim to the grass my horses have eaten, because you had enclosed it with a fence: now tell me, who caused the grass to grow? Can *you* make the grass grow? I think not, and no body can except the great Mannitto. He it is who causes it to grow both for my horses and for yours! See, friend! the grass which grows out of the earth is common to all; the game in the woods is common to all. Say, did you ever eat venison and bear's meat?" "Yes, very often." "Well, and did you ever hear me or any other Indian complain about that? No; then be not disturbed at my horses having eaten only once, of what you call *your* grass, though the grass my horses did eat, in like manner as the meat you did eat, was given to the Indians by the Great Spirit. Besides, if you will but consider, you will find that my horses did not eat *all* your grass. For friendship's sake, however, I shall never put my horses in your meadow again."

—FROM *ACCOUNT OF THE HISTORY, MANNERS AND CUSTOMS OF THE INDIAN NATIONS, WHO ONCE INHABITED PENNSYLVANIA AND THE NEIGHBORING STATES*, 1819

Workers' Utopia, The Bronx

KATE SIMON

For a time I enjoyed the "coops," as the new houses were called. Our apartment was light and fresh and the atmosphere as impassioned in its own way as that of Lafontaine Avenue, my childhood street. This was to be Utopia, a workers' Utopia, run justly and lovingly, truly democratically. It was culturally avid, education of all sorts organized before the last toilets were placed in the bathrooms. There were dance classes, classes in Russian, in English, in political science, in crafts. There was a cafeteria that served huge Jewish-kitchen portions with generous slabs of bread and side orders of pickles and beet salad. There was a large food shop, run cooperatively, to which I refused to go after a comrade clerk laughed at me when I asked for Oscar Wilde sardines. I should have asked for King Oscar but hated him for correcting me, although my error proved the superior quality of my thoughts. In time the food store failed, partially as a result of excessive democracy: a committee of cutters, bookkeepers, and Yiddish journalists, in spite of—or because of—their lengthy discussions, failed to catch the freshest crates of spinach at the most advantageous prices, were bilked by capitalist canned soup suppliers, and blamed each other for costly errors. The cafeteria closed; too many disputes among the cooking comrades, the serving comrades, the cleaning-up comrades, and prices didn't stay idealistically low.

In spite of difficulties and disappointments, spirits stayed high and hot. Rent strikes in the neighborhood were signaled by a banging on apartment doors. "Come! Out! Run! Leave everything, the cossacks [cops] are here!" Whether they wanted to or not, many ran, not always sure they knew where or why, especially the unenlightened housewives caught elbow-deep in washtubs or frying the delicate, perishable crepes of blintzes. Others, always at the ready, dashed with revolutionary fervor. My mother never responded. She said the women who did were *mishigoyim*[1] looking for excitement, anything to get away from their sinks and kids. She might have been somewhat right. The children of the most vigorous rent-strike militants, the most insistent shouters and bangers on doors, were the shabbiest, most neglected children, free of bourgeois traits like socks that matched and regular meals. They were often renamed, to their bewilderment, from Solly, Benny, Davy, to Lenin, Marx, Trotsky, which, with the addition of the inescapable diminutive, became Leninel, Marxele, Trotskele. Their mothers, married to the same passive husbands for twenty years, redesigned their lives as well; now members of a new world, they discarded the word "husband" and spoke of their bland men as "mein comrade"—a stormer of barricades, the bearer of the reddest banner.

—FROM *A WIDER WORLD: PORTRAITS IN AN ADOLESCENCE*, 1986

Knoxville Revisited

NIKKI GIOVANNI

Gay Street is to Knoxville what Fifth Avenue is to New York. Something special, yes? And it looked the same. But Vine Street, where I would sneak to the drugstore to buy *Screen Stories* and watch the men drink wine and play pool—all gone. A wide, clean, military-looking highway has taken its place. Austin Homes is cordoned off. It looked like a big prison. The Gem Theatre is now some sort of nightclub and Mulvaney Street is gone. Completely wiped out. Assassinated along with the old people who made it live. I looked over and saw that the lady who used to cry "HOT FISH! GOOD HOT FISH!" no longer had a Cal Johnson Park to come to and set up her stove in. Grandmother would not say, "Edith White! I think I'll send Gary for a sandwich. You want one?" Mrs. Abrum and her reverend husband from rural Tennessee wouldn't bring us any more goose eggs from across the street. And Leroy wouldn't chase his mother's boyfriend on Saturday night down the back alley anymore. All gone, not even to a major highway but to a cutoff of a cutoff. All the old people who died from lack of adjustment died from a cutoff of a cutoff.

---

[1] Crazy people; *goyim* is a derogatory Yiddish term for Gentiles or non-Jews. (Ed.)

And I remember our finding Grandmother the house on Linden Avenue and constantly reminding her it was every bit as good as if not better than the little ole house. A bigger back yard and no steps to climb. But I knew what Grandmother knew, what we all knew. There was no familiar smell in that house. No coal ashes from the fireplaces. Nowhere that you could touch and say, "Yolande threw her doll against this wall," or "Agnes fell down these steps." No smell or taste of biscuits Grandpapa had eaten with the Alaga syrup he loved so much. No Sunday chicken. No sound of "Lord, you children don't care a thing 'bout me after all I done for you," because Grandmother always had the need to feel mistreated. No spot in the back hall weighted down with lodge books and no corner where the old record player sat playing Billy Eckstine crooning, "What's My Name?" till Grandmother said, "Lord! Any fool know his name!" No breeze on dreamy nights when Mommy would listen over and over again to "I Don't See Me in Your Eyes Anymore." No pain in my knuckles where Grandmother had rapped them because she was determined I would play the piano, and when that absolutely failed, no effort on Linden for us to learn the flowers. No echo of me being the only person in the history of the family to curse Grandmother out and no Grandpapa saying, "Oh, my," which was serious from him, "we can't have this." Linden Avenue was pretty but it had no life.

—FROM *GEMINI*, 1971

Las Vegas

JOAN DIDION

Las Vegas is the most extreme and allegorical of American settlements, bizarre and beautiful in its venality and in its devotion to immediate gratification, a place the tone of which is set by mobsters and call girls and ladies' room attendants with amyl nitrite poppers in their uniform pockets. Almost everyone notes that there is no "time" in Las Vegas, no night and no day and no past and no future (no Las Vegas casino, however, has taken the obliteration of the ordinary time sense quite so far as Harold's Club in Reno, which for a while issued, at odd intervals in the day and night, mimeographed "bulletins" carrying news from the world outside); neither is there any logical sense of where one is. One is standing on a highway in the middle of a vast hostile desert looking at an eighty-foot sign which blinks "STARDUST" or "CAESAR'S PALACE." Yes, but what does that explain? This geographical implausibility reinforces the sense that what happens there has no connection with "real" life; Nevada cities like Reno and Carson are ranch towns, Western towns, places behind which there is some historical imperative. But Las Vegas seems to exist only in the eye of the beholder.

—FROM "MARRYING ABSURD," *SLOUCHING TOWARDS BETHLEHEM*, 1967

Alaska, the Last Frontier

TREVOR FISHLOCK

In Alaska there is all the ambiguity of the frontier. The Last Frontier slogan is invested with self-consciousness and sadness. It is meant to sound robustly all-American and celebratory, but it has, too, a note of nostalgic longing, regret for vanishing youth. Otherwise, surely, Alaskans would have called their land, in a more forward-looking way, the New Frontier. Men still journey here to be frontiersmen. They grow their whiskers especially for the purpose. They ransack the trading post catalogues for thick wool shirts, thermal underwear, rifles, Bowie knives and books on how to build log cabins and bear-proof larders. They buy devices to get solar electricity "free from the midnight sun" and consider whether to invest in "the world's most powerful hand gun, 2000 foot-pounds of raw power! Alaska's answer to bear protection." Thus equipped they thrust their eager bushy faces towards the challenging wilderness—and are dismayed to find parking tickets on their windscreens. Anchorage and Fairbanks have traffic jams, parking congestion and severe carbon monoxide pollution. Even in distant Nome, population 2500, there are irksome regulations. *The Nome Nugget*, Alaska's oldest newspaper (the motto on its masthead states: There's no place like Nome), commented regretfully on the installation of the town's first traffic signal in 1984: "It doesn't make us do anything we weren't already supposed to do. So, no cause for alarm yet. It just makes one wonder who will get the first ticket and how long before the first bullet hole shows up. Big city life is creeping up on us."

—FROM *THE STATE OF AMERICA*, 1986

Melting Pot in Lewellen, Nebraska

MALGORZATA NIEZABITOWSKA

We met a lot of people and heard many stories. All of them compose that extraordinary mosaic called America, but now as I get ready for my trip back to Poland, one memory keeps returning particularly often. One night during a sudden storm we stopped over in a small town in Nebraska. The motel was the only one in town, and we were the only guests. In the morning we discovered that the town had one paved street and about 300 inhabitants. It was called Lewellen.

For breakfast we went to the only cafe in town. The manager, three days' growth on his face, stood behind the counter. The customers, all men, were seated around the tables. In the middle stood a round, large and empty table. And that was where we sat to have our cinnamon rolls. Our entrance caused a sensation. All conversations died down, and everybody stared at us in silence. Finally a tall, red-bearded man brought over the coffeepot from the counter and offered to refill our cups, which were still full.

In a moment our table was teeming with people, all of them asking us questions and talking about themselves. It turned out that among these 15 or so Lewellen citizens there were a Greek, an Italian, an Irishman, a Hungarian, a German, and a Pole—if not in the first, then in the second or third generation. They teased each other good-humoredly about the supposed foibles of different nationalities, and we quickly joined in the fun.

Obviously life in Lewellen is no idyll, and everybody isn't always joking. Yet the image of this big table and the people gathered around it, whose ancestors came to a lost-in-the-prairie town from different parts of the world, has for me great charm and importance.

—FROM "DISCOVERING AMERICA," IN *NATIONAL GEOGRAPHIC*, 1988

Colonia Mexicana

ERNESTO GALARZA

In the hotels and rooming houses scattered about the *barrio* the Filipino farm workers, riverboat stewards, and houseboys made their homes. Like the Mexicans they had their own poolhalls, which they called clubs. Hindus from the rice and fruit country north of the city stayed in the rooming houses when they were in town, keeping to themselves. The Portuguese and Italian families gathered in their own neighborhoods along Fourth and Fifth Streets southward toward the Y-street levee. The Poles, Yugo-Slavs, and Koreans, too few to take over any particular part of it, were scattered throughout the *barrio*. Black men drifted in and out of town, working the waterfront. It was a kaleidoscope of colors and languages and customs that surprised and absorbed me at every turn. . . .

For the Mexicans the *barrio* was a colony of refugees. We came to know families from Chihuahua, Sonora, Jalisco, and Durango. Some had come to the United States even before the revolution, living in Texas before migrating to California. Like ourselves, our Mexican neighbors had come this far moving step by step, working and waiting, as if they were feeling their way up a ladder. They talked of relatives who had been left behind in Mexico, or in some far-off city like Los Angeles or San Diego. From whatever place they had come, and however short or long the time they had lived in the United States, together they formed the *colonia mexicana*. In the years between our arrival and the First World War, the *colonia* grew and spilled out from the lower part of town. Some families moved into the alley shacks east of the Southern Pacific tracks, close to the canneries and warehouses and across the river among the orchards and rice mills.

The *colonia* was like a sponge that was beginning to leak along the edges, squeezed between the levee, the railroad tracks, and the river front. But it wasn't squeezed dry, because it kept filling with newcomers who found families who took in boarders: basements, alleys, shanties, run-down rooming houses and flop joints where they could live.

—FROM *BARRIO BOY*, 1971

My First Day

JAMAICA KINCAID

It was my first day. I had come the night before, a gray-black and cold night before—as it was expected to be in the middle of January, though I didn't know that at the time—and I could not see anything clearly on the way in from the airport, even though there were lights everywhere. As we drove along, someone would single out to me a fabulous building, an important street, a park, a bridge that when built was thought to be a spectacle. In a daydream I used to have, all these places were points of happiness to me; all these places were lifeboats to my small drowning soul, for I would imagine myself entering and leaving them, and just that—entering and leaving over and over again—would see me through a bad feeling I did not have a name for. I only knew it felt a little like sadness. Now that I saw these places, they looked ordinary, dirty, worn down by so many people entering and leaving them in real life, and it occurred to me that I could not be the only person in the world for whom they were a fixture of fantasy. It was not my first bout with the disappointment of reality and it would not be my last. The undergarments that I wore were all new, bought for my journey, and as I sat in the car, twisting this way and that to get a good view of the sights before me, I was reminded of how uncomfortable the new can make you feel.

—FROM "POOR VISITOR," IN *THE NEW YORKER,* 1989

Ann Banks, Army Brat

STUDS TERKEL

The way you know an army brat is when you ask them: "Where are 1
you from?" A normal question. There's a silence. I've trained myself
to say Florida. That's where my family's from and where I was born.
But I didn't grow up there and I don't really feel from there. Usually, there's just a silence. You're gathering your energy to say:
"Well, nowhere really." . . .

I was sheltered from growing up, on those army posts. You had 2
to go through a sentry gate to get in. I lived on this little protected
island in the middle of America. It was sort of an enchanted princess
atmosphere. The one thing that struck me is that all these army
posts look alike. That's probably very carefully orchestrated. Even in
the middle of the desert in Oklahoma, the residential section is
green. Grass, very carefully trimmed, and shade trees. It's a beautiful way to grow up—in a way. It's like a vast playground. It's a very
safe place and the kids can run wild. I think very early I knew this
wasn't real America.

You go to schools on army posts, too, so your world is self- 3
contained. When you go off the army posts, there are commercial
strips of bars and tattoo parlors and used-car joints. So you go from
this extremely ordered environment to a total honky-tonk chaos.

When you're an army brat, it means your entire environment is 4
conditioned by much more than what your father does for a living.
You grow up in a total institution. I always thought of it as being
like a circus child. There are many second- and third-generation military families. Every need is taken care of and you're not expected to
ever leave. If you're a woman, you're an army wife in training. If
you're a man, you're expected to go to West Point.

My father, who had a lot of interest in my marrying an army 5
officer (laughs), would have been totally appalled if I had said I
want to make the army my life, I want to join the women's army
corps. I think he would have fainted. (Laughs.) He had a certain image of the WACs' being not what he wanted his daughter to be.

Studs Terkel (1912-   ), from Chicago, is the author of several
collections of oral histories including *Working* (1974) and *"The Good
War"* (1984). "Ann Banks, Army Brat" is from *American Dreams: Lost
and Found* (1980).

My father would say to us: "You're going to visit your cousins.   6
Poor them. They have to live in one place all their lives. Doesn't that
sound boring? We've gotten to live all over. We've had a lot of different experiences. Doesn't that sound more interesting?" We'd say:
"It sure does." And we really felt it. Obviously, he felt a little guilty
about schlepping us all over all the time. The odd thing was, until I
went to college, I had no idea that anybody could have thought differently.

My father was at the embassy in Bonn, and I went to a boarding   7
school for military and embassy kids in Frankfurt. The first week, I
met this guy who had grown up in one place, Miami, all his life.
"How many times did you move?" he said. "I moved fourteen,
fifteen times," I told him. "Oh, poor you," he said. I said: "Poor *you*,
that had to live in one place all your life." (Laughs.)

You grow up a certain way. You never realize other people grow   8
up different. I had this epiphany about five years ago. I was in California, driving down Highway One, which bisects Fort Ord. Sometimes you hear something and it's intensely familiar before you quite
understand what it is. You're overwhelmed with emotion before
you know what it is. I heard this sound. It was reassuring, like a lul-
laby. Then I realized what it was. It was artillery practice. It was the
distant sound of these guns, booming.

The first song I was taught was the artillery song: *Over hill, over*   9
dale. There were the flag ceremonies. Very compelling. They'd play
taps at five o'clock every afternoon. Wherever you're going on the
post, you have to stop your car and stand facing the flag. How you
knew where it was, I don't know, but everybody did it.

When I was six, we lived in Carlisle Barracks, Pennsylvania, and   10
then we moved to Fort Sill, Oklahoma. It was a city surrounded by
walls. I think the army tries to make it seem like a small town. You
have the commissary, you have the movie theater, you have the
bowling alley. You have stables, you have a swimming pool, you
have lots of swimming pools. Nobody can drive fast. If you drive
over fifteen miles an hour, they send you to jail. You have the
houses. The lieutenant colonels' houses are all alike. The colonels'
houses are all alike. Your grass has to be mowed a certain way or
you'd get a letter from the quartermaster corps. At this point, I was
beginning to understand there were other ways of living. I was
learning to read.

I was in fourth grade when my father went to Korea. My mother   11
decided that we'd live on Anna Maria Island, off the coast of Sara-
sota. I felt this was my one chance to see what real American life
was like. I watched everything. This one family, with six kids, lived

right down the street. I thought: Boy, I've got myself a typical American family. I was a little ten-year-old anthropologist. The mother was trying to get the kids into growing avocados or taking care of the goldfish. She'd try to interest me in the constructive projects, too, and I used to think: My project is watching you. (Laughs.)

I thought Anna Maria Island was typical America. What's funny 12 is the place was so bizarre. (Laughs.) It was the kind of odd conglomeration of people who end up in some warm climate, drifters and runaways. A lot of alcoholics there. It was a place where every sort of drifter and ne'er-do-well, you'd tilt the country and they'd all float to California or float to Florida, all the ones who weren't attached. I loved the place. They had these little ticky-tacky houses right on the ocean. Whenever there'd be a storm, there'd be sandbagging parties. I remember sneaking out and watching them. There they were, all night in a howling storm, getting drunker and drunker. What was funny about it was that I was convinced this was the real heart of the country.

I remember reading a *Saturday Evening Post* or a *Life* that year. 13 There was a corporate ad for Bell Telephone. It was a charcoal drawing of a soldier. It said something about husbands, fathers, brothers, boyfriends, who might be killed at any moment, blah, blah, blah. It never crossed my mind that my father might be killed. That never, never occurred to me. I thought: What are they doing, telling me this? I'm not supposed to know. Nobody told me that before. It's a very protective environment for kids, very idyllic.

There were problems, as part of a total institution. If you were 14 an adolescent and got into trouble as adolescents do, there'd be a file on you, and your father's career would be affected. Certain demerits. When we were in Germany at the embassy, my sister told me of a club some kids belonged to, the Mercedes Club. The way to get in was to break the silver star off the car. Mercedes has this hood ornament. It was their daredevil exploit, a typical delinquent act. When it was found out, whole families were sent home.

When I was sixteen, two things happened. I was doing a term 15 paper on the Hungarian revolution. I used the American Embassy library and I read the U.N. transcripts. About the American role: the Voice of America and Radio Free Europe giving the Hungarian rebels false hope. I knew some Hungarian refugees. I interviewed one. I thought: This is an outrage.

The other thing. I was in Livorno, northern Italy. I went dancing 16 with these two Italian men one Saturday night. I was sixteen, just completely the belle. We were frolicking around the town. It was, by this time, eleven-thirty or twelve o'clock at night. We walked by this little tiny cubicle. It was a shoe repair stand. There was a young man, extremely handsome, pounding these shoes. He looked so full of energy and vitality, and yet he looked so angry. It looked like the anger of everyone in the world who was at the bottom that he was pounding out into these shoes. I had just been on top of the world, we'd been drinking champagne and dancing. I was just so caught up by this sight. The world was beautiful. Then I saw this man hammering these shoes. I still remember it. It's like a photograph.

It still took me a long time to become aware. At Fort Bragg, I'm a   17
lifeguard at the officers' club swimming pool. I'm nineteen. It's in the early sixties. People were being trained to go to Vietnam as advisors. I remember one young man finishing something called HALO school. That's an acronym for high altitude, low opening. You jump out of an airplane at a very high altitude, you free fall, then you open. He was learning jungle survival skills. Then he was sent to a language school to learn Burmese. It didn't take much to figure out the plans for him to parachute into the jungles of Burma. The feeling I had was these men who got to lord it over others, just because they jumped out of airplanes, were macho. My only weapon was to make fun of it. I've tried to trace back my feelings about American imperialism. It was no one thing. A lot of people who were army brats ended up being against the war.

There's a man I went to high school with. He was an army brat.   18
Brilliant, incredibly egotistical, and abrasive. He was in the class at West Point that was like *the* Vietnam class. He had graduated and was a Rhodes scholar, a brilliant lunatic. He was killed in Vietnam. He had written his own obituary for *The New York Times* Op-Ed page. He felt the war was totally justified and didn't want anybody making political capital out of his death. I felt on reading it: That goddamn Alex, grandstanding again, just the way he always did. (Laughs.) Yet the moral authority of a person who's written something which he knows will be published only posthumously was indisputable. He was talking about the life I'd known, the life of an army brat. I thought: Unfair, unfair advantage. (Laughs.) My reaction was really bizarre. He's making unfair points 'cause he had to go and get himself killed.

The funny thing is that I feel I'm very American even though I   19
spent seven years of my young life out of the country. Though I'm opposed to what we do politically around the world, I'm emotionally and culturally very American. I like jazz, country and folk music, and open roads and the desert and space.

The military tries to promote a sense of community and a sense   20
of shared purpose above and beyond one's individual family. It's a

terrifically pleasing life in a certain way. I think it's a deadly life for the wives. There are all these traditions and all this protocol. Yet there's a kind of ceremonial quality to the life that is satisfying to the children.

But, I think, the shared purpose is a spurious one, an evil one. I 21 want no part of it.

It's My Country Too

JUAN CADENA

I work for the Muscatine Migrant Committee. We're a government- 1
funded organization that's been in existence for over twenty years.
We provide medical help for migrants and seasonal farm workers.
I've been the director of the program since 1971.

"Migrant" and "immigrant" are not synonymous. Our definition 2
of a migrant is someone who has earned half of their income within
a twelve-consecutive-month period in the past twenty-four months.
And the fact that they're from Mexico or any other country or are
white or speak Spanish or don't speak Spanish is really not relevant.
On the other hand, 99 percent of the migrants are Mexican-Americans and *mexicanos*. With seasonal farm workers it's just the opposite, 90 percent are white, European-Americans from Iowa. I don't
know what percentage of the migrants are Mexican citizens. Fifteen
years ago, a great percentage of our migrants were from Texas and
were American citizens by birth. In the last three or four years we
have had a higher proportion of Mexican citizens than before.

I grew up in the Midwest. I was born in Texas, but we moved to 3
Saginaw, Michigan, when I was ten years old. When we first moved
to Carleton, just across the Saginaw River, there was a little—what
we call *colonia*. It didn't amount to much, there were only eight migrant houses, and we lived right down the tracks in another little
house near the sugar beet company. We made friends with everybody in the *colonia*. We all went to the same school. Well, a couple of
years later my father bought a house about three or four miles from
there, in the Buena Vista neighborhood. We were only half a block
from Saginaw, but I kept in contact with the people from the *colonia*.

We used to have Mexican dances. First in a real small hall, then 4
we graduated to the auditorium, then to the armory. By the 1960s,
"Los Relámpagos del Norte" came and there were two thousand
people at the dance. It just grew and grew. After I left Saginaw in

Juan Cadena (1935–   ), from Muscatine, Iowa, is outreach coordinator for the Muscatine School District and former director of the
Muscatine Migrant Committee. "It's My Country Too" originally
appeared in *Mexican Voices/American Dreams: An Oral History of Mexican Immigration to the United States*, edited by Marilyn P. Davis
(1990).

the seventies, Vincente Fernández came to the Civic Center and
they had a real turnout.

So there is a substantial number of Hispanics in Saginaw. The   5
community college, when we left, had over 200 Mexicans enrolled.
A few years ago, I went back and they had 400 in the community
college.

When I was a community organizer we had clubs in each of the   6
high schools for Mexican kids, to encourage them to go to college.
One school had over 250 kids. The Graduation Club was started
back in the forties for all the Mexicans who are going to graduate
from high school. They have their own prom and bring speakers
such as Senator Chavez and Senator Montoya, to give a special com-
mencement. The kids still go to graduation with their respective
schools, but they also have a separate one just for Mexicans.

I don't know if they still do, but in Saginaw they used to cele-   7
brate the *diez de septiembre*[1] and *cinco de mayo*.[2] I don't think half of
them know what the heck's being celebrated. That's the truth. I was
in San Antonio and these Mexicans, my wife, Martha's cousins, live
in an affluent, nice neighborhood on the north side. They were all
excited because they were going to this Festival San Jacinto and
Martha says, "Well what is the celebration about?" And they didn't
know. *¿Verdad, Martha?*[3] They didn't know. I knew, but I didn't say
nothing. They said, *"No sabemos lo que es,*[4] but we have a lot of fun."
But this whole holiday is about when the *mexicanos* got whipped by
the whites here in San Jacinto and they don't even know. They're
going out there to celebrate. So you know they don't even care.
Even the whites don't know what the San Jacinto's about anymore,
and nobody gives a hoot.

In Saginaw I had no real close friends that were not Mexicans. I   8
wasn't unfriendly with anyone, but I really never got associated
with whites very much until I went in the army. Actually in those
year I never paid any attention to who was from Mexico and who
was from Texas, who was from Saginaw, who was from out of
town, no attention whatsoever. I never even thought about it until I
came here.

And here, when we first came to Muscatine it was like I was   9
wearing a sign on my forehead, "I'm Mexican." It wasn't just my
perception, because when my relations would come down from Sag-

---

[1] *diez de septiembre:* September 10, the Festival of San Jacinto. (Ed.)
[2] *cinco de mayo:* May 5, Mexican national holiday recognizing the anniversary of the Battle of
Puebla (1862), in which outnumbered Mexican troops under General Ignacio Zaragoza defeated
the French forces of Napoleon III. (Ed.)
[3] *¿Verdad?:* Right? Isn't that so? (Ed.)
[4] *No sabemos lo que es:* We do not know what it is. (Ed.)

inaw to visit, they would say, "What's wrong with the people in
Muscatine? They stare at you." Well, that's not true anymore, but
that was the situation when we first came here in '71. It was like a
little cultural shock for me too, because I was confronted with this,
"You're a Mexican." I knew I was a Mexican, but I didn't want people to be looking at me like, "Hey, Mexican!" They didn't say it, but
that's the feeling you got. In Saginaw it wasn't that way at all—the
relationship between whites and Mexicans is real good. There's really not that obvious discrimination. There was a little bit in the forties but not after that. Now there's even a lot of intermarriage.

See here, it was pretty bad. I was standing in line at the bank 10
one day—this is one example—and this guy says, "This is the way
Mexicans line up for food stamps," and everybody was ha-ha-ha.
Well I didn't laugh. I felt like grabbing the guy and throwing him
through the window. But I was going to a church council meeting, I
was president. Now how would I be getting into a fight? I was getting a little more religious, so I started thinking and acting different.
A few years before I probably would have tried to throw him
through the window.

Another time I called this number for a house to rent. I guess he 11
was busy and didn't notice that I had an accent. So when we got
there he said, "Stop right there, I'm not renting to no Mexicans!"
You know it was kind of comical.

I said, "Did I hear what you said?"   12

He said, "That's right, I don't rent to Mexicans."   13

I said, "Oh Christ!" So I called the civil rights commission, I was 14
going to do something, but I never followed up on it.

A couple, Anglo friends, did a consumers' report here. We 15
would send a Mexican couple, or pretend-to-be couple, to rent an
apartment, and the landlord would say there wasn't any place to
rent. Then our Anglo friends would come right behind them an
hour later and, like magic, they would have a vacancy. After about
twenty cases, they wrote a report. Those landlords were mad! But
see we started exposing all that foolishness. Then in the schools
there was also a lot of discrimination. I'm sure there still is, to some
extent, but it has changed a lot. ¿Verdad, Martha? There's a lot of
good Anglos in this community.

I was considered real militant in Saginaw, and when I came here 16
I was in the mood that I could do anything. That's the way I was. I
sort of enjoyed it, you know. I was thirty-four, so I was no young
kid. But nothing scared me, nothing.

I don't know. We had this old Mexican guy that was being 17
ripped off in West Liberty. This was a long time ago, but this justice
of the peace had rented a place to the Mexican. In the first place it

was small, a real shack. But beyond that there's no way that any thinking person could have expected the old guy to pay this kind of rent for the amount of money he was earning. So a friend and I, he was a law student, we went over there. Out comes this justice of the peace, and this guy looks like he's from *Petticoat Junction*, had his striped coveralls with this little hat and the whole bit. He said, "We don't want all those Mexicans coming into town. They park their cars and half of the time they're leaking oil and they leave all those oil spots all over and all that." My friend was saying, "Write that down, Juan." And I was writing notes, writing notes.

The justice of the peace would tell his lawyer, "They're gonna get me. They're gonna get us, Ernie." 18

"Ah, don't worry about it." But you could see he was all worried. So finally the lawyer said, "Juan, I'll talk to you, I don't want to talk to your friend. I'll talk to you, just you and I." 19

See, we were playing the good cop, bad cop. I went in but told my friend, "You stay out of here." Then I told the justice's lawyer, "Well, I'll keep this lawyer away from here if you cut the rent in half and . . ." And this is exactly what the man had wanted. He agreed to everything. 20

"You're not going to take it any further than this?" 21

I said, "No, we'll forget the whole thing." 22

So we went back for the old goat to sign the papers and he said, "Well, I'm sorry what I said about Mexicans, it's not only Mexicans that do that, niggers and Puerto Ricans do the same." 23

Can you believe that? He was serious. God, I'll never forget that. How can you get angry with somebody like that? You can't, these people are crazy. He was apologizing and insulting us at the same time. I've noticed that people are like that. If you really look at them, they're hilarious. The only time I'm really worried about a racist person is if they're in a position to determine someone's economic or social future. 24

Before I came here I was a coordinator for the grape boycott, for Cesar Chavez in the Saginaw area. We confronted a lot of people, people who would spit on us and say, "Go back to Mexico, you wetbacks!" And we were all from the United States. A lot of Anglos were helping us out, but in a way I was a racist. I wanted Mexicans to be doing something for Mexicans, but we were all American citizens. When I joined the grape boycott movement it was being led by some seventeen-year-old Anglo girl, and 99 percent of the people doing the marching were Anglos, nuns, and priests. I took it over and chased them all out. I didn't tell them directly to leave, but in a month or so they were all gone except the real hard-nosed. I would have 100 or 150 and they were all Mexicans. *¿Verdad, Martha?* The 25

Anglos didn't want me because I was coming across too hard. They wanted to make waves but not BIG waves, and I was making REAL BIG waves.

But here in Muscatine it was a different ballgame than Saginaw. 26 If you're really trying to do something useful and to really help or change conditions, you have to adapt to the conditions that you're dealing with. You can't just sing the same songs.

In Saginaw there really wasn't that many poor people. Now I'm 27 used to it, but when we came here, we went riding around to the southside. We saw Anglos, blue-eyed, blond kids with stringy hair and dirty faces, scroungy looking, and I said, "Well wait a minute, I thought I would have to go to the Ozarks to see this. Not Iowa, the breadbasket of America." I thought everybody would be like you know, *Ozzie and Harriet.* But you see a lot of poor people, and really I don't know how you would say it, riff-raff maybe.

We don't have that in Saginaw. There's a large middle class, and 28 everybody works in the plants, and they all make a lot of money. There I could say, "Look at the way the poor Mexicans live here." Because there were a few poor Mexicans. But here, I can't say that because we have as many poor whites.

Another difference, in Saginaw everybody works side by side 29 there at the plants, and it doesn't matter whether you're white, yellow, or blue. You earn the same kind of money, the same kind of education and everything else.

People wanted me to get involved with the union here too, like 30 the grape boycott. But I said, "It isn't going to work. In Saginaw we used to go to a supermarket. I would take six people and we would turn away 50 percent of the people. Here you can take 200 people and you aren't going to turn 5 percent of the people away. They don't identify with the union. In Saginaw everybody was union." I don't care if they were Polish or Mexican or black, they were all union people. So it was real easy to close down a store. Here it wouldn't work. People are not union oriented. Cesar Chavez came and people said. "Let's get him down to organize." It isn't going to work. The whole thing was a different world, and I found that out real quick.

I've read a lot of books. The bible has influenced me. I've read 31 Espinoza, Jung, Marx, Ché Guevara, Fidel Castro, Mao Tse-tung, Gandhi, and Franz Fanon. Spicer, an anthropologist, influenced me too.

In school when I was growing up in Texas, the history books 32 were always lying. My dad would correct the history like Pancho Villa and the Alamo, and say, "This is a bunch of lies. These *gringos* are telling you a bunch of lies." So I started thinking for myself. I remember once the nuns wanted us to sign some papers they were going to drop over China and I didn't sign them. My sister Lupe didn't sign it either. She was the only one in her class and I was the only one in mine. I said, "How do I know communism is wrong? How do I know that they're not right and I'm wrong?" White people have been lying to us all these years, and they have discriminated against us in Texas, so how come they're supposed to be so good? They broke all those treaties with the Indians and treated them like dogs, and now they're going to tell me that they're good and the Chinese are bad. I said, "No. I hope the Chinese come and take this country over." That's what I told them.

And the nuns would say, "We're going to have Father come and 33 talk to you because you're a communist." I said, "How can I be a communist? You don't even know what a communist is." I didn't completely buy that little trick of the land of the free and the home of the brave. The United States, I do agree, is probably the best country in the world. And I'm glad I'm an American citizen and was born in this country. But the point is, you can't just swallow everything that they try to tell us, especially when it comes to minorities. I always saw the United States was an extension of Europe, and if you were not of European ancestry somehow you weren't American. What the heck, I was born here, but if I said anything against the United States they would say, "Why don't you go back to Mexico." Well, why don't you go back to Europe. Why should you be trying to send me to Mexico. What's the difference?

Like one guy—we were at a school board hearing where I was 34 pushing for bilingual education—he told the superintendent of schools, "You mean to tell me this man"—talking about me, I was sitting right in front of him—"expects us to teach his kids Spanish in school?"

And then I told the superintendent, "You mean to tell me that 35 this man here expects me to teach his kid English in school?"

He said, "What do you mean, you speak Spanish at home, don't 36 you?"

I said, "Well what do you speak at home, Chinese? If you expect 37 me to teach my kid Spanish at home, then you teach your kid English at home."

He said, "Well I don't mind, maybe you people already living 38 here have the right to speak Spanish, but I'm talking about the other people coming in."

"Fine, I'm okay if you speak English, but all new people coming 39 in should speak Spanish. What makes you right and me wrong?"

He said, "Well because we're the majority."   40

I said, "No, no, no, what about Zimbabwe? You white Eu- 41

ropeans want to push your culture and your language everywhere. In Zimbabwe you're the minority." I wanted to make the same argument. If he would say my argument wasn't right, it would be because he thought I was a second-class citizen, but why should he be more of a citizen than me? I'm a taxpayer. It's my money too. It's my country too. It's my school system too. It's a matter of perceiving what we're all about here in the United States.

A Letter to My Daughter

SIU WAI ANDERSON

August 1989, Boston

Dear Maya Shao-ming,

You were born at Mt. Auburn Hospital in Cambridge on June 6, 1 1989, an auspicious date, and for me, the end of a long, long travail. Because you insisted on being breech, with your head always close to my heart, you came into the world by C-section into a chilly O.R. at the opposite end of the labor and delivery suite where, exhausted yet exuberant, I pushed out your brother in a birthing room nearly four years ago.

I couldn't believe my ears when your father exclaimed, "A girl!" 2 All I could do was cry the tears of a long-awaited dream come true. You are so beautiful, with your big dark eyes and silky black hair. Your skin is more creamy than golden, reflecting your particular "happa haole" blend. But your long elegant fingers are those of a Chinese scholar, prized for high intelligence and sensitivity.

You are more than just a second child, more than just a girl to 3 match our boy, to fit the demographical nuclear family with the proverbial 2.5 children. No, ten years ago I wrote a song for an unborn dream: a dark-haired, dark-eyed child who would be my flesh-and-blood link to humanity. I had no other until your brother came. He was my first Unborn Song. But you, little daughter, are the link to our female line, the legacy of another woman's pain and sacrifice thirty-one years ago.

Let me tell you about your Chinese grandmother. Somewhere in 4 Hong Kong, in the late fifties, a young waitress found herself pregnant by a cook, probably a co-worker at her restaurant. She carried the baby to term, suffered to give it birth, and kept the little girl for the first three months of her life. I like to think that my mother— your grandmother—loved me and fought to raise me on her own, but that the daily struggle was too hard. Worn down by the demands of the new baby and perhaps the constant threat of starva-

---

Siu Wai Anderson (1958–   ), born in Hong Kong and raised in the United States, is the author of book reviews and short stories. "A Letter to My Daughter" is from *Making Face, Making Soul/Haciendo Caras: Creative and Critical Perspectives by Women of Color*, edited by Gloria Anzaldúa (1990).

tion, she made the agonizing decision to give away her girl so that both of us might have a chance for a better life.

More likely, I was dumped at the orphanage steps or forcibly re- 5 moved from a home of abuse and neglect by a social welfare worker. I will probably never know the truth. Having a baby in her unmarried state would have brought shame on the family in China, so she probably kept my existence a secret. Once I was out of her life, it was as if I had never been born. And so you and your brother and I are the missing leaves on an ancestral tree.

Do they ever wonder if we exist?   6

I was brought to the U.S. before I was two, and adopted by the 7 Anglo parents who hail you as their latest beautiful grandchild. Raised by a minister's family in postwar American prosperity and nourished on three square meals a day, I grew like a wild weed and soaked up all the opportunities they had to offer—books, music, education, church life and community activities. Amidst a family of blue-eyed blonds, though, I stood out like a sore thumb. Whether from jealousy or fear of someone who looked so different, my older brothers sometimes tormented me with racist name-calling, teased me about my poor eyesight and unsightly skin, or made fun of my clumsy walk. Moody and impatient, gifted and temperamental, burdened by fears and nightmares that none of us realized stemmed from my early years of deprivation, I was not an easy child to love. My adoptive mother and I clashed countless times over the years, but gradually came to see one another as real human beings with faults and talents, and as women of strength in our own right. Now we love each other very much, though the scars and memories of our early battles will never quite fade. Lacking a mirror image in the mother who raised me, I had to seek my identity as a woman on my own. The Asian American community has helped me reclaim my dual identity and enlightened my view of the struggles we face as minorities in a white-dominated culture. They have applauded my music and praised my writings.

But part of me will always be missing: my beginnings, my per- 8 sonal history, all the subtle details that give a person her origin. I don't know how I was born, whether it was vaginally or by Cesarean. I don't know when, or where exactly, how much I weighed, or whose ears heard my first cry of life. Was I put to my mother's breast and tenderly rocked, or was I simply weighed, cleaned, swaddled and carted off to a sterile nursery, noted in the hospital records as "newborn female"?

Someone took the time to give me a lucky name, and write the 9 appropriate characters in neat brush strokes in the Hong Kong city register. "Siu" means "little." My kind of "wai" means "clever" or "wise." Therefore, my baby name was "Clever little one." Who chose those words? Who cared enough to note my arrival in the world?

I lost my Chinese name for eighteen years. It was Americanized [10] for convenience to "Sue." But like an ill-fitting coat, it made me twitch and fret and squirm. I hated the name. But even more, I hated being Chinese. It took many years to become proud of my Asian heritage and work up the courage to take back my birthname. That plus a smattering of classroom Cantonese, are all the Chinese culture I have to offer you, little one. Not white, certainly, but not really Asian, I straddle the two worlds and try to blaze your trails for you. Your name, "Shao-ming," is very much like mine—"Shao" is the Mandarin form of "Siu," meaning "little." And "ming" is "bright," as in a shining sun or moon. Whose lives will you brighten, little Maya? Your past is more complete than mine, and each day I cradle you in your babyhood, lavishing upon you the tender care I lacked for my first two years. When I console you, I comfort the lost baby inside me who still cries out for her mother. No wonder so many adoptees desperately long to have children of their own.

Sweet Maya, it doesn't matter what you "become" later on. You [11] have already fulfilled my wildest dreams.

I love you,

Mommy

The Wild Man of the Green Swamp

MAXINE HONG KINGSTON

For eight months in 1975, residents on the edge of Green Swamp, 1
Florida, had been reporting to the police that they had seen a Wild
Man. When they stepped toward him, he made strange noises as in
a foreign language and ran back into the saw grass. At first, authorities said the Wild Man was a mass hallucination. Man-eating animals lived in the swamp, and a human being could hardly find a
place to rest without sinking. Perhaps it was some kind of a bear the
children had seen.

In October, a game officer saw a man crouched over a small fire, 2
but as he approached, the figure ran away. It couldn't have been a
bear because the Wild Man dragged a burlap bag after him. Also,
the fire was obviously man-made.

The fish-and-game wardens and the sheriff's deputies entered 3
the swamp with dogs but did not search for long; no one could live
in the swamp. The mosquitoes alone would drive him out.

The Wild Man made forays out of the swamp. Farmers encoun- 4
tered him taking fruit and corn from the turkeys. He broke into a
house trailer, but the occupant came back, and the Wild Man escaped out a window. The occupant said that a bad smell came off
the Wild Man. Usually, the only evidence of him were his abandoned campsites. At one he left the remains of a four-foot-long alli-
gator, of which he had eaten the feet and tail.

In May a posse made an air and land search; the plane signaled 5
down to the hunters on the ground, who circled the Wild Man. A
fish-and-game warden "brought him down with a tackle," according
to the news. The Wild Man fought, but they took him to jail. He
looked Chinese, so they found a Chinese in town to come translate.

The Wild Man talked a lot to the translator. He told him his 6
name. He said he was thirty-nine years old, the father of seven children, who were in Taiwan. To support them, he had shipped out on

Maxine Hong Kingston (1940–   ), born in Stockton, California,
of Chinese immigrant parents and now living in Hawaii, is the author of *The Woman Warrior: Memoirs of a Girlhood among Ghosts*
(1975). "The Wild Man of the Green Swamp" is from *China Men*
(1980).

a Liberian freighter. He had gotten very homesick and asked everyone if he could leave the ship and go home. But the officers would not let him off. They sent messages to China to find out about him. When the ship landed, they took him to the airport and tried to put him on an airplane to some foreign place. Then, he said, the white demons took him to Tampa Hospital, which is for insane people, but he escaped, just walked out and went into the swamp.

The interpreter asked how he lived in the swamp. He said he ate 7 snakes, turtles, armadillos, and alligators. The captors could tell how he lived when they opened up his bag, which was not burlap but a pair of pants with the legs knotted. Inside, he had carried a pot, a piece of sharpened tin, and a small club, which he had made by sticking a railroad spike into a section of aluminum tubing.

The sheriff found the Liberian freighter that the Wild Man had 8 been on. The ship's officers said that they had not tried to stop him from going home. His shipmates had decided that there was something wrong with his mind. They had bought him a plane ticket and arranged his passport to send him back to China. They had driven him to the airport, but there he began screaming and weeping and would not get on the plane. So they found him a doctor, who sent him to Tampa Hospital.

Now the doctors at the jail gave him medicine for the mosquito 9 bites, which covered his entire body, and medicine for his stomachache. He was getting better, but after he'd been in jail for three days, the U. S. Border Patrol told him they were sending him back. He became hysterical. That night, he fastened his belt to the bars, wrapped it around his neck, and hung himself.

In the newspaper picture he did not look very wild, being led by 10 the posse out of the swamp. He did not look dirty, either. He wore a checkered shirt unbuttoned at the neck, where his white undershirt showed; his shirt was tucked into his pants; his hair was short. He was surrounded by men in cowboy hats. His fingers stretching open, his wrists pulling apart to the extent of the handcuffs, he lifted his head, his eyes screwed shut, and cried out.

There was a Wild Man in our slough too, only he was a black 11 man. He wore a shirt and no pants, and some mornings when we walked to school, we saw him asleep under the bridge. The police came and took him away. The newspaper said he was crazy; it said the police had been on the lookout for him for a long time, but we had seen him every day.

Los Angeles

CHRISTOPHER ISHERWOOD

In order to get the worst possible first impression of Los Angeles 1
one should arrive there by bus, preferably in summer and on a Saturday night. That is what I did, eight years ago, having crossed the
country via Washington, New Orleans, El Paso, Albuquerque and
Flagstaff, Arizona. As we passed over the state-line at Needles (one
of the hottest places, outside Arabia, in the world) a patriotic lady
traveler started to sing "California, here I come!" In America you can
do this kind of thing unselfconsciously on a long-distance bus: a
good deal of the covered wagon atmosphere still exists. Nevertheless, the effect was macabre. For ahead of us stretched the untidy
yellow desert, quivering in its furnace-glare, with, here and there,
among the rocks at the roadside, the rusty skeleton of an abandoned
automobile, modern counterpart of the pioneer's dead mule. We
drove forward into the Unpromising Land.

Beyond the desert, the monster market-garden begins: thou- 2
sands of acres of citrus-groves, vineyards, and flat fields planted
with tomatoes and onions. The giant billboards reappear. The Coca
Cola advertisement: "Thirst ends here." The girl telling her friend:
"He's tall, dark . . . and owns a Ford V-8." The little towns seem almost entirely built of advertisements. Take these away, you feel,
and there would be scarcely anything left: only drugstores, filling-
stations and unpainted shacks. And fruit: Himalayas of fruit. To the
European immigrant, this rude abundance is nearly as depressing as
the desolation of the wilderness. The imagination turns sulky. The
eye refuses to look and the ear to listen.

Downtown Los Angeles is at present one of the most squalid 3
places in the United States. Many of the buildings along Main Street
are comparatively old but they have not aged gracefully. They are
shabby and senile, like nasty old men. The stifling sidewalks are
crowded with sailors and Mexicans, but there is none of the glamour

Christopher Isherwood (1904–1986) was born in England and lived
in many different countries before settling in the United States. He
is the author of novels, travel books, and memoirs including *All the
Conspirators* (1928), *Goodbye to Berlin* (1939), *The Condor and the Cows*
(1949), and *Christopher and His Kind* (1976). "Los Angeles" is from
Exhumations (1966).

of a port and none of the charm of a Mexican city. In twenty-five years this section will probably have been torn down and rebuilt; for Los Angeles is determined to become at all costs a metropolis. Today, it is still an uncoordinated expanse of townlets and suburbs, spreading wide and white over the sloping plain between the mountains and the Pacific Ocean. The Angeleno becomes accustomed to driving great distances in his car between his work, his entertainment and his home: eighty miles a day would not be very unusual. Most people have a car or the use of one. It is an essential, not a luxury, for the bus services are insufficient and there is no subway. I would scarcely know how to "show" Los Angeles to a visitor. Perhaps the best plan would be to drive quite aimlessly, this way and that, following the wide streets of little stucco houses, gorgeous with flowering trees and bushes—jacaranda, oleander, mimosa and eucalyptus—beneath a technicolor sky. The houses are ranged along communal lawns, unfenced, staring into each other's bedroom windows, without even a pretense of privacy. Such are the homes of the most inquisitive nation in the world; a nation which demands, as its unquestioned right, the minutest details of the lives of its movie stars, politicians and other public men. There is nothing furtive or unfriendly about this American curiosity, but it can sometimes be merciless.

It should not be supposed, from what I have written above, that   4
the architecture of Los Angeles is uniform or homogeneous. On the contrary, it is strongly, and now and then insanely, individualistic. Aside from all the conventional styles—Mexican, Spanish, French Chateau, English Tudor, American Colonial and Japanese—you will find some truly startling freaks: a witch's cottage with nightmare gables and eaves almost touching the ground, an Egyptian temple decorated with hieroglyphics, a miniature medieval castle with cannon on the battlements. Perhaps the influence of the movies is responsible for them. Few of the buildings look permanent or entirely real. It is rather as if a gang of carpenters might be expected to arrive with a truck and dismantle them next morning.

North of Hollywood rises a small steep range of hills. In the   5
midst of the city, they are only half-inhabited; many of their canyons are still choked with yuccas, poison oak and miscellaneous scrub. You find rattlesnakes there and deer and coyotes. At dusk, or in the first light of dawn, the coyotes can be mistaken for dogs as they come trotting along the trail in single file, and it is strange and disconcerting to see them suddenly turn and plunge into the undergrowth with the long, easy leap of the wild animal. Geologically speaking, the Hollywood hills will not last long. Their decomposed

granite breaks off in chunks at a kick and crumbles in your hand. Every year the seasonal rains wash cartloads of it down into the valley.

In fact, the landscape, like Los Angeles itself, is transitional. Impermanence haunts the city, with its mushroom industries—the aircraft perpetually becoming obsolete, the oil which must one day be exhausted, the movies which fill America's theaters for six months and are forgotten. Many of its houses—especially the grander ones—have a curiously disturbing atmosphere, a kind of psychological dankness which smells of anxiety, overdrafts, uneasy lust, whisky, divorce and lies. "Go away," a wretched little ghost whispers from the closet, "go away before it is to late. I was vain. I was silly. They flattered me. I failed. You will fail, too. Don't listen to their promises. Go away. Now, at once." But the new occupant seldom pays any attention to such voices. Indeed he is deaf to them, just as the pioneers were deaf to the ghosts of the goldfields. He is quite sure that he knows how to handle himself. He will make his pile; and he will know when to stop. No stupid mistakes for *him*. No extravagance, no alimony, no legal complications. . . . And then the lawyer says: "Never mind all that small print: it doesn't mean a thing. All you have to do is sign here." And he signs.

California is a tragic country—like Palestine, like every Promised Land. Its short history is a fever-chart of migrations—the land rush, the gold rush, the oil rush, the movie rush, the Okie fruit-picking rush, the wartime rush to the aircraft factories—followed, in each instance, by counter-migrations of the disappointed and unsuccessful, moving sorrowfully homeward. You will find plenty of people in the Middle West and in the East who are very bitter against California in general and Los Angeles in particular. They complain that the life there is heartless, materialistic, selfish. But emigrants to Eldorado have really no right to grumble. Most of us come to the Far West with somewhat cynical intentions. Privately, we hope to get something for nothing—or, at any rate, for very little. Well, perhaps we shall. But if we don't, we have no one to blame but ourselves.

The movie industry—to take the most obvious example—is still very like a goldmining camp slowly and painfully engaged in transforming itself into a respectable, ordered community. Inevitably, the process is violent. The anarchy of the old days, with every man for himself and winner take the jackpot, still exercises an insidious appeal. It is not easy for the writer who earns 3,000 dollars a week to make common cause with his colleague who only gets 250. The original tycoons were not monsters; they were merely adventurers, in the best and worst sense of the word. They had risked everything and won—often after an epic and ruthless struggle—and they thought themselves entitled to every cent of their winnings. Their attitude toward their employees, from stars down to stagehands, was possessive and paternalistic. Knowing nothing about art and very little about technique, they did not hesitate to interfere in every stage of film production—blue-pencilling scripts, dictating casting, bothering directors and criticizing camera angles. The specter of the Box Office haunted them night and day. This was their own money, and they were madly afraid of losing it. "There's nothing so cowardly," a producer once told me, "as a million dollars." The paternalist is a sentimentalist at heart, and the sentimentalist is always potentially cruel. When the studio operatives ceased to rely upon their bosses' benevolence and organized themselves into unions, the tycoon became an injured papa, hurt and enraged by their ingratitude. If the boys did not trust him—well, that was just too bad. He knew what was good for them, and to prove it he was ready to use strike-breakers and uniformed thugs masquerading as special police. But the epoch of the tycoons is now, happily, almost over. The financier of today has learnt that it pays better to give his artists and technicians a free hand, and to concentrate his own energies on the business he really understands: the promotion and distribution of the finished product. The formation of independent units within the major studios is making possible a much greater degree of cooperation between directors, writers, actors, composers and art-directors. Without being childishly optimistic, one can foresee a time when quite a large proportion of Hollywood's films will be entertainment fit for adults, and when men and women of talent will come to the movie colony not as absurdly overpaid secretaries resigned to humoring their employers but as responsible artists free and eager to do their best. Greed is, however, only one of two disintegrating forces which threaten the immigrant's character: the other, far more terrible, is sloth. Out there, in the eternal lazy morning of the Pacific, days slip away into months, months into years; the seasons are reduced to the faintest nuance by the great central fact of the sunshine; one might pass a lifetime, it seems, between two yawns, lying bronzed and naked on the sand. The trees keep their green, the flowers perpetually bloom, beautiful girls and superb boys ride the foaming breakers. They are not always the same boys, girls, flowers and trees; but that you scarcely notice. Age and death are very discreet there; they seem as improbable as the Japanese submarines which used to lurk up and down the coast during the war and sometimes sink ships within actual sight of the land. I need not describe the de luxe, parklike cemeteries which so hospitably invite you to the final act of relaxation: Aldous Huxley has done this classically already in *After Many a Summer*. But it is worth recalling one of their advertisements, in which a charming, well-groomed elderly lady (presumably risen from the dead) assured the public: "It's better at Forest Lawn. *I speak from experience.*"

To live sanely in Los Angeles (or, I suppose, in any other large   9 American city) you have to cultivate the art of staying awake. You must learn to resist (firmly but not tensely) the unceasing hypnotic suggestions of the radio, the billboards, the movies and the newspapers; those demon voices which are forever whispering in your ear what you should desire, what you should fear, what you should wear and eat and drink and enjoy, what you should think and do and be. They have planned a life for you—from the cradle to the grave and beyond—which it would be easy, fatally easy, to accept. The least wandering of the attention, the least relaxation of your awareness, and already the eyelids begin to droop, the eyes grow vacant, the body starts to move in obedience to the hypnotist's command. Wake up, wake up—before you sign that seven-year contract, buy that house you don't really want, marry that girl you secretly despise. Don't reach for the whisky, that won't help you. You've got to think, to discriminate, to exercise your own free will and judgment. And you must do this, I repeat, without tension, quite rationally and calmly. For if you give way to fury against the hypnotists, if you smash the radio and tear the newspapers to shreds, you will only rush to the other extreme and fossilize into defiant eccentricity. Hollywood's two polar types are the cynically drunken writer aggressively nursing a ten-year-old reputation and the theatrically self-conscious hermit who strides the boulevard in sandals, home-made shorts and a prophetic beard, muttering against the Age of the Machines.

An afternoon drive from Los Angeles will take you up into the   10 high mountains, where eagles circle above the forests and the cold blue lakes, or out over the Mojave Desert, with its weird vegetation and immense vistas. Not very far away are Death Valley, and Yosemite, and the Sequoia Forest with its giant trees which were growing long before the Parthenon was built; they are the oldest living things in the world. One should visit such places often, and be conscious, in the midst of the city, of their surrounding presence. For this is the real nature of California and the secret of its fascination; this untamed, undomesticated, aloof, prehistoric landscape which relentlessly reminds the traveler of his human condition and the circumstances of his tenure upon the earth. "You are perfectly welcome," it tells him, "during your short visit. Everything is at your disposal. Only, I must warn you, if things go wrong, don't blame me. I accept no responsibility. I am not part of your neurosis. Don't cry to me for safety. There is no home here. There is no security in your mansions or your fortresses, your family vaults or your banks or your double beds. Understand this fact, and you will be free. Accept it, and you will be happy."

Gay Freedom Day Parade, San Francisco

FRANCES FITZGERALD

It was one of those days in San Francisco when the weather is so 1
perfect there seems to be no weather. The sun shone out of a
cerulean sky lighting the streets to a shadowless intensity. It was a
Sunday morning, and the streets were almost empty, so our pickup
truck sped uninterrupted up and down the hills, giving those of us
in the back a Ferris wheel view of the city. In Pacific Heights the
roses were blooming, the hollies were in berry, and enormous
clumps of daisies billowed out from under palm trees. On Russian
Hill the Victorian houses with their ice-cream-colored facades
seemed to reflect this bewilderment of seasons. At the bottom of the
hill the skyscrapers of the financial district wheeled through our
horizon, and the truck careened through the deserted canyons of
the financial district heading for the waterfront.

"Don't worry," said Armistead. "We're on gay time, so the pa- 2
rade won't have started yet."

He was right, of course. Rounding a corner, we came upon a 3
line of stationary floats. The balloons were flying—the lavender,
pink and silver bouquets crowding the sky—and the bands were
just warming up. People in costumes milled about amid a crowd of
young men and women in blue jeans. The Gay Freedom Day Parade
had not yet begun.

Our truck nosed itself into the parade lineup behind a group of 4
marchers with signs reading LUTHERANS CONCERNED FOR GAY
PEOPLE and a hay wagon advertising a gay rodeo in Reno, Nevada.
Our truck had no sign on it, but it carried in addition to myself and
another journalist, two people well known to the gay community of
the city: the writer and humorist Armistead Maupin and the professional football player Dave Kopay. In the front seat were Ken Maley
and a couple of other friends of Armistead's.

Frances FitzGerald (1940–   ), from New York, is the author of
Fire in the Lake: The Vietnamese and Americans in Vietnam (1972) and
America Revised: History Schoolbooks in the Twentieth Century (1979).
"Gay Freedom Day Parade, San Francisco" is from "The Castro," in
Cities on a Hill: A Journey through Contemporary American Cultures
(1986).

In a few minutes our part of the parade began to move forward;   5
a country-and-western band struck up somewhere behind us, and a
number of men dressed as cowboys and clowns took their places in
and around the hay wagon. A clown in whiteface with baggy overalls came and walked alongside our truck. I asked about the rodeo,
and he said matter-of-factly, "This is only our second year, so we
don't expect any bulldogging, but we've got a lot of calf ropers,
some bronc riders, and some really wonderful Dale Evans imitations. You've *got* to come."

The clown paused, distracted by the sight of a huge person in   6
velvet robes with ermine trim and red velvet hat to match hurrying
along the sidewalk. "Just *who* does she think *she* is?" he asked
rhetorically. The "Boris Gudunov" personage was followed by what
seemed to be a frowsy middle-aged woman with an enormous bosom. The woman was wearing a kerchief and a cheap cloth coat,
and she was having some trouble with her high heels—so the red-
robed person kept having to go back to right her and pull her along.
"Well, it's certainly not the Empress," the clown said. "Far too
tacky."

The clown drifted off, and I turned to watch a man in a Batman   7
cape and a sequined jockstrap roller-skating by. He had the torso of
a dancer, and he moved with liquid, dreamlike movements, crossing
and recrossing the street. He glided through the Lutheran contingent and then swept through another group of clergymen carrying
large placards of Christ on the cross. At the intersection he looped
around a yellow taxicab filled with young women in T-shirts. The
young women were leaning out of the windows cheering and
bouncing about a sign that read LESBIAN TAXI DRIVERS OF SAN
FRANCISCO. One of them, a slim young woman with long blond
hair, I recognized as the taxi driver who had brought me in from the
airport a few weeks before.

Eventually our pickup truck turned onto Market Street, the main   8
thoroughfare of the city, and we had suddenly a view of the whole
first half of the parade—its floats and lines of marchers filling the
street in front of us—on its way to City Hall. The sun was now
harsh as a kleig light overhead; it burnished the streets and set the
windows of the skyscrapers on fire. Nearby an elderly Chinese man
with a dog walked along the sidewalk close to the buildings, his
head bowed, his eyes averted from the marchers. A block away a
woman in a baggy coat and kerchief scuttled into a doorway—just in
time to avoid the sight of the transvestite copy of herself hulking
down the avenue. Otherwise the sidewalks and the streets leading
off into the downtown were deserted—as empty as if a neutron
bomb had hit, cleaning away the weekday mass of humanity and

leaving the skyscrapers perfectly intact for a new civilization to move in. At this point there were no spectators; there was no one to watch this horde in its outlandish costumes march into the city.

That summer—it was 1978—estimates of the gay population of   9
San Francisco ranged from 75,000 to 150,000. If the off-cited figure of 100,000 were correct, this meant that in this city of less than 700,000 people, approximately one out of every five adults and one out of every three or four voters was gay. A great proportion of these people—half of them or more—had moved into the city within the past eight years. And most of these new immigrants were young, white, and male. There were now some 90 gay bars in the city and perhaps 150 gay organizations including church groups, social services, and business associations. There were 9 gay newspapers, 2 foundations, and 3 Democratic clubs. While the gay men and women had settled all over the city, they had created an almost exclusive area of gay settlement in the Eureka Valley, in a neighborhood known as the Castro. The previous year the Castro had elected a city supervisor, Harvey Milk, who ran as a gay candidate—against 16 opponents including another gay man. Now, quite visibly, this area of settlement was spreading in all directions: up into the hills above the Castro, down into the Mission District, and across into the lower Haight Street neighborhood. While New York and Los Angeles probably had more gay residents, the proportions were nowhere as high as they were in San Francisco. Possibly the sheer concentration of gay people in San Francisco had no parallel in history.

At that time most San Franciscans still contrived to ignore the   10
growing gay population in their midst. The local press reported on gay events and on the growth of the Castro, but most San Franciscans I talked to seemed not to have noticed these pieces—or they had forgotten them. Small wonder, perhaps, for the articles were not sensational in any sense. The local reporters seemed to have gotten quite used to the gay community without ever giving it its due. They now took certain things for granted. Earlier that year a young journalist from out of town had gone with the mayor and other city officials to the annual Beaux Arts Costume Ball. The event had shaken him, but the local newspapers had reported it as they would a mayoral visit to a Knights of Columbus dinner. It was, after all, the third year the mayor had gone to a drag ball in the civic auditorium.

The program in my press kit showed that there were 138 contin-   11
gents in the parade, and that with a few exceptions, such as Straights for Gay Rights and the San Francisco Commission on the Status of Women, all of them represented gay organizations of one sort or another. With the program it was possible to sort these organizations into certain categories: political organizations, human rights

groups, professional associations, social-service organizations, ethnic minority groups, religious organizations, college groups, out-of-town contingents, such as the Napa Gay People's Coalition, fraternal organizations, such as those for transsexuals and bisexuals for gay rights, sports groups, and commercial enterprises. Perhaps for variety's sake, however, the organizers had chosen to mix up the categories to some degree, so that the actual order of the parade might have come from the pages of Claude Lévi-Strauss.[1]

By the time our truck turned onto Market Street, I was in fact 12 too late to see the head of the parade: the Gay American Indian contingent followed by Disabled Gay People and Friends, followed by a ninety-piece marching band and the gay political leaders of the city. But leaving my truck to walk along the sidelines where a crowd was now gathering, I was able to make my way up to number forty-one: the Gay Latino Alliance, or GALA, a group of young men dancing down the street to mariachi music. Just behind them was a group representing the gay Jewish synagogue, a rather serious group of people, the men with yarmulkes on carrying a banner with the Star of David. This contingent was closely followed by a Marilyn Monroe look-alike on stilts batting six-inch-long eyelashes and swaying to the music of the disco float just behind her. Farther back there were people in country work clothes with a sign for the Order of Displaced Okies. The Local Lesbian Association Kazoo Marching Band led a number of women's groups, including the San Francisco Women's Center, UC Berkeley Women's Studies, and Dykes on Bikes. This latter group could be easily located, as every time they came to an intersection, the six or seven petite women in tight jeans, men's undershirts, and boots would rev up their motorcycles, bringing loud applause from the crowd. Farther back, behind the Gay Pagans, the Free Beach Activists, the Zimbabwe Medical Drive, and the Alice B. Toklas Democratic Club, came the float that many had been waiting for: the sequined, spangled, and tulle-wrapped chariot of the Council of Grand Dukes and Duchesses of San Francisco. Somewhere in this neighborhood there was a truly unfortunate juxtaposition. The Women Against Violence in Pornography and the Media had taken their proper places in line, but then somehow, perhaps as a result of some confusion in the Society of Janus, elements of the sadomasochistic liberation front had moved in just behind them. The pallid-looking men in uniforms were not dragging chains—the parade organizers had counseled against it—but they

---

[1] French anthropologist (1908–   ); see Brief Encounters, Chapters 1 and 5. (Ed.)

were carrying a sign of questionable grammar that read BLACK AND BLUE IS BEAUTIFUL.

At that time—the very height of gay liberation—many Ameri- 13 cans believed that the homosexual population of the United States had greatly increased in the past ten or twenty years. And they were willing to explain it. Some said the country was going soft: there was no discipline anymore, and no morality. Others, including a number of gay men, said that the country was finding its ecological balance and creating natural limits to population growth. There was, however, no evidence for the premise—never mind for the theories built upon it. What demographic studies there were showed that male homosexuals had remained a fairly stable percentage of the population since 1948 when the first Kinsey study came out. What had happened since then, but particularly in the past decade, was that homosexuals had assumed much greater visibility. Gay libera- tion was, more than anything else, a move into consciousness. The movement "created" some homosexuals in that it permitted some people to discover their homosexual feelings and to express them. But its main effect was to bring large numbers of homosexuals out of the closet—and into the consciousness of others. Its secondary effect was to create a great wave of migration into the tolerant cities of the country. All the gay immigrants I talked to said that they had always known they were attracted to the same sex; their decision was not to become a homosexual but to live openly as one and in a gay commu- nity. "I lived in Rochester," a young political consultant told me. "I was white, male, and middle class, and I had gone to Harvard. I thought I could do anything I wanted, so I resented having to con- ceal something as basic as sex. I resented being condemned to re- press or ignore my homosexuality and to live in turmoil for the rest of my life. The solution was to move here."

The parade was moving slowly, but the farther we went up Mar- 14 ket Street, the more spectators there were. First there was a line of people and then a crowd filling the sidewalks and spilling out into the streets behind. Many of the spectators were young men, and though we had no sign on our truck, it now happened frequently that one of them would call out, "Hey, it's Armistead!" or, "Look, it's Dave Kopay!"

Kopay, tall, broad-shouldered, and lantern-jawed, was not hard 15 to recognize: he looked like a movie version of a football player. A veteran running back, he had played pro ball for eight years with the 49ers, the Lions, the Redskins, the Saints, and the Green Bay Packers. He retired in 1975 and three years later, convinced that ru- mors of his homosexuality had denied him a coaching job, he de- cided to come out to a newspaper reporter doing a story on homosexuality in professional sports. The reporter had talked to a number of gay athletes, but only Kopay permitted his name to be used. His gesture created a scandal in the sports world, for while everyone knew there were homosexuals in professional sports, no one wanted the evidence of it. But Kopay became something of a hero among gay men.

Armistead Maupin might have been more difficult to recognize,   16 as he was wearing a lavender-and-yellow hockey jersey with a matching cap pulled down over his bright blue eyes. But in San Francisco he was just as well known as Kopay. A journalist and fiction writer, he was the author of *Tales of the City*, a humorous serial on San Francisco life that had appeared in the *San Francisco Chronicle*. The terrain he mapped in his *Tales* was the world of young single people, gay and straight, who came to San Francisco to change their lives. It was a world he knew well. Maupin, as it happened, came from an aristocratic and ultraconservative North Carolina family. On graduating from the University of North Carolina at Chapel Hill, he had joined the Navy, gone through officers' school, and served a tour of duty in Vietnam. He had then spent another summer in Vietnam as a volunteer building refugee housing with some fellow officers. On his return, President Richard Nixon invited him to the White House and honored him as the very model of patriotic young Republicanism. A year later Maupin left for San Francisco.

Because of his writing but also because of his enormous south-   17 ern charm, Armistead had become the Gay Personality of San Francisco. The year before he had been master of ceremonies at the gay parade, and he had opened the annual game between the San Francisco Sheriff's Department and the Gay Softball League by throwing out an orange. Once, to demonstrate that nothing is sacred, including *amour-propre*,[2] he turned up in a white rabbit suit to sell jockstraps for a gay charity. The epigraph for his book was a quotation from Oscar Wilde: "It's an odd thing, but anyone who disappears is said to be seen in San Francisco."

Most of the spectators crowding the sidewalks appeared to be in   18 their twenties or thirties. Dressed California-style in natural fibers and hiking or jogging shoes, both the men and women looked lean, tan, and athletic. Many of the men, now shirtless in the sun, had admirably muscled chests. "Just think," Armistead said, looking out at a row of them sunbathing on a wall, "of all the fortunes spent in bodybuilding equipment." There were some older people, including

---

[2] *amour-propre:* self-esteem or self-respect. (Ed.)

a group of four women with butch haircuts and lined faces and a couple of men with identical beards and canes, but not very many. And apart from a few glum-looking tourist families, there were hardly any mixed couples or children. To the expert observers on my truck, most of the spectators appeared to be gay.

The majority of San Franciscans could still ignore the growing 19 gay population in their midst in part because the city—in spite of the endless views of self afforded by its hills—was still decentralized, its residential neighborhoods a series of ethnic villages: black, Hispanic, Irish, Italian, and Chinese. Like all the other minorities, the gays had their own neighborhoods and places of entertainment which other San Franciscans circumnavigated as they went from work to home. But then, too, unlike the rest, gay people had no distinguishing marks, no permanent badges of color, class, or accent. Going to work in the downtown, gay people, black or white, men or women, were invisible to others for as long as they wanted to be. Politically speaking, they acted like a highly organized ethnic group—indeed this year (1978) they had persuaded the city government to give the gay parade the same sum it gave ethnic parades for the purpose of encouraging tourism. Yet this minority, being defined by desire alone, materialized only once a year, in June, on Gay Freedom Day.

From time to time during the slow march up Market Street it 20 came to me to see the gay parade as the unfurling of a municipal dream sequence—the clowns, the drag queens, and the men in their leather suits being the fantastic imagery of the city's collective unconscious. Sigmund Freud, after all, had believed that man was born bisexual and that every human being had homosexual desires in some degree. From this perspective it seemed unreasonable that the parade should not include everyone in San Francisco. On the other hand, Freud believed that each individual's inner world was quite unique—individual desires having different qualities or textures, different degrees of intensity and modes of expression. And from this perspective it seemed unreasonable that all these thousands of people should pick up a banner labeled GAY and march with it to City Hall. What made the experience more bewildering still was that to watch the contingents pass by was to watch a confusion of categories something like that of Borges's[3] Chinese list: Dykes on Bikes, California Human Rights Advocates, Sutro Baths, Lesbian Mothers, the Imperial Silver Fox Court. Looking at the cos-

---

[3] Jorge Luis Borges (1899–1986), Argentinian fiction writer. (Ed.)

tumes—the leather and the tulle—I wondered which were new and which had been worn for decades, even centuries, in the undergrounds of Paris or London. Which were the permanent archetypes of desires, and which merely fashions or the jokes of the young? My friends on the truck would answer with the counterculture koan that everyone—all of us—were in drag. And yet some of these costumes and dream images had settlement patterns in the city. There were in fact four gay centers in San Francisco, each geographically distinct, each containing what appeared to be distinct subcultures or culture parts.

The oldest gay center in the city lay in the Tenderloin—that tri- 21 angle of sleazy bars and cheap hotels bordered by the business district, the theater district, and Market Street. The Tenderloin, like its counterparts in other cities, was far from exclusively gay. The home of winos and bums, it was the transit station for sailors and other impecunious travelers, and it harbored most of the prostitution, both gay and straight, for the entire city. In the late afternoon female prostitutes, male hustlers, and transvestite whores could be seen performing a complicated street corner ballet as they tried at once to evade the police and sort out their initially undifferentiated customers. In the fifties the district had harbored most of the gay bars in the city—but now only hustler and drag queen bars were left. The Kokpit, owned by a queen called Sweet Lips, had been in operation for about a decade. Now lined with trophies and photographs of countless drag balls, it had become a kind of Toots Shor's of drag San Francisco. A few blocks away there was a bar of a professional and much more highly specialized nature, where six- to seven-foot-tall black transvestites hustled white men in business suits, who were, necessarily, shorter.

Chronologically speaking, Polk Street, or Polk Gulch, was the 22 second gay center of the city. It was the decorators' district, and in the sixties a number of gay bars had moved into the blocks lined with antique shops and furniture stores. Since then it had been the major site of the Halloween festivities. On that one night a year the police stood by, leaving the street to a carnival of witches, clowns, nuns on roller skates, and Jackie Kennedy look-alikes or Patty Hearst look-alikes with toy machine guns. Polk Street was a mixed neighborhood—both gay and straight people lived there, and its restaurants catered to both crowds. Its gay bars were thus not conspicuous except at night when groups of young hustlers stood out on the sidewalks around them. A number of them still catered to the stylish and the well-to-do. They had low lights, expensive furniture, and music by the old favorites: Marlene Dietrich, Noel Coward, and

Judy Garland. Even to outsiders their patrons would be recognizable, for Polk Street was still the land of good taste and attitude: the silk scarf so perfectly knotted, the sentimentality, the witty little jab.

A newer gay center lay around Folsom Street in the old warehouse district south of Market. At night Folsom Street was the complement to Polk Street—the raw, as it were, to the cooked—for it was lined with leather bars: the Stud, the Brig, the Ramrod, the Black and Blue. Late at night groups of men in blue jeans, motorcycle jackets, and boots would circle around ranks of Triumphs and Harley-Davidsons, eyeing each other warily. The bars had sawdust on the floors, and men drank beer standing up, shoulder to shoulder, in a din of heavy metal and hard rock. In the Black and Blue some of them wore studded wristbands, studded neckbands, and caps with Nazi insignia; above the bar a huge motorcycle was suspended in a wash of psychedelic lights. On Wednesday nights the Arena bar had a slave auction: men would be stripped almost naked, chained up by men in black masks with whips, prodded, and sold off to the highest bidder. Such was the theater of Folsom Street. The men in leather came from Polk Street and other quiet neighborhoods, the money went to charity, and the "slave" put on a business suit and went to work the next day. 23

Folsom Street was a night town—the Valley of the Kings, it was called, as opposed to the Valley of the Queens in the Tenderloin and the Valley of the Dolls on Polk Street. But in addition to the leather bars, a variety of gay restaurants, discotheques, bathhouses, and sex clubs had moved into its abandoned warehouses and manufacturing lofts. It was an entertainment place, and few people lived there. 24

The Castro, by contrast, was a neighborhood. Though first settled by gays—homesteaded, as it were—in the early seventies, it was now the fulcrum of gay life in the city. At first glance it was much like other neighborhoods: a four-block main street with a drugstore, corner groceries, a liquor store, dry cleaners, and a revival movie house whose facade had seen better days. Here and there upscale money was visibly at work: a café advertised Dungeness crab, a store sold expensive glass and tableware, and there were two banks. But there was nothing swish about the Castro. The main street ran off into quiet streets of two- and three-story white-shingle houses; the main haberdashery, The All-American Boy, sold clothes that would have suited a conservative Ivy Leaguer. In fact the neighborhood was like other neighborhoods except that on Saturdays and Sundays you could walk for blocks and see only young men dressed as it were for a hiking expedition. Also the bookstore was a gay bookstore, the health club a gay health club; and behind the shingles hung out on the street there was a gay real-estate bro- 25 kerage, a gay lawyer's office, and the office of a gay psychiatrist. The bars were, with once exception, gay bars, and one of them, the Twin Peaks bar near Market Street, was, so Armistead told me, the first gay bar in the country to have picture windows on the street.

Armistead and his friends liked to take visitors to the Castro and point out landmarks such as the Twin Peaks. But in fact the only remarkable-looking thing on the street was the crowd of young men. Even at lunchtime on a weekday there would be dozens of good-looking young men crowding the café tables, hanging out at the bars, leaning against doorways, or walking down the streets with their arms around each other. The sexual tension was palpable. "I'd never live here," Armistead said. "Far too intense. You can't go to the laundromat at ten A.M. without the right pair of jeans on." The Castro was the place where most of the young gay men came. Fifty to a hundred thousand came as tourists each summer, and of these, thousands decided to settle, leaving Topeka and Omaha for good. New York and Los Angeles had their Polk Streets and Folsom Districts, but the Castro was unique: it was the first settlement built by gay liberation.

The denizens of the Castro were overwhelmingly male, but occasionally in a crowd of men on the street you would see two or three young women dressed in jeans or jumpsuits. Some gay women lived in the Castro—they considered it safe—and close by there were a few small lesbian settlements in the Haight, the Duboce Triangle and the Mission District. But you could not find these settlements unless you knew where to look, so inconspicuous were they. On one quiet street there was a comfortable neighborhood bar with a jukebox and a pool table; on the walls were framed photographs of the softball team its regulars organized each summer. This was Maud's Study, and the bartender plus all of the customers were women. But there were only five or six lesbian bars in the entire city. There were many more women's organizations, theater groups, social-service organizations, and so on—but there was no female equivalent of the Castro. In Berkeley and north Oakland across the Bay, young political women had taken over some of the big, slightly run-down, shingle houses and started a newspaper, a crafts cooperative, a recording company, and various other enterprises. And there were a number of lesbian farm communes up the coast in northern California. But nowhere did gay women congregate the way gay men did. In the city—feeling themselves vulnerable—they took on protective colorings and melted into the landscape. No one ever knew how many of them there were in San Francisco, as no research money was ever allotted to finding that out. They appeared in large numbers only on Gay Freedom Day.

The front of the parade had long ago reached its terminus at 28
City Hall when our truck pulled into the Civic Center Plaza. A ro-
tunda building like the U.S. Capitol, the San Francisco City Hall
looked large and imposing, fronted, as it was, by tree-lined malls
and a reflecting pool. At the same time, recently cleaned and bright
white against a bright blue sky, it looked like an enormous wedding
cake of the sort displayed in old-fashioned Italian bakeries. As we
arrived, a tall, handsome woman standing on the dais before its
steps was chanting something like a prayer. She was saying:

"In the memory of the recorded nine million women, many of 29
whom were lesbians, who were executed on charges of witchcraft,
we invoke the name of the Great Goddess.

"In memory of the uncounted number of gay men who were 30
thrown into the fire as faggots to light the pyres of their sisters, we
invoke the name of the Great Goddess, the Mother of all living
things."

The speaker, I discovered later, called herself Bayta Podos. She 31
was a secretary and an instructor in women's studies at San Francisco State University. She was also the priestess of a feminist religion that she herself had conceived out of her research into matriar-
chal or matrilineal societies. She practiced magic and invented
rituals to be used on ceremonial occasions. Recently she had closed
a feminist conference on violence against women by producing a
large wooden sword and instructing the women to meditate upon it,
filling it with all their fears and all the anger they felt against the pa-
triarchate. Then she broke the sword in two.

"We invoke you, Great One," she continued. "You whose 32
names have been sung from time beyond time: You who are Inanni,
Isis, Ishtar, Anath, Ashtoreth, Amaterasu, Neith, Selket, Turquoise
Woman, White Shell Woman, Cihuacotl, Tonantzin, Demeter,
Artemis, Earthquake Mother, Kail . . ."

Next to the dais Harvey Milk was standing with a lei of purple 33
orchids around his neck and a bunch of daisies in one hand, giving
interviews to a small group of radio and television correspondents.
He had already made his speech—a strong one, I was told—denouncing the so-called Briggs Initiative, a proposition on the California ballot which, if passed, would drive all openly gay teachers and
all discussions of gay rights out of the public schools. He was now
calling for a national gay march on Washington for the following
year. Nearby, beside the dais, a woman in a gypsy costume was
swinging her child around through the air; a man in a tuxedo with
makeup on and long red fingernails strolled past her humming to
himself.

In front of the dais a large crowd had assembled—a very large 34 crowd. Indeed, it seemed to me when I looked at it from the top of City Hall steps that I must be looking at all the twenty- to thirty-year-olds in northern California. The young people in front were following the proceedings on the dais enthusiastically. Some were waving banners; others were standing with linked arms, chanting and cheering. Behind them groups of people were lying on the grass, their heads pillowed on backpacks, talking and rolling joints while other groups of young people drifted around them. From the front the crowd looked like an early antiwar demonstration; from the back it looked like the Woodstock nation. Both seemed to be crowds of the sixties returned, only now, both of them were gay.

The next day, June 26, 1978, the *San Francisco Chronicle* reported 35 that 240,000 people turned out for the annual Gay Freedom Day Parade. It quoted the police estimate rather than the chamber of commerce estimate of 300,000 made later in the day or the figure of 375,000 quoted by the *Los Angeles Times*. Even the second figure would make the turnout one of the largest in San Francisco's history and would equal nearly half of the adult population of the city. The local press tended to avoid figures leading to such arithmetic. It did not like to advertise that San Francisco had become the gay capital of the country, if not of the world.

The Subway Is a Madhouse

PAUL THEROUX

We were at Flushing Avenue, on the GG line, talking about rules for 1
riding the subway. You need rules: the subway is like a complex—
and diseased—circulatory system. Some people liken it to a sewer
and others hunch their shoulders and mutter about being in the
bowels of the earth. It is full of suspicious-looking people.

I said, "Keep away from isolated cars, I suppose," and my 2
friend, a police officer, said, "Never display jewelry."

Just then, a man walked by, and he had Chinese coins—the old 3
ones with a hole through the middle—woven somehow into his
hair. There were enough coins in that man's hair for a swell night
out in old Shanghai, but robbing him would have involved scalping
him. There was a woman at the station, too. She was clearly crazy,
and she lived in the subway the way people live in railway stations
in India, with stacks of dirty bags. The police in New York call such
people "skells" and are seldom harsh with them. "Wolfman Jack" is
a skell, living underground at Hoyt-Schermerhorn, also on the GG
line; the police in that station give him food and clothes, and if you
ask him how he is, he says, "I'm getting some calls." Call them colorful characters and they don't look so dangerous or pathetic.

This crazy old lady at Flushing Avenue was saying, "I'm a mem- 4
ber of the medical profession." She had no teeth, and plastic bags
were taped around her feet. I glanced at her and made sure she kept
her distance. The previous day, a crazy old lady just like her, came
at me and shrieked, "Ahm goon cut you up!" This was at Pelham
Parkway, on the IRT-2 line in the Bronx. I left the car at the next
stop, Bronx Park East, where the zoo is, though who could be
blamed for thinking that, in New York City, the zoo is everywhere?

Then a Muslim unflapped his prayer mat—while we were at 5
Flushing Avenue, talking about Rules—and spread it on the platform and knelt on it, just like that, and was soon on all fours, be-

Paul Theruox (1941–   ), born in Medford, Massachusetts, but
living most of his adult life overseas, is the author of travel books
and novels including *The Great Railway Bazaar: By Train through Asia*
(1975), *The Old Patagonian Express: By Train through the Americas*
(1979), and *The Mosquito Coast* (1982). "The Subway Is a Madhouse"
is from "Subterranean Gothic," originally published as "Subway
Odyssey" in *The New Yorker* (1981).

seeching Allah and praising the Prophet Mohammed. This is not remarkable. You see people praying, or reading the Bible, or selling
religion on the subway all the time. "Hallelujah, brothers and sisters," the man with the leaflets says on the BMT-RR line at Prospect
Avenue in Brooklyn. "I love Jesus! I used to be a wino!" And Muslims beg and push their green plastic cups at passengers, and try to
sell them copies of something called *Arabic Religious Classics*. It is December and Brooklyn, and the men are dressed for the Great Nafúd
Desert, or Jiddah or Medina—skullcap, gallabieh, sandals.

"And don't sit next to the door," the second police officer said.   6
We were still talking about Rules. "A lot of these snatchers like to
play the doors."

The first officer said, "It's a good idea to keep near the conduc-   7
tor. He's got a telephone. So does the man in the token booth. At
night, stick around the token booth until the train comes in."

"Although, token booths," the second officer said. "A few years   8
ago, some kids filled a fire extinguisher with gasoline and pumped it
into a token booth at Broad Channel. There were two ladies inside,
but before they could get out the kids set the gas on fire. The booth
just exploded like a bomb, and the ladies died. It was a revenge
thing. One of the kids had gotten a summons for Theft of Service—
not paying his fare."

Just below us, at Flushing Avenue, there was a stream running   9
between the tracks. It gurgled and glugged down the whole length
of the long platform. It gave the station the atmosphere of a sewer—
dampness and a powerful smell. The water was flowing towards
Myrtle and Willoughby. And there was a rat. It was only my third
rat in a week of riding the subway, but this one was twice the size of
rats I've seen elsewhere. I thought, *Rats as big as cats.*

"Stay with the crowds. Keep away from quiet stairways. The   10
stairways at 41st and 43rd are usually quiet, but 42nd is always
busy—that's the one to use."

So many rules! It's not like taking a subway at all; it's like walk-   11
ing through the woods—through dangerous jungle, rather: Do this,
Don't do that . . .

"It reminds me," the first officer said. "The burning of that to-   12
ken booth at Broad Channel. Last May, six guys attempted to murder someone at Forest Parkway, on the 'J' line. It was a whole gang
against this one guy. Then they tried to burn the station down with
molotov cocktails. We stopped that, too."

The man who said this was six-feet four, two hundred and   13
eighty-one pounds. He carried a .38 in a shoulder holster and wore
a bullet-proof vest. He had a radio, a can of Mace and a blackjack.
He was a plainclothesman.

The funny thing is that, one day, a boy—five feet six, one hun-   14
dred and thirty-five pounds—tried to mug him. The boy slapped
him across the face while the plainclothesman was seated on a train.
The boy said, "Give me your money," and then threatened the man
in a vulgar way. The boy still punched at the man when the man
stood up; he still said, "Give me all your money!" The plainclothesman then took out his badge and his pistol and said, "I'm a police
officer and you're under arrest." "I was just kidding!" the boy said,
but it was too late.

I laughed at the thought of someone trying to mug this well-   15
armed giant.

"Rule one for the subway," he said. "Want to know what it is?"   16
He looked up and down the Flushing Avenue platform, at the old
lady and the Muslim and the running water and the vandalized
signs. "Rule one is—don't ride the subway if you don't have to."

A lot of people say that. I did not believe it when he said it, and af-   17
ter a week of riding the trains I still didn't. The subway is New York
City's best hope. The streets are impossible, the highways are a failure, there is nowhere to park. The private automobile has no future
in this city. This is plainest of all to the people who own and use
cars in the city; they know, better than anyone, that the car is the
last desperate old-fangled fling of a badly planned transport system.
What is amazing is that back in 1904 a group of businessmen solved
New York's transport problems for centuries to come. What vision!
What enterprise! What an engineering marvel they created in this
underground railway! And how amazed they would be to see what
it has become, how foul-seeming to the public mind.

The subway is a gift to any connoisseur of superlatives. It has   18
the longest rides of any subway in the world, the biggest stations,
the fastest trains, the most track, the most passengers, the most police officers. It also has the filthiest trains, the most bizarre graffiti,
the noisiest wheels, the craziest passengers, the wildest crimes.
Some New Yorkers have never set foot in the subway, other New
Yorkers actually live there, moving from station to station, whining
for money and eating yesterday's bagels and sleeping on benches.
These "skells" are not merely down-and-out. Many are insane,
chucked out of New York hospitals in the early 1970s when it was
decided that long-term care was doing them little good. "They were
resettled in rooms or hotels," Ruth Cohen, a psychiatric social-
worker at Bellevue Hospital, told me. "But many of them can't follow through. They get lost, they wander the streets. They're not violent, suicidal or dangerous enough for Bellevue—this is an

acute-care hospital. But these people who wander the subway, once they're on their own they begin to decompensate—"

Ahm goon cut you up: that woman who threatened to slash me 19 was decompensating. Here are a few more decompensating—one is weeping on a wooden bench at Canal Street, another has wild hair and is spitting into a Coke can. One man who is decompensating in a useful way, has a bundle of brooms and is setting forth to sweep the whole change area at Grand Central; another is scrubbing the stairs with scraps of paper at 14th Street. They drink, they scream, they gibber like monkeys. They sit on subway benches with their knees drawn up, just as they do in mental hospitals. A police officer told me, "There are more serious things than people screaming on trains." This is so, and yet the deranged person who sits next to you and begins howling at you seems at the time very serious indeed.

The subway, which is many things, is also a madhouse.   20

Wyoming: The Solace of Open Spaces

GRETEL EHRLICH

It's May, and I've just awakened from a nap, curled against sage-brush the way my dog taught me to sleep—sheltered from the wind. A front is pulling the huge sky over me, and from the dark a hailstone has hit me on the head. I'm trailing a band of 2000 sheep across a stretch of Wyoming badland, a fifty-mile trip that takes five days because sheep shade up in hot sun and won't budge until it cools. Bunched together now, and excited into a run by the storm, they drift across dry land, tumbling into draws like water and surging out again onto the rugged, choppy plateaus that are the building blocks of this state.

The name Wyoming comes from an Indian word meaning "at the great plains," but the plains are really valleys, great arid valleys, 1600 square miles, with the horizon bending up on all sides into mountain ranges. This gives the vastness a sheltering look.

Winter lasts six months here. Prevailing winds spill snowdrifts to the east, and new storms from the northwest replenish them. This white bulk is sometimes dizzying, even nauseating, to look at. At twenty, thirty, and forty degrees below zero, not only does your car not work but neither do your mind and body. The landscape hardens into a dungeon of space. During the winter, while I was riding to find a new calf, my legs froze to the saddle, and in the silence that such cold creates I felt like the first person on earth, or the last.

Today the sun is out—only a few clouds billowing. In the east, where the sheep have started off without me, the benchland tilts up in a series of red-earthed, eroded mesas, planed flat on top by a million years of water; behind them, a bold line of muscular scarps rears up 10,000 feet to become the Big Horn Mountains. A tidal pattern is engraved into the ground, as if left by the sea that once cov-

Gretel Ehrlich (1946–   ), raised in California and now living in Wyoming, is the author of the poetry volumes *Geode/Rock Body* (1970) and *To Touch the Water* (1981). "Wyoming: The Solace of Open Spaces" is from Ehrlich's personal memoir *The Solace of Open Spaces* (1985).

ered this state. Canyons curve down like galaxies to meet the oncoming rush of flat land.

To live and work in this kind of open country, with its hundred-mile views, is to lose the distinction between background and foreground. When I asked an older ranch hand to describe Wyoming's openness, he said, "It's all a bunch of nothing—wind and rattlesnakes—and so much of it you can't tell where you're going or where you've been and it don't make much difference." John, a sheepman I know, is tall and handsome and has an explosive temperament. He has a perfect intuition about people and sheep. They call him "Highpockets," because he's so long-legged; his graceful stride matches the distances he has to cover. He says, "Open space hasn't affected me at all. It's all the people moving in on it." The huge ranch he was born on takes up much of one county and spreads into another state; to put 100,000 miles on his pickup in three years and never leave home is not unusual. A friend of mine has an aunt who ranched on Powder River and didn't go off her place for eleven years. When her husband died, she quickly moved to town, bought a car, and drove around the States to see what she'd been missing.

Most people tell me they've simply driven through Wyoming as if there were nothing to stop for. Or else they've skied in Jackson Hole, a place Wyomingites acknowledge uncomfortably, because its green beauty and chic affluence are mismatched with the rest of the state. Most of Wyoming has a "lean-to" look. Instead of big, roomy barns and Victorian houses, there are dugouts, low sheds, log cabins, sheep camps, and fence lines that look like driftwood blown haphazardly into place. People here still feel pride because they live in such a harsh place, part of the glamorous cowboy past, and they are determined not to be the victims of a mining-dominated future.

Most characteristic of the state's landscape is what a developer euphemistically describes as "indigenous growth right up to your front door"—a reference to waterless stands of salt sage, snakes, jackrabbits, deerflies, red dust, a brief respite of wildflowers, dry washes, and no trees. In the Great Plains, the vistas look like music, like kyries of grass, but Wyoming seems to be the doing of a mad architect—tumbled and twisted, ribboned with faded, deathbed colors, thrust up and pulled down as if the place had been startled out of a deep sleep and thrown into a pure light.

I came here four years ago. I had not planned to stay, but I couldn't make myself leave. John, the sheepman, put me to work immediately. It was spring, and shearing time. For fourteen days of fourteen hours each, we moved thousands of sheep through sorting corrals to be sheared, branded, and deloused. I suspect that my original motive for coming here was to "lose myself" in new and unpopulated territory. Instead of producing the numbness I thought I wanted, life on the sheep ranch woke me up. The vitality of the people I was working with flushed out what had become a hallucinatory rawness inside me. I threw away my clothes and bought new ones; I cut my hair. The arid country was a clean slate. Its absolute indifference steadied me.

Sagebrush covers 58,000 square miles of Wyoming. The biggest   9 city has a population of 50,000, and there are only five settlements that could be called cities in the whole state. The rest are towns, scattered across the expanse with as much as sixty miles between them, their populations 2000, fifty, or ten. They are fugitive-looking, perched on a barren, windblown bench, or tagged onto a river or a railroad, or laid out straight in a farming valley with implement stores and a block-long Mormon church. In the eastern part of the state, which slides down into the Great Plains, the new mining settlements are boomtowns, trailer cities, metal knots on flat land.

Despite the desolate look, there's a coziness to living in this   10 state. There are so few people (only 470,000) that ranchers who buy and sell cattle know each other statewide; the kids who choose to go to college usually go to the state's one university, in Laramie; hired hands work their way around Wyoming in a lifetime of hirings and firings. And, despite the physical separation, people stay in touch, often driving two or three hours to another ranch for dinner.

Seventy-five years ago, when travel was by buckboard or horse-   11 back, cowboys who were temporarily out of work rode the grub line—drifting from ranch to ranch, mending fences or milking cows, and receiving in exchange a bed and meals. Gossip and messages traveled this slow circuit with them, creating an intimacy between ranchers who were three and four weeks' ride apart. One old-time couple I know, whose turn-of-the-century homestead was used by an outlaw gang as a relay station for stolen horses, recall that if you were traveling, desperado or not, any lighted ranch house was a welcome sign. Even now, for someone who lives in a remote spot, arriving at a ranch or coming to town for supplies is cause for celebration. To emerge from isolation can be disorienting. Everything looks bright, new, vivid. After I had been herding sheep for only three days, the sound of the camp-tender's pickup flustered me. Longing for human company, I felt a foolish grin take over my face, yet I had to resist an urgent temptation to run and hide.

Things happen suddenly in Wyoming: the change of seasons   12 and weather; for people, the violent swings in and out of isolation. But goodnaturedness is concomitant with severity. Friendliness is a tradition. Strangers passing on the road wave hello. A common sight is two pickups stopped side by side far out on a range, on a dirt track winding through the sage. The drivers will share a cigarette, uncap their thermos bottles, and pass a battered cup, steaming with coffee, between windows. These meetings summon up the details of several generations, because in Wyoming, private histories are largely public knowledge.

Because ranch work is a physical and, these days, economic 13 strain, being "at home on the range" is a matter of vigor, self-reliance, and common sense. A person's life is not a series of dramatic events for which he or she is applauded or exiled but a slow accumulation of days, seasons, years, fleshed out by the generational weight of one's family and anchored by a land-bound sense of place.

In most parts of Wyoming, the human population is visibly out- 14 numbered by the animal. Not far from my town of fifty, I rode into a narrow valley and startled a herd of 200 elk. Eagles look like small people as they eat car-killed deer by the road. Antelope, moving in small, graceful bands, travel at 60 miles an hour, their mouths open as if drinking in the space.

The solitude in which westerners live makes them quiet. They 15 telegraph thoughts and feelings by the way they tilt their heads and listen; pulling their Stetsons into a steep dive over their eyes, or pigeon-toeing one boot over the other, they lean against a fence with a fat wedge of snoose beneath their lower lips and take the whole scene in. These detached looks of quiet amusement are sometimes cynical, but they can also come from a dry-eyed humility as lucid as the air is clear.

Conversation goes on in what sounds like a private code; a few 16 phrases imply a complex of meanings. Asking directions, you get a curious list of details. While trailing sheep, I was told to "ride up to that kinda upturned rock, follow the pink wash, turn left at the dump, and then you'll see the waterhole." One friend told his wife on roundup to "turn at the salt lick and the dead cow," which turned out to be a scattering of bones and no salt lick at all.

Sentence structure is shortened to the skin and bones of a 17 thought. Descriptive words are dropped, even verbs: a cowboy looking over a corral full of horses will say to a wrangler, "Which one needs rode?" People hold back their thoughts in what seems to be a dumbfounded silence, then erupt with an excoriating, perceptive remark. Language, so compressed, becomes metaphorical. A rancher ended a relationship with one remark: "You're a bad check," meaning bouncing in and out was intolerable, and even coming back would be no good.

What's behind this laconic style is shyness. There is no vocabu- 18 lary for the subject of feelings. It's not a hangdog shyness, or anything coy—always there's a robust spirit in evidence behind the restraint, as if the earth-dredging wind that pulls across Wyoming had carried its people's voices away but everything else in them had shouldered confidently into the breeze.

I've spent hours riding to sheep camp at dawn in a pickup when 19 nothing was said; eaten meals in the cookhouse when the only words spoken were a mumbled "Thank you, ma'am" at the end of dinner. The silence is profound. Instead of talking, we seem to share one eye. Keenly observed, the world is transformed. The landscape is engorged with detail, every movement on it chillingly sharp. The air between people is charged. Days unfold, bathed in their own music. Nights become hallucinatory; dreams, prescient.

Spring weather is capricious and mean. It snows, then blisters 20 with heat. There have been tornadoes. They lay their elephant trunks out in the sage until they find houses, then slurp everything up and leave. I've noticed that melting snowbanks hiss and rot, viperous, then drip into calm pools where ducklings hatch and livestock, being trailed to summer range, drink. With the ice cover gone, rivers churn a milkshake brown, taking culverts and small bridges with them. Water in such an arid place (the average annual rainfall where I live is less than eight inches) is like blood. It festoons drab land with green veins: a line of cottonwoods following a stream; a strip of alfalfa; and on ditchbanks, wild asparagus growing.

I've moved to a small cattle ranch owned by friends. It's at the 21 foot of the Big Horn Mountains. A few weeks ago, I helped them deliver a calf who was stuck halfway out of his mother's body. By the time he was freed, we could see a heartbeat, but he was straining against a swollen tongue for air. Mary and I held him upside down by his back feet, while Stan, on his hands and knees in the blood, gave the calf mouth-to-mouth resuscitation. I have a vague memory of being pneumonia-choked as a child, my mother giving me her air, which may account for my romance with this windswept state.

If anything is endemic to Wyoming, it is wind. This big room of 22 space is swept out daily, leaving a boneyard of fossils, agates, and carcasses in every stage of decay. Though it was water that initially shaped the state, wind is the meticulous gardener, raising dust and pruning the sage.

I try to imagine a world of uncharted land, in which one could   23
look over an uncompleted map and ride a horse past where all the
lines have stopped. There is no wilderness left; wilderness, yes, but
true wilderness has been gone on this continent since the time of
Lewis and Clark's overland journey.

Two hundred years ago, the Crow, Shoshone, Arapaho,   24
Cheyenne, and Sioux roamed the intermountain West, orchestrating
their movements according to hunger, season, and warfare. Once
they acquired horses, they traversed the spines of all the big Wyoming ranges—the Absarokas, the Wind Rivers, the Tetons, the Big
Horns—and wintered on the unprotected plains that fan out from
them. Space was life. The world was their home.

What was life-giving to Native Americans was often nightmarish   25
to sodbusters who arrived encumbered with families and ethnic
pasts to be transplanted in nearly uninhabitable land. The great distances, the shortage of water and trees, and the loneliness created
unexpected hardships for them. In her book *O Pioneers!* Willa Cather
gives a settler's version of the bleak landscape:

> The little town behind them had vanished as if it had never been,
> had fallen behind the swell of the prairie, and the stern frozen
> country received them into its bosom. The homesteads were few
> and far apart; here and there a windmill gaunt against the sky, a
> sod house crouching in a hollow.

The emptiness of the West was for others a geography of possi-   26
bility. Men and women who amassed great chunks of land and
struggled to preserve unfenced empires were, despite their self-serv-
ing motives, unwitting geographers. They understood the lay of the
land. But by the 1850s, the Oregon and Mormon trails sported
bumper-to-bumper traffic. Wealthy landowners, many of them aristocratic absentee landlords, known as remittance men because they
were paid to come West and get out of their families' hair, over-
stocked the range with more than a million head of cattle. By 1885,
the feed and water were desperately short, and the winter of 1886
laid out the gaunt bodies of dead animals so closely together that
when the thaw came, one rancher from Kaycee claimed to have
walked on cowhide all the way to Crazy Woman Creek, twenty
miles away.

Territorial Wyoming was a boy's world. The land was generous   27
with everything but water. At first there was room enough, food
enough, for everyone. And, as with all beginnings, an expansive
mood set in. The young cowboys, drifters, shopkeepers, schoolteachers, were heroic, lawless, generous, rowdy, and tenacious. The

individualism and optimism generated during those times have endured.

John Tisdale rode north with the trail herds from Texas. He was 28 a college-educated man with enough money to buy a small outfit near the Powder River. While driving home from the town of Buffalo with a buckboard full of Christmas toys for his family and a winter's supply of food, he was shot in the back by an agent of the cattle barons who resented the encroachment of small-time stockmen like him. The wealthy cattlemen tried to control all the public grazing land by restricting membership in the Wyoming Stock Growers Association, as if it were a country club. They ostracized from roundups and brandings cowboys and ranchers who were not members, then denounced them as rustlers. Tisdale's death, the second such cold-blooded murder, kicked off the Johnson County cattle war, which was no simple good-guy-bad-guy shootout but a complicated class struggle between landed gentry and less affluent settlers—a shocking reminder that the West was not an egalitarian sanctuary after all.

Fencing ultimately enforced boundaries, but barbed wire abro- 29 gated space. It was stretched across the beautiful valleys, into the mountains, over desert badlands, through buffalo grass. The "anything is possible" fever—the lure of any new place—was constricted. The integrity of the land as a geographical body, and the freedom to ride anywhere on it, was lost.

I punched cows with a young man named Martin, who is the 30 great-grandson of John Tisdale. His inheritance is not the open land that Tisdale knew and prematurely lost but a rage against restraint.

Wyoming tips down as you head northeast; the highest 31 ground—the Laramie Plains—is on the Colorado border. Up where I live, the Big Horn River leaks into difficult, arid terrain. In the basin where it's dammed, sandhill cranes gather and, with delicate legwork, slice through the stilled water. I was driving by with a rancher one morning when he commented that cranes are "old-fashioned." When I asked why, he said, "Because they mate for life." Then he looked at me with a twinkle in his eyes, as if to say he really did believe in such things but also understood why we break our own rules.

In all this open space, values crystallize quickly. People are 32 strong on scruples but tenderhearted about quirky behavior. A friend and I found one ranch hand, who's "not quite right in the head," sitting in front of the badly decayed carcass of a cow, shaking his finger and saying, "Now, I don't want you to do this ever again!" When I asked what was wrong with him, I was told, "He's goofier than hell, just like the rest of us." Perhaps because the West is historically new, conventional morality is still felt to be less important than rock-bottom truths. Though there's always a lot of teasing and sparring around, people are blunt with each other, sometimes even cruel, believing honesty is stronger medicine than sympathy, which may console but often conceals.

The formality that goes hand in hand with the rowdiness is 33 known as "the Western Code." It's a list of practical dos and don'ts, faithfully observed. A friend, Cliff, who runs a trapline in the winter, cut off half his foot while axing a hole in the ice. Alone, he dragged himself to his pickup and headed for town, stopping to open the ranch gate as he left, and getting out to close it again, thus losing, in his observance of rules, precious time and blood. Later, he commented, "How would it look, them having to come to the hospital to tell me their cows had gotten out?"

Accustomed to emergencies, my friends doctor each other from 34 the vet's bag with relish. When one old-timer suffered a heart attack in hunting camp, his partner quickly stirred up a brew of red horse liniment and hot water and made the half-conscious victim drink it, then tied him onto a horse and led him twenty miles to town. He regained consciousness and lived.

The roominess of the state has affected political attitudes as well. 35 Ranchers keep up with world politics and the convulsions of the economy but are basically isolationists. Being used to running their own small empires of land and livestock, they're suspicious of big government. It's a "don't fence me in" holdover from a century ago. They still want the elbow room their grandfathers had, so they're strongly conservative, but with a populist twist.

Summer is the season when we get our "cowboy tans"—on the 36 lower parts of our faces and on three fourths of our arms. Excessive heat, in the nineties and higher, sends us outside with the mosquitoes. In winter, we're tucked inside our houses, and the white wasteland outside appears to be expanding, but in summer, all the greenery abridges space. Summer is a go-ahead season. Every living thing is off the block and in the race: battalions of bugs in flight and biting; bats swinging around my log cabin as if the bases were loaded and someone had hit a home run. Some of summer's high-speed growth is ominous: larkspur, death camas, and green greasewood can kill sheep—an ironic idea, dying in this desert from eating what is too verdant. With sixteen hours of daylight, farmers and ranchers irrigate feverishly. There are first, second, and third cuttings of hay, some crews averaging only four hours of sleep a night for weeks. And, like the cowboys who in summer ride the night rodeo circuit, nighthawks make daredevil dives at dusk with an eerie whirring that sounds like a plane going down on the shimmering horizon.

In the town where I live, they've had to board up the dance-hall 37 windows because there have been so many fights. There's so little to do except work that people wind up in a state of idle agitation that becomes fatalistic, as if there were nothing to be done about all this untapped energy. So the dark side to the grandeur of these spaces is the small-mindedness that seals people in. Men become hermits; women go mad. Cabin fever explodes into suicides, or into grudges and lifelong family feuds. Two sisters in my area inherited a ranch but found they couldn't get along. They fenced the place in half. When one's cows got out and mixed with the other's, the women went at each other with shovels. They ended up in the same hospital room, but never spoke a word to each other for the rest of their lives.

Eccentricity ritualizes behavior. It's a shortcut through unman- 38 ageable emotions and strict social conventions. I knew a sheepherder named Fred who, at seventy-eight, still had a handsome face, which he kept smooth by plastering it each day with bag balm and Vaseline. He was curious, well-read, and had a fact-keeping mind to go along with his penchant for hoarding. His reliquary of gunnysacks, fence wire, wood, canned food, unopened Christmas presents, and magazines matched his odd collages of meals: sardines with maple syrup; vegetable soup garnished with Fig Newtons. His wagon was so overloaded that he had to sleep sitting up because there was no room on the bed. Despite his love of up-to-date information, Fred died from gangrene when an old-timer's remedy of fresh sheep manure, applied as a poultice to a bad cut, failed to save him.

After the brief lushness of summer, the sun moves south. The 39 range grass is brown. Livestock has been trailed back down from the mountains. Waterholes begin to frost over at night. Last fall Martin asked me to accompany him on a pack trip. With five horses, we followed a river into the mountains behind the tiny Wyoming town of Meeteetse. Groves of aspen, red and orange, gave off a light that made us look toasted. Our hunting camp was so high that clouds skidded across our foreheads, then slowed to sail out across the warm valleys. Except for a bull moose who wandered into our camp and mistook our black gelding for a rival, we shot at nothing.

One of our evening entertainments was to watch the night sky. 40 My dog, who also came on the trip, a dingo bred to herd sheep, is so used to the silence and emtpy skies that when an airplane flies over he always looks up and eyes the distant intruder quizzically. The sky, lately, seems to be much more crowded than it used to be. Satellites make their silent passes in the dark with great regularity. We counted eighteen in one hour's viewing. How odd to think that while they circumnavigated the planet, Martin and I had moved only six miles into our local wilderness, and had seen no other human for the two weeks we stayed there.

At night, by moonlight, the land is whittled to slivers—a ridge, 41 a river, a strip of grassland stretching to the mountains, then the huge sky. One morning a full moon was setting in the west just as the sun was rising. I felt precariously balanced between the two as I loped across a meadow. For a moment, I could believe that the stars, which were still visible, work like cooper's bands, holding everything above Wyoming together.

Space has a spiritual equivalent, and can heal what is divided 42 and burdensome in us. My grandchildren will probably use space shuttles for a honeymoon trip or to recover from heart attacks, but closer to home we might also learn how to carry space inside ourselves in the effortless way we carry our skins. Space represents sanity, not a life purified, dull, or "spaced out" but one that might accommodate intelligently any idea or situation.

From the clayey soil of northern Wyoming is mined bentonite, 43 which is used as a filler in candy, gum, and lipstick. We Americans are great on fillers, as if what we have, what we are, is not enough. We have a cultural tendency toward denial, but, being affluent, we strangle ourselves with what we can buy. We have only to look at the houses we build to see how we build *against* space, the way we drink against pain and loneliness. We fill up space as if it were a pie shell, with things whose opacity further obstructs our ability to see what is already there.

Revival Meeting in Stamps, Arkansas

MAYA ANGELOU

The cloth tent had been set on the flatlands in the middle of a field   1
near the railroad tracks. The earth was carpeted with a silky layer of
dried grass and cotton stalks. Collapsible chairs were poked into the
still-soft ground and a large wooden cross was hung from the center
beam at the rear of the tent. Electric lights had been strung from behind the pulpit to the entrance flap and continued outside on poles
made of rough two-by-fours.

Approached in the dark the swaying bulbs looked lonely and   2
purposeless. Not as if they were there to provide light or anything
meaningful. And the tent, that blurry bright three-dimensional A,
was so foreign to the cotton field, that it might just get up and fly
away before my eyes.

People, suddenly visible in the lamplight, streamed toward the   3
temporary church. The adults' voices relayed the serious intent of
their mission. Greetings were exchanged, hushed.

"Evening, sister, how you?"   4

"Bless the Lord, just trying to make it in."   5

Their minds were concentrated on the coming meeting, soul to   6
soul, with God. This was no time to indulge in human concerns or
personal questions.

"The good Lord give me another day, and I'm thankful." Noth-   7
ing personal in that. The credit was God's, and there was no illusion
about the Central Position's shifting or becoming less than Itself.

Teenagers enjoyed revivals as much as adults. They used the   8
night outside meetings to play at courting. The impermanence of a
collapsible church added to the frivolity, and their eyes flashed and
winked and the girls giggled little silver drops in the dusk while the
boys postured and swaggered and pretended not to notice. The
nearly grown girls wore skirts as tight as the custom allowed and

Maya Angelou (1928–   ), originally from St. Louis, Missouri, is
the author of poetry collections and memoirs including *Gather Together in My Name* (1974), *Shaker, Why Don't You Sing?* (1983), and
All God's Children Need Traveling Shoes (1986). "Revival Meeting in
Stamps, Arkansas" is from *I Know Why the Caged Bird Sings* (1969).

the young men slicked their hair down with Moroline Hairdressing and water.

To small children, though, the idea of praising God in a tent was 9 confusing, to say the least. It seemed somehow blasphemous. The lights hanging slack overhead, the soft ground underneath and the canvas wall that faintly blew in and out, like cheeks puffed with air, made for the feeling of a country fair. The nudgings and jerks and winks of the bigger children surely didn't belong in a church. But the tension of the elders—their expectation, which weighted like a thick blanket over the crowd—was the most perplexing of all.

Would the gentle Jesus care to enter into that transitory setting? 10 The altar wobbled and threatened to overturn and the collection table sat at a rakish angle. One leg had yielded itself to the loose dirt. Would God the Father allow His only Son to mix with this crowd of cotton pickers and maids, washerwomen and handymen? I knew He sent His spirit on Sundays to the church, but after all that was a church and the people had had all day Saturday to shuffle off the cloak of work and the skin of despair.

Everyone attended the revival meetings. Members of the hoity- 11 toity Mount Zion Baptist Church mingled with the intellectual members of the African Methodist Episcopal and African Methodist Episcopal Zion, and the plain working people of the Christian Methodist Episcopal. These gatherings provided the one time in the year when all of those good village people associated with the followers of the Church of God in Christ. The latter were looked upon with some suspicion because they were so loud and raucous in their services. Their explanation that "the Good Book say, 'Make a joyful noise unto the Lord, and be exceedingly glad'" did not in the least minimize the condescension of their fellow Christians. Their church was far from the others, but they could be heard on Sunday, a half mile away, singing and dancing until they sometimes fell down in a dead faint. Members of the other churches wondered if the Holy Rollers were going to heaven after all their shouting. The suggestion was that they were having their heaven right here on earth.

This was their annual revival. 12

Mrs. Duncan, a little woman with a bird face, started the ser- 13 vice. "I know I'm a witness for my Lord ... I know I'm a witness for my Lord, I know I'm a witness ..."

Her voice, a skinny finger, stabbed high up in the air and the 14 church responded. From somewhere down front came the jangling sound of a tambourine. Two beats on "know," two beats on "I'm a" and two beats on the end of "witness."

Other voices joined the near shriek of Mrs. Duncan. They 15 crowded around and tenderized the tone. Handclaps snapped in the roof and solidified the beat. When the song reached its peak in sound and passion, a tall, thin man who had been kneeling behind the altar all the while stood up and sang with the audience for a few bars. He stretched out his long arms and grasped the platform. It took some time for the singers to come off their level of exaltation, but the minister stood resolute until the song unwound like a child's playtoy and lay quieted in the aisles.

"Amen." He looked at the audience. 16

"Yes, sir, amen." Nearly everyone seconded him. 17

"I say, Let the church say 'Amen.'" 18

Everyone said, "Amen." 19

"Thank the Lord. Thank the Lord." 20

"That's right, thank the Lord. Yes, Lord. Amen." 21

"We will have prayer, led by Brother Bishop." 22

Another tall, brown-skinned man wearing square glasses 23 walked up to the altar from the front row. The minister knelt at the right and Brother Bishop at the left.

"Our Father"—he was singing—"You who took my feet out the 24 mire and clay—"

The church moaned, "Amen." 25

"You who saved my soul. One day. Look, sweet Jesus. Look 26 down, on these your suffering children—"

The church begged, "Look down, Lord." 27

"Build us up where we're torn down . . . Bless the sick and the 28 afflicted . . ."

It was the usual prayer. Only his voice gave it something new. 29 After every two words he gasped and dragged the air over his vocal cords, making a sound like an inverted grunt. "You who"—grunt—"saved   my"—gasp—"soul   one"—inhalation—"day"—humph.

Then the congregation, led again by Mrs. Duncan, flew into 30 "Precious Lord, take my hand, lead me on, let me stand." It was sung at a faster clip than the usual one in the C.M.E. Church, but at that tempo it worked. There was a joy about the tune that changed the meaning of its sad lyrics. "When the darkness appears, and the night draweth near and my life is almost gone . . ." There seemed to be an abandon which suggested that with all those things it should be a time for great rejoicing.

The serious shouters had already made themselves known, and 31 their fans (cardboard advertisements from Texarkana's largest Negro funeral home) and lacy white handkerchiefs waved high in the air. In their dark hands they looked like small kites without the wooden frames.

The tall minister stood again at the altar. He waited for the song 32 and the revelry to die.

He said, "Amen. Glory." 33

The church skidded off the song slowly. "Amen. Glory." 34

He still waited, as the last notes remained in the air, staircased 35 on top of each other. "At the river I stand—" "I stand, guide my feet—" "Guide my feet, take my hand." Sung like the last circle in a round. Then quiet descended.

The Scripture reading was from Matthew, twenty-fifth chapter, 36 thirtieth verse through the forty-sixth.

His text for the sermon was "The least of these." 37

After reading the verses to the accompaniment of a few Amens 38 he said, "First Corinthians tells me, 'Even if I have the tongue of men and of angels and have not charity, I am as nothing. Even if I give all my clothes to the poor and have not charity, I am as nothing. Even if I give my body to be burned and have not charity it availeth me nothing. Burned, I say, and have not charity, it availeth nothing.' I have to ask myself, what is this thing called Charity? If good deeds are not charity—"

The church gave in quickly. "That's right, Lord." 39

"—if giving my flesh and blood is not charity?" 40

"Yes, Lord." 41

"I have to ask myself what is this charity they talking so much 42 about."

I had never heard a preacher jump into the muscle of his sermon 43 so quickly. Already the humming pitch had risen in the church, and those who knew had popped their eyes in anticipation of the coming excitement. Momma sat tree-trunk still, but she had balled her handkerchief in her hand and only the corner, which I had embroidered, stuck out.

"As I understand it, charity vaunteth not itself. Is not puffed 44 up." He blew himself up with a deep breath to give us the picture of what Charity was not. "Charity don't go around saying 'I give you food and I give you clothes and by rights you ought to thank me.'"

The congregation knew whom he was talking about and voiced 45 agreement with his analysis. "Tell the truth, Lord."

"Charity don't say, 'Because I give you a job, you got to bend 46 your knee to me.'" The church was rocking with each phrase. "It don't say, 'Because I pays you what you due, you got to call me master.' It don't ask me to humble myself and belittle myself. That ain't what Charity is."

Down front to the right, Mr. and Mrs. Stewart, who only a few 47 hours earlier had crumbled in our front yard, defeated by the cotton rows, now sat on the edges of their rickety-rackety chairs. Their faces shone with the delight of their souls. The mean whitefolks was going to get their comeuppance. Wasn't that what the minister said, and wasn't he quoting from the words of God Himself? They had been refreshed with the hope of revenge and the promise of justice.

"Aaagh. Raagh. I said...Charity. Wooooo, a Charity. It don't 48 want nothing for itself. It don't want to be bossman...Waah...It don't want to be headman...Waah...It don't want to be fore-man...Waah...It...I'm talking about Charity...It don't want...Oh Lord...help me tonight...It don't want to be bowed to and scraped at..."

America's historic bowers and scrapers shifted easily and hap- 49 pily in the makeshift church. Reassured that although they might be the lowest of the low they were at least not uncharitable, and "in that great Gettin' Up Morning, Jesus was going to separate the sheep (them) from the goats (the white-folks)."

"Charity is simple." The church agreed, vocally.   50

"Charity is poor." That was us he was talking about.   51

"Charity is plain." I thought, that's about right. Plain and sim- 52 ple.

"Charity is...Oh, Oh, Oh. Cha-ri-ty. Where are you? 53 Wooo...Charity...Hump."

One chair gave way and the sound of splintering wood split the 54 air in the rear of the church.

"I call you and you don't answer. Woooh, oh Charity."   55

Another holler went up in front of me, and a large woman 56 flopped over, her arms above her head like a candidate for baptism. The emotional release was contagious. Little screams burst around the room like Fourth of July firecrackers.

The minister's voice was a pendulum. Swinging left and down 57 and right and down and left and—"How can you claim to be my brother, and hate me? Is that Charity? How can you claim to be my sister and despise me? Is that supposed to be Charity? How can you claim to be my friend and misuse and wrongfully abuse me? Is that Charity? Oh, my children, I stopped by here—"

The church swung on the end of his phrases. Punctuating. 58 Confirming. "Stop by here, Lord."

"—to tell you, to open your heart and let Charity reign. Forgive 59 your enemies for His sake. Show the Charity that Jesus was speaking of to this sick old world. It has need of the charitable giver." His voice was falling and the explosions became fewer and quieter.

"And now I repeat the words of the Apostle Paul, and 'now 60 abideth faith, hope, and charity, these three; but the greatest of these is charity.'"

The congregation lowed with satisfaction. Even if they were so- 61
ciety's pariahs, they were going to be angels in a marble white
heaven and sit on the right hand of Jesus, the Son of God. The Lord
loved the poor and hated those cast high in the world. Hadn't He
Himself said it would be easier for a camel to go through the eye of a
needle than for a rich man to enter heaven? They were assured that
they were going to be the only inhabitants of that land of milk and
honey, except of course a few whitefolks like John Brown who history books said was crazy anyway. All the Negroes had to do generally, and those at the revival especially, was bear up under this life
of toil and cares, because a blessed home awaited them in the far-off
bye and bye.

"Bye and bye, when the morning come, when all the saints of 62
God's are gathering home, we will tell the story of how we overcome and we'll understand it better bye and bye."

A few people who had fainted were being revived on the side 63
aisles when the evangelist opened the doors of the church. Over the
sounds of "Thank you, Jesus," he started a long-meter hymn:

> I came to Jesus, as I was,
> Worried, wounded, and sad,
> I found in Him a resting place,
> And He has made me glad.

The old ladies took up the hymn and shared it in tight harmony. 64
The humming crowd began to sound like tired bees, restless and
anxious to get home.

"All those under the sound of my voice who have no spiritual 65
home, whose hearts are burdened and heavy-ladened, let them
come. Come before it's too late. I don't ask you to join the Church of
God in Christ. No. I'm a servant of God, and in this revival, we are
out to bring straying souls to Him. So if you join this evening, just
say which church you want to be affiliated with, and we will turn
you over to a representative of that church body. Will one deacon of
the following churches come forward?"

That was revolutionary action. No one had ever heard of a min- 66
ister taking in members for another church. It was our first look at
Charity among preachers. Men from the A.M.E., A.M.E.Z., Baptist
and C.M.E. churches went down front and assumed stances a few
feet apart. Converted sinners flowed down the aisles to shake hands
with the evangelist and stayed at his side or were directed to one of
the men in line. Over twenty people were saved that night.

There was nearly as much commotion over the saving of the sin- 67
ners as there had been during the gratifying melodic sermon.

The Mothers of the Church, old ladies with white lace disks 68
pinned to their thinning hair, had a service all their own. They
walked around the new converts singing,

> Before this time another year,
> I may be gone,
> In some lonesome graveyard,
> Oh, Lord, how long?

When the collection was taken up and the last hymn given to 69
the praise of God, the evangelist asked that everyone in his presence
rededicate his soul to God and his life's work to Charity. Then we
were dismissed.

Outside and on the way home, the people played in their magic, 70
as children poke in mud pies, reluctant to tell themselves that the
game was over.

"The Lord touched him tonight, didn't He?"   71

"Surely did. Touched him with a mighty fire."   72

"Bless the Lord. I'm glad I'm saved."   73

"That's the truth. It make a whole lot of difference."   74

"I wish them people I works for could of heard that sermon. 75
They don't know what they letting theyselves in for."

"Bible say, 'He who can hear, let him hear. He who can't, shame 76
on 'em.'"

They basked in the righteousness of the poor and the exclusive- 77
ness of the downtrodden. Let the whitefolks have their money and
power and segregation and sarcasm and big houses and schools and
lawns like carpets, and books, and mostly—mostly—let them have
their whiteness. It was better to be meek and lowly, spat upon and
abused for this little time than to spend eternity frying in the fires of
hell. No one would have admitted that the Christian and charitable
people were happy to think of their oppressors' turning forever on
the Devil's spit over the flames of fire and brimstone.

But that was what the Bible said and it didn't make mistakes. 78
"Ain't it said somewhere in there that 'before one word of this
changes, heaven and earth shall fall away?' Folks going to get what
they deserved."

When the main crowd of worshipers reached the short bridge 79
spanning the pond, the ragged sound of honky-tonk music assailed
them. A barrelhouse blues was being shouted over the stamping of
feet on a wooden floor. Miss Grace, the good-time woman, had her
usual Saturday-night customers. The big white house blazed with
lights and noise. The people inside had forsaken their own distress
for a little while.

Passing near the din, the godly people dropped their heads and   80
conversation ceased. Reality began its tedious crawl back into their
reasoning. After all, they were needy and hungry and despised and
dispossessed, and sinners the world over were in the driver's seat.
How long, merciful Father? How long?

A stranger to the music could not have made a distinction be-   81
tween the songs sung a few minutes before and those being danced
to in the gay house by the railroad tracks. All asked the same questions. How long, oh God? How long?

The Way to Rainy Mountain

N. SCOTT MOMADAY

A single knoll rises out of the plain in Oklahoma, north and west of 1
the Wichita Range. For my people, the Kiowas, it is an old land-
mark, and they gave it the name Rainy Mountain. The hardest
weather in the world is there. Winter brings blizzards, hot tornadic
winds arise in the spring, and in summer the prairie is an anvil's
edge. The grass turns brittle and brown, and it cracks beneath your
feet. There are green belts along the rivers and creeks, linear groves
of hickory and pecan, willow and witch hazel. At a distance in July
or August the steaming foliage seems almost to writhe in fire. Great
green-and-yellow grasshoppers are everywhere in the tall grass,
popping up like corn to sting the flesh, and tortoises crawl about on
the red earth, going nowhere in the plenty of time. Loneliness is an
aspect of the land. All things in the plain are isolate; there is no confusion of objects in the eye, but *one* hill or *one* tree or *one* man. To
look upon that landscape in the early morning, with the sun at your
back, is to lose the sense of proportion. Your imagination comes to
life, and this, you think, is where Creation was begun.

I returned to Rainy Mountain in July. My grandmother had died 2
in the spring, and I wanted to be at her grave. She had lived to be
very old and at last infirm. Her only living daughter was with her
when she died, and I was told that in death her face was that of a
child.

I like to think of her as a child. When she was born, the Kiowas 3
were living that last great moment of their history. For more than a
hundred years they had controlled the open range from the Smoky
Hill River to the Red, from the headwaters of the Canadian to the
fork of the Arkansas and Cimarron. In alliance with the Comanches,
they had ruled the whole of the southern Plains. War was their sacred business, and they were among the finest horsemen the world
has ever known. But warfare for the Kiowas was preeminently a
matter of disposition rather than of survival, and they never understood the grim, unrelenting advance of the U.S. Cavalry. When at

---

N. Scott Momaday (1934–   ), born in Lawton, Oklahoma, is professor of English at the University of Arizona and the author of the
novel *House Made of Dawn* (1968) and *Angle of Geese and Other Poems*
(1974). "The Way to Rainy Mountain" is from his memoir *The Way
to Rainy Mountain* (1969).

last, divided and ill-provisioned, they were driven onto the Staked Plains in the cold rains of autumn, they fell into panic. In Palo Duro Canyon they abandoned their crucial stores to pillage and had nothing then but their lives. In order to save themselves, they surrendered to the soldiers at Fort Sill and were imprisoned in the old stone corral that now stands as a military museum. My grandmother was spared the humiliation of those high gray walls by eight or ten years, but she must have known from birth the affliction of defeat, the dark brooding of old warriors.

Her name was Aho, and she belonged to the last culture to ₄ evolve in North America. Her forebears came down from the high country in western Montana nearly three centuries ago. They were a mountain people, a mysterious tribe of hunters whose language has never been positively classified in any major group. In the late seventeenth century they began a long migration to the south and east. It was a long journey toward the dawn, and it led to a golden age. Along the way the Kiowas were befriended by the Crows, who gave them the culture and religion of the Plains. They acquired horses, and their ancient nomadic spirit was suddenly free of the ground. They acquired Tai-me, the sacred Sun Dance doll, from that moment the object and symbol of their worship, and so shared in the divinity of the sun. Not least, they acquired the sense of destiny, therefore courage and pride. When they entered upon the southern Plains, they had been transformed. No longer were they slaves to the simple necessity of survival; they were a lordly and dangerous society of fighters and thieves, hunters and priests of the sun. According to their origin myth, they entered the world through a hollow log. From one point of view, their migration was the fruit of an old prophecy, for indeed they emerged from a sunless world.

Although my grandmother lived out her long life in the shadow ₅ of Rainy Mountain, the immense landscape of the continental interior lay like memory in her blood. She could tell of the Crows, whom she had never seen, and of the Black Hills, where she had never been. I wanted to see in reality what she had seen more perfectly in the mind's eye, and traveled fifteen hundred miles to begin my pilgrimage.

Yellowstone, it seemed to me, was the top of the world, a region ₆ of deep lakes and dark timber, canyons and waterfalls. But, beautiful as it is, one might have the sense of confinement there. The skyline in all directions is close at hand, the high wall of the woods and deep cleavages of shade. There is a perfect freedom in the mountains, but it belongs to the eagle and the elk, the badger and the bear. The Kiowas reckoned their stature by the distance they could see, and they were bent and blind in the wilderness.

Descending eastward, the highland meadows are a stairway to ⁷
the plain. In July the inland slope of the Rockies is luxuriant with
flax and buckwheat, stonecrop and larkspur. The earth unfolds and
the limit of the land recedes. Clusters of trees and animals grazing
far in the distance cause the vision to reach away and wonder to
build upon the mind. The sun follows a longer course in the day,
and the sky is immense beyond all comparison. The great billowing
clouds that sail upon it are shadows that move upon the grain like
water, dividing light. Farther down, in the land of the Crows and
Blackfeet, the plain is yellow. Sweet clover takes hold of the hills
and bends upon itself to cover and seal the soil. There the Kiowas
paused on their way; they had come to the place where they must
change their lives. The sun is at home on the plains. Precisely there
does it have the certain character of a god. When the Kiowas came
to the land of the Crows, they could see the dark lees of the hill at
dawn across the Bighorn River, the profusion of light on the grain
shelves, the oldest deity ranging after the solstices. Not yet would
they veer southward to the caldron of the land that lay below; they
must wean their blood from the northern winter and hold the
mountains a while longer in their view. They bore Tai-me in procession to the east.

A dark mist lay over the Black Hills, and the land was like iron. ⁸
At the top of a ridge I caught sight of Devil's Tower upthrust against
the gray sky as if in the birth of time the core of the earth had broken through its crust and the motion of the world was begun. There
are things in nature that engender an awful quiet in the heart of
man; Devil's Tower is one of them. Two centuries ago, because they
could not do otherwise, the Kiowas made a legend at the base of the
rock. My grandmother said:

> Eight children were there at play, seven sisters and their brother.
> Suddenly the boy was struck dumb; he trembled and began to run
> upon his hands and feet. His fingers became claws, and his body
> was covered with fur. Directly there was a bear where the boy had
> been. The sisters were terrified; they ran, and the bear after them.
> They came to the stump of a great tree, and the tree spoke to them.
> It bade them climb upon it and as they did so, it began to rise into
> the air. The bear came to kill them, but they were just beyond its
> reach. It reared against the tree and scored the bark all around with
> its claws. The seven sisters were borne into the sky, and they be-
> came the stars of the Big Dipper.

From that moment, and as long as the legend lives, the Kiowas have
kinsmen in the night sky. Whatever they were in the mountains,
they could be no more. However tenuous their well-being, however

much they had suffered and would suffer again, they had found a way out of the wilderness.

My grandmother had a reverence for the sun, a holy regard that 9 now is all but gone out of mankind. There was a wariness in her and an ancient awe. She was a Christian in her later years, but she had come a long way about, and she never forgot her birthright. As a child she had been to the Sun Dances; she had taken part in those annual rites, and by them she had learned the restoration of her people in the presence of Tai-me. She was about seven when the last Kiowa Sun Dance was held in 1887 on the Washita River above Rainy Mountain Creek. The buffalo were gone. In order to consummate the ancient sacrifice—to impale the head of a buffalo bull upon the medicine tree—a delegation of old men journeyed into Texas, there to beg and barter for an animal from the Goodnight herd. She was ten when the Kiowas came together for the last time as a living Sun Dance culture. They could find no buffalo; they had to hang an old hide from the sacred tree. Before the dance could begin, a company of soldiers rode out from Fort Sill under orders to disperse the tribe. Forbidden without cause the essential act of their faith, having seen the wild herds slaughtered and left to rot upon the ground, the Kiowas backed away forever from the medicine tree. That was July 20, 1890, at the great bend of the Washita. My grandmother was there. Without bitterness, and for as long as she lived, she bore a vision of deicide.

Now that I can have her only in memory, I see my grandmother 10 in the several postures that were peculiar to her: standing at the wood stove on a winter morning and turning meat in a great iron skillet; sitting at the south window, bent above her beadwork, and afterwards, when her vision had failed, looking down for a long time into the fold of her hands; going out upon a cane, very slowly as she did when the weight of age came upon her; praying. I remember her most often at prayer. She made long, rambling prayers out of suffering and hope, having seen many things. I was never sure that I had the right to hear, so exclusive were they of all mere custom and company. The last time I saw her she prayed standing by the side of her bed at night, naked to the waist, the light of a kerosene lamp moving upon her dark skin. Her long, black hair, always drawn and braided in the day, lay upon her shoulders and against her breasts like a shawl. I do not speak Kiowa, and I never understood her prayers, but there was something inherently sad in the sound, some merest hesitation upon the syllables of sorrow. She began in a high and descending pitch, exhausting her breath to silence; then again and again—and always the same intensity of effort, of something that is, and is not, like urgency in the human

voice. Transported so in the dancing light among the shadows of
her room, she seemed beyond the reach of time. But that was illusion; I think I knew then that I should not see her again.

Houses are like sentinels in the plain, old keepers of the weather   11
watch. There, in a very little while, wood takes on the appearance of
great age. All colors wear soon away in the wind and rain, and then
the wood is burned gray and the grain appears and the nails turn
red with rust. The windowpanes are black and opaque; you imagine
there is nothing within, and indeed there are many ghosts, bones
given up to the land. They stand here and there against the sky, and
you approach them for a longer time than you expect. They belong
in the distance; it is their domain.

Once there was a lot of sound in my grandmother's house, a lot   12
of coming and going, feasting and talk. The summers there were full
of excitement and reunion. The Kiowas are a summer people; they
abide the cold and keep to themselves; but when the season turns
and the land becomes warm and vital, they cannot hold still; an old
love of going returns upon them. The aged visitors who came to my
grandmother's house when I was a child were made of lean and
leather, and they bore themselves upright. They wore great black
hats and bright ample shirts that shook in the wind. They rubbed fat
upon their hair and wound their braids with strips of colored cloth.
Some of them painted their faces and carried the scars of old and
cherished enmities. They were an old council of warlords, come to
remind and be reminded of who they were. Their wives and daughters served them well. The women might indulge themselves; gossip
was at once the mark and compensation of their servitude. They
made loud and elaborate talk among themselves, full of jest and gesture, fright and false alarm. They went abroad in fringed and
flowered shawls, bright beadwork and German silver. They were at
home in the kitchen, and they prepared meals that were banquets.

There were frequent prayer meetings, and great nocturnal   13
feasts. When I was a child, I played with my cousins outside, where
the lamplight fell upon the ground and the singing of the old people
rose up around us and carried away into the darkness. There were a
lot of good things to eat, a lot of laughter and surprise. And afterwards, when the quiet returned, I lay down with my grandmother
and could hear the frogs away by the river and feel the motion of
the air.

Now there is a funeral silence in the rooms, the endless wake of   14
some final word. The walls have closed in upon my grandmother's
house. When I returned to it in mourning, I saw for the first time in
my life how small it was. It was late at night, and there was a white
moon, nearly full. I sat for a long time on the stone steps by the

kitchen door. From there I could see out across the land; I could see the long row of trees by the creek, the low light upon the rolling plains, and the stars of the Big Dipper. Once I looked at the moon and caught sight of a strange thing. A cricket had perched upon the handrail, only a few inches away from me. My line of vision was such that the creature filled the moon like a fossil. It had gone there, I thought, to live and die, for there of all places, was its small definition made whole and eternal. A warm wind rose up and purled like the longing within me.

The next morning I awoke at dawn and went out on the dirt 15 road to Rainy Mountain. It was already hot, and the grasshoppers began to fill the air. Still, it was early in the morning, and the birds sang out of the shadows. The long yellow grass on the mountain shone in the bright light, and a scissortail hied above the land. There, where it ought to be, at the end of a long and legendary way, was my grandmother's grave. Here and there on the dark stones were ancestral names. Looking back once, I saw the mountain and came away.

READING AND WRITING
ABOUT AMERICAN PLACES AND PEOPLE

1. Reread several of the Brief Encounters, then jot down one sentence about each that summarizes your overall dominant impression about the place being described (Walpi Village, Knoxville, and the Sacramento *barrio* described by Galarza, for example). How much of this impression comes from explicit statements by the writer, and how much do you infer or read between the lines? Study how the details the writer has selected contribute to this dominant effect.

2. Think about a place you've visited that left a lasting impression on you, and freewrite or brainstorm about why. Then write your own one-page description, using details to recreate this impression. Assume that your readers have not been to this place or, if they have, that they didn't experience it the same way you did. If you read your description to your class or small group, find out how successfully you've communicated the dominant impression you intended.

3. Did you grow up in a single place or move around a lot? How do you think this affected your sense of your culture, American or otherwise? Compare your experiences with those of your classmates, "Ann Banks," or Juan Cadena.

4. Interview a classmate, on tape, about the place or places where he or she grew up. Use the Terkel and Cadena selections to help plan your questions; you might ask, for example, "At what point did you begin 'to understand there were other ways of living' (Terkel, paragraph 10) than the way you grew up?" or "What experiences with prejudice or discrimination have you had in your hometown?" Transcribe the interview, then edit it to make it more focused or coherent. Share the results, before and after, with the subject of your interview and other classmates. Explain the editing decisions you made.

5. Write a letter to your daughter or son (your imaginary child if you don't have one) about your background or family heritage, as Siu Wai Anderson does.

6. The characters involved in the Wild Man incident described by Maxine Hong Kingston include the residents of Green Swamp, the police, the "authorities," the game officer, fish-and-game wardens, sheriff's deputies, farmers, the occupant of the house trailer, the posse, the translator, the ship's officers of the Liberian freighter, doctors, the U.S. Border Patrol, newspaper reporters, the Wild Man himself, Kingston the writer, and you the reader. Divide your class so as to represent a variety of these roles, then have each person or group re-tell the incident from that particular viewpoint. Discuss how the story changes according to which character is telling it.

7. Which of Christopher Isherwood's observations and predictions about Los Angeles seem relevant today, almost fifty years after he wrote this essay? Which observations still apply not just to Los Angeles or California but to American culture in general? Do you agree, for instance, that "They have planned a life for you—from the cradle to the grave and beyond—which it would be easy, fatally easy, to accept" (paragraph 9)? Who are "they"?

8. Frances FitzGerald says that most of the gay people she observes are young, white, and male. What additional characteristics of the gay subculture of San Francisco in 1978 can you infer from her colorful description of the floats, costumed marchers, and other people? How does her description of the four different "gay centers" enhance or change your picture of the gay subculture?

9. Describe Paul Theroux's tone—the attitude he seems to reveal towards his subject matter. How would the subway, the police officers, and the other underground characters be portrayed differently through the eyes of one of the "skells"? Compare Theroux's tone to Kingston's or Isherwood's.

10. What does Gretel Ehrlich mean when she writes, "Space has a spiritual equivalent" (paragraph 42)? Analyze how Ehrlich links the behavior and values of Wyoming residents with their geography and environment.

11. Compare or contrast how Los Angelenos are affected by their environment (according to Isherwood) with how Wyoming residents are affected by theirs (according to Ehrlich). Use this comparison and your experience to formulate your own thesis about the relationship between cultural values and space or geography.

12. "All the Negroes had to do," writes Maya Angelou, describing the general opinion of the congregation at the revival meeting, "was bear up under this life of toil and cares, because a blessed home awaited them in the far-off bye and bye" (paragraph 61). How do you think Angelou feels about this "blessed home"? How can you tell? What should black people do, if not "bear up"?

13. Ann Banks says, in Terkel's piece, "I was a little ten-year-old anthropologist" (paragraph 11). Anthropologists study social and cultural development and behavior; like other scientists and social scientists, they may make observations, gather data, propose and test hypotheses, and draw conclusions. Discuss the ways both Banks and Angelou act as "ten-year-old anthropologists," or the ways other writers in this chapter (such as FitzGerald, Theroux, or Ehrlich) act at least partly as social scientists.

14. Scott Momaday's "The Way to Rainy Mountain" was originally published as "The Journey of Tai-me." How do these two titles affect your interpretation of the essay? How many different "journeys" does Momaday write about?

15. Based on Momaday's and Ehrlich's essays, compare the ways the Kiowa Indians and the white setters of Wyoming related to the land.

16. Many of the authors or the characters described in this chapter feel to some extent like outsiders, like strangers in their own land. Write about this theme, integrating two or more of the readings and, if relevant, your own experience.

MAKING FURTHER CONNECTIONS

1. Analyze Angelou's essay in terms of the debate, engaged by Michelle Cliff and Rachel Jones in Chapter 1, about "the King's English" (or standard American English) and Black English. Judging from both her rendering of black speech and her own narrative, what position would Angelou likely take in this debate?

2. How does the language Momaday uses to write about the Kiowas specifically challenge the "language of Indian derision" catalogued by Haig Bosmajian in Chapter 1?

3. Read the Brief Encounters in Chapter 3 and compare the sense of strangeness abroad conveyed by one of these authors with the sense of domestic alienation or estrangement conveyed by one of the authors in Chapter 2. For example, compare Darwin's description of the Fuegians (Chapter 3) to Theroux's description of the subway-dwellers (Chapter 2); or try applying Theroux's Chapter 3 Brief

Encounter, "Living among Strangers," to Anderson's, Kingston's, or Momaday's essay in Chapter 2.

4. Compare the experience of any two authors from Chapter 2, using one or more of the Brief Encounters in Chapter 4 to help you find a purpose and framework for the comparison. Some possible pairings include Cadena and Anderson (using Margaret Mead's or Mark Twain's selection from Chapter 4 to focus on the immigrant experience) and Ehrlich and Momaday (using Henry David Thoreau or Paula Gunn Allen from Chapter 4 to focus on historical attitudes toward the land).

5. Tell your classmates about your name—first and/or last name. What does it mean, what story or family history lies behind it, how do you feel about it? Like Anderson in "A Letter to My Daughter" and Sandra Cisneros in her Brief Encounter, "My Name" (Chapter 6), write about your name or a relative's name. (If you're not sure what it means, trace its etymology in the reference section of your library.)

6. How do FitzGerald's journalistic account and David Leavitt's fictional treatment (in the Chapter 6 story "Territory") of San Francisco's Gay Freedom Parade affect you differently and similarly? What conclusions can you draw about the different or overlapping purposes and techniques of nonfiction and fiction in general?

7. Compare Juan Cadena with Sancho Salazar, the father character in Arturo Islas's "Thanksgiving Border Crossing" (Chapter 6). What are their attitudes towards the Anglo culture and their Mexican roots? How does each work within or against the legal system? Or choose a different author or character from Chapter 2 and a fictional character from Chapter 6 to compare. The purpose of your comparison should be to make a larger point about the essay or story or American culture, not simply to point out similarities and differences.

EXPLORING NEW SOURCES

1. How have the Jewish neighborhoods of New York City changed since Kate Simon's childhood? Augment your library research, if possible, by interviewing classmates from New York or professors with expertise in the area.

2. What has been the legacy for the people and culture of Alaska of the *Exxon Valdez* oil spill of 1989? One approach to this question would be to analyze the different reports on the spill and recommendations made by the State of Alaska, the federal government, the Exxon Corporation, and environmental groups.

3. Collect oral histories from several family members and neighbors about the place where you grew up. Transcribe and edit these interviews (as Terkel has done for "Ann Banks" and Marilyn Davis has done for Juan Cadena). Then conduct library research to find any objective measures about this locale, such as demographic and economic statistics. Write an essay, incorporating these various sources, that explains to outsiders why your hometown is—or is perceived—a certain way.

4. Explore the recent history of public transportation in Los Angeles or another city. Or pick another current transportation issue that concerns you, and address a proposal to the appropriate government agency or directly to the voters.

5. The AIDS epidemic has brought major changes to the gay subculture and to the larger culture in general. Investigate one aspect of these changes. For example, you might compare a late-'80s Gay Pride Day with the 1978 San Francisco parade described by FitzGerald; write about cultural changes in a particular gay neighborhood such as the Castro, Los Angeles's West Hollywood, New York's Greenwich Village, Chicago's New Town, or Houston's Westheimer district; or consider how attitudes towards gay people have changed in one of these cities as a result of AIDS. How will you measure these changes or attitudes?

6. Update Theroux's essay by researching some aspect of the New York subway system, such as the effects of recent station renovations on crime rates or the current relations between homeless people and the transit police.

7. Read several books by Maya Angelou, including her poetry and memoirs. Write about either the autobiographical aspects of her poetry or the poetic aspects of her autobiographical writing.

3

THE WRITER AS TRAVELER: DISCOVERING FOREIGN PLACES AND PEOPLE

A generation ago, the stereotype of "the Ugly American"[1] was prevalent around the world: the condescending brute who expected everyone to speak English wherever he (the stereotype is a man) traveled. He complained about the inadequate service and lack of amenities, such as his accustomed booming hot water in the shower, and generally acted as though all people ought to be more like Americans—presumably affluent white male Americans.

A new generation of American travelers—including more students and young people, more women, more immigrants and people of color—has been reshaping this image, and as a result you won't find any Ugly Americans in this chapter. Generally, the writers here approach foreign places and people with curiosity, sensitivity, and acute powers of observation. As in Chapter 2, the distinction between tourists and travelers may illuminate this approach. Whereas tourists produce and consume guidebooks about "destinations," travelers read and write thoughtful reflections about personal experience. As author and University of Pennsylvania English professor Paul Fussell has written,

> Successful travel writing mediates between two poles: the individual physical things it describes, on the one hand, and the larger theme that it is "about," on the other. That is, the particular and the universal.[2]

---

[1] The name comes from a best-selling 1958 novel by William J. Lederer and Eugene Burdick about American diplomats in Southeast Asia.

[2] Paul Fussell, ed., *The Norton Book of Travel* (W. W. Norton, 1987), p. 16.

Openness to foreign cultures cannot, however, insulate travelers from all the preconceptions and biases of their own culture, nor can grappling with universal human themes make them immune from global social and historical forces. In the late twentieth century, the United States, with only about 5 percent of the world's population, routinely consumes more than a quarter (some estimates run higher) of the world's resources, a large portion of which come from the poorer countries of the Southern Hemisphere. Some of these poorer countries, in a kind of vicious circle, have become dependent on tourism to generate the cash to buy the products of Western technology that their own natural resources or human labor made possible. When Americans meet the world in the 1980s and 1990s, as they do in this and later chapters, we must view them at least partly in this global context.

To the tension between subjectivity and objectivity introduced in Chapter 2, in Chapter 3 we add the push and pull between the limited perspective afforded by our culture and the struggle to exceed that limitation. As the reader of today, only you can finally decide how well these authors represent or challenge your approach to foreign places and people; as the traveler of tomorrow, you will help determine what happens when the United States meets the world of the next century.

Chapter 3's Brief Encounters focus on meetings with strangers and indicate a broader historical and international context for the main selections. For Paul Theroux, an American who has lived abroad for many years, "living among strangers" sharpens his memory of the past. Nigerian Chinua Achebe recounts the apparent blindness of that most famous European traveler of the thirteenth century, Marco Polo. Charles Darwin and Isabella Bird express some fear or condescension towards those different from themselves, reflecting colonial attitudes prevalent in nineteenth-century Europe. Such fears seem to be overcome to different degrees in our century by Edith Wharton, Isak Dinesen, and Colin Thubron in their encounters with strangers or strange places. Finally, Evelyn Waugh takes a wry look at an earlier generation of American tourists.

After reading the main selections, you might re-read Waugh and ask yourself whether, as he suggests, "the laugh . . . is [still] on us":

- John Krich reacts to the poverty of India by "turning clinician" and studying "the human flow."

- Mary Morris, traveling by bus in Mexico, meets other Americans and begins "another journey inside [her] head, a journey of memory and sensation" involving her relationships with men.

- Herbert Gold encounters deep-seated stereotypes and prejudices in Haiti—where Jews are not evident even in the cemeteries— before coming across Jacmel, a Haitian-Jewish tailor.

- Alex Haley, returning to the ancient Gambian village of Kunte Kinte, finds that his best-selling book *Roots* has had very different effects on Africans than on African Americans.
- Andrea Lee attends a B. B. King concert in Leningrad and recounts the various reactions of the Soviet audience, the musicians, and King himself.
- Pico Iyer encounters in the Philippines not an exotic foreign culture, but "Dick Clark, Ronald McDonald, and Madonna," reminding him of "desolate small towns of the American West."
- John Updike describes, with calculated objectivity, the rich and poor inhabitants of Venezuela through the eyes of an unnamed visitor.
- Joan Didion, using powerful images along with documentary evidence, tries to reconstruct "the exact mechanism of terror" in the U.S.–backed political regime in power in El Salvador.
- Kate Millett brings an American feminist agenda with her to post-revolutionary Iran, where she encounters black veils, submachine guns, and the women and men behind them.

BRIEF ENCOUNTERS

Living among Strangers

PAUL THEROUX

Living among strangers in a foreign place I am like an unexpected guest waiting in a tropical parlor. My mind is especially alert to differences of smell and sound, the shape of objects, and I am apprehensive about what is going to happen next. I sit with my knees together in the heat, observing the surfaces of things. At the same time, the place is so different I can indulge myself in long unbroken reflections, for the moments of observation are still enough to allow the mind to travel in two directions: recording mentally the highly colored things one sees is simple; the mind then wanders. The reflection may be a reminiscence of early youth, a piecing-together of an episode out of the distant past; it is not contradicted or interrupted by anything near. In a foreign country I can live in two zones of time, the immediate and apprehensible, and in that vaguer zone I thought I had forgotten. Since I do not write autobiographically, I am able to see the past more clearly; I haven't altered it in fiction. That detail of the goiters in Ohio, the forsythia bush behind our Medford house, our large family; slowly, in a foreign place, the memory whirs and gives back the past. It is momentarily a reassurance, the delay of any daydream, but juxtaposed with the vivid present it is an acute reminder of my estrangement.

—FROM "A LOVE-SCENE AFTER WORK," IN NORTH AMERICAN REVIEW, 1971

What Marco Polo Failed to See

CHINUA ACHEBE

One of the greatest and most intrepid travelers of all time, Marco Polo, journeyed to the Far East from the Mediterranean in the thirteenth century and spent twenty years in the court of Kublai Khan in China. On his return to Venice he set down in his book entitled *Description of the World* his impressions of the peoples and places and customs he had seen. There are at least two extraordinary omissions in his account. He says nothing about the art of printing unknown as yet in Europe but in full flower in China. He either did not notice it at all or if he did, failed to see what use Europe could possibly have for it. Whatever reason, Europe had to wait another hundred years for Gutenberg. But even more spectacular was Marco Polo's omission of any reference to the Great Wall of China, nearly 4000 miles long and already more than 1000 years old at the time of his visit. Again, he may not have seen it; but the Great Wall of China is the only structure built by man which is visible from the moon![1] Indeed, travelers can be blind.

—FROM "AN IMAGE OF AFRICA," *CHANT OF SAINTS*, 1979

Natives of Tierra del Fuego

CHARLES DARWIN

While going one day on shore near Wollaston Island, we pulled alongside a canoe with six Fuegians. These were the most abject and miserable creatures I anywhere beheld. On the east coast the natives, as we have seen, have guanaco cloaks, and on the west, they possess seal-skins. Amongst these central tribes the men generally have an otter-skin, or some small scrap about as large as a pocket-handkerchief, which is barely sufficient to cover their backs as low down as their loins. It is laced across the breast by strings, and according as the wind blows, it is shifted from side to side. But these Fuegians in the canoe were quite naked, and even one full-grown woman was absolutely so. It was raining heavily, and the fresh water, together with the spray, trickled down her body. In another harbor not far distant, a woman, who was suckling a recently born child, came one day alongside the vessel, and remained there out of mere curiosity, whilst the sleet fell and thawed on her naked bosom, and on the skin of her naked baby! These poor wretches were stunted in their growth, their hideous faces bedaubed with white paint, their skins filthy and greasy, their hair entangled, their voices discordant, and their gestures violent. Viewing such men, one can hardly make oneself believe that they are fellow-creatures, and inhabitants of the same world. It is a common subject of conjecture what pleasure in life some of the lower animals can enjoy: how much more reasonably the same question may be asked with respect to these barbarians! At night, five or six human beings, naked and scarcely protected from the wind and rain of this tempestuous climate, sleep on the wet ground coiled up like animals. Whenever it is

[1] About the omission of the Great Wall of China, I am indebted to *The Journey of Marco Polo* as re-created by artist Michael Foreman, published by *Pegasus* magazine, 1974.

low water, winter or summer, night or day, they must rise to pick shellfish from the rocks; and the women either dive to collect sea-eggs, or sit patiently in their canoes, and with a baited hair-line without any hook, jerk out little fish. If a seal is killed, or the floating carcass of a putrid whale discovered, it is a feast; and such miserable food is assisted by a few tasteless berries and fungi.

—FROM *VOYAGE OF THE BEAGLE*, 1839

Eating Lunch in Yusowa, Japan

ISABELLA BIRD

Yusowa is a specially objectionable-looking place. I took my lunch— a wretched meal of a tasteless white curd made from beans, with some condensed milk added to it—in a yard, and the people crowded in hundreds to the gate, and those behind, being unable to see me, got ladders and climbed on the adjacent roofs, where they remained till one of the roofs gave way with a loud crash, and precipitated about fifty men, women, and children into the room below, which fortunately was vacant. Nobody screamed—a noteworthy fact—and the casualties were only a few bruises. Four policemen then appeared and demanded my passport, as if I were responsible for the accident, and failing, like all others, to read a particular word upon it, they asked me what I was traveling for, and on being told "to learn about the country," they asked if I was making a map! Having satisfied their curiosity they disappeared, and the crowd surged up again in fuller force. The Transport Agent begged them to go away, but they said they might never see such a sight again! One old peasant said he would go away if he were told whether "the sight" were a man or a woman, and, on the agent asking if that were any business of his, he said he should like to tell at home what he had seen, which awoke my sympathy at once, and I told Ito to tell them that a Japanese horse galloping night and day without ceasing would take five and a half weeks to reach my country—a statement which he is using lavishly as I go along.

—FROM *UNBEATEN TRACKS IN JAPAN*, 1880

Merinid Court, Morocco

EDITH WHARTON

But the crown of El Kairouiyin is the Merinid court of ablutions. This inaccessible wonder lies close under the Medersa Attarine, one of the oldest and most beautiful collegiate buildings of Fez; and through the kindness of the Director of Fine Arts, who was with us, we were taken up to the roof of the Medersa and allowed to look down into the enclosure.

It is so closely guarded from below that from our secret coign of vantage we seemed to be looking down into the heart of forbidden things. Spacious and serene the great tiled cloister lay beneath us, water spilling over from a central basin of marble with a cool sound to which lesser fountains made answer from under the pyramidal green roofs of the twin pavilions. It was near the prayer-hour, and worshippers were flocking in, laying off their shoes and burnouses, washing their faces at the fountains and their feet in the central tank, or stretching themselves out in the shadow of the enclosing arcade.

This, then, was the famous court "so cool in the great heats that seated by thy beautiful jet of water I feel the perfection of bliss"—as the learned doctor Abou Abd Allah el Maghili sang of it; the court in which the students gather from the adjoining halls after having committed to memory the principles of grammar in prose and verse, the "science of the reading of the Koran," the invention, exposition, and ornaments of style, law, medicine, theology, metaphysics, and astronomy, as well as the talismanic numbers, and the art of ascertaining by calculation the influences of the angels, the spirits, and the heavenly bodies, "the names of the victor and the vanquished, and of the desired object and the person who desires it."

Such is the twentieth-century curriculum of the University of Fez. Repetition is the rule of Arab education as it is of Arab ornament. The teaching of the University is based entirely on the medieval principle of mnemonics; and as there are no examinations, no degrees, no limits to the duration of any given course, nor is any disgrace attached to slowness in learning, it is not surprising that many students, coming as youths, linger by the fountain of Kairouiyin till their hair is gray. One well-known *oulama*[1] has lately finished his studies after twenty-seven years at the University, and is justly proud of the length of his stay. The life of the scholar is easy, the way of knowledge is long, the contrast exquisite between the foul lanes and noisy bazaars outside and this cool heaven of learning.

—FROM *IN MOROCCO*, 1920

---

[1] *oulama:* learner. (Ed.)

Kamante and Odysseus

ISAK DINESEN

"Msabu, what is there in books?"

As an illustration, I told him the story from the Odyssey of the hero and Polyphemus, and of how Odysseus had called himself Noman, had put out Polyphemus' eye, and had escaped tied up under the belly of a ram.

Kamante listened with interest and expressed as his opinion, that the ram must have been of the same race as the sheep of Mr. Long, of Elmentaita, which he had seen at the cattle show in Nairobi. He came back to Polyphemus, and asked me if he had been black, like the Kikuyu. When I said no, he wanted to know if Odysseus had been of my own tribe or family.

"How did he," he asked, "say the word, *Noman,* in his own language? Say it."

"He said *Outis,*" I told him. "He called himself Outis, which in his language means Noman."

"Must you write about the same thing?" he asked me.

"No," I said, "people can write of anything they like. I might write of you."

Kamante who had opened up in the course of the talk, here suddenly closed again, he looked down himself and asked me in a low voice, what part of him I would write about.

"I might write about the time when you were ill and were out with the sheep on the plain," I said, "what did you think of then?"

His eyes wandered over the room, up and down; in the end he said vaguely: "*Sejur*"—I know not.

"Were you afraid?" I asked him.

After a pause, "Yes," he said firmly, "all the boys on the plain are afraid sometimes."

"Of what were you afraid?" I said.

Kamante stood silent for a little while, his face became collected and deep, his eyes gazed inward. Then he looked at me with a little wry grimace:

"Of Outis," he said. "The boys on the plain are afraid of Outis."

—FROM *OUT OF AFRICA,* 1937

Mushroom Hunting in the Soviet Union

COLIN THUBRON

Mushroom-hunting . . . I wish I could express it to you." Volodya's face became filled with this obscure national excitement. "It's like this. You get into the forests and you know instinctively if the conditions are right for them. You can sense it. It gives you a strange thrill. Perhaps the grass is growing at the right thickness, or there's the right amount of sun. You can even smell them. You just know that here there'll be mushrooms"—he spoke the word "mushrooms" in a priestly hush—"so you go forward in the shadows, or in a light clearing perhaps, and there they are, under the birches!" He reached out in tender abstraction and plucked a ghostly handful from the air. "Have you ever sniffed mushrooms? The poisonous ones smell bitter, but the good ones—you'll remember that fragrance for ever!"

He went on to talk about the different kinds and qualities of mushroom, and how they grew and where to find them—delicate white mushrooms with umbrellaed hats, which bred in the pine forests; red, strong-tasting birch-mushrooms with whitish stems and feverish black specks; the yellow "little foxes," which grew in huddles all together; and the sticky, dark-tipped mushroom called "butter-covered," delicate and sweet. Then there was the *apyata* which multiplied on shrubs—"you can pick a whole bough of them!"—and at last, in late autumn, came a beautiful green-capped mushroom which it was sacrilege to fry. All these mushrooms, he said, might be boiled in salt and pepper, laced with garlic and onions, and the red ones fried in butter and cut into bits until they appeared to have shrunk into nothing, then gobbled down with vodka all winter.

We sat on the verge for a little longer, talking of disconnected things. He was going to Brest, and I to Smolensk, and it was futile to pretend that we would ever meet again. This evanescence haunted all my friendships here. Their intimacy was a momentary triumph over the prejudice and fear which had warped us all our lives; but it could never be repeated.

Volodya clasped my hand in parting, and suddenly said: "Isn't it all ridiculous—I mean propaganda, war. Really I don't understand." He stared at where we'd been sitting—an orphaned circle of crushed grass. "If only I were head of the Politburo, and you were President of America, we'd sign eternal peace at once"—he smiled sadly— "and go mushroom-picking together!"

I never again equated the Russian system with the Russian people.

—FROM *WHERE NIGHTS ARE LONGEST*, 1983

American Tourists in Egypt

EVELYN WAUGH

One day I went alone to Sakkara, the enormous necropolis some way down the Nile from Mena. There are two pyramids there, and a number of tombs; one of them, named unpronounceably the Mastaba of Ptahhotep, is exquisitely decorated in low relief. Another still more beautifully sculptured chamber is called more simply the Mastaba of Ti. As I emerged from this vault I came upon a large party of twenty or thirty indomitable Americans dragging their feet, under the leadership of a dragoman, across the sand from a chara-banc. I fell in behind this party and followed them underground again, this time into a vast subterranean tunnel called the Serapeum, which, the guide explained, was the burial place of the sacred bulls. It was like a completely unilluminated tube-railway station. We were each given a candle, and our guide marched on in front with a mag-nesium flare. Even so, the remote corners were left in impenetrable darkness. On either side of our path were ranged the vast granite sarcophagi; we marched very solemnly the full length of the tunnel, our guide counting the coffins aloud for us; there were twenty-four of them, each so massive that the excavating engineers could devise no means of removing them. Most of the Americans counted aloud with him.

One is supposed, I know, to think of the past on these occa-sions; to conjure up the ruined streets of Memphis and to see in one's mind's eye the sacred procession as it wound up the avenue of sphinxes, mourning the dead bull; perhaps even to give license to one's fancy and invent some personal romance about the lives of these garlanded hymn-singers, and to generalize sagely about the mutability of human achievement. But I think we can leave all that to Hollywood. For my own part I found the present spectacle infinitely stimulating. What a funny lot we looked, trooping along that obscure gallery! First the Arab with his blazing white ribbon of magnesium, and behind him, clutching their candles, like penitents in procession, this whole rag-tag and bobtail of self-improvement and uplift. Some had been bitten by mosquitoes and bore swollen, asymmetrical faces; many were footsore, and limped and stumbled as they went; one felt faint and was sniffing "salts"; one coughed with dust; another had her eyes inflamed by the sun; another wore his arm in a sling, injured in heaven knows what endeavor; every one of the party in some way or another was bruised and upbraided by the thundering surf of education. And still they plunged on. One, two, three, four . . . twenty-four dead bulls; not twenty-three or twenty-five. How could they remember twenty-four? Why, to be sure, it was the number of Aunt Mabel's bedroom at Luxor. "How did the bulls die?" one of them asks.

"What did he ask?" chatter the others.

"What did the guide answer?" they want to know.

"How *did* the bulls die?"

"How much did it cost?" asks another. "You can't build a place like this for nothing."

"We don't spend money that way nowadays."

"Fancy spending all that burying bulls . . ."

Oh, ladies and gentlemen, I longed to declaim, dear ladies and gentlemen, fancy crossing the Atlantic Ocean, fancy coming all this way in the heat, fancy enduring all these extremities of discomfort and exertion; fancy spending all this money, to see a hole in the sand where, three thousand years ago, a foreign race whose motives must forever remain inexplicable interred the carcasses of twenty-four bulls. Surely the laugh, dear ladies and gentlemen, is on us.

But I remembered I was a gate-crasher in this party and remained silent.

—FROM *LABELS: A MEDITERRANEAN JOURNAL,* 1930

Calcutta Is Forever

JOHN KRICH

What makes a city a city when all benefits are gone? What purpose 1
in swarming when the honey's been licked clean, siphoned off to
officials, exported, or bartered for lapidary work meant to invoke the
presence of honey past? When all that beckons now are reports of
black market goo, traces of stick, the maddening twitch of antennae
up ahead, beyond reach, which indicates the fleeting appearance of
sweet? And where the sustenance in gathering with so many other
pilgrims of the stomach, when what most have in common is a
dwindling of the stamina required to console? Kindness is one commodity that cannot be hoarded. Progress, when it just means cen-
tralization, an enlargement of the undernourished hive, is nothing
more than proof that misery loves company.

In Calcutta, one cannot lack for company. Each night, you're in- 2
vited to the world's least exclusive, no-host pajama party. Moment
the heat falters, charpoys, those hammocks on stubby legs, are
pulled from some communal closet, materialize out of a snake
charmer's bottomless basket, to redecorate the sidewalks. A civic
scramble for bedtime turf, with no ideals motivating, no services
provided beyond pumps for washing and drinking and laundering.
This outdoor show is no longer mere housing overflow; the claims
staked here are for permanent quarters in the flux. The only item in
Calcutta of which there's no shortage are these portable hospital cots
and bodies to fill the ward. An evening stroll here is but a bedcheck,
an obstacle course through the prone.

The electricity in Victorian streetlamps is tentative, giving a si- 3
lent-movie flicker to the proceedings. The sleepers' only blanket is a
murky fog that clings to the pavement—suggesting the old Lime-
house, and reminding us that this place rests on a swamp, reclaimed
by the British East India Trading Company in order to create this
other swamp. What's being played out is Dickens in brown skins.
But these characters aren't scheming to stay out of debtors' prison,
they're already in it. The colonialists have played Indian-givers to
the Indians, taking away all the goodies and leaving behind an

---

John Krich (1951–   ), from San Francisco, is the author of the
novels *A Totally Free Man* (1981) and *One Big Bed* (1987). "Calcutta Is
Forever" is a chapter from the travel memoir *Music in Every Room:
Around the World in a Bad Mood* (1984).

aborted industrialism's dislocations. Stodgy and imperturbable government buildings also remain, blood red armories the pillows for bled people with one bowl and ten kids' belongings wrapped in single indigo-colored cloth square. Picnics laid across sewer lines, there's a curious intimacy to the subsistence rituals on view, and no intimacy to what comes after. No goodnight whispers, campers' pranks, no fondling after lights out. Absolutely no undressing, for modesty's sake and so folds of dhoti can serve as sheets, best sandals can't be stolen off the feet. Just nutshell bodies with itches all over and no compunction about scratching them.

Or is this a slaughterhouse haze through which swoop the 4 crows immortalized by Kipling? Smirking black tyrants, so privileged to be winged. Occasional baboons waltz by, or tarry on ledges overhead, pondering suicidal leaps, goaded senselessly to the city, driven from their natural habitat like the rest, except that they know when to screech and go berserko. To run from the gradual kill. On makeshift platforms, agitators harangue their captive audience, albino devils all in white with white beards before lecterns strewn with white petals. Bare bulbs sway hypnotically over them; the amplification is too great and fanatic waftings carry for blocks around, swabbing the tear-stained sidewalks with promises. These demagogues sell ideologies like elixirs. The solution, one zealot claims, is mass immigration to Bangladesh. The land of opportunity! Where the only consensus is malnutrition, political acts are consigned to the agenda of the surreal. On each lamppost above the dormitory, the placards of Mrs. Gandhi's "emergency"—like, "Punctuality for the Railways? No, For You Also!"—exhort further sacrifice from those who've already given everything.

"Emergency?" goes the folk wisdom. "There is always an emer- 5 gency in Calcutta!" Here, waking hours are the bad dream and sleep's the only time for realism, really. The best city to live in is the one that's made and unmade as public snores mingle. It's a pointless exercise to plumb the actual when there's no possibility of control, and once the morning traffic of bullock-carts serves as their alarm, this snoozing citizenry relinquishes all to duty lack of options and the marching orders of appetite. Change is a business unsuited to these avenues of exhaustion where sleepers turn and turn trying to find buoyancy in their netting, a soft spot in the concrete. One more turn and they may slip into purgatory. Is that what makes them do it so gingerly, what constricts their restlessness? Or is it the sheer quantity of snoozers and groomers and mothers crouching to protect handfuls of rice or half moons of silver nose rings that every other woman hoards as well? What schemes circulate in all these districts turned indoors-out? Is there at least lust for affection, approval, status, birthday parties, new underwear, an afternoon at the picture show, a front door, something to do? How about an urge to escape?

I'd like to know the secret of such obtuse contentment. Or would I? I cope with this place by turning clinician. I observe the fiendish experiment in hopes of reporting my findings to someone, anyone. I have to think these subjects' travail must lead to discoveries. I feel a curious lack of personal despair. I sleep long, rich hours, uninterrupted by nightmare. The day's thick broth of images never boils over, just bubbles away and gives off reassuring steam. At formal dining services in our colonial relic of a boarding house, I eat as much as the uniformed bearers will allow, even though I can look down from my room on their barracks where, stripped of white gloves, braided turbans and epaulets, they reveal apalling skinniness, drift into between-meals myopia. I take second helpings of Yorkshire pies and starchy curries, I nurse the contents of my cozy at high tea. My pulse is regular as the climate allows. And I feel this sahib's itch to catalogue. I have no illusions about rescuing people with words, only hopes that the rescue of words will keep leading me back to these people. After all, the streets are so dirty and my notebook is so clean. My fingers burn from the pen as a throat burns from crying.

I have to know: Do human beings have a center of gravity? Could they lose it without noticing? Can they be toppled over, cast down, just when they think they're most steady, upstanding and confidently striding forward? There is deceptive activity here, in the morning markets, steeplechase jockeying between taxis and oxendrivers. Plenty of rickshawers, runners, cobblers, bobblers, chattel and rattle. Is this commerce or just the proliferation of cancer cells? Witnessing it makes the corners of the retina singe and curl up like burnt paper. And rooftops likewise shrivel in. At least, a town turning shanty makes for a fix-it-man's heaven. Plenty of trickling leaks needing new washers, lots of opportunity for unsupervised tinkering. In Calcutta, big changes would be wrought by a dozen nails. In Calcutta, no one can find a hammer.

In Calcutta, the most genial stroll is always uphill, the surest ventures impossible, the flattest and broadest boulevards logjammed with vertigo. Also, despite appearances, loneliness: not just the ordinary tragic variety, since tragedy too requires privacy, but a generalized furtiveness that turns each day into one great scalding hot sigh. It's those who've lost their way longing for the old ways, the present hankering after the past. Whether it's the command and costumes of caste, or the more mundane dreck of Victoriana, clogging the rusted shopwindows with sets of wooden false teeth beside

duck blinds beside mustache wax beside shuttlecocks beside how-
dahs beside shaving brushes beside "Try Once Our Betel Nut!," the
past is so much more vivid than the present.

Like that mausoleum of the raj called the Victoria Memorial,   9
where portraits of viceroys have a crispness that's startling beside
Calcutta's frayed condition; like the zoo, where the elephants Sam-
bari and Sawazdi look so much better fed than their keepers; like a
steam-powered steamroller with rusted wheels that's probably an
original Fulton design but is still a new-fangled wonderment used
for Calcutta street repair; like goatherds leading their braying
charges across Dalhousie Square, oblivious to the traffic and packed
trolleys; like the leftover English commons, the maidan, that forms
Calcutta's civic apron, gripping the heat to its greens; like the park's
plotters who huddle in closed circles (no women allowed), underneath soccer stadium bleachers, on abandoned cricket pitches, their
work not mere sedition but seeds of sinister vigilantism, religious
seething spread across Etonian fields turned fiery at sunset. Poor
lonesome suitors! Which past do they court? Under what flag?

Day's end is rope's end, and like everyone else, we find   10
ourselves unraveling in the direction of Howrah Bridge. Just slide
with the shift in mass weight toward Calcutta's only way out, a
squat piece of crochetwork in metal that's nonetheless the singular
bit of past that still supports and exemplifies the crossing to the future. Along the embankments nearby, massages *en plein air*[1] are offered by healers; swamis attempt to out-dissolve the lozenge sun; ac-
robats cartwheel in celebration of open space; beggars are so
plentiful they seek hazard pay; makeshift villages form, stage feuds,
disperse. Aboriginal kids roam in khakis tattered to loincloths, eyes
puffed with hunger, pausing to shit out the pure luminescent green
of chronic dysentery anyplace on the stone expanse. Following Iris
and me, they stage games of barefoot chase, but when I dare to photograph them, we become their playthings. They skip along, taunt-
ing us by imitating a camera with circles of fingers, then empty cans
picked from the garbage and held to their eyes. I'm Mister Specs to
them, and the kids get full entertainment value from it. Though they
may not know exactly what I'm up to, they sense something's inherently wrong, that documentation is a denial of life, which consists of
feces and river and tag in the twilight.

We climb the utilitarian girders of this gangplank for six million.   11
Off either end, the sharks wait, a city with fangs. This one funnel
for all human traffic is Calcutta's roost, agora, exercise yard, hatch.

---

[1] *en plein air:* in the open. (Ed.)

The scramble does not exactly end here, on sagging truncated black-as-Blackfriars causeway, but at least is forced to move in definite tos and fros. A few cars climb up, too, all of them the rolling bowler hats called Ambassadors, made-in-India and consequently the only kind available. They're instant antiques, brand-new 1947 models, churned out on assembly lines that haven't been retooled since the British left. Such improvements are irrelevant where time is suspended, as on this suspension. Once on it, stray cars and the two of us must fight the waves of commuters who come twenty across, a stampede in both directions. From afar, this mass had been indiscernible from the bridge's underpinnings, a current of living buttress no less unbroken than the arms of iron. At what points does a crowd become a multitude? It is enough to say that people hold up Howrah Bridge as much as they burden it.

Leaning over the railings, we're surprised at the lack of jagged 12 skyline in either direction. Just a neon sign for "GWALIOR SUITING" on the far side, outlines of the railway station, and Calcutta a Zuni pueblo out of control, a worn-to-smoothness jumble in the deepening haze. The crows are all that's distinct against brown banks meeting brown water. Docks fall in staircases chiseled with erosion. The Hooghly, sluggish tributary of the Ganges, turns deep wheat then rouge then a blue without iciness. Barges powered by bony oarsmen ply the shallows. While a dash of coriander falls from the pitiless sky, half-sunken cradles push off from the ghats in one century and return to shore millennia later.

The human flow on the bridge is the one that bears us off. Don't 13 call it a rush hour, though. No one's rushing their salute to the cast-off sun, this funeral for another dirty day. In the barrage of brown wiry legs in ten-thousand fabric folds, starched but going amber in the dusk, of cheap, sticky plastic shoes that come to Sultanic points at the end, of wrapped homespun and amulets and holy man body paint, what colors exude, what strata of evocation! The resulting spectrum's as constant as from any perfect crystal. Each man who passes is a duplicate, triplicate exemplar. Every crease of dhoti reflects in a series of invisible mirrors, cascading back through generations, as though someone's always been there to take up each pedestrian's exact space and form. And someone always will be. The names don't matter: Gopal and Krishna, Chatterjee and Narayan. They may not be terribly pleased about it, but they're all one.

These trampers comprise the fortunate set, with portmanteaus 14 to grip and hovel homes awaiting, but all are punished by a hovering spirituality that won't go away. Where life's but a passing annoyance with flies circling 'round, no man can be at peace, yet all go in peace. The pack is kept moving by wandering dazed shepherds who prod their flock with piercing stares. The sulk, the scowl, the glare, the glower: there's no site in Hindustan to compare with the sight of one's own self reflected in saddhu eyes deep as wells of the soul.

Meeting those eyes, we're invited inside a trance state that tells 15 us we're of this place, not just at it. Having come westward, westward with the discovering sun, we're finally East as we can get— and don't mind if that restless sun abandons us here. The here-ness is all around, a here-ness of which we've heard so much. Iris and I must hold hands, shameful public display, so we won't be swept off into the parade and become separated amidst the earth's largest lost and found. Where lost is found. We also grab tight so we can share Howrah Bridge's momentary lack-of-present that is present, lack-of-change that is change, lack-of-wisdom that is wisdom. "Calcutta Is Forever," the Tourist Bureau billboards dare to boast, and a claim like that has no way of being proved false.

Traveling Alone in Mexico

MARY MORRIS

Women who travel as I travel are dreamers. Our lives seem to be 1
lives of endless possibility. Like readers of romances we think that
anything can happen to us at any time. We forget that this is not our
real life—our life of domestic details, work pressures, attempts and
failures at human relations. We keep moving. From anecdote to
anecdote, from hope to hope. Around the next bend something new
will befall us. Nostalgia has no place for the woman traveling alone.
Our motion is forward, whether by train or daydream. Our sights
are on the horizon, across strange terrain, vast desert, unfordable
rivers, impenetrable ice peaks.

I wanted to keep going forever, to never stop, that morning 2
when the truck picked me up at five a.m. It was like a drug in me.
As a traveler I can achieve a kind of high, a somewhat altered state
of consciousness. I think it must be what athletes feel. I am transported out of myself, into another dimension in time and space.
While the journey is on buses and across land, I begin another journey inside my head, a journey of memory and sensation, of past
merging with present, of time growing insignificant.

My journey was now filled with dreams of other journeys to 3
cool, breezy places. The plateaus of Tibet, the altiplano of Bolivia,
cold places, barren, without tropical splendor. I did not dream of
Africa and its encompassing heat. I longed for white Siberia, for
Tierra del Fuego, the Arctic tundra, vast desolate plains. I longed for
what came next. Whatever the next stop, the next love, the next
story might be.

Josh was sitting in the back of the truck when it pulled up to my 4
pension. "I thought you were going to Guatemala City," I said.

"Well," he said, smiling, "there are other ways to get to 5
Panama." He grabbed my duffel and pulled me on. Then we sat
across from each other as we set out through a lush pass in the
mountains, bouncing in the back through a very misty morning,

---

Mary Morris (1947–   ), born in Chicago, is the author of short
story collections and novels including *The Bus of Dreams* (1985) and
The Waiting Room (1989). "Traveling Alone in Mexico" is from *Nothing to Declare: Memoirs of a Woman Traveling Alone* (1988).

past charging rivers, herds of cattle and goats, toward the border of Honduras.

At about five-thirty the driver stopped to pick up two women. 6 They were teachers who worked in one-room schoolhouses in the hills. One of them told us she walked an hour from where the truck would drop her to her school and she did this twice a day every day.

"You must be exhausted every day," I said.   7

She had a bright smile, sleek black hair, and dark eyes. "Oh, 8 no." She laughed. "The walk is beautiful and I always arrive feeling refreshed."

"You never get tired of it?" I asked, incredulous.   9

"There is always something to see," she said, smiling. At six- 10 thirty, she got off, heading toward the mountains, waving, then disappeared along a trail.

At seven we reached the frontier and found it closed. We took 11 our bags, waved good-bye to our pickup, and waited for the border to open and for some other vehicle, which we assumed would materialize, to appear. For an hour or so we clomped around, taking pictures of an enormous cow that was nearby. At last the border opened. "You want to go into Honduras?" the guard said with a bit of a sneer.

"Yes, we're going to the ruins." I have no idea why I felt the 12 need to say that, but I did.

"Well, if you want to go into Honduras, that's your problem." 13 He stamped our passports just as another minibus arrived, heading for Copán.

We spent the day at the ruins. We had no plan, really, no sense of 14 whether we would stay there or try to get out of the jungle and to some city by night. The ruins were fairly deserted and we spent the day climbing around. We had not gone far when we startled an enormous blue-black snake that had been asleep. The snake rose up on its side, then chased us along the path for several feet. I had never been chased by a snake before and was amazed at how fast it could move. Josh hurled a stone at it and the snake disappeared into the jungle.

We walked deeper into the jungle and a wasp stung me twice on 15 the knee. Josh scooped wet mud and packed it around the bites. My knee became very stiff and I thought I couldn't go on, but he coaxed me and I did.

We came to a pyramid. It was hardly excavated. The steps were 16 broken, stones were covered with moss, but we climbed. My knee hurt, but I didn't care. We climbed and climbed. It was a very high pyramid and when we reached the top, we were silent. We sat still on the top of this unexcavated pyramid, looking at the tremendous jungle that stretched before us.

I liked Josh. What more can I say. I liked him. I wanted to go 17 with him to Panama. I had only just met him and I hadn't thought it through, but I wanted to go. Thinking about it now, I'm not sure what it was that I liked about him so much—he was, in fact, rather ordinary—but I think it had something to do with the fact that he was an American. He was an intelligent American male and he represented for me all those things that were now missing in my life. He could have dinner with my parents at my father's club. The men would wear suits and ties and discuss the market over Scotch and soda. My mother would wink at me across the table. Later she'd take me aside and say what a nice man he was and how they hoped they'd be seeing more of him.

I thought about Alejandro, sitting in that dark apartment, wait- 18 ing for my return, telegram in hand, but all I could think about was going on with Josh to Panama. That afternoon as we walked, we spoke of more personal things. I told him I had a boyfriend in Mexico City. He said he had just broken up with a woman in Berkeley.

We checked into the Mayan Copán and had dinner on the patio. 19 Sitting there with Josh in the steam of the jungle brought back to me what until now had seemed farthest away—the hot summer days and nights of Manhattan. Suddenly I found myself longing for a dripping ice cream cone while the plaintive song of a saxophonist echoed up the avenue. I longed for the heat of the pavement, cheap wine during a concert in the park, and black children jumping double-Dutch while illegal aliens sold assorted ices—pineapple, anise, coconut. I wanted to be transplanted, to feel the pace of the city in summer—an afternoon spent at the matinee, a weekend flight to Jones Beach. I even longed for what repulsed me—the garbage, the stench of urine, the homeless, the yellow smogged sky. All the things I swore I'd never miss.

After dinner we sat on the porch of the hotel, drinking rum and 20 Cokes and speaking of our travels. Josh told me about trekking through Afghanistan and hiking across the Khyber Pass, about wanting to walk to Turkistan and getting captured by rebels somewhere along the way. He said that he had talked his way into and out of every situation you could imagine. "But if I were a woman," he said, "I don't know if I'd do it alone."

"It has its ups and downs," I said.   21

"Have you ever had anything bad happen to you?"   22

I shrugged. "Some near-misses, that's all."   23

He sipped his rum contemplatively. "I've heard terrible stories." 24

"Like what?"   25

He leaned over and kissed me on the lips. "I don't want to ruin   26
your evening."

"You may as well tell me now."   27

He pulled his chair closer. "Well, this happened to a friend of a   28
friend of mine. Not someone I really know. I met him once, that's
all. I'm not even sure it happened the way my friend said. This man
went to Turkey with his wife. To Istanbul. He never talks about it,
but they went to Istanbul. It was a kind of second honeymoon. They
wanted to start a family, so anyway, they went on this second honeymoon—"

I reached across, touching his hand. "Just tell me the story." He   29
held onto my fingers and did not let go until he was done.

"All right. So they went. They were at the bazaar one day and   30
his wife wanted to buy a dress. She was a pretty woman, blond. So
they went into a store and after a while he got bored and said he
wanted to take a walk. He said he'd go have a cigarette and be back
in half an hour. They had a little fight about this, but he went anyway. When he came back, the dress shop was closed and no one
was there. So he thought they'd closed early and he went to the hotel and waited for his wife to meet him there. But she never went
back to the hotel. He waited and waited, but she never came back.
He talked to the police and the next day they went to the shop, but
the people, people he recognized from the day before, said they had
never seen the woman and she'd never been there. He stayed in Istanbul for weeks, but they never found his wife."

"And he thinks she was kidnapped by the people who owned   31
the dress shop?"

Josh nodded. "Kidnapped. And sold."   32

"Sold?"   33

"That's right. Sold."   34

We sat in silence for a long time, listening to the jungle noises.   35
After a while, Josh pulled me by my hand. "Come on," he said.
"Let's go to sleep."

In the morning we boarded the minibus. The women who got on all   36
had holes cut in their dresses where their nipples hung out and
small children suckled. The men carried machetes, which they
checked with the bus driver by tucking them under his seat. Many
of the men had slash marks on their arms or faces and many were
missing fingers and limbs, so it appeared that this precaution was a
necessary one. I was reminded of the movies about the Wild West,
where the gunslingers check their guns at the saloon door.

Several hours later we reached La Entrada. Everyone there car-   37 ried a machete. We went to a bar to have a beer and a man walked in. Both his hands had been chopped off above the wrist and his nose was missing. "A machete did that," Josh said.

Suddenly I could not bear the thought of spending a moment 38 alone. The story he had told me of the woman in Istanbul stayed in my mind and I knew that having heard it, I'd never be quite the same.

Josh was undecided about which direction he would take and I 39 was undecided as to whether or not I would go with him. I wanted him to ask me. I thought that if he asked me, I'd go. From La Entrada there were buses to either coast and points east and west. The choices were infinite. But Josh had taken a liking to inland Honduras and the guidebook said there were some things to see in a neighboring town called Florida. "Look," Josh said. "How often are you going to be in this part of Honduras?"

"Not often," I said. And we hitched a ride with a farmer in the 40 back of his pickup truck.

Josh had heard about a gas station attendant in Florida who 41 knew everything there was to know about the Mayan ruins in the vicinity.

"I thought you were tired of ruins."   42

"Well, we're here. We may as well make the most of it."   43

We found the gas station attendant and he sent us in the direc- 44 tion of some ruins not far from the border. We crawled around in the heat of the day while Josh tried to decide what kind of people lived in this place. A dog that was skin and bones followed us. I threw him scraps of sandwich, but Josh kept trying to chase the dog away.

Later that night while a tropical breeze blew in through the win- 45 dows of our small room, Josh told me he was going to go to Salvador. I thought to myself how, having lost all sense of proportion, I'd follow this man anywhere, and after about thirty seconds I said, "Mind if I come with you?"

"Not at all," he said. "But what about your boyfriend in Mex- 46 ico?"

"What about him?"   47

"Well, won't he be upset?"   48

"Do you want me to go with you or not?" I asked, pressing the 49 point.

"I want you to do whatever makes you happy," he said.   50

"Well, then I'm going with you."   51

He drifted right to sleep, but I stayed awake. I could not stop 52 thinking about that woman he'd told me about the night before, a captive in some harem, a woman used and tossed aside, trying endlessly to plan her escape. A blonde among dark people. A woman who could not speak their tongue. Perhaps she had been ingenious, learning their ways, and had made a life for herself wherever her prison was. Perhaps she had fallen into the hands of a benevolent sheik who took pity on her, and though his pride would not permit him to release her, he would not abuse her, either.

But I think the scenario is much darker than this. That woman 53 would never be free. She would never return. If it were me, when I realized that rescue wouldn't come, that I would not be found, that I would never go home and would always be a prisoner of men, I would lose my mind. I would die of grief or by my own hand.

In the morning we stood at the crossroads at La Entrada, waiting for 54 the bus for Salvador. Until the bus arrived, I wasn't sure what I was going to do, but as soon as I saw it, kicking up dust, puffing in the distance, I knew what lay before me. When the driver stopped and opened the ancient door, I kissed Josh. "Have a safe journey," I said.

"What? Aren't you coming?"   55

"I'm going to Tegucigalpa." If he begs me, I told myself, I'll go. 56

"Well, whatever suits you."   57

He wasn't begging. He wasn't even asking. "Yes, I guess this 58 suits me." I waved good-bye. Sitting on my duffel in the sun— though dreaming of the way I could have gone with him—I felt sure I was on the right road. About an hour later the bus for Tegucigalpa approached. The bus driver asked me if I was a *gente de la sandía*, a watermelon person. A joke on the Sandinistas, and I said no, I was a tourist from the United States. He nodded and I took a seat in the rear.

It was a big bus this time, heading for the capital. Not long after 59 I boarded a young girl and her father got on, and they sat near the front. After about an hour the bus stopped and the father got off. He kissed his daughter good-bye and waved as the bus drove away. The girl was perhaps thirteen or fourteen and after a few moments she began to cry. She cried uncontrollably and the driver stopped. Women rushed to her, then came away shaking their heads. She was an idiot, one of the women told me. Her father had abandoned her here on this bus. "Too expensive to feed," the man behind me muttered. "Too expensive to keep."

Jews in a Land without Jews

HERBERT GOLD

As a student in the mid-'50s, I spent two years in the Republic of 1
Haiti—a land without Jews except in myth and memory. There was
no Jewish community, no Jewish life. Even that most final sign of
Jewish history, as of all histories, was lacking—no Jewish cemetery,
no Jewish place in a cemetery. A Jew might run and hide—history is
full of that—but the cemetery remains, or the place where the cemetery once stood, or the memory of this place. None. No graveyard,
no place, no memory of the place that never was.

And yet, as it happened, even here, in this lovely, forsaken cor- 2
ner of the world, Jews had come. Since my student days, I have
been returning for the past 35 years as a writer enchanted by this
place of the best nightmares on earth.

Before I found the vivid traces of Jews, I found the anti-Semites, 3
refugees from their crimes. The Gestapo informer from Paris who
became my friend and companion ("Get me into the States, can't
you? Surely *you* can!"), and the Petainist colonel who had left France
for a Haitian exile after collaborating with the Nazi occupation. Odd
to meet the evidence of my history first in the form of its enemy, the
exiles biting their nails, biding their time in a backwater. And I
found Haitians like Jean Weiner, as handsome and lofty as a Watusi,
who cackled hysterically as he described the origins of his distinguished Roman Catholic family: "A Jew from Vienna came here to
trade in coffee!"

Through Jean, I met a morose accountant with a degree from a 4
school of business in Philadelphia and a mania for recounting the
days of his persecution. Restaurants, doormen, professors, women
had all treated him like a *Negro*—"*Moi qui est Haitien!*"[1] he cried. Re-

---

[1] *Moi qui est Haitien!*: I who am Haitian! (Ed.)

Herbert Gold (1924–   ), born in Cleveland, is the author of essays, stories, and novels including *Biafra Goodbye* (1970), *A Girl of
Forty* (1986), and *Travels in San Francisco* (1990). "Jews in a Land
without Jews" first appeared in *This World*, the Sunday magazine of
the *San Francisco Chronicle* (1990), and is adapted from the memoir
Best Nightmare on Earth (1991).

membering the purgatory of Philadelphia, he despised Haiti, the peasantry and the Jews, and his name was Cohen.

When he confided one evening that the Jews are at the root of 5 all the trouble in Haiti and the world, I said to him, "I'm a Jew." He peered at me blankly through his red-rimmed eyes as if he had never seen one before. "And you, with your name," I said.

"My grandfather came from Jamaica."   6

"You must have had a Jewish grandfather in there someplace."   7

"You're making that up! . . . How did you know?"   8

"Cohen."   9

"*Cohen?*" he asked. To him Cohen was the name of a Mass-go- 10 ing Haitian accountant. I explained that the Cohanim were priests and he was descended from priests and princes.

"Priests don't have children," he said irritably.   11

"Do you really think Jews caused all the trouble in Haiti?"   12

"No, not all," he said, "but the wars, the world wars they 13 started, all the wars hurt us, too."

There was a double ledger for his secret Jewish grandfather and 14 his need to find an explanation for trouble and sin. I could nag at him with facts, scandalize him with my own history, but I could never change his accounting and put Cohen, the Haitian accountant, in touch with Cohen, the man with an ancestor who did not begin the line of Cohens in Jamaica. He was horn-rimmed glasses, owlish eyes with reddened conjunctiva, pockmarked black skin, and a Jew-hating heart that was outraged by the information—which he knew already—that his name meant something drastic in his past. He was not descended from an infinite line of Jamaican mulattos.

"If you knew more about the troubles of the world," I told him, 15 "you'd be safer from them."

"I've had them, *des difficultés.* "   16

I was only confusing the black Roman Catholic Cohen in search 17 of clear definitions.

There were others like him, of course, good Mass-going Haitians 18 with names like Goldenberg or Levi, or with Sephardic names like Mendes or Silvera. In Jacmel, a tiny town on the sea with an unpaved Grand Rue, perhaps once a week a police jeep scattered the traffic jams of black Haitian pigs, flailing dust—the *cochons noirs* as skinny and speedy as dogs. There was a *pension*, telephones and electricity that rarely worked, the mud huts of an African village—and in this place, Jacmel, I found a Jewish tailor.

A few elegantly carpentered Haitian dream houses floated above 19 reality like candy visions—slats and shutters, parapets and magic cages filled with lizards or birds—but Monsieur Schneider lived in a dwelling separated only by a few boards and nails from *caille-paille*, the country shelter of mud and straw.

He did his work at a hand-treadled machine in the dusty street, 20 his head tilted to one side to favor his good eye, his joints swollen and his body twisted by arthritis. He was old and wore rags, like many Haitians, but the rags were sewn into the blurred shape of a European shirt and suit. It was too hot for such formality. He was one of three white people in the town. In the air around him, like the insects and the animals, eddied the members of his extended family—the mixed African and Semitic—some dark and some light, children and adults, wives and grandchildren.

"Mister Schneider," I began, first in English. No English, but he 21 understood what I was asking. Was *I*? Yes. *Oui*. A flood of Yiddish poured out of his head. I spoke no Yiddish.

He looked at me as if to doubt my sanity. A Jew, I said, and 22 spoke no Yiddish? He tried Creole. We settled on French, which he spoke in a Yiddish accent, with Creole words and phrases. He believed I was what I said I was, for otherwise what gain for either of us? Who needed to tell lies here, so far from the Czar's police? He kicked amiably at the grandchildren—children?—playing about the treadles of his Singer machine. The treadle was cast with ironwork scrolls and Art Nouveau symbols polished by his bare feet.

He did not have the look of a person who asked deep questions, 23 but he stared at me from his one good eye. "What's a Jew doing in Jacmel?" he asked.

His face was shriveled against sunlight, shrunken by age, 24 blotched and deeply freckled. It looked like a dog's muzzle. "Why is a Jew *living* here?" I asked him in return.

"My home," he said. "You call this a life? My wife is dead. I 25 have another wife. My children and grandchildren are here."

"Would you forgive the question? How did you happen to settle 26 in Jacmel?"

He pumped furiously at the machine. He was fixing a seam, a 27 simple matter, but he gave it all his concentration. Then he squinted around at me. I had moved so he wouldn't be staring into the sun. He winked, Jew to Jew.

"And where else?" 28

Jeremie, St.-Marc, Cap Haitian, Port-au-Prince, Port-de-Paix— 29 that's all. So he settled in Jacmel.

"Were you Polish?" 30

"Russian." 31

"So were my parents. Why didn't you go to the United States?" 32

"Ah," he said. "Because I wished to learn the French and Creole 33
languages, *c'est vrai?*"

"*Non.*" 34

"Because"—and he spread wide his arms—"I had adventure in 35
my heart?"

"No." 36

He put down his cloth and stood up. 37

He put his face close to mine, pulled at the lid of the dead eye as 38
if he were stretching a piece of cloth, and said, "I went to Ellis Isle,
maybe your father did too. But he didn't have a sick eye. It was in-
fected from the filth. They sent me away. And then I wandered, no
place left. So instead of killing myself I came to Haiti."

"I'm sorry," I said, although it seemed foolish to be oppressed 39
by a sick eye from a generation before I was born.

He started to laugh. It was not the dry, old man's laughter of my 40
uncles in Cleveland. It was a rich, abandoned, Haitian old man's
laughter. He clutched at his crotch for luck. "You see these children? You see all the brown Schneider children in Jacmel? Many
died—my wives often die—but look what I have done. I have
proved God is not malevolent. He let me live. He let some of these
children live. God is indifferent, but I have shown, not proved, of
course, but *demonstrated* that he is not malevolent."

"If you believe, God is not evil, merely all-powerful." 41

He put his face down. He reached for a packet of sugar and held 42
it up to my face. "If he were all-powerful, then he would be evil. He
could not allow what he allows. You like good Haitian coffee, *Monsieur?* Martie!" he shouted into the *caille-paille.* "*Blanc v'le café—poté.*"

I drank coffee with the tailor and his new wife, who said not a 43
word as she sat with us. He sucked at sugar and sipped his coffee
through it.

"I have a few books," he said. "A scholar I was not. My uncle 44
was a rabbi. I think my brother was going to be a rabbi, but"—he
shrugged—"I never found out what he became. You're not a rabbi?"

"No." 45

"It's not so stupid to ask. I heard of rabbis now who don't speak 46
Yiddish."

"I don't speak Hebrew, either." 47

"Then you couldn't be a rabbi, could you?" 48

I wanted to give him answers and ask questions, but we made 49
mere conversation. We were two Jews speaking a peculiar polyglot
in the town of Jacmel. At that time there was no paved road from
Port-au-Prince, and when it rained, even jeeps couldn't pass the
streams. Jacmel was a port at the end of the world.

His wife watched us with mournful eyes, as if I might take him 50
away from her, but time was taking him away faster than I could.
We had little to say across the years and history between us except
to give each other greetings.

When I said good-by, dizzy with coffee, he stood up painfully, a 51
small thin bent brown man, a creature neither Russian nor Jewish
nor Haitian, something molded in time's hands like a clay doll. He
put out his hand and said in a cracked voice, laughing at the peculiar word he must have pronounced for the first time in years:
"Shalom!"

Return to the Land of Roots

ALEX HALEY

"Alex! It's Alex!," shouted some of Juffure Village's children, run- 1
ning toward us. They had just recognized me as one of the three
men unloading our car's back seat and trunk of four 100 pound bags
of sugar and rice and the traditional visitor's gift packets of kola nuts
wrapped in big dark-green palm leaves. *Geo* photographer Guido
Mangold and I had been driven from Banjul, the capital of The Gambia, by the dark, good-looking, fiftyish Kebba Saidy, who would
also be our interpreter. I had purposely sent the Juffure Village folk
no advance word of my coming. I knew they would have put themselves to much trouble to give me an extravagant welcome, as they'd
done on my previous visits.

I just wanted this to be a quiet arrival on a non-tourist, normal 2
day for the villagers—or, anyhow, whatever had become normal for
them since the world-wide reception given my book *Roots* and its accompanying television film. In part because of the publicity, the previously little-known Republic of The Gambia suddenly began receiving more than 20,000 tourists annually. Hot, dusty, back-country
Juffure Village (population 75) simultaneously found itself the country's principal tourist attraction, because *Roots* had described it as
the circa-1750s home of a Mandinka youth named Kunta Kinte. The
book told of Kunta's capture and abduction on a slave ship to the
United States, where on a Virginia plantation he began a family—
and in the process became my maternal great-great-great-great-
grandfather.

The children's noisy commotion roused the elders, who had 3
been escaping the sun within their small mud-walled, thatch-roofed
homes. They came popping through their doorways; then they, too,
rushed toward us, waving their arms and exclaiming that I'd returned again. Gratitude toward them engulfed me, and I felt guilty
that nearly two years had passed since my last visit. I wished I knew
a way to convey to them the irony that when a writer is lucky
enough to achieve a major success, then his previous life-style,

---

Alex Haley (1921–   ), from Ithaca, New York, is the author of
Roots: The Saga of an American Family (1976) and was Malcolm X's
collaborator for *The Autobiography of Malcom X* (1965). "Return to the
Land of *Roots*" was originally published in the journal *Geo: The
Earth Diary* (1981).

which in my case would have permitted more visits, is radically changed. That had happened to me since the publication of *Roots*. Then it occurred to me that I probably could not fully understand to what degree the once quiet lives of Juffure's people had also been changed.

Hurrying toward us among the villagers were two tall uni- 4 formed policemen. I remembered hearing in the United States how Juffure's swiftly increasing tourism had required the Gambian government to assign a permanent police force there. Even so, daily tourism so disturbed the people's normal way of living that finally tourism within the village as well as its environs was officially permitted only three days a week.

Someone halloed loudly and repetitively to signal the women 5 and younger men, who were tilling their food crops in the nearby fields. Soon Guido, Kebba and I were the center of an animated crowd of people. Conspicuous among them was a short, brusque, middle-aged man of determined look and manner who was wearing a blue knit cap under the hot sun. He pushed and shoved ahead of the others until he had posted himself directly in front of us. Looking anxious that we acknowledge his mission, he pumped up and down before us what seemed to be a gray metal tool case with a thick steel lock. Cut through the top of the case was a finger-size slot.

Pointing at the slot, the man spoke rapid Mandinka to Kebba 6 Saidy. Kebba translated the message, which was that visitors were expected to drop donations of money into the case: each month the case was unlocked and opened with all observing, and the villagers shared its contents.

It was so different from the Juffure I had first visited. The 7 portable cashbox and its bearer's manner—and the way both appeared to be taken for granted—were at odds with the utter dignity and reserve of the Juffure Village I had known.

Across the intervening thirteen years, I had learned only too 8 well—from considerable travel and some brief periods of residence in underdeveloped countries—that in spending or displaying relative wealth, tourists and other visitors only heighten local perception of relative poverty. I knew that the process had inevitably evolved in so many other places, but I felt no less badly that now it had also happened in Juffure. And where Juffure was concerned, it was harder yet for me to face the fact that I had played the undeniable role of catalyst in the process.

Bursting through my thoughts, the squealing, rail-thin Mrs. 9 Binta Kinte rushed to embrace me, her head and shoulders bound up in one of her trademarked brightly iridescent scarves. Just behind her was the very old, very black *alcala* (village headman), Mr. Bakaryding Taal, a tall, spare man clad in a white pillbox hat and long black robe. I knew the nature of the rivalry between them. Traditionally, nobody ever dares to challenge an alcala's position in the village, but the natural flair and charisma of Mrs. Binta Kinte had long since made her such a tourist favorite that her photograph adorned many thousands of postcards on sale all over The Gambia. Moreover, in 1967 it had been her late husband, the *griot* (oral historian) of Juffure Village, who had told me the ancestral Kinte clan history, of which I had written in *Roots*. And Mrs. Binta Kinte, most aware of all these assets, employs her own subtle ways to require the somber, aged Mr. Bakaryding Taal to compete for such recognition as he can get. It was no accident that the alcala's only alternative was to stand and wait, leaning sourly on his cane, as I sought physically to disengage myself from the practically adhesive arms of Mrs. Binta Kinte before I could grasp and shake his gnarled, wrinkled hands.

Behind Mr. Bakaryding Taal were the village's two policemen. 10 "You are Mr. Alex Haley?" asked the taller one, who spoke with a precise formality. He was Constable Ebrima Jammeh, 23, a six-footer of the Jola tribe from Bulock Village. Affirming that I was, I introduced Guido Mangold as my photographer friend and guest from Germany, and Kebba Saidy as the driver having been kind enough to bring us that morning from Banjul. The policemen exchanged glances and appeared briefly to consider the situation. Then Constable Jammeh said, "Well, this is not a permitted visiting day, but as it is you, sir, I believe exception can be made." He paused, handing me a printed card, and added, "However, these are the rules."

As I scanned the card, my sense of concern was only refueled. 11 Had my book helped or hurt this village? There could be no question that *Roots* had accomplished many desirable things. It had replaced black Africa's long, onerous "Tarzan and Jane" image with the far more accurate and certainly much more appropriate images of Kunta Kinte of Juffure and his people. It was generally conceded that among some 27 million black Americans, *Roots* had generated a new sense of ethnic and ancestral pride. In addition, from black Africa itself there had come praise from heads of state, and the Educational Federation of West Africa had even requested a special primary-school edition spanning only Kunta Kinte's growing-up years. The teachers felt that this part of *Roots* would convey to contemporary African students a greater knowledge and appreciation of the old African culture.

There was all this and much more, yet inescapably, it was also a 12 fact that on the card Constable Jammeh had handed me, each of those printed rules for visitors sought to cope with real dilemmas that now threatened the quality of life in Juffure.

Rule number one directed that tourists give no money or gifts to 13 anyone but the village headman, whose courier bore the portable cashbox. I'd heard about the background for this in America. The initial waves of tourists into Juffure had set the villagers vying with one another for gifts, until each night brought heated discussions and residual bad feelings. All this when the amiable, caring and sharing characteristics of rural Gambians are well-known (even city-dwelling Gambians are noted throughout West Africa for their peacefulness).

Another rule printed on the card prohibited any TV or movie 14 cameras: Juffure had been visited by unscrupulous filmmakers encouraging bared breasts or anything else they could photograph to strike a prurient note. A third rule stipulated a maximum of 25 visitors at any one time, with each person required to have spent at least one night in the Gambian capital of Banjul. I knew this rule was intended to foil shrewd Senegalese speedboat operators who took large tourist parties directly up the wide Gambia River, first to visit Juffure Village and then to circle the ancient Fort James Island slave headquarters; they would then whisk their clients back to Senegal, leaving The Gambia without a single cent reaped from its visitors.

I thanked Constable Jammeh for the card, assuring him that 15 we'd respect the rules. I was again embraced by Mrs. Binta Kinte, who told me something in Mandinka; the gathered people nodded vigorously. Kebba Saidy translated: they were filled with embarrassment because, not knowing I was coming, they had prepared no suitable welcome. For the umpteenth time, I felt like kicking myself for never having learned to communicate even a little in my ancestral tongue so that I wouldn't always be utterly dependent on an interpreter. Now I was again asking Kebba Saidy if he'd please relay that I deeply respected their welcoming custom and that I hoped my not sending advance word had in no way offended them but that I would never need further assurance of their welcome than that which they had given me when I returned soon after *Roots* was published.

And indeed I never could forget that welcome. I had brought 16 several American family members and friends with me, and even before we reached The Gambia, on arrival in neighboring Senegal, we had received the red-carpet treatment and a special audience with Léopold Senghor, who was then the president. In The Gambia,

President Dawda Jawara had ordered that his yacht sail all of us up-
river to Juffure.

The village adjacent to Juffure, Albreda, joined in the celebration 17
as our party disembarked at the mooring pier. I remember being
physically buffeted between leaping, shouting, dancing celebrants
as the ragged, dusty parade wended its way back toward Juffure. At
the entrance to the village, some men sprang from roadside bushes
and fired off ancient-looking muskets that set masked *kankurang*
dancers, their bodies covered with leafy green branches, into frenzied motion.

Now, lacking advance notice, some younger men appeared 18
spontaneously, playing drums, *koras*[1] and balaphons; women and
children were singing, dancing and beating dried gourds with
sticks. Some women, sweating profusely because they'd just hurried
in from the fields, joined in with abrupt bursts of short, stomping
steps. Mr. Bakaryding Taal took commanding lead of the procession, punctuating each of his labored steps with his stafflike cane,
whose middle was shiny from long use. Mrs. Binta Kinte clung
tightly to my left arm.

We reached the village clearing. Mr. Bakaryding Taal, turning, 19
raised his robed arm until all the voices became silent. Brusquely, he
issued an order. I knew without translation that it was for the chairs
and benches to be brought out and positioned beneath the big tree,
the village meeting place.

Mr. Bakaryding Taal, pointing, indicated my seat of honor. Mrs. 20
Binta Kinte had so intertwined her arm with mine that wherever I
went, *we* went. Together, we shared the chair.

Guido was moving deftly, photographing the assembly from all 21
angles. Young men had brought up the bags of sugar and rice and
the packets of kola nuts. The ceremonial acceptance was brief and
formal. Mr. Bakaryding Taal sat facing me. As is usual when a
group is involved in a translation, he would speak as the alcala, then
dramatically lean back in his chair as the villagers chorused an explosive "Hah!" in agreement.

Kebba Saidy translated for me: Allah had blessed us to gather 22
here once again. Some whom I had previously seen as members of
the village family were no longer present to the eyes. But their spirits were no less present.

I asked Kebba to say for me that I indeed felt blessed to be 23
among them again, and that I distinctly felt the spirits of those others among us.

---

[1] *koras:* West African stringed instruments, similar to a harp. (Ed.)

The alcala cleared his throat. He sat arrow-straight in his chair. 24
A sense of expectancy hung in the air. He spoke more crisply this
time: since I was a son of the village and Allah had blessed me to
find great wealth in faraway America, they were certain I would not
want to forget that but for the evil known as slavery, I would have
been born and christened into my family compound there in Juffure.

"Hah!" 25

I sat for a moment, studying my shoes against the hard-packed 26
brown African earth. I turned to Kebba Saidy to translate for me.

I said that I felt I understood what they had said to me. Yes, but 27
for slavery, I might have been born in Africa rather than in America.
I said that my book actually told the general history of all black
Americans. We all descend from some African forefather who was
born and reared in some African village like Juffure and was later
kidnapped onto some slave ship bound for America or the
Caribbean, where by now that original African's family has lived for
many generations. My own ancestor, Kunta Kinte of Juffure, lived
seven generations ago, I said, and I felt great pride in returning as a
son of Juffure Village.

It seemed to me that this was the perfect setting in which to tell 28
the villagers why I had returned again.

I said that I had come to ask their approval for building a new 29
mosque in Juffure Village. It would replace the old patched and
weathered one in which they had long worshiped. I said that
though I was Protestant, a Methodist, I deeply respected every human being's personal faith. They were Muslim, as was my ancestor
Kunta Kinte. I said that if they approved, I would like this mosque
to be dedicated to Kunta Kinte's memory.

Again, I watched their faces closely. Every expression I saw re- 30
minded me, hopefully, of something I'd read somewhere: native
black Africans, if deeply moved, will try hard not to show it.

Mr. Bakaryding Taal briefly addressed his fellow villagers. There 31
was a short, agitated discussion. He turned, his deep-set eyes
squarely meeting mine. Yes, the Juffure people would be most
happy to have a new mosque dedicated to Kunta Kinte.

The sound of the people's "Hah!" was delightful to hear, but 32
then almost immediately I was confused by the ensuing restlessness
and murmuring, which seemed to convey that they still awaited
something else. Then the alcala spoke again:

They were all sure I would want to be told that the farming had 33
been especially poor that year, so that the village people's needs
were many. And the people were sure that as a son of the village
whom Allah had blessed with wealth, I would not knowingly permit
my family in Juffure to continue in want and need—

"Hah!"   34

I felt a sense of helplessness. The radical changes that had al-   35
ready affected Juffure within the relatively short span since the first
tourists had come there bearing gifts made it clear that the most
damaging thing I could do would be to give a sum of money to every person in the village. That, at best, could only apply a temporary
balm to a far deeper problem. As I saw it, Juffure's ancient tradition
of self-reliance and self-pride was in danger of giving way to a new
sense of communal dependency—upon tourists, upon me, upon
things beyond the villagers' own resources.

My mind searched again for the way I could best express my   36
earnest desire to be as genuinely helpful to them and to all Gambians as I possibly knew how.

I asked them to understand that I personally thought that the   37
benefits of education were matchless. Hoping that my feelings
would thus be more clearly illustrated, I told them of the number of
Gambian young people whom I was helping to educate in the
United States.

Watching the expressions of the Juffure villagers, I could tell that   38
it really held little meaning for them that several Gambian young
men would return trained as teachers or agriculturists; or that Sonha
Sallah, from Banjul, was pursuing her master's degree in communi-
cations; or that Seni Sise, from a village not much bigger than Juffure, was achieving honors in pharmacology, determined to become
The Gambia's first woman pharmacist.

Perhaps, I thought, if any of those students had come from Juf-   39
fure, then my efforts to help might have been better conveyed to the
people. But it was clear that as things stood, the Juffure people
wanted something they could look at and feel in their hands, something tangible; this made me very sad, for I had really tried to do
what I felt was the best thing.

Soon, I told them through Kebba's translations, we would have   40
to be leaving. I explained that we had to visit Fort James Island, just
offshore in the Gambia River, and following that, we'd have to hasten along the roads if we were to make the last night ferryboat at
Barra and reach Banjul and our hotel.

Now the Juffure villagers were perplexed and disappointed.   41
Kebba began to translate as one after another of them abruptly
thrust himself forward and spoke to me in rapid, intense Mandinka.

The first one, a stout, middle-aged man, said I'd returned so   42
dramatically to them years before, but afterward I'd never seemed to
have much time for them. Why was that?

Asked another: why must I always leave so quickly? In fact, why   43
couldn't I spend at least a few weeks in the village among them?

"After all, we are your family," wailed Mrs. Binta Kinte. "Your 44
cousins are here! This is your home."

I thought of my schedule book, with its blur of business ap- 45
pointments and lectures awaiting in Los Angeles, New York,
Chicago, Detroit, Miami and other cities. Even if this could be explained to them, how could I possibly ask them to understand that
though my schedule always saw me quickly "leaving them," I loved
the village, the people and Africa; and that an anticipation of
"coming home" was something I always carried with me.

But aloud, via the translator, I only apologized and expressed to 46
the Juffure villagers my sincere desire to try to make my visits more
frequent.

Then we all trooped for perhaps an eighth of a mile to the vil- 47
lage of Albreda, on the bank of the Gambia River. Protocol demanded that we reassemble under Albreda's big tree, where their alcala presided. He stressed how the two villages had always been
close neighbors, which meant that our ancestors had surely played
together as childhood friends.

Albreda's welcome included a small itinerant troupe of Sene- 48
galese entertainers, featuring a plump young woman of about 25.
She danced with her whole body, sinuously responding to every nuance of the drums' rhythms. Some people threw her money, which
she gracefully retrieved, continuing to dance with the money
pressed between her extended fingers.

Mostly, I sat there staring out across the river at Fort James Is- 49
land: it held the silhouetted ruins of the fort from which so many
slave ships had sailed during the trade in human beings that lasted
two centuries.

Kebba Saidy was arguing loudly with some boatmen. Their ex- 50
changes grew more heated, and I knew that both they and he were
engaging in a traditional bargaining ritual. Finally, an agreement
having been reached, Kebba indignantly stalked away as if he had
just been robbed. Now our little party moved out to the boats that
were moored to the timbers of the long planked pier extending into
the river.

We sailed out, the outboard puttering smoothly, and I recalled 51
the first day I had ever seen the Gambia River. En route to The
Gambia from Dakar, Senegal, I was flying over the wide, brown
river in a small Nigeria Airways plane. My face was pressed against
the window, and it seemed that I could see the slave ships sailing
those waters I had read so much about. It seemed that I could hear
the moans and wails within their holds, and I became so angry up
there in the air that I felt like fighting somebody.

But I didn't feel that way now, not anymore. Working for years 52 with slavery records had taught me that in order to be emotionally able to continue, I would do best to deal clinically and abstractly with slavery, adopting something like a surgeon's approach at the operating table.

We landed on Fort James Island. Walking among the familiar ru- 53 ins of the fort, which had once been a bastion of iron, stone, and concrete, I found myself studying the comparative sizes of the underground slave pens and the far larger, above-ground rooms that had housed the European soldiers who had guarded the fort against enemy fleets trying to take over the lucrative trade in flesh.

The keeper of Fort James Island was Mr. Kebba Jabang, a short 54 man wearing a dark robe; he carried like a Bible a book in which all visitors were required to enter their names and addresses. He said that many of the name-filled books were now stored in the Banjul offices of Mr. Bakari Sidibe, The Gambia's chief archivist.

"Many black people from your country who come here cry as if 55 their hearts will break," Mr. Jabang said. I said that I knew. I had cried there, too.

We were back in Kebba Saidy's black Ford sedan, returning to- 56 ward Banjul, when Guido Mangold said, "Alex, I am a German, a white man. I don't have to question why I'm an outsider here. But you, in a different way, you're also an outsider. You're no longer the true black color of these people you claim as ancestors."

Guido's observation brought flashing back to me the experience 57 of my first visit to The Gambia, when I had rented a small motor launch to take a party of 15 from Banjul to Juffure. We had not gone too far along the river when for some reason I began glancing around at all the others. Suddenly the realization hit me that I was the only person on board with a brown complexion, that the skin color of every other person there was really black. I had felt alien and confused; I had even felt, among them, that I was impure. I told no one, of course, but it took me quite some time to cope with that unpleasant, queasy feeling.

And I knew that many other American black people had been 58 affected in later years by some variation of my experience when they had gone to Africa in fulfillment of a driving desire to visit the motherland. Some blacks of light complexion had even been shocked when Africans, especially children, innocently referred to them as *toubob*, the Mandinka word meaning "white man." And indeed, I remembered my father's tales of *his* grandparents, who had been Irish on the paternal side and black slaves on the maternal side. It was impossible for me to be less than honest—I am, after all, a born-and-reared, acculturated product of the United States.

Guido's comment had hung in the air as I thought of these 59 things, and I finally said, "Guido, I understand what you mean, but just let yourself imagine. Across two centuries of slavery, nobody can ever know the countless times that white males impregnated black slave women." I thought for a moment. "But we all began from pure Africans. Guido, being brown doesn't make me any less black. I could never be an outsider to what I am."

Guido was thoughtful. After a while he said, "I can understand 60 what you say."

Kebba Saidy was pushing the Ford pretty hard. We had to make 61 the ferry at Barra, the site of one of the most bitter pills of my entire nine years of research before writing *Roots*. For as thousands of whites had played roles in the taking of Africans into slavery, so had an infamous few Africans—among them the black king of Barra. He tricked, trapped, imprisoned, then sold—as "punishment"—many of his own people. I remember how bitterly I'd hated the man, who had been dead for more than 200 years. He coated his treachery, cruelty, and avarice with an egomaniacal pomp that saw him demand 17 and 21-gun salutes from every slave ship entering the river in pursuit of black human cargo. I wished hard that some slaver captain had got the chance—which all of them would have gleefully seized—to grab the king of Barra and sail out with *him* in chains, as just one more item of cargo.

After a night's sleep back in Banjul's brand-new Atlantic Hotel, I 62 took a taxicab to the Gloucester Street home of Alhaji Malik Manga. The Manga family, of the Wolof tribe, have been my close friends since early 1967, when I met the student Ebou Manga at Hamilton College in Clinton, New York. Ebou had accompanied me to The Gambia and had introduced me to his father, Alhaji Manga, who became my mentor in matters Gambian. Ebou's younger brother, Joe, was then about 14 years old. Joe is now 29, a Gambian district engineer who knows the village of Juffure very well. Now once again I talked in Banjul with the Mangas, and with his father's approval, I asked Joe to take over both the architectural design and the physical building of the new mosque for Juffure. After he queried my basic ideas, Joe made some rough first sketches. I liked them and thought the Juffure villagers would, too. Alhaji Manga, Joe and I discussed the probable cost, and I wrote Joe a check with which to get started.

Since my return to the United States, Joe Manga has sent me 63 beautifully detailed blueprints of the Juffure mosque, with which, he writes, the villagers are "very happy." Exactly on the site of the old mosque, the somewhat larger new one will service the worshipers from Juffure, Albreda and elsewhere.

I am anxious to return to Juffure as soon as the mosque is 64 finished and ready for dedication to the memory of my ancestor Kunta Kinte. I feel deeply that he would approve.

The Blues Abroad

ANDREA LEE

A few weeks ago we were lucky enough to attend a B. B. King con- 1
cert in the Gorky Palace of Culture in Leningrad. B. B. King, correctly described by his publicity as the best-known blues musician in
the world, had been touring the Soviet Union for three weeks, generating waves of enthusiasm among its citizens—who know jazz
well but have little exposure to the blues. The tour began with a concert in the capital of Azerbaijan; it moved on to Yerevan and then to
Tbilisi, where, according to a State Department aide, the impulsive
Georgians nearly started a riot, shoving into the theater until two
people sat in every seat. In Leningrad, the excitement had been
building up long before we reached the Culture Palace. There had
been absolutely no advance publicity in the city, but all our Russian
friends knew about the concert from Voice of America (another, not
always facetious, nickname for this broadcast is "Voice of the Enemy"). The afternoon of the concert, a subtle excitement diffused itself through the crowds of Nevsky Prospekt. On the metro, groups
of well-dressed people were eying one another and anxiously demanding the time. The horde of ticket scalpers encountered on the
way to any Soviet performance extended this time all the way down
into the subway. "Do you have extra tickets?" people were shouting
on all sides. Our friend Tolya, who was with us, said that the street
tickets were going for between fifty and a hundred rubles apiece.

Inside the performance hall, we found an ample display of So- 2
viet fashion. There were endless pairs of American jeans, which
women wore with the skinny-heeled Italian ankle boots that are the
dernier cri[1] of Russian style. The curious thing about the crowd was
that it consisted not mainly of young people, as one might expect,
but of people of all ages. There were many middle-aged men and
women, dressed in their best baggy suits and polyester dresses.

---

[1] *dernier cri:* latest thing. (Ed.)

Andrea Lee (1953–   ), born in Philadelphia, is the author of
short stories and the novel *Sarah Phillips* (1985). "The Blues
Abroad" is from her memoir of a year spent as a student in the Soviet Union, *Russian Journal* (1981).

There were small children, and there were some of the oldest *babushki* I had ever seen, walking slowly, with pleased grins, their heads wrapped in shawls.

A slick-haired Soviet M.C. announced B. B. King ("A great   3 *Negritanski* musician"), and then King was onstage with his well-known guitar—Lucille—and a ten-man ensemble. As King and the ensemble swung into "Why I Sing the Blues," one could sense the puzzlement of the Soviet audience. "Negro" music to them meant jazz or spirituals, but this was something else. Also, there was the question of response. B. B. King is a great, warm presence when he performs, and he asks his audiences to pour themselves out to him in return. King teases his audiences, urging them to clap along, to whistle, to hoot their appreciation, like the congregations in the Southern churches in which he grew up. But to Russians, such behavior suggests a lack of culture and an almost frightening disorder. Though obviously impressed, the audience at first kept a respectful silence during the numbers, as it might at the symphony. (Only the foreigners shouted and stomped out the beat; we found the Russians around us staring at us open-mouthed.) Then King played an irresistible riff, stopped, and leaned toward the audience with his hand cupped to his ear. The audience caught on and began to clap. King changed the beat, and waited for the audience to catch up. Then he changed it again. Soon the whole place was clapping along to "Get off My Back, Woman," and there were even a few timid shouts and whistles. King, who has carried the blues to Europe, Africa, and the Far East, had broken the ice one more time.

At intermission we were fortunate enough to talk to B. B. King.   4 He rose when we came into his dressing room, a large dark-skinned man with sweat glistening on his forehead. King is one of the few performers whom it is not a revelation to see close up; he presents himself onstage exactly as he is, and his conversation has the same warmth and intermittent playfulness as his music. We asked him about his experiences in the Soviet Union, and he answered carefully, glancing occasionally at his manager, Sid Seidenberg, who stood by the door, and at an Intourist guide sitting nearby. (The backstage area was bristling with security people and Intourist personnel; Tolya said, "This place is full of KGB.") King said that although he preferred capitalism, he respected the Soviet system, and that he had been impressed by the cordial hospitality of the Soviet people. Audiences all over the Soviet Union, he said, had received his music enthusiastically. "The blues is likely something they've never heard before," he said. "I like to help them understand." He told us a bit about touring Georgia and Armenia—his favorite parts of the Soviet Union. His best memory, he said, was driving up to a

mountain lake in Armenia, eating a fish dinner, and meeting the local farm people. "I grew up working on farms," he added.

We asked him what he felt he'd learned from touring the Soviet   5
Union, and he seemed to give the question serious thought.

"I've learned two things," he said finally, leaning toward us.   6
"The first is patience. The Soviet people are very patient. When
things don't happen on time—if a plane doesn't take off for three
hours, if a meal doesn't come—they wait. I've learned how to wait.
The second thing I've learned here is that you can be a great musician and an amateur. I didn't think that was possible before I came
to the Soviet Union. But we have listened to—and in one case actually jammed with—some very fine jazz musicians in Baku and Tbilisi. None of them were professionals."

When we asked him what he thought of Soviet jazz in general,   7
he said he was impressed by what he heard.

"They were good technically—sure, that you'd expect," he said.   8
"But these fellows felt the music, and that's what impressed me. I
don't know where they got the feeling, but they felt it."

We said goodbye to B. B. King and left the dressing room to talk   9
with some of his back-up musicians. These musicians were less
guarded in their comments. Like King, they were happy about the
audience response, and they praised the jazz musicians of Baku and
Tbilisi. But they generally agreed that for a touring musician, the Soviet Union is a boring place.

"There's nothing to do here," said one. "At home we'd finish up   10
the show and go to some little after-hours joint and listen to some
music or something. But there's nothing like that here. Everything
closes down. It's hard to meet women. It's hard to meet *anybody*."

Another player complained, "It's like a damn prison here. We   11
go down to dinner in a big group, we go up to our rooms in a
group, and there's two, three Russians watching us all the time. Are
we followed? Hell, yes. I live in New York. I know the fuzz when I
see it. Guides, they call them. They don't like us to do one thing on
our own. I like the people, man. The people—especially those Georgians—are something else, if you can just get away from the
guides."

By the second half of the performance, the audience was looser   12
than any other Soviet audience I'd ever seen. People whistled, they
hooted with delight, they clapped along, answering King's playful
coaxing on the guitar. The guards standing against the auditorium
walls looked uneasy. "This is exactly what they don't like," whispered Tolya. "This rowdiness. They're terrified of a riot." The music, already superb, got better and better. By the time King swung
into his final song—the show-stopper—"The Thrill Is Gone," the au-

dience was in love. Following the number, there was tumultuous applause, flowers were flung on the stage, and three Soviet hippies forced their way up onto the stage to kiss King's hands and to get his autograph. They were quickly wrestled away by a combination of American and Soviet security forces. King bent to shake hands from the stage, and the guards frowned some more as the crowd broke out into a roaring chant of "B. B. King! B. B. King!"

Quickly the guards fanned out through the audience, pushing 13 people toward the cloakrooms and ending the wild applause before it really got going. At one point, during a lull, Tom and I had a chance to talk to our neighbor, a woman who had initially stared at our clapping. She was a well-dressed middle-aged woman who hadn't taken part in any of the "rowdy" behavior. Nevertheless, she had seemed deeply moved by the performance, and when we asked her how she had enjoyed it, we saw that she had tears in her eyes. "I have been studying American Negro music for years," she said. "I have listened to hundreds of records. It has been a kind of dream of mine to attend a live performance. Now—all that I can say is that I understand the music. One performance is worth a thousand records."

In the cloakroom line, we talked to other local people. The reac- 14 tions were all enthusiastic and emotional. One girl said, "This is one of the greatest things that ever happened to me in my life! A friend gave me the tickets; I never expected to go. It's almost impossible for an ordinary person like me to see something like this. You have to be special—to have a lot of money or some Party connections—to get to a performance like this."

An older man in a baggy suit looked thoughtful as we talked to 15 him. "B. B. King," he said, pronouncing the syllables distinctly, "B. B. King astounded me. This blues music—it's not like jazz. He poured his whole heart and soul out there on the stage. Such feeling is very Russian—we believe in emotion, in the soul. I never thought that an American could feel that way."

Music in the Philippines

PICO IYER

"Where There Is Music," said a T-shirt in a Mabini gift shop, "There   1
Can't Be Misery." "Music," said another in the same store, "Is the
Medicine of a Troubled Mind."

Such wishful slogans were not difficult to believe so long as I   2
was inside some folk-music club, watching a smiling singer under
flashing orange lights. But as soon as I was back on the streets, amid
the clutch of urchins and the cracked fences, it was harder to imagine that music could change the world. And as the days passed, the
gray skies of Manila, its sense of peeling dereliction, began to wear
me down. I did not know how to cope with the beggars, how to be
of assistance to the large-eyed girls in the restaurants. I did not
know what to make of glossy ads for the Manila Casino (on Imelda
Avenue), which offered free entrance to tourists and cried, "Game
and Gain in U.S. Dollars. Watch that hot dice dance! Tumble at the
table!" I needed some fresh air.

And so one day I took a bus out to Angeles City, the small town   3
around Clark Air Force Base, one of the two American bases that
help bind the ties between the United States and the only country it
has ever directly ruled.

It was not hard to tell when we had arrived. For an hour or so,   4
the bus drove through rice fields and small villages, past huts
guarded by wide-eyed gamins. Then it drew up to an unkempt T-
junction surrounded by vacant lots, gas stations and fading billboards. On one side of the road was Shakey's and Kentucky Fried
Chicken; on the other a Dunkin' Donuts outlet ("Open 24 Hours.
World's Finest Coffee") and a Drive-Thru Donut King. On the far
side of the junction stood a rusted roadside shack called the Jail-
house Rock Disco and next to it the Café Valenzuela ("Pride of the
Highway"). In the near gray distance gleamed the Golden Arches.

Inside, the walls of McDonald's were decorated in the style of an   5
Arizona coffee shop; a faded picture of John Wayne; another of the
Lone Ranger and of Chief Red Cloud; a drawing of a Typical Cow-

---

Pico Iyer (1957–   ), born in England of Indian parents and now
living in California, is a journalist and the author of *Video Night in
Kathmandu* (1988), about his travels across Asia. "Music in the
Philippines" is from the chapter in that book called "The Philippines: Born in the U.S.A."

boy; a map representing "Guns of the West." Opposite me, frowning over his breakfast of burger and fries, was a big American kid, with blue eyes and a broad, open face. Above his snakeskin boots and jeans he wore a short-sleeved blue shirt made up of a collage of headlines from the *New York Times* and the *Miami Herald*. And seeping sweetly out of the music system I heard, yet again, the willful optimism of "We Are the World."

I waited to hear the end of the song and then went out along the town's main drag, the MacArthur Highway (sometimes spelled McArthur, sometimes spelled Hi-way). It was, I thought, the saddest-looking place in all the world—one long, gray strip of cardboard signs and cocktail lounges and beat-up bars with neon signs for beer in their windows, all lined by a rickety wooden porch. The stores had electric guitars in their windows, and "Harley-Davidson" warm-up jackets; sometimes they had baseball caps with "Playboy Club" on the front, or "Hillcrest Baptist Church"; sometimes they had army shields that said "Eternal Vigilance" and "Ready to Report" and "Pride in Uniform." 6

There were plenty of motels too, all with air conditioning, swimming pools and wall-to-wall carpeting, some advertising such additional frills as Betamaxes, Magic Mirrors, Drive-Thru service and free transportation to the base. There were also billboards advertising "bold movies" at the local cinemas. Mostly, though, there were bars—the Valley of the Dolls, the Spanish Fly, the Lovers Inn. The sign outside one of them said simply, "Wanted: Girls Immediately." 7

I could, I imagined, have been in any of the desolate small towns of the American West, where used-car lots and twinkling motels and dilapidated cafés run all the way out to the desert. But here there were not stores, but shacks; and here there were shanties, not houses, along the riverbank. There were "Pickup for Hire" signs in all the hardware stores, but there were also signs that said "Goat for Hire." And the children playing in the streets were not exactly All-American: the little boys bouncing tennis balls had black skins with Oriental features; the little girls at the candy stores were dark, but their hair was sandy. 8

As I continued looking around, a plane rumbled through the heavens and a few minutes later it began to rain, pouring down hard on the stucco roof of the Question Mark Lounge, on Louisa's Patio ("Tourists and Returnees Hangout"), on the bar that promised Candy's Models and the Sunshine Café ("No Hustlers / Shoeshine Boys / Poofters / Dunces"). I hailed a jeepney (the souped-up secondhand U.S. jeep that provides mass transport in the Philippines) and took shelter on one of its benches, looking out into the grayness as we juddered past the Ponderosa Club, Mark and Donald's ham- 9 burger joint, the Harlem Disco À-Go-Go, Coney Island ("the All-American ice cream"). Most of my fellow passengers were little girls just out of school, eyes dark and faces bright in their tidy Holy Angels uniforms.

The jeepney bounced me off to the far side of town, and then 10 turned around and took me back to the Friendship Highway. I got out, though the rain had yet to abate, and began walking again. "Born in the U.S.A." was thumping out of one of the bars, accompanied by a steady pattering on the rooftops. A gangly American teenager in a crew cut was leading a pretty little Filipina into one of the motels. Another tall man with a blond crew cut and a clean white shirt was marching purposefully through the downpour, a badge on his heart saying "Church of Latter-day Saints."

And as the rain kept coming down, I took shelter on the street- 11 side patio. Beside me, under a falling roof, a jukebox stood forlornly against the wall. A teenage Filipina in pink curlers strolled out of a pool hall and pressed a selection. Then, as the first chords of "We Are the World" began to come through, she started to sing along with it softly, rocking her baby in her arms as the rain continued to fall.

The Philippines is not just the site of the largest U.S. military instal- 12 lations in the world. It is also perhaps the world's largest slice of the American Empire, in its purest impurest form. The first time I landed in Hong Kong, I felt a thrill of recognition to see the pert red letterboxes, the blue-and-white road signs, the boxes of Smarties that had been the props of my boyhood in England; upon arriving in Manila, I felt a similar pang as my eye caught Open 24-Hour gas stations, green exit signs on the freeways, Florida-style license plates and chains of grocery stores called "Mom and Pop." The deejay patter bubbling from the radios, the Merle Haggard songs drifting out of jukeboxes, the Coke signs and fast-food joints and grease-smeared garages—all carried me instantly back home, or, if not home, at least to some secondhand, beat-up image of the Sam Shepard Southwest, to Amarillo, perhaps, or East L.A.

Most of all, the Philippines took me back to the junk-neon flash 13 of teen America, the rootless Western youth culture of drive-ins and jukeboxes, junior proms, cheap cutoffs, and custom dragsters. Many of the young dudes here, in their long hair and straw hats and bushy mustaches, had the cocky strut of aspiring rock stars, and many of the girls, saucing up their natural freshness, the apprehensive flair of would-be models. The jeepneys they rode, plastered with girlie pictures, Rolling Stones tongues, garish stickers and religious symbols, looked like nothing so much as graffitied pinball machines on wheels. And everyone here had a nickname (Wee-Wee, Baby, Boy and even Apple Pie), which made them seem even younger than they really were, little brown siblings to the big Americans across the sea. As it was, the average age in the entire country was only seventeen (in Japan, by contrast, it was over thirty). Small wonder, perhaps, that I felt myself living in a chrome-and-denim Top 40 world.

America's honorary fifty-second state had received much more, 14 of course, from its former rulers than star-spangled love songs and hand-me-down jeans. The commercial area of Manila, Makati, looked not at all like Bakersfield or Tucson, but more like some textbook upper-middle-class California suburban tract. Jaguars lurked in the driveways of white split-level homes, maids sprinklered the lawns along leafy residential streets. The shopping strips were neatly laid out with a mall-to-mall carpeting of coffee shops and department stores. And though the area's jungle of high-rise office blocks seemed hardly to merit its title of "the Wall Street of Asia," it did resemble the kind of financial district you might find in the Sunbelt—the downtown area of Salt Lake City, say, or San Diego.

Baguio too, the hill station designed as a summer retreat for the 15 American rulers—a kind of New World Simla—revealed the American Empire in a more pastoral mood. I could not easily discern the town's resemblance to Washington, D.C.—on which, many Filipinos proudly informed me, it had been modeled—save for the fact that both places had roads and trees, as well as a quorum of American servicemen, scientists and missionaries ("Most people in the U.S., I think," said a local cabbie, "are Christians and Mormons"). But Baguio was still a glistening vision of silver and green, graced with its own distinctive charm—white villas set among the thickly forested slopes of pine, quiet parks verdant in the mist. In the mild drizzle of a dark afternoon, the place had a cozy market-town feel of hot cakes and light rain; on a calm Sunday morning, the peal of church bells through the mist took me back to an English village. In Baguio, I settled down with an Elizabeth Bowen novel in the teapot snugness of a small café, and went on a gray afternoon to a crowded kiddies' matinee.

For all its silvered, foggy charm, though, Baguio did not seem to 16 have the imperiousness of a British hill station, or its weighted dignity. And in much the same way, I did not sense in the Philippines anything comparable to the kind of stately legacy that the British, for example, had bequeathed to India. India seemed to have gained, as a colony, a sense of ritual solemnity, a feeling for the language of Shakespeare, a polished civil service, a belief in democracy and a sonorous faith in upstanding legal or educational institutions; it had, in some respects, been steadied by the chin-up British presence. By contrast, the most conspicuous institutions that America had bequeathed to the Philippines seemed to be the disco, the variety show, and the beauty pageant. Perhaps the ideas and ideals of America had proved too weighty to be shipped across the seas, or perhaps they were just too fragile. Whatever, the nobility of the world's youngest power and the great principles on which it had been founded were scarcely in evidence here, except in a democratic system that seemed to parody the chicanery of the Nixon years. In the Philippines I found no sign of Lincoln or Thoreau or Sojourner Truth; just Dick Clark, Ronald McDonald and Madonna.

On a human level, of course, the relation between America and her 17 former colony was altogether more complex, and best seen, I thought, just by watching the slow mating dances that filled the smoky country-and-western joints of Ermita every night.

As I entered Club 21 one rainy evening, a small and perky Fili- 18 pina in a red-and-white-checked shirt and tight jeans—a kind of dusky Joey Heatherton—was leading a country band through songs of lost love and heartbreak. The minute the group struck up the opening chords of another sad song, one of the American GI types seated at the bar, a craggy man in his sixties, six feet tall perhaps, slowly stood up and extended his hand to a pretty teenage girl in a white frock and white pumps. "Today," drawled the singer, "is the darkest day of my life," and the pedal steel wailed and the man put one hand around the girl's tiny waist and the other on her shoulder and led her, with great courtliness, through a slow, slow dance.

As the next ballad began, the vocalist went into a perfect Dolly 19 Parton rasp, and a man in a bushy ginger mustache with sad eyes behind his thick glasses stood up, hitched up his trousers and walked over to a table in the corner where eight young Filipinas were staring idly into the distance. Crouching down, he whispered something to a beautiful young lady in a yellow-and-red ruffled skirt and she followed him back to the bar. "What's your name?" he said softly as they sat down, extending his hand. "I'm an American."

A couple of barstools away, another old-timer was gently strok- 20 ing the long hair of his doll-like companion. "Hey," he chuckled, looking over her head to a colleague. "I'm going to marry her in a minute." And the band went through another plaintive ballad, then vanished through a back door that said "George's Massage Special."

A man got up from the bar and walked out, and as the door 21 slammed behind him, his sweet-faced companion stuck out her tongue at his memory, then straightened her skirt and went off to sit in another man's lap. The door swung open again, and a lady came

in with a basket full of roses. A red-faced Australian hailed her from
where he sat and bought ten flowers. Then, very slowly, he walked
around the place and, very tenderly, presented a rose to every girl
in the room. The band came back again, and sailed into more sad
songs from the West. "I warned you not to love me," wailed the
singer, "I'm not going to be here very long."

If I had closed my eyes, I could have believed myself in Tucum- 22
cari, New Mexico, or listening to some jukebox in Cheyenne. But
my eyes were wide open and in front of me two couples were glid-
ing around the dance floor, tiny arms wrapped around large backs
as two pretty young girls, eyes closed, buried their silky heads in
their partners' burly chests.

A couple of minutes later, the band went into a faster number. 23
"Yee-hah," cried a man with the frame of a construction worker,
standing up at the bar, shaking his fanny and pumping his elbows.
He swirled a high school girl in high heels out onto the dance floor,
and she flashed a smile back at him, shimmying like a dream.
"Shake it," cried out the singer. "Yee-hah!" The dance floor started
to get crowded. The Australian pulled his companion out onto the
floor. Two girls in jeans began dancing together. A young girl in a
flounced skirt swayed happily opposite an old girl with too much
makeup. "Welcome to my world," sang the girls as they danced,
smiling at their partners and clapping. "Welcome to my world."
And as I went out, the singer was just breaking into a perfect replica
of Loretta Lynn, while singing, with flawless anguish, "You know,
it's only make-believe."

The professionalism of music in Manila had impressed me almost as 24
soon as I arrived. But as I stayed longer in town, I was hit more
forcibly by a different aspect of the local singing. It struck me first
one night in Baguio, in one of the city's many "Minus One" sing-
along pubs, where customers take turns coming onstage and delivering the latest hits, accompanied by a tape to provide backup in-
strumentation. "I would like to dedicate this song to a special
someone," a girl was whispering huskily into the mike as I walked
in. Then she adjusted the stand, put on her tape and proceeded to
deliver a note-perfect version of Madonna's "Like a Virgin," absolutely identical to the original, down to the last pause and tic. Song
complete, she whispered "Thank you" to the mike, sauntered off-
stage and went home with her special someone.

As the evening went on, the scene was repeated again and again 25
and again and again. Almost everyone in the pub came up to deliver
flawless imitations of some American hit. And almost everyone had
every professional move down perfectly. They knew not only how

to trill like Joan Baez and rasp like the Boss, but also how to play on the crowd with their eyes, how to twist the microphone wire in their hands, how to simulate every shade of heartbreak. They were wonderfully professional amateurs. But they were also professional impersonators.

When I walked into another pub down the street I got to witness   26 an even greater display of virtuoso mimicry: the Chinese singer onstage was able to modulate his voice so as to muster a gruff warmth for a Kenny Rogers number, a high earnestness for Graham Nash, a kind of operatic bombast for Neil Diamond and a bland sincerity for Lionel Richie. His Paul Simon was perfect in its boyish sweetness. Yet what his own voice sounded like, and what his own personality might have been, were impossible to tell. And when it came to improvising, adding some of the frills or flourishes that his culture relished, making a song his own, he—like every other singer I had heard—simply did not bother.

"Sure," an American correspondent based in Manila told me   27 when I mentioned this. "Music is definitely the single best thing here. But there's no way you're going to hear any local tunes, or variations on the recorded versions of the American hits. There's one singer in Davao they call the Stevie Wonder of the Philippines, because he sounds exactly—*exactly*—like Stevie Wonder. And there's another woman locally who's the Barbra Streisand of the Philippines. That's how they make it big here. You know one reason why the Filipinos love 'We Are the World' so much? Because it gives one member of the group the chance to do Michael Jackson, and another Cyndi Lauper and a third Bruce Springsteen. Some guy even gets to do Ray Charles."

Finally, in Baguio one night, I came upon a happy exception to   28 the rule: a pudgy singer who slyly camped up Julio Iglesias's song "To All the Girls I Know" by delivering it in a perfect simulation of Iglesias's silky accent, while substituting "boys" for "girls." But then, a few days later, back in Manila, I heard another singer at the Hobbit House do exactly the same trick, with exactly the same words (and, a few months later, I was told, local minstrels were delivering the same song, in honor of the fallen Imelda, to the words: "To all the shoes I had before / I wore them once, and then no more"). Likewise, at a free public concert one afternoon I was surprised to hear a professionally trained singer transform the revved-up anarchy and energy of the Beatles' "Help" into a slow, soulful ballad of lovelorn agony. But then I heard the song delivered in exactly the same way, with exactly the same heartrent inflections, in a small club in Baguio, and then again at another bar: all the singers, I realized, were not in fact creating a new version, but simply copying some cover version quite different from the Beatles' original. All the feelings were still borrowed.

This development of musical mannequins struck me as strange, especially in a country that understandably regarded its musical gifts as a major source of national pride. I could certainly see how the Filipinos' brilliance at reproducing their masters' voices, down to the very last burr, had made them the musical stars of Asia—the next-best thing, in fact, to having a real American. But as a form of self-expression, this eerie kind of ventriloquism made me sad.

It was the same kind of sadness I felt when I read that the national hero José Rizal had described his home as "a country without a soul" or when I opened *What's On in Manila* to find the first ad in the personals section begin: "I would like to meet an American. Looks are not important but he must be kind and cheerful." It was the same kind of sadness I felt when I went to Pistang Pilipino, the capital's main tourist center, and found that the highlight of its show of local culture was a splashy Hollywood-style spectacular in which chorus lines of handsome young men whipped through some brassy choreography and six-year-old girls in bikinis performed acrobatics while a fat man with greasy hair in an open shirt crooned "House of the Rising Sun." Mostly, it was the sadness I felt, when an intelligent Filipino friend in New York told me, with a happy smile, "Every Filipino dreams that he will grow up to be an American."

While I was in Manila, there was plenty of token opposition to the U.S. presence. Nationalists railed against the country's still justified image as the world's great center of mail-order brides and chambermaids. The Marcos-run paper, in a show of ill-considered braggadocio, printed Manuel Quezon's famous cry: "I prefer to see a government run like hell by Filipinos than a government run like heaven by Americans." And when foreign newsmen flooded into town for the election a few months later, an opposition paper greeted them as "two-bit, white-skinned, hirsute, AIDS-predisposed visitors." But the "two-bit," I thought, said it all. In the Philippines, anti-American guerrillas drew up their strategies in Michael Jackson notebooks. And a respected newspaper greeted the suggested removal of the American bases with the headline "Bye, Bye, American Pie."

Venezuela for Visitors

JOHN UPDIKE

All Venezuela, except for the negligible middle class, is divided be- 1
tween the Indians (*los indios*) and the rich (*los ricos*). The Indians are
mostly to be found in the south, amid the muddy tributaries of the
Orinoco and the god-haunted *tepuys* (mesas) that rear their fearsome
mile-high crowns above the surrounding jungle, whereas the rich
tend to congregate in the north, along the sunny littoral, in the bur-
geoning metropolis of Caracas, and on the semicircular shores of
Lake Maracaibo, from which their sumptuous black wealth is
drawn. The negligible middle class occupies a strip of arid savanna
in the center of the nation and a few shunned enclaves on the suburban slopes of Monte Avila.

The Indians, who range in color from mocha to Dentyne, are 2
generally under five feet tall. Their hair style runs to pageboys and
severe bangs, with some tonsures in deference to lice. Neither sex is
quite naked: the males wear around their waists a thong to which
their foreskins are tied, pulling their penises taut upright; the females, once out of infancy, suffer such adornments as three pale
sticks symmetrically thrust into their lower faces. The gazes of both
sexes are melting, brown, alert, canny. The visitor, standing among
them with his Nikon FE and L. L. Bean fannypack, is shy at first,
but warms to their inquisitive touches, which patter and rub across
his person with a soft, sandy insistence unlike both the fumblings of
children and the caresses one Caucasian adult will give another.
There is an infectious, wordless ecstasy in their touches, and a blank
eagerness with yet some parameters of tact and irony. *These are human presences*, the visitor comes to realize.

The rich, who range in color from porcelain to mocha, are gener- 3
ally under six feet tall. Their hair style runs to chignons and blow-
dried trims. Either sex is elegantly clad: the males favor dark suits of
medium weight (nights in Caracas can be cool), their close English
cut enhanced by a slight Latin flare, and shirts with striped bodies

John Updike (1932–   ), born in Shillington, Pennsylvania, is the
author of essays, criticism, poetry, short stories, and novels including *Rabbit, Run* (1960), *A Month of Sundays* (1975), and *The Witches of
Eastwick* (1984). "Venezuela for Visitors" is from his collection *Hugging the Shore* (1983).

but stark-white collars and French cuffs held by agates and gold; the females appear in a variety of gowns and mock-military pants suits, Dior and de la Renta originals flown in from Paris and New York. The gazes of both sexes are melting, brown, alert, canny. The visitor, standing among them in his funky Brooks Brothers suit and rumpled blue button-down, is shy at first, but warms to their excellent English, acquired at colleges in London or "the States," and to their impeccable manners, which conceal, as their fine clothes conceal their skins, rippling depths of Spanish and those dark thoughts that the mind phrases to itself in its native language. They tell anecdotes culled from their rich international lives; they offer, as the evening deepens, confidences, feelers, troubles. These, too, are human presences.

The Indians live in *shabonos*—roughly circular lean-tos woven   4 beautifully of palm thatch in clearings hacked and burned out of the circumambient rain forest. A *shabono* usually rots and is abandoned within three years. The interiors are smoky, from cooking fires, and eye diseases are common among the Indians. They sleep, rest, and die in hammocks (*cinchorros*) hung as close together as pea pods on a vine. Their technology, involving in its pure state neither iron nor the wheel, is yet highly sophisticated: the chemical intricacies of curare have never been completely plumbed, and with their blowpipes of up to sixteen feet in length the Indians can bring down prey at distances of over thirty meters. They fish without hooks, by employing nets and thrashing the water with poisonous lianas. All this sounds cheerier than it is. It is depressing to stand in the gloom of a *shabono,* the palm thatch overhead infested with giant insects, the Indians drooping in their hammocks, their eyes diseased, their bellies protuberant, their faces and limbs besmirched with the same graybrown dirt that composes the floor, their possessions a few brown baskets and monkey skins. Their lives are not paradise but full of anxiety—their religion a matter of fear, their statecraft a matter of constant, nagging war. To themselves, they are "the people" (*Yanomami*); to others, they are "the killers" (*Waikás*).

The rich dwell in *haciendas*—airy long ranch houses whose roofs   5 are of curved tile and, surprisingly, dried sugar-cane stalks. Some *haciendas* surviving in Caracas date from the sixteenth century, when the great valley was all but empty. The interiors are smoky, from candlelit dinners, and contact lenses are common among the rich. The furniture is solid, black, polished by generations of servants. Large paintings by Diebenkorn, Stella, Baziotes, and Botero adorn the white plaster walls, along with lurid religious pictures in the colonial Spanish style. The appliances are all modern and paid for; even if the oil in Lake Maracaibo were to give out, vast deposits of heavy crude have been discovered in the state of Bolívar. All this sounds cheerier than it is. The rich wish they were in Paris, London, New York. Many have condominiums in Miami. *Haute couture* and abstract painting may not prove bulwark enough. Constitutional democracy in Venezuela, though the last dictator fled in 1958, is not so assured as may appear. Turbulence and tyranny are traditional. Che Guevara is still idealized among students. To themselves, the rich are good, decent, amusing people; to others, they are *"reaccionarios."*

Missionaries, many of them United States citizens, move among   6 the Indians. They claim that since Western civilization, with all its diseases and detritus, must come, it had best come through them. Nevertheless, Marxist anthropologists inveigh against them. Foreign experts, many of them United States citizens, move among the rich. They claim they are just helping out, and that anyway the oil industry was nationalized five years ago. Nevertheless, Marxist anthropologists are not mollified. The feet of the Indians are very broad in front, their toes spread wide for climbing avocado trees. The feet of the rich are very narrow in front, their toes compressed by pointed Italian shoes. The Indians seek relief from tension in the use of *ebene,* or *yopo,* a mind-altering drug distilled from the bark of the *ebene* tree and blown into the user's nose through a hollow cane by a colleague. The rich take cocaine through the nose, and frequent mind-altering discotheques, but more customarily imbibe cognac, *vino blanco,* and Scotch, in association with colleagues.

These and other contrasts and comparisons between the Indians   7 and the rich can perhaps be made more meaningful by the following anecdote: A visitor, after some weeks in Venezuela, was invited to fly to the top of a *tepuy* in a helicopter, which crashed. As stated, the *tepuys* are supposed by the Indians to be the forbidden haunts of the gods; and, indeed, they present an exotic, attenuated vegetation and a craggy geology to the rare intruder. The crash was a minor one, breaking neither bones nor bottles (a lavish picnic, including *mucho vino blanco,* had been packed). The bottles were consumed, the exotic vegetation was photographed, and a rescue helicopter arrived. In the Cessna back to Caracas, the survivors couldn't get enough of discussing the incident and their survival, and the red-haired woman opposite the visitor said, "I *love* the way you pronounce '*tepuy.*'" She imitated him: tupooey. "Real zingy," she said. The visitor slowly realized that he was being flirted with, and that therefore *this woman was middle-class.* In Venezuela, only the negligible middle class flirts. The Indians kidnap or are raped; the rich commandeer, or languorously give themselves in imperious surrender.

The Indians tend to know only three words of Spanish: "*¿Cómo* 8 *se llama?*" ("What is your name?"). In Indian belief, to give one's name is to place oneself in the other's power. And the rich, when one is introduced, narrow their eyes and file one's name away in their mysterious depths. Power among them flows along lines of kinship and intimacy. After an imperious surrender, a rich female gazes at her visitor with new interest out of her narrowed, brown, melting, kohl-ringed eyes. He has become someone to be reckoned with, if only as a potential source of financial embarrassment. "Again, what is your name?" she asks.

Los indios and *los ricos* rarely achieve contact. When they do, *mes-* 9 *tizos* result, and the exploitation of natural resources. In such lies the future of Venezuela.

El Salvador: The Mechanism of Terror

JOAN DIDION

The three-year-old El Salvador International Airport is glassy and   1
white and splendidly isolated, conceived during the waning of the
Molina "National Transformation" as convenient less to the capital
(San Salvador is forty miles away, until recently a drive of several
hours) than to a central hallucination of the Molina and Romero
regimes, the projected beach resorts, the Hyatt, the Pacific Paradise,
tennis, golf, water-skiing, condos, *Costa del Sol;* the visionary invention of a tourist industry in yet another republic where the leading
natural cause of death is gastrointestinal infection. In the general absence of tourists these hotels have since been abandoned, ghost resorts on the empty Pacific beaches, and to land at this airport built to
service them is to plunge directly into a state in which no ground is
solid, no depth of field reliable, no perception so definite that it
might not dissolve into its reverse.

The only logic is that of acquiescence. Immigration is negotiated   2
in a thicket of automatic weapons, but by whose authority the
weapons are brandished (Army or National Guard or National Police or Customs Police or Treasury Police or one of a continuing proliferation of other shadowy and overlapping forces) is a blurred
point. Eye contact is avoided. Documents are scrutinized upside
down. Once clear of the airport, on the new highway that slices
through green hills rendered phosphorescent by the cloud cover of
the tropical rainy season, one sees mainly underfed cattle and mongrel dogs and armored vehicles, vans and trucks and Cherokee
Chiefs fitted with reinforced steel and bulletproof Plexiglas an inch
thick. Such vehicles are a fixed feature of local life, and are popularly
associated with disappearance and death. There was the Cherokee
Chief seen following the Dutch television crew killed in Cha-
latenango province in March of 1982. There was the red Toyota

---

Joan Didion (1934—   ), born in Sacramento, California, is the
author of novels, including *Play It as It Lays* (1970) and *Democracy*
(1984); short stories; screenplays; and the essay collections *Slouching
towards Bethlehem* (1968) and *The White Album* (1979). "El Salvador:
The Mechanism of Terror" is from *Salvador* (1983).

three-quarter-ton pickup sighted near the van driven by the four American Catholic workers on the night they were killed in 1980. There were, in the late spring and summer of 1982, the three Toyota panel trucks, one yellow, one blue, and one green, none bearing plates, reported present at each of the mass detentions (a "detention" is another fixed feature of local life, and often precedes a "disappearance") in the Amatepec district of San Salvador. These are the details—the models and the colors of armored vehicles, the makes and calibers of weapons, the particular methods of dismemberment and decapitation used in particular instances—on which the visitor to Salvador learns immediately to concentrate, to the exclusion of past or future concerns, as in a prolonged amnesiac fugue.

Terror is the given of the place. Black-and-white police cars   3
cruise in pairs, each with the barrel of a rifle extruding from an open window. Roadblocks materialize at random, soldiers fanning out from trucks and taking positions, fingers always on triggers, safeties clicking on and off. Aim is taken as if to pass the time. Every morning *El Diario de Hoy* and *La Prensa Gráfica* carry cautionary stories. *"Una madre y sus dos hijos fueron asesinados con arma cortante (corvo) por ocho sujetos desconocidos el lunes en la noche"*: A mother and her two sons hacked to death in their beds by eight *desconocidos*, unknown men. The same morning's paper: the unidentified body of a young man, strangled, found on the shoulder of a road. Same morning, different story: the unidentified bodies of three young men, found on another road, their faces partially destroyed by bayonets, one face carved to represent a cross.

It is largely from these reports in the newspapers that the United   4
States embassy compiles its body counts, which are transmitted to Washington in a weekly dispatch referred to by embassy people as "the grim-gram." These counts are presented in a kind of tortured code that fails to obscure what is taken for granted in El Salvador, that government forces do most of the killing. In a January 15, 1982 memo to Washington, for example, the embassy issued a "guarded" breakdown on its count of 6909 "reported" political murders between September 16, 1980, and September 15, 1981. Of these 6909, according to the memo, 922 were "believed committed by security forces," 952 "believed committed by leftist terrorists," 136 "believed committed by rightist terrorists," and 4889 "committed by unknown assailants," the famous *desconocidos* favored by those San Salvador newspapers still publishing. (The figures actually add up not to 6909 but to 6899, leaving ten in a kind of official limbo.) The memo continued:

The uncertainty involved here can be seen in the fact that responsibility cannot be fixed in the majority of cases. We note, however, that it is generally believed in El Salvador that a large number of the unexplained killings are carried out by the security forces, officially or unofficially. The Embassy is aware of dramatic claims that have been made by one interest group or another in which the security forces figure as the primary agents of murder here. El Salvador's tangled web of attack and vengeance, traditional criminal violence and political mayhem make this an impossible charge to sustain. In saying this, however, we make no attempt to lighten the responsibility for the deaths of many hundreds, and perhaps thousands, which can be attributed to the security forces. . . .

The body count kept by what is generally referred to in San Salvador as "the Human Rights Commission" is higher than the embassy's, and documented periodically by a photographer who goes out looking for bodies. These bodies he photographs are often broken into unnatural positions, and the faces to which the bodies are attached (when they are attached) are equally unnatural, sometimes unrecognizable as human faces, obliterated by acid or beaten to a mash of misplaced ears and teeth or slashed ear to ear and invaded by insects. *"Encontrado en Antiguo Cuscatlán el día 25 de Marzo 1982: camison de dormir celeste,"* the typed-caption reads on one photograph: found in Antiguo Cuscatlán March 25, 1982, wearing a sky-blue nightshirt. The captions are laconic. Found in Soyapango May 21, 1982. Found in Mejicanos June 11, 1982. Found at El Playon May 30, 1982, white shirt, purple pants, black shoes. 5

The photograph accompanying that last caption shows a body with no eyes, because the vultures got to it before the photographer did. There is a special kind of practical information that the visitor to El Salvador acquires immediately, the way visitors to other places acquire information about the currency rates, the hours for the museums. In El Salvador one learns that vultures go first for the soft tissue, for the eyes, the exposed genitalia, the open mouth. One learns that an open mouth can be used to make a specific point, can be stuffed with something emblematic; stuffed, say, with a penis, or, if the point has to do with land title, stuffed with some of the dirt in question. One learns that hair deteriorates less rapidly than flesh, and that a skull surrounded by a perfect corona of hair is a not uncommon sight in the body dumps. 6

All forensic photographs induce in the viewer a certain protective numbness, but dissociation is more difficult here. In the first place these are not, technically, "forensic" photographs, since the evidence they document will never be presented in a court of law. In the second place the disfigurement is too routine. The locations are 7 too near, the dates too recent. There is the presence of the relatives of the disappeared: the women who sit every day in this cramped office on the grounds of the archdiocese, waiting to look at the spiral-bound photo albums in which the photographs are kept. These albums have plastic covers bearing soft-focus color photographs of young Americans in dating situations (strolling through autumn foliage on one album, recumbent in a field of daisies on another), and the women, looking for the bodies of their husbands and brothers and sisters and children, pass them from hand to hand without comment or expression.

> One of the more shadowy elements of the violent scene here [is] the death squad. Existence of these groups has long been disputed, but not by many Salvadorans. . . .Who constitutes the death squads is yet another difficult question. We do not believe that these squads exist as permanent formations but rather as ad hoc vigilante groups that coalesce according to perceived need. Membership is also uncertain, but in addition to civilians we believe that both on- and off-duty members of the security forces are participants. This was unofficially confirmed by right-wing spokesman Maj. Roberto D'Aubuisson who stated in an interview in early 1981 that security force members utilize the guise of the death squad when a potentially embarrassing or odious task needs to be performed.
> —From the confidential but later declassified January 15, 1982, memo previously cited, drafted for the State Department by the political section at the embassy in San Salvador.

The dead and pieces of the dead turn up in El Salvador every- 8 where every day, as taken for granted as in a nightmare, or a horror movie. Vultures of course suggest the presence of a body. A knot of children on the street suggests the presence of a body. Bodies turn up in the brush of vacant lots, in the garbage thrown down ravines in the richest districts, in public rest rooms, in bus stations. Some are dropped in Lake Ilopango, a few miles east of the city, and wash up near the lakeside cottages and clubs frequented by what remains in San Salvador of the sporting bourgeoisie. Some still turn up in El Playón, the lunar lava field of rotting human flesh visible at one time or another on every television screen in America but characterized in June of 1982 in the *El Salvador News Gazette*, an English-language weekly edited by an American named Mario Rosenthal, as an "uncorroborated story . . . dredged up from the files of leftist propaganda." Others turn up at Puerta del Diablo, above Parque Balboa, a national *Turicentro* described as recently as the April–July 1982 issue of *Aboard TACA*, the magazine provided passengers on the national airline of El Salvador, as "offering excellent subjects for color photography."

I drove up to Puerta del Diablo one morning in June of 1982, 9
past the Casa Presidencial and the camouflaged watch towers and
heavy concentrations of troops and arms south of town, on up a
narrow road narrowed further by landslides and deep crevices in the
roadbed, a drive so insistently premonitory that after a while I began
to hope that I would pass Puerta del Diablo without knowing it, just
miss it, write it off, turn around and go back. There was however no
way of missing it. Puerta del Diablo is a "view site" in an older and
distinctly literary tradition, nature as lesson, an immense cleft rock
through which half of El Salvador seems framed, a site so romantic
and "mystical," so theatrically sacrificial in aspect, that it might be a
cosmic parody of nineteenth-century landscape painting. The place
presents itself as pathetic fallacy: the sky "broods," the stones
"weep," a constant seepage of water weighting the ferns and moss.
The foliage is thick and slick with moisture. The only sound is a
steady buzz, I believe of cicadas.

Body dumps are seen in El Salvador as a kind of visitors' must- 10
do, difficult but worth the detour. "Of course you have seen El
Playón," an aide to President Alvaro Magaña said to me one day,
and proceeded to discuss the site geologically, as evidence of the
country's geothermal resources. He made no mention of the bodies.
I was unsure if he was sounding me out or simply found the
geothermal aspect of overriding interest. One difference between El
Playón and Puerta del Diablo is that most bodies at El Playón appear
to have been killed somewhere else, and then dumped; at Puerta del
Diablo the executions are believed to occur in place, at the top, and
the bodies thrown over. Sometimes reporters will speak of wanting
to spend the night at Puerta del Diablo, in order to document the actual execution, but at the time I was in Salvador no one had.

The aftermath, the daylight aspect, is well documented. 11
"Nothing fresh today, I hear," an embassy officer said when I mentioned that I had visited Puerta del Diablo. "Were there any on top?"
someone else asked. "There were supposed to have been three on
top yesterday." The point about whether or not there had been any
on top was that usually it was necessary to go down, to see bodies.
The way down is hard. Slabs of stone, slippery with moss, are set
into the vertiginous cliff, and it is down this cliff that one begins the
descent to the bodies, or what is left of the bodies, pecked and mag-
goty masses of flesh, bone, hair. On some days there have been helicopters circling, tracking those making the descent. Other days
there have been militia at the top, in the clearing where the road
seems to run out, but on the morning I was there the only people on
top were a man and a woman and three small children, who played
in the wet grass while the woman started and stopped a Toyota

pickup. She appeared to be learning how to drive. She drove forward and then back toward the edge, apparently following the man's signals, over and over again.

We did not speak, and it was only later, down the mountain and back in the land of the provisionally living, that it occurred to me that there was a definite question about why a man and a woman might choose a well-known body dump for a driving lesson. This was one of a number of occasions, during the two weeks my husband and I spent in El Salvador, on which I came to understand, in a way I had not understood before, the exact mechanism of terror.

Whenever I had nothing better to do in San Salvador I would walk up in the leafy stillness of the San Benito and Escalón districts, where the hush at midday is broken only by the occasional crackle of a walkie-talkie, the click of metal moving on a weapon. I recall a day in San Benito when I opened my bag to check an address, and heard the clicking of metal on metal all up and down the street. On the whole no one walks up here, and pools of blossoms lie undisturbed on the sidewalks. Most of the houses in San Benito are more recent than those in Escalón, less idiosyncratic and probably smarter, but the most striking architectural features in both districts are not the houses but their walls, walls built upon walls, walls stripped of the usual copa de oro and bougainvillea, walls that reflect successive generations of violence: the original stone, the additional five or six or ten feet of brick, and finally the barbed wire, sometimes concertina, sometimes electrified; walls with watch towers, gun ports, closed-circuit television cameras, walls now reaching twenty and thirty feet.

San Benito and Escalón appear on the embassy security maps as districts of relatively few "incidents," but they remain districts in which a certain oppressive uneasiness prevails. In the first place there are always "incidents"—detentions and deaths and disappearances—in the *barrancas,* the ravines lined with shanties that fall down behind the houses with the walls and the guards and the walkie-talkies; one day in Escalón I was introduced to a woman who kept the lean-to that served as a grocery in a *barranca* just above the Hotel Sheraton. She was sticking prices on bars of Camay and Johnson's baby soap, stopping occasionally to sell a plastic bag or two filled with crushed ice and Coca-Cola, and all the while she talked in a low voice about her fear, about her eighteen-year-old son, about the boys who had been taken out and shot on successive nights recently in a neighboring *barranca.*

In the second place there is, in Escalón, the presence of the Sheraton itself, a hotel that has figured rather too prominently in certain local stories involving the disappearance and death of Americans. The Sheraton always seems brighter and more mildly festive than either the Camino Real or the Presidente, with children in the pool and flowers and pretty women in pastel dresses, but there are usually several bulletproofed Cherokee Chiefs in the parking area, and the men drinking in the lobby often carry the little zippered purses that in San Salvador suggest not passports or credit cards but Browning 9-mm. pistols.

It was at the Sheraton that one of the few American *desapare-* 16 *cidos,* a young free-lance writer named John Sullivan, was last seen, in December of 1980. It was also at the Sheraton, after eleven on the evening of January 3, 1981, that the two American advisers on agrarian reform, Michael Hammer and Mark Pearlman, were killed, along with the Salvadoran director of the Institute for Agrarian Transformation, José Rodolfo Viera. The three were drinking coffee in a dining room off the lobby, and whoever killed them used an Ingram MAC-10, without sound suppressor, and then walked out through the lobby, unapprehended. The Sheraton has even turned up in the investigation into the December 1980 deaths of the four American churchwomen, Sisters Ita Ford and Maura Clarke, the two Maryknoll nuns; Sister Dorothy Kazel, the Ursuline nun; and Jean Donovan, the lay volunteer. In *Justice in El Salvador: A Case Study,* prepared and released in July of 1982 in New York by the Lawyers' Committee for International Human Rights, there appears this note:

> On December 19, 1980, the [Duarte government's] Special Investigative Commission reported that 'a red Toyota $\frac{3}{4}$-ton pickup was seen leaving (the crime scene) at about 11:00 P.M. on December 2' and that 'a red splotch on the burned van' of the churchwomen was being checked to determine whether the paint splotch 'could be the result of a collision between that van and the red Toyota pickup.' By February 1981, the Maryknoll Sisters' Office of Social Concerns, which has been actively monitoring the investigation, received word from a source which it considered reliable that the FBI had matched the red splotch on the burned van with a red Toyota pickup belonging to the Sheraton hotel in San Salvador. . . . Subsequent to the FBI's alleged matching of the paint splotch and a Sheraton truck, the State Department has claimed, in a communication with the families of the churchwomen, that 'the FBI could not determine the source of the paint scraping.'

There is also mention in this study of a young Salvadoran busi- 17 nessman named Hans Christ (his father was a German who arrived in El Salvador at the end of World War II), a part owner of the Sheraton. Hans Christ lives now in Miami, and that his name should have even come up in the Maryknoll investigation made many people uncomfortable, because it was Hans Christ, along with his brother-in-law, Ricardo Sol Meza, who, in April of 1981, was first charged with the murders of Michael Hammer and Mark Pearlman and José Rodolfo Viera at the Sheraton. These charges were later dropped, and were followed by a series of other charges, arrests, releases, expressions of "dismay" and "incredulity" from the American embassy, and even, in the fall of 1982, confessions to the killings from two former National Guard corporals, who testified that Hans Christ had led them through the lobby and pointed out the victims. Hans Christ and Ricardo Sol Meza have said that the dropped case against them was a government frameup, and that they were only having drinks at the Sheraton the night of the killings, with a National Guard intelligence officer. It was logical for Hans Christ and Ricardo Sol Meza to have drinks at the Sheraton because they both had interests in the hotel, and Ricardo Sol Meza had just opened a roller disco, since closed, off the lobby into which the killers walked that night. The killers were described by witnesses as well dressed, their faces covered. The room from which they walked was at the time I was in San Salvador no longer a restaurant, but the marks left by the bullets were still visible, on the wall facing the door.

Whenever I had occasion to visit the Sheraton I was apprehensive, and this apprehension came to color the entire Escalón district for me, even its lower reaches, where there were people and movies and restaurants. I recall being struck by it on the canopied porch of a restaurant near the Mexican embassy, on an evening when rain or sabotage or habit had blacked out the city and I became abruptly aware, in the light cast by a passing car, of two human shadows, silhouettes illuminated by the headlights and then invisible again. One shadow sat behind the smoked glass windows of a Cherokee Chief parked at the curb in front of the restaurant; the other crouched between the pumps at the Esso station next door, carrying a rifle. It seemed to me unencouraging that my husband and I were the only people seated on the porch. In the absence of the headlights the candle on our table provided the only light, and I fought the impulse to blow it out. We continued talking, carefully. Nothing came of this, but I did not forget the sensation of having been in a single instant demoralized, undone, humiliated by fear, which is what I meant when I said that I came to understand in El Salvador the mechanism of terror. [18]

Arriving in Tehran

KATE MILLETT

The first sight of them was terrible. Like black birds, like death, like 1
fate, like everything alien. Foreign, dangerous, unfriendly. There
were hundreds of them, specters crowding the barrier, waiting their
own. A sea of chadori, the long terrible veil, the full length of it, like
a dress descending to the floor, ancient, powerful, annihilating us.
And the men beside them too, oddly enough, nondescript in their
badly cut Western suits, a costume that had none of the power of an
Arab robe. And in giving themselves this bit of "Westernism," this
suit that looks, like the suits on men in Japan, never really right
since it is an adopted clothing, a deference to the wealth and political force of another section of persons, the men announce their alliance with the "new," the world of business and technology, currency and bureaucratic forms and industrialism. Relegating women
to the old, the traditional, the tribal garment. In Japan it is ceremonial and decorative, here merely punitive and abject. The men control them, insignificant as they appear, hardly visible before the
splendor and drama of the chador.

Yet if the women were alone they would be wonderful; awe- 2
some, even frightening—for there is a mana of antiquity in the sight
of their chador, the length, the ferocity of that fall of black cloth, the
masses of them like the chorus in Greek tragedy. You would never
be close to it: these women seem utterly closed to women. Here in
this public place defended by their robes, the fabric held tightly under the chin, much of the face hidden by the fold of cloth as it peaks
over the forehead or is folded hard against forehead obscuring it altogether. And the hair hidden, the friendliness of hair, from woman
to woman, its personality, its sexual innocence, the signal of animal
humanity.

Yet the chador is theater, some theater of women so old I no 3
longer know it. Before this garment was forced upon us for our
shame, it must have been our pride; before it was compelled upon
us, we must have worn it out of self-love, vanity, grace, thoroughly
conscious how glamorous it could be in evening, how seductive. A

Kate Millett (1934–   ), born in St. Paul, Minnesota, is the author
of *Sexual Politics* (1970), *Flying* (1974), and other nonfiction books.
"Arriving in Tehran" is from *Going to Iran* (1982), about a trip to
meet with Iranian feminists shortly after the 1979 Islamic revolution.

glance thrown from it, the way it frames the face, reveals the bones, accentuates, turns every face into mystery, eyes, eyebrows speaking. Effective. As all frames are. As all costume heightens. And it is surely costume, the thrill of theater in it. But the threat too.

Look at them and they do not look back, even the friendly curiosity with which women regard each other. Still wearing the cloth of their majesty, they have become prisoners in it. The bitterness, the driven rage behind these figures, behind these yards of black cloth. They are closed utterly. The small, hardly visible men in their suits have absolute control here.

I wonder if the women on the airplane on the way here have ducked back into their headscarves or have dared to enter this crowd without them. I understand now their fear. This is real, and I had only thought they were squeamish, sissy. The crowd before us is adamant, like an ancient obdurate wall of conformity. And behind them you already see the guns. Big ones. Machine guns carried in the arms of militia, some in uniform, some not, but equally ferocious, insanely proud of the object they hold, its authority; new, superbly new, the importance it gives them, the masculinity in a country now in a paroxysm of masculinity. Here is the crowning emblem. Always just about to go off. From the way they hold it you doubt their knowledge of the weapon, are sure it is recently acquired. Their fingers are on the trigger, actually on the trigger, they even carry it and walk along with their fingers on the trigger, naive belief in the magic of the safety catch. Out hunting I once nearly shot a friend by that sort of credulity. The way guns are carried here, displayed, the arrogance of it, the swagger, has even in the half-hour going through customs made me angry and frightened ten times over. How oppressive the size of these weapons, not your policeman's little pistol covered by a holster, but huge, bigger than carbines, faster, more delightful to their possessor, more intimidating to all others.

There are guns everywhere, and when you look around, you discover that they are often pointed at you. In a moment our friends will appear, we'll be out of this, our eyes darting along the faces at the barricade. That moment of truth when you reach the barricade after customs and your friend calls out your name and you smile and people watch you and you are both self-consciously embarrassed and delighted. And saved, crossing over into their arms, you become a private person, no longer stared at, but claimed. For everyone stares at us, we are foreigners, foreign women, the men staring in thousands of ways, the women staring inscrutably from the chador but when we look at them they look away; shut, disapproving.

We are even becoming something of a public spectacle; the fact   7
that we are not being met is becoming public knowledge, the fact of
our being unclaimed. When it is so obvious we expect it, our look of
anticipation, or assurance that Kateh will be here, that Khalil will
have called her. An article of faith to us. And of course she won't be
wearing a chador, she'll look like us, she'll be easy to recognize. The
people are pressing behind us, we cannot stand here forever searching the crowd behind the barrier, examined and rejected by each of
them as we scan one after another for a fellow spirit. Perhaps Kateh
sent someone else, Caifi are always doing things like that, one person's busy, another one is dispatched to an airport to pick up an arrival. Who looks the right type? Sort of hip, radical young, student-
like, the appropriate clothing. There are only two young women
without chador in the whole crowd. We are examining it from the
back now, having so spectacularly failed the applause moment of
being greeted before the throng. In fact we are trying to disappear in
it, so intense are the stares.

I stand by the bags, feeling absurd in my English bobby's cape,   8
in shape a chador without a hood, my head an object of reproach,
my very existence somehow an affront. The happy traveler. With a
submachine gun trained on her from the guard at the front door. He
is actually pointing this thing at me, I say to myself, Sophie gone off
to page our friends; here is your adventure in Iran you were so crazy
to have against all your friends' better judgment, your mother's
warning, trying to grin at the guard, trying to be so obviously harmless he will dismiss me and get on to something better.

Travelers are trying to leave through his door, he is giving them   9
the runaround, insisting they use another door, strutting his petty
power, being a nuisance, exciting himself to wrath with that weapon
in his hands. His superior comes over, dashing type in a jumpsuit,
smaller but more glamorous gun, probably Air Force paratrooper,
the crack troops here, they armed the insurgents on the great day of
the Revolution—21 Bahman (February).

See it all historically; a newly armed populace of course will be   10
fascinated, even childishly fascinated with its weapons, the power
they represent, having been shoved around for years by creeps with
guns, they will all too easily strut and be insolent having their
own—but not in the same entire abuse of power. These are the militia, not the Shah's Savak.[1] You would never have been permitted to

---

[1] *Savak* is the acronym for *Sazman-e Amniyat Va Ettelaat-e Keshvar* (the Security and Information Agency of the State), a secret police organization created in the 1950s which received training
by the American CIA and the Israeli intelligence agency, MOSSAD, and was responsible for im-
prisoning and torturing large numbers of Iranians. (Ed.)

enter this airport at all in the old days; and you are an oddity, so calm down. Sit down, in fact, if you want to stop drawing attention. There are other unfortunates whose friends have failed to arrive, it's probably just traffic. I console myself with tobacco and smile at the woman on the next bench. She smiles back. We have arrived in the late evening, the exhange is closed, we have no Iranian money, only one phone number and address in Tehran. If this is not just a little mix-up, it could be a dead end. Rather humbling. Very frightening.

Sophie says it's a little more serious than that, she has begged a 11 coin to use the phone; Kateh's mother had no idea we were coming, Kateh isn't home. Though she speaks little English, Kateh's mother has conveyed her sense that we are dangerous, she recognizes her daughter knows us but it is unwise to speak on the phone, and it would be more graceful perhaps to betake ourselves to a hotel and straighten everything out in the morning. Well, all right, a hotel, I seem to have forgotten that there are hotels, though without money it may be hard to get to one. Sophie dispatches me to the travelers' aid, where a good-looking man with a gun hears my sad tale and changes a twenty-dollar bill. He is going to "The States" in two weeks, he can use the money. Going to Virginia, he says. I tell him Virginia is lovely just now, the blossoms should be out. He says they won't be out here for quite a while, it's been a very cold winter. We are getting along famously, it is almost normal.

Even the guns and the checkpoints on the way to the hotel he 12 has sent us to seem plausible. The hotel itself is overly so—a Sheraton. All one's fantasies of real Persian hotels, heautiful and subtle as Japanese inns—all that out the window. That we have a roof over our heads, running water, a bed after two days of airplane. That is enough. Though it sets the teeth on edge to look at the Arya Sheraton. Awful monumental concrete pile, American anonymous modern transported here, in fact the whole neighborhood is such, and in the days after, as we drove through the city we discovered more dismal "new" buildings than I have ever seen anywhere else in the world. The Shah was in a rage of producing this stuff, to make an entire city of totalitarian modern, a monument to himself, to the conquerors who sponsored him, a tribute to Western imperialism, destroying all indigenous buildings, leaving only these skeletons of half-built towers we see through the windows of our room.

The Sheraton is sandbagged in front. More sandbags in the 13 lobby. Young men with machine guns lolling about to "defend" it from some anonymous attackers. The hotel is nearly deserted. Merely a dozen guests lost in its towers. The hotel staff seem unhappy. Under guard. This is no way to run a place of hostelry, they seem to say. One is even quite open with Sophie over his dissatisfaction. We call Kateh again. She had not expected us, or certainly not so soon. Khalil had waited till the last moment to call Tehran and say we were coming. His paranoia, his precaution, his plain old error, perhaps—but arriving like this, unexpected, or not expected for several days, seems to make us a bit less welcome, a bit of a nuisance. There is little room at Kateh's house, they are crowded with family, her brother Khosrow and his wife and children, Kateh herself and her husband, Babak, are there as well; but we are welcome to sleep on the floor. Awkward. We should stay here, even though we hate it and can't really afford it. Nor did we come all the way to Tehran to live in a hotel; a friend's floor is better. It would be better to be with Kateh tonight; she thinks there is still someplace open where we can all get dinner. "No, on second thought, eat at your hotel and we will send someone to pick you up there when you're finished."

A man comes to bring us towels and we mistake him for a sub- 14 versive force, howling, "Holy, holy, holy," outside our door. We say we don't want any. Further awkwardness in checking out, the room immaculate, still without towels. At the elevator we meet the towel man having another go at it. A go at us too, elaborate attempts to shake our hands, then to kiss us; we tire of international goodwill and close the elevator door, expecting the worst from the management. Our sudden departure. Explain it as best we can.

Dinner is in the basement, Sheraton's Italian-grotto motif, ar- 15 ranged somewhere else for somewhere else or nowhere at all. The swimming pool just outside the windows is equally "international" in flavor, equally flavorless. Its invitation to the sun, to drinks by poolside, to languor and relaxation, are now only symptoms of decadence. It is also decadent to ask the waiter for a drink. "Alcohol is no longer served," he rebukes me. "But it's on the menu." Until a few days ago you could have a drink here, now it's against the law. Doesn't that seem a pity? I ask him, acknowledging the power of the state over our lives, but curious to know if there is any sense of how arbitrary it all is. Doesn't he think many of the people having dinner here would like to have a beer or a glass of wine with their food, even a little whiskey beforehand? Does he drink himself, does he know how it relaxes you when you're tired, nervous, frustrated? What will it do to a whole population to be without this little pleasure, to have it made against the law? I wheedle, but he's not buying any. The very fact that I dare to discuss Muslim law is impiety. The people at the next table stare and then smile; they are in agreement with us probably as he reports our scandalous remarks.

We suffer through dinner: everything one would hate about a 16 Western multinational corporation is here: the mediocre tasteless food (neither Western nor Eastern nor food), the showy swimming pool to intimidate the poor, the hot, the dusty, the millions who would never be permitted in the door, even the phony decor. And nothing redeemable is left either; the food seems deliberately disimproved and carelessly served, the pleasure of the pool is lost forever since you are sure they will never fill it again. Two corny Western-style bars and you can't have even one drink. As if everything that might be fun is now governmentally interdict. What an odd way to liberate a place. Instead of confiscating the imperialist fat-cat stuff and democratizing the enjoyment of it—instead, what few pleasures it offered have all been forbidden. To everyone.

The just resentment against foreign things, foreign money, foreign arrogance has run its course to a kind of xenophobia. The young militiamen surround us up at the desk and demand to know where we are going. Are we American? Sophie is quick to claim her Canadian dispensation. I answer that I am American, as if it were a crime for which I am expected to take responsibility. Why are we going out at night? Our friends are coming to get us. We are bourgeois foreigners according to them. We ask if they are socialists, leftists. We get little satisfaction here. They are the Islamic revolution, they are from the Komiteh. An earlier bunch—they have just changed guard—had felt like leftist students; these now feel like Khomeini types, the good boys at the mosque who Khalil says are replacing the leftists—but to a woman both give off the same threat, the same obdurate male stance. I ask them about the women. Becoming suspicious thereby. Why ask about that? I want to know what the women will gain by the revolution. "We got rid of the Shah." "Of course, and the women helped to do it, but what will it be like for women now?" "Our women are happy. They do what we want." Another laughs. How easy and infuriating this humor over women, how universal. "That's happiness?" "Why you ask about this?" a third demands, gun in hand. "Because I'm a feminist." A dangerous thing to say, but I risk it, having talked to them long enough now to have established contact, they are unlikely even to arrest me. 17

We are waiting for our friends, hours of waiting; we still don't know it, but it is only the beginning of our days of waiting. Sophie is talking to the desk clerk, a very different conversation from mine with the militia. Pouring out to her all his detestation of the new regime, his frustration and that of his colleagues—no one comes to the hotel anymore, no one wants to be bossed by the soldiers, denied a drink. The Intercontinental is getting all their business, it is still almost a hotel rather than a branch of the police and the state, it still sells alcohol, it is full of reporters. Sophie makes a mental note to stay at the Intercontinental if she is ever in need of a hotel. She's 18 a reporter; he must tell her what it's like here. And listens to the man's woes. He develops a great interest in her. Becoming inquisitive, becoming forward, offering his services, would we like him to act as our interpreter during our visit here? Sophie decides he's a spy. I decide our friends are never coming long before one of them, Bahram, calls to say there are thirty-two checkpoints to get through between us, and they think it too dangerous. It has taken them this long just to locate a car.

"Are they always this inefficient, these friends of yours in   19
Caifi?" Sophie is miffed. We have been two hours in the lobby exposed to hotel clerks and soldiery. The humiliation of reregistering lies ahead of us; having checked out, we must now check in again. "I can't understand what's the matter, they're always wonderful to work with." Trying to imagine what it means to get through thirty-two checkpoints; coming here, they didn't stop our cab, but would they stop Caifi, search, question? Thirty-two times. Of course they couldn't come. We are being inconsiderate, we are failing to notice that this is a country under armed guard only a few weeks after an insurrection; if we are not in the midst of a revolution, we are at least in the midst of a counterrevolution, which, because so much is still in flux, might still come out all right.

We have only to wait and see, we have only to be patient, going   20
to bed at the Sheraton, talking into our tape recorder, the day a confusing mass behind us. We are rather alone in Tehran.

READING AND WRITING
ABOUT FOREIGN PLACES AND PEOPLE

1. Discuss an experience you have had with another culture or another way of life. What do you remember most vividly about the experience? How did you feel about the place or people at the time? Do you feel differently about the experience now?

2. Describe, in a few words each, the attitudes of Charles Darwin, Isabella Bird, Edith Wharton, Isak Dinesen, and Colin Thubron towards the strangers or foreign culture they encounter. Which writers have the most similar attitudes, which the most different? Which of these Brief Encounters comes closest to capturing your own attitude towards an experience you've had with another culture?

3. To what audience do you think Darwin is addressing his description of the Fuegians? Speculate about the social class and values of this audience. How does Darwin shape his evidence that the Fuegians are "abject and miserable" for this particular audience? On what preconceptions or assumptions from his home culture does his evidence seem to be based?

4. Study the ways Dinesen, Thubron, and Evelyn Waugh use dialogue in their brief action scenes. Notice in particular when they choose to quote someone directly (direct discourse), and when they summarize or paraphrase a speech instead (indirect discourse). How do you account for these choices? Experiment with direct and indirect discourse in your own narrative writing.

5. John Krich says of Calcutta, "I cope with this place by turning clinician." What does he mean by this? How successful do you think he is at maintaining this perspective? Compare the kinds of observations Krich makes about Calcutta with those Mary Morris makes about Mexico. What differences do you detect in their approaches to the places they're visiting, and how do you account for these differences? How would you describe Morris's coping, if she's not also "turning clinician"?

6. Herbert Gold, Alex Haley, and Andrea Lee all relate experiences in which the people from two different cultures have difficulty communicating, at least at first. Discuss to what extent this difficulty is overcome, and how, in each case. What role does stereotyping— relying on fixed, oversimplified ideas about groups or types of people— play in the process?

7. Gold is Jewish, Haley and Lee are African Americans, and Pico Iyer is Anglo Indian. To what extent does the writer's ethnic or racial heritage affect his or her travel experience in each case?

8. Do you think Haley did the right thing in refusing to contribute to the Juffure Village money box? Why, or why not?

9. How does Iyer justify his characterization of the Philippines as "the world's largest slice of the American Empire" and "America's fifty-second state"? Are you convinced?

10. Describe John Updike's tone or attitude towards his subjects— *los indios, los ricos,* and "the visitor." What overall point do you think he's trying to make? Imitate Updike's comparison and contrast with your own essay entitled "The United States for Visitors," "[Your college] for Visitors," or "[Your home town] for Visitors."

11. Without looking back, write down images or details that stick in your mind after reading Joan Didion's essay. Why are these particularly memorable? Why do you think she included them? After re-reading, decide how these images or details contribute to your understanding of Didion's overall purpose in the essay.

12. Look back over the passages relating to guns in both Didion's and Kate Millett's essays. How are the two writers' attitudes towards the guns or the people carrying them similar? How are they different? How would you compare the atmosphere of the San Salvador Sheraton with that of the Tehran Sheraton?

13. Based on her narrative, what women's issues seem of greatest concern to Millett? What women's issues seem of greatest concern to Morris? How do their different styles of writing illuminate their different priorities? You might present your analysis in the form of a dialogue between Morris and Millett.

14. When Chinua Achebe says that "travelers can be blind," he implies that they may miss something besides just physical manifestations of culture, like the Great Wall of China unnoticed (or ignored) by Marco Polo. Discuss what one or more of the other writers in this chapter fail to notice about the places they visit. What do these omissions reveal about the travelers' home culture? What peculiarly American preconceptions about the way people ought to look, think, or behave to you detect? Try answering the same questions about something you have written previously or earlier in the term.

15. Which of the writers in this chapter discover the most about themselves personally during their adventure abroad? What, specifically, do they discover? Choose one author, and analyze his or her interior journey as it parallels, or coincides with, the exterior journey.

MAKING FURTHER CONNECTIONS

1. If you speak the native language of any of the places visited by Chapter 3 authors—such as Japanese, Russian, Spanish, Tagalog, Arabic, or Farsi (Persian)—speculate about how the conceptual labels and categories of English, as discussed by Peter Farb in Chapter 1, may have affected the author's perception of the place.

2. Some differences between tourists and travelers are suggested in the introductions to Chapters 2 and 3. What is your view of this distinction, and how might you modify or enlarge upon it? Base your response on selections from Chapters 2 and 3 and your own experience.

3. Compare or contrast a traveler from this chapter with a "domestic traveler" from Chapter 2. You might focus your comparison on the writers' interior journeys, cultural preconceptions or biases, ethnic experiences, or writing styles.

4. Read the Brief Encounters by Philip L. Pearce and Peter S. Adler in Chapter 5. How would you classify various travelers of Chapter 3 according to Pearce's "fifteen types"? Apply Adler's "five stages of culture shock" to an experience from Chapter 3 and/or your own experience. Which stages most closely describe the experience? How does this model illuminate or change your view of the experience?

5. Morris, Didion, and Millett encounter the threat of violence or terror when they visit developing countries. Discuss the different forms of violence and their causes in one or two of these essays and in Paul Bowles's story, "A Distant Encounter," in Chapter 6. How might your causal analysis help explain the violence in our own country?

6. Haley, Iyer, and Updike explore the influence that affluent Western nations—the United States in particular—are having on poor countries or former colonies in the Third World. List, from these writers' essays, some of the symptoms and effects of this

"Westernization," then analyze the Westernization the fictional Dang tribe undergoes in George P. Elliott's (Chapter 6) story, "Among the Dangs."

7. What differences and similarities do you find between the imaginary city Omelas, in Ursula K. LeGuin's story, "The Ones Who Walk away from Omelas" (Chapter 6), and one of the real places described in Chapter 3?

EXPLORING NEW SOURCES

1. Research some aspect of the staggering poverty encountered by one of Chapter 3's authors, focusing on particular government or international programs in Third World countries. For example, evaluate Indian government efforts to address the homelessness in Calcutta described by Krich; or explore the short-term and long-term effects of the *maquilladora* system—an economic arrangement between the United States and Mexico for employing factory workers in American-owned businesses.

2. Read Haley's book *Roots;* if your media library has a copy, see a videotape of the television drama as well. Read some secondary sources, such as reviews and magazine articles, about the book and its impact. One controversy surrounding *Roots* that you could address is whether it should be classified as nonfiction or fiction. How does your research change, or reinforce, your view of the dilemma Haley faces in his essay regarding Juffure Village?

3. How has popular music in the Soviet Union—or another art or cultural form that interests you—been influenced by *glasnost* and *perestroika*?

4. How have U.S.–Philippines relations changed since the downfall of the Marcos regime? Choose a specific issue, such as the debate about the U.S. military presence in the Philippines, to focus your research.

5. How successfully can you substantiate or dispute any of the claims that Updike makes about the rich or the Indians in Venezuela? If you focus on the Yanomami Indians, you might begin with Florinda Donner's 1982 book *Shabono: A True Adventure in the Remote and Magical Heart of the South American Jungle.* How does the kind of knowledge you get from this personal narrative differ from

that offered in the professional anthropological studies you find about the Yanomami?

6. How has the condition of political terror in El Salvador changed since the time of Didion's 1982 book *Salvador* (from which her essay comes)? To what extent is U.S. aid a good or bad influence on "the mechanism of terror"?

7. How have Iranian women been affected by the Islamic revolution in their country? You might investigate how Muslim women themselves feel about veiling or other Islamic traditions; if possible, talk with women and men from Islamic countries as part of your research. Record your interviews with them, and cite them as primary sources.

4

THE CRITICAL JOURNEY: ENCOUNTERING DIVERSITY AT HOME

The United States and the land it occupies, like all places but more than most, has always been inhabited by people who came from somewhere else. The very first '"Americans" were Asian immigrants—Mongol peoples who journeyed across the Bering Strait, between present-day Alaska and the Soviet Union's Chukchi Peninsula, at least fifty thousand years ago. As they migrated south and east, these Amerindians gave rise to widely diverse cultures and civilizations, estimated to comprise more than two thousand distinct languages by the time Columbus landed in 1492.[1]

Much of this native cultural diversity was eliminated (along with most of the natives) by the European conquest of the "New World," which provided new sources of ethnic diversity. The English, Scots, Irish, Germans, and other Europeans came to the future United States in large numbers from the sixteenth to the eighteenth centuries—as did the Africans they imported as slaves.[2] During the largest wave of U.S. immigration from 1890 to 1915, some sixteen million people—the majority from continental Europe—were processed through the Ellis Island complex in New York Harbor. Today almost half of all Americans can trace their ancestry directly to Ellis Island,[3] and about one-tenth have African roots from the slave

---

[1] Harry Hoijer, "American Aboriginal Languages," *Encyclopaedia Britannica*, 1970.
[2] Scholars disagree over whether to classify slaves as immigrants. But the fact remains that of the first million foreigners who came to the historical United States from colonial times until 1820, about 600,000 were from Europe (350,000 from England) and 400,000 from Africa. See Roger Daniels, *Coming to America* (New York: HarperCollins, 1990), p. 6.
[3] Bartholomew P. Lahiff, "A Plea for Selfishness," *America*, July 21, 1990.

trade. Of the latest wave of immigrants mentioned in Chapter 1—more than six million in the 1980s alone—more than eighty percent are from Asia and Latin America.[4] Estimates of the number of illegal immigrants living in the United States (mostly from Latin America and the Caribbean) range from about three million to twelve million.

Why have all these people come to the United States? The answer is certainly complex, but it's safe to say that, with the notable exception of enslaved Africans, most have sought the economic opportunity that has come to be associated with "the American dream." Precisely what constitutes this dream, who has been able to achieve it, and to what extent it is a worthy ideal—these are important questions for you to consider as you read this chapter.

The popular "melting pot" metaphor suggests that America's millions of immigrants—regardless of why they came—both influence and become assimilated to an evolving national identity. During the past generation, however, this model has been challenged by one emphasizing cultural pluralism, in which America's various ethnic and other subcultures are seen to retain their individual characters and flavors—more like a stew or salad than a melting pot. You can test these models, or perhaps even devise your own metaphor for American diversity, as you read Chapter 4. Which model most accurately describes our history or present condition? Which, as an ideal, holds out the best hope for our future?

In Chapter 4, the kinds of American places and people "discovered" in Chapter 2 are encountered more critically—that is, more analytically or argumentatively. Analyses and arguments take many forms here, from a transcribed and unedited speech to newspaper or magazine articles, literary essays, social criticism, and academic writing. But the critical journey these selections represent should be taken by you as well as by their authors. You will undoubtedly not share some of the views or values regarding American diversity that they present; but agree or disagree, you will have many opportunities to examine and defend your opinions, challenge your beliefs, or explore new ideas.

The Brief Encounters sample an historical range of opinions about America's immigrant ethnic groups. Alex de Tocqueville and Henry David Thoreau offer contrasting nineteenth-century views of the first white settlers of New England, and Paula Gunn Allen suggests that Native American contributions to the revolutionary ideals

---

[4] See James Paul Allen and Eugene James Turner, *We the People: An Atlas of America's Ethnic Identity* (New York: Macmillan, 1988).

of these colonists have been ignored. Anthropologist Margaret Mead analyzes American culture in terms of the adjustments made by the children and grandchildren of immigrants. Mark Twain criticizes his fellow Americans for their treatment of a "Chinaman" worker, while a hundred years later Robert Claiborne—tired of being criticized— argues that stereotypes about WASPs are unfounded. Alice Walker, in defining the term "womanist," asserts certain values she associates with women of color. Finally, Charles Kuralt refers to several of these other writers in offering his verdict on the melting pot model.

The main selections of Chapter 4 examine U.S. diversity from a variety of current and recent perspectives, emphasizing interactions between ethnic and other social groups or subcultures:

- Ishmael Reed criticizes the cultural values of the Puritans and argues that the limited notion of "Western civilization" inadequately addresses the complexity of our multinational society.

- Joan Didion analyzes "the precise angle at which Miami Anglos and Miami Cubans were failing to connect" in a real-life case study of the melting pot model.

- Maria Moreno, in a 1961 talk on behalf of the Agricultural Workers' Organizing Committee, makes a plea for growers to give lettuce workers a raise to $1.25 an hour.

- Richard Rodriguez argues that the culture shock of college is not limited to ethnic minorities, so "scholarship boys" of all stripes must largely sacrifice their home culture in order to succeed in academia.

- Ellyn Bache uses her experience as an American sponsor of Vietnamese refugees to address current attempts—based on "fear that some groups will become long-term welfare burdens"—to limit the numbers of foreigners coming to the United States.

- Alexandra Tantranon-Saur penetrates the "Asian mask" by directly confronting the common stereotypes held by the white majority and offering specific advice for communicating with Asian and Pacific Islander people.

- Julia Gilden analyzes the phenomenon of "garbage people"— middle-class dropouts who live in abandoned buildings and, like punk rockers, defiantly criticize "the Good Life."

- Phyllis McGinley makes the case for middle-class suburbia as an ideal, conscious compromise between the dangers of big cities and the disadvantages of rural small towns.

- James Baldwin, warning in the 1960s about problems that are still with us, claims that ghetto housing projects fail because of the deep frustration with "the white man's world" felt by "many strong, admirable men and women whose only crime is color."

- Shelby Steele argues that the "pattern of racial identification that emerged in the sixties" is at odds with the middle-class values of many blacks today, and he explores this dilemma of dual identities.

- Randall E. Majors analyzes the outward manifestations of an emerging homosexual culture in the United States—gay neighborhoods, social groups, symbols, and meeting behavior—and speculates about the human needs driving these changes.

- Edith A. Folb offers definitions and a framework for analyzing all the domestic "nondominant groups" discussed in this chapter, those for whom there is "no room at the top."

BRIEF ENCOUNTERS

The Founding of New England

ALEXIS DE TOCQUEVILLE

The foundation of New England was something new in the world, all the attendant circumstances being both peculiar and original.

In almost all other colonies the first inhabitants have been men without wealth or education, driven from their native land by poverty or misconduct, or else greedy speculators and industrial entrepreneurs. Some colonies cannot claim even such an origin as this; San Domingo was founded by pirates, and in our day the English courts of justice are busy populating Australia.

But all the immigrants who came to settle on the shores of New England belonged to the well-to-do classes at home. From the start, when they came together on American soil, they presented the unusual phenomenon of a society in which there were no great lords, no common people, and, one may almost say, no rich or poor. In proportion to their numbers, these men had a greater share of accomplishments than could be found in any European nation now. All, perhaps without a single exception, had received a fairly advanced education, and several had made a European reputation by their talents and their knowledge. The other colonies had been founded by unattached adventurers, whereas the immigrants to New England brought with them wonderful elements of order and morality; they came with their wives and children to the wilds. But what most distinguished them from all others was the very aim of their enterprise. No necessity forced them to leave their country; they gave up a desirable social position and assured means of livelihood; nor was their object in going to the New World to better their position or accumulate wealth; they tore themselves away from home comforts in obedience to a purely intellectual craving; in facing the inevitable sufferings of exile they hoped for the triumph of *an idea.*

The immigrants, or as they so well named themselves, the Pilgrims, belonged to that English sect whose austere principles had led them to be called Puritans. Puritanism was not just a religious doctrine; in many respects it shared the most absolute democratic and republican theories. That was the element which had aroused its most dangerous adversaries. Persecuted by the home government, and with their strict principles offended by the everyday ways of the society in which they lived, the Puritans sought a land so barbarous and neglected by the world that there at last they might be able to live in their own way and pray to God in freedom.

—FROM *DEMOCRACY IN AMERICA*, 1835

Growing up in Immigrant America

MARGARET MEAD

Our children are given years of cultural nonparticipation in which they are permitted to live in a world of their own. They are allowed to say what they like, when they like, how they like, to ignore many of the conventions of their adults. Those who try to stem the tide are derided as "old fogies," "old-fashioned," "hidebound," and flee in confusion before these magic words of exorcism. This state of discipline is due to very real causes in American society. In an immigrant country, the children are able to make a much better adjustment than have their parents. The rapid rate of invention and change in the material side of life has also made each generation of children relatively more proficient than their parents. So the last generation use the telephone more easily than their parents: the present generation are more at home in automobiles than are their fathers and mothers. When the grandparent generation has lived through the introduction of the telegraph, telephone, wireless, radio and telephotography, automobiles and airplanes, it is not surprising that control should slip through their amazed fingers into the more readily adaptable hands of children. While adults fumbled helplessly with daylight saving time, missed appointments and were late to dinner, children of six whose ideas of time had not yet become crystallized rapidly assimilated the idea that ten o'clock was not necessarily ten o'clock, but might be nine or eleven. In a country where the most favored are the ones to take up the newest invention, and old things are in such disrepute that one encounters humorless signs, which advertise, "Antiques old and new" and "Have your wedding ring renovated," the world belongs to the new generation. They can learn the new techniques far more easily than can their more culturally set elders. So the young in America seize their material world, almost from birth, without any practice in humility, and their parade of power becomes a shallow jugglery with things, phrases, catchwords.

—FROM "BEQUEATHING OUR TRADITION GRACIOUSLY," *GROWING UP IN NEW GUINEA*, 1930

The Yankee and the Red Man

HENRY DAVID THOREAU

Some spring the white man came, built him a house, and made a clearing here, letting in the sun, dried up a farm, piled up the old gray stones in fences, cut down the pines around his dwelling, planted orchard seeds brought from the old country, and persuaded the civil apple tree to blossom next to the wild pine and the juniper, shedding its perfume in the wilderness. Their old stocks still remain. He culled the graceful elm from out the woods and from the river-side, and so refined and smoothed his village plot. And thus he plants a town. He rudely bridged the stream, and drove his team afield into the river meadows, cut the wild grass, and laid bare the homes of beaver, otter, muskrat, and with the whetting of his scythe scared off the deer and bear. He set up a mill, and fields of English grain sprang in the virgin soil. And with his grain he scattered the seeds of the dandelion and the wild trefoil over the meadows, min-gling his English flowers with the wild native ones. The bristling burdock, the sweet scented catnip, and the humble yarrow, planted themselves along his woodland road, they too seeking "freedom to worship God" in their way. The white man's mullein soon reigned in Indian corn-fields, and sweet scented English grasses clothed the new soil. Where, then, could the red man set his foot? The honey bee hummed through the Massachusetts woods, and sipped the wild flowers round the Indian's wigwam, perchance unnoticed, when, with prophetic warning, it stung the red child's hand, fore-runner of that industrious tribe that was to come and pluck the wild flower of his race up by the root.

The white man comes, pale as the dawn, with a load of thought, with a slumbering intelligence as a fire raked up, knowing well what he knows, not guessing but calculating; strong in community, yield-ing obedience to authority; of experienced race; of wonderful, won-derful common sense; dull but capable, slow but persevering, severe but just, of little humor but genuine; a laboring man, despising game and sport; building a house that endures, a framed house. He buys the Indian's moccasins and baskets, then buys his hunting grounds, and at length forgets where he is buried, and plows up his bones. And here town records, old, tattered, time-worn, weather-stained chronicles, contain the Indian sachem's mark, perchance an arrow or a beaver, and the few fatal words by which he deeded his hunting grounds away. He comes with a list of ancient Saxon, Nor-man, and Celtic names, and strews them up and down this river,— Framingham, Sudbury, Bedford, Carlisle, Billerica, Chelmsford—

and this is New Angle-land, and these are the new West Saxons, whom the red men call, not Angle-ish or English, but Yengeese, and so at last they are known for Yankees.

—FROM *A WEEK ON THE CONCORD AND MERRIMACK RIVERS*, 1849

American History and Native Americans

PAULA GUNN ALLEN

The belief that rejection of tradition and of history is a useful response to life is reflected in America's amazing loss of memory concerning its origins in the matrix and context of Native America. America does not seem to remember that it derived its wealth, its values, its food, much of its medicine, and a large part of its "dream" from Native America. It is ignorant of the genesis of its culture in this Native American land, and that ignorance helps to perpetuate the long-standing European and Middle Eastern monotheistic, hierarchical, patriarchal cultures' oppression of women, gays, and lesbians, people of color, working class, unemployed people, and the elderly. Hardly anyone in America speculates that the constitutional system of government might be as much a product of American Indian ideas and practices as of colonial American and Anglo-European revolutionary fervor.

Even though Indians are officially and informally ignored as intellectual movers and shapers in the United States, Britain, and Europe, they are peoples with ancient tenure on this soil. During the ages when tribal societies existed in the Americas largely untouched by patriarchal oppression, they developed elaborate systems of thought that included science, philosophy, and government based on a belief in the central importance of female energies, autonomy of individuals, cooperation, human dignity, human freedom, and egalitarian distribution of status, goods, and services. Respect for others, reverence for life, and, as a by-product, pacifism as a way of life; importance of kinship ties in the customary ordering of social interaction; a sense of the sacredness and mystery of existence; balance and harmony in relationships both sacred and secular were all features of life among the tribal confederacies and nations. And in those that lived by the largest number of these principles, gynarchy was the norm rather than the exception. Those systems are as yet unmatched in any contemporary industrial, agrarian, or postindustrial society on earth.

—FROM "WHO IS YOUR MOTHER? RED ROOTS OF FEMINISM," *THE SACRED HOOP: RECOVERING THE FEMININE IN AMERICAN INDIAN TRADITIONS*, 1986

John Chinaman in New York

MARK TWAIN

As I passed along by one of those monster American tea stores in New York, I found a Chinaman sitting before it acting in the capacity of a sign. Everybody that passed by gave him a steady stare as long as their heads would twist over their shoulders without dislocating their necks, and a group had stopped to stare deliberately.

Is it not a shame that we, who prate so much about civilization and humanity, are content to degrade a fellow-being to such an office as this? Is it not time for reflection when we find ourselves willing to see in such a being matter for frivolous curiosity instead of regret and grave reflection? Here was a poor creature whom hard fortune had exiled from his natural home beyond the seas, and whose troubles ought to have touched these idle strangers that thronged about him; but did it? Apparently not. Men calling themselves the superior race, the race of culture and of gentle blood, scanned his quaint Chinese hat, with peaked roof and ball on top, and his long queue dangling down his back; his short silken blouse, curiously frogged and figured (and, like the rest of his raiment, rusty, dilapidated, and awkwardly put on); his blue cotton, tight-legged pants, tied close around the ankles; and his clumsy blunt-toed shoes with thick cork soles; and having so scanned him from head to foot, cracked some unseemly joke about his outlandish attire or his melancholy face, and passed on. In my heart I pitied the friendless Mongol. I wondered what was passing behind his sad face, and what distant scene his vacant eye was dreaming of. Were his thoughts with his heart, ten thousand miles away, beyond the billowy wastes of the Pacific? among the ricefields and the plumy palms of China? under the shadows of remembered mountain peaks, or in groves of bloomy shrubs and strange forest trees unknown to climes like ours? And now and then, rippling among his visions and his dreams, did he hear familiar laughter and half-forgotten voices, and did he catch fitful glimpses of the friendly faces of a bygone time? A cruel fate it is, I said, that is befallen this bronzed wanderer. In order that the group of idlers might be touched at least by the words of the poor fellow, since the appeal of his pauper dress and his dreary exile was lost upon them, I touched him on the shoulder and said:

"Cheer up—don't be downhearted. It is not America that treats you in this way, it is merely one citizen, whose greed of gain has eaten the humanity out of his heart. America has a broader hospitality for the exiled and oppressed. America and Americans are always ready to help the unfortunate. Money shall be raised—you shall go back to China—you shall see your friends again. What wages do they pay you here?"

"Divil a cint but four dollars a week and find meself; but it's aisy, barrin' the troublesome furrin clothes that's so expinsive."

The exile remains at his post. The New York tea merchants who need picturesque signs are not likely to run out of Chinamen.

—FROM *SKETCHES NEW AND OLD*, 1873

The WASP Stereotype

ROBERT CLAIBORNE

I come of a long line of WASPs; if you disregard my French great-great-grandmother and a couple of putatively Irish ancestors of the same vintage, a rather pure line. My mother has long been one of the Colonial Dames, an organization some of whose members consider the Daughters of the American Revolution rather parvenu. My umpty-umpth WASP great-grandfather, William Claiborne, founded the first European settlement in what is now Maryland (his farm and trading post were later ripped off by the Catholic Lord Baltimore, Maryland politics being much the same then as now).

As a WASP, the mildest thing I can say about the stereotype emerging from the current wave of anti-WASP chic is that I don't recognize myself. As regards emotional uptightness and sexual inhibition, modesty forbids comment—though I dare say various friends and lovers of mine could testify on these points if they cared to. I will admit to enjoying work—because I am lucky enough to be able to work at what I enjoy—but not, I think, to the point of compulsiveness. And so far as ruling America, or even New York, is concerned, I can say flatly that (a) it's a damn lie because (b) if I *did* rule them, both would be in better shape than they are. Indeed I and all my WASP relatives, taken in a lump, have far less clout with the powers that run this country than any one of the Buckleys or Kennedys (Irish Catholic), the Sulzbergers or Guggenheims (Jewish), or the late A. P. Giannini (Italian) of the Bank of America.

Admittedly, both corporate and (to a lesser extent) political America are dominated by WASPs—just as (let us say) the garment industry is dominated by Jews, and organized crime by Italians. But to conclude from this that The WASPs are the American elite is as silly as to say that The Jews are cloak-and-suiters or The Italians are gangsters. WASPs, like other ethnics, come in all varieties, including criminals—political, corporate, and otherwise.

—FROM "A WASP STINGS BACK," IN *NEWSWEEK*, 1974

Definition of Womanist

ALICE WALKER

Womanist

From *womanish*. (Opp. of "girlish," i.e., frivolous, irresponsible, not serious.) A black feminist or feminist of color. From the black folk expression of mothers to female children, "You acting womanish," i.e., like a woman. Usually referring to outrageous, audacious, courageous, or *willful* behavior. Wanting to know more and in greater depth than is considered "good" for one. Interested in grown-up doings. Acting grown up. Being grown up. Interchangeable with another black folk expression: "You trying to be grown." Responsible. In charge. *Serious.*

2. *Also:* A woman who loves other women, sexually and/or nonsexually. Appreciates and prefers women's culture, women's emotional flexibility (values tears as a natural counterbalance of laughter), and women's strength. Sometimes loves individual men, sexually and/or nonsexually. Committed to survival and wholeness of entire people, male *and* female. Not a separatist, except periodically, for health. Traditionally universalist, as in: "Mama, why are we brown, pink, and yellow, and our cousins are white, beige, and black?" Ans.: "Well, you know the colored race is just like a flower garden, with every color flower represented." Traditionally capable, as in: "Mama, I'm walking to Canada and I'm taking you and a bunch of other slaves with me." Reply: "It wouldn't be the first time."

3. Loves music. Loves dance. Loves the moon. *Loves* the Spirit. Loves love and food and roundness. Loves struggle. *Loves* the Folk. Loves herself. *Regardless.*

4. Womanist is to feminist as purple is to lavender.

—FROM IN SEARCH OF OUR MOTHERS' GARDENS, 1983

Different Drummers

CHARLES KURALT

I love to read about the travels of those who wandered the country before me, de Tocqueville, Mark Twain, John Steinbeck, and all the rest. Each of them caught a little bit of the truth about America and wrote it down. Even the best of them never got it all into one book, because the country is too rich and full of contradictions. Newspaper columnists, on slow days, write columns about "the mood of

America." That takes a lot of nerve, I think. The mood of America is infinitely complex and always changing and highly dependent on locale and circumstance. The mood of Tribune, Kansas, depends on whether that black cloud to the west becomes a hailstorm that flattens the wheat crop or passes harmlessly. The mood of Haines, Alaska, depends on whether the lumber mill is hiring. The mood of Altoona rises and falls with the fortunes of the high school football team. The mood of New York City is much affected by heat and rain and the percentage of taxis with their off-duty signs lighted at any given time. You can't get your thumb on America's mood. I never try.

Even the clearest-eyed observers of the country, like Alexis de Tocqueville, got into trouble by overgeneralizing. "As they mingle," de Tocqueville wrote, "the Americans become assimilated. . . . They all get closer to one type." Right there, the great de Tocqueville stubbed his toe. The assimilation never came to pass; the "Melting Pot," so much written about, never succeeded in melting us. Americans are made of some alloy that won't be melted. To this day we retain a dread of conformity.

Henry Thoreau, who never traveled at all (except, as he said, "a good deal in Concord"), composed us a credo in 1854: "If a man does not keep pace with his companions, perhaps it is because he hears a different drummer. Let him step to the music which he hears. . . ."

We admire de Tocqueville, but it was Thoreau we listened to.

—FROM *ON THE ROAD WITH CHARLES KURALT*, 1985

America: The Multinational Society

ISHMAEL REED

At the annual Lower East Side Jewish Festival yesterday, a Chinese woman ate a pizza slice in front of Ty Thuan Duc's Vietnamese grocery store. Beside her a Spanish-speaking family patronized a cart with two signs: "Italian Ices" and "Kosher by Rabbi Alper." And after the pastrami ran out, everybody ate knishes.

—*New York Times*, June 23, 1983

On the day before Memorial Day, 1983, a poet called me to describe a city he had just visited. He said that one section included mosques, built by the Islamic people who dwelled there. Attending his reading, he said, were large numbers of Hispanic people, forty thousand of whom lived in the same city. He was not talking about a fabled city located in some mysterious region of the world. The city he'd visited was Detroit.

A few months before, as I was leaving Houston, Texas, I heard it announced on the radio that Texas's largest minority was Mexican-American, and though a foundation recently issued a report critical of bilingual education, the taped voice used to guide the passengers on the air trams connecting terminals in Dallas Airport is in both Spanish and English. If the trend continues, a day will come when it will be difficult to travel through some sections of the country without hearing commands in both English and Spanish; after all, for some Western states, Spanish was the first written language and the Spanish style lives on in the Western way of life.

Shortly after my Texas trip, I sat in an auditorium located on the campus of the University of Wisconsin at Milwaukee as a Yale professor—whose original work on the influence of African cultures upon those of the Americas has led to his ostracism from some monocultural intellectual circles—walked up and down the aisle, like an old-time Southern evangelist, dancing and drumming the top

Ishmael Reed (1938–   ), born in Chattanooga, Tennessee, is the author of essays, poetry, and novels including *Mumbo Jumbo* (1972) and *Reckless Eyeballing* (1986). "America: The Multinational Society" is from his collection, *Writin' Is Fightin': Thirty-Seven Years of Boxing on Paper* (1988).

1

2

3

264

of the lectern, illustrating his points before some serious Afro-American intellectuals and artists who cheered and applauded his performance and his mastery of information. The professor was "white." After his lecture, he joined a group of Milwaukeeans in a conversation. All of the participants spoke Yoruban, though only the professor had ever traveled to Africa.

One of the artists told me that his paintings, which included   4
African and Afro-American mythological symbols and imagery, were hanging in the local McDonald's restaurant. The next day I went to McDonald's and snapped pictures of smiling youngsters eating hamburgers below paintings that could grace the walls of any of the country's leading museums. The manager of the local McDonald's said, "I don't know what you boys are doing, but I like it," as he commissioned the local painters to exhibit in his restaurant.

Such blurring of cultural styles occurs in everyday life in the   5
United States to a greater extent than anyone can imagine and is probably more prevalent than the sensational conflict between people of different backgrounds that is played up and often encouraged by the media. The result is what the Yale professor, Robert Thompson, referred to as a cultural bouillabaisse, yet members of the nation's present educational and cultural Elect still cling to the notion that the United States belongs to some vaguely defined entity they refer to as "Western civilization," by which they mean, presumably, a civilization created by the people of Europe, as if Europe can be viewed in monolithic terms. Is Beethoven's Ninth Symphony, which includes Turkish marches, a part of Western civilization, or the late nineteenth- and twentieth-century French paintings, whose creators were influenced by Japanese art? And what of the cubists, through whom the influence of African art changed modern painting, or the surrealists, who were so impressed with the art of the Pacific Northwest Indians that, in their map of North America, Alaska dwarfs the lower forty-eight in size?

Are the Russians, who are often criticized for their adoption of   6
"Western" ways by Tsarist dissidents in exile, members of Western civilization? And what of the millions of Europeans who have black African and Asian ancestry, black Africans having occupied several countries for hundreds of years? Are these "Europeans" members of Western civilization, or the Hungarians, who originated across the Urals in a place called Greater Hungary, or the Irish, who came from the Iberian Peninsula?

Even the notion that North America is part of Western civiliza-   7
tion because our "system of government" is derived from Europe is being challenged by Native American historians who say that the founding fathers, Benjamin Franklin especially, were actually

influenced by the system of government that had been adopted by the Iroquois hundreds of years prior to the arrival of large numbers of Europeans.

Western civilization, then, becomes another confusing category 8 like Third World, or Judeo-Christian culture, as man attempts to impose his small-screen view of political and cultural reality upon a complex world. Our most publicized novelist[1] recently said that Western civilization was the greatest achievement of mankind, an attitude that flourishes on the street level as scribbles in public restrooms: "White Power," "Niggers and Spics Suck," or "Hitler was a prophet," the latter being the most telling, for wasn't Adolph Hitler the archetypal monoculturalist who, in his pigheaded arrogance, believed that one way and one blood was so pure that it had to be protected from alien strains at all costs? Where did such an attitude, which has caused so much misery and depression in our national life, which has tainted even our noblest achievements, begin? An attitude that caused the incarceration of Japanese-American citizens during World War II, the persecution of Chicanos and Chinese-Americans, the near-extermination of the Indians, and the murder and lynchings of thousands of Afro-Americans.

Virtuous, hardworking, pious, even though they occasionally 9 would wander off after some fancy clothes, or rendezvous in the woods with the town prostitute, the Puritans are idealized in our schoolbooks as "a hardy band" of no-nonsense patriarchs whose discipline razed the forest and brought order to the New World (a term that annoys Native American historians). Industrious, responsible, it was their "Yankee ingenuity" and practicality that created the work ethic. They were simple folk who produced a number of good poets, and they set the tone for the American writing style, of lean and spare lines, long before Hemingway. They worshiped in churches whose colors blended in with the New England snow, churches with simple structures and ornate lecterns.

The Puritans were a daring lot, but they had a mean streak. 10 They hated the theater and banned Christmas. They punished people in a cruel and inhuman manner. They killed children who disobeyed their parents. When they came in contact with those whom they considered heathens or aliens, they behaved in such a bizarre and irrational manner that this chapter in the American history comes down to us as a late-movie horror film. They exterminated the Indians, who taught them how to survive in a world unknown

---

[1] A reference to Saul Bellow (1915–　), American novelist born in Canada. (Ed.)

to them, and their encounter with the calypso culture of Barbados resulted in what the tourist guide in Salem's Witches' House refers to as the Witchcraft Hysteria.

The Puritan legacy of hard work and meticulous accounting led 11 to the establishment of a great industrial society; it is no wonder that the American industrial revolution began in Lowell, Massachusetts, but there was the other side, the strange and paranoid attitudes toward those different from the Elect.

The cultural attitudes of that early Elect continue to be voiced in 12 everyday life in the United States: the president of a distinguished university, writing a letter to the *Times*, belittling the study of African civilizations; the television network that promoted its show on the Vatican art with the boast that this art represented "the finest achievements of the human spirit." A modern up-tempo state of complex rhythms that depends upon contacts with an international community can no longer behave as if it dwelled in a "Zion Wilderness" surrounded by beasts and pagans.

When I heard a schoolteacher warn the other night about the in- 13 vasion of the American educational system by foreign curriculums, I wanted to yell at the television set, "Lady, they're already here." It has already begun because the world is here. The world has been arriving at these shores for at least ten thousand years from Europe, Africa, and Asia. In the late nineteenth and early twentieth centuries, large numbers of Europeans arrived, adding their cultures to those of the European, African, and Asian settlers who were already here, and recently millions have been entering the country from South America and the Caribbean, making Yale Professor Bob Thompson's bouillabaisse richer and thicker.

One of our most visionary politicians said that he envisioned a 14 time when the United States could become the brain of the world, by which he meant the repository of all of the latest advanced information systems. I thought of that remark when an enterprising poet friend of mine called to say that he had just sold a poem to a computer magazine and that the editors were delighted to get it because they didn't carry fiction or poetry. Is that the kind of world we desire? A humdrum homogeneous world of all brains and no heart, no fiction, no poetry; a world of robots with human attendants bereft of imagination, of culture? Or does North America deserve a more exciting destiny? To become a place where the cultures of the world crisscross. This is possible because the United States is unique in the world: The world is here.

Miami: The Cuban Presence

JOAN DIDION

On the 150th anniversary of the founding of Dade County, in February of 1986, the *Miami Herald* asked four prominent amateurs of local history to name "the ten people and the ten events that had the most impact on the county's history." Each of the four submitted his or her own list of "The Most Influential People in Dade's History," and among the names mentioned were Julia Tuttle ("pioneer businesswoman"), Henry Flagler ("brought the Florida East Coast Railway to Miami"), Alexander Orr, Jr. ("started the research that saved Miami's drinking water from salt"), Everest George Sewell ("publicized the city and fostered its deepwater seaport"). . . . There was Dr. James M. Jackson, an early Miami physician. There was Napoleon Bonaparte Broward, the governor of Florida who initiated the draining of the Everglades. There appeared on three of the four lists the name of the developer of Coral Gables, George Merrick. There appeared on one of the four lists the name of the coach of the Miami Dolphins, Don Shula.

On none of these lists of "The Most Influential People in Dade's History" did the name Fidel Castro appear, nor for that matter did the name of any Cuban, although the presence of Cubans in Dade County did not go entirely unnoted by the *Herald* panel. When it came to naming the Ten Most Important "Events," as opposed to "People," all four panelists mentioned the arrival of the Cubans, but at slightly off angles ("Mariel Boatlift of 1980" was the way one panelist saw it), and as if the arrival had been just another of those isolated disasters or innovations which deflect the course of any growing community, on an approximate par with the other events mentioned, for example the Freeze of 1895, the Hurricane of 1926, the opening of the Dixie Highway, the establishment of Miami International Airport, and the adoption, in 1957, of the metropolitan form of government, "enabling the Dade County Commission to provide urban services to the increasingly populous unincorporated area."

Joan Didion (1934–   ), born in Sacramento, California, is the author of several novels including *Play It as It Lays* (1970) and *Democracy* (1984), short stories, screenplays, and the essay collections *Slouching towards Bethlehem* (1968) and *The White Album* (1979). "Miami: The Cuban Presence" is from *Miami* (1987).

This set of mind, in which the local Cuban community was seen 3
as a civic challenge determinedly met, was not uncommon among
Anglos to whom I talked in Miami, many of whom persisted in the
related illusions that the city was small, manageable, prosperous in
a predictable broad-based way, Southern in a progressive Sunbelt
way, American, and belonged to them. In fact 43 percent of the population of Dade County was by that time "Hispanic," which meant
mostly Cuban. Fifty-six percent of the population of Miami itself was
Hispanic. The most visible new buildings on the Miami skyline, the
Arquitectonica buildings along Brickell Avenue, were by a firm with
a Cuban founder. There were Cubans in the board rooms of the major banks, Cubans in clubs that did not admit Jews or blacks, and
four Cubans in the most recent mayoralty campaign, two of whom,
Raul Masvidal and Xavier Suarez, had beaten out the incumbent and
all other candidates to meet in a runoff, and one of whom, Xavier
Suarez, a thirty-six-year-old lawyer who had been brought from
Cuba to the United States as a child, was by then mayor of Miami.

The entire tone of the city, the way people looked and talked 4
and met one another, was Cuban. The very image the city had begun presenting of itself, what was then its newfound glamour, its
"hotness" (hot colors, hot vice, shady dealings under the palm
trees), was that of prerevolutionary Havana, as perceived by Americans. There was even in the way women dressed in Miami a
definable Havana look, a more distinct emphasis on the hips and
décolletage, more black, more veiling, a generalized flirtatiousness
of style not then current in American cities. In the shoe departments
at Burdine's and Jordan Marsh there were more platform soles than
there might have been in another American city, and fewer displays
of the running shoe ethic. I recall being struck, during an afternoon
spent at La Liga Contra el Cancer, a prominent exile charity which
raises money to help cancer patients, by the appearance of the volunteers who had met that day to stuff envelopes for a benefit. Their
hair was sleek, of a slightly other period, immaculate pageboys and
French twists. They wore Bruno Magli pumps, and silk and linen
dresses of considerable expense. There seemed to be a preference
for strictest gray or black, but the effect remained lush, tropical, like
a room full of perfectly groomed mangoes.

This was not, in other words, an invisible 56 percent of the pop- 5
ulation. Even the social notes in *Diario Las Americas* and in *El Herald*,
the daily Spanish edition of the *Herald* written and edited for *el exilio*,
suggested a dominant culture, one with money to spend and a notable willingness to spend it in public. La Liga Contra el Cancer alone
sponsored, in a single year, two benefit dinner dances, one benefit
ball, a benefit children's fashion show, a benefit telethon, a benefit

exhibition of jewelry, a benefit presentation of Miss Universe contestants, and a benefit showing, with Saks Fifth Avenue and chicken *vol-au-vent*, of the Adolfo (as it happened, a Cuban) fall collection.

One morning *El Herald* would bring news of the gala at the   6
Pavillon of the Amigos Latinamericanos del Museo de Ciencia y Planetarium; another morning, of an upcoming event at the Big Five Club, a Miami club founded by former members of five fashionable clubs in prerevolutionary Havana: a *coctel*, or cocktail party, at which tables would be assigned for yet another gala, the annual "Baile Imperial de las Rosas" of the American Cancer Society, Hispanic Ladies Auxiliary. Some members of the community were honoring Miss America Latina with dinner dancing at the Doral. Some were being honored themselves, at the Spirit of Excellence Awards Dinner at the Omni. Some were said to be enjoying the skiing at Vail; others to prefer Bariloche, in Argentina. Some were reported unable to attend (but sending checks for) the gala at the Pavillon of the Amigos Latinamericanos del Museo de Ciencia y Planetarium because of a scheduling conflict, with *el coctel de* Paula Hawkins.

Fete followed fete, all high visibility. Almost any day it was pos-   7
sible to drive past the limestone arches and fountains which marked the boundaries of Coral Gables and see little girls being photographed in the tiaras and ruffled hoop skirts and maribou-trimmed illusion capes they would wear at their *quinces*, the elaborate fifteenth-birthday parties at which the community's female children come of official age. The favored facial expression for a *quince* photograph was a classic smolder. The favored backdrop was one suggesting Castilian grandeur, which was how the Coral Gables arches happened to figure. Since the idealization of the virgin implicit in the *quince* could exist only in the presence of its natural foil, *machismo*, there was often a brother around, or a boyfriend. There was also a mother, in dark glasses, not only to protect the symbolic virgin but to point out the better angle, the more aristocratic location. The *quinceanera* would pick up her hoop skirts and move as directed, often revealing the scuffed Jellies she had worn that day to school. A few weeks later there she would be, transformed in *Diario Las Americas*, one of the morning battalion of smoldering fifteen-year-olds, each with her arch, her fountain, her borrowed scenery, the gift if not exactly the intention of the late George Merrick, who built the arches when he developed Coral Gables.

Neither the photographs of the Cuban *quinceaneras* nor the notes   8
about the *coctel* at the Big Five were apt to appear in the newspapers read by Miami Anglos, nor, for that matter, was much information at all about the daily life of the Cuban majority. When, in the fall of 1986, Florida International University offered an evening course

called "Cuban Miami: A Guide for Non-Cubans," the *Herald* sent a staff writer, who covered the classes as if from a distant beat. "Already I have begun to make some sense out of a culture, that, while it totally surrounds us, has remained inaccessible and alien to me," the *Herald* writer was reporting by the end of the first meeting, and, by the end of the fourth:

> What I see day to day in Miami, moving through mostly Anglo corridors of the community, are just small bits and pieces of that other world, the tip of something much larger than I'd imagined. . . . We may frequent the restaurants here, or wander into the occasional festival. But mostly we try to ignore Cuban Miami, even as we rub up against this teeming, incomprehensible presence.

Only thirteen people, including the *Herald* writer, turned up for   9 the first meeting of "Cuban Miami: A Guide for Non-Cubans" (two more appeared at the second meeting, along with a security guard, because of telephone threats prompted by what the *Herald* writer called "somebody's twisted sense of national pride"), an enrollment which suggested a certain willingness among non-Cubans to let Cuban Miami remain just that, Cuban, the "incomprehensible presence." In fact there had come to exist in South Florida two parallel cultures, separate but not exactly equal, a key distinction being that only one of the two, the Cuban, exhibited even a remote interest in the activities of the other. "The American community is not really aware of what is happening in the Cuban community," an exiled banker named Luis Botifoll said in a 1983 *Herald* Sunday magazine piece about ten prominent local Cubans. "We are clannish, but at least we know who is whom in the American establishment. They do not." About another of the ten Cubans featured in this piece, Jorge Mas Canosa, the *Herald* had this to say:

> He is an advisor to U.S. senators, a confidant of federal bureaucrats, a lobbyist for anti-Castro U.S. policies, a near unknown in Miami. When his political group sponsored a luncheon speech in Miami by Secretary of Defense Caspar Weinberger, almost none of the American business leaders attending had ever heard of their Cuban host.

The general direction of this piece, which appeared under the   10 cover line "THE CUBANS: *They're ten of the most powerful men in Miami. Half the population doesn't know it*," was, as the *Herald* put it,

> to challenge the widespread presumption that Miami's Cubans are not really Americans, that they are a foreign presence here, an exile community that is trying to turn South Florida into North Cuba.

. . . The top ten are not separatists; they have achieved success in the most traditional ways. They are the solid, bedrock citizens, hard-working humanitarians who are role models for a community that seems determined to assimilate itself into American society.

This was interesting. It was written by one of the few Cubans 11 then on the *Herald* staff, and yet it described, however unwittingly, the precise angle at which Miami Anglos and Miami Cubans were failing to connect: Miami Anglos were in fact interested in Cubans only to the extent that they could cast them as aspiring immigrants, "determined to assimilate," a "hard-working" minority not different in kind from other groups of resident aliens. (But had I met any Haitians, a number of Anglos asked when I said that I had been talking to Cubans.) Anglos (who were, significantly, referred to within the Cuban community as "Americans") spoke of cross-culturalization, and of what they believed to be a meaningful second-generation preference for hamburgers, and rock-and-roll. They spoke of "diversity," and of Miami's "Hispanic flavor," an approach in which 56 percent of the population was seen as decorative, like the Coral Gables arches.

Fixed as they were on this image of the melting pot, of immi- 12 grants fleeing a disruptive revolution to find a place in the American sun, Anglos did not on the whole understand that assimilation would be considered by most Cubans a doubtful goal at best. Nor did many Anglos understand that living in Florida was still at the deepest level construed by Cubans as a temporary condition, an accepted political option shaped by the continuing dream, if no longer the immediate expectation, of a vindicatory return. *El exilio* was for Cubans a ritual, a respected tradition. *La revolución* was also a ritual, a trope fixed in Cuban political rhetoric at least since José Martí, a concept broadly interpreted to mean reform, or progress, or even just change. Ramón Grau San Martín, the president of Cuba during the autumn of 1933 and from 1944 until 1948, had presented himself as a revolutionary, as had his 1948 successor, Carlos Prío. Even Fulgencio Batista had entered Havana life calling for *la revolución*, and had later been accused of betraying it, even as Fidel Castro was now.

This was a process Cuban Miami understood, but Anglo Miami 13 did not, remaining as it did arrestingly innocent of even the most general information about Cuba and Cubans. Miami Anglos for example still had trouble with Cuban names, and Cuban food. When the Cuban novelist Guillermo Cabrera Infante came from London to lecture at Miami-Dade Community College, he was referred to by several Anglo faculty members to whom I spoke as "Infante." Cuban food was widely seen not as a minute variation on that eaten throughout both the Caribbean and the Mediterranean but as "exotic," and full of garlic. A typical Thursday food section of the *Herald* included recipes for Broiled Lemon-Curry Cornish Game Hens, Chicken Tetrazzini, King Cake, Pimiento Cheese, Raisin Sauce for Ham, Sauteed Spiced Peaches, Shrimp Scampi, Easy Beefy Stir-Fry, and four ways to used dried beans ("Those cheap, humble beans that have long sustained the world's poor have become the trendy set's new pet"), none of them Cuban.

This was all consistent, and proceeded from the original con-   14
struction, that of the exile as an immigration. There was no reason to be curious about Cuban food, because Cuban teenagers preferred hamburgers. There was no reason to get Cuban names right, because they were complicated, and would be simplified by the second generation, or even by the first. "Jorge L. Mas" was the way Jorge Mas Canosa's business card read. "Raul Masvidal" was the way Raul Masvidal y Jury ran for mayor of Miami. There was no reason to know about Cuban history, because history was what immigrants were fleeing.

Even the revolution, the reason for the immigration, could be   15
covered in a few broad strokes: "Batista," "Castro," "26 Julio," this last being the particular broad stroke that inspired the Miami Springs Holiday Inn, on July 26, 1985, the thirty-second anniversary of the day Fidel Castro attacked the Moncada Barracks and so launched his six-year struggle for power in Cuba, to run a bar special on Cuba Libres, thinking to attract local Cubans by commemorating their holiday. "It was a mistake," the manager said, besieged by outraged exiles. "The gentleman who did it is from Minnesota."

There was in fact no reason, in Miami as well as in Minnesota,   16
to know anything at all about Cubans, since Miami Cubans were now, if not Americans, at least aspiring Americans, and worthy of Anglo attention to the exact extent that they were proving themselves, in the *Herald*'s words, "role models for a community that seems determined to assimilate itself into American society"; or, as George Bush put it in a 1986 Miami address to the Cuban American National Foundation, "the most eloquent testimony I know to the basic strength and success of America, as well as to the basic weakness and failure of Communism and Fidel Castro."

The use of this special lens, through which the exiles were seen   17
as a tribute to the American system, a point scored in the battle of the ideologies, tended to be encouraged by those outside observers who dropped down from the Northeast corridor for a look and a

column or two. George Will, in *Newsweek*, saw Miami as "a new installment in the saga of America's absorptive capacity," and Southwest Eighth Street as the place where "these exemplary Americans," the seven Cubans who had been gotten together to brief him, "initiated a columnist to fried bananas and black-bean soup and other Cuban contributions to the tanginess of American life." George Gilder, in *The Wilson Quarterly*, drew pretty much the same lesson from Southwest Eighth Street, finding it "more effervescently thriving than its crushed prototype," by which he seemed to mean Havana. In fact Eighth Street was for George Gilder a street that seemed to "percolate with the forbidden commerce of the dying island to the south . . . the Refrescos Cawy, the Competidora and El Cuño cigarettes, the *guayaberas*,[1] the Latin music pulsing from the storefronts, the pyramids of mangoes and tubers, gourds and plantains, the iced coconuts served with a straw, the new theaters showing the latest anti-Castro comedies."

There was nothing on this list, with the possible exception of the "anti-Castro comedies," that could not most days be found on Southwest Eighth Street, but the list was also a fantasy, and a particularly *gringo* fantasy, one in which Miami Cubans, who came from a culture which had represented western civilization in this hemisphere since before there was a United States of America, appeared exclusively as vendors of plantains, their native music "pulsing" behind them. There was in any such view of Miami Cubans an extraordinary element of condescension, and it was the very condescension shared by Miami Anglos, who were inclined to reduce the particular liveliness and sophistication of local Cuban life to a matter of shrines on the lawn and love potions in the *botanicas*, the primitive exotica of the tourist's Caribbean. 18

Cubans were perceived as most satisfactory when they appeared most fully to share the aspirations and manners of middle-class Americans, at the same time adding "color" to the city on appropriate occasions, for example at their *quinces* (the *quinces* were one aspect of Cuban life almost invariably mentioned by Anglos, who tended to present them as evidence of Cuban extravagance, i.e., Cuban irresponsibility, or childishness), or on the day of the annual Calle Ocho Festival, when they could, according to the *Herald*, "samba" in the streets and stir up a paella for two thousand (ten cooks, two thousand mussels, two hundred and twenty pounds of 19

---

[1] *guayaberas:* summer shirts. (Ed.)

lobster, and four hundred and forty pounds of rice), using rowboat oars as spoons. Cubans were perceived as least satisfactory when they "acted clannish," "kept to themselves," "had their own ways," and, two frequent flash points, "spoke Spanish when they didn't need to" and "got political"; complaints, each of them, which suggested an Anglo view of what Cubans should be at significant odds with what Cubans were.

This question of language was curious. The sound of spoken 20 Spanish was common in Miami, but it was also common in Los Angeles, and Houston, and even in the cities of the Northeast. What was unusual about Spanish in Miami was not that it was so often spoken, but that it was so often heard: In, say, Los Angeles, Spanish remained a language only barely registered by the Anglo population, part of the ambient noise, the language spoken by the people who worked in the car wash and came to trim the trees and cleared the tables in restaurants. In Miami Spanish was spoken by the people who ate in the restaurants, the people who owned the cars and the trees, which made, on the socio-auditory scale, a considerable difference. Exiles who felt isolated or declassed by language in New York or Los Angeles thrived in Miami. An entrepreneur who spoke no English could still, in Miami, buy, sell, negotiate, leverage assets, float bonds, and, if he were so inclined, attend galas twice a week, in black tie. "I have been after the *Herald* ten times to do a story about millionaires in Miami who do not speak more than two words in English," one prominent exile told me. " 'Yes' and 'no.' Those are the two words. They come here with five dollars in their pockets and without speaking another word of English they are millionaires."

The truculence a millionaire who spoke only two words of En- 21 glish might provoke among the less resourceful native citizens of a nominally American city was predictable, and manifested itself rather directly. In 1980, the year of Mariel, Dade County voters had approved a referendum requiring that county business be conducted exclusively in English. Notwithstanding the fact that this legislation was necessarily amended to exclude emergency medical and certain other services, and notwithstanding even the fact that many local meetings continued to be conducted in that unbroken alternation of Spanish and English which had become the local patois ("I will be in Boston on Sunday and *desafortunadamente yo tengo un compromiso en* Boston *qu no puedo romper y yo no podre estar con Vds.*," read the minutes of a 1984 Miami City Commission meeting I had occasion to look up. "*En espiritu, estaré, pero* the other members of the commission I am sure are invited . . ."),[1] the very existence of this referendum was seen by many as ground regained, a point made. By 1985 a St. Petersburg optometrist named Robert Melby was launching his third attempt in four years to have English declared the official language of the state of Florida, as it would be in 1986 of California. "I don't know why your legislators here are so, how should I put it?— spineless," Robert Melby complained about those South Florida politicians who knew how to count. "No one down here seems to want to run with the issue."

Even among those Anglos who distanced themselves from such efforts, Anglos who did not perceive themselves as economically or socially threatened by Cubans, there remained considerable uneasiness on the matter of language, perhaps because the inability or the disinclination to speak English tended to undermine their conviction that assimilation was an ideal universally shared by those who were to be assimilated. This uneasiness had for example shown up repeatedly during the 1985 mayoralty campaign, surfacing at odd but apparently irrepressible angles. The winner of that contest, Xavier Suarez, who was born in Cuba but educated in the United States, a graduate of Harvard Law, was reported in a wire service story to speak, an apparently unexpected accomplishment, "flawless English."   22

A less prominent Cuban candidate for mayor that year had unsettled reporters at a televised "meet the candidates" forum by answering in Spanish the questions they asked in English. "For all I or my dumbstruck colleagues knew," the *Herald* political editor complained in print after the event, "he was reciting his high school's alma mater or the ten Commandments over and over again. The only thing I understood was the occasional *Cubanos vota Cubano* he tossed in." It was noted by another *Herald* columnist that of the leading candidates, only one, Raul Masvidal, had a listed telephone number, but: ". . . if you call Masvidal's 661-0259 number on Kiaora Street in Coconut Grove—during the day, anyway—you'd better speak Spanish. I spoke to two women there, and neither spoke enough English to answer the question of whether it was the candidate's number."   23

On the morning this last item came to my attention in the *Herald* I studied it for some time. Raul Masvidal was at that time the chairman of the board of the Miami Savings Bank and the Miami Savings   24

---

[2] I will be in Boston on Sunday and unfortunately I have an appointment in Boston that I can't break and I won't be able to be with you. In spirit, I will be, but the other members of the commission I am sure are invited . . ."

Corporation. He was a former chairman of the Biscayne Bank, and a minority stockholder in the M Bank, of which he had been a founder. He was a member of the Board of Regents for the state university system of Florida. He had paid $600,000 for the house on Kiaora Street in Coconut Grove, buying it specifically because he needed to be a Miami resident (Coconut Grove is part of the city of Miami) in order to run for mayor, and he had sold his previous house, in the incorporated city of Coral Gables, for $1,100,000.

The Spanish words required to find out whether the number 25 listed for the house on Kiaora Street was in fact the candidate's number would have been roughly these: "*¿Es la casa de Raul Masvidal?*" The answer might have been "*Si,*" or the answer might have been "*No.*" It seemed to me that there must be very few people working on daily newspapers along the southern borders of the United States who would consider this exchange entirely out of reach, and fewer still who would not accept it as a commonplace of American domestic-life that daytime telephone calls to middle-class urban households will frequently be answered by women who speak Spanish.

Something else was at work in this item, a real resistance, a 26 balkiness, a coded version of the same message Dade County voters had sent when they decreed that their business be done only in English: WILL THE LAST AMERICAN TO LEAVE MIAMI PLEASE BRING THE FLAG, the famous bumper stickers had read the year of Mariel. "It was the last American stronghold in Dade County," the owner of the Gator Kicks Longneck Saloon, out where Southwest Eighth Street runs into the Everglades, had said after he closed the place for good the night of Super Bowl Sunday, 1986. "Fortunately or unfortunately, I'm not alone in my inability," a *Herald* columnist named Charles Whited had written a week or so later, in a column about not speaking Spanish. "A good many Americans have left Miami because they want to live someplace where everybody speaks one language: theirs." In this context the call to the house on Kiaora Street in Coconut Grove which did or did not belong to Raul Masvidal appeared not as a statement of literal fact but as shorthand, a glove thrown down, a stand, a cry from the heart of a beleaguered raj.

I'm Talking for Justice

MARIA MORENO

I am Maria Moreno, forty years old, mother of twelve children. Born 1
in Karnes City, Texas. Raised in Corpus Christi. Since 1928 I start
working in agricultural work. I been a worker all my life. I know
how to handle a man's job like a man and I'm not ashamed to say it.
I'm American citizen, and I'm talking for justice. I'm asking for justice. Not only for me or for my family, but all the migrant workers.
We been suffering for so long. Waiting and hoping, but it seems like
that our hope been lost. I guess we got the right to do it. I guess we
got the right because we are human beings as everybody.

For so many long years ago our children been suffering. I'm go- 2
ing to tell a little of my life with my own children. My first child was
born, had no doctor. Was born alone, me and my husband. And I
didn't know that a woman supposed to go to the doctor. Second
child born, me and my husband alone. The third one born. Same
thing.

We were working in Texas. Picking cotton, chopping cotton. 3
nineteen thirty-two we're picking cotton, twenty-five cents a hundred. We're chopping cotton, ten cents a row. And have to support
the children who in those days did never know what shoes were on
their feet. Our children didn't know that they have to drink milk every day. Our children drink milk once a week. Our children eat
meat once a week. Why? We can't afford it. That is the reason we
are working, trying to get the agricultural workers organized.

I guess we got rights. I guess we been suffering so much. It is 4
time to ask for justice. We're demanding $1.25, which is, I think, not
very much for a grower to give us. We're asking, we're waiting and
we're hoping for get this $1.25.

Nineteen forty, we came to California. Waiting and hoping to 5
find a better living, a better living condition for ourselves and for

---

Maria Moreno (1922–   ), born in Karnes City, Texas, had only
six months' formal education before becoming a speaker and organizer for the Agricultural Workers' Organizing Committee (AFL-
CIO) in the 1960s. "I'm Talking for Justice," a speech she delivered
in Berkeley in 1961 to raise money for striking California lettuce
workers, appeared unedited in the journal *Regeneracion* (1971).

our family. The braceros[1] came in. We had to move on from the Imperial Valley. We hit Salinas. Here come the braceros. Well, we're tickled anyway when we work a little. We can earn a little money. We can feed our children. Half eat. Don't you think that our children [should have] their stomachs full of food like the rest of you people, the rest of you people that have a union or a better decent wage than we got? The road is our home. The ground is our table.

I've got a twenty-three-year-old son. When he was nineteen 6 years old, he was blind because he was without eat. Nineteen fifty-eight it start raining so hard we can't earn very much money. The little money that we earn. It start raining and raining. And kept on raining a month. We couldn't go to work. All our food was gone. All our money was gone. No hope held.

One day I decided to go to the welfare and ask for something to 7 eat. They refused to help out. Some people think that the welfare help everybody, but they help them when they want to and when they like. If they help them, the food they give we have to work for. They don't give it to us. We have to work and pay for it.

I went to the welfare and they refused to help me. We already 8 had when I went to the welfare no hope and no place to get money or food or anything, so I went to the welfare. We had three weeks without eating more than once a day. Three weeks. I had my baby, three month. I was feeding him water and sugar. The days sped on.

The investigator came home and I told her that she might as 9 well come in the home and search and see what she can find. Anyhow, she did it, and she was satisfied. There was not a thing to eat in that place. Said, "Mrs. Moreno, if you don't get the food for Thursday, you're not going to get anything."

Three days passed by three weeks which we were eating once a 10 day. Three days, my son got blind. He got so weak, he lost all his strength. He was blind for three days. The day that he was blind, my heart was broken in pieces. When I see a strong American. I see how richest America will live. And the real miserable life that we're living. I'm not ashamed to say this in front of nobody because it's truth.

I've got nothing to do. Nowhere to go. All my hopes were lost. 11 Went, called the police and brought them home. Said, "I want you to look at my son. He is real blind." He got surprised. Said, "What happened?" Said, "He lost his strength. He went blind."

We were leading him by his hand. Nineteen-year-old boy. Just 12 imagine what a mother has to pass by. How you think I feel, my son

---

[1] Migrant fieldworkers from Mexico. (Ed.)

blind only because we got nothing to eat while some other tables are full and wasting food? The days pass on, then the door was opened.

Said, "Mrs. Moreno, we didn't know that you really need the 13 food." They did know because I went and knock the doors but got no answer because the agricultural workers been ignored, been forgotten for so many long years.

People been forgotten. They don't care about us. Our home is 14 under the tree. That's the way that we have been treated. We never screamed. We never had a word until now. Like I said, I'm mother of twelve children and I'm working for discovering the things that been hiding for so long—that people must know what we been suffering, what we been through.

People think that because somebody else have something to eat, 15 they think that the whole world have some. But, people, I want you to understand that my family been suffering greatest mockery in the world that I ever seen. When every flame goes out, when you hear no fry pan noise at the stove. Potatoes and beans are gone. The only hope we have is God. We call for Him because we been calling to the people. They don't hear. They don't care. We have an old piano that we bought for $25 with a lot of sacrifice. We get together at that piano and we rejoice and we feel happy.

But the thing that really hurts me is this: that we are living in a 16 rich America, that the people been sending food, the clothing overseas. And then forgotten us. That we are citizens, and we're living in America. That's what really hurts me, but like I said, I hope that you people help us do something for this situation. You won't have to go very far. You travel a little up here to Mendota. Woodlake. Visalia. Firebaugh. Huron. All places around here. You can find out. People sleeping on the floor for so long.

This is the way the agricultural worker lives. This is the way that 17 we have been treated. This is the way that we have been keeping on going.

We're asking for a little different wages. And I hope we'll get it. 18 Growers said that we don't need the $1.25, that we got enough. I'm not trying to say that we're taking away the bread of the ranchers or the farmers. The ranchers say they don't make any money, but one thing I know for sure; they're lying. I never heard about a rancher go and knock at the welfare doors and ask for something to eat like the agricultural workers do.

What I say it's truth, and I'm not afraid to say it. For too long 19 the agricultural workers been afraid. When somebody hollers, we jump. We never answer back. Well, I'm not afraid no more. These are the things I have to say and I'm hope that you understand the things that I say.

Going Home Again: The New American Scholarship Boy

RICHARD RODRIGUEZ

At each step, with every graduation from one level of education to the next, the refrain from bystanders was strangely the same: "Your parents must be so proud of you." I suppose that my parents were proud, although I suspect, too, that they felt more than pride alone as they watched me advance through my education. They seemed to know that my education was separating us from one another, making it difficult to resume familiar intimacies. Mixed with the instincts of parental pride, a certain hurt also communicated itself—too private ever to be adequately expressed in words, but real nonetheless.

The autobiographical facts pertinent to this essay are simply stated in two sentences, though they exist in somewhat awkward juxtaposition to each other. I am the son of Mexican-American parents, who speak a blend of Spanish and English, but who read neither language easily. I am about to receive a Ph.D. in English Renaissance literature. What sort of life—what tensions, feelings, conflicts—connects these two sentences? I look back and remember my life from the time I was seven or eight years old as one of constant movement away from a Spanish-speaking folk culture toward the world of the English-language classroom. As the years passed, I felt myself becoming less like my parents and less comfortable with the assumption of visiting relatives that I was still the Spanish-speaking child they remembered. By the time I began college, visits home became suffused with silent embarrassment: there seemed so little to share, however strong the ties of our affection. My parents would tell me what happened in their lives or in the lives of relatives; I would respond with news of my own. Polite questions would follow. Our conversations came to seem more like interviews.

A few months ago, my dissertation nearly complete, I came upon my father looking through my bookcase. He quietly fingered the volumes of Milton's tracts and Augustine's theology with that

Richard Rodriguez (1944–   ), from San Francisco, is an associate editor for Pacific News Service and author of *Hunger of Memory: The Education of Richard Rodriguez* (1982). "Going Home Again: The New American Scholarship Boy" first appeared in the journal *The American Scholar* (1974).

combination of reverence and distrust those who are not literate sometimes show for the written word. Silently, I watched him from the door of the room. However much he would have insisted that he was "proud" of his son for being able to master the texts, I knew, if pressed further, he would have admitted to complicated feelings about my success. When he looked across the room and suddenly saw me, his body tightened slightly with surprise, then we both smiled.

For many years I kept my uneasiness about becoming a success 4 in education to myself. I did so in part because I wanted to avoid vague feelings that, if considered carefully, I would have no way of dealing with; and in part because I felt that no one else shared my reaction to the opportunity provided by education. When I began to rehearse my story of cultural dislocation publicly, however, I found many listeners willing to admit to similar feelings from their own pasts. Equally impressive was the fact that many among those I spoke with were *not* from nonwhite racial groups, which made me realize that one can grow up to enter the culture of the academy and find it a "foreign" culture for a variety of reasons, ranging from economic status to religious heritage. But why, I next wondered, was it that, though there were so many of us who came from childhood cultures alien to the academy's, we voiced our uneasiness to one another and to ourselves so infrequently? Why did it take *me* so long to acknowledge publicly the cultural costs I had paid to earn a Ph.D. in Renaissance English literature? Why, more precisely, am I writing these words only now when my connection to my past barely survives except as nostalgic memory?

Looking back, a person risks losing hold of the present while be- 5 ing confounded by the past. For the child who moves to an academic culture from a culture that dramatically lacks academic traditions, looking back can jeopardize the certainty he has about the desirability of this new academic culture. Richard Hoggart's description, in *The Uses of Literacy*, of the cultural pressures on such a student, whom Hoggart calls the "scholarship boy," helps make the point. The scholarship boy must give nearly unquestioning allegiance to academic culture, Hoggart argues, if he is to succeed at all, so different is the milieu of the classroom from the culture he leaves behind. For a time, the scholarship boy may try to balance his loyalty between his concretely experienced family life and the more abstract mental life of the classroom. In the end, though, he must choose between the two worlds: if he intends to succeed as a student, he must, literally and figuratively, separate himself from his family, with its gregarious life, and find a quiet place to be alone with his thoughts.

After a while, the kind of allegiance the young student might 6
once have given his parents is transferred to the teacher, the new
parent. Now without the support of the old ties and certainties of
the family, he almost mechanically acquires the assumptions, practices, and style of the classroom milieu. For the loss he might otherwise feel, the scholarship boy substitutes an enormous enthusiasm
for nearly everything having to do with school.

How readily I read my own past into the portrait of Hoggart's 7
scholarship boy. Coming from a home in which mostly Spanish was
spoken, for example, I had to decide to forget Spanish when I began
my education. To succeed in the classroom, I needed psychologically to sever my ties with Spanish. Spanish represented an alternate
culture as well as another language—and the basis of my deepest
sense of relationship to my family. Although I recently taught myself to read Spanish, the language that I see on the printed page is
not quite the language I heard in my youth. That other Spanish, the
spoken Spanish of my family, I remember with nostalgia and guilt:
guilt because I cannot explain to aunts and uncles why I do not answer their questions any longer in their own idiomatic language.
Nor was I able to explain to teachers in graduate school, who regularly expected me to read and speak Spanish with ease, why my
very ability to reach graduate school as a student of English literature in the first place required me to loosen my attachments to a language I spoke years earlier. Yet, having lost the ability to speak
Spanish, I never forgot it so totally that I could not understand it.
Hearing Spanish spoken on the street reminded me of the community I once felt a part of, and still cared deeply about. I never forgot
Spanish so thoroughly, in other words, as to move outside the range
of its nostalgic pull.

Such moments of guilt and nostalgia were, however, just that— 8
momentary. They punctuated the history of my otherwise successful
progress from *barrio* to classroom. Perhaps they even encouraged it.
Whenever I felt my determination to succeed wavering, I tightened
my hold on the conventions of academic life.

Spanish was one aspect of the problem, my parents another. 9
They could raise deeper, more persistent doubts. They offered encouragement to my brothers and me in our work, but they also
spoke, only half jokingly, about the way education was putting "big
ideas" into our heads. When we would come home, for example,
and challenge assumptions we earlier believed, they would be
forced to defend their beliefs (which, given our new verbal skills,
they did increasingly less well) or, more frequently, to submit to our
logic with the disclaimer, "It's what we were taught in our time to
believe. . . ." More important, after we began to leave home for col-

lege, they voiced regret about how "changed" we had become, how much further away from one another we had grown. They partly yearned for a return to the time before education assumed their children's primary loyalty. This yearning was renewed each time they saw their nieces and nephews (none of whom continued their education beyond high school, all of whom continued to speak fluent Spanish) living according to the conventions and assumptions of their parents' culture. If I was already troubled by the time I graduated from high school by that refrain of congratulations ("Your parents must be so proud. . . ."), I realize now how much more difficult and complicated was my progress into academic life for my parents, as they saw the cultural foundation of their family erode, than it was for me.

Yet my parents were willing to pay the price of alienation and   10 continued to encourage me to become a scholarship boy because they perceived, as others of the lower classes had before them, the relation between education and social mobility. Lacking the former themselves made them acutely aware of its necessity as prerequisite for the latter. They sent their children off to school in the hopes of their acquiring something "better" beyond education. Notice the assumption here that education is something of a tool or license—a means to an end, which has been the traditional way the lower or working classes have viewed the value of education in the past. That education might alter children in more basic ways than providing them with skills, certificates of proficiency, and even upward mobility, may come as a surprise for some, but the financial cost is usually tolerated.

Complicating my own status as a scholarship boy in the last ten   11 years was the rise, in the mid-1960s, of what was then called "the Third World Student Movement." Racial minority groups, led chiefly by black intellectuals, began to press for greater access to higher education. The assumption behind their criticism, like the assumption of white working-class families, was that educational opportunity was useful for economic and social advancement. The racial minority leaders went one step further, however, and it was this step that was probably most revolutionary. Minority students came to the campus feeling that they were representative of larger groups of people—that, indeed, they were advancing the condition of entire societies by their matriculation. Actually, this assumption was not altogether new to me. Years before, educational success was something my parents urged me to strive for precisely because it would reflect favorably on *all* Mexican-Americans—specifically, my intellectual achievement would help deflate the stereotype of the "dumb Pancho." This early goal was only given greater currency by the rhetoric of the Third World spokesmen. But it was the fact that I felt myself suddenly much more a "public" Mexican-American, a representative of sorts, that was to prove so crucial for me during these years.

One college admissions officer assured me one day that he rec- 12 ognized my importance to his school precisely as deriving from the fact that, after graduation. I would surely be "going back to [my] community." More recently, teachers have urged me not to trouble over the fact that I am not "representative" of my culture, assuring me that I can serve as a "model" for those still in the *barrio* working toward academic careers. This is the line that I hear, too, when being interviewed for a faculty position. The interviewer almost invariably assumes that, because I am racially a Mexican-American, I can serve as a special counselor to minority students. The expectation is that I still retain the capacity for intimacy with "my people."

This new way of thinking about the possible uses of education is 13 what has made the entrance of minority students into higher education so dramatic. When the minority group student was accepted into the academy, he came—in everyone's mind—as part of a "group." When I began college, I barely attracted attention except perhaps as a slightly exotic ("Are you from India?") brown-skinned student; by the time I graduated, my presence was annually noted by, among others, the college public relations office as "one of the fifty-two students with Spanish surnames enrolled this year." By having his presence announced to the campus in this way, the minority group student was unlike any other scholarship boy the campus had seen before. The minority group student now dramatized more publicly, if also in new ways, the issues of cultural dislocation that education forces, issues that are not solely racial in origin. When Richard Rodriguez *became* a Chicano, the dilemmas he earlier had as a scholarship boy were complicated but not decisively altered by the fact that he had assumed a group identity.

The assurance I heard that, somehow, I was being useful to my 14 community by being a student was gratefully believed, because it gave me a way of dealing with the guilt and cynicism that each year came my way along with the scholarships, grants, and, lately, job offers from schools which a few years earlier would have refused me admission as a student. Each year, in fact, it became harder to believe that my success had anything to do with my intellectual performance, and harder to resist the conclusion that it was due to my minority group status. When I drove to the airport, on my way to London as a Fulbright Fellow last year, leaving behind cousins of my age who were already hopelessly burdened by financial insecurity and dead-end jobs, momentary guilt could be relieved by the thought that somehow my trip was beneficial to persons other than myself. But, of course, if the thought was a way of dealing with the guilt, it was also the reason for the guilt. Sitting in a university library, I would notice a janitor of my own race and grow uneasy; I was, I knew, in a rough way a beneficiary of his condition. Guilt was accompanied by cynicism. The most dazzlingly talented minority students I know today refuse to believe that their success is wholly based on their own talent, or even that when they speak in a classroom anyone hears them as anything but *the* voice of their minority group. It is scarcely surprising, then, though initially it probably seemed puzzling, that so many of the angriest voices on the campus against the injustices of racism came from those not visibly its primary victims.

It became necessary to believe the rhetoric about the value of 15 one's presence on campus simply as a way of living with one's "success." Among ourselves, however, minority group students often admitted to a shattering sense of loss—the feeling that, somehow, something was happening to us. Especially from students who had not yet become accustomed, as by that time I had, to the campus, I remember hearing confessions of extreme discomfort and isolation. Our close associations, the separate dining-room tables, and the special dormitories helped to relieve some of the pain, but only some of it.

Significant here was the development of the ethnic studies concept—black studies, Chicano studies, etcetera—and the related assumption held by minority group students in a number of departments that they could keep in touch with their old cultures by making these cultures the subject of their study. Here again one notices how different the minority student was from other comparable students: other scholarship boys—poor Jews and the sons of various immigrant cultures—came to the academy singly, much more inclined to accept the courses and material they found. The ethnic studies concept was an indication that, for a multitude of reasons, the new racial minority group students were not willing to give up so easily their ties with their old cultures.

The importance of these new ethnic studies was that they introduced the academy to subject matter that generally deserved to be studied, and at the same time offered a staggering critique of the academy's tendency toward parochialism. Most minority group intellectuals never noted this tendency toward academic parochialism. They more often saw the reason for, say, the absence of a course on black literature in an English department as a case of simple racism. That it might instead be an instance of the fact that academic culture can lose track of human societies and whole areas of human experience was rarely raised. Never asking such a question, the minority group students never seemed to wonder either if as teachers their own courses might suffer the same cultural limitations other seminars and classes suffered. Consequently, in a peculiar way the new minority group critics of higher education came to justify the academy's assumptions. The possibility that academic culture could encourage one to grow out of touch with cultures beyond its conceptual horizon was never seriously considered.

Too often in the last ten years one heard minority group stu- 18 dents repeat the joke, never very funny in the first place, about the racial minority academic who ended up sounding more "white" than white academics. Behind the scorn for such a figure was the belief that the new generation of minority group students would be able to avoid having to make similar kinds of cultural concessions. The pressures that might have led to such conformity went unexamined.

For the last few years my annoyance at hearing such jokes was 19 doubtless related to the fact that I was increasingly beginning to sense that I was the "bleached" academic the minority group students found so laughable. I suppose I had always sensed that my cultural allegiance was undergoing subtle alterations as I was being educated. Only when I finished my course work in graduate school and went off to England for my dissertation year did I grasp how far I had traveled from my cultural origins. My year in England was actually my first opportunity to write and reflect upon the kind of material that I would spend my life producing. It was my first chance, too, to be free simultaneously of the distractions of course-work and of the insecurities of trying to find my niche in academic life. Sitting in the reading room of the British Museum, I no longer doubted that I had joined academic society. Ironically, this feeling of having finally arrived allowed me to look back to the community whence I came. That I was geographically farther away from my home than I had ever been lent a metaphorical resonance to the cultural distance I suddenly felt.

But that feeling was not pleasing. The reward of feeling a part of 20 the world of the British Museum was an odd one. Each morning I would arrive at the reading room and grow increasingly depressed by the silence and what the silence implied—that my life as a scholar would require self-absorption. Who, I wondered, would find my work helpful enough to want to read it? Was not my dissertation—whose title alone would puzzle my relatives—only my grandest exercise thus far in self-enclosure? The sight of the heads around me bent over their texts and papers, many so thoroughly engrossed that they wouldn't look up at the silent clock overhead for hours at a stretch, made me recall the remarkable noises of life in my family home. The tedious prose I was writing, a prose constantly qualified by footnotes, reminded me of the capacity for passionate statement those of the culture I was born into commanded—and which, could it be, I had now lost.

As I remembered it during those gray English afternoons, the 21 past rushed forward to define more precisely my present condition. Remembering my youth, a time when I was not restricted to a chair but ran barefoot under a summer sun that tightened my skin with its white heat, made the fact that it was only my mind that "moved" each hour in the library painfully obvious.

I did need to figure out where I had lost touch with my past. I 22 started to become alien to my family culture the day I became a scholarship boy. In the British Museum the realization seemed obvious. But later, returning to America, I returned to minority group students who were still speaking of their cultural ties to their past. How was I to tell them what I had learned about myself in England?

A short while ago, a group of enthusiastic Chicano undergradu- 23 ates came to my office to ask me to teach a course to high school students in the *barrio* on the Chicano novel. This new literature, they assured me, has an important role to play in helping to shape the consciousness of a people currently without adequate representation in literature. Listening to them I was struck immediately with the cultural problems raised by their assumption. I told them that the novel is not capable of dealing with Chicano experience adequately, simply because most Chicanos are not literate, or are at least not yet comfortably so. This is not something Chicanos need to apologize for (though, I suppose, remembering my own childhood ambition to combat stereotypes of the Chicano as mental menial, it is not something easily admitted). Rather the genius and value of those Chicanos who do not read seem to me to be largely that their reliance on voice, the spoken word, has given them the capacity for intimate conversation that I, as someone who now relies heavily on the written word, can only envy. The second problem, I went on, is more in the nature of a technical one: the novel, in my opinion, is not a form capable of being true to the basic sense of communal life that typifies Chicano culture. What the novel as a literary form is best capable of representing is solitary existence set against a large social background. Chicano novelists, not coincidentally, nearly always fail to capture the breathtakingly rich family life of most Chicanos, and instead often describe only the individual Chicano in transit between Mexican and American cultures.

I said all of this to the Chicano students in my office, and could 24 see that little of it made an impression. They seemed only frustrated by what they probably took to be a slick, academic justification for evading social responsibility. After a time, they left me, sitting alone. . . .

There is a danger of being misunderstood here. I am not sug- 25 gesting that an academic cannot reestablish ties of any kind with his old culture. Indeed, he can have an impact on the culture of his childhood. But as an academic, one exists by definition in a culture separate from one's nonacademic roots and, therefore, any future ties one has with those who remain "behind" are complicated by one's new cultural perspective.

Paradoxically, the distance separating the academic from his 26 nonacademic past can make his past seem, if not closer, then clearer. It is possible for the academic to understand the culture from which he came "better" than those who still live within it. In my own experience, it has only been as I have come to appraise my past through categories and notions dervied from the social sciences that I have been able to think of Chicano life in cultural terms at all. Characteristics I took for granted or noticed only in passing—the spontaneity, the passionate speech, the trust in concrete experience, the willingness to think communally rather than individually—these are all significant phenomena to me now as aspects of a total culture. (My parents have neither the time nor the inclination to think about their culture as a culture.) Able to conceptualize a sense of Chicano culture, I am now also more attracted to that culture than I was before. The temptation now is to try to preserve those traits of my old culture that have not yet, in effect, atrophied.

The racial self-consciousness of minority group students during 27 the last few years evident in the ethnic costumes, the stylized gestures, and the idiomatic though often evasive devices for insisting on one's continuing membership in the community of the past, are also indications that the minority group student has gained a new appreciation of the culture of his origin precisely because of his earlier alienation from it. As a result, Chicano students sometimes become more Chicano than most Chicanos. I remember, for example, my father's surprise when, walking across my college campus one afternoon, we came upon two Chicano academics wearing serapes. He and my mother were also surprised—indeed offended—when they earlier heard student activists use the word "Chicano." For them the term was a private one, primarily descriptive of persons they knew. It suggested intimacy. Hearing the word shouted into a microphone by a stranger left them bewildered. What they could not understand was that the student activist finds it easier than they to use "Chicano" in a more public way, for his distance from their culture and his membership in academic culture permits a wider and more abstract view.

The Mexican-Americans who begin to call themselves Chicanos 28 in this new way are actually forming a new version of what it means to be a Chicano. The culture that didn't see itself as a culture is suddenly prized and identified for being one. The price one pays for this new self-consciousness is the knowledge of just that—it is *new*—and this knowledge is not available to those who remain at home. So it is knowledge that separates as well as unites people. Wanting more desperately than ever to assert his ties with the newly visible culture, the minority group student is tempted to exploit those characteristics of that culture that might yet survive in him. But the self-consciousness never allows one to feel completely at ease with the old culture. Worse, the knowledge of the culture of the past often leaves one feeling strangely solitary. At home, I hear relatives speak and find myself analyzing too much of what they say. It is embarrassing being a cultural anthropologist in one's own family kitchen. I keep feeling myself little more than a cultural voyeur. I often come away from family gatherings suspecting, in fact, that what conceptions of my culture I carry with me are no more than illusions. Because they were never there before, because no one back home shares them, I grow less and less to trust their reliability: too often they seem no more than mental bubbles floating before an academic's eye.

Many who have taught minority group students in the last 29 decade testify to sensing characteristics of a childhood culture still very much alive in these students. Should the teacher make these students aware of these characteristics? Initially, most of us would probably answer negatively. Better to trust the unconscious survival of the past than the always problematical, sometimes even clownish, re-creations of it. But the cultural past cannot be assured of survival; perhaps many of its characteristics are lost simply because the student is never encouraged to look for them. Even those that do survive do so tenuously. As a teacher, one can only hope that the best qualities in his minority group students' cultural legacy aren't altogether snuffed out by academic education.

More easy to live with and distinguishable from self-conscious 30 awareness of the past are the ways the past unconsciously survives—perhaps even yet survives in me. As it turns out, the issue becomes less acute with time. With each year, the chance that the student is unaware of his cultural legacy is diminished as the habit of academic reflectiveness grows stronger. Although the culture of the academy makes innocence about one's cultural past less likely, this same culture, and the conceptual tools it provides, increases the desire to want to write and speak about the past. The paradox persists.

Awaiting the scholarship boy who finally acknowledges the fact 31 that his perceptions of reality have changed is the dilemma of action. The sentimental reaction to this knowledge entails merely a refusal to renew contact with one's nonacademic culture lest one contaminate it. The problem, however, with this sentimental solution is that it overlooks the way academic culture renders one capable of dealing with the transactions of mass society. Academic culture, with its habits of conceptualization and abstraction, allows those of us from other cultures to deal with each other in a mass society. In this sense academic culture does have a profound political impact. Although people intent upon social mobility think of education as a means to an end, education does become an end: its culture allows one to exist more easily in a society increasingly anonymous and impersonal. The truth is, the academic's distance from his own experience brings the capacity for communicating with bureaucracies and understanding one's position in society—a prerequisite for political action.

If the sentimental reaction to nonacademic culture is to fear 32 changing it, the political response, typical especially of working-class and lately minority group leaders, is to see higher education solely in terms of its political and social possibilities. Its cultural consequences, in this view, are disregarded. At this time when we are so keenly aware of social and economic inequality, it might seem beside the point to warn those who are working to bring about equality that education alters culture as well as economic status. And yet, if there is one main criticism that I, as a minority group student, must make of minority group leaders in their past attacks on the "racism" of the academy, it is that they never distinguished between my right to higher education and the desirability of my actually entering the academy—which is another way of saying again that they never recognized that there were things I could lose by becoming a scholarship boy.

Certainly, the academy changes those from alien cultures more 33 than it is changed by them. While minority groups had an impact on higher education, largely because of their advantage in coming as a group, within the last few years students such as myself, who finally ended up certified as academics, also ended up sounding very much like the academics we found when we came to the campus. I do not enjoy making such admissions. But perhaps now the time has come when questions about the cultural costs of education ought to be delayed no longer. Those of us who have been scholarship boys know in our bones that our education has exacted a large price in exchange for the large benefits it has conferred upon us. And what is sadder to consider, after we have paid that price, we go home and casually change the cultures that nurtured us. My parents today understand how they are "Chicanos" in a large and impersonal sense. The gains from such knowledge are clear. But so, too, are the reasons for regret.

Vietnamese Refugees: Overcoming Culture Clash

ELLYN BACHE

Ten years have passed since the last chapter of this journal was writ- 1
ten, and more than fourteen since Kim and Quang escaped from
Vietnam along with 125,000 of their countrypeople. Not surprisingly, the situation for both refugees and sponsors today is vastly
different from what it was then.

The postwar mood that greeted Kim and Quang was not entirely 2
sympathetic—not just in the "pull up the drawbridge" sense that always makes life difficult for newcomers, but also because they were
obviously Vietnamese, obviously "different," at a time when many
people didn't want to look at refugees and be reminded of recent
events in Vietnam. Also, unemployment was high, causing some to
feel that existing jobs should go to Americans, not to foreigners. The
policy of scattering the refugees to sponsors throughout the country
was partly a reaction to these sentiments—a hope that if the Vietnamese were spread widely enough, they would not be too visible
in any one job market and might conveniently blend into the landscape. As everyone knows, within a year they began to make what
has continued to be a pilgrimage to California and other selected
pockets of the country, where they have become very visible indeed.
The initial scattering of the refugees turned out to be one of the inherent cruelties of the program. Penniless and without the means to
travel independently at first, they were at the mercy of Americans
who bewildered them and made them long for other countrypeople
to whom they could turn for support.

As time passed, problems like this were addressed and the trial- 3
and-error lessons of those first efforts gradually incorporated into a
formal policy. In the years after 1975, continuing upheaval in Southeast Asia brought not only more Vietnamese into the country, but
also Cambodians and Laotians. Between 1979 and 1981 alone, sev-

---

Ellyn Bache (1942–   ), born in Washington, D.C., is the author
of articles, reviews, short stories, and the novel *Safe Passage* (1988).
"Vietnamese Refugees: Overcoming Culture Clash" is the epilogue
from *Culture Clash* (second edition, 1989), about her experiences as
American sponsor of a refugee family.

eral hundred thousand "boat people" arrived. Others were coming from elsewhere around the globe including Afghanistan, Latin America, and Eastern Europe. Events contributed to bring in nearly 12,000 Ethiopians between 1983 and 1988. With each new group, refugee resettlement became more sophisticated. Overseas Refugee Training Programs were set up in the Philippines and Thailand to provide newcomers with six months of English language instruction, cultural training, and job information before they arrived in the United States. American sponsors were given more orientation. Federal policies were devised to forestall long-term dependence on welfare by encouraging early economic self-sufficiency. The goal became a job within four months of arrival. When it became apparent that groups from certain areas of the world did not do well scattered and isolated from their countrypeople, efforts were made to cluster them in communities where they could draw strength from each other's presence. At this writing nearly a million Indochinese live in this country. A newcomer is often sponsored by his own relatives; there is also help available from both the Indochinese (or Ethiopian, Amerasian, etc.) community and a host of social service organizations. The transition still isn't easy, but it is often more humane.

What hasn't changed is the friction that inevitably arises between new Americans and traditional American culture. This clashing of cultures is not much different today than it was for us and for Kim and Quang fourteen years ago. The difficulties seem to be much the same no matter where the refugees come from and don't seem to be prevented by most orientation programs. We had a glimpse of this when Kim and Quang, having been through all the ups and downs of resettlement, later became sponsors themselves—of Kim's uncle, his wife, and children, who came with the 1979 boat people. Though Kim and Quang spoke his language and could tell him about their own experiences, the uncle complained bitterly about his expenses that first year, especially his fuel bills (about which he had been forewarned). His sympathetic landlord finally gave him half a tank of oil as a gift. Later, as soon as he saved some money, the uncle hooked up to cable TV and paid extra for the HBO option. He and Quang had a bitter fight about this. HBO could wait until later, Quang said. Basic cable service gave him plenty of channels; he didn't need an extra bill for a few movies. The uncle ignored him; he wanted HBO *now*. Nor could he understand why he couldn't afford a house when Quang had one, or a new car. 4

"I tell him you work, you save money, then you buy," Quang told us, "but he no understand." The uncle believed Quang had been given a large sum of subsidy money that he (the uncle) wasn't getting (in fact, the rules had changed and the uncle didn't get the 5 small cash subsidy Quang had been given a few years before). The uncle also thought he was entitled to something extra because he had fought on the American side in Vietnam and spent two years in jail afterwards as a result. He was certain there was some information—or more particularly, some available money—he wasn't being told about.

This time, Kim and Quang bore the brunt of that first year of disappointment and distrust, even though they were relatives with a shared language and culture. Even Quang's counsel, which certainly must have seemed more reliable than Ben's advice seemed to Quang at first, couldn't overcome a lifetime of habits and expectations. It took the uncle about the same time it had taken Kim and Quang to realize he had come to the U.S. with unrealistic expectations. But as with Kim and Quang, he gradually adjusted like many others before and since.

Kim and Quang's ongoing experience since the end of this journal is in many ways typical of the success of the 1975 Vietnamese refugees. The fear that the refugees would become a long-term welfare burden had been calmed by the fact that 94 percent of the heads of household were working. By 1979, Kim and Quang owned a house and two cars. That year, they had their second son, Bobby. Kim put him into daycare with his brother and went back to work to save money for the second, more modern house the family bought in 1980. Instead of selling the first house, they turned it into a rental property to generate more income. By then Minh was attending the University of Maryland, and Lan was in school in California. Kim and Quang were helping both of them financially and also sending goods to their families in Vietnam. When, in the early 1980s, Kim's father and younger brother escaped from Vietnam, they soon joined the family in Maryland.

As the household grew, the family considered going into a business that would provide work for the men just arriving in this country as well as for Quang himself. Briefly, Quang considered opening a home remodeling firm in California, to serve the Vietnamese community. (Kim's father wanted to be in a warmer climate and near friends on the west coast.) But eventually, they went in another direction entirely, into a business they knew virtually nothing about but which they approached with the same survival skills that had served them earlier. By selling both their houses, Kim and Quang were able to buy a shrimp boat in a Gulf coast town in Mississippi, where they moved their entire family.

The move wasn't—and hasn't been—easy. At the swimming pool of the apartment complex where they lived, their children were teased and bullied for being Vietnamese—a problem they hadn't anticipated. Their shrimp boat was old, in need of repairs, and so slow that when they heard of an area where shrimp were running, they were among the last to reach it. Once Quang learned enough of the business to be competitive, storms ruined an entire shrimping season. Kim's father decided to leave Mississippi to resettle in California, taking some of Quang's "help" with him.

But as they had done before, Kim and Quang persevered. One 10 thing that served them well was their fluency in English, which some of the other immigrant shrimpers lacked. This put Quang into the position of spokesman in situations that required dealing with the English-speaking population and earned him the respect of his new colleagues. He repaired his boat and later replaced it with a newer one. The family rented a house away from the rabble who teased their children—a house that served their purposes although it was never as comfortable as their homes in Maryland. Kim had two more babies and took a part-time job in a restaurant. Eventually, the family bought a small Oriental grocery which Kim now runs full-time and where Quang helps during the off-season. Their children, like most children of those 1975 refugees, are bright and cheerful; they excel in school and think in English though they speak rapid and (they tell us) "very bad" Vietnamese. During a visit last year, their three-year-old daughter gleefully called Ben an "uggie-face"—a term, Kim assured us, she learned from her three unruly brothers. Kim has not forgotten her good manners, and her daughter, it seems, has inherited her gumption and high spirits.

Kim's sister, Lan, married another Vietnamese refugee about a 11 year after her move to California. Today they live and work near Los Angeles and are raising a daughter. Minh received her degree in computer science from the University of Maryland and entered the job market as a professional. She works for a high-tech company in North Carolina and will soon be married. Incredibly—to us—she is now a woman of twenty-eight. When she came here, she was a child of fourteen.

Condensed like this, Kim and Quang's story sounds like the 12 Great American Dream retold—the story of immigrant groups before them as well as that of the 1975 Vietnamese. Part of the reason for their coming was to achieve a comfortable standard of living and it shouldn't surprise anyone that they did. What is more significant is that they opted to put it at risk when they moved to Mississippi in their effort to provide a better situation not just for themselves but for their extended family. Their efforts, however, have required no small sacrifice. They have lived since the move in modest rented quarters, only recently buying a lot on which Quang hopes to build a house from one of Ben's plans. They continue to spend countless hours and dollars helping their family overseas and their relatives in this country. For years, depending on the political situation abroad, they have sent cash, jeans and bicycles to be sold on the black market. In this country, they have provided housing, guidance, money and shrimping work to friends and family who need it, some of them young men wanting summer jobs to finance the college educations Kim and Quang themselves will never have. We feel honored to have known people of such grit, determination, and character.

We live a thousand miles from each other now, and though our visits seem too infrequent, we feel as if we are being reunited not just with friends but with family. Kim makes her famous spring rolls, which everyone downs by the handful. We reminisce about our early years together, telling stories Mike and Lisa (now in their late teens) and Kim's oldest son, Tommy (in his early teens) like to hear because they claim to remember some of what happened. Ben and Quang discuss the housing market and interest rates. Kim and I fill each other in on people we keep in touch with in Maryland. We are genuinely happy to see each other. Because of what we went through together, we share a common history, many memories (both painful and pleasant), and many friends. 13

Our son, Mike, was four when Kim and Quang arrived. He has never seen Vietnamese people as "different" and, in fact, has often seemed to identify with his Vietnamese friends and to be more comfortable with them than he is with his American ones, both in Maryland and now since our move to coastal North Carolina, where the Vietnamese population is small. I particularly remember an incident when he was about ten when he and a companion got into a fight with a third boy who called Mike's friend a "chink." What infuriated both boys most was that the name-caller had not been able to see that Mike's friend was Vietnamese, not Chinese. I could never understand why this was the salient point, but to them it seemed obvious. There are probably many subtleties of this sort that I will never understand; I'm glad my children do. 14

Rocky as the beginning of the resettlement program was for both us as individual sponsors for the refugees and for the organizations which administered it, the program was nevertheless served well by the underlying conviction that people escaping from oppression should be helped as quickly as possible. Today, the emphasis has taken a disturbing turn to defining terms instead of offering aid. Is one who seeks political asylum (that is, one who flees because of "a well-founded fear of persecution" based on political or other criteria) more a refugee than one who hopes for a better life overseas? The "economic migrant" is often sent back or kept in refugee camps indefinitely. Should we really take more refugees when not all the 15 groups already here have "done well"? (Someone who has "done well" is generally defined as someone who is self-supporting; someone who has "done poorly" is on welfare.)

To us, this kind of thinking is chilling. Is the "true refugee's" potential life in a political prison worse than the "economic migrant's" slow starvation? If someone has the courage to take a fishing boat into storm- or pirate-ridden waters to escape an intolerable situation, isn't that the kind of person we want in the U.S.? Do well-fed bureaucrats have the right to define "intolerable"? Because of the efforts of American Jews to keep the memory of the Holocaust alive, we have recently seen memorialized the refugee boat that landed in Florida during World War II and was sent back to Germany, where its passengers died in concentration camps. Despite such efforts, in May 1988, one of our own U.S. Navy ships turned away a floundering boat with over a hundred refugees on it. Before it was rescued by Filipino fishermen a month later, the bodies of the dead were cannibalized, and some of the passengers were allegedly drowned to provide food for the others; ultimately, only fifty-two people survived. Does history teach us anything? 16

As countries like ours quibble over definitions, countries like Thailand, Malaysia, and Indonesia, where the refugees go first— countries of "first asylum"—become reluctant to accept refugees, fearing that they will be stuck with them rather than simply moving them through. This is not an unfounded concern. Thousands of refugees sit for years in stark and inhumane camps with little hope of getting out. As regulations in the resettlement countries have tightened, first-asylum countries have pushed boats back into international waters, located refugee camps on dangerous borders, or made life in the campus increasingly harsh, hoping word will get back to the homeland and stem the refugee tide. In this respect, the situation is far more grim than it was in 1975. 17

Compared to the sheer inhumanity of what is happening on an international scale, the justification that is sometimes put forth for limiting the influx of refugees into the U.S. seems almost ludicrous. Many fear that some groups will become long-term welfare burdens, developing a welfare mentality that will result in generation after generation on public support. But in the relatively few years that have passed since the recent refugee movement began, how can accurate predictions be made? Short-term dependency is to be expected; it isn't necessarily indicative of what is to come. Like many of the desperate "economic migrants" we are so unwilling to take, my great-grandmother was illiterate when she arrived in the United States from Russia. She lived here forty years, never spoke a word of English, and had to be supported all her life. There was no wel- 18 fare in those days, but if there had been, she would have been considered one of those who did not "do well." But her children were neither illiterate nor welfare recipients; like most of their generation, they gave to American society far more than they took. So it is likely to be with the children of the refugees in this country today. The offspring of the 1975 Vietnamese are thriving; they provide a disproportionate number of high school valedictorians, outdistance their peers in math, and promise to become the brightest in scientific fields. Other groups who came later, from less advantaged backgrounds, may take longer to catch up. But there is evidence that, despite the fears of long-term dependency, they are often doing better than expected. The Hmong from the mountains of Laos, long targeted as a group that "struggles" (that is, takes welfare), are "doing well" in some communities. Even where the statistics aren't promising—as in Fresno, California, where more Hmong live than anywhere else outside Southeastern Asia—innovative local programs have been helping improve a dismal unemployment rate in a still-sluggish economy. Teenage Hmong students are surprising everyone by scoring as well as or better than their American counterparts on certain standardized tests, though so far few are continuing on to college because of cultural traditions. Historically, every incoming group has made ours a more complex and richer culture. Our experience with Kim and Quang is one small example of how understanding and appreciation can occur between peoples whose cultures clash. Their experience demonstrates the changes that are possible in the refugees themselves as they become self-reliant and contribute to the larger community. The past fourteen years have made aspects of resettlement smoother for all concerned; that is something to build on. Our hope is that we will remain the strong, resourceful nation we have always been and leave the doors open.

What's behind the "Asian Mask"?

ALEXANDRA TANTRANON-SAUR

First the "yellow peril," now the "model minority"—most of you 1
know enough to scoff at these racist stereotypes. Some are beginning to know the violence and sorrow visited upon the Asian and
Pacific peoples in this country by ordinary white people blinded by
stereotypes, and mourn and rage with us as we demand justice.

But there is yet another layer to penetrate, a layer of seemingly 2
innocuous assumptions, that clouds your vision of us, and confuses
your attempts to find, work with, experience us. You see us wearing
masks; we see you imagining we should prefer your cultures to
ours! Let's take a look at this "Asian mask."

Asian/Pacific people are quiet. Asian/Pacific people are not quiet! 3
Certainly in this area[1] most of us have had a chance to visit one Chinatown or another; is it quiet? Lots of Chinese, especially the older
immigrants, walking on the streets having loud and musical conversations with each other. Chinese working-class women waiting tables and shouting to each other and the cooks. Pushing their carts of
dim sum through the aisles, tempting the weekend brunch crowd
with *"Ha gow! Shui mei! Cha-shu bow!"*[2] For the Chinese, as for many
other peoples, the issue of speaking quietly versus loudly is a class
issue.

And as for the volume of spoken words—no one can tell me 4
Asian/Pacific people don't say much. My mother, sister and I outtalk
my non-Asian father hands down. My Asian/Pacific friends can
outtalk me. Go into the Thai Buddhist temple during service. The
monks have to chant over the microphone; everyone else is talking.
In language class, the children talk and the teachers talk louder.

---

[1] The San Francisco Bay area.
[2] Different types of Chinese hors d'oeuvres. (Ed.)

Alexandra Tantranon-Saur (1952–   ), born in New York City of
Thai and English-Swedish parents, is a computer consultant and
luthier (builder of musical instruments) in Oakland, California.
"What's behind the 'Asian Mask' " was first published in the journal *Our Asian Inheritance* (1986).

Don't get me wrong; I'm sure there are some quiet Asian/Pacific 5
people. I've heard there are. (Even I occasionally like to be quiet.) I
just don't know any.

So why does it appear to non-Asian/Pacific people (and in fact to 6
many Asian/Pacific Americans as well) that we are quiet? A closer
look at some common Asian/Pacific-American conversational habits
may surprise you.

The *pause.* I learned the proper way to speak was to leave pauses 7
in between thoughts and even sentences. We sculpt the flow of our
words with silences; spaces for thinking, reflecting, relaxing. Get together with people who talk like this, hold your tongue, and you'll
see how comfortably a conversation goes. You can think with
pauses! You can see that, from a purely mechanical point of view,
most people who speak without pauses will be constantly interrupting us; and while we wait for the longer pause which signals that
the speaker has finished a thought and that the next speaker may
start, the non-Asian/Pacific people will talk on and on, marveling
that they have found such a good listener who seems to have nothing to say.

But this is more than just a mechanical speech pattern. I was 8
taught, and I observe this in other Asian/Pacific Americans, to be
constantly aware of the attention level of my listener, in fact to monitor and nurture it. The *pause* is part of this. If someone else immediately grabs the moment of silence, then that person must not have
been listening with much attention, right? In fact, they may have
been waiting desperately to get a chance to unload. So of course
they should get the attention if they're that desperate.

The pause is also often lengthened into the *question pause.* That 9
is: from time to time it is good to stop in the middle and see if a listener asks, "What else? Say more!" This is a useful check to see if
they are listening and interested. If they don't ask, why continue to
talk?

In addition to monitoring the attention level in our listener, the 10
start-off question is the most clear example of actively building our listener's attention level. You all know this one. I want to tell you what
I think about the World Bank (we have been talking about canoe-
ing), so I ask you what *you* think about the World Bank. Why don't I
just start out on the World Bank? Well, why should I assume that
you'll be able to listen to that? First I check, and I listen to you, and
by the time you have gotten whatever you need to off your chest,
you will probably realize that you want to know what *I* think about
the World Bank.

You may notice another attention-maintaining technique we use 11
in conversations. It is the frequent *sorry*'s you hear. If you find this

irritating, it's no wonder—you probably think we are apologizing! Many people were apparently raised to think that "I'm sorry" is an admission of guilt or statement of contriteness or self-denigration. I'm sorry, it's not true. It simply means, "no offense intended by what I have to say to you." It means, "listen to me knowing that you are not being personally attacked"; it means, "listen attentively with an open mind."

You will notice that my behavior is based on the assumption 12 that I pay better attention to others than do non-Asian/Pacific people. Can this be true? In the sense of having the habit of thinking about others in uncomfortable situations, it is true. How can this happen, that we pay better attention?

Part of this is a survival technique, not unique to Asian/Pacific 13 Americans: the experience of an oppressed people is that we have to pay more attention to the feelings of our oppressors than vice versa. Everyone knows this one—how much time do we spend talking about the boss? We know the boss's habits, preferences, moods, ir-rationalities—we have to! But the boss is unlikely to know ours. The same thing happens between people of color and white people.

But the primary reason that Asian/Pacific people pay more atten- 14 tion to others has to do with the principles of cooperation and ex-change, which form the basis of our societies and cultures. Consider typical Asian/Pacific group behavior:

Asian/Pacific people have a pattern of going last ("invisibility"). If you 15 could be a fly on my shoulder in an Asian/Pacific group, you would notice the conversational customs I mentioned above. If you look also at how the group attention flows from subject to subject, you would see that our number one priority is to take care of the group as a whole. You will notice us attending to business matters first. We will rarely risk the integrity of the group by presenting "personal" needs or demands before all the group needs are taken care of. This cooperative behavior functions quite well in the Asian/ Pacific context.

Let me tell you a story illustrating what often happens in the 16 mixed context. In a group dealing with issues of internalized racism, we first separated into our "racial" groups (Asian/Pacific, African, European, Latino/a[3, 4] with a list of questions to answer and two lists to make and present to the larger group. The schedule allowed forty-five minutes total for presentations. Back in the larger group, we Asians made our presentation first, and for the most part simply

---

[3] We unfortunately had no Native American group.
[4] These terms are not inclusive or descriptive enough. African Americans, Latinos, and Lati-nas are working hard to find names that define themselves accurately and respectfully.

read through the two lists. That took about five minutes. The African group was next. They had decided not to do the assigned questions and lists, and instead made up four different lists, and presented them, each member of the group speaking several times. That took about twenty minutes. It was important for the African group to make the exercise useful by changing it as needed, and to express to the group the feelings that had come up for them. The schedule would just have to give. It was important to us to make sure things moved along as planned (i.e., time-wise and assignment-wise); instead of changing the assignment and schedule, we would wait with our feelings.

Both fine approaches. But again, simply the mechanics of mixing 17 the two approaches means that, without thoughtful intervention, our personal needs will come last, if at all. If others are unaware of our approach, and are carrying around "quiet/unemotional Asian" stereotypes of us, it may never occur to them to ask us, after everything else is done, "Well, what about *your* feelings?"

Asian/Pacific people are "nice" and "polite." These so-called Asian 18 traits are praised by those who would like to keep us in line (teachers and employers, for example) and damned by our loving supporters who wish we would assimilate to Western-style bumper-car social interactions. I'm sorry, folks (see above), but I just have to complain about labeling being "nice" and "polite" as a problem. Why don't we use the right words? Gracious and hospitable. Cultural strengths which help us maintain the functioning and integrity of our families and groups. It sure never stopped us from making war on each other, exploiting each other, defending ourselves, or making revolution! The problem is not the behavior itself; it is the inability to choose another behavior when more appropriate. Obviously *that* has nothing to do with being Asian or Pacific, but rather with the experience of being immigrant minorities and being murdered in large numbers.

A variation on this is *Asian/Pacific people don't show their feelings.* 19 Just like anyone else, we will laugh, cry, rage, shiver, and melt with love, as soon as we get enough loving attention. And, just like anyone else, our feelings are written all over our faces and bodies. Not seeing how we express it is part of the "they all look the same to me" syndrome. "But what if someone always has the same look on their face?" you say. Put on your thinking cap! What does it mean if your friend has the same feelings frozen into her face all the time she's around you? That's a rather eloquent message, I would say. "But she can't/won't tell me what she's feeling!" Nope, we sure do resist translating for you, don't we?

Asian/Pacific people need assertiveness training. It sure might look 20 like that to someone accustomed to bumper-car social interactions. But welcome, ye weary bumper cars, to another cultural setting. Interactions between Asian/Pacific people are based to a great extent upon cooperation and exchange. Consider the group behavior—cooperation before individualism. Consider the *start-off question*—I give you attention first, then you offer it back to me. Exchange is an important cultural principle. A non-Asian/Pacific American was counseling an Indian woman on a decision she needed to make. The conversation went something like this:

"After all, who's the most important?" 21
"My mother." 22
"Wrong!" 23
"My father?" 24
"No!" 25
"My sister??" 26
"*You* are!" 27
"???" 28

In the Indian social system, you make someone else the most 29 important; watch out for their welfare, make decisions based on their needs. *You* get to be the most important for someone else; you have someone thinking about *your* needs. You give and you get, and it all evens out.

Several Japanese and Japanese-American customs also illustrate 30 this exchange principle. You don't split up the bill at a restaurant; you treat your friends, knowing that the next time they will treat you back. People pay attention to each other through *exchange of appreciations*. The woman who has spent three days preparing a feast offers it to her guests with "This isn't much, but please help yourselves." This is a signal for the guests to express their appreciation of her. They respond without rancor, because they, too, will get validated by the same mechanism. This extends to speaking about the children—"My daughter, she isn't very good at that." "But she's so good at these other things. You have a fine daughter!" Of course, sometimes it is important that you let someone know what you can do. In that case, your friend speaks for you. You never have to toot your own horn.

This is not to say that people don't get squished by these rules. 31 The Japanese have a saying, "The nail that stands above the others will get hammered down to the same level." The historical lack of natural resources required cooperation and discouraged individualism, there having been no excess to cover the risks of individual mistakes. Now the Japanese are far beyond survival level, and the cultural survival techniques have not been discarded. But within the cultural context, the exchange principle functions well.

What's a friend to do? How can you put your new-found insights ³²
into action? These suggestions and exercises will not only bring you
closer to us, but will also challenge you to act clearly and decisively
in groups and one-to-one relationships.

1. Take responsibility for equal time-sharing, especially in mixed
   groups.

2. Notice and deal with the feelings that come up for you when
   there is silence in a conversation. There is often desperation behind the habit of filling every second with words. An appreciation of silence will allow you to awarely encourage us to break
   the silence when we choose.

3. Notice when Asian/Pacific people are not talking. Assume that
   when we are not talking, you are interrupting us. It will become
   obvious what to do. Also, don't assume we are finished when
   we stop talking. It may be a *thinking pause* or a *question pause,* instead of an *end-of-thought pause.* It is perfectly acceptable to simply ask if we are finished.

4. Don't try to assist us by taking the perspective that we should
   change our behavior, but rather that we need to have more
   choices. Remember the exchange principle. We need to deal
   with the hurt we experience when other people don't come
   through on the exchange, but instead simply take from us. Encourage us to have the highest expectations of our allies, to require your attention, in fact to demand it, instead of always giving it first and waiting for it to be offered back.

5. Talk and listen Asian/Pacific-style with us. Practice recognizing
   and using the various *pauses.*

6. Remember that our "politeness," "apologies," etcetera, are not
   necessarily forms of self-invalidation. In European-American
   culture, these habits are often also considered to be signs of the
   weakness of the female. In this way, acting out sexism/internal-
   ized sexism by wishing us to give up our "weak" habits can turn
   out to be racist. Don't buy it! These are women's cultural
   strengths as well as Asian/Pacific cultural strengths.

7. Remember that, just like anyone else, we will express and release the full range of emotions as soon as we get enough caring
   attention. And, just like anyone else, our feelings are written all
   over our faces and bodies. We will do you the favor of not translating. Trust your thinking, make lots of mistakes, and pretty
   soon you'll be able not only to translate, but to think and see
   Asian/Pacific-style, too.

Warehouse Tribes: Living in the Cracks of Civilization

JULIA GILDEN

On a nippy evening in a warehouse in San Francisco, urban sur- 1
vivors gather around candles and a space heater. Like tired warriors,
they swap stories of their days at get-by jobs. Lupe cleans; Patrick
paints houses. Bubba, the family dog, and Sir Lawrence, a six-toed
cat that insisted on joining the tribe in Seattle, join the circle.

This scene is replicated in big cities all over the country. Young 2
refugees from middle-class America have left their comfortable
homes and predictable futures to forge lives that closely resemble
homelessness. They scavenge in curbside dumpsters and free boxes
to create temporary homes in warehouses or abandoned buildings.
Some groups just sneak in and "squat"; most pay rent to absentee
landlords. The impermanence of their groupings makes their numbers difficult to estimate. They live for the short term.

At the same time, they mean to forge new societal bonds, and 3
find a new kind of family closeness, through living by their wits.

For them, living in the shadows of the city is guerrilla training 4
for surviving in a brittle society, soon to be shattered. "We are making ourselves tough," says Laurie Spencer, a member of an ad hoc
collective who call themselves the Killgood Gang or, generically,
"garbage people."

The Killgood Gang's living room is on the second floor of a di- 5
lapidated warehouse that has been sectioned off into sleeping lofts,
a bathroom and a kitchen area, leaving a large center space with several used sofas for frequently staged performance art pieces. On the
ground-floor level are elaborate skateboard ramps, a soundproofed
room with two full drum sets facing each other, and an assortment
of bottles and boxes labeled "Stuff" and "Junk."

People live in these collectives or "squats" for different reasons. 6
For Laurie, the life is a dynamic experiment in sharing—sometimes

Julia Gilden (1943–   ), born in Caruthersville, Missouri, is a
free-lance writer in San Francisco and author of magazine articles
and feature stories. "Warehouse Tribes: Living in the Cracks of Civilization" was written for *This World,* the Sunday magazine of the
San Francisco Chronicle (1989).

food, sometimes space—with a goal of "personal empowerment." Others in this and similar warehouses feel they are waging a political struggle. Jeff Curtis, who lives in Project Artaud, wishes to battle "systemic forces that deprive communities of organic life." Project Artaud, a housing collective owned by the artists who live and work there, was originally a squat.

A collective, for garbage people, means "doing it without money." "Garbage people" implies being dirty, even being human refuse, but it's really just lower-end economics—using up what is considered waste. 7

"We put on three plays with no budget. Free," says Patrick Shade, who studied theater arts at the University of Arizona. "We got theater-quality lights. People didn't have to pay. They could bring dumpster food, or whatever they wanted. 8

"We went to a garbage performance in Tucson where all the patrons were in their 40s. The artist lay in chopped glass and passed out dumpster fruit. No one knew where it came from. It was delicious." 9

For a while, "garbage was the only thing that was free," says Andrew Vermont, a Cornell University dropout who now studies English literature at San Francisco State University and works in a community thrift shop to augment an education stipend from his parents. "But now garbage is less and less free. People drive around at night and collect boxes and cans. In fact, when I drink a can of Coke now, I leave the can on the street where it will be easy to pick up." 10

Andrew compares his life to that of an extraterrestrial: He might not know the monetary value of things, but would evaluate each object by how it could be used. "Everything here came from the streets. We brought little and stole nothing—well, maybe a few planks of wood. We wanted to build our own bathroom from scratch. We wanted to decide where the walls of each bedroom would be." 11

Freedom from imposed boundaries is part of the garbage people's self-definition. "Our dog is a garbage dog, not on a leash like other people's dogs," says Andrew. "People walking their dogs on leashes are on leashes themselves. You just can't see them." 12

Warehouse people build their survival skills by dropping out of comfortable life-styles, becoming invisible in the urban tapestry, and then finding the creative forces they believe were deadened during their formative years in an overprotective environment. At the same time, they are reluctant to speak unkindly of their parents' middle-class, goal-oriented lives, which they see as parents' misguided attempts to provide the best for their children. 13

Laurie, Patrick, and Andrew are all in their mid-twenties. 14
Patrick first lived in a warehouse in Tucson. He and Laurie have a
new daughter named Rogue. His performance art is a statement
against, in his words, "the consumer mentality, the wholesale acceptance of some developer's greed—a way of life that is not about
discovery, that is insulated from the difficulties of life."

"We lived in a cocoon," said Andrew, originally from Philadel- 15
phia. "I had to get out and find real life."

What they seek seems the antithesis of the American Dream. In- 16
stead of staking their own turf, they purposely move frequently
from one abandoned industrial property to another. Instead of collecting inventories of household goods, they choose to salvage cast-
offs, which they often destroy in acts of performance art.

Although each warehouse tribe develops its own subtle philo- 17
sophical variations, it is generally understood that they are not skin-
heads, not heavy metal rockers, and not hippies. "Hippies were the
last big alternative movement. But they were unrealistic," says Andrew's sister, Lupe. "They used a lot of drugs, did a lot of experi-
menting, and lost their momentum."

Two common denominators among warehouse tribes—transient 18
living and rejection of social control—are reminiscent of ideas found
in the 1987 TV series "Max Headroom," which portrayed survival
society after The Bomb. In the series, "Fringers" exist on the edges
of society in any kind of dwelling they can scrape together; "Blanks"
are intentional outlaws who have avoided the computerized number
identities mandated by the system, and who live by their own code
of honor. Warehouse tribes seem to be acting out these Orwellian
fantasies, except that the system they try to escape is not a totalitarian government but the benign devouring marshmallow of The
Good Life.

But the most seminal ideas of warehouse life and art come from 19
punk rock, whose lyrics discourage most forms of permanence and
hero worship. "One of the most important things about punk rock is
not to immortalize stars," says Andrew. "Most groups that are famous don't even have records." Andrew says he listened as a
teenager to Minor Threat and The Bad Brains, both East Coast
groups, and to Stiff Little Fingers, of Ireland.

In Europe, in a parallel movement, industrial sites and aban- 20
doned warehouses attract a cross-section of disaffected young people. But there are differences. The movement is more overtly political, and at the same time the European squats are better tolerated by
mainstream society. People are sometimes even paid by landlords to
refurbish old buildings, or they may set up rent-free households in

abandoned buildings whose owners look the other way. The only city known for tolerating squatters in America is New York, according to underground travelers.

Bernd Gruenwald lives in a squat in Cologne, Germany, where 21 he says the motivations for warehouse living are similar to those in America, but more formalized. "The movement is old and quite established; the groups are drawn together from all walks of life for radical political purposes," Bernd says. "There is a historical perspective. In America, people are not so involved in larger movements. They are on more individual trips."

Bruce Momich, a twenty-eight-year-old former Navy sailor, 22 house painter, and veteran of warehouse life in Philadelphia and San Francisco, agrees. "Here, each person can have his own rendition of how he wants to live. Some warehouses are drugs, art, noise. In others, everybody works and goes to bed early."

Lupe Vermont, who has spent years in European and American 23 warehouses and squats, says the problem here is that everything is so spread out. "In Europe people don't give up so easily; they're more persistent. They fight for low-rent or no-rent housing as a basic human right. In the United States there's more financial necessity"—fewer "safety net" benefits—"and it's harder to piece together a movement because we're so spaced out geographically."

In his book *Lipstick Traces*, music critic Greil Marcus has com- 24 pared the punk rock movement to earlier European nihilism and Dadaism, which aimed to destroy everything, including oneself, and start over. People now in their twenties grew up with predictions of global nuclear holocaust and environmental collapse, giving some of them a kind of cheerful hopelessness. Punk is anarchic and anti-egocentric, striving to tear down Western civilization's self-centered structures and build more organic communities in their place. These are strong themes in European and American warehouse collectives. Squats and warehouses often house organizers for the new environmental Green political parties in Europe and America. And in San Francisco, Food Not Bombs—a collective that sets up mobile soup kitchens for the homeless in Golden Gate Park—has used the Killgood Gang's warehouse kitchen to prepare meals.

Like most tribes, warehouse dwellers revel in their distinctive 25 costume. Most often they can be seen weaving their way through cities on skateboards like urban jackrabbits, wearing ragged layers of sweats and '50s-era print shirts and dresses, all of which become unisex clothing. They sport tattoos and nose rings, personalized high-top sneakers, and an amazing variety of Mohawks.

Though everyone might not agree that such an outrageous style 26 lends itself to camouflage, there is a conspiratorial feeling among warehouse tribes that they succeed in being invisible to most outsiders. "We are surrounded by people who don't know what's going on here," says Andrew. "I never knew about warehouse life in Philly until I left. I was living in the middle of it and never saw it."

Bruce says, "You can find [us] in every town in America, but especially in the Rust Belt, where there is so much industry. I can go to any town and within two hours find my people just by standing on the corner in the right part of town." 27

"We recognize that a number of people are using industrial buildings for residential purposes," says Paul Lord of the San Francisco City Planning Department, but neither his department nor other city agencies nationwide know how large the number is. Margie O'Driscoll of Art House, a nonprofit organization created three years ago as a joint project of the San Francisco Arts Commission and California Lawyers for the Arts to help artists find living space, estimates that there are two hundred legal live-work spaces and five hundred illegal spaces in the city. The Killgood Gang estimates there are fifteen hundred. 28

Laurie, a twenty-six-year-old Purdue University dropout who has supported herself as a masseuse, recalls a visit to Anchorage, Alaska, where she found a local variation of a warehouse tribe. "After a few hours in town, we went to a bar, and there they were—Mohawks, colored hair, very friendly. They lived in a garbage house. It was full of trash, the walls and windows were trashed, and they had found a 'Model Home' sign to put out in front. They were out of there within two weeks, but it was totally cool while it lasted." 29

American warehouse people do not aspire to be identified with residents of formalized live-work lofts—long-established domiciles on the East Coast that are considered upwardly mobile, refined "artist" spaces, controlled by individuals and passed along through friends. Instead, warehouse collectives are amorphous and unpredictable. "There's no long-term potential," says Laurie. 30

Recently Art House presented a seminar on "How to Legalize Your Living Space." A bunch of tribe members walked out before it was over. 31

On the other side of the city, in the abandoned Plaza West public housing project at Divisadero and Eddy streets, warehouse tribe ideas are being acted out by a performance art group called Contraband. For several weekends the artists have re-created a piece originally staged in the former Gartland Pit, a vacant lot at 16th and Valencia streets whose deep walls were covered for years with angry 32 neighborhood grafitti. The Gartland Pit was what remained after a seedy hotel for transients was destroyed by arson thirteen years ago. The pit itself is now gone, too, filled in by the foundations of a new apartment building.

Contraband chose the Plaza West site, in the shadow of St. Ig- 33 natius Church, because it has, according to member Keith Hennessy, "a history of community rights violations." The piece, called "Religare," explores the helplessness of people deprived of dwelling space due to social forces beyond their control, and the inherent tendencies of humans to bind together for protection and definition. The piece comments on the displacement of indigenous peoples by San Francisco settlers, the forced evacuation of Japanese to concentration camps during World War II, the eviction of blacks in the 1960s from the Western Addition and, finally, the ongoing routing of transient "homesteaders" from the abandoned project itself.

The Latin word *religare* means "to bind back together"—in this 34 case to reconstruct the tribe and find its home. Contraband's flyer announces: "Admission by sliding scale. No one turned away for lack of funds."

Contraband has performed in the Killgood Gang's warehouse, 35 bringing more formalized politics to their amiable anarchy. Many of the performers themselves live in warehouses and feel at the mercy of the implacable forces of modern society. Director Sara Shelton Mann lives in Project Artaud. Even though her home is relatively "respectable" and her company has received grants to perform here and abroad, living space is as much an issue for her and her group as it is for the transient warehouse tribes. "Contraband is obsessed with housing and real estate," Mann says.

It is an open question whether warehouse people will someday 36 return to the mainstream, making the same kinds of compromises earlier radicals have frequently made.

Laurie says she has been thinking a lot about her life, and the 37 kinds of controls her daughter will face as she grows up. "I don't know what will happen to me, and I don't know how much this way of life will affect Rogue, but I expect to keep finding creative ways to live. Being able to define my space, to change it if I want to—that's very important to me."

The warehouse tribe interviewed for this story no longer exists. All the Killgood Gang have regrouped, and several new tribes have been born.

Suburbia: Of Thee I Sing

PHYLLIS McGINLEY

Twenty miles east of New York City as the New Haven Railroad   1
flies sits a village I shall call Spruce Manor. The Boston Post Road,
there, for the length of two blocks, becomes Main Street, and on one
side of that thundering thoroughfare are the grocery stores and the
drug stores and the Village Spa where teen-agers gather of an afternoon to drink their cokes and speak their curious confidences. There
one finds the shoe repairers and the dry cleaners and the secondhand stores which sell "antiques" and the stationery stores which
dispense comic books to ten-year-olds and greeting cards and lend-
ing library masterpieces to their mothers. On the opposite side stand
the bank, the fire house, the public library. The rest of this town of
perhaps four or five thousand people lies to the south and is
bounded largely by Long Island Sound, curving protectively on
three borders. The movie theater (dedicated to the showing of second-
run, single-feature pictures) and the grade schools lie north, beyond
the Post Road, and that is a source of worry to Spruce Manorites.
They are always a little uneasy about the children, crossing, perhaps, before the lights are safely green. However, two excellent
policemen—Mr. Crowley and Mr. Lang—station themselves at the
intersections four times a day, and so far there have been no acci-
dents.

Spruce Manor in the spring and summer and fall is a pretty   2
town, full of gardens and old elms. (There are few spruces, but the
village Council is considering planting a few on the station plaza,
out of sheer patriotism.) In the winter, the houses reveal themselves
as comfortable, well-kept, architecturally insignificant. Then one can
see the town for what it is and has been since it left off being farm
and woodland some sixty years ago—the epitome of Suburbia, not
the country and certainly not the city. It is a commuter's town, the
living center of a web which unrolls each morning as the men swing
aboard the locals, and contracts again in the evening when they re-

Phyllis McGinley (1905–1978), born in Ontario, Oregon, was the
author of *One More Manhattan* (1937), *Times Three* (1961), and other
books of poems, as well as the essay collections *Sixpence in Her Shoe*
(1964) and *Saint-Watching* (1969). "Suburbia: Of Thee I Sing" is from
her essay collection *The Province of the Heart* (1959).

turn. By day, with even the children pent in schools, it is a village of women. They trundle mobile baskets at the A&P, they sit under driers at the hairdressers, they sweep their porches and set out bulbs and stitch up slip covers. Only on weekends does it become heterogeneous and lively, the parking places difficult to find.

Spruce Manor has no country club of its own, though devoted   3 golfers have their choice of two or three not far away. It does have a small yacht club and a beach which can be used by anyone who rents or owns a house here. The village supports a little park with playground equipment and a counselor, where children, unattended by parents, can spend summer days if they have no more pressing engagements.

It is a town not wholly without traditions. Residents will point   4 out the two-hundred-year-old manor house, now a minor museum; and in the autumn they line the streets on a scheduled evening to watch the Volunteer Firemen parade. That is a fine occasion, with so many heads of households marching in their red blouses and white gloves, some with flaming helmets, some swinging lanterns, most of them genially out of step. There is a bigger parade on Memorial Day with more marchers than watchers and with the Catholic priest, the rabbi, and the Protestant ministers each delivering a short prayer when the paraders gather near the War Memorial. On the whole, however, outside of contributing generously to the Community Chest, Manorites are not addicted to municipal get-togethers.

No one is very poor here and not many families rich enough to   5 be awesome. In fact, there is not much to distinguish Spruce Manor from any other of a thousand suburbs outside of New York City or San Francisco or Detroit or Chicago or even Stockholm, for that matter. Except for one thing. For some reason, Spruce Manor has become a sort of symbol to writers and reporters familiar only with its name or trivial aspects. It has become a symbol of all that is middle-class in the worst sense, of settled-downness or rootlessness, according to what the writer is trying to prove; of smug and prosperous mediocrity—or even, in more lurid novels, of lechery at the country club and Sunday morning hangovers.

To condemn Suburbia has long been a literary cliché, anyhow. I   6 have yet to read a book in which the suburban life was pictured as the good life or the commuter as a sympathetic figure. He is nearly as much a stock character as the old stage Irishman: the man who "spends his life riding to and from his wife," the eternal Babbitt[1]

---

[1] Middle-class protagonist in Sinclair Lewis's 1922 novel *Babbitt*. (Ed.)

who knows all about Buicks and nothing about Picasso, whose sanctuary is the club locker room, whose ideas spring readymade from
the illiberal newspapers. His wife plays politics at the P.T.A. and
keeps up with the Joneses. Or—if the scene is more gilded and less
respectable—the commuter is the high-powered advertising executive with a station wagon and an eye for the ladies, his wife a restless baggage given to too many cocktails in the afternoon.

These clichés I challenge. I have lived in the country, I have 7
lived in the city. I have lived in an average Middle Western small
town. But for the best eleven years of my life I have lived in Suburbia and I like it.

"Compromise!" cried our friends when we came here from an 8
expensive, inconvenient, moderately fashionable tenement in Manhattan. It was the period in our lives when everyone was moving
somewhere. Farther uptown, farther downtown, across town to Sut-
ton Place, to a half-dozen rural acres in Connecticut or New Jersey
or even Vermont. But no one in our rather rarefied little group was
thinking of moving to the suburbs except us. They were aghast that
we could find anything appealing in the thought of a middle-class
house on a middle-class street in a middle-class village full of middle-class people. That we were tired of town and hoped for children,
that we couldn't afford both a city apartment and a farm, they put
down as feeble excuses. To this day they cannot understand us. You
see, they read the books. They even write them.

Compromise? Of course we compromise. But compromise, if not 9
the spice of life, is its solidity. It is what makes nations great and
marriages happy and Spruce Manor the pleasant place it is. As for
its being middle-class, what is wrong with acknowledging one's
roots? And how free we are! Free of the city's noise, of its ubiquitous
doormen, of the soot on the windowsill and the radio in the next
apartment. We have released ourselves from the seasonal hegira to
the mountains or the seashore. We have only one address, one
house to keep supplied with paring knives and blankets. We are free
from the snows that block the countryman's roads in winter and his
electricity which always goes off in a thunderstorm. I do not insist
that we are typical. There is nothing really typical about any of our
friends and neighbors here, and therein lies my point. The true sub-
urbanite needs to conform less than anyone else; much less than the
gentleman farmer with his remodeled salt-box or than the determined cliff dweller with his necessity for living at the right address.
In Spruce Manor all addresses are right. And since we are fairly numerous here, we need not fall back on the people nearest us for total
companionship. There is not here, as in a small city away from truly
urban centers, some particular family whose codes must be ours.

And we could not keep up with the Joneses even if we wanted to, for we know many Joneses and they are all quite different people leading the most various lives.

The Albert Joneses spend their weekends sailing, the Bertram Joneses cultivate their delphinium, the Clarence Joneses—Clarence being a handy man with a cello—are enthusiastic about amateur chamber music. The David Joneses dote on bridge, but neither of the Ernest Joneses understands it, and they prefer staying home of an evening so that Ernest Jones can carve his witty caricatures out of pieces of old fruit wood. We admire each other's gardens, applaud each other's sailing records; we are too busy to compete. So long as our clapboards are painted and our hedges decently trimmed, we have fulfilled our community obligations. We can live as anonymously as in a city or we can call half the village by their first names.

On our half-acre or three-quarters, we can raise enough tomatoes for our salads and assassinate enough beetles to satisfy the gardening urge. Or we can buy our vegetables at the store and put the whole place to lawn without feeling that we are neglecting our property. We can have privacy and shade and the changing of the seasons and also the Joneses next door from whom to borrow a cup of sugar or a stepladder. Despite the novelists, the shadow of the country club rests lightly on us. Half of us wouldn't be found dead with a golf stick in our hands, and loathe Saturday dances. Few of us expect to be deliriously wealthy or world-famous or divorced. What we do expect is to pay off the mortgage and send our healthy children to good colleges.

For when I refer to life here, I think, of course, of living with children. Spruce Manor without children would be a paradox. The summer waters are full of them, gamboling like dolphins. The lanes are alive with them, the yards overflow with them, they possess the tennis courts and the skating pond and the vacant lots. Their roller skates wear down the asphalt, and their bicycles make necessary the twenty-five-mile speed limit. They converse interminably on the telephones and make rich the dentist and the pediatrician. Who claims that a child and a half is the American middle-class average? A nice medium Spruce Manor family runs to four or five, and we count proudly, but not with amazement, the many solid households running to six, seven, eight, even up to twelve. Our houses here are big and not new, most of them, and there is a temptation to fill them up, let the décor fall where it may.

Besides, Spruce Manor seems designed by providence and town planning for the happiness of children. Better designed than the city; better, I say defiantly, than the country. Country mothers must be constantly arranging and contriving for their children's leisure time. There is no neighbor child next door for playmate, no school within walking distance. The ponds are dangerous to young swimmers, the woods full of poison ivy, the romantic dirt roads unsuitable for bicycles. An extra acre or two gives a fine sense of possession to an adult; it does not compensate children for the give-and-take of our village, where there is always a contemporary to help swing the skipping rope or put on the catcher's mitt. Where in the country is the Friday evening dancing class or the Saturday morning movie (approved by the P.T.A.)? It is the greatest fallacy of all time that children love the country as a year-around plan. Children would take a dusty corner of Washington Square or a city sidewalk, even, in preference to the lonely sermons in stones and books in running brooks which their contemporaries cannot share.

As for the horrors of bringing up progeny in the city, for all its 14 museums and other cultural advantages (so perfectly within reach of suburban families if they feel strongly about it), they were summed up for me one day last winter. The harried mother of one, speaking to me on the telephone just after Christmas, sighed and said, "It's been a really wonderful time for me, as vacations go. Barbara has had an engagement with a child in our apartment house every afternoon this week. I have had to take her almost nowhere." Barbara is eleven. For six of those eleven years, I realized, her mother must have dreaded Christmas vacation, not to mention spring, as a time when Barbara had to be entertained. I thought thankfully of my own daughters whom I had scarcely seen since school closed, out with their skis and their sleds and their friends, sliding down the roped-off hill half a block away, coming in hungrily for lunch and disappearing again, hearty, amused, and safe—at least as safe as any sled-borne child can be.

Spruce Manor is not Eden, of course. Our taxes are higher than 15 we like, and there is always that eight-eleven in the morning to be caught, and we sometimes resent the necessity of rushing from a theater to a train on a weekday evening. But the taxes pay for our really excellent schools and for our garbage collections (so that the pails of orange peels need not stand in the halls overnight as ours did in the city) and for our water supply which does not give out every dry summer as it frequently does in the country. As for the theaters—they are twenty miles away and we don't get to them more than twice a month. But neither, I think, do many of our friends in town. The eight-eleven is rather a pleasant train, too, say the husbands; it gets them to work in thirty-four minutes and they read the papers restfully on the way.

"But the suburban mind!" cry our die-hard friends in Manhattan 16
and Connecticut. "The suburban conversation! The monotony!"
They imply that they and I must scintillate or we perish. Let me
anatomize Spruce Manor, for them and for the others who envision
Suburbia as a congregation of mindless housewives and amoral go-
getters.

From my window, now, on a June morning, I have a view. It 17
contains neither solitary hills nor dramatic skyscrapers. But I can see
my roses in bloom, and my foxglove, and an arch of trees over the
lane. I think comfortably of my friends whose houses line this and
other streets rather like it. Not one of them is, so far as I know, doing any of the things that suburban ladies are popularly supposed to
be doing. One of them, I happen to know, has gone bowling for her
health and figure, but she had already tidied up her house and arranged to be home before the boys return from school. Some, undoubtedly, are ferociously busy in the garden. One lady is on her
way to Ellis Island, bearing comfort and gifts to a Polish boy—a
seventeen-year-old stowaway who did slave labour in Germany and
was liberated by a cousin of hers during the war—who is being held
for attempting to attain the land of which her cousin told him. The
boy has been on the Island for three months. Twice a week she
takes this tedious journey, meanwhile besieging courts and immigration authorities on his behalf. This lady has a large house, a part-
time maid, and five children.

My friend around the corner is finishing her third novel. She 18
writes daily from nine-thirty until two. After that her son comes
back from school and she plunges into maternity; at six, she combs
her pretty hair, refreshes her lipstick, and is charming to her doctor
husband. The village dancing school is run by another neighbor, as
it has been for twenty years. She has sent a number of ballerinas on
to the theatrical world as well as having shepherded for many a successful season the white-gloved little boys and full-skirted little girls
through their first social tasks.

Some of the ladies are no doubt painting their kitchens or a 19
nursery; one of them is painting the portrait, on assignment, of a
very distinguished personage. Some of them are nurses' aides and
Red Cross workers and supporters of good causes. But all find time
to be friends with their families and to meet the 5:32 five nights a
week. They read something besides the newest historical novel,
Braque is not unidentifiable to most of them, and their conversation
is for the most part as agreeable as the tables they set. The tireless
bridge players, the gossips, the women bored by their husbands live
perhaps in our suburb, too. Let them. Our orbits need not cross.

And what of the husbands, industriously selling bonds or prac- 20
ticing law or editing magazines or looking through microscopes or
managing offices in the city? Do they spend their evenings and their
weekends in the gaudy bars of Fifty-second Street? Or are they the
perennial householders, their lives a dreary round of taking down
screens and mending drains? Well, screens they have always with
them, and a man who is good around the house can spend happy
hours with the plumbing even on a South Sea island. Some of them
cut their own lawns and some of them try to break par and some of
them sail their little boats all summer with their families for crew.
Some of them are village trustees for nothing a year and some listen
to symphonies and some think Milton Berle ought to be President.
There is a scientist who plays wonderful bebop, and an insurance
salesman who has bought a big old house nearby and with his own
hands is gradually tearing it apart and reshaping it nearer to his
heart's desire. Some of them are passionate hedge-clippers and
some read Plutarch for fun. But I do not know many—though there
may be such—who either kiss their neighbor's wives behind doors
or whose idea of sprightly talk is to tell you the plot of an old movie.

It is June, now, as I have said. This afternoon my daughters will 21
come home from school with a crowd of their peers at their heels.
They will eat up the cookies and drink up the ginger ale and go
down for a swim at the beach if the water is warm enough, that
beach which is only three blocks away and open to all Spruce
Manor. They will go unattended by me, since they have been swimming since they were four, and besides there are lifeguards and no
big waves. (Even our piece of ocean is a compromise.) Presently it
will be time for us to climb into our very old Studebaker—we are not
car-proud in Spruce Manor—and meet the 5:32. That evening expedition is not vitally necessary, for a bus runs straight down our principal avenue from the station to the shore, and it meets all trains.
But it is an event we enjoy. There is something delightfully ritualistic about the moment when the train pulls in and the men swing off,
with the less sophisticated children running squealing to meet them.
The women move over from the driver's seat, surrender the keys,
and receive an absent-minded kiss. It is the sort of picture that
wakes John Marquand[1] screaming from his sleep. But, deluded people that we are, we do not realize how mediocre it all seems. We will
eat our undistinguished meal, probably without even a cocktail to
enliven it. We will drink our coffee at the table, not carry it into the
living room; if a husband changes for dinner here it is into old and
spotty trousers and more comfortable shoes. The children will then

---

[1] American novelist (1893–1960). (Ed.)

go through the regular childhood routine—complain about their homework, grumble about going to bed, and finally accomplish both ordeals. Perhaps later the Gerard Joneses will drop in. We will talk a great deal of unimportant chatter and compare notes on food prices; we will also discuss the headlines and disagree. (Some of us in the Manor are Republicans, some are Democrats, a few lean plainly leftward. There are probably anti-Semites and anti-Catholics and even anti-Americans. Most of us are merely anti-antis.) We will all have one highball, and the Joneses will leave early. Tomorrow and tomorrow and tomorrow the pattern will be repeated. This is Suburbia.

But I think that some day people will look back on our little interval here, on our Spruce Manor way of life, as we now look back on the Currier and Ives kind of living, with nostalgia and respect. In a world of terrible extremes, it will stand out as the safe, important medium.

Suburbia, of thee I sing!   23

Fifth Avenue, Uptown: A Letter from Harlem

JAMES BALDWIN

There is a housing project standing now where the house in which 1
we grew up once stood, and one of those stunted city trees is
snarling where our doorway used to be. This is on the rehabilitated
side of the avenue. The other side of the avenue—for progress takes
time—has not been rehabilitated yet and it looks exactly as it looked
in the days when we sat with our noses pressed against the win-
dowpane, longing to be allowed to go "across the street." The grocery store which gave us credit is still there, and there can be no
doubt that it is still giving credit. The people in the project certainly
need it—far more, indeed, than they ever needed the project. The
last time I passed by, the Jewish proprietor was still standing among
his shelves, looking sadder and heavier but scarcely any older. Farther down the block stands the shoe-repair store in which our shoes
were repaired until reparation became impossible and in which,
then, we bought all our "new" ones. The Negro proprietor is still in
the window, head down, working at the leather.

These two, I imagine, could tell a long tale if they would (per- 2
haps they would be glad to if they could), having watched so many,
for so long, struggling in the fishhooks, the barbed wire, of this avenue.

The avenue is elsewhere the renowned and elegant Fifth. The 3
area I am describing, which, in today's gang parlance, would be
called "the turf," is bounded by Lenox Avenue on the west, the
Harlem River on the east, 135th Street on the north, and 130th Street
on the south. We never lived beyond these boundaries; this is where
we grew up. Walking along 145th Street—for example—familiar as it
is, and similar, does not have the same impact because I did not
know any of the people on the block. But when I turn east on 131st
Street and Lenox Avenue, there is first a soda-pop joint, then a

---

James Baldwin (1924–1987), born in New York but a resident of
France most of his adult life, was the author of poetry, plays, essays, and novels including *Go Tell It on the Mountain* (1953), *Notes of
a Native Son* (1955), and *Another Country* (1962). "Fifth Avenue, Uptown: A Letter from Harlem," from *Nobody Knows My Name: More
Notes of a Native Son* (1961); originally appeared in *Esquire* (1960).

shoeshine "parlor," then a grocery store, then a dry cleaners', then the houses. All along the street there are people who watched me grow up, people who grew up with me, people I watched grow up along with my brothers and sisters; and, sometimes in my arms, sometimes underfoot, sometimes at my shoulder—or on it—their children, a riot, a forest of children, who include my nieces and nephews.

When we reach the end of this long block, we find ourselves on wide, filthy, hostile Fifth Avenue, facing that project which hangs over the avenue like a monument to the folly, and the cowardice, of good intentions. All along the block, for anyone who knows it, are immense human gaps, like craters. These gaps are not created merely by those who have moved away, inevitably into some other ghetto; or by those who have risen, almost always into a greater capacity for self-loathing and self-delusion; or yet by those who, by whatever means—War II, the Korean war, a policeman's gun or billy, a gang war, a brawl, madness, an overdose of heroin, or, simply, unnatural exhaustion—are dead. I am talking about those who are left, and I am talking principally about the young. What are they doing? Well, some, a minority, are fanatical churchgoers, members of the more extreme of the Holy Roller sects. Many, many more are "moslems," by affiliation or sympathy, that is to say that they are united by nothing more—and nothing less—than a hatred of the white world and all its works. They are present, for example, at every Buy Black street-corner meeting—meetings in which the speaker urges his hearers to cease trading with white men and establish a separate economy. Neither the speaker nor his hearers can possibly do this, of course, since Negroes do not own General Motors or RCA or the A&P, nor, indeed, do they own more than a wholly insufficient fraction of anything else in Harlem (those who *do* own anything are more interested in their profits than in their fellows). But these meetings nevertheless keep alive in the participators a certain pride of bitterness without which, however futile this bitterness may be, they could scarcely remain alive at all. Many have given up. They stay home and watch the TV screen, living on the earnings of their parents, cousins, brothers, or uncles, and only leave the house to go to the movies or to the nearest bar. "How're you making it?" one may ask, running into them along the block, or in the bar. "Oh, I'm TV-ing it"; with the saddest, sweetest, most shame-faced of smiles, and from a great distance. This distance one is compelled to respect; anyone who has traveled so far will not easily be dragged again into the world. There are further retreats, of course, than the TV screen or the bar. There are those who are simply sitting on their stoops, "stoned," animated for a moment only, and hideously, by

4

the approach of someone who may lend them the money for a "fix."
Or by the approach of someone from whom they can purchase it,
one of the shrewd ones, on the way to prison or just coming out.

And the others, who have avoided all of these deaths, get up in   5
the morning and go downtown to meet "the man." They work in
the white man's world all day and come home in the evening to this
fetid block. They struggle to instill in their children some private
sense of honor or dignity which will help the child survive. This
means, of course, that they must struggle, stolidly, incessantly, to
keep this sense alive in themselves, in spite of the insults, the indifference, and the cruelty they are certain to encounter in their working day. They patiently browbeat the landlord into fixing the heat,
the plaster, the plumbing; this demands prodigious patience; nor is
patience usually enough. In trying to make their hovels habitable,
they are perpetually throwing good money after bad. Such frustration, so long endured, is driving many strong, admirable men and
women whose only crime is color to the very gates of paranoia.

One remembers them from another time—playing handball in   6
the playground, going to church, wondering if they were going to
be promoted at school. One remembers them going off to war—
gladly, to escape this block. One remembers their return. Perhaps
one remembers their wedding day. And one sees where the girl is
now—vainly looking for salvation from some other embittered,
trussed, and struggling boy—and sees the all-but-abandoned children in the streets.

Now I am perfectly aware that there are other slums in which   7
white men are fighting for their lives, and mainly losing. I know that
blood is also flowing through those streets and that the human damage there is incalculable. People are continually pointing out to me
the wretchedness of white people in order to console me for the
wretchedness of blacks. But an itemized account of the American
failure does not console me and it should not console anyone else.
That hundreds of thousands of white people are living, in effect, no
better than the "niggers" is not a fact to be regarded with compla-
cency. The social and moral bankruptcy suggested by this fact is of
the bitterest, most terrifying kind.

The people, however, who believe that this democratic anguish   8
has some consoling value are always pointing out that So-and-So,
white, and So-and-So, black, rose from the slums into the big time.
The existence—the public existence—of, say, Frank Sinatra and
Sammy Davis, Jr. proves to them that America is still the land of opportunity and that inequalities vanish before the determined will. It
proves nothing of the sort. The determined will is rare—at the mo-

ment, in this country, it is unspeakably rare—and the inequalities suffered by the many are in no way justified by the rise of a few. A few have always risen—in every country, every era, and in the teeth of regimes which can by no stretch of the imagination be thought of as free. Not all of these people, it is worth remembering, left the world better than they found it. The determined will is rare, but it is not invariably benevolent. Furthermore, the American equation of success with the big times reveals an awful disrespect for human life and human achievement. This equation has placed our cities among the most dangerous in the world and has placed our youth among the most empty and most bewildered. The situation of our youth is not mysterious. Children have never been very good at listening to their elders, but they have never failed to imitate them. They must, they have no other models. That is exactly what our children are doing. They are imitating our immorality, our disrespect for the pain of others.

All other slum dwellers, when the bank account permits it, can 9 move out of the slum and vanish altogether from the eye of persecution. No Negro in this country has ever made that much money and it will be a long time before any Negro does. The Negroes in Harlem, who have no money, spend what they have on such gimcracks as they are sold. These include "wider" TV screens, more "faithful" hi-fi sets, more "powerful" cars, all of which, of course, are obsolete long before they are paid for. Anyone who has ever struggled with poverty knows how extremely expensive it is to be poor; and if one is a member of a captive population, economically speaking, one's feet have simply been placed on the treadmill forever. One is victimized, economically, in a thousand ways—rent, for example, or car insurance. Go shopping one day in Harlem—for anything—and compare Harlem prices and quality with those downtown.

The people who have managed to get off this block have only 10 got as far as a more respectable ghetto. This respectable ghetto does not even have the advantages of the disreputable one—friends, neighbors, a familiar church, and friendly tradesmen; and it is not, moreover, in the nature of any ghetto to remain respectable long. Every Sunday, people who have left the block take the lonely ride back, dragging their increasingly discontented children with them. They spend the day talking, not always with words, about the trouble they've seen and the trouble—one must watch their eyes as they watch their children—they are only too likely to see. For children do not like ghettos. It takes them nearly no time to discover exactly why they are there.

The projects in Harlem are hated. They are hated almost as 11
much as policemen, and this is saying a great deal. And they are
hated for the same reason: both reveal, unbearably, the real attitude
of the white world, no matter how many liberal speeches are made,
no matter how many lofty editorials are written, no matter how
many civil-rights commissions are set up.

The projects are hideous, of course, there being a law, appar- 12
ently respected throughout the world, that popular housing shall be
as cheerless as a prison. They are lumped all over Harlem, colorless,
bleak, high, and revolting. The wide windows look out on Harlem's
invincible and indescribable squalor: the Park Avenue railroad
tracks, around which, about forty years ago, the present dark community began; the unrehabilitated houses, bowed down, it would
seem, under the great weight of frustration and bitterness they contain; the dark, the ominous schoolhouses from which the child may
emerge maimed, blinded, hooked, or enraged for life; and the
churches, churches, block upon block of churches, niched in the
walls like cannon in the walls of a fortress. Even if the administra-
tion of the projects were not so insanely humiliating (for example:
one must report raises in salary to the management, which will then
eat up the profit by raising one's rent; the management has the right
to know who is staying in your apartment; the management can ask
you to leave, at their discretion), the projects would still be hated because they are an insult to the meanest intelligence.

Harlem got its first private project, Riverton[1]—which is now, 13
naturally, a slum—about twelve years ago because at that time Negroes were not allowed to live in Stuyvesant Town. Harlem watched
Riverton go up, therefore, in the most violent bitterness of spirit,
and hated it long before the builders arrived. They began hating it at
about the time people began moving out of their condemned houses
to make room for this additional proof of how thoroughly the white
world despised them. And they had scarcely moved in, naturally,
before they began smashing windows, defacing walls, urinating in
the elevators, and fornicating in the playgrounds. Liberals, both
white and black, were appalled at the spectacle. I was appalled by
the liberal innocence—or cynicism, which comes out in practice as

---

[1] The inhabitants of Riverton were much embittered by this description; they have, apparently, forgotten how their project came into being; and have repeatedly informed me that I cannot
possibly be referring to Riverton, but to another housing project which is directly across the
street. It is quite clear, I think, that I have no interest in accusing any individuals or families of the
depredations herein described: but neither can I deny the evidence of my own eyes. Nor do I
blame anyone in Harlem for making the best of a dreadful bargain. But anyone who lives in
Harlem and imagines that he has *not* struck this bargain, or that what he takes to be his status (in
whose eyes?) protects him against the common pain, demoralization, and danger, is simply self-
deluded.

much the same thing. Other people were delighted to be able to point to proof positive that nothing could be done to better the lot of the colored people. They were, and are, right in one respect: that nothing can be done as long as they are treated like colored people. The people in Harlem know they are living there because white people do not think they are good enough to live anywhere else. No amount of "improvement" can sweeten this fact. Whatever money is now being earmarked to improve this, or any other ghetto, might as well be burnt. A ghetto can be improved in one way only: out of existence.

Similarly, the only way to police a ghetto is to be oppressive. 14 None of the Police Commissioner's men, even with the best will in the world, have any way of understanding the lives led by the people they swagger about in twos and threes controlling. Their very presence is an insult, and it would be, even if they spent their entire day feeding gumdrops to children. They represent the force of the white world, and the world's real intentions are, simply, for the world's criminal profit and ease, to keep the black man corraled up here, in his place. The badge, the gun in the holster, and the swinging club make vivid what will happen should his rebellion become overt. Rare, indeed, is the Harlem citizen, from the most circumspect church member to the most shiftless adolescent, who does not have a long tale to tell of police incompetence, injustice, or brutality. I myself have witnessed and endured it more than once. The businessmen and racketeers also have a story. And so do the prostitutes. (And this is not, perhaps, the place to discuss Harlem's very complex attitude toward black policemen, nor the reasons, according to Harlem, that they are nearly all downtown.)

It is hard, on the other hand, to blame the policeman, blank, 15 good-natured, thoughtless, and insuperably innocent, for being such a perfect representative of the people he serves. He, too, believes in good intentions and is astounded and offended when they are not taken for the deed. He has never, himself, done anything for which to be hated—which of us has?—and yet he is facing, daily and nightly, people who would gladly see him dead, and he knows it. There is no way for him not to know it: there are few things under heaven more unnerving than the silent, accumulating contempt and hatred of a people. He moves through Harlem, therefore, like an occupying soldier in a bitterly hostile country; which is precisely what, and where, he is, and is the reason he walks in twos and threes. And he is not the only one who knows why he is always in company: the people who are watching him know why, too. Any street meeting, sacred or secular, which he and his colleagues uneasily cover has as its explicit or implicit burden the cruelty and injustice of the white domination. And these days, of course, in terms increasingly vivid and jubilant, it speaks of the end of that domination. The white policeman standing on a Harlem street corner finds himself at the very center of the revolution now occurring in the world. He is not prepared for it—naturally, nobody is—and, what is possibly much more to the point, he is exposed, as few white people are, to the anguish of the black people around him. Even if he is gifted with the merest mustard grain of imagination, something must seep in. He cannot avoid observing that some of the children, in spite of their color, remind him of children he has known and loved, perhaps even of his own children. He knows that he certainly does not want *his* children living this way. He can retreat from his uneasiness in only one direction: into a callousness which very shortly becomes second nature. He becomes more callous, the population becomes more hostile, the situation grows more tense, and the police force is increased. One day, to everyone's astonishment, someone drops a match in the powder keg and everything blows up. Before the dust has settled or the blood congealed, editorials, speeches, and civil-rights commissions are loud in the land, demanding to know what happened. What happened is that Negroes want to be treated like men.

Negroes want to be treated like men: a perfectly straightforward 16 statement, containing only seven words. People who have mastered Kant, Hegel, Shakespeare, Marx, Freud, and the Bible find this statement utterly impenetrable. The idea seems to threaten profound, barely conscious assumptions. A kind of panic paralyzes their features, as though they found themselves trapped on the edge of a steep place. I once tried to describe to a very well-known American intellectual the conditions among Negroes in the South. My recital disturbed him and made him indignant; and he asked me in perfect innocence, "Why don't all the Negroes in the South move North?" I tried to explain what *has* happened, unfailingly, whenever a significant body of Negroes move North. They do not escape Jim Crow: they merely encounter another, not-less-deadly variety. They do not move to Chicago, they move to the South Side; they do not move to New York, they move to Harlem. The pressure within the ghetto causes the ghetto walls to expand, and this expansion is always violent. White people hold the line as long as they can, and in as many ways as they can, from verbal intimidation to physical violence. But inevitably the border which has divided the ghetto from the rest of the world falls into the hands of the ghetto. The white people fall back bitterly before the black horde; the landlords make a tidy profit by raising the rent, chopping up the rooms, and all but dispensing with the upkeep; and what has once been a neighbor-

hood turns into a "turf." This is precisely what happened when the
Puerto Ricans arrived in their thousands—and the bitterness thus
caused is, as I write, being fought out all up and down those streets.

Northerners indulge in an extremely dangerous luxury. They 17
seem to feel that because they fought on the right side during the
Civil War, and won, they have earned the right merely to deplore
what is going on in the South, without taking any responsibility for
it; and that they can ignore what is happening in Northern cities because what is happening in Little Rock or Birmingham is worse.
Well, in the first place, it is not possible for anyone who has not endured both to know which is "worse." I know Negroes who prefer
the South and white Southerners, because "At least there, you
haven't got to play any guessing games!" The guessing games referred to have driven more than one Negro into the narcotics ward,
the madhouse, or the river. I know another Negro, a man very dear
to me, who says with conviction and with truth, "The spirit of the
South is the spirit of America." He was born in the North and did
his military training in the South. He did not, as far as I can gather,
find the South "worse"; he found it, if anything, all too familiar. In
the second place, though, even if Birmingham *is* worse, no doubt Jo-
hannesburg, South Africa, beats it by several miles, and Buchen-
wald was one of the worst things that ever happened in the entire
history of the world. The world has never lacked for horrifying examples; but I do not believe that these examples are meant to be
used as justification for our own crimes. This perpetual justification
empties the heart of all human feeling. The emptier our hearts become, the greater will be our crimes. Thirdly, the South is not
merely an embarrassingly backward region, but a part of this country, and what happens there concerns every one of us.

As far as the color problem is concerned, there is but one differ- 18
ence between the Southern white and the Northerner: the Southerner remembers, historically and in his own psyche, a kind of Eden
in which he loved black people and they loved him. Historically, the
flaming sword laid across this Eden is the Civil War. Personally,
it is the Southerner's sexual coming of age, when, without any
warning, unbreakable taboos are set up between himself and his
past. Everything, thereafter, is permitted him except the love he remembers and has never ceased to need. The resulting, indescribable
torment affects every Southern mind and is the basis of the Southern hysteria.

None of this is true for the Northerner. Negroes represent noth- 19
ing to him personally, except, perhaps, the dangers of carnality. He
never sees Negroes. Southerners see them all the time. Northerners
never think about them whereas Southerners are never really think-

ing of anything else. Negroes are, therefore, ignored in the North and are under surveillance in the South, and suffer hideously in both places. Neither the Southerner nor the Northerner is able to look on the Negro simply as a man. It seems to be indispensable to the national self-esteem that the Negro be considered either as a kind of ward (in which case we are told how many Negroes, comparatively, bought Cadillacs last year and how few, comparatively, were lynched), or as a victim (in which case we are promised that he will never vote in our assemblies or go to school with our kids). They are two sides of the same coin and the South will not change—*cannot* change—until the North changes. The country will not change until it reexamines itself and discovers what it really means by freedom. In the meantime, generations keep being born, bitterness is increased by incompetence, pride, and folly, and the world shrinks around us.

It is terrible, an inexorable, law that one cannot deny the hu- 20 manity of another without diminishing one's own: in the face of one's victim, one sees oneself. Walk through the streets of Harlem and see what we, this nation, have become.

On Being Black and Middle Class

SHELBY STEELE

Not long ago a friend of mine, black like myself, said to me that the 1
term "black middle class" was actually a contradiction in terms.
Race, he insisted, blurred class distinctions among blacks. If you
were black, you were just black and that was that. When I argued,
he let his eyes roll at my naiveté. Then he went on. For us, as black
professionals, it was an exercise in self-flattery, a pathetic preten-
sion, to give meaning to such a distinction. Worse, the very idea of
class threatened the unity that was vital to the black community as a
whole. After all, since when had white America taken note of anything but color when it came to blacks? He then reminded me of an
old Malcolm X line that had been popular in the sixties. Question:
What is a black man with a Ph.D.? Answer: A nigger.

For many years I had been on my friend's side of this argument. 2
Much of my conscious thinking on the old conundrum of race and
class was shaped during my high school and college years in the
race-charged sixties, when the fact of my race took on an almost religious significance. Progressively, from the mid-sixties on, more and
more aspects of my life found their explanation, their justification,
and their motivation in race. My youthful concerns about career, romance, money, values, and even styles of dress became subject to
consultation with various oracular sources of racial wisdom. And
these ranged from a figure as ennobling as Martin Luther King, Jr.,
to the underworld elegance of dress I found in jazz clubs on the
South Side of Chicago. Everywhere there were signals, and in those
days I considered myself so blessed with clarity and direction that I
pitied my white classmates who found more embarrassment than
guidance in the fact of *their* race. In 1968, inflated by my new power,
I took a mischievous delight in calling them culturally disadvantaged.

But now, hearing my friend's comment was like hearing a priest 3
from a church I'd grown disenchanted with. I understood him, but
my faith was weak. What had sustained me in the sixties sounded

---

Shelby Steele (1946–   ), born in Chicago, is professor of English
at San Jose State University and author of *The Content of Our Character: A New Vision of Race in America* (1991). "On Being Black and
Middle Class" first appeared in the journal *Commentary* (1988).

monotonous and off the mark in the eighties. For me, race had lost much of its juju, its singular capacity to conjure meaning. And today, when I honestly look at my life and the lives of many other middle-class blacks I know, I can see that race never fully explained our situation in American society. Black though I may be, it is impossible for me to sit in my single-family house with two cars in the driveway and a swing set in the back yard and *not* see the role class has played in my life. And how can my friend, similarly raised and similarly situated, not see it?

Yet despite my certainty I felt a sharp tug of guilt as I tried to explain myself over my friend's skepticism. He is a man of many comedic facial expressions and, as I spoke, his brow lifted in extreme moral alarm as if I were uttering the unspeakable. His clear implication was that I was being elitist and possibly (dare he suggest?) anti-black—crimes for which there might well be no redemption. He pretended to fear for me. I chuckled along with him, but inwardly I did wonder at myself. Though I never doubted the validity of what I was saying, I felt guilty saying it. Why?   4

After he left (to retrieve his daughter from a dance lesson) I realized that the trap I felt myself in had a tiresome familiarity and, in a sort of slow-motion epiphany, I began to see its outline. It was like the suddenly sharp vision one has at the end of a burdensome marriage when all the long-repressed incompatibilities come undeniably to light.   5

What became clear to me is that people like myself, my friend, and middle-class blacks generally are caught in a very specific double bind that keeps two equally powerful elements of our identity at odds with each other. The middle-class values by which we were raised—the work ethic, the importance of education, the value of property ownership, of respectability, of "getting ahead," of stable family life, of initiative, of self-reliance—are, in themselves, raceless and even assimilationist. They urge us toward participation in the American mainstream, toward integration, toward a strong identification with the society—and toward the entire constellation of qualities that are implied in the word "individualism." These values are almost rules for how to prosper in a democratic, free-enterprise society that admires and rewards individual effort. They tell us to work hard for ourselves and our families and to seek our opportunities whenever they appear, inside or outside the confines of whatever ethnic group we may belong to.   6

But the particular pattern of racial identification that emerged in the sixties and that still prevails today urges middle-class blacks (and all blacks) in the opposite direction. This pattern asks us to see ourselves as an embattled minority, and it urges an adversarial   7 stance toward the mainstream, an emphasis on ethnic consciousness over individualism. It is organized around an implied separatism.

The opposing thrust of these two parts of our identity results in 8 the double bind of middle-class blacks. There is no forward movement on either plane that does not constitute backward movement on the other. This was the familiar trap I felt myself in while talking with my friend. As I spoke about class, his eyes reminded me that I was betraying race. Clearly, the two indispensable parts of my identity were a threat to each other.

Of course when you think about it, class and race are both similar in some ways and also naturally opposed. They are two forms of 9 collective identity with boundaries that intersect. But whether they clash or peacefully coexist has much to do with how they are defined. Being both black and middle class becomes a double bind when class and race are defined in sharply antagonistic terms, so that one must be repressed to appease the other.

But what is the "substance" of these two identities, and how 10 does each establish itself in an individual's overall identity? It seems to me that when we identify with any collective we are basically identifying with images that tell us what it means to be a member of that collective. Identity is not the same thing as the fact of membership in a collective; it is, rather, a form of self-definition, facilitated by images of what we wish our membership in the collective to mean. In this sense, the images we identify with may reflect the aspirations of the collective more than they reflect reality, and their content can vary with shifts in those aspirations.

But the process of identification is usually dialectical. It is just as 11 necessary to say what we are *not* as it is to say what we are—so that finally identification comes about by embracing a polarity of positive and negative images. To identify as middle class, for example, I must have both positive and negative images of what being middle class entails; then I will know what I should and should not be doing in order to be middle class. The same goes for racial identity.

In the racially turbulent sixties the polarity of images that came 12 to define racial identification was very antagonistic to the polarity that defined middle-class identification. One might say that the positive images of one lined up with the negative images of the other, so that to identify with both required either a contortionist's flexibility or a dangerous splitting of the self. The double bind of the black middle class was in place.

The black middle class has always defined its class identity by 13 means of positive images gleaned from middle- and upper-class white society, and by means of negative images of lower-class blacks. This habit goes back to the institution of slavery itself, when "house" slaves both mimicked the whites they served and held themselves above the "field" slaves. But in the sixties the old bourgeois impulse to dissociate from the lower classes (the "we-they" distinction) backfired when racial identity suddenly called for the celebration of this same black lower class. One of the qualities of a double bind is that one feels it more than sees it, and I distinctly remember the tension and strange sense of dishonesty I felt in those days as I moved back and forth like a bigamist between the demands of class and race.

Though my father was born poor, he achieved middle-class 14 standing through much hard work and sacrifice (one of his favorite words) and by identifying fully with solid middle-class values— mainly hard work, family life, property ownership, and education for his children (all four of whom have advanced degrees). In his mind these were not so much values as laws of nature. People who embodied them made up the positive images in his class polarity. The negative images came largely from the blacks he had left behind because they were "going nowhere."

No one in my family remembers how it happened, but as time 15 went on, the negative images congealed into an imaginary character named Sam, who, from the extensive service we put him to, quickly grew to mythic proportions. In our family lore he was sometimes a trickster, sometimes a boob, but always possessed of a catalogue of sly faults that gave up graphic images of everything we should not be. On sacrifice: "Sam never thinks about tomorrow. He wants it now or he doesn't care about it." On work: "Sam doesn't favor it too much." On children: "Sam likes to have them but not to raise them." On money: "Sam drinks it up and pisses it out." On fidelity: "Sam has to have two or three women." On clothes: "Sam features loud clothes. He likes to see and be seen." And so on. Sam's persona amounted to a negative instruction manual in class identity.

I don't think that any of us believed Sam's faults were accurate 16 representations of lower-class black life. He was an instrument of self-definition, not of sociological accuracy. It never occurred to us that he looked very much like the white racist stereotype of blacks, or that he might have been a manifestation of our own racial self-hatred. He simply gave us a counterpoint against which to express our aspirations. If self-hatred was a factor, it was not, for us, a matter of hating lower-class blacks but of hating what we did not want to be.

Still, hate or love aside, it is fundamentally true that my middle- 17 class identity involved a dissociation from images of lower-class black life and a corresponding identification with values and pat-

terns of responsibility that are common to the middle class everywhere. These values sent me a clear message: be both an individual
and a responsible citizen; understand that the quality of your life
will approximately reflect the quality of effort you put into it; know
that individual responsibility is the basis of freedom and that the
limitations imposed by fate (whether fair or unfair) are no excuse for
passivity.

Whether I live up to these values or not, I know that my accep-   18
tance of them is the result of lifelong conditioning. I know also that I
share this conditioning with middle-class people of all races and that
I can no more easily be free of it than I can be free of my race.
Whether all this got started because the black middle class modeled
itself on the white middle class is no longer relevant. For the middle-
class black, conditioned by these values from birth, the sense of
meaning they provide is as immutable as the color of his skin.

I started the sixties in high school feeling that my class-conditioning   19
was the surest way to overcome racial barriers. My racial identity
was pretty much taken for granted. After all, it was obvious to the
world that I was black. Yet I ended the sixties in graduate school a
little embarrassed by my class background and with an almost desperate need to be "black." The tables had turned. I knew very
clearly (though I struggled to repress it) that my aspirations and my
sense of how to operate in the world came from my class background, yet "being black" required certain attitudes and stances that
made me feel secretly a little duplicitous. The inner compatibility of
class and race I had known in 1960 was gone.

For blacks, the decade between 1960 and 1969 saw racial   20
identification undergo the same sort of transformation that national
identity undergoes in times of war. It became more self-conscious,
more narrowly focused, more prescribed, less tolerant of opposition.
It spawned an implicit party line, which tended to disallow compet-
ing forms of identity. Race-as-identity was lifted from the relative
slumber it knew in the fifties and pressed into service in a social and
political war against oppression. It was redefined along sharp adversarial lines and directed toward the goal of mobilizing the great mass
of black Americans in this warlike effort. It was imbued with a
strong moral authority, useful for denouncing those who opposed it
and for celebrating those who honored it as a positive achievement
rather than as a mere birthright.

The form of racial identification that quickly evolved to meet this   21
challenge presented blacks as a racial monolith, a singular people
with a common experience of oppression. Differences within the
race, no matter how ineradicable, had to be minimized. Class dis-

tinctions were one of the first such differences to be sacrificed, since they not only threatened racial unity but also seemed to stand in contradiction to the principle of equality which was the announced goal of the movement for racial progress. The discomfort I felt in 1969, the vague but relentless sense of duplicity, was the result of a historical necessity that put my race and class at odds, that was asking me to cast aside the distinction of my class and identify with a monolithic view of my race.

If the form of this racial identity was the monolith, its substance 22 was victimization. The civil rights movement and the more radical splinter groups of the late sixties were all dedicated to ending racial victimization, and the form of black identity that emerged to facilitate this goal made blackness and victimization virtually synonymous. Since it was our victimization more than any other variable that identified and unified us, moreover, it followed logically that the purest black was the poor black. It was images of him that clustered around the positive pole of the race polarity; all other blacks were, in effect, required to identify with him in order to confirm their own blackness.

Certainly there were more dimensions to the black experience 23 than victimization, but no other had the same capacity to fire the indignation needed for war. So, again out of historical necessity, victimization became the overriding focus of racial identity. But this only deepened the double bind for middle-class blacks like me. When it came to class we were accustomed to defining ourselves against lower-class blacks and identifying with at least the values of middle-class whites; when it came to race we were now being asked to identify with images of lower-class blacks and to see whites, middle class or otherwise, as victimizers. Negative lining up with positive, we were called upon to reject what we had previously embraced and to embrace what we had previously rejected. To put it still more personally, the Sam figure I had been raised to define myself against had now become the "real" black I was expected to identify with.

The fact that the poor black's new status was only passively 24 earned by the condition of his victimization, not by assertive, positive action, made little difference. Status was status apart from the means by which it was achieved, and along with it came a certain power—the power to define the terms of access to that status, to say who was black and who was not. If a lower-class black said you were not really "black"—a sellout, an Uncle Tom—the judgment was all the more devastating because it carried the authority of his status. And this judgment soon enough came to be accepted by many whites as well.

In graduate school I was once told by a white professor, "Well, 25 but . . . you're not really black. I mean, you're not disadvantaged." In his mind my lack of victim status disqualified me from the race itself. More recently I was complimented by a black student for speaking reasonably correct English, "proper" English as he put it. "But I don't know if I really want to talk like that," he went on. "Why not?" I asked. "Because then I wouldn't be black no more," he replied without a pause.

To overcome his marginal status, the middle-class black had to 26 identify with a degree of victimization that was beyond his actual experience. In college (and well beyond) we used to play a game called "nap matching." It was a game of one-upmanship, in which we sat around outdoing each other with stories of racial victimization, symbolically measured by the naps of our hair. Most of us were middle class and so had few personal stories to relate, but if we could not match naps with our own biographies, we would move on to those legendary tales of victimization that came to us from the public domain.

The single story that sat atop the pinnacle of racial victimization 27 for us was that of Emmett Till, the Northern black teenager who, on a visit to the South in 1955, was killed and grotesquely mutilated for supposedly looking at or whistling at (we were never sure which, though we argued the point endlessly) a white woman. Oh, how we probed his story, finding in his youth and Northern upbringing the quintessential embodiment of black innocence, brought down by a white evil so portentous and apocalyptic, so gnarled and hideous, that it left us with a feeling not far from awe. By telling his story and others like it, we came to *feel* the immutability of our victimization, its utter indigenousness, as a thing on this earth like dirt or sand or water.

Of course, these sessions were a ritual of group identification, a 28 means by which we, as middle-class blacks, could be at one with our race. But why were we, who had only a moderate experience of victimization (and that offset by opportunities our parents never had), so intent on assimilating or appropriating an identity that in so many ways contradicted our own? Because, I think, the sense of innocence that is always entailed in feeling victimized filled us with a corresponding feeling of entitlement, or even license, that helped us endure our vulnerability on a largely white college campus.

In my junior year in college I rode to a debate tournament with three 29 white students and our faculty coach, an elderly English professor. The experience of being the lone black in a group of whites was so familiar to me that I thought nothing of it as our trip began. But then halfway through the trip the professor casually turned to me and, in an isn't-the-world-funny sort of tone, said that he had just refused to rent an apartment in a house he owned to a "very nice" black couple because their color would "offend" the white couple who lived downstairs. His eyebrows lifted helplessly over his hawkish nose, suggesting that he too, like me, was a victim of America's racial farce. His look assumed a kind of comradeship: he and I were above this grimy business of race, though for expediency we had occasionally to concede the world its madness.

My vulnerability in this situation came not so much from the [30] professor's blindness to his own racism as from his assumption that I would participate in it, that I would conspire with him against my own race so that he might remain comfortably blind. Why did he think I would be amenable to this? I can only guess that he assumed my middle-class identity was so complete and all-encompassing that I would see his action as nothing more than a trifling concession to the folkways of our land, that I would in fact applaud his decision not to disturb propriety. Blind to both his own racism and to me— one blindness serving the other—he could not recognize that he was asking me to betray my race in the name of my class.

His blindness made me feel vulnerable because it threatened to [31] expose my own repressed ambivalence. His comment pressured me to choose between my class identification, which had contributed to my being a college student and a member of the debating team, and my desperate desire to be "black." I could have one but not both; I was double-bound.

Because double binds are repressed there is always an element [32] of terror in them: the terror of bringing to the conscious mind the buried duplicity, self-deception, and pretense involved in serving two masters. This terror is the stuff of vulnerability, and since vulnerability is one of the least tolerable of all human feelings, we usually transform it into an emotion that seems to restore the control of which it has robbed us; most often, that emotion is anger. And so, before the professor had even finished his little story, I had become a furnace of rage. The year was 1967, and I had been primed by endless hours of nap-matching to feel, at least consciously, completely at one with the victim-focused black identity. This identity gave me the license, and the impunity, to unleash upon this professor one of those volcanic eruptions of racial indignation familiar to us from the novels of Richard Wright. Like Cross Damon in *Outsider*, who kills in perfectly righteous anger, I tried to annihilate the man. I punished him not according to the measure of his crime but according to the measure of my vulnerability, a measure set by the cumulative tension of years of repressed terror. Soon I saw that terror in *his* face, as he stared hollow-eyed at the road ahead. My white friends in the back seat, knowing no conflict between their own class and race, were astonished that someone they had taken to be so much like themselves could harbor a rage that for all the world looked murderous.

Though my rage was triggered by the professor's comment, it 33 was deepened and sustained by a complex of need, conflict, and repression in myself of which I had been wholly unaware. Out of my racial vulnerability I had developed the strong need of an identity with which to defend myself. The only such identity available was that of me as victim, him as victimizer. Once in the grip of this paradigm, I began to do far more damage to myself than he had done.

Seeing myself as a victim meant that I clung all the harder to my 34 racial identity, which, in turn, meant that I suppressed my class identity. This cut me off from all the resources my class values might have offered me. In those values, for instance, I might have found the means to a more dispassionate response, the response less of a victim attacked by a victimizer than of an individual offended by a foolish old man. As an individual I might have reported this professor to the college dean. Or I might have calmly tried to reveal his blindness to him, and possibly won a convert. (The flagrancy of his remark suggested a hidden guilt and even self-recognition on which I might have capitalized. Doesn't confession usually signal a willingness to face oneself?) Or I might have simply chuckled and then let my silence serve as an answer to his provocation. Would not my composure, in any form it might take, deflect into his own heart the arrow he'd shot at me?

Instead, my anger, itself the hair-trigger expression of a long- 35 repressed double bind, not only cut me off from the best of my own resources, it also distorted the nature of my true racial problem. The righteousness of this anger and the easy catharsis it brought buoyed the delusion of my victimization and left me as blind as the professor himself.

As a middle-class black I have often felt myself *contriving* to be 36 "black." And I have noticed this same contrivance in others—a certain stretching away from the natural flow of one's life to align oneself with a victim-focused black identity. Our particular needs are out of sync with the form of identity available to meet those needs. Middle-class blacks need to identify racially; it is better to think of ourselves as black and victimized than not black at all; so we contrive (more unconsciously than consciously) to fit ourselves into an identity that denies our class and fails to address the true source of our vulnerability.

For me this once meant spending inordinate amounts of time at 37 black faculty meetings, though these meetings had little to do with my real racial anxieties or my professional life. I was new to the university, one of two blacks in an English department of over seventy, and I felt a little isolated and vulnerable, though I did not admit it to myself. But at these meetings we discussed the problems of black faculty and students within a framework of victimization. The real vulnerability we felt was covered over by all the adversarial drama the victim/victimized polarity inspired, and hence went unseen and unassuaged. And this, I think, explains our rather chronic ineffectiveness as a group. Since victimization was not our primary problem—the university had long ago opened its doors to us—we had to contrive to make it so, and there is not much energy in contrivance. What I got at these meetings was ultimately an object lesson in how fruitless struggle can be when it is not grounded in actual need.

At our black faculty meetings, the old equation of blackness with 38 victimization was ever present—to be black was to be a victim; therefore, not to be a victim was not to be black. As we contrived to meet the terms of this formula there was an inevitable distortion of both ourselves and the larger university. Through the prism of victimization the university seemed more impenetrable than it actually was, and we more limited in our powers. We fell prey to the victim's myopia, making the university an institution from which we could seek redress but which we could never fully join. And this mind-set often led us to look more for compensations for our supposed victimization than for opportunities we could pursue as individuals.

The discomfort and vulnerability felt by middle-class blacks in the 39 sixties, it could be argued, was a worthwhile price to pay considering the progress achieved during that time of racial confrontation. But what may have been tolerable then is intolerable now. Though changes in American society have made it an anachronism, the monolithic form of racial identification that came out of the sixties is still very much with us. It may be more loosely held, and its power to punish heretics has probably diminished, but it continues to catch middle-class blacks in a double bind, thus impeding not only their own advancement but even, I would contend, that of blacks as a group.

The victim-focused black identity encourages the individual to 40 feel that his advancement depends almost entirely on that of the group. Thus he loses sight not only of his own possibilities but of the inextricable connection between individual effort and individual advancement. This is a profound encumbrance today, when there is more opportunity for blacks than ever before, for it reimposes limitations that can have the same oppressive effect as those the society has only recently begun to remove.

It was the emphasis on mass action in the sixties that made the 41 victim-focused black identity a necessity. But in the eighties and beyond, when racial advancement will come only through a multitude of individual advancements, this form of identity inadvertently adds itself to the forces that hold us back. Hard work, education, individual initiative, stable family life, property ownership—these have always been the means by which ethnic groups have moved ahead in America. Regardless of past or present victimization, these "laws" of advancement apply absolutely to black Americans also. There is no getting around this. What we need is a form of racial identity that energizes the individual by putting him in touch with both his possibilities and his responsibilities.

It has always annoyed me to hear from the mouths of certain ar- 42 biters of blackness that middle-class blacks should "reach back" and pull up those blacks less fortunate than they—as though middle-class status were an unearned and essentially passive condition in which one needed a large measure of noblesse oblige to occupy one's time. My own image is of reaching back from a moving train to lift on board those who have no tickets. A noble enough sentiment—but might it not be wiser to show them the entire structure of principles, effort, and sacrifice that puts one in a position to buy a ticket any time one likes? This, I think, is something members of the black middle class can realistically offer to other blacks. Their example is not only a testament to possibility but also a lesson in method. But they cannot lead by example until they are released from a black identity that regards that example as suspect, that sees them as "marginally" black, indeed that holds *them* back by catching them in a double bind.

To move beyond the victim-focused black identity we must learn 43 to make a difficult but crucial distinction: between actual victimization, which we must resist with every resource, and identification with the victim's status. Until we do this we will continue to wrestle more with ourselves than with the new opportunities which so many paid so dearly to win.

America's Emerging Gay Culture

RANDALL E. MAJORS

A gay culture, unique in the history of homosexuality, is emerging   1
in America. Gay people from all walks of life are forging new self-
identity concepts, discovering new political and social power, and
building a revolutionary new life style. As more people "come out,"
identify themselves as gay, and join with others to work and live as
openly gay people, a stronger culture takes shape with each passing
year.

There have always been homosexual men and women, but   2
never before has there emerged the notion of a distinct "culture"
based on being gay.[1] A useful way to analyze this emerging gay culture is to observe the communication elements by which gay people
construct their life styles and social institutions. Lesbians and gay
men, hereafter considered together as gay people, are creating a
new community in the midst of the American melting pot.[2] They are
building social organizations, exercising political power, and solidi-
fying a unique sense of identity—often under repressive and sometimes dangerous conditions. The following essay is an analysis of
four major communicative elements of the American gay culture: the
gay neighborhood, gay social groups, gay symbols, and gay meeting
behavior. These communication behaviors will demonstrate the vi-
brancy and joy that a new culture offers the American vision of individual freedom and opportunity.

The Gay Neighborhood

Most cultural groups find the need to mark out a home "turf."   3
American social history has many examples of ethnic and social
groups who create their own special communities, whether by with-
drawing from the larger culture or by forming specialized groups
within it. The utopian communities of the Amish or Shakers are ex-

---

Randall E. Majors (1949–   ), born in Greenfield, Indiana, is associate professor of marketing at California State University, Hayward, and author of college textbooks including *Basic Speech Communication* (1986) and *Business Communication* (1989). "America's
Emerging Gay Culture" is from *Intercultural Communication: A
Reader*, sixth edition, edited by Larry A. Samovar and Richard E.
Porter (1988).

amples of the first, and "ghetto" neighborhoods in large urban areas are examples of the latter.

This need to create a group territory fulfills several purposes for gay people. First, a gay person's sense of identity is reinforced if there is a special place that is somehow imbued with "gayness." When a neighborhood becomes the home of many gay people, the ground is created for a feeling of belonging and sharing with others. Signs of gayness, whether overt symbols like rainbow flags or more subtle cues such as merely the presence of other gay people on the street, create the feeling that a certain territory is special to the group and hospitable to the group's unique values.

How do you know when a neighborhood is gay? As with any generality, the rule of thumb is that "enough gay people in a neighborhood and it becomes a gay neighborhood." Rarely do gay people want to paint the streetlamps lavender, but the presence of many more subtle factors gives a gay character to an area. The most subtle cues are the presence of gay people as they take up residence in a district. Word spreads in the group that a certain area is starting to look attractive and open to gay members. There is often a move to "gentrify" older, more affordable sections of a city and build a new neighborhood out of the leftovers from the rush to the suburbs. Gay businesses, those operated by or catering to gay people, often develop once enough clientele is in the area. Social groups and services emerge that are oriented toward the members of the neighborhood. Eventually, the label of "gay neighborhood" is placed on an area, and the transformation is complete. The Castro area in San Francisco, Greenwich Village in New York, New Town in Chicago, the Westheimer district in Houston, and West Hollywood or Silver Lake in Los Angeles are examples of the many emergent gay neighborhoods in cities across America.[3]

A second need fulfilled by the gay neighborhood is the creation of a meeting ground. People can recognize and meet each other more easily when a higher density of population is established. It is not easy to grow up gay in America, gay people often feel "different" because of their sexual orientations. The surrounding heterosexual culture often tries to imprint sexual behaviors and expectations that do not suit gay natures. Because of this pressure, gay people often feel isolated and alienated, and the need for a meeting ground is very important.[4] Merely knowing that there is a specific place where other gay people live and work and play does much to anchor the psychological aspect of gayness in a tangible, physical reality. A gay person's sense of identity is reinforced by knowing that there is a home base, or a safe place where others of a similar persuasion are nearby.

Gay neighborhoods reinforce individual identity by focusing ac- 7
tivities and events for members of the group. Celebrations of group
unity and pride, demonstrations of group creativity and accomplishment, and services to individual members' needs are more easily developed when centralized. Gay neighborhoods are host to all the
outward elements of a community—parades, demonstrations, car
washes, basketball games, petition signing, street fairs, and garage
sales.

A critical purpose for gay neighborhoods is that of physical and 8
psychological safety. Subcultural groups usually experience some
degree of persecution and oppression from the larger surrounding
culture. For gay people, physical safety is a very real concern—
incidences of homophobic assaults or harassment are common in
most American cities.[5] By centralizing gay activities, some safe-
guards can be mounted, as large numbers of gay people living in
proximity create a deterrence to violence. This may be informal
awareness of the need to take extra precautions and to be on the
alert to help other gay people in distress or in the form of actual
street patrols or social groups, such as Community United Against
Violence in San Francisco. A sense of psychological safety follows
from these physical measures. Group consciousness raising on
neighborhood safety and training in safety practices create a sense of
group cohesion. The security inspired by the group creates a psychic
comfort that offsets the paranoia that can be engendered by alienation and individual isolation.

Another significant result of gay neighborhoods is the political 9
reality of "clout."[6] In the context of American grassroots democracy,
a predominantly gay population in an area can lead to political
power. The concerns of gay people are taken more seriously by
politicians and elected officials representing an area where voters
can be registered and mustered into service during elections. In
many areas, openly gay politicians represent gay constituencies directly and voice their concerns in ever-widening forums. The impact
of this kind of democracy-in-action is felt on other institutions as
well: police departments, social welfare agencies, schools, churches,
and businesses. When a group centralizes its energy, members can
bring pressure to bear on other cultural institutions, asking for and
demanding attention to the unique needs of that group. Since American culture has a strong tradition of cultural diversity, gay neighborhoods are effective agents in the larger cultural acceptance of gay
people. The gay rights movement, which attempts to secure housing, employment, and legal protection for gay people, finds its
greatest support in the sense of community created by gay neighborhoods.

Gay Social Groups

On a smaller level than the neighborhood, specialized groups fulfill 10
the social needs of gay people. The need for affiliation—to make
friends, to share recreation, to find life partners, or merely to while
away the time—is a strong drive in any group of people. Many gay
people suffer from an isolation caused by rejection by other people
or by their own fear of being discovered as belonging to an unpopu-
lar group. This homophobia leads to difficulty in identifying and
meeting other gay people who can help create a sense of dignity and
caring. This is particularly true for gay teenagers who have limited
opportunities to meet other gay people.[7] Gay social groups serve the
important function of helping gay people locate each other so that
this affiliation need can be met.

The development of gay social groups depends to a large degree 11
on the number of gay people in an area and the perceived risk factor. In smaller towns and cities, there are often no meeting places,
which exacerbates the problem of isolation. In some small towns a
single business may be the only publicly known meeting place for
gay people within hundreds of miles. In larger cities, however, an
elaborate array of bars, clubs, social groups, churches, service agencies, entertainment groups, stores, restaurants, and the like add to
the substance of a gay culture.

The gay bar is often the first public gay experience for a gay per- 12
son, and the gay bar serves as a central focus in gay life for many
people. Beyond the personal need of meeting potential relationship
partners, the gay bar also serves the functions of entertainment and
social activity. Bars offer a wide range of attractions suited to gay
people: movies, holiday celebrations, dancing, costume parties, live
entertainment, free meals, boutiques, and meeting places for social
groups. Uniquely gay forms of entertainment, such as drag shows
and disco dancing, were common in gay bars before spreading into
the general culture. Bars often become a very central part of a community's social life by sponsoring athletic teams, charities, community services, and other events as well as serving as meeting places.

The centrality of the bar in gay culture has several drawbacks, 13
however. Young gay people are denied entrance because of age re-
strictions, and there may be few other social outlets for them. A
high rate of alcoholism among urban gay males is prominent. With
the spread of Acquired Immune Deficiency Syndrome (AIDS), the
use of bars for meeting sexual partners has declined dramatically as
gay people turn to developing more permanent relationships.[8]

Affiliation needs remain strong despite these dangers, however, 14
and alternative social institutions arise that meet these needs. In

'large urban areas, where gay culture is more widely developed, social groups include athletic organizations that sponsor teams and tournaments; leisure activity clubs in such areas as country-and-western dance, music, yoga, bridge, hiking, and recreation; religious groups such as Dignity (Roman Catholic), Integrity (Episcopal), and the Metropolitan Community Church (MCC); volunteer agencies such as information and crisis hotlines and charitable organizations; and professional and political groups such as the Golden Gate Business Association of San Francisco or the national lobby group, the Gay Rights Task Force. A directory of groups and services is usually published in urban gay newspapers, and their activities are reported on and promoted actively. Taken together, these groups compose a culture that supports and nourishes a gay person's life.

Gay Symbols

Gay culture is replete with symbols. These artifacts spring up and   15 constantly evolve as gayness moves from being an individual, personal experience into a more complex public phenomenon. All groups express their ideas and values in symbols, and the gay culture, in spite of its relatively brief history, has been quite creative in symbol making.

The most visible category of symbols is in the semantics of gay   16 establishment names. Gay bars, bookstores, restaurants, and social groups want to be recognized and patronized by gay people, but they do not want to incur hostility from the general public. This was particularly true in the past when the threat of social consequences was greater. In earlier days, gay bars, the only major form of gay establishment, went by code words such as "blue" or "other"—the Blue Parrot, the Blue Goose, the Other Bar, and Another Place.

Since the liberalization of culture after the 1960s, semantics have   17 blossomed in gay place names. The general trend is still to identify the place as gay, either through affiliation (Our Place or His 'N' Hers), humor (the White Swallow or Uncle Charley's), high drama (the Elephant Walk or Backstreet), or sexual suggestion (Ripples, Cheeks, or Rocks). Lesbians and gay men differ in this aspect of their cultures. Lesbian place names often rely upon a more personal or classical referent (Amanda's Place or the Artemis Cafe), while hypermasculine referents are commonly used for gay male meeting places (the Ramrod, Ambush, Manhandlers, the Mine Shaft, the Stud, or Boots). Gay restaurants and nonpornographic bookstores usually reflect more subdued names, drawing upon cleverness or historical associations: Dos Hermanos, Women and Children First, Diana's, the Oscar Wilde Memorial Bookstore, and Walt Whitman

Bookstore. More commonly, gay establishments employ general naming trends of location, ownership, or identification of product or service similar to their heterosexual counterparts. The increasing tendency of businesses to target and cater to gay markets strengthens the growth and diversity of gay culture.

A second set of gay symbols are those that serve as member- [18] recognition factors. In past ages such nonverbal cues were so popular as to become mythic: the arched eyebrow of Regency England, the green carnation of Oscar Wilde's day, and the "green shirt on Thursday" signal of mid-century America. A large repertoire of identifying characteristics have arisen in recent years that serve the functions of recognizing other gay people and focusing on particular interests. In the more sexually promiscuous period of the 1970s, popular identifying symbols were a ring of keys worn on the belt, either left or right depending upon sexual passivity or aggressiveness, and the use of colored handkerchiefs in a rear pocket coded to desired types of sexual activity. Political sentiments are commonly expressed through buttons, such as the "No on 64" campaign against the LaRouche initiative in California in 1986. The pink triangle as a political symbol recalls the persecution and annihilation of gay people in Nazi Germany. The lambda symbol, an ancient Greek referent, conjures up classical images of gay freedom of expression. Stud earrings for men are gay symbols in some places, though such adornment has evolved and is widely used for the expression of general countercultural attitudes. The rainbow and the unicorn, mythical symbols associated with supernatural potency, also are common signals of gay enchantment, fairy magic, and spiritual uniqueness by the more "cosmic" elements of the gay community.

Another set of gay symbols to be aware of are the images of gay [19] people as portrayed in television, film, literature, and advertising. The general heterosexual culture controls these media forms to a large extent, and the representations of gay people in those media take on a straight set of expectations and assumptions. The results are stereotypes that often oversimplify gay people and their values and do not discriminate the subtleties of human variety in gay culture. Since these stereotypes are generally unattractive, they are often the target of protests by gay people. Various authors have addressed the problem of heterosexual bias in the areas of film and literature.[9] As American culture gradually becomes more accepting of and tolerant toward gay people, these media representations become more realistic and sympathetic, but progress in this area is slow.

One hopeful development in the creation of positive gay role [20] models has been the rise of an active gay market for literature. Most large cities have bookstores which stock literature supportive of gay culture. A more positive image for gay people is created through gay characters, heros, and stories that deal with the important issues of family, relationship, and social responsibility. This market is constantly threatened by harsh economic realities, however, and gay literature is not as well developed as it might be.[10]

Advertising probably has done the most to popularize and inte- 21 grate gay symbols into American culture. Since money making is the goal of advertising, the use of gay symbols has advanced more rapidly in ad media than in the arts. Widely quoted research suggests that gay people, particularly men, have large, disposable incomes, so they become popular target markets for various products: tobacco, body-care products, clothing, alcohol, entertainment, and consumer goods. Typical gay-directed advertising in these product areas includes appeals based upon male bonding, such as are common in tobacco and alcohol sales ads, which are attractive to both straight and gay men since they stimulate the bonding need that is a part of both cultures.

Within gay culture, advertising has made dramatic advances in 22 the past ten years, due to the rise of gay-related businesses and products. Gay advertising appears most obviously in media specifically directed at gay markets, such as gay magazines and newspapers, and in gay neighborhoods. Gay products and services are publicized with many of the same means as are their straight counterparts. Homoerotic art is widely used in clothing and body-care product ads. The male and female body are displayed for their physical and sexual appeal. This eroticizing of the body may be directed at either women or men as a desirable sexual object, and perhaps strikes at a subconscious homosexual potential in all people. Prominent elements of gay advertising are its use of sexuality and the central appeal of hypermasculinization. With the rise of sexual appeals in general advertising through double entendre, sexual punning, subliminal seduction, and erotic art work, it may be that gay advertising is only following suit in its emphasis on sexual appeals. Hugely muscled bodies and perfected masculine beauty adorn most advertising for gay products and services. Ads for greeting cards, billboards for travel service, bars, hotels, restaurants, and clothing stores tingle to the images of Hot 'N' Hunky Hamburgers, Hard On Leather, and the Brothel Hotel or its crosstown rival, the Anxious Arms. Some gay writers criticize this use of advertising as stereotyping and distorting of gay people, and certainly, misconceptions about the diversity in gay culture are more common than understanding. Gay people are far more average and normal than the images that appear in public media would suggest.

Gay Meeting Behavior

The final element of communication in the gay culture discussed 23
here is the vast set of behaviors by which gay people recognize and
meet one another. In more sexually active days before the concern
for AIDS, this type of behavior was commonly called cruising. Currently, promiscuous sexual behavior is far less common than it once
was, and cruising has evolved into a more standard meeting behavior that helps identify potential relationship partners.

Gay people meet each other in various contexts: in public situa- 24
tions, in the workplace, in gay meeting places, and in the social contexts of friends and acquaintances. Within each context, a different
set of behaviors is employed by which gay people recognize someone else as gay and determine the potential for establishing a relationship. These behaviors include such nonverbal signaling as frequency and length of interaction, posture, proximity, eye contact,
eye movement and facial gestures, touch, affect displays, and
paralinguistic signals.[11] The constraints of each situation and the
personal styles of the communicators create great differences in the
effectiveness and ease with which these behaviors are displayed.

Cruising serves several purposes besides the recognition of 25
other gay people. Most importantly, cruising is an expression of joy
and pride in being gay. Through cruising, gay people communicate
their openness and willingness to interact. Being gay is often compared to belonging to a universal—though invisible—fraternity or
sorority. Gay people are generally friendly and open to meeting
other gay people in social contexts because of the common experience of rejection and isolation they have had growing up. Cruising
is the means by which gay people communicate their gayness and
bridge the gap between stranger and new-found friend.

Cruising has become an integral part of gay culture because it is 26
such a commonplace behavior. Without this interpersonal skill—and
newcomers to gay life often complain of the lack of comfort or ease
they have with cruising—a gay person can be at a distinct disadvantage in finding an easy path into the mainstream of gay culture.
While cruising has a distinctly sexual overtone, the sexual subtext is
often a symbolic charade. Often the goals of cruising are no more
than friendship, companionship, or conversation. In this sense,
cruising becomes more an art form or an entertainment. Much as the
"art of conversation" was the convention of a more genteel cultural
age, gay cruising is the commonly accepted vehicle of gay social interaction. The sexual element, however, transmitted by double
meaning, clever punning, or blatant nonverbal signals, remains a
part of cruising in even the most innocent of circumstances.

In earlier generations, a common stereotype of gay men focused 27
on the use of exaggerated, dramatic, and effeminate body language—the "limp wrist" image. Also included in this negative image of gay people was cross-gender dressing, known as "drag," and
a specialized, sexually suggestive argot called "camp."[12] Some gay
people assumed these social roles because that was the picture of
"what it meant to be gay," but by and large these role behaviors
were overthrown by the gay liberation of the 1970s. Gay people became much less locked into these restraining stereotypes and developed a much broader means of social expression. Currently, no
stereotypic behavior would adequately describe gay communication
style—it is far too diverse and integrated into mainstream American
culture. Cruising evolved from these earlier forms of communication, but as a quintessential gay behavior, cruising has replaced the
bitchy camp of an earlier generation of gay people.

The unique factor in gay cruising, and the one that distinguishes 28
it from heterosexual cruising, is the level of practice and refinement
the process receives. All cultural groups have means of introduction
and meeting, recognition, assessment, and negotiation of a new relationship. In gay culture, however, the "courtship ritual" or friendship ritual of cruising is elaborately refined in its many variants and
contexts. While straight people may use similar techniques in relationship formation and development, gay people are uniquely self-
conscious in the centrality of these signals to the perpetuation of
their culture. There is a sense of adventure and discovery in being
"sexual outlaws," and cruising is the shared message of commitment to the gay life style.[13]

Conclusion

These four communication elements of gay culture comprise only a 29
small part of what might be called gay culture. Other elements have
been more widely discussed elsewhere: literature, the gay press, religion, politics, art, theater, and relationships. Gay culture is a marvelous and dynamic phenomenon. It is driven and buffeted by the
energies of intense feeling and creative effort. Centuries of cultural
repression that condemned gay people to disgrace and persecution
have been turned upside down in a brief period of history. The results of this turbulence have the potential for either renaissance or
cataclysm. The internalized fear and hatred of repression is balanced
by the incredible joy and idealism of liberation. Through the celebration of its unique life style, gay culture promises to make a great
contribution to the history of sexuality and to the rights of the indi-

vidual. Whether it will fulfill this promise or succumb to the pressures that any creative attempt must face remains to be seen.

Notes

1. Several good reviews of "famous homosexuals" include the following: Barbara Grier and Coletta Reid, *Lesbian Lives* (Oakland, Calif.: Diana Press, 1976); Noel I. Garde, *Jonathan to Gide: The Homosexual in History* (New York: Nosbooks, 1969); and A. L. Rowse, *The Homosexual in History* (Metuchen, N.J.: Scarecrow Press, 1975).

2. The relative differences and similarities between gay men and lesbians is a hotly debated issue in the gay/lesbian community. For the purposes of this paper, I have chosen to speak of them as a single unit. For an introduction to this issue, see Celia Kitzinger, *The Social Construction of Lesbianism* (Newbury Park, Calif.: Sage Publications, 1987).

3. An excellent analysis of the role of the Castro in California's gay culture is in Frances FitzGerald, *Cities on a Hill* (New York: Simon and Schuster, 1986). An entertaining source that discusses gay neighborhoods across America is Edmund White, *States of Desire: Travels in Gay America* (New York: E. P. Dutton, 1980).

4. For more information on the problems of gay self-identity, see Don Clark, *(The New) Loving Someone Gay* (Berkeley: Celestial Arts, 1987) and George Weinberg, *Society and the Healthy Homosexual* (New York: Doubleday, 1973).

5. A discussion of violence and its effects on gay people is in Dennis Altman, *The Homosexualization of America: The Americanization of Homosexuality* (New York: St. Martin's Press, 1982), pp. 100–101.

6. For a discussion of emerging gay politics, see Peter Fisher, *The Gay Mystique* (New York: Stein and Day, 1972) and Laud Humphreys, *Out of the Closets: The Sociology of Homosexual Liberation* (Englewood Cliffs, N.J.: Prentice-Hall, 1972).

7. Problems of young gay people are discussed in Mary V. Borhek, *Coming Out to Parents* (New York: Pilgrim Press, 1983) and in story form in Mary V. Borhek, *My Son Eric* (New York: Pilgrim Press, 1979) and Aaron Fricke, *Reflections of a Rock Lobster* (New York: Alyson, 1981).

8. Gay relationships are discussed in Betty Berzon, *Permanent Partners: Building Gay and Lesbian Relationships That Last* (New York: E. P. Dutton, 1988) and David P. McWirter and Andrew M. Mattison, *The Male Couple* (Englewood Cliffs, N.J.: Prentice-Hall, 1984).

9. The treatment of gay people in literature is discussed in Barbara Grier, *The Lesbian in Literature* (Iowa City, Iowa: Naiad, 1988); George-Michel Sarotte, *Like a Brother, Like a Lover* (New York: Doubleday, 1978); Ian Young (Ed.), *The Male Homosexual in Literature: A Bibliography* (Metuchen, N.J.: Scarecrow Press, 1975); and Roger Austen, *Playing the Game: The Homosexual Novel in America* (Indianapolis: Bobbs-Merrill Press, 1977). Gay people in films are discussed in Parker Tyler, *Screening the Sexes: Homosexuality in the Movies* (New York: Holt, Rinehart, & Winston, 1972) and Vito Russo, *The Celluloid Closet: Lesbians and Gay Men in American Film* (New York: Harper & Row, 1980).

10. The emergence of positive roles is discussed in Betty Berzon, *Positively Gay* (Los Angeles: Mediamix Associates, 1979).

11. An excellent reference source for more information on gay communication research is Wayne R. Dynes, *Homosexuality: A Research Guide* (New York: Garland, 1987). He covers nonverbal communciation in his section on "Social Semiotics," pp. 372 ff.

12. Camp is discussed in Susan Sontag, "Notes on Camp," *Against Interpretation* (New York: Dell, 1969). For a dictionary of antique camp language, see Bruce Rodgers, *The Queen's Vernacular: A Gay Lexicon* (New York: Simon and Schuster, 1972).

13. Altman discusses cruising in *The Homosexualization of America*, p. 176.

Who's Got the Room at the Top? A Nomenclature for Intracultural Communication

EDITH A. FOLB

By "nondominant groups" I mean those constellations of people 1 who have not historically or traditionally had continued access to or influence upon or within the dominant culture's (that is, those who dominate culture) social, political, legal, economic, and/or religious structures and institutions. Nondominant groups include people of color, women, gays, the physically challenged[1] and the aged, to name some of the most prominent. I use the expression "nondominant" to characterize these people because, as suggested, I am referring to power and dominance, not numbers and dominance. Within the United States, those most likely to hold and control positions of real—not token—power and those who have the greatest potential ease of access to power and high status are still generally white, male, able-bodied, heterosexual, and youthful in appearance if not in age.[2]

Nondominant people are also those who, in varying degrees 2 and various ways, have been "invisible" within the society of which they are a part and at the same time bear a visible caste mark. Furthermore, it is this mark of caste identity that is often consciously or habitually assigned low or negative status by members of the dominant culture.

The dimensions of invisibility and marked visibility are keen in- 3 dicators of the status hierarchy in a given society. In his book, *The Invisible Man*, Ralph Ellison instructs us in the lesson that nondomi-

---

Edith A. Folb (1938–   ), born in Los Angeles, is professor of speech communication at San Francisco State University and author of books and articles on communication and culture including *A Comparative Study of Urban Black Argot* (1972) and *Runnin' Down Some Lines: The Language and Culture of Black Teenagers* (1980). "Who's Got the Room at the Top? A Nomenclature for Intracultural Communication" is from "Who's Got the Room at the Top? Issues of Dominance and Nondominance in Intracultural Communication," which first appeared in *Intercultural Communication: A Reader*, third edition, edited by Larry A. Samovar and Richard E. Porter (1982).

nant people—in this instance, black people—are figuratively "invisible." They are seen by the dominant culture as no one, nobody and therefore go unacknowledged and importantly unperceived.[3] Furthermore, nondominant peoples are often relegated to object status rather than human status. They are viewed as persons of "no consequence," literally and metaphorically. Expressions such as, "If you've seen one, you've seen them all"; "They all look alike to me"; "If you put a bag over their heads, it doesn't matter who you screw" attest to this level of invisibility and dehumanization of nondominant peoples, such as people of color or women. Indeed, one need only look at the dominant culture's slang repertory for a single nondominant group, women, to see the extent of this object status: "tail," "piece of ass," "side of beef," "hole," "gash," "slit," and so on.

At the same time that nondominant peoples are socially invisible, they are often visibly caste marked. Though we tend to think of caste in terms, say, of East Indian culture, we can clearly apply the concept to our own culture. One of the important dimensions of a caste system is that it is hereditary—you are born into a given caste and are usually marked for life as a member. In fact, we are all born into a caste, we are all caste marked. Indeed, some of us are doubly or multiply caste marked. In the United States, the most visible marks of caste relate to gender, race, age, and the degree to which one is able-bodied. 4

As East Indians do, we too assign low to high status and privilege to our people. The fact that this assignment of status and privilege may be active or passive, conscious or unconscious, malicious or unthinking does not detract from the reality of the act. And one of the major determinants of status, position, and caste marking relates back to who has historically or traditionally had access to or influence upon or within the power elite and its concomitant structures and institutions. So, historically blacks, Native Americans, Chicanos, women, the old, the physically challenged have at best been neutrally caste marked and more often negatively identified when it comes to issues of power, dominance, and social control.[4] 5

Low status has been assigned to those people whom society views as somehow "stigmatized." Indeed, we have labels to identify such stigmatization: "deviant," "handicapped," "abnormal," "substandard," "different"—that is, different from those who dominate. As already suggested, it is the white, male, heterosexual, able-bodied, youthful person who both sets the standards for caste marking and is the human yardstick by which people within the United States are importantly measured and accordingly treated. As Porter and Samovar (1976) remind us, "We [in the United States] have gen- 6 erally viewed racial minorities as less than equal; they have been viewed as second-class members of society—not quite as good as the white majority—and treated as such. . . . Blacks, Mexican-Americans, Indians, and Orientals are still subject to prejudice and discrimination and treated in many respects as colonized subjects" (p. 11). I would add to this list of colonized, low-status subjects women, the physically challenged, and the aged. Again, our language is a telling repository for illuminating status as it relates to subordination in the social hierarchy: "Stay in your place," "Don't get out of line," "Know your place," "A woman's place is chained to the bed and the stove," "Know your station in life," are just a few sample phrases.

It is inevitable that nondominant peoples will experience, indeed 7 be subjected to and suffer from, varying degrees of fear, denial, and self-hatred of their caste marking. Frantz Fanon's (1963) characterization of the "colonized native"—the oppressed native who has so internalized the power elite's perception of the norm that he or she not only serves and speaks for the colonial elite but is often more critical and oppressive of her or his caste than is the colonial—reveals this depth of self-hatred and denial.

In a parallel vein, the concept of "passing" which relates to a 8 person of color attempting to "pass for" white, is a statement of self-denial. Implicit in the act of passing is the acceptance, if not the belief, that "white is right" in this society, and the closer one can come to the likeness of the privileged caste, the more desirable and comfortable one's station in life will be. So, people of color have passed for white—just as Jews have passed for Gentile or gay males and females have passed for straight, always with the fear of being discovered "for what they are." Physical impairment, too, has been a mark of shame in this country for those so challenged. Even so powerful a figure as F.D.R. refused to be photographed in any way that would picture him to be a "cripple."

If the act of passing is a denial of one's caste, the process of 9 "coming out of the closet" is a conscious acceptance of one's caste. It is an important political and personal statement of power, a vivid metaphor that literally marks a rite of passage. Perhaps the most striking acknowledgement of one's caste marking in our society relates to sexual preference. For a gay male or lesbian to admit their respective sexual preferences is for them to consciously take on an identity that our society has deemed abnormal and deviant—when measured against the society's standard of what is appropriate. They become, quite literally, marked people. In an important way, most of our domestic liberation movements are devoted to having their membership come out of the closet. That is, these movements seek not only to have their people heard and empowered by the power elite, but to have them reclaim and assert their identity and honor their caste. Liberation movement slogans tell the story of positive identification with one's caste: "Black is beautiful," "brown power," "Sisterhood is powerful," "gay pride," "I am an Indian and proud of it."

The nature and disposition of the social hierarchy in a given so- 10 ciety, such as the United States, is reflected not only in the caste structure, but also in the class structure and the role prescriptions and expectations surrounding caste and class. Although the power structure in the United States is a complex and multileveled phenomenon, its predominant, generating force is economic. That is, the power elite is an elite that controls the material resources and goods in this country as well as the means and manner of production and distribution. Though one of our national fictions is that the United States is a classless society, we have, in fact, a well-established class structure based largely on economic power and control. When we talk of lower, middle, and upper classes in this country, we are not usually talking about birth or origins, but about power and control over material resources, and the attendant wealth, privilege, and high status.

There is even a kind of status distinction made within the upper- 11 class society in this country that again relates to wealth and power, but in a temporal rather than a quantitative way—how long one has had wealth, power, and high-class status. So, distinctions are made between the old rich (the Harrimans, the Gores, the Pews) and the new rich (the Hunt family, Norton Simon, and their like).

Class, then, is intimately bound up with matters of caste. Not 12 all, or even most, members of our society have the opportunity—let alone the caste credentials—to get a "piece of the action." It is no accident of nature that many of the nondominant peoples in this country are also poor peoples. Nor is it surprising that nondominant groups have been historically the unpaid, low-paid, and/or enslaved work force for the economic power elite.

Finally, role prescriptions are linked to both matters of status 13 and expectations in terms of one's perceived status, class, and caste. A role can be defined simply as a set of behaviors. The set of behaviors we ascribe to a given role is culture-bound and indicative of what has been designated as appropriate within the culture vis-à-vis that role. They are prescriptive, not descriptive, behaviors. We hold certain behavioral expectations for certain roles. It is a mark of just how culture-bound and prescriptive these roles are when someone is perceived to behave inappropriately—for example, the mother who gives up custody of her children in order to pursue her career; she has "stepped out of line."

Furthermore, we see certain roles as appropriate or inappropri- 14
ate to a given caste. Though another of our national myths—the Horatio Alger myth—tells us that there is room at the top for the industrious, bright go-getter, the truth of the matter is that there is room
at the top if you are appropriately caste marked (that is, are white,
male, able-bodied, and so on). The resistance, even outright hostility, nondominant peoples have encountered when they aspire to or
claim certain occupational roles, for example, is a mark of the power
elite's reluctance to relinquish those positions that have been traditionally associated with privileged status and high caste and class
ranking. Though, in recent years, there has been much talk about a
woman Vice-President of the United States, it has remained just
talk. For that matter, there has not been a black Vice-President or a
Hispanic or a Jew. The thought of the Presidency being held by
most nondominant peoples is still "unspeakable."

The cultural prescription to keep nondominant peoples "in their 15
place" is reinforced by and reinforces what I refer to as the
"subterranean self"—the culture-bound collection of prejudices,
stereotypes, values, and beliefs that each of us embraces and employs to justify our world view and the place of people in that
world. It is, after all, our subterranean selves that provide fuel to fire
the normative in our lives—what roles people ought and ought not
to perform, what and why certain individuals are ill- or well-
equipped to carry out certain roles, and our righteously stated ration-
alizations for keeping people in their places as we see them. Again,
it should be remembered that those who dominate the culture reinforce and tacitly or openly encourage the perpetuation of those cultural prejudices, stereotypes, values, and beliefs that maintain the
status quo, that is, the asymmetrical nature of the social hierarchy.
Those who doubt the fervent desire of the power elite to maintain
things as they are need only ponder the intense and prolonged resistance to the Equal Rights Amendment. If women are already
"equal," why not make their equality a matter of record?

The foregoing discussion has been an attempt to illuminate the 16
meaning of nondominance and the position of the nondominant
person within our society. By relating status in the social hierarchy
to matters of caste, class, and role, it has been my intention to highlight what it means to be a nondominant person within a culture
that is dominated by the cultural precepts and artifacts of a power
elite. It has also been my intention to suggest that the concept of
"dominant culture" is something of a fiction, as we in communication studies traditionally use it. Given my perspective, it is more accurate to talk about those who dominate a culture rather than a
dominant culture per se. Finally, I have attempted to point out that

cultural dominance is not necessarily, or even usually, a matter of the numbers of people in a given society, but of those who have real power in a society.

Geopolitics

The viewpoint being developed in this essay highlights still another [17] facet of dominance and nondominance as it relates to society and the culture it generates and sustains—namely, the geopolitical facet. The United States is not merely a territory with certain designated boundaries—a geographical entity—it is a geopolitical configuration. It is a country whose history reflects the clear-cut interrelationship of geography, politics, economics, and the domination and control of people. For example, the westward movement and the subsequent takeover of the Indian nations and chunks of Mexico were justified by our doctrine of Manifest Destiny, not unlike the way Hitler's expansionism was justified by the Nazi doctrine of "geopolitik." It is no accident that the doctrine of Manifest Destiny coincides with the rapid growth and development of U.S. industrialization. The U.S. power elite wanted more land in which to expand and grow economically, so it created a rationalization to secure it.

Perhaps nowhere is a dominant culture's (those who dominate [18] culture) ethnocentrism more apparent than in the missionarylike work carried on by its members—whether it be to "civilize" the natives (that is, to impose the conquerors' cultural baggage on them), to "educate them in the ways of the white man," or to "Americanize" them. Indeed, the very term *America* is a geopolitical label as we use it. It presumes that those who inhabit the United States are the center of the Western hemisphere, indeed its only residents.[5] Identifying ourselves as "Americans" and our geopolitical entity as "America," in light of the peoples who live to the north and south of our borders, speaks to both our economic dominance in this hemisphere and our ethnocentrism.

Identifying the United States in geopolitical terms is to identify it [19] as a conqueror and controller of other peoples, and suggests both the probability of nondominant groups of people within that territory as well as a polarized, even hostile relationship between these groups and those who dominate culture. What Rich and Ogawa (1982) have pointed out in their model of interracial communication is applicable to most nondominant peoples: "As long as a power relationship exists between cultures where one has subdued and dominated the other . . . hostility, tension and strain are introduced into the communicative situation" (p. 46). Not only were the Indian nations[6] and parts of Mexico conquered and brought under the colonial rule of the United States, but in its industrial expansionism, the United States physically enslaved black Africans to work on the farms and plantations of the South. It also economically enslaved large numbers of East European immigrants, Chinese, Irish, Hispanics (and more recently, Southeast Asians) in its factories, on its railroads, in its mines and fields through low wages and long work hours. It co-opted the cottage industries of the home and brought women and children into the factories under abysmal conditions and the lowest of wages.

Indeed, many of the nondominant peoples in this country today [20] are the very same ones whom the powerful have historically colonized, enslaved, disenfranchised, dispossessed, discounted, and relegated to poverty and low caste and class status. So, the asymmetrical relationship between the conquerer and the conquered continues uninterrupted. Although the form of oppression may change through time, the fact of oppression—and coexistent nondominance—remains.

Notes

1. The semantic marker "physically challenged" is used in lieu of other, more traditional labels such as "handicapped," "physically disabled," or "physically impaired," because it is a designation preferred by many so challenged. It is seen as a positive, rather than a negative, mark of identification.

2. In a country as youth-conscious as our own, advanced age is seen as a liability, not as a mark of honor and wisdom as it is in other cultures. Whatever other reservations people had about Ronald Reagan's political aspirations in 1980, the one most discussed was his age. His political handlers went to great lengths—as did Reagan himself—to "prove" he was young in spirit and energy if not in years. It was important that he align himself as closely as possible with the positive mark of youth we champion and admire in this country.

3. It is no mere coincidence that a common thread binds together the domestic liberation movements in this country. It is the demand to be seen, heard, and empowered.

4. See Nancy Henley's *Body Politics* (1977) for a provocative look at the interplay of the variables power, dominance, and sex as they affect nonverbal communication.

5. The current bumper sticker, "Get the United States Out of North America," is a pointed reference to our hemispheric self-centeredness.

6. Neither the label "Indian" nor the label "Native American" adequately identifies those people who inhabited the North American continent before the European conquest of this territory. Both reflect the point of view of the labeler, not those so labeled. That is why many who fought for the label "Native American" now discount it as not significantly different from "Indian."

References

Fanon, Frantz. *Wretched of the Earth.* New York: Grove Press, Inc., 1963.

Porter, Richard E. and Larry A. Samovar, "Communicating Interculturally." In *Intercultural Communication: A Reader*, 2nd ed., ed. Larry A. Samovar and Richard E. Porter. Belmont, Calif.: Wadsworth, 1976.

Rich, Andrea L., and Dennis M. Ogawa. "Intercultural and Interracial Communication: An Analytical Approach." In *Intercultural Communication: A Reader*, 3rd ed., ed. Larry A. Samovar and Richard E. Porter. Belmont, Calif.: Wadsworth, 1982.

READING AND WRITING
ABOUT DIVERSITY AT HOME

1. Contrast the various opinions about America's first immigrants offered by Alex de Tocqueville, Henry David Thoreau, Paula Gunn Allen, and Ishmael Reed.

2. Identify some of the assumptions or values underlying Reed's argument about America's "cultural bouillabaisse" and Robert Claiborne's defense of WASPs. What does each author evidently believe that he doesn't state directly? How well does each support his position with evidence or reasoning?

3. What, according to Joan Didion, is "the precise angle at which Miami Anglos and Miami Cubans were failing to connect" (paragraph 11)? How does she demonstrate Anglos' misunderstanding of Cubans in Miami?

4. Working with a partner or small group, edit Maria Moreno's transcribed speech into grammatical standard American English. Read aloud passages from both the original and your revised version. What, if anything, gets lost in the "translation" into standard English? Which version do you find more persuasive, and why?

5. Margaret Mead suggests that later-generation immigrants "make a much better adjustment [to American culture] than their parents" but then perform merely a "parade of power." Test her analysis by applying it to the Cubans of Miami (with reference to Didion's essay), to Richard Rodriguez's "scholarship boys," or to the Vietnamese refugees discussed by Ellyn Bache.

6. To what extent do you agree with Rodriguez that (a) academia is a kind of "foreign culture" for students of all ethnicities, and (b) in order to succeed in the academic world, "scholarship boys" (or girls) must lose touch with the culture they came from? How distant from your home culture have you become since you started college?

7. What specifically is Bache arguing for or against in paragraphs 15 to 18? What kinds of evidence does she offer, here and elsewhere in the essay, for her views on U.S. refugee policies and resettlement programs?

8. Make a list of common stereotypes about another ethnic group, as Alexandra Tantranon-Saur does for Asian/Pacific people in general then ask members of that group to help you evaluate the validity, causes, or effects of these stereotypes. Finally, "put your newfound insights into action" (as Tantranon-Saur says) by addressing a list of suggestions or exercises to the white majority or to another racial or ethnic group.

9. Do you agree with "Andrew Cornell," in Julia Gilden's essay, that "people walking their dogs on leashes are on leashes themselves"? What leashes does he mean? What is "the benign devouring marshmallow of the The Good Life," and how appropriate do you find this image for modern society?

10. Imagine a conversation between Phyllis McGinley and one of Gilden's "garbage people" about a current social issue, such as homelessness. How would each challenge the other's basic values and assumptions about society? Try playing both roles with a partner or small group, then write an essay in the form of a dialogue. Express your own position by including yourself, or a moderator representing your views, in the dialogue.

11. Aside from the fairly obvious fact that McGinley was not "a black feminist or feminist of color," in what ways does she fulfill and not fulfill Alice Walker's definition of *womanist*?

12. What different audiences are McGinley, James Baldwin, and Shelby Steele writing for? How can you tell? Discuss how each writer deals with opposition to his or her opinion.

13. What would Steele say is missing from Baldwin's analysis of Harlem's problems? How else might he criticize the "Letter from Harlem," and how would Baldwin respond to this criticism?

14. Which features of gay culture analyzed by Randall Majors—neighborhoods, social groups, symbols, and meeting behavior—are most relevant to another group with which you're familiar? To what degree are the psychological and social needs of gay people suggested by Majors shared by heterosexuals in our society?

15. Test Edith Folb's ideas about social class, caste, and role in one of this chapter's other essays. One angle would be to apply her concept of the "subterranean self" (paragraph 15), which she says is responsible for perpetuating our cultural prejudices and stereotypes, to another Chapter 4 author or essay.

16. Majors and Folb both maintain an ostensibly objective, social-scientific tone. To what extent does each advocate a political position in his or her scholarly article? Cite specific passages that show how Majors himself feels about the emerging gay culture and about gay people in general, or cite passages that reveal Folb's opinion of the dominant and nondominant groups she discusses.

17. The "Melting Pot," Charles Kuralt writes, "never succeeded in melting us." Several writers in this chapter (such as Reed, Baldwin, and Majors) would seem to agree with him, while others (including Rodriguez, Bache, and Steele) seem to demonstrate the assimilation of immigrant and minority groups implied by the melting pot metaphor. To what extent do you agree with Kuralt that "Americans are made of some alloy that won't be melted"? Use your own experiences and your previous outside reading, in addition to Chapter 4's selections, to support your views.

18. "Kim and Quang's story sounds like the Great American Dream retold," Bache writes about the Vietnamese refugees her family sponsored. "What they seek," says Gilden of warehouse-tribe dropouts, "seems the antithesis of the American Dream." How do you define "the American Dream"? How well is this dream working out for the various ethnic and other social groups in America, especially those you belong to? Use evidence from any of the essays in this chapter both to support your thesis and to anticipate—and deal with—objections to your views.

MAKING FURTHER CONNECTIONS

1. Based on the academic writing of Majors or Folb, do you agree with Michael Ventura (Chapter 1) that "the university is where language goes to die"? Do you think Moreno's lack of academic fluency excludes her, as Rachel Jones (Chapter 1) says of Black English speakers, "from full participation" in our society? Or do you agree with Kit Yuen Quan (Chapter 1) that academic "abstractions like 'oppression,' 'sexism,' 'racism,' etc." (paragraph 15) can themselves be oppressive?

2. Rodriguez in this chapter and Michelle Cliff in Chapter 1 both write about working on Ph.D. dissertations in London and the conflicts they felt in this context as members of racial minorities. Whose reactions to these conflicts do you sympathize with more, and why?

3. Focusing on her descriptions of gay neighborhoods, social groups, or symbols, consider Frances FitzGerald's Chapter 2 essay in terms of Majors's sociological analysis of U.S. gay culture. What can you add to, or how might you modify, Majors's analysis? For example, of San Francisco's "four gay centers," FitzGerald considers only the Castro to be a true neighborhood; how well does this jibe with Majors' definition of the "gay neighborhood"?

4. How does David Leavitt, in his story "Territory" in Chapter 6, try to break down hurtful stereotypes about gay men? Is he more or less successful at this than FitzGerald (Chapter 2) or Majors?

5. Test your notion of "the American Dream" from this chapter (see Question 18 above) against a different notion from a Chapter 2 author such as Studs Terkel, Juan Cadena, Christopher Isherwood, or Gretel Ehrlich.

6. Use Steele's ideas about the relationship of race to economic class to help you analyze Alex Haley's dilemma on his return visit to The Gambia (Chapter 3).

7. Baldwin's and Steele's arguments about the condition of American blacks offer different ways to interpret the meeting of cultures that takes place in Grace Paley's story "The Long-Distance Runner" in Chapter 6. Test your own view of the story against these different social criticisms.

8. The assimilation or Americanization of various minority groups (see Question 17 in the first section) is an issue in several of Chapter 6's stories—including Arturo Islas's "Thanksgiving Border Crossing," Frank Chin's "Railroad Standard Time," Bharati Mukherjee's "Tamurlane," and Louise Erdrich's "American Horse." Write about this theme in one or more of these stories; compare the "melting pot" experiences of an author from Chapter 4.

9. Compare the different assumptions about the roles of men and women made by McGinley in her essay and by the male and female characters of Joanna Russ's story "When It Changed" in Chapter 6.

EXPLORING NEW SOURCES

1. Try to prove or disprove some of the conflicting claims made in this chapter about early American settlers, such as Tocqueville's claim that the settlers of New England were all affluent and well educated; Allen's claim that our "constitutional system of government might be as much a product of American Indian ideas and practices as of colonial American and Anglo-European" ideas; or Reed's claim that the Puritans killed children who misbehaved. Include some primary sources in your research, such as newspaper articles or personal memoirs from the seventeenth century, if these are available in your library.

2. Do some background research on the U.S. government's current policies regarding refugees and resettlement programs. If possible, interview refugees living in your area, their American sponsors, or government officials involved with these programs. After your research, take a position on one of the controversies addressed by Bache and write an essay defending your position.

3. Compare the punk movement, cited by Gilden as a major influence on the urban dropouts she writes about, with a previous social protest movement in the United States (such as the hippie counterculture or the beat movement). Focus on a particular aspect of the movements that interests you, such as their music or prevalent life-style habits.

4. Talk with your family and identify at least one of your relatives or ancestors who came from somewhere outside the United States. If you can't identify the relative or relatives who first came to the U.S., find someone who immigrated somewhere else. Determine, at least, the person's place of origin and destination and the approximate dates. Research the social conditions in both places at that time, and speculate on the reasons for your ancestor's immigration.

5. With the most recent information you can find, including the 1990 census report, determine the relative socioeconomic situation of an ethnic or social group to which you belong or in which you're interested. Analyze the causes or effects of this current status. To what extent has this group achieved, or can it hope to achieve, some version of "the American Dream"?

6. What issues relating to ethnic and cultural diversity are currently being debated at your college or university? Possibilities include: changes in the curriculum or required courses (such as ethnic studies), support services for ethnic or other minority-group students (such as gay people or disabled people), and ethnic theme dormitories

at residence-based schools. In addition to consulting relevant scholarly studies, arrange interviews with school administrators, members of student groups, and professors with expertise in this area. Write a letter to the editor of the student newspaper summarizing your argument, then write a proposal, presenting your evidence in detail, to the responsible administrator or faculty group.

5

THE CRITICAL JOURNEY: ENCOUNTERING CULTURES ABROAD

The global context that has been more or less implicit in previous chapters is made explicit in this chapter. If we saw the writer as a traveler in Chapter 3, now we view the "traveler" as a social critic. Americans are still discovering foreign places and meeting strangers here, but at the same time they are more consciously encountering—interpreting, evaluating, judging—the larger culture that gives those places and people an international context. So the selections in Chapter 5, like those in Chapter 4, are increasingly analytical and argumentative.

The tensions introduced in previous chapters—between language and culture, between subjectivity and objectivity, between culture-bound limitations and their transcendence, and between assimilationist and pluralistic models for cross-cultural relations—still find expression in this chapter. In addition, another broad theme appears in Chapter 5: the problem of generalizing about national groups. When is stereotyping necessary and even desirable? When is it not useful, when does it become harmful, and at what point does it degenerate into prejudice or racism?

To begin addressing this theme, you might explore your own stereotypical beliefs, and those held about whatever racial, ethnic, social, or national groups you belong to. For example, according to a long-time advisor of foreign students, Gary Althen, in his book *American Ways*, common stereotypes held about Americans by foreigners include that:

> . . . American women are nearly all readily available for sexual activity. . . .

Most American women are beautiful . . . and most American men are handsome. . . . Those who are not beautiful or handsome are criminals, deceitful people, and members of the lower class.

Violent crime is an ever-present threat in all parts of the country.

Average Americans are rich and usually do not have to work to get money.

Average Americans live in large, modern, shiny houses or apartments. . . .

There is a stratum of American society in which most people are nonwhite, physically ugly, uneducated, and dedicated to violence.

High-speed automobile chases are frequently seen on American streets.

[Americans believe that] nonwhite people are inferior to white people.[1]

To the extent that you disagree with or object to these stereotypes, you should also question your own beliefs about other cultures. To the extent that these stereotypes result partly from the way Americans are presented in movies and television programs broadcast overseas, you should examine the basis for your own generalizations about people from other countries.

The diversity of authors encountering other cultures in Chapter 5 is reflected, as in previous chapters, in a variety of writing styles and techniques. To support their claims, these authors may make lists and charts, draw analogies, offer examples, make comparisons, trace causes, quote authorities, cite facts and scientific studies, reason logically, appeal to emotions, tell stories, or use humor, irony, and exaggerations. As you read this chapter, consider which kinds of arguments and analyses you find most persuasive. Challenge yourself, when you find an essay especially convincing or unconvincing, to explain why—and to apply this strategic lesson to your own analytical and argumentative writing.

The Brief Encounters open with a paradox posed by French anthropologist Claude Lévi-Strauss about the difficulty of studying other cultures without corrupting them. Philip L. Pearce and Peter S. Adler offer two social science frameworks you can use to test selections from this and other chapters, classifying travelers into "fifteen types" and culture shock into "five stages." Isak Dinesen, writing earlier in this century, speculates about how long it will take Africans "to catch up with" European civilization; Chinua Achebe, from Nigeria, argues that such comparisons reveal the West's "deep

---

[1] Gary Althen, *American Ways: A Guide for Foreigners in the United States* (Yarmouth, Maine: Intercultural Press, 1988), pp. 75–76.

anxieties about the precariousness of its civilization." Lawrence Durrell introduces the concept of national character and its connection to geography, and Gary Snyder, Jan Morris, and Margaret Atwood generalize about national character in comparisons involving India, Japan, China, the United States, and Canada.

In the main selections:

- Nancy Masterson Sakamoto uses tennis and bowling analogies to portray the differences between Western-style and Japanese-style conversation.

- Stanley Meisler analyzes the common perception of the French as "the coldest and least welcoming people of Europe."

- Alice Bloom tries to move beyond the "imaginary natives" of the travel posters by comparing a dignified Greek peasant woman she observes on the beach to a "nearly naked" blond tourist walking nearby.

- Paul Theroux uses the Tarzan myth, as portrayed in the comic books of his youth, to criticize his fellow expatriate Americans and Europeans living in Africa—racists and "liberals" alike.

- Michelle Cliff combines personal experience, history, and politics in Jamaica, England, and the United States to address the relationship between domestic oppression and colonialism.

- Calvin Trillin takes a humorous stab at gender issues in Japan and Saudi Arabia by arguing with a friend who "always wants to understand everything in its cultural context."

- Margaret K. Nydell tries to promote cross-cultural understanding by outlining some basic, deeply ingrained differences in the ways Arab peoples and Westerners see themselves and the world.

- Pico Iyer argues that two popular views of global relations—that the First World is corrupting the Third World, and that the Third World "is hustling the First"—are both too simplistic.

- Robert Lado offers examples such as a bullfight, tarpon fishing, and milk consumption at dinner to scientifically compare behaviors in different cultures in terms of their "forms," "meanings," and "distributions."

- Genelle G. Morain, presenting evidence from a variety of cultures, analyzes nonverbal communication behaviors including posture, facial expression, eye movement, and gestures.

- Renato Rosaldo argues for a new paradigm for cultural studies, one that rejects the imperialist notion of Western scientists studying "their natives" and that legitimizes the study of "cultural borderlands."

BRIEF ENCOUNTERS

The Traveler's Dilemma

CLAUDE LÉVI-STRAUSS

I should have liked to live in the age of *real* travel, when the spectacle on offer had not yet been blemished, contaminated, and confounded; then I could have seen Lahore not as I saw it, but as it appeared to Bernier, Tavernier, Manucci. . . . There's no end, of course, to such conjectures. When was the right moment to see India? At what period would the study of the Brazilian savage have yielded the purest satisfaction and the savage himself been at his peak? Would it have been better to have arrived at Rio in the eighteenth century, with Bougainville, or in the sixteenth, with Léry and Thevet? With every decade that we traveled further back in time, I could have saved another costume, witnessed another festivity, and come to understand another system of belief. But I'm too familiar with the texts not to know that this backward movement would also deprive me of much information, many curious facts and objects, that would enrich my meditations. The paradox is irresoluble: the less one culture communicates with another, the less likely they are to be corrupted, one by the other; but, on the other hand, the less likely it is, in such conditions, that the respective emissaries of these cultures will be able to seize the richness and significance of their diversity. The alternative is inescapable: either I am a traveler in ancient times, and faced with a prodigious spectacle which would be almost entirely unintelligible to me and might, indeed, provoke me to mockery or disgust; or I am a traveler of our own day, hastening in search of a vanished reality. In either case I am the loser—and more heavily than one might suppose; for today, as I go groaning among the shadows, I miss, inevitably, the spectacle that is now taking shape. My eyes, or perhaps my degree of humanity, do not equip me to witness that spectacle; and in the centuries to come, when another traveler revisits this same place, he too may groan aloud at the disappearance of much that I should have set down, but cannot. I am the victim of a double infirmity: what I see is an affliction to me; and what I do not see, a reproach.

—FROM *TRISTES TROPIQUES*, 1955

Fifteen Types of Travelers

PHILIP L. PEARCE

Traveler Category	The Five Clearest Role-Related Behaviours (in order of relative importance)
Tourist	Takes photos, buys souvenirs, goes to famous places, stays briefly in one place, does not understand the local people
Traveler	Stays briefly in one place, experiments with local food, goes to famous places, takes photos, explores places privately
Holidaymaker	Takes photos, goes to famous places, is alienated from the local society, buys souvenirs, contributes to the visited economy
Jet-setter	Lives a life of luxury, concerned with social status, seeks sensual pleasures, prefers interacting with people of his/her own kind, goes to famous places
Businessperson	Concerned with social status, contributes to the economy, does not take photos, prefers interacting with people of his/her own kind, lives a life of luxury
Migrant	Has language problems, prefers interacting with people of his/her own kind, does not understand the local people, does not live a life of luxury, does not exploit the local people
Conservationist	Interested in the environment, does not buy souvenirs, does not exploit the local people, explores places privately, takes photos
Explorer	Explores places privately, interested in the environment, takes physical risks, does not buy souvenirs, keenly observes the visited society
Missionary	Does not buy souvenirs, searches for the meaning of life, does not live in luxury, does not seek sensual pleasures, keenly observes the visited society
Overseas student	Experiments with local food, does not exploit the people, takes photos, keenly observes the visited society, takes physical risks
Anthropologist	Keenly observes the visited society, explores places privately, interested in the environment, does not buy souvenirs, takes photos
Hippie	Does not buy souvenirs, does not live a life of luxury, is not concerned with social status, does not take photos, does not contribute to the economy
International athlete	Is not alienated from own society, does not exploit the local people, does not understand the local people, explores places privately, searches for the meaning of life
Overseas journalist	Takes photos, keenly observes the visited society, goes to famous places, takes physical risks, explores places privately
Religious pilgrim	Searches for the meaning of life, does not live a life of luxury, is not concerned with social status, does not exploit the local people, does not buy souvenirs

—FROM *THE SOCIAL PSYCHOLOGY OF TOURIST BEHAVIOR*, 1982

Five Stages of Culture Shock

PETER S. ADLER

Stage	Perception	Emotional Range	Behavior	Interpretation
Contact	Differences are intriguing Perceptions are screened and selected	Excitement Stimulation Euphoria Playfulness Discovery	Curiosity Interest Assured Impressionistic	The individual is insulated by his or her own culture. Differences as well as similarities provide rationalization for continuing confirmation of status, role, and identity.
Disintegration	Differences are impactful Contrasted cultural reality cannot be screened out	Confusion Disorientation Loss Apathy Isolation Loneliness Inadequacy	Depression Withdrawal	Cultural differences begin to intrude. Growing awareness of being different leads to loss of self-esteem. Individual experiences loss of cultural support ties and misreads new cultural cues.
Reintegration	Differences are rejected	Anger Rage Nervousness Anxiety Frustration	Rebellion Suspicion Rejection Hostility Exclusive Opinionated	Rejection of second culture causes preoccupation with likes and dislikes; differences are projected. Negative behavior, however, is a form of self-assertion and growing self-esteem.
Autonomy	Differences and similarities are legitimized	Self-assured Relaxed Warm Empathic	Assured Controlled Independent "Old hand" Confident	The individual is socially and linguistically capable of negotiating most new and different situations; he or she is assured of ability to survive new experiences.
Independence	Differences and similarities are valued and significant	Trust Humour Love Full range of previous emotions	Expressive Creative Actualizing	Social, psychological and cultural differences are accepted and enjoyed. The individual is capable of exercising choice and responsibility and able to *create* meaning for situations.

—FROM "THE TRANSITIONAL EXPERIENCE: AN ALTERNATIVE VIEW OF CULTURE SHOCK," IN THE *JOURNAL OF HUMANISTIC PSYCHOLOGY*, 1975

Of Natives and History

ISAK DINESEN

The people who expect the Natives to jump joyfully from the stone age to the age of the motor cars, forget the toil and labor which our own fathers have had, to bring us all through history up to where we are.

We can make motor-cars and aeroplanes, and teach the Natives to use them. But the true love of motor cars cannot be made, in human hearts, in the turn of a hand. It takes centuries to produce it, and it is likely that Socrates, the Crusades, and the French Revolution, have been needed in the making. We of the present day, who love our machines, cannot quite imagine how people in the old days could live without them. But we could not make the Athanasian Creed, or the technique of the Mass, or of a five-act tragedy, and perhaps not even of a sonnet. And if we had not found them there ready for our use, we should have had to do without them. Still we must imagine, since they have been made at all, that there was a time when the hearts of humanity cried out for these things, and when a deeply felt want was relieved when they were made.

The modern white people in Africa believe in evolution and not in any sudden creative act. They might then run the Natives through a short practical lesson of history to bring them up to where we are. We took these nations over not quite forty years ago; if we compare that moment to the moment of the birth of the Lord, and allow them, to catch up with us, three years to our hundred, it will now be time to send them out Saint Francis of Assisi, and in a few years Rabelais. They would love and appreciate both better than we do, of our century. They liked Aristophanes when some years ago I tried to translate to them the dialogue between the farmer and his son, out of "The Clouds." In twenty years they might be ready for the Encyclopaedists, and then they would come, in another ten years, to Kipling. We should let them have dreamers, philosophers and poets out, to prepare the ground for Mr. Ford.

Where shall they find us then? Shall we in the meantime have caught them by the tail and be hanging on to it, in our pursuit of some shade, some darkness, practicing upon a tomtom? Will they be able to have our motor cars at cost price then, as they can now have the doctrine of the Transubstantiation?

—FROM *OUT OF AFRICA*, 1937

Old Prejudices

CHINUA ACHEBE

For reasons which can certainly use close psychological inquiry, the West seems to suffer deep anxieties about the precariousness of its civilization and to have a need for constant reassurance by comparing itself to Africa. If Europe, advancing in civilization, could cast a backward glance periodically at Africa trapped in primordial barbarity, it could say with faith and feeling: There, but for the grace of God, go I. . . . I had thought to . . . suggest from my privileged position in African and Western culture some advantages the West might derive from Africa once it rid its mind of old prejudices and began to look at Africa not through a haze of distortions and cheap mystification but quite simply as a continent of people—not angels, but not rudimentary souls either—just people, often highly gifted people and often strikingly successful in their enterprise with life and society. But as I thought more about the stereotype image, about its grip and pervasiveness, about the willfull tenacity with which the West holds it to its heart; when I thought of your television and the cinema and newspapers, about books read in schools and out of school, of churches preaching to empty pews about the need to send help to the heathen in Africa, I realized that no easy optimism was possible. And there is something totally wrong in offering bribes to the West in return for its good opinion of Africa. Ultimately, the abandonment of unwholesome thoughts must be its own and only reward.

—FROM "AN IMAGE OF AFRICA," *CHANT OF SAINTS*, 1979

Landscape and Character

LAWRENCE DURRELL

I believe you could exterminate the French at a blow and resettle the country with Tartars, and within two generations discover, to your astonishment, that the national characteristics were back at norm— the restless metaphysical curiosity, the tenderness for good living and the passionate individualism: even though their noses were now flat. This is the invisible constant in a place with which the ordinary tourist can get in touch just by sitting quite quietly over a glass of wine in a Paris *bistrot*. He may not be able to formulate it very clearly to himself in literary terms, but he will taste the unmistakable keen knife-edge of happiness in the air of Paris: the pristine brilliance of a national psyche which knows that art is as important as love or food. He will not be blind either to the hard metallic rational sense, the irritating *coeur raisonnable*[1] of the men and women. When the French want to be *malins*,[2] as they call it, they can be just as we can be when we stick our toes in over some national absurdity.

Yes, human beings are expressions of their landscape, but in order to touch the secret springs of a national essence you need a few moments of quiet with yourself. Truly the intimate knowledge of landscape, if developed scientifically, could give us a political science—for half the political decisions taken in the world are based on what we call national character. We unconsciously acknowledge this fact when we exclaim, "How typically Irish" or "It would take a Welshman to think up something like that." And indeed we all of us jealously guard the sense of minority individuality in our own nations—the family differences. The great big nations like say the Chinese or the Americans present a superficially homogeneous appearance; but I've noticed that while we Europeans can hardly tell one American from another, my own American friends will tease each other to death at the lunch-table about the intolerable misfortune of being born in Ohio or Tennessee—a recognition of the validity of place which we ourselves accord to the Welshman, Irishman and Scotsman at home. It is a pity indeed to travel and not get this essential sense of landscape values. You do not need a sixth sense for it. It is there if you just close your eyes and breathe softly through your nose; you will hear the whispered message, for all landscapes ask the same question in the same whisper. "I am watching you— are you watching yourself in me?" Most travelers hurry too much. But try just for a moment sitting on the great stone omphalos, the navel of the ancient Greek world, at Delphi. Don't ask mental questions, but just relax and empty your mind. It lies, this strange amphora-shaped object, in an overgrown field above the temple. Everything is blue and smells of sage. The marbles dazzle down below you. There are two eagles moving softly softly on the sky, like distant boats rowing across an immense violet lake.

Ten minutes of this sort of quiet inner identification will give you the notion of the Greek landscape which you could not get in twenty years of studying ancient Greek texts.

—FROM "LANDSCAPE AND CHARACTER," IN *THE NEW YORK TIMES MAGAZINE*, 1960

---

[1] *coeur raisonnable*—reasonable heart. (Ed.)
[2] *malins*—cunning or shrewd. (Ed.)

Comparing India with Japan

GARY SNYDER

Now we are about to leave India, and feeling very lucky to have come through it all intact, with nothing worse than diarrhea a few times, quite elated really. And glad to be leaving, then, because India is not comfortable, nor is the food really good enough to stay healthy on forever. If you were settled in one spot and could do your own cooking and fix up your own quarters to suit yourself it would be different, of course.

But India in any case is not a comfortable country, the way Japan is. The contrasts are very sharp. Japanese culture is basically hedonistic, and even at its poorest, provides comforts: like the universal public baths, where you can get all the hot water you want to wash yourself clean, any time of the year. Cleanliness. Clean houses, clean inns, no matter how inexpensive. Toilet paper. (India doesn't use toilet paper, in part, because no one can *afford* it!) And of course, bars, sake stalls, teahouses, young pretty girl hostesses, all that sort of thing—which exists in limited quantity in India, and is much more degraded and dirty than it is in Japan. To understand the problem in part just picture the consequences of having various groups of people who will not dine together, bathe together, or even use the same water supply. How can you have a public life with castes? In India we always bathed by standing near a tap and pouring pans of water over ourselves. In the country one does this by standing in a stream or pond; and it was not uncommon to see people standing in filthy murky-looking water pouring panful after panful over themselves happily washing. The public manners of Indians are much noisier and more argumentative than the Japanese too (and Japanese public manners are lots worse than private manners). Dishonesty, cheating, hostility, rudeness, loudness, thoughtlessness, etc., on all sides in India. Again perhaps part of being a country overrun by so many aggressors, and full of so many groups constantly confronting each other. Yet there is a kind of honesty in India which is ultimately lacking in Japan; straightforwardness though rude, and a general refusal to play roles.

There's nothing phony there (even the phony holy men are *really* doing ascetic practices, *really* celibate, *really* vegetarian; their phoniness is that their understanding may not be as great as people or their own literature ascribes to them). The people, the landscape, even the religion, sticks to essentials. Part of this is just the poverty and suffering, I suppose, which cannot be acted over. But more than that: even the poverty-stricken areas of Japan, or poor periods of

history, never removed the constant playing of social roles by which
Japanese society exists. I think the difference is simply that for the
Japanese person (average) there is no substance or reality he can
conceive of outside the social fabric. For the Indian, all reality is outside the social fabric, which exists at best as a kind of disciplinary religious system for laymen, so that if you follow it properly ultimately
you'd be born into the Brahman caste and from there can be reborn
into nonhuman higher realms.

—FROM "NOW INDIA," IN *CATERPILLAR*, 1972

Progress in China

JAN MORRIS

The airline magazine on CAAC Flight 1502, Shanghai to Beijing, was
six months old (and reported the self-criticism of a Chinese women's
volley-ball team defeated by Americans in 1982—"they were desperate with fiery eyes, whereas we were passive and vulnerable to attack"). It was like flying in a dentist's waiting-room, I thought. Also
the seats in the 707 seemed to be a job lot from older, dismembered
aircraft, some of them reclining, some of them rigid, while people
smoked unrestrictedly in the non-smoking section, and our in-flight
refreshment was a mug of lukewarm coffee brought by a less than
winning stewardess. I was not surprised by all this. I was lucky, I
knew, that there were no wicker chairs in the middle of the aisle, to
take care of over-booking, and at least we were not called upon, as
passengers on other flights have been, to advance *en masse* upon re-
actionary hijackers, bombarding them with lemonade bottles.

The enigmas were mounting. Why, I wondered, were the Chinese modernizing themselves with such remarkable ineptitude? Did
they not invent the wheelbarrow a thousand years before the West?
Had they not, for that matter, split the atom and sent rockets into
space? Were they not brilliantly quick on the uptake, acute of observation, subtle of inference? The broad-minded Deng Xiaoping is
boss man of China these days, and he is dedicated to technical progress of any derivation—as he once said in a famous phrase, what
does it matter whether a cat is black or white, so long as it catches
mice? China simmers all over with innovation and technology from
the West: yet still the coffee's cold on Flight 1502.

The brick-laying of contemporary China would shame a backyard amateur in Arkansas. The architecture is ghastly. In the newest
and grandest buildings cement is cracked, taps don't work, escala-

tors are out of order. *Respect Hygiene,* proclaim the street posters, but the public lavatories are vile, and they have to put spittoons in the tombs of the Ming Emperors. Western architects, I am told, often despair to find air-conditioning connected to heating ducts, or fire-escapes mounted upside-down, and though it is true that the Chinese-made elevators in my Shanghai hotel were the *politest* I have ever used, with buttons marked Please Open and Please Close, still I felt that all the courtesy in the world would not much avail us if we ever got stuck halfway.

Why? What happened to the skills and sensibilities that built the Great Wall, molded the exquisite dragon-eaves, dug out the lovely lakes of *chinoiserie*? Feudalism stifled them, the official spokesmen say. Isolation atrophied them, the historians maintain. Maoism suppressed them, say the pragmatists. Communism killed them, that's what, say the tourists knowingly. But perhaps it goes deeper than that: perhaps the Chinese, deprived of their ancient magics, observing that nothing lasts, come Ming come Mao, have no faith in mere materialism, and put no trust in efficiency. *Feng shui,* the ancient Chinese geomancy which envisaged a mystic meaning to the form of everything, is banned from the People's Republic; and dear God, it shows, it shows.

Never mind: with an incomprehensible splutter over the public address system, and a bit of a struggle among those who could not get their tables to click back into their sockets, we landed safely enough in Beijing.

—FROM "VERY STRANGE FEELING: A CHINESE JOURNEY," *JOURNEYS,* 1984

Over the Fence in Canada

MARGARET ATWOOD

The noses of a great many Canadians resemble Porky Pig's. This comes from spending so much time pressing them against the longest undefended one-way mirror in the world. The Canadians looking through this mirror behave the way people on the hidden side of such mirrors usually do: They observe, analyze, ponder, snoop and wonder what all the activity on the other side means in decipherable human terms.

The Americans, bless their innocent little hearts, are rarely aware that they are even being watched, much less by the Canadians. They just go on doing body language, playing in the sandbox of the world, bashing one another on the head and planning how to blow things up, same as always. If they think about Canada at all, it's only when things get a bit snowy, or the water goes off, or the Canadians start fussing over some piddly detail, such as fish. Then they regard them as unpatriotic; for Americans don't really see Canadians as foreigners, not like the Mexicans, unless they do something weird like speak French or beat the New York Yankees at baseball. Really, think the Americans, the Canadians are just like us, or would be if they could.

Or we could switch metaphors and call the border the longest undefended backyard fence in the world. The Canadians are the folks in the neat little bungalow with the tidy little garden and the duck pond. The Americans are the other folks, the ones in the sprawly mansion with the bad-taste statues on the lawn. There's a perpetual party, or something, going on there—loud music, raucous laughter, smoke billowing from the barbecue. Beer bottles and Coke cans land among the peonies. The Canadians have their own beer bottles and barbecue smoke, but they tend to overlook it. Your own mess is always more forgivable than the mess someone else makes on your patio.

The Canadians can't exactly call the police—they suspect that the Americans are the police—and part of their distress, which seems permanent, comes from their uncertainty as to whether or not they've been invited. Sometimes they do drop by next door, and find it exciting but scary. Sometimes the Americans drop by their house and find it clean. This worries the Canadians. They worry a lot. Maybe that Americans want to buy up their duck pond, with all the money they seem to have, and turn it into a cesspool or a water-skiing emporium.

—FROM "THE VIEW FROM THE BACKYARD," IN *THE NATION*, 1986

Conversational Ballgames

NANCY MASTERSON SAKAMOTO

After I was married and had lived in Japan for a while, my Japanese   1
gradually improved to the point where I could take part in simple
conversations with my husband and his friends and family. And I
began to notice that often, when I joined in, the others would look
startled, and the conversational topic would come to a halt. After
this happened several times, it became clear to me that I was doing
something wrong. But for a long time, I didn't know what it was.

Finally, after listening carefully to many Japanese conversations,   2
I discovered what my problem was. Even though I was speaking
Japanese, I was handling the conversation in a western way.

Japanese-style conversations develop quite differently from   3
western-style conversations. And the difference isn't only in the languages. I realized that just as I kept trying to hold western-style conversations even when I was speaking Japanese, so my English students kept trying to hold Japanese-style conversations even when
they were speaking English. We were unconsciously playing entirely different conversational ballgames.

A western-style conversation between two people is like a game   4
of tennis. If I introduce a topic, a conversational ball, I expect you to
hit it back. If you agree with me, I don't expect you simply to agree
and do nothing more. I expect you to add something—a reason for
agreeing, another example, or an elaboration to carry the idea further. But I don't expect you always to agree. I am just as happy if
you question me, or challenge me, or completely disagree with me.
Whether you agree or disagree, your response will return the ball to
me.

And then it is my turn again. I don't serve a new ball from my   5
original starting line. I hit your ball back again from where it has
bounced. I carry your idea further, or answer your questions or ob-

---

Nancy Masterson Sakamoto (1931–   ), born in Los Angeles, is a
former English teacher and teacher trainer in Japan. She is currently professor of American Studies at Shitennoji Gakuen University, Hawaii Institute, and coauthor of *Mutual Understanding of Different Cultures* (1981). "Conversational Ballgames" is from her
textbook *Polite Fictions* (1982).

jections, or challenge or question you. And so the ball goes back and forth, with each of us doing our best to give it a new twist, an original spin, or a powerful smash.

And the more vigorous the action, the more interesting and exciting the game. Of course, if one of us gets angry, it spoils the conversation, just as it spoils a tennis game. But getting excited is not at all the same as getting angry. After all, we are not trying to hit each other. We are trying to hit the ball. So long as we attack only each other's opinions, and do not attack each other personally, we don't expect anyone to get hurt. A good conversation is supposed to be interesting and exciting. 6

If there are more than two people in the conversation, then it is like doubles in tennis, or like volleyball. There's no waiting in line. Whoever is nearest and quickest hits the ball, and if you step back, someone else will hit it. No one stops the game to give you a turn. You're responsible for taking your own turn. 7

But whether it's two players or a group, everyone does his best to keep the ball going, and no one person has the ball for very long. 8

A Japanese-style conversation, however, is not at all like tennis or volleyball. It's like bowling. You wait for your turn. And you always know your place in line. It depends on such things as whether you are older or younger, a close friend or a relative stranger to the previous speaker, in a senior or junior position, and so on. 9

When your turn comes, you step up to the starting line with your bowling ball, and carefully bowl it. Everyone else stands back and watches politely, murmuring encouragement. Everyone waits until the ball has reached the end of the alley, and watches to see if it knocks down all the pins, or only some of them, or none of them. There is a pause, while everyone registers your score. 10

Then, after everyone is sure that you have completely finished your turn, the next person in line steps up to the same starting line, with a different ball. He doesn't return your ball, and he does not begin from where your ball stopped. There is no back and forth at all. All the balls run parallel. And there is always a suitable pause between turns. There is no rush, no excitement, no scramble for the ball. 11

No wonder everyone looked startled when I took part in Japanese conversations. I paid no attention to whose turn it was, and kept snatching the ball halfway down the alley and throwing it back at the bowler. Of course the conversation died. I was playing the wrong game. 12

This explains why it is almost impossible to get a western-style conversation or discussion going with English students in Japan. I used to think that the problem was their lack of English language 13 ability. But I finally came to realize that the biggest problem is that they, too, are playing the wrong game.

Whenever I serve a volleyball, everyone just stands back and 14 watches it fall, with occasional murmurs of encouragement. No one hits it back. Everyone waits until I call on someone to take a turn. And when that person speaks, he doesn't hit my ball back. He serves a new ball. Again, everyone just watches it fall.

So I call on someone else. This person does not refer to what the 15 previous speaker has said. He also serves a new ball. Nobody seems to have paid any attention to what anyone else has said. Everyone begins again from the same starting line, and all the balls run parallel. There is never any back and forth. Everyone is trying to bowl with a volleyball.

And if I try a simpler conversation, with only two of us, then the 16 other person tries to bowl with my tennis ball. No wonder foreign English teachers in Japan get discouraged.

Now that you know about the difference in the conversational 17 ballgames, you may think that all your troubles are over. But if you have been trained all your life to play one game, it is no simple matter to switch to another, even if you know the rules. Knowing the rules is not at all the same thing as playing the game.

Even now, during a conversation in Japanese I will notice a star- 18 tled reaction, and belatedly realize that once again I have rudely interrupted by instinctively trying to hit back the other person's bowling ball. It is no easier for me to "just listen" during a conversation, than it is for my Japanese students to "just relax" when speaking with foreigners. Now I can truly sympathize with how hard they must find it to try to carry on a western-style conversation.

If I have not yet learned to do conversational bowling in 19 Japanese, at least I have figured out one thing that puzzled me for a long time. After his first trip to America, my husband complained that Americans asked him so many questions and made him talk so much at the dinner table that he never had a chance to eat. When I asked him why he couldn't talk and eat at the same time, he said that Japanese do not customarily think that dinner, especially on fairly formal occasions, is a suitable time for extended conversation.

Since westerners think that conversation is an indispensable part 20 of dining, and indeed would consider it impolite not to converse with one's dinner partner, I found this Japanese custom rather strange. Still, I could accept it as a cultural difference even though I didn't really understand it. But when my husband added, in explanation, that Japanese consider it extremely rude to talk with one's mouth full, I got confused. Talking with one's mouth full is certainly not an American custom. We think it very rude, too. Yet we still manage to talk a lot and eat at the same time. How do we do it?

For a long time, I couldn't explain it, and it bothered me. But after I discovered the conversational ballgames, I finally found the answer. Of course! In a western-style conversation, you hit the ball, and while someone else is hitting it back, you take a bite, chew, and swallow. Then you hit the ball again, and then eat some more. The more people there are in the conversation, the more chances you have to eat. But even with only two of you talking, you still have plenty of chances to eat.

Maybe that's why polite conversation at the dinner table has never been a traditional part of Japanese etiquette. Your turn to talk would last so long without interruption that you'd never get a chance to eat.

Are the French Really Rude?

STANLEY MEISLER

After five years in France, an American still has a puzzling time 1
figuring out the French. Are they really rude? Does their school system stifle many of them? Do they posture foolishly on the world
stage?

There are short answers to each of these questions: no; maybe; 2
yes; no. But there are long, complex, and contradictory answers as
well, for a myriad of ambiguities befuddle any American trying to
make out the French.

To many foreigners, for example, it is not surprising that the pa- 3
tron saint of Paris is St. Genevieve, a nun who fasted and prayed in
the 6th century to keep Paris safe from foreigners. She fits an image
that France cannot shake off. All studies show that outsiders look on
the French as the coldest and least welcoming people of Europe.

Yet there are few countries in the world that have welcomed and 4
embraced so many foreigners, from the Italian Renaissance genius
Leonardo Da Vinci to the Spanish painter Pablo Picasso to the Irish
writer James Joyce to the black American singer Josephine Baker.
Some of the most celebrated French of the 20th century, such as Nobel Prize physicist Marie Curie, actor-singer Yves Montand and novelist Romain Gary, were born outside France.

Contradictions like these seem even more puzzling because the 5
French at heart ought not to be so puzzling. To an American, the
French are not really exotic like Australian bushmen or the Maya or
even the Japanese. French culture seems familiar. French Champagne and perfume and cheese and ballads and movies conjure up
old and warm images. Yet, although Americans sometimes feel they
have France in their reach, they rarely can grasp it. No other people
so close seem so far.

A mood, a spirit set the French apart, and moods and spirits are 6
difficult to fathom. Take the French concern for language and ideas.
The French respect for intellect is breathtaking, far beyond the experience of any American.

Politicians and civil servants speak and write with unequaled 7

Stanley Meisler (1931–   ), from New York City, is a journalist,
author of magazine articles, and former foreign correspondent and
chief of the Paris Bureau for the *Los Angeles Times*. "Are the French
Really Rude?" first appeared in the *Los Angeles Times* (1988).

style, sophistication, flair for literature and grounding in history. Daily newspapers devote far more space to philosophy and sociology than sports. The French first came up with the term *intellectuel* at the turn of the century to describe writers, artists and philosophers with influence. Intellectuals still have influence and still matter.

8   Throughout this year, for example, a controversy has raged over the late German philosopher Martin Heidegger, a controversy set off by a Chilean professor who wrote a book accusing Heidegger of unswerving loyalty to Hitler's Nazi party from 1933 to 1945.

9   Heidegger is regarded as one of the most influential philosophers of the 20th century, but it is hard to conceive of the same fuss taking place anywhere else. Heidegger has a special place in France because his views influenced those of the great French writer Jean-Paul Sartre. But that does not really explain why the French media have devoted so much attention to him. Heidegger, after all, is unintelligible to the average reader in any language, even French. But the average French reader, whether he reads Heidegger or not, knows that philosophers are important and therefore worth fussing about.

10   Intellectual achievement is so prized that the smartest secondary students are treated like celebrities. *Le Monde*, France's most influential newspaper, published the full text in July of the student essay that won the annual prize of the Ministry of Education for the best composition in French. These annual prizes, which began in 1747, are major events. The news weekly *Le Point*, in a cover story a few weeks ago, profiled nine of this year's winners in various subjects, revealing their family backgrounds, study habits, heroes and favorite dishes.

11   The best graduates of the French educational system have a precision of mind, command of language and store of memory that would make the heart of most American educators ache with envy. It is doubtful that any school system in the world teaches more logic and grammar or offers more courses.

12   But a sobering price is paid. Precision in thought and beauty of language are the products of an elite French school system that is repressive, frightening and stifling to many pupils who cannot keep up. There is no tolerance or time for spontaneity or weakness.

13   An elite few do well and uphold the glory and grandeur of French culture. But many other students are shunted aside by the system. Almost two-thirds of French pupils who enter secondary school fail to win the baccalaureate degree that is the crowning achievement of their secondary education. Some feel that failure for the rest of their lives.

Dr. Philippe Guran, director of pediatrics at the Richaud Hospi- 14
tal in Versailles, once described the school system as "hazardous to
children's health and well-being." The children, he said, are moti-
vated by "the fear of failure rather than the pursuit of success."

Although some French educators question the rigidity and 15
elitism of the school system, most politicians and parents do not.
These kinds of schools, after all, have produced a dozen winners of
the Nobel Prize in literature this century, far more than any other
country, including the United States, with all its emphasis on creativity.

Parents, concerned that their children may fail the national bac- 16
calaureate examinations, complain that a school's standards are not
tough enough. Politicians denounce principals for offering too many
frills. President François Mitterrand insists that teachers should force
pupils to memorize more dates in French history.

No one seems to think of the school system when the French 17
government launches one of its periodic campaigns to persuade the
French to show more hospitality to tourists. Yet the schools, in
many ways, must be blamed for the hoary tourist cliché that the
French are rude.

French education fosters a defensive attitude in those fearful of 18
failure. It is not surprising that foreigners sometimes run into a defensive waiter or store clerk or lower-level bureaucrat. After years of
trying to avoid the strictures of their teachers, people like this handle every hint of a complaint by blaming someone else.

French education also makes it very difficult for the French to under- 19
stand foreigners who do not speak French well. It has been drilled
into the French for years that they must not mispronounce words or
mangle grammar. Their minds cannot make much of an adjustment
for a foreigner who misses the mark; many French simply do not
understand.

In English, linguists, trying to assess how well a foreigner 20
speaks, measure the level at which he or she will be understood by
"a sympathetic native speaker." The concept of such a speaker simply does not exist in French.

"The cultural capital of the world is a provincial place," a Boliv- 21
ian writer said in Paris recently. "Nowhere else in the world do people treat you like the French do if you cannot speak their language.
It would not happen in New York or even London. Paris is a city
suspicious of foreigners; it is like the Middle Ages."

The problem is compounded because the French, especially in 22
Paris, are not an open, gregarious people like Americans or Latins.

They are inward and undemonstrative. They do not like to commit themselves quickly; they do not like to show their feelings openly.

The truth is that the cliché about French rudeness, like most 23 clichés, is exaggerated, sometimes in a spiteful way. Most French are not defensive, intolerant and insensitive. Most are not rude.

It is true that most French do not open up quickly to people they 24 do not know, whether foreign or French. But, once contact is made and renewed, they are as kind and loyal as any other people. They show their friendship and emotion, however, with simple civil gestures—a small gift or favor or act of kindness—but not in any extravagant way.

There is another puzzle. The French, in the eyes of many for- 25 eigners, refuse to accept their role as a middling power. On an official and diplomatic level, many Americans grow irritated with French leaders for what the Americans look on as posturing on the world stage.

France was once a great power. Even as late as the eve of World 26 War II, many analysts thought that the French army was the most powerful in the world. But such notions died in the defeat and disgrace of World War II.

Now, France is a European country of moderate strength, with 27 enough nuclear weapons to count in some councils of war and peace but hardly enough to qualify as a superpower. Yet its leaders, unlike the leaders of Britain, never seem to accept this. The French sometimes sound as if World War II had never come to dash the pretensions of France.

At economic summit conferences, for example, President Mitter- 28 rand is one of the few foreign leaders who stands up to the United States and refuses to bow to its power and influence. French officials act not as if they were trying to pose as more than they are but as if past French grandeur and the potential for future French leadership in Europe entitles them to more of a voice than a middling power might expect. The past and future ought to count for something.

The concept is novel, but it may make a lot of sense. It certainly 29 enhances a sense of nationalism and makes the French, as ever, somewhat larger than life.

On a Greek Holiday

ALICE BLOOM

. . . I am unable to "go on a vacation." To borrow the parlance of 1
travel ads, I don't go to "get away," I go to get into. In addition to
following [one's] love—lovers of place being such a trustworthy
sort, an enviable sort—one travels not to enjoy oneself, or to repeat
oneself, or to cosset oneself, or—past a certain age—to find oneself,
but to find the distinctly other. That other, that is there, and is
loved. The only interesting question on a trip for me is—what sustains life elsewhere? How deep does it go? Can one see it? This
hope, this anticipation, is forcibly blocked. Henry Miller, in 193–,
stood in Epidaurus, alone, in a "weird solitude," and felt the "great
heart of the world beat." We stand at Epidaurus with several thousand others, some of whom are being called "my chickens" by their
tour guide who calls herself "your mother hen," whose counterpart,
this time at Delphi, explains several times that what is being looked
at is the "bellybutton of the world, okay? The Greeks thought, this is
the bellybutton of the world, okay?" "These stones all look alike to
me," someone grumbles. There is no help for it; we're there with
guidebooks ourselves; but this fact—tourism is big business—and
others, throw us back, unwilling, into contemplation of our own
dull home-soul, our dull bodily comforts, our own dull dwindling
purse, our own dull resentments; because the other—in this case,
Greece—is either rapidly disappearing or else, self-protective, is re-
treating so far it is disappeared. You can get there, but you can't get
at it.

For instance, a study of travel posters and brochures, which in 2
the process of setting dates and buying tickets always precedes a
trip, shows us, by projection into these pictured, toothy, tourist
bodies, having some gorgeous piece of ingestion: the yellow beach,
the mossy blue ruin, a dinner table laden with food and red wine of
the region, dancing, skiing, golfing, shopping, waving to roadside
natives as our rented car sails by, as though we only go to play, as

Alice Bloom (1941–   ), born in Belleville, Illinois, teaches in the
English Department at the University of Maine, Farmington, and is
the author of essays and reviews. "On a Greek Holiday" is excerpted from her essay of the same title in *The Hudson Review*
(1983).

though all we do here at home is work, as though, for two or four weeks abroad, we seek regression.

Also in the posters, but as part of the landscape, there are the natives—whether Spanish, Greek, Irish, etc.—costumed as attractions, performing in bouzouki or bag-pipe bands, or doing some picturesque and nonindustrial piece of work such as fishing, weaving, selling colorful cheap goods in open-air markets, herding sheep or goats. The journey promised by the posters and brochures is a trip into everyone's imaginary past: one's own, drained of the normal childhood content of fear, death, space, hurt, abandonment, perplexity, and so forth, now presented as the salesmen think we think it should have been: one in which we only ate, slept, and played in the eternal sun under the doting care of benevolent elders.

And we are shown the benevolent elders, the imaginary natives who also, for a handsome fee, exist now, in the present of the trip we are about to take. ("Take" is probably a more telling verb here than we think.) They exist in a past where they are pictured having grown cheerfully old and wise doing only harmless, enjoyable, preindustrial, clean, self-employed, open-air work, in pink crinkled cheeks, merry eyes, and wonderful quaint clothes, with baskets, nets, toy-shaped boats, flower boxes, cottages, sheep crooks, country roads, whitewashed walls, tea shop signs, and other paraphernalia of the pastoral wish. I have never seen a travel poster showing natives of the country enjoying their own food or beaches or ski-jumps or hotel balconies; nor have I ever seen a travel poster showing the natives working the night-shift in the Citroën factory, either.

The natives in the posters (are they Swiss, Mexican, Chilean, Turkish models?) are happy parent figures, or character dolls, and their faces, like the faces of the good parents we are supposed to have dreamed, show them pleased with their own lot, busy but not too busy with a job that they obviously like, content with each other, and warmly indulgent of our need to play, to be fed good, clean food on time, and to be tucked into a nice bed at the end of our little day. They are the childhood people that also existed in early grammar-school readers, and nowhere else: adults in your neighborhood, in the identifiable costumes of their humble tasks, transitional-object people, smiling milkman, friendly aproned store-owner in his small friendly store, happy mailman happy to bring your happy mail, happy mommy, icons who make up a six-year-old's school-enforced dream town, who enjoy doing their nonindustrial, unmysterious tasks: mail, milk, red apple, cooky, just for you, so you can learn to decipher: See, Jip, see.

A travel remark I have always savored came from someone surprised in love for a place, just returned from a month in the Far East (no longer tagged "the mysterious," I've noticed), and who was explaining this trip at a party. She said, "I just loved Japan. It was so authentic and Oriental." Few people would go quite so naked as that, but the charm of her feelings seemed just right. Perhaps she had expected Tokyo to be more or less a larger version of the Japanese Shop in the Tokyo Airport. It is somewhat surprising that she found it to be anything much more.

One of the hushed-tone moral superiority stories, the aren't-we-advanced stories told by those lucky enough to travel in Soviet Russia, has to do with that government's iron management of the trip. There are people who can't be met, buildings that can't be entered, upper story windows that can't be photographed, streets that can't be strolled, districts that can't be crossed, cities in which it is impossible to spend the night, and so on. However, our notions of who we are and what comforts we demand and what conditions we'll endure, plus any country's understandably garbled versions of who we are, what we want, and what we'll pay for, are far more rigid than the strictures of any politburo because such strictures don't say "This is you, this is what you must want," but "This is what you can't, under any circumstances, do." That, though it inhibits movement, and no doubt in some cases prevents a gathering of or understanding of some crucial or desired bit of information, has at least the large virtue of defining the tourist as potentially dangerous. What we meet most of the time, here and abroad, is a definition of ourselves as harmless, spoiled babies, of low endurance and little information, minimal curiosity, frozen in infancy, frozen in longing, terrified for our next square meal and clean bed, and whose only potential danger is that we might refuse to be separated from our money.

Suppose, for a moment, that tourism—the largest "industry" in 8 Greece (it employs, even more than shipping, the most people)—were also the largest industry in America. Not just in Manhattan or Washington, D.C., or Disneyland or Disneyworld or at the Grand Canyon or Niagara Falls, but in every motel, hotel, restaurant, in every McDonald's and Colonel Sanders and Howard Johnson's and Mom & Pop's, in every bar and neighborhood hang-out, truck stop, gas station, pharmacy, department store, museum, church, historical site, battleground, in every taxi, bus, subway, train, plane, in every public building, in post offices and banks and public bathrooms, on every street in every city, town, village and hamlet from West Jonesport, Maine, to Centralia, Illinois, to Parachute, Colorado, and every stop in between and beyond, just as it is in Greece: tourists.

Suppose that every other business establishment across the 9 country therefore found it in their best interest to become a souvenir shop, selling cheap, mass-produced "gifts" for the tourists to take back home that, back home, would announce that they had visited America. What images would we mass produce for them? Millions of little bronzed Liberty Bells? Tepees? St. Louis Arches? Streetcars named "Desire"? Statues of Babe Ruth? of Liberty? of Daniel Boone? In Greece we saw miniature bottles of ouzo encased in tiny plastic replicas of the temple of Athena Nike. Could we do something so clever, and immediately recognizable, with miniatures of bourbon? Encase them in tiny plastic Washington Monuments? Lincoln Memorials? Would we feel misrepresented?

Third, suppose that a sizable portion of these tourists wanting 10 gifts, toilets, rooms, baths, meals, dollars, film, drinks, stamps, directions, are Greek; or else, let us suppose that we assumed, that whether actually Greek or not, wherever they come from they speak Greek as a second language. Assume, therefore, that our map and traffic and road signs, postings of instruction and information, advertisements, timetables, directions—"stop," "go," "hot," "cold," "men," "women," "open," "closed," "yes," "no,"—to name a few rudiments of life, plus all the menus in all those sandwich counters, truck stops, fast-food outlets, lunch rooms, and so forth, had to be in Greek as well as in English. We have never been, so far, an occupied country, whether by forces enemy or not. Undoubtedly, if we were, as an ongoing fact of our "in-season" summer months, we Americans, having to offer our multitudinous wares in Greek, would come up with items as hilarious as those we collected from the English side of Greek menus: baygon and egs. Xamberger steake. Veat. Orange juise. Rost beef. Shrimp carry. Potoes. Spaggeti. Morcoroni. And our favorite, Fried Smooth Hound. (This turned out to be a harmless local fish, much to the disappointment of our children, born surrealists.)

Suppose that we had to post Bar Harbor, Plum Island, Chin- 11 coteague, Key West, Bay St. Louis, Galveston, Big Sur and Seattle beaches with "No Nakedness Allowed" signs, but that the Greeks and other tourists, freed from the cocoons of air-conditioned tour buses, armed with sun-oil in every degree of protection, rushed beachwards past the signs and stripped to their altogether, anyway? Would our police sit quietly in the shade and drink with other men and turn, literally, their khaki-clad rumps to the beach, as did the Greek police?

And food. Suppose we had to contrive to feed them, these hun- 12 gry hordes? They will come here, as we go there, entrenched in their habits and encumbered with fears of being cheated, fears of indigestion, of recurrent allergies, of breaking their diets, of catching

American trots, of being poisoned by our water, fattened by our
grease and starch, put off by our feeding schedules, sickened by
something weird or local. Suppose we decided, out of some semi-
conscious, unorganized, but national canniness, that what these
tourists really want is our cobbled version of their national foods.
Whom will we please: the English who want their teas at four, or
the Italians who want supper at nine at night? Or both? And what
will we cook and serve, and how will we spell it?

Or suppose they want to eat "American" food. What tastes like 13
us? What flavors contain our typicality, our history, our heroes, our
dirt, our speeches, our poets, our battles, our national shames? The
hot dog? Corn on the cob? I have eaten, barring picnics and occasional abstention, probably about 130 meals in Greece. And Greek
food, I feel somewhat qualified to say, contains their history, and
tastes of sorrow and triumph, of olive oil and blood, in about equal
amounts. It is the most astounding and the most boring food that I,
an eater, have ever eaten. . . .

Two women are walking towards us, at noon, across the nearly 14
deserted rocks. Most of the other swimmers and sunbathers are up
in the café, eating lunch under the fig trees, the grapevine. These
two women are not together, they walk several feet apart, and they
do not look at each other. One is tall and blond, dressed in a
flowered bikini and clogs, a tourist, English or American or Scandi-
navian or German. The other woman, a Greek, is carrying a basket,
walking quickly, and gives the impression of being on a neighborhood errand. She is probably from one of the small old farms—
sheep, olive trees, hens, gardens, goats—that border this stretch of
sea and climb a little way into the pine and cypress woods.

Both are smoking and both walk upright. Beyond that, there is 15
so little similarity they could belong to different planets, eras, species, sexes. The tourist looks young, the Greek looks old; actually,
she looks as old as a village well and the blond looks like a drawn-
out infant, but there could be as little as five or ten years difference
between them.

The Greek woman is short and heavy, waistless, and is wearing 16
a black dress, a black scarf pulled low around her eyes, a black
sweater, thick black stockings, black shoes. She is stupendously
there, black but for the walnut of her face, in the white sun, against
the white space. She looks, at once, as if she could do everything
she's ever done, anything needed, and also at once, she gives off an
emanation of humor, powers, secrets, determinations, acts. She is
moving straight ahead, like a moving church, a black peaked roof, a
hot black hat, a dark tent, like a doom, a government, a force for

good and evil, an ultimatum, a determined animal. She probably can't read, or write; she may never in her life have left this island; but she is beautiful, she could crush you, love you, mend you, deliver you of child or calf or lamb or illusion, bleed a pig, spear a fish, wring a supper's neck, till a field, coax an egg into life. Her sex is like a votive lamp flickering in a black, airless room. As she comes closer, she begins to crochet—that's what's in her basket, balls of cotton string and thick white lace coming off the hook and her brown fingers.

The blond tourist, struggling along the hot pebbles in her clogs, 17 is coming back to her beach mat and friends. She looks as though she couldn't dress a doll without having a fit of sulks and throwing it down in a tantrum. It may not be the case, of course. She is on holiday, on this Greek island, which fact means both money and time. She is no doubt capable, well-meaning, and by the standards and expectations of most of the world's people, well-educated and very rich and very comfortable. She can undoubtedly read and write, most blond people can, and has, wherever she comes from, a vote, a voice, a degree of some kind, a job, a career perhaps, money certainly, opinions, friends, health, talents, habits, central heating, living relatives, personalized checks, a return ticket, a summer wardrobe, the usual bits and clamor we all, tourists, have. But presence, she has not. Nor authority, nor immediacy, nor joy for the eye, nor a look of adding to the world, not of strength nor humor nor excitement. Nearly naked, pretty, without discernible blemish, blond, tall, tan, firm, the product of red meat and whole milk, vitamins, orange juice, women's suffrage, freedom of religion, child labor laws, compulsory education, the anxious, dancing, lifelong attendance of uncounted numbers of furrow-browed adults, parents, teachers, pediatricians, orthodontists, counselors, hairdressers, diet and health and career and exercise and fashion consultants, still, she is not much to look at. She looks wonderful, but your eye, your heart, all in you that wants to look out on the substance of the people of the day, doesn't care, isn't interested long, is, in fact, diminished a little.

She could be anything—a professor of Romance Languages at a 18 major university, a clerk in a Jermyn Street shop, a flight attendant, a Stockholm lawyer, but nothing shows of that life or luck or work or history, not world, not pain or freedom or sufficiency. What you think of, what her person walking towards you in the fierce noon light forces you to think of, after the momentary, automatic envy of her perfections, is that she looks as though she's never had enough—goods or rights or attention or half-decent days. Whether she is or not, she looks unutterably dissatisfied and peevish. And yet, in order to be here on this blue white beach on this July day, unless you are chasing your own stray goat across the rocks, requires a position of luxury, mobility, and privilege common to us but beyond any imagining of the Greek woman who walks here too with a basket of string and her hot, rusty clothes but who, however, and not at all paradoxically, exudes a deep, sustained bass note of slumbering, solid contentment.

Insofar as ignorance always makes a space, romance rushes in to 19 people it. With so little fact at hand about either of these lives, fact which might make things plain and profound as only fact can do, there is little but romance, theories, guess work, and yet, it seems, this accidental conjunction of women in the sun, considered, says it is not a matter of the one, the blond, being discontent in spite of much and the other, the farm woman in black, being smugly, perhaps ignorantly content with little. That theory is too much the stuff of individual virtue, and of fairy tales: grateful peasant, happy with scraps and rags, and querulous, bitchy princess, untried, suffering every pea, pursued by frogs, awaiting a magic deliverance. Because in literal, daily fact, the Greek woman has more than the tourist, and the tourist, wherever she comes from and despite her list of equipment and privileges, is also, in literal daily fact, deprived. To see this as a possible deciphering of this scene means to stop thinking of the good life strictly in terms of goods, services, and various rights, and think instead, insofar as we can, of other, almost muted because so nearly lost to us, needs of life.

Beyond seeing that she has two arms, two good legs, a tanned 20 skin, blond hair and friends, I know nothing about this particular tourist. Beyond knowing that she has two arms, two good legs, a face that could stop or move an army, a black dress, and can crochet lace, I know nothing about this particular peasant woman. I don't even know, it's only a clumsy guess, that "peasant" should be the qualifying adjective. I can only talk about these women as they appeared, almost a mirage in the shimmer of beach heat, almost icons, for a moment and walked past; and as they are on an island where I, too, have spent a notch of time. Whatever the Greek woman, and her kind, has enjoyed or missed, has suffered or lost in war, under dictatorship, under occupation, from men, in poverty or plenty, I don't know. The other woman, I won't describe, won't further guess at, for she is familiar to us; she is us.

I don't know in what order of importance, should that order exist or be articulable, the Greek woman would place what occurs on the visible street of her life. For that is all I do see, all that we can see, and it wrings the heart, that visible street. For one thing, in most places, the street is not yet given over to the demands of the motor. The Greek is still a citizen and a large part of his day is given to whatever life goes on in public, and that life takes place on the street. Much of what we do in private, in isolation, in small personally chosen groups—eating, drinking, talking, staring into space—is, in Greece, done on the impersonal, random street. This habit of daily gathering, which is done for no particular reason, that is, there is no special occasion, lends to every day and night the feel of mild, but lively festival.

Second, among the other visible things that "underdeveloped" means, it means that—due either to a generous wisdom that has survived, or else funding that is not yet available—there is not enough money for the fit to invent shelters for the unfit. For whatever reasons, the Greek woman still lives in a culture where this has not yet happened. That is, not only are the streets used by and for people, but all sorts of people are on them, still privileged to their piece of the sun, the common bread, the work, the gossip, the ongoing parade. Our children are pitying and amazed. After several days on these streets they assume that in Greece there are more fat and slow and old, more crippled and maimed, more feeble of mind and body, more blind and begging, more, in general, outcast folks than we, Americans, have. They are especially amazed at how *old* people get to be in Greece. Being young and American, and not living in New York, the only city we have that approximates the fullness and variety of a village, they assume this is evidence of extreme longevity on the one hand, and evidence of extreme bad health on the other. It was as hard to explain about American nursing homes and other asylums and institutions as it was to explain about public nudity, how archaeologists find hidden ruins, and other questions that came up on the trip.

A "developed" country is seldom mysterious but always mystifying. Where do things come from and where do they go? Life can be looked at, but not often comprehended in any of its ordinary particulars: food, shelter, work, money, producing and buying and selling. The Greek woman on the beach, again for many reasons, does still live in a world that, in those particulars—food, shelter, work, product, etc.—is comprehensible. Outside the few urban, industrial areas in Greece, it is still possible to build and conduct life without the benefit of technicians, specialists, explainers, bureaucrats, middlemen, and other modern experts. This means that there is possible an understanding of, a connection with, and a lack of technological mystification to many of the elements, objects, and products commonly lived with in any day. A typical Greek house is so simple and cunning that it could be built, or destroyed, by almost anyone. This may mean less convenience, but it also means more comprehension.

For the ordinary person, there is relatively little of the multiform, continual, hardly-much-thought-about incomprehensibility of daily things—where does this lamb chop come from? where does this wash water go?—that most people in developed countries live with, or manage to ignore, every day. Therefore, for this Greek woman on the beach and her kind, there is another mind possible, one which sees, and understands, and in most instances can control many details; and a mind in which, therefore, many mysteries can grow a deeper root.

Food, to take another example, is eaten in season and most of it 24 is locally grown, harvested or butchered, processed, sold and consumed. There is no particular moral virtue in this fact, but this fact does signify the possibility of a sharper, more acute (it sees, it has to see and comprehend more details) and more satisfied intelligence. Having money means being able to buy the end product; therefore, money replaces the need for intricate knowledge of processes; therefore, money replaces knowledge. The understanding of a glass of water or wine, a melon, an onion, or a fried fish, from inception to end, does mean living with a different kind of mind than the one which results from having merely bought and consumed the wine or fish or onion at the end. In that sense, therefore, it is possible that the unhappy peevishness and dissatisfaction on the face of the pretty tourist comes in part from a life of being left out of knowledge of the intricate details of the complete cycle of any single thing she is able to consume.

Including the country of Greece. 25

There is a new world everywhere now that money will buy. It is 26 a world without a nation, though it exists as an overlay of life, something on the order of the computer, in almost any country of the globe. It is an international accommodation, and wherever it exists— whether in Madrid, London, Istanbul, Athens, Cleveland—it resembles a large airport lounge. In this way, the new world specially constructed everywhere for tourists is something like the thousands of Greek churches, as alike as eggs, and no matter what their size all modeled on the single great discovered design of Constantine's Hagia Sophia.

Inside this international accommodation is allowed only so 27 much of any specific country as lends itself as background, decor, and trinkets. In this sense, the travel posters are an accurate portrayal of exactly how little can happen on a well-engineered trip: scenery and "gifts." Because most of the world is still what would be termed "poor," the more money you can spend, nearly any place, the more you are removed from the rich, complex life of that place. It is possible to buy everything that puts an average American life—

taps that mix hot and cold, flush toilets, heating and cooling systems, menus in English—on top of any other existing world. It is possible to pay for every familiar security and comfort and, as the posters show, still have been *there* having it. At the end of the trip, you can say that you were there.

However, the extent to which one buys familiarity, in most of 28 the world today, is also the extent to which one will not see, smell, taste, feel, or in any way be subjected to, enlightened by, or entered by that piece of the world and its people. The world's people are not blind to this fear of the unfamiliar and uncomfortable, nor insensitive to the dollars that will be paid to ward it off. In the winter months, when life returns to normal, the friendly Greek "waiters" resume their lives as masons, carpenters, builders, mechanics, schoolteachers, and so forth, a fact unknown to or overlooked by many tourists who assume, for example, that many unfinished buildings, seen languishing in the summer season, are due to neglect, laziness, disinterest, or what have you.

We all assume, and usually safely, that the more money you 29 have the more you can buy. In travel, however, the opposite is true. The less money you spend, the less money you have to spend, perhaps, the more your chances of getting a whiff, now and then, of what another place is like. There are the ideals: walking a country, living there, learning its language. Short of that, those conditions which most of us cannot meet, one can try spending as little as possible: class D hotels, public transportation, street meals. And then one must try to be as brave and patient and good-humored and healthy as possible because, without a doubt, the less money you spend the closer you come to partaking of very annoying, confusing, exhausting, foreign, debilitating, sometimes outrageous discomfort.

For instance, the two things one would most want to avoid in 30 Greece in the summer are the intense heat and the unworldly, unimaginable, unforeseeable amount of din. Pandemonium is, after all, a Greek idea, but in actual life, it is hardly confined to the hour of noon. Silence is a vacuum into which, like proverbial nature, a single Greek will rush with a pure love of noise. Two Greeks together produce more noise than 200 of any other Western nation. Greeks love above all else the human voice, raised in any emotion; next to that they love their actions with objects. One Greek with any object—a string of beads, a two-cylinder engine, preferably one on the eternal blink, a rug to beat, a single child to mind, a chair to be moved—will fill all time and space with his operation; it will be the Platonic scrape of metal chair leg on stone street; it will be the one explanation to last for all eternity why the child should not torture

the cat in the garden. A generalization: Greeks love horns, bells, animal cries, arguments, dented fenders, lengthy explanations, soccer
games, small motors, pots and pans, cases of empty bottles, vehicles
without mufflers, cups against saucers, fireworks, political songs,
metal awnings, loud-speakers, musical instruments, grandmothers,
the Orthodox liturgy, traffic jams, the sound of breaking glass, and
Mercedes taxi cabs that tootle "Mary Had A Little Lamb."

A further generalization: the above generalization is one that 31
only *not* spending money will buy. That is, you have to be in a class
F room, in a hotel on the harbor, one flight above a taverna frequented by fishermen, 120 degrees in the room, no screens,
mosquito coils burning in the unmoving air through the night, and
through the night—a donkey in heat tethered in the walled garden
below your shuttered, only shuttered, window. In other words, it's
quiet, and cool, at the Hilton; and there are, God and international
capitalism be thanked, no donkeys.

Tarzan Is an Expatriate

PAUL THEROUX

Consider the following quotation, from *The Man-Eaters of Tsavo* by 1
Lt. Col. J. H. Patterson, D.S.O.

". . . Shortly I saw scores of lights twinkling through the 2
bushes; every man in camp turned out, and with tom-toms beating
and horns blowing came running to the scene. They surrounded my
eyrie, and to my amazement prostrated themselves on the ground
before me, saluting me with cries of 'Mabarak! Mabarak!' which I believe means 'blessed one' or 'Savior' . . . We all returned in triumph
to the camp, where great rejoicings were kept up for the remainder
of the night, the Swahili and other African natives celebrating the
occasion by an especially wild and savage dance. For my part I anxiously awaited the dawn . . ."

There is a human shape that stands astride this description and 3
a thousand others like it. It is the shape of Tarzan, prime symbol of
Africa.

My knowledge of Tarzan is that of a person who, fifteen years 4
ago, spent Sunday afternoons on the living room floor on his elbows
reading that serious comic inspired by Edgar Rice Burrough's novels. Tarzan may be gone from the comics; I have no way of knowing. But I do know that he is here, in Africa, in the flesh. I see him
every day.

The Tarzan I remember was a strong white man in a leather loin- 5
cloth, always barefoot; and he was handsome, a wise mesomorph,
powerful, gentle and humorless. The animals all knew him. He
spoke to them cryptically, in a sort of private Kitchen Swahili (two of
the words he frequently used were *bundolo* and *tarmangani*). The animals replied in bubbles which only Tarzan understood. Although he
was known as Tarzan, "The Ape-Man," he was undeniably a man
and bore not the slightest trace of simian genes.

There was Jane. She aroused me: her enormous breasts strained 6
the makeshift knots on her monkeyskin brassière; she was also bare-

---

Paul Theroux (1941–   ), born in Medford, Massachusetts, but
living most of his adult life overseas, is the author of travel books
and novels including *The Great Railway Bazaar: By Train through Asia*
(1975), *The Old Patagonian Express: By Train through the Americas*
(1979), and *The Mosquito Coast* (1982). "Tarzan Is an Expatriate" was
originally published in the Ugandan journal *Transition* (1967).

foot, an added nakedness that in the case of a woman is certainly erotic, and she walked on the balls of her feet. She was watchful, worried that Tarzan might be in danger. When she sniffed trouble she had a sexy habit of thrusting out those breasts of hers, cocking her head to the side and cupping her hand to her ear. Boy, the odd epicene child, appeared on the living room floor one week and stayed, as pubescent as the day I first laid eyes on him: slender, hairless little boy scout with his child-sized spear.

And my Tarzan, real or the result of a dim recollection dimmed 7
even further by my being remote in time and place, defined his society and implied its close limits when he said, pointing, "Me Tarzan . . . You Jane . . . Him Boy . . ."

In spite of the fact that there was a green parrot with his claws 8
dug into Tarzan's shoulder, a monkey holding his hand and a lion faithfully dogging his tracks, Tarzan did not admit these creatures to his definition. In the most politic way, by not mentioning them, he excluded the animals from the society of the intimate white three. There was no question of equality: the fact remained that the animals simply were not the same and could therefore never have the same rights as the humans. Tarzan did not aggravate the situation; he asserted his authority over the animals very passively. When there was trouble the animals rallied round, they served Tarzan, grunted their bubble-messages and assisted him. Except in a time of jungle crisis Tarzan had little or nothing to do with them. Distance was understood. Tarzan never became bestial; he ate cooked food and, to my knowledge, never bit or clawed any of his enemies or buggered his functionaries. Yes, of course he swung on vines, beat his chest and roared convincingly, but these gestures were not an expression of innate animalism as much as they were the signal of a certain solidarity with the animals; as gestures they demonstrated futility as well as sympathy, and it was this sympathy that made them seem genuine. But, still, even the skillful pose which the gestures ultimately comprised was not a pose which anyone could bring off. Only Tarzan could beat his chest and win respect. Others would be laughed at.

Having defined his society (a small superior group; white, hu- 9
man, strong) Tarzan still recognized that he was in the jungle. His definition therefore was an assertion of exclusiveness which, coupled with the fact that he did not want to leave the jungle, seemed to indicate that he wanted to be a king; or, if "king" is objectionable, then he wanted to be special, lordly, powerful. We have established the fact that he was not an "ape-man" and we know that he was above the lion and the elephant, both of which are known as King of the Jungle, according to who has faced them (the lion-hunters

plump for the lion, the elephant-hunters for the elephant). Above all, he had conquered the animals with an attitude, an air; no force was involved in the conquering and so it was the easiest and most lasting victory. This gave rise to Tarzan's master-servant relationship with the animals rather than a master-slave relationship (the slave does not know his master, the servant does; the servant is over-powered by an attitude, the slave by a whip).

Tarzan was contemptuous of all outsiders, especially those who 10 were either hunters or technicians. When the old scientist and his daughter lose their way in the bush and are confronted by Tarzan, it turns out that Tarzan is wiser than the scientist and Jane has bigger breasts than the daughter; if there is a boy involved, he is a simpleton compared with Boy. The animals feared the botanist in the cork helmet, the anthropologist in the Landrover; Tarzan had either hatred or contempt for them. But though he hated these people who had a special knowledge of the jungle fauna and flora, Tarzan was still interested, in a highly disorganized way, in preserving wildlife and keeping the jungle virgin. Tarzan knew about the jungle: each root, tree, animal and flower, the composition of soil, the yank of the quicksand, the current of rivers. He had conquered by knowing and he was knowledgeable because he lived in the jungle. There was very little brainwork in this. It was a kind of savage osmosis: he took the knowledge through his skin and he was able to absorb this wisdom because he was in Africa. All that was necessary in this learning-experience was his physical presence.

He did not harm the animals; this was enough. He knew every- 11 thing any animal knew; he lived among the animals but not with them. The animals traipsed after him and sometimes he followed them; still the relationship was a master-servant one, with an important distance implied (no one, for example, ever suspected Tarzan of bestiality). He did not kill as outsiders did; at most he wounded or crippled, though usually he sprang an ingenious trap, embarrassing the enemy with helplessness instead of allowing him the dignity of a violent jungle death. He led a good vegetarian life, a life made better because he had no ambition except to prevent the interruption of his passive rule. He was indolent, but still there was nothing in the jungle Tarzan could not do.

The phrase *in the jungle* is important. Take Tarzan out of the jun- 12 gle and he would be powerless. His element was the jungle and yet he was not of the jungle. He was clearly an outsider, obviously a man; much more than Robinson Crusoe who was inventive, impatient and self-conscious, Tarzan was the first expatriate.

We should not wonder why Tarzan came to the jungle. The rea- 13 sons Tarzan had could be the same as those of any white expatriate in Africa. There are five main reasons: an active curiosity in things strange; a vague premonition that Africa rewards her visitors; a disgust with the anonymity of the industrial setting; a wish to be special; and an unconscious desire to stop thinking and let the body take over. All of these reasons are selfish in a degree. Mixed with them may be the desire to do a little good, to help in some way; but this is desire together with the knowledge that the good deeds will be performed in a pleasant climate. This, in the end, is not so much a reason for coming as it is an excuse. The wish to be special (and rewarded) is dominant; the need for assertion—the passive assertion, the assertion of color—by a man's mere physical presence eventually dominates the life of the expatriate. Tarzan must stand out; he is nonviolent but his muscles show.

Curiosity is the first to go. It may draw a person away from 14 home but in Africa it diminishes and finally dies. When the expatriate feels he knows the country in which he is working he loses interest. There is a simple level at which the expatriate learns quickly and easily about his surroundings (and no one is more in his surroundings than the expatriate; the lack of privacy is almost total, but privacy is something upon which very few in Africa place a high value). He learns the settler anecdotes and racial jokes, the useful commands for the servants, the endless dialect stories about the habits of Africans and the rules of conduct which are expected of him as a white man in a black country. All of this information is slanted toward white superiority, the African as animal and, again, the kind of assertion that is based on color. A sample Kenyan story concerns a white man who sees an African walking a dog. "Where are you going with that baboon?" the white man asks. "This isn't a baboon, it's a dog," says the African. "I'm not talking to you!" the white man snaps. There are the expatriate truisms: never give an African anything; Africans really don't want anything; if you run over an African on the road you must drive away as fast as you can or you'll be killed by the murderous mob that gathers (this is not refuted even by the staunchest liberals); Africans smell, have rhythm, don't wash, are terribly happy and so forth. There are the vernacular commands, all of which can be learned in a matter of a few days: "Cut the wood," "Dry the dishes," "Mop the floor," "Get bwana's slippers," "Don't be sulky to Memsahib." The rules of conduct for whites are aimed at keeping up expatriate morale: never argue with a fellow expatriate in the presence of an African; always offer a lift to whites you see walking in the road; never be a loner or exclude other whites from your society, especially in up-country places; feel free to drop in on fellow expatriates—expect them to drop in on you; when traveling, get the names of all the whites on your route; develop an anti-Indian prejudice; fornication, conversation and general truck with Africans must be covert and kept to a minimum—sleeping with tribeswomen is bad for the morale of expatriate wives. The jokes, the racial stereotypes, the vernacular commands, the rules of conduct—all of these tell the expatriate that he is different, he is superior, he is Tarzan. This information is sought by the recently arrived expatriate; his confidence is built on such information. When he knows enough so that he won't blunder unknowingly into liberalism and so that he is able to dominate everyone except those in his rigidly defined society, he stops seeking.

He wants to do more than merely stay alive; he *does* want to be 15 special, visible, one of the few. But this is the easiest thing of all, and so surprising in its ease that the result is a definite feeling of racial superiority. His color alone makes him distinct. He does not have to lift a finger. The great moment in the life of every expatriate comes when he perceives that, for the first time in his life, people are watching him; he is not anonymous in a crowd, in a line, in a theater or a bar. With the absence of strict segregation he is even more distinct: he is *among* but not *with*, drinking in a bar where there are many Africans he will stand out. His color sets him apart and those he is among nearly always respect him and keep their distance: the Indian shopkeeper rubs his hands and scurries around trying to please him; the African carries his shopping for twenty cents, singles him out in a crowd and offers to wash his car while the expatriate watches a film, takes his place for a penny in the stamp line at the post office and a hundred other things.

The realization that he is white in a black country, and respected 16 for it, is the turning point in the expatriate's career. He can either forget it or capitalize on it. Most choose the latter. It is not only the simplest path, it is the one that panders most to his vanity and material well-being. He may even decide to fortify his uniqueness by carefully choosing affectations: odd clothes, a walking stick, a lisp, a different accent; he may develop a penchant for shouting at his servants, losing his temper or drinking a quart of whisky a day; he may take to avocados, afternoon siestas or small boys. When the expatriate goes too far with his affectations, his fellow expatriates say he is a victim of "bush fever." But they know better. What the expatriate is doing is preparing his escape, not out of the jungle, but escape to retirement—that long sleep until death comes to kill—within the jungle. Having proven his uniqueness by drawing attention to his color, by hinting through his presence that he is different, by suggesting through a subtle actionless language that he is a racist, and perhaps demonstrating one or two feats of physical or intellectual strength, he retires to a quiet part of the jungle and rests. He is fairly sure that no one will bother him and that he will be comfortable.

Reward is a certainty. I speak about East and Central Africa. 17 There are very few expatriates in these parts of Africa who do not make more money here than they would make at home. The standard of expatriate living is always very high: here the watchful parrot is a Nubian night watchman for the house, and the rest of Tarzan's useful animal servants have their equally talented counterparts in the cook, houseboy, steward, driver, gardener, and so forth. There is a functionary at every turn: carpenters, tailors, garage mechanics, baby-sitters and carwashers—each of whom will work for a song. They have been trained by other Tarzans; there are always more candidates to be trained who are jobless, poor with large families and small gardens and not the slightest notion of either comfort or salary. It is easy to train them, to keep them employed and, especially, to dominate them. If they work poorly they can be fired on the spot. It is unlikely that the Labor Office will get after the former employer and intercede on the fired man's behalf. If the Labor Office did care to make an issue of it, it would probably lose. In the parts of Africa I have lived whites do not lose arguments.

There are further rewards, equally as tempting for Tarzan as the 18 servants and functionaries. There are baggage allowances, expatriation allowances, subsidized housing, squash courts, golf courses, swimming pools and mostly white clubs. The sun shines every day of the year on the flowers. There are holidays: a car trip to Mombasa, climbing and camping in the snow-covered Mountains of the Moon with a score of bearers, a visit to the volcanoes of Rwanda or the brothels of Nairobi, a sail in a dhow, a golfing vacation in the Northern Region. One day's drive from where I write this can take me to pygmies, elephants, naked Karamojong warriors (who, for a shilling, will let themselves be photographed glowering into the lens), leopards, the Nile River, a hydroelectric dam, Emin Pasha's fort, palatial resorts, Murchison Falls or the Congo.

The expatriate has all of these rewards together with a distinct 19 conviction that no one will bother him; he will be helped by the Africans and overrated by his friends who stayed in England or the United States. He is Tarzan, the King of the Jungle. He will come to expect a degree of adulation as a matter of course. He is no longer hurrying down a filthy subway escalator, strewn with ads for girdles, to a crowded train in which he will be breathed upon by dozens of sweating over-dressed people; he is no longer stumbling up another escalator to his home where his children are croaking and shrieking on the floor. Tarzan had his vine, the expatriate has his car and, very likely, driver. The idea of using public transportation does not occur to the expatriate: it exists for the public, not him. Africans will wave to him as he drives by in his car; some, in up-country places, will fall to their knees as he passes. He will have few enemies, but even if he had many, none would matter. Everyone else is on his side. He is Tarzan.

There is the death of the mind. The expatriate does not have to 20 think; he has long since decided that nothing should change, the jungle should not alter. In Africa he is superior and should remain so. Most agree with him; all the people he works with agree with him; Africans with money and position are the most convinced of all that change means upsetting the nature of society.

These Africans have come around to the expatriate point of 21 view; they have been conquered with an attitude and a little money; they settle tribal disputes by saying to the tribesmen, "Let's be English about this" and ask the expatriate's indulgence in not being critical of the brutal and bloody suppression of a tribe or opposition party or minority group. "These are difficult transitional years for our developing country," is the excuse for these purges.

The expatriate does not enter any fray; he takes Tarzan's view: it 22 is wrong—because it is unnatural—to try and settle jungle quarrels. It proves nothing. The animals may chatter and squabble, but this is of no concern to Tarzan; this is nature at her purest and should not be interfered with.

The mind dies and Tarzan discovers flesh. The suspicion about 23 Africa that the expatriate had in a cold English or American suburb is confirmed in a Mombasa bar or a Lagos nightclub when three or four slim black girls begin fighting over him. They also fight for the fat bald man sitting in the corner, for the Italian merchant marine jigging in the center of the floor, with his pants down, for the Yugoslavian ape-man who has just stumbled in and is now tearing the pinball machine apart. The expatriate has gone away from home to give his flesh freedom. He never guessed how simple the whole process was. What makes it all the simpler is that there is no blame attached. Even if there were blame or reprisals, only the embassy would suffer. The expatriate is soon ardently dealing in skin and this, with the death of the mind and the conscious assertion of color, is the beginning of the true Tarzan Complex. The expatriate has been served, waited on, pandered to, pimped for and overpaid; he has fed the image of his uniqueness and his arrogance has reached its full vigor.

There is a plain truth that must be stated as well. This Tarzan, 24

like the Tarzan of the comics, is not an objectionable man. He is not
Mr. Kurtz,[1] "Mad" Mike Hoare[2] or Cecil Rhodes.[3] There is very little
that can be called sinister about him. There was little duplicity in his
reasons for coming to Africa, but overthrowing the government by
force is the furthest thing from his mind. What is most striking
about him is his ordinariness: he is a very ordinary white person in
an extraordinary setting. He is a white man starting to wilt, sweating profusely, among millions of black men, frangipanis, wild animals and bush foliage.

The liberal has it both ways. He enjoys all the privileges of Tar-   25
zan and still is able to say that he is a nationalist. He is the reversible
Tarzan. His speech is entirely at odds with his actions: he bullies his
servants in one breath and advocates class struggle in the next.
When there is trouble he becomes Tarzan, with all of Tarzan's characteristic passivity. He does not fight, and yet the schizoid nature of
his existence drives him occasionally to apologize for a brutal black
regime. The archetypal Tarzan never apologizes; he accepts the behavior of the animals insofar as it does not bother him, Jane or Boy.
The liberal Tarzan denies that there are differences in the jungle and
insists that his color means nothing. But his life is much the same as
the Tarzan expatriate, and his motives for coming to Africa are likewise the same. He is the most fortunate liberal on earth. He makes a
virtue of keeping silent while the jungle is spattered with gunfire.
He knows he will lose his job and have to go home if he criticizes
the ruling party. Although he may say he is concerned with freedom, he knows that certain topics are taboo: in Kenya he cannot defend the Asians when they are under attack; in Tanzania, Malawi
and a dozen other countries he cannot be critical of the one-party
form of government; in Uganda he cannot mention that, one year
ago, there was a forcible and bloody suppression of the largest tribe
in the country. He believes that he has won over the Africans by
saying the right things and praising the injustices. But the African
attitude toward him, because it is based on color, is no different
from the attitude toward the average nonpolitical expatriate.

The liberal's paradise seems to be a place where he can hold left-   26
ist opinions in a lovely climate. Sub-Saharan Africa is one of these
paradises: the old order does not alter, the revolutions change nothing and still to be white is to be right; being British is an added
bonus. The liberal quacking may continue, and the liberal may pre-

---

[1] White European character who reverts to savagery in Joseph Conrad's novel *Heart of Darkness* (1902). (Ed.)
[2] A.k.a. William Halfpenny (?–?), eighteenth-century English architectural designer. (Ed.)
[3] English financier, colonizer, and South African mining magnate (1853–1902). (Ed.)

tend that he is not Tarzan, but he is Tarzan as much as any tightlipped civil servant admiring his jacarandas. The Tory Tarzan keeps silent; the liberal Tarzan says "Hear, hear" when the preventive detention legislation is passed.

A person should not agree to work in a country that demands silence of him. This rids the person of any human obligations and helps him to become Tarzan, the strong white man who has what he wants at the expense of millions of people who serve him in one way or another; he has everything, those around him have nothing. The very fact that silence is a condition of getting the job should indicate, especially to the academics, that the government is not ready for him. With this release from any feelings of sympathy or any real obligations toward the people he is among, the expatriate has a lot of free time to think, but no set standard for reflection except the excesses of past Tarzans. In this climate, with no sensible limits on thought, fascism is easy. This is the extreme no one expected before he came. The simple selfishness that was a part of all his reasons for coming to Africa had nothing to do with fascism, but within the slowly decaying condition of mind that is realized after years of sun and crowds, disorder and idleness, is a definite racial bias. It is not a scientific thing; rather, it is the result of being away, being idle among those he does not know. His voice gets shrill, unrecognizable, but he cannot speak; he has taken a vow of silence; his bad temper increases. An extended time in this unnatural pose can make him hateful; a black face laughing in the heat or screaming, a knot of black people merely standing muttering on the street corner can make him a killer. 27

The sun should make no one a fascist, but it is more than the sun. It is a whole changed way of looking and feeling: "I now understand *apartheid,*" says the Israeli hotel-owner who has spent two years in Nigeria; "Frankly, I like the stupid Africans best," says the white army officer in Malawi; "I wouldn't give you a shilling for the whole lot of them," says the businessman in Kenya; "Oh, I know they're frightfully inefficient and hopeless at politics—but, you know, they're terribly sweet," says the liberal English lady. If I stay here much longer I will begin to talk like this as well. I do not want that to happen. I do not want to be Tarzan and cannot think of anything drearier or more stupid and barbarous than racism. The last thing I want to be is the King of the Jungle, any jungle, and that includes Boston as much as it does Bujumbura. 28

Somewhere along the way there was an understanding reached between Tarzan and his followers. Either it was a collaboration (don't bother me and I won't bother you) or it was true conquering that was in some ways permanent. There must have been this un- 29 derstanding or there would not be so many Tarzans today. I refuse to collaborate or conquer and further refuse to sit by while the double talk continues. Someone must convince the African governments that fascism is not the special property of the Italians and Germans, and ask why independent African rule has made it infinitely easier for Tarzan, complete with *fasces,* to exist undisturbed and unchallenged.

If I Could Write This in Fire, I Would Write This in Fire

MICHELLE CLIFF

I

We were standing under the waterfall at the top of Orange River.   1
Our chests were just beginning to mound—slight hills on either
side. In the center of each were our nipples, which were losing their
sideways look and rounding into perceptible buttons of dark flesh.
Too fast it seemed. We touched each other, then, quickly and almost
simultaneously, raised our arms to examine the hairs growing underneath. Another sign. Mine was wispy and light-brown. My
friend Zoe had dark hair curled up tight. In each little patch the riverwater caught the sun so we glistened.

The waterfall had come about when my uncles dammed up the river   2
to bring power to the sugar mill. Usually, when I say "sugar mill" to
anyone not familiar with the Jamaican countryside or for that matter
my family, I can tell their minds cast an image of tall smokestacks,
enormous copper cauldrons, a man in a broad-brimmed hat with a
whip, and several dozens of slaves—that is, if they have any idea of
how large sugar mills once operated. It's grandiose expression—like
plantation, verandah, out-building. (Try substituting farm, porch,
outside toilet.) To some people it even sounds romantic.

Our sugar mill was little more than a round-roofed shed, which con-   3
tained a wheel and woodfire. We paid an old man to run it, tend the
fire, and then either bartered or gave the sugar away, after my
grandmother had taken what she needed. Our canefield was about
two acres of flat land next to the river. My grandmother had six
acres in all—one donkey, a mule, two cows, some chickens, a few
pigs, and stray dogs and cats who had taken up residence in the
yard.

Michelle Cliff (1946–   ), born in Kingston, Jamaica, and now living in California, is the author of the poetry collection *Claiming an
Identity They Taught Me to Despise* (1980) and the novel *Abeng* (1984).
"If I Could Write This in Fire, I Would Write This in Fire" is from
her prose and poetry collection *The Land of Look Behind* (1985).

Her house had four rooms, no electricity, no running water. The 4
kitchen was a shed in the back with a small pot-bellied stove. Across
from the stove was a mahogany counter, which had a white enamel
basin set into it. The only light source was a window, a small space
covered partly by a wooden shutter. We washed our faces and
hands in enamel bowls with cold water carried in kerosene tins from
the river and poured from enamel pitchers. Our chamber pots were
enamel also, and in the morning we carefully placed them on the
steps at the side of the house where my grandmother collected them
and disposed of their contents. The outhouse was about thirty yards
from the back door—a "closet" as we called it—infested with lizards
capable of changing color. When the door was shut it was totally
dark, and the lizards made their presence known by the noise of
their scurrying through the torn newspaper, or the soft shudder
when they dropped from the walls. I remember most clearly the
stench of the toilet, which seemed to hang in the air in that climate.

But because every little piece of reality exists in relation to another 5
little piece, our situation was not that simple. It was to our yard that
people came with news first. It was in my grandmother's parlor that
the Disciples of Christ held their meetings.

Zoe lived with her mother and sister on borrowed ground in a place 6
called Breezy Hill. She and I saw each other almost every day on our
school vacations over a period of three years. Each morning early—
as I sat on the cement porch with my coffee cut with condensed
milk—she appeared: in her straw hat, school tunic faded from blue
to gray, white blouse, sneakers hanging around her neck. We had
coffee together, and a piece of hard-dough bread with butter and
cheese, waited a bit and headed for the river. At first we were shy
with each other. We did not start from the same place.

There was land. My grandparents' farm. And there was color. 7

(My family was called *red*. A term which signified a degree of white- 8
ness. "We's just a flock of red people," a cousin of mine said once.)
In the hierarchy of shades I was considered among the lightest. The
countrywomen who visited my grandmother commented on my
"tall" hair—meaning long. Wavy, not curly.

I had spent the years from three to ten in New York and spoke—at 9
first—like an American. I wore American clothes: shorts, slacks,
bathing suit. Because of my American past I was looked upon as the

creator of games. Cowboys and Indians. Cops and Robbers. Peter Pan.

(While the primary colonial identification for Jamaicans was English, 10
American colonialism was a strong force in my childhood—and of course continues today. We were sent American movies and American music. American aluminum companies had already discovered bauxite on the island and were shipping the ore to their mainland. United Fruit bought our bananas. White Americans came to Montego Bay, Ocho Rios, and Kingston for their vacations and their cruise ships docked in Port Antonio and other places. In some ways America was seen as a better place than England by many Jamaicans. The farm laborers sent to work in American agribusiness came home with dollars and gifts and new clothes; there were few who mentioned American racism. Many of the middle class who emigrated to Brooklyn or Staten Island or Manhattan were able to pass into the white American world—saving their blackness for other Jamaicans or for trips home; in some cases, forgetting it altogether. Those middle-class Jamaicans who could not pass for white managed differently—not unlike the Bajans in Paule Marshall's *Brown Girl, Brownstones*—saving, working, investing, buying property. Completely separate in most cases from Black Americans.)

I was someone who had experience with the place that sent us triple 11
features of B-grade westerns and gangster movies. And I had tall hair and light skin. And I was the granddaughter of my grandmother. So I had power. I was the cowboy, Zoe was my sidekick, the boys we knew were Indians. I was the detective, Zoe was my "girl," the boys were the robbers. I was Peter Pan, Zoe was Wendy Darling, the boys were the lost boys. And the terrain around the river—jungled and dark green—was Tombstone, or Chicago, or Never-Never Land.

This place and my friendship with Zoe never touched my life in 12
Kingston. We did not correspond with each other when I left my grandmother's home.

I never visited Zoe's home the entire time I knew her. It was a 13
given: never suggested, never raised.

Zoe went to a state school held in a country church in Red Hills. It 14
had been my mother's school. I went to a private all-girls school where I was taught by white Englishwomen and pale Jamaicans. In

her school the students were caned as punishment. In mine the harshest punishment I remember was being sent to sit under the *lignum vitae* to "commune with nature." Some of the girls were out-and-out white (English and American), the rest of us were colored—only a few were dark. Our uniforms were blood-red gabardine, heavy and hot. Classes were held in buildings meant to recreate England: damp with stone floors, facing onto a cloister, or quad as they called it. We began each day with the headmistress leading us in English hymns. The entire school stood for an hour in the zinc-roofed gymnasium.

Occasionally a girl fainted, or threw up. Once, a girl had a grand 15
mal seizure. To any such disturbance the response was always "keep singing." While she flailed on the stone floor, I wondered what the mistresses would do. We sang "Faith of Our Fathers," and watched our classmate as her eyes rolled back in her head. I thought of people swallowing their tongues. This student was dark—here on a scholarship—and the only woman who came forward to help her was the gamesmistress, the only dark teacher. She kneeled beside the girl and slid the white web belt from her tennis shorts, clamping it between the girl's teeth. When the seizure was over, she carried the girl to a tumbling mat in a corner of the gym and covered her so she wouldn't get chilled.

Were the other women unable to touch this girl because of her 16
darkness? I think that now. Her darkness and her scholarship. She lived on Windward Road with her grandmother; her mother was a maid. But darkness is usually enough for women like those to hold back. Then, we usually excused that kind of behavior by saying they were "ladies." (We were constantly being told we should be ladies also. One teacher went so far as to tell us many people thought Jamaicans lived in trees and we had to show these people they were mistaken.) In short, we felt insufficient to judge the behavior of these women. The English ones (who had the corner on power in the school) had come all this way to teach us. Shouldn't we treat them as the missionaries they were certain they were? The creole Jamaicans had a different role: they were passing on to those of us who were light-skinned the creole heritage of collaboration, assimilation, loyalty to our betters. We were expected to be willing subjects in this outpost of civilization.

The girl left school that day and never returned. 17

After prayers we filed into our classrooms. After classes we had 18
games: tennis, field hockey, rounders (what the English call base-ball), netball (what the English call basketball). For games we were

divided into "houses"—groups named for Joan of Arc, Edith Cavell, Florence Nightingale, Jane Austen. Four white heroines. Two martyrs. One saint. Two nurses. (None of us knew then that there were Black women with Nightingale at Scutari.) One novelist. Three involved in white men's wars. Two dead in white men's wars. *Pride and Prejudice.*[1]

Those of us in Cavell wore red badges and recited her last words before a firing squad in W. W. I: "Patriotism is not enough. I must have no hatred or bitterness toward anyone." 19

Sorry to say I grew up to have exactly that. 20

Looking back: To try and see when the background changed places with the foreground. To try and locate the vanishing point: where the lines of perspective converge and disappear. Lines of color and class. Lines of history and social context. Lines of denial and rejection. When did *we* (the light-skinned middle-class Jamaicans) take over for *them* as oppressors? I need to see when and how this happened. When what should have been reality was overtaken by what was surely unreality. When the house nigger became master. 21

"What's the matter with you? You think you're white or something?" 22

"Child, what you want to know 'bout Garvey[2] for? The man was nothing but a damn fool." 23

"They not our kind of people." 24

Why did we wear wide-brimmed hats and try to get into Oxford? Why did we not return? 25

Great Expectations:[3] a novel about origins and denial, about the futility and tragedy of that denial, about attempting assimilation. We learned this novel from a light-skinned Jamaican woman—she concentrated on what she called the "love affair" between Pip and Estella. 26

Looking back: Through the last page of *Sula.*[4] "And the loss pressed down on her chest and came up into her throat. 'We was girls together,' she said as though explaining something." It was Zoe, and 27

[1] 1813 novel by English author Jane Austen (1775–1817). (Ed.)
[2] Marcus Garvey (1887–1940), Jamaican nationalist deported from the United States. (Ed.)
[3] 1861 novel by English author Charles Dickens (1812–1870). (Ed.)
[4] 1973 novel by American author Toni Morrison (1931–   ). (Ed.)

Zoe alone, I thought of. She snapped into my mind and I remembered no one else. Through the greens and blues of the riverbank. The flame of red hibiscus in front of my grandmother's house. The cracked grave of a former landowner. The fruit of the ackee which poisons those who don't know how to prepare it.

"What is to become of us?"   28

We borrowed a baby from a woman and used her as our dolly.   29
Dressed and undressed her. Dipped her in the riverwater. Fed her
with the milk her mother had left with us: and giggled because we
knew where the milk had come from.

A letter: "I am desperate. I need to get away. I beg you one fifty- 30
dollar."

I send the money because this is what she asks for. I visit her on a 31
trip back home. Her front teeth are gone. Her husband beats her
and she suffers blackouts. I sit on her chair. She is given birth control pills which aggravate her "condition." We boil up sorrel and
ginger. She is being taught by Peace Corps volunteers to embroider
linen mats with little lambs on them and gives me one as a keep-
sake. We cool off the sorrel with a block of ice brought from the
shop nearby. The shopkeeper immediately recognizes me as my
grandmother's granddaughter and refuses to sell me cigarettes. (I
am twenty-seven.) We sit in the doorway of her house, pushing
back the colored plastic strands which form a curtain, and talk about
Babylon and Dred.[5] About Manley[6] and what he's doing for Jamaica.
About how hard it is. We walk along the railway tracks—no longer
used—to Crooked River and the post office. Her little daughter
walks beside us and we recite a poem for her: "Mornin' buddy/Me
no buddy fe wunna/Who den, den I saw?" and on and on.

I can come and go. And I leave. To complete my education in Lon- 32
don.

II

Their goddam kings and their goddam queens. Grandmotherly Vic- 33
toria spreading herself thin across the globe. Elizabeth II on our TV
screens. We stop what we are doing. We quiet down. We pay our
respects.

---

[5]Babylon and Dred: references to Rastafarianism, black Jamaican religion whose members
worship Haile Selassie (aka Ras Tafari) of Ethiopia (1892–1975); see paragraphs 57–59, 84. (Ed.)
[6]Michael Manley, former Jamaican prime minister; see paragraph 75. (Ed.)

1981: In Massachusetts I get up at 5 A.M. to watch the royal wed- 34
ding. I tell myself maybe the IRA[7] will intervene. It's got to be better
than starving themselves to death. Better to be a kamikaze in St.
Paul's Cathedral than a hostage in Ulster. And last week Black and
white people smashed storefronts all over the United Kingdom. But
I really don't believe we'll see royal blood on TV. I watch because
they once ruled us. In the back of the cathedral a Maori woman
sings an aria from Handel, and I notice that she is surrounded by
the colored subjects.

To those of us in the commonwealth the royal family was the perfect 35
symbol of hegemony. To those of us who were dark in the dark nations, the prime minister, the parliament barely existed. We believed
in royalty—we were convinced in this belief. Maybe it played on
some ancestral memories of West Africa—where other kings and
queens had been. Altars and castles and magic.

The faces of our new rulers were everywhere in my childhood. Cal- 36
endars, newsreels, magazines. Their presences were often among
us. Attending test matches between the West Indians and South
Africans. They were our landlords. Not always absentee. And no
matter what Black leader we might elect—were we to choose independence—we would be losing something almost holy in our impu-
dence.

WE ARE HERE BECAUSE YOU WERE THERE
BLACK PEOPLE AGAINST STATE BRUTALITY
BLACK WOMEN WILL NOT BE INTIMIDATED
WELCOME TO BRITAIN . . . WELCOME TO SECOND-CLASS
CITIZENSHIP
                         (slogans of the Black movement in Britain)

Indian women cleaning the toilets in Heathrow airport. This is the 37
first thing I notice. Dark women in saris trudging buckets back and
forth as other dark women in saris—some covered by loosefitting
winter coats—form a line to have their passports stamped.

The triangle trade: molasses/rum/slaves. Robinson Crusoe was on a 38
slave-trading journey, Robert Browning[8] was a mulatto. Holding
pens. Jamaica was a seasoning station. Split tongues. Sliced ears.
Whipped bodies. The constant pretense of civility against rape. Still.

---

[7] Irish Republican Army. (Ed.)
[8] English poet (1812–1889). (Ed.)

Iron collars. Tinplate masks. The latter a precaution: to stop the slaves from eating the sugar cane.

A pregnant woman is to be whipped—they dig a hole to accommo-   39
date her belly and place her face down on the ground. Many of us became light-skinned very fast. Traced ourselves through bastard lines to reach the duke of Devonshire. The earl of Cornwall. The lord of this and the lord of that. Our mothers' rapes were the things unspoken.

You say: But Britain freed her slaves in 1833. Yes.   40

Tea plantations in India and Ceylon. Mines in Africa. The Cape-to-   41
Cairo Railroad. Rhodes scholars. Suez Crisis. The white man's bloody burden. Boer War. Bantustans. Sitting in a theatre in London in the seventies. A play called *West of Suez*.[9] A lousy play about British colonials. The finale comes when several well-known white actors are machine-gunned by several lesser-known Black actors. (As Nina Simone says: "This is a show tune but the show hasn't been written for it yet.")

The red empire of geography classes. "The sun never sets on the   42
British empire and you can't trust it in the dark." Or with the dark peoples. "Because of the Industrial Revolution European countries went in search of markets and raw materials." Another geography (or was it a history) lesson.

Their bloody kings and their bloody queens. Their bloody peers.   43
Their bloody generals. Admirals. Explorers. Livingstone.[10] Hillary.[11]
Kitchener.[12] All the bwanas. And all their beaters, porters, sherpas.
Who found the source of the Nile. Victoria Falls. The tops of mountains. Their so-called discoveries reek of untruth. How many dark people died so they could misname the physical features in their blasted gazetteer. A statistic we shall never know. Dr. Livingstone, I presume you are here to rape our land and enslave our people.

There are statues of these dead white men all over London.   44

---

[9] By John Osborne (1929–   ), published in 1971. (Ed.)
[10] David Livingstone (1813–1873), Scottish missionary and explorer in Africa. (Ed.)
[11] Sir Edmund Hillary (1919–   ), explorer from New Zealand, first Westerner to climb Mt. Everest. (Ed.)
[12] Horatio Kitchener (1850–1916), British earl, soldier, and colonial administrator in Africa. (Ed.)

An interesting fact: The swear word "bloody" is a contraction of "by   45
my lady"—a reference to the Virgin Mary. They do tend to use their
ladies. Name ages for them. Places for them. Use them as screens,
inspirations, symbols. And many of the ladies comply. While the
national martyr Edith Cavell was being executed by the Germans in
1915 in Belgium (called "poor little Belgium" by the allies in the
war), the Belgians were engaged in the exploitation of the land and
peoples of the Congo.

And will we ever know how many dark peoples were "imported" to   46
fight in white men's wars. Probably not. Just as we will never know
how many hearts were cut from African people so that the Christian
doctor might be a success—i.e., extend a white man's life. Our Sister Killjoy observes this from her black-eyed squint.

Dr. Schweitzer—humanitarian, authority on Bach, winner of the   47
Nobel Peace Prize—on the people of Africa: "The Negro is a child,
and with children nothing can be done without the use of authority.
We must, therefore, so arrange the circumstances of our daily life
that my authority can find expression. With regard to Negroes,
then, I have coined the formula: 'I am your brother, it is true, but
your elder brother.'" (*On the Edge of the Primeval Forest*, 1961)

They like to pretend we didn't fight back. We did: with obeah, poi-   48
son, revolution. It simply was not enough.

"Colonies . . . these places where 'niggers' are cheap and the earth   49
is rich." (W. E. B. Du Bois, "The Souls of White Folk")

A cousin is visiting me from Cal Tech where he is getting a degree in   50
engineering. I am learning about the Italian Renaissance. My cousin
is recognizably Black and speaks with an accent. I am not and do
not—unless I am back home, where the "twang" comes upon me.
We sit for some time in a bar in his hotel and are not served. A light-
skinned Jamaican comes over to our table. He is an older man—a
professor at the University of London. "Don't bother with it, you
hear. They don't serve us in this bar." A run-of-the-mill incident for
all recognizably Black people in this city. But for me it is not.

Henry's eyes fill up, but he refuses to believe our informant. "No,   51
man, the girl is just busy." (The girl is a fifty-year-old white woman,
who may just be following orders. But I do not mention this. I have
chosen sides.) All I can manage to say is, "Jesus Christ, I hate the

fucking English." Henry looks at me. (In the family I am known as the "lady cousin." It has to do with how I look. And the fact that I am twenty-seven and unmarried—and for all they know, unattached. They do not know that I am really the lesbian cousin). Our informant says—gently, but with a distinct tone of disappointment—"My dear, is that what you're studying at the university?"

You see—the whole business is very complicated.   52

Henry and I leave without drinks and go to meet some of his white 53
colleagues at a restaurant I know near Covent Garden Opera House. The restaurant caters to theatre types and so I hope there won't be a repeat of the bar scene—at least they know how to pretend. Besides, I tell myself, the owners are Italian *and* gay; they *must* be halfway decent. Henry and his colleagues work for an American company which is paying their way through Cal Tech. They mine bauxite from the hills in the middle of the island and send it to the United States. A turnaround occurs at dinner: Henry joins the white men in a sustained mockery of the waiters: their accents and the way they walk. He whispers to me: "Why you want to bring us to a batty-man's den, lady?" (*Battyman* = *faggot* in Jamaican.) I keep quiet.

We put the white men in a taxi and Henry walks me to the under- 54
ground station. He asks me to sleep with him. (It wouldn't be incest. His mother was a maid in the house of an uncle and Henry has not seen her since his birth. He was taken into the family. She was let go.) I say that I can't. I plead exams. I can't say that I don't want to. Because I remember what happened in the bar. But I can't say that I'm a lesbian either—even though I want to believe his alliance with the white men at dinner was forced: not really him. He doesn't buy my excuse. "Come on, lady, let's do it. What's the matter, you 'fraid?" I pretend I am back home and start patois to show him somehow I am not afraid, not English, not white. I tell him he's a married man and he tells me he's a ram goat. I take the train to where I am staying and try to forget the whole thing. But I don't. I remember our different skins and our different experiences within them. And I have a hard time realizing that I am angry with Henry. That to him—no use in pretending—a queer is a queer.

1981: I hear on the radio that Bob Marley is dead and I drive over the 55
Mohawk Trail listening to a program of his music and I cry and cry and cry. Someone says: "It wasn't the ganja that killed him, it was poverty and working in a steel foundry when he was young."

I flash back to my childhood and a young man who worked for an   56
aunt I lived with once. He taught me to smoke ganja behind the
house. And to peel an orange with the tip of a machete without cutting through the skin—"Love" it was called: a necklace of orange
rind the result. I think about him because I heard he had become a
Rastaman. And then I think about Rastas.

We are sitting on the porch of an uncle's house in Kingston—the   57
family and I—and a Rastaman comes to the gate. We have guns but
they are locked behind a false closet. We have dogs but they are tied
up. We are Jamaicans and know that Rastas mean no harm. We let
him in and he sits on the side of the porch and shows us his brooms
and brushes. We buy some to take back to New York. "Peace, mis-
sis."

There were many Rastas in my childhood. Walking the roadside   58
with their goods. Sitting outside their shacks in the mountains. The
outsides painted bright—sometimes with words. Gathering at Pal-
isadoes Airport to greet the Conquering Lion of Judah. They were
considered figures of fun by most middle-class Jamaicans. Harmless—like Marcus Garvey.

Later: white American hippies trying to create the effect of dred in   59
their straight white hair. The ganja joint held between their straight
white teeth. "Man, the grass is good." Hanging out by the Sheraton
pool. Light-skinned Jamaicans also dred-locked, also assuming the
ganja. Both groups moving to the music but not the words. Harmless. "Peace, brother."

III

My grandmother: "Let us thank God for a fruitful place."   60
My grandfather: "Let us rescue the perishing world."   61

This evening on the road in western Massachusetts there are pock-   62
ets of fog. Then clear spaces. Across from a pond a dog staggers in
front of my headlights. I look closer and see that his mouth is foaming. He stumbles to the side of the road—I go to call the police.

I drive back to the house, radio playing "difficult" piano pieces. And   63
I think about how I need to say all this. This is who I am. I am not
what you allow me to be. Whatever you decide me to be. In a bookstore in London I show the woman at the counter my book and she

stares at me for a minute, then says: "You're a Jamaican." "Yes." "You're not at all like our Jamaicans."

Encountering the void is nothing more nor less than understanding 64 invisibility. Of being fogbound.

Then: It was never a question of passing. It was a question of 65 hiding. Behind Black and white perceptions of who we were—who they thought we were. Tropics. Plantations. Calypso. Cricket. We were the people with the musical voices and the coronation mugs on our parlor tables. I would be whatever figure these foreign imaginations cared for me to be. It would be so simple to let others fill in for me. So easy to startle them with a flash of anger when their visions got out of hand—but never to sustain the anger for myself.

It could become a life lived within myself. A life cut off. I 66 know who I am but you will never know who I am. I may in fact lose touch with who I am.

I hid from my real sources. But my real sources were also 67 hidden from me.

Now: It is not a question of relinquishing privilege. It is a ques- 68 tion of grasping more of myself. I have found that in the real sources are concealed my survival. My speech. My voice. To be colonized is to be rendered insensitive. To have those parts necessary to sustain life numbed. And this is in some cases—in my case—perceived as privilege. The test of a colonized person is to walk through a shanty-town in Kingston and not bat an eye. This I cannot do. Because part of me lives there—and as I grasp more of this part I realize what needs to be done with the rest of my life.

Sometimes I used to think we were like the Marranos—the Se- 69 phardic Jews forced to pretend they were Christians. The name was given to them by the Christians, and meant "pigs." But once out of Spain and Portugal, they became Jews openly again. Some settled in Jamaica. They knew who the enemy was and acted for their own survival. But they remained Jews always.

We also knew who the enemy was—I remember jokes about the En- 70 glish. Saying they stank. saying they were stingy. that they drank too much and couldn't hold their liquor. that they had bad teeth. were dirty and dishonest. were limey bastards. and horse-faced bitches. We said the men only wanted to sleep with Jamaican women. And that the women made pigs of themselves with Jamaican men.

But of course this was seen by us—the light-skinned middle class— 71 with a double vision. We learned to cherish that part of us that was them—and to deny the part that was not. Believing in some cases that the latter part had ceased to exist.

None of this is as simple as it may sound. We were colorists and we 72 aspired to oppressor status. (Of course, almost any aspiration instilled by Western civilization is to oppressor status: success, for example.) Color was the symbol of our potential: color taking in hair "quality," skin tone, freckles, nose-width, eyes. We did not see that color symbolism was a method of keeping us apart: in the society, in the family, between friends. Those of us who were light-skinned, straight-haired, etc., were given to believe that we could actually attain whiteness—or at least those qualities of the colonizer which made him superior. We were convinced of white supremacy. If we failed, we were not really responsible for our failures: we had all the advantages—but it was that one persistent drop of blood, that single rogue gene that made us unable to conceptualize abstract ideas, made us love darkness rather than despise it, which was to be blamed for our failure. Our dark part had taken over: an inherited imbalance in which the doom of the creole was sealed.

I am trying to write this as clearly as possible, but as I write I realize 73 that what I say may sound fabulous, or even mythic. It is. It is insane.

Under this system of colorism—the system which prevailed in my 74 childhood in Jamaica, and which has carried over to the present— rarely will dark and light people co-mingle. Rarely will they achieve between themselves an intimacy informed with identity. (I should say here that I am using the categories light and dark both literally and symbolically. There are dark Jamaicans who have achieved lightness and the "advantages" which go with it by their successful pursuit of oppressor status.)

Under this system light and dark people will meet in those ways in 75 which the light-skinned person imitates the oppressor. But imitation goes only so far: the light-skinned person becomes an oppressor in fact. He/she will have a dark chauffeur, a dark nanny, a dark maid, and a dark gardener. These employees will be paid badly. Because of the slave past, because of their dark skin, the servants of the middle class have been used according to the traditions of the slavocracy. They are not seen as workers for their own sake, but for the sake of the family who has employed them. It was not until Michael Manley became prime minister that a minimum wage for houseworkers was enacted—and the indignation of the middle class was profound.

During Manley's leadership the middle class began to abandon the island in droves. Toronto. Miami. New York. Leaving their houses and businesses behind and sewing cash into the tops of suitcases. Today—with a new regime—they are returning: "Come back to the way things used to be" the tourist advertisement on American TV says. "Make it Jamaica again. Make it your own." 76

But let me return to the situation of houseservants as I remember it: They will be paid badly, but they will be "given" room and board. However, the key to the larder will be kept by the mistress in her dresser drawer. They will spend Christmas with the family of their employers and be given a length of English wool for trousers or a few yards of cotton for dresses. They will see their children on their days off: their extended family will care for the children the rest of the time. When the employers visit their relations in the country, the servants may be asked along—oftentimes the servants of the middle class come from the same part of the countryside their employers have come from. But they will be expected to work while they are there. Back in town, there are parts of the house they are allowed to move freely around; other parts they are not allowed to enter. When the family watches the TV, the servant is allowed to watch also, but only while standing in a doorway. The servant may have a radio in his/her room, also a dresser and a cot. Perhaps a mirror. There will usually be one ceiling light. And one small square louvered window. 77

A true story: One middle-class Jamaican woman ordered a Persian rug from Harrod's in London. The day it arrived so did her new maid. She was going downtown to have her hair touched up, and told the maid to vacuum the rug. She told the maid she would find the vacuum cleaner in the same shed as the power mower. And when she returned she found that the fine nap of her new rug had been removed. 78

The reaction of the mistress was to tell her friends that the "girl" was backward. She did not fire her until she found that the maid 79 had scrubbed the teflon from her new set of pots, saying she thought they were coated with "nastiness."

The houseworker/mistress relationship in which one Black woman is 80 the oppressor of another Black woman is a cornerstone of the experience of many Jamaican women.

I remember another true story: In a middle-class family's home one 81 Christmas, a relation was visiting from New York. This woman had brought gifts for everybody, including the housemaid. The maid had been released from a mental institution recently, where they had "treated" her for depression. This visiting light-skinned woman had brought the dark woman a bright red rayon blouse and presented it to her in the garden one afternoon, while the family was having tea. The maid thanked her softly, and the other woman moved toward her as if to embrace her. Then she stopped, her face suddenly covered with tears, and ran into the house, saying, "My God, I can't, I can't."

We are women who come from a place almost incredible in its 82 beauty. It is a beauty which can mask a great deal and which has been used in that way. But that the beauty is there is a fact. I remember what I thought the freedom of my childhood, in which the fruitful place was something I took for granted. Just as I took for granted Zoe's appearance every morning on my school vacations— in the sense that I knew she would be there. That she would always be the one to visit me. The perishing world of my grandfather's graces at the table, if I ever seriously thought about it, was somewhere else.

Our souls were affected by the beauty of Jamaica, as much as they 83 were affected by our fears of darkness.

There is no ending to this piece of writing. There is no way to end it. 84 As I read back over it, I see that we/they/I may become confused in the mind of the reader: but these pronouns have always co-existed in my mind. The Rastas talk of the "I and I"—a pronoun in which they combine themselves with Jah. Jah is a contraction of Jahweh and Jehova, but to me always sounds like the beginning of Jamaica. I and Jamaica is who I am. No matter how far I travel—how deep the ambivalence I feel about ever returning. And Jamaica is a place in which we/they/I connect and disconnect—change place.

Saudi Woman Driver Alert!

CALVIN TRILLIN

You may be wondering why I haven't gotten around to discussing 1
the question of whether or not female reporters have a right to be in
the locker rooms of the National Football League. As it happens, I'm
still trying to deal with a news report of several weeks ago that a
Japanese construction company barred a female reporter from a tunnel completion ceremony because, in the word of the project supervisor, "the presence of women could anger the jealous Goddess of
the Mountain." After that, I have to get to the issue of whether or
not the Saudis should allow women to hold drivers' licenses. In
other words, I'm working up to this.

Before we proceed, I'd better state my position clearly on the 2
general question of equality between the sexes. In previous comments, which are on the public record, I have made it clear that I believe there to be no essential differences between men and women
except that women tend to believe new slipcovers are needed in the
spring and men have, deep in the chromosomes, an absolute com-
pulsion to take out the garbage. That's where I stand.

You'd think that someone with a position that forthright would 3
have no patience at all for the argument by Japanese construction
workers at the Sakazukiyama Tunnel that all women be banned
from tunneling sites or with the response of the project supervisor,
one Hatsuo Sato, who said of the banning of the female reporter, "I
see nothing discriminatory in the action."

You would be absolutely right. My first response to the news 4
from Japan was, "Nothing discriminatory! Give me a break, Hatsuo!
How would you feel if you wanted to pop down to your local for a
pick-me-up and you were banned because the proprietor said that
the presence of a tunnel-construction project-supervisor would
make the God of Saki feel woozy? Also, even if there is a Goddess of
the Mountain, what makes these construction guys think they know
that the presence of women makes her jealous? Maybe she's the sort

Calvin Trillin (1935–   ), born in Kansas City, Missouri, and living in New York City, is the author of stories, novels, and
nonfiction including *Runestruck* (1977), *Alice, Let's Eat: Further Adventures of a Happy Eater* (1978), and *Uncivil Liberties* (1982). "Saudi
Woman Driver Alert!" is from his syndicated newspaper column
(1990).

of goddess who likes the presence of women—the sort who enjoys kaffee-klatsches and pajama parties where they all get together and talk about how ratty the slipcovers are beginning to look."

Unfortunately, I uttered my criticism of Hatsuo Sato's position 5 in front of my friend Barton, who explained to me that I was failing to understand this matter in its cultural context. Barton always wants to understand everything in its cultural context. I can't tell you what a pain he is.

Let me give you an example. Several weeks ago, I returned from 6 a short visit to Istanbul and, in speaking within Barton's earshot of the increasing traffic problem in that otherwise noble metropolis, I said, "I mean this in the most constructive way and I wouldn't for a moment want to interfere in Turkish internal affairs, but it seems to me that it might help the traffic situation over there if they used lanes."

Barton told me that I was trying to impose an essentially West- 7 ern notion on a Muslim nation that has one foot in Asia. I don't know how a country can have a foot anywhere, but that's the way Barton talks. Also, I don't know what the religion of a country has to do with traffic lanes. It's not as if it says in the Koran somewhere that cars should all move at the same time toward a narrow opening, like restless cattle moving toward the one hole in the fence.

Barton is the same way about the question of women not being 8 permitted to drive in Saudi Arabia. What I suggested is that the Saudis could gradually phase in the right of women to drive. First they'd let women drive but Saudi men would be allowed to tell woman-driver jokes. Then, after a decent interval, the men would have to give up the woman-driver jokes. I think they could do it. I read somewhere that the Saudis managed to give up slavery 28 years ago, so it's not as if they're that set in their ways.

Barton says that putting it in terms of woman-driver jokes is just 9 another indication that I, as a Westerner, can't understand the situation. But I understand the situation perfectly: A Saudi woman wants to go out and comparison-shop slipcover fabrics. Her husband says the slipcovers they've got are practically brand-new. So she tells him to empty the garbage. While he's out there, she jumps in the car and is about to go downtown to the fabric store. Then she remembers: She's not allowed to drive. It doesn't have anything to do with the cultural context. It's against nature.

Beliefs and Values, Emotion and Logic in the Arab World

MARGARET K. NYDELL

Beliefs and Values

When we set ourselves the task of coming to a better understanding   1
of groups of people and their culture, it is useful to begin by identifying their most basic beliefs and values. It is these beliefs and values which determine their outlook on life and govern their social behavior.

Westerners tend to believe, for instance, that the individual is   2
the focal point of social existence, that laws apply equally to everyone, that people have a right to certain kinds of privacy, and that
the environment can be controlled by humans through technological
means. These beliefs have a strong influence on what Westerners
think about the world around them and how they behave toward
each other.

Arabs characteristically believe that many if not most things in   3
life are controlled, ultimately, by fate rather than by humans, that
everyone loves children, that wisdom increases with age, and that
the inherent personalities of men and women are vastly different.
As with Westerners, these beliefs play a powerful role in determining the nature of Arab culture.

One might wonder whether there is in fact such a thing as   4
"Arab culture," given the diversity and geographic disparateness of
the Arab World. Looking at a map, one realizes how much is en-
compassed by the phrase "the Arab World." The twenty Arab countries cover considerable territory, much of which is desert or
wilderness. Sudan is larger than all of Western Europe, yet its population is less than that of France; Saudi Arabia is larger than Texas
and Alaska combined, yet has fewer people than New York City.
Egypt, with forty-two million people, is 95% desert. One writer has
stated: "A true map of the Arab World would show it as an

Margaret K. Nydell (1943–   ), born in New York City, is former
director of Arabic language training at the Foreign Service Institute
of the U.S. State Department and coauthor of *Update: Saudi Arabia*
(1990). "Beliefs and Values, Emotion and Logic in the Arab World"
is from *Understanding Arabs: A Guide for Westerners* (1987).

archipelago: a scattering of fertile islands through a void of sand and sea. The Arabic word for desert is 'sahara' and it both divides and joins."[1] The political diversity among the Arab countries is notable; governmental systems include monarchies, military governments, and socialist republics.

But despite these differences, the Arabs are more homogeneous   5 than Westerners in their outlook on life. All Arabs share basic beliefs and values which cross national or social class boundaries. Social attitudes have remained relatively constant because Arab society is conservative and demands conformity from its members. Their beliefs are influenced by Islam even if they are not Moslems, child-rearing practices are nearly identical, and the family structure is essentially the same. Arabs are not as mobile as people in the West, and they have a high regard for tradition.

Initially foreigners may feel that Arabs are difficult to under-   6 stand, that their behavior patterns are not logical. In fact their behavior is quite comprehensible, even predictable. For the most part it conforms to certain patterns which make Arabs consistent in their reactions to other people.

It is important for the foreigner to be able to identify these cultural pat-   7 *terns and to distinguish them from individual traits.* By becoming aware of patterns, one can achieve a better understanding of what to expect and thereby cope more easily. The following lists of Arab values, religious attitudes and self-perceptions are central to the fundamental patterns of Arab culture. . . .

Basic Arab Values

- A person's dignity, honor, and reputation are of paramount importance and no effort should be spared to protect them, especially one's honor.
- It is important to behave at all times in a way which will create a good impression on others.
- Loyalty to one's family takes precedence over personal needs.
- Social class and family background are the major determining factors of personal status, followed by individual character and achievement.

Basic Arab Religious Attitudes

- Everyone believes in God, acknowledges His power and has a religious affiliation.

- Humans cannot control all events; some things depend on God (i.e., "fate").
- Piety is one of the most admirable characteristics in a person.
- There should be no separation between "church and state"; religion should be taught in schools and promoted by governments.
- Religious tenets should not be subjected to "liberal" interpretations or modifications which can threaten established beliefs and practices.

Basic Arab Self-perceptions

- Arabs are generous, humanitarian, polite, and loyal. Several studies have demonstrated that Arabs see these traits as characteristic of themselves and as distinguishing them from other groups.[2]
- Arabs have a rich cultural heritage. This is illustrated by their contributions to religion, philosophy, literature, medicine, architecture, art, mathematics, and the natural sciences.[3]
- Although there are many differences among Arab countries, the Arabs are a clearly defined cultural group, members of the "Arab nation" (al-umma al-'arabiyya).
- The Arab peoples have been victimized and exploited by the West. For them, the experience of the Palestinians represents the most painful and obvious example.
- Indiscriminate imitation of Western culture, by weakening traditional family ties and social and religious values, will have a corrupting influence on Arab society.
- Arabs are misunderstood and wrongly characterized by most Westerners.

Arabs feel that they are often portrayed in the Western media as [8] excessively wealthy, irrational, sensuous, and violent, and there is little counterbalancing information about ordinary people who live family- and work-centered lives on a modest scale. One observer has remarked, "The Arabs remain one of the few ethnic groups who can still be slandered with impunity in America."[4] Another has stated, "In general, the image of the Arabs in British popular culture seems to be characterized by prejudice, hostility, and resentment. The mass media in Britain have failed to provide an adequate representation of points of view for the consumer to judge a real world of the Arabs."[5]

Emotion and Logic

How people deal with emotion or what value they place on objective 9
vs. subjective behavior is culturally conditioned. *While objectivity is
given considerable emphasis in Western culture, the opposite is true in Arab
culture.*

Objectivity and Subjectivity

Westerners are taught that objectivity, the examination of facts 10
in a logical way without the intrusion of emotional bias, is the mature and constructive approach to human affairs. One of the results
of this belief is that in Western culture, subjectivity, a willingness to
allow personal feelings and emotions to influence one's view of
events, represents immaturity. Arabs believe differently. They place
a higher value on the display of emotion, sometimes to the embarrassment or discomfort of foreigners. It is not uncommon to hear
Westerners label this behavior as "immature," imposing their own
values on what they have observed.

A British office manager in Saudi Arabia once described to me 11
his problems with a Palestinian employee. "He is too sensitive, too
emotional about everything," he said. "The first thing he should do
is *grow up.*" While Westerners label Arabs as "too emotional," Arabs
find Westerners "cold" and inscrutable.

Arabs consciously reserve the right to look at the world in a subjective 12
way, particularly if a more objective assessment of a situation would
bring to mind a too-painful truth. There is nothing to gain, for example, by pointing out Israel's brilliant achievements in land reclama-
tion or in comparing the quality of Arab-made consumer items with
imported ones. Such comments will generally not lead to a substantive discussion of how Arabs could benefit by imitating others; more
likely, Arab listeners will become angry and defensive, insisting that
the situation is not as you describe it and bringing up issues such as
Israeli occupation of Arab lands or the moral deterioration of technological societies.

Fatalism

Fatalism, or a belief that people are helpless to control events, is 13
part of traditional Arab culture. It has been much over-emphasized
by Westerners, however, and is far more prevalent among traditional, uneducated Arabs than it is among the educated elite today.
It nevertheless still needs to be considered, since it will usually be
encountered in one form or another by the Western visitor.

For Arabs, fatalism is based on the religious belief that God has 14
direct and ultimate control of all that happens. If something goes
wrong, a person can absolve himself of blame or justify doing nothing to make improvements or changes by assigning the cause to
God's will. Indeed, too much self-confidence about controlling
events is considered a sign of arrogance tinged with blasphemy. The
legacy of fatalism in Arab thought is most apparent in the oft heard
and more or less ritual phrase "Inshallah" (if God wills).

Western thought has essentially rejected fatalism. Though God 15
is believed by many Westerners to intervene in human affairs, Greek
logic, the humanism of the Enlightenment and cause-and-effect em-
piricism have inclined the West to view humans as having the ability
to control their environment and destinies.

What Is Reality?

Reality is what you perceive—if you believe something exists, it 16
is real to you. If you select or rearrange facts, and repeat these to
yourself often enough, they eventually become reality.

The cultural difference between Westerners and Arabs arises not 17
from the fact that this selection takes place, but from how each
makes the selection. *Arabs are more likely to allow subjective perceptions
to direct their actions.* This is a common source of frustration for Westerners, who often fail to understand why people in the Middle East
act as they do.

If an Arab feels that something threatens his personal dignity, 18
he may be obliged to deny it, even in the face of facts to the contrary. A Westerner can point out flaws in his argument, but that is
not the point. If he does not want to accept the facts, he will reject
them and proceed according to his own view of the situation. An
Arab will rarely admit to an error openly if it will cause him to lose
face. *To Arabs, honor is more important than facts.*

An American woman in Tunis realized, when she was packing 19
to leave, that some of her clothes and a suitcase were missing. She
confronted the maid, who insisted that she had no idea where they
could be. When the American found some of her clothes under a
mattress, she called the company's Tunisian security officer. They
went to the maid's house and found more missing items. The maid
was adamant that she could not account for the items being in her
home. The security officer said that he felt the matter should not be
reported to the police—the maid's humiliation in front of her neighbors was sufficient punishment.

In 1974 an Israeli entered a small Arab-owned cafe in Jerusalem 20
and asked for some watermelon, pointing at it and using the He-

brew word. The Arab proprietor responded that it should be called by the Arabic name, but the Israeli insisted on the Hebrew name. The Arab took offense at this point. He paused, shrugged, and instead of serving his customer, said, "There isn't any!"

At a conference held to discuss Arab and American cultures, Dr. Laura Nader related this incident: 21

> The mistake people in one culture often make in dealing with another culture is to transfer their functions to the other culture's functions. A political scientist, for example, went to the Middle East to do some research one summer and to analyze Egyptian newspapers. When he came back, he said to me, "But they are all just full of emotions. There is no data in these newspapers." I said, "What makes you think there should be?"[6]

Another way of influencing the perception of reality is by the choice of descriptive words and names. The Arabs are very careful in naming or referring to places, people, and events; slogans and labels are popular and provide an insight into how things are viewed. The Arabs realize that *names have a powerful effect on perception.*   22

There is a big psychological gap between opposing labels like "Palestine/Israel," "The West Bank/Judea and Samaria," and "freedom fighters ('hero martyrs' if they are killed)/terrorists." The 1967 Arab-Israeli War is called "The War of the Setback" in Arabic—in other words, it was *not* a "defeat." The 1973 War is called "The War of Ramadan" or "The Sixth of October War," *not* "The Yom Kippur War."   23

Be conscious of names and labels—they matter a great deal to the Arabs. If you attend carefully to what you hear in conversations with Arabs and what is written in their newspapers, you will note how precisely they select descriptive words and phrases. You may find yourself being corrected by Arab acquaintances, and you will soon learn which terms are acceptable and which are not.   24

The Human Dimension

Arabs look at life in a personalized way. They are concerned about people and feelings and place emphasis on "human factors" when they make decisions or analyze events. They feel that Westerners are too prone to look at events in an abstract or theoretical way, and that most Westerners lack sensitivity toward people.   25

In the Arab World, a manager or official is always willing to reconsider a decision, regulation, or problem in view of someone's personal situation. Any regulation can be modified or avoided by someone with enough persuasive influence, particularly if the request   26 is justified on the grounds of unusual personal need. This is unlike most Western societies, which emphasize the equal application of laws to all citizens. *In the Arab culture, people are more important than rules.*

T. E. Lawrence stated it succinctly: "Arabs believe in persons, not in institutions."[7] They have a long tradition of personal appeal to authorities for exceptions to rules. This is commonly seen when they attempt to obtain special permits, exemptions from fees, acceptance into a school when preconditions are not met, or employment when qualifications are inadequate. They do not accept predetermined standards if these standards are a personal inconvenience. 27

Arabs place great value on personal interviews and on giving people the opportunity to state their case. They are not comfortable filling out forms or dealing with an organization impersonally. They want to know the name of the top person who makes the final decision and are always confident that the rejection of a request may be reversed if top-level personal contact can be made. Frequently, that is exactly what happens. 28

Persuasion

Arabs and Westerners place a different value on certain types of statements, which may lead to decreased effectiveness on both sides when they negotiate with each other. Arabs respond much more readily to personalized arguments than to attempts to impose "logical" conclusions. When you are trying to make a persuasive case in your discussions with Arabs, you will find it helpful to supplement your arguments with personal comments. You can refer to your mutual friendship, or emphasize the effect which approval or disapproval of the action will have on other people. 29

In the Middle East negotiation and persuasion have been developed into a fine art. Participants in negotiations enjoy long, spirited discussions and are usually not in any hurry to conclude them. Speakers feel free to add to their points of argument by demonstrating their verbal cleverness, using their personal charm, applying personal pressure, and engaging in personal appeals for consideration of their point of view. 30

The display of emotion also plays its part; indeed, one of the most commonly misunderstood aspects of Arab communication involves their "display" of anger. Arabs are not usually as angry as they appear to Westerners. Raising the voice, repeating points, even pounding the table for emphasis may sound angry but, in the speaker's mind, indicate sincerity. A Westerner overhearing such a conversation (especially if it is in Arabic) may wrongly conclude that 31 an argument is taking place. *Emotion connotes deep and sincere concern for the outcome of the discussion.*

Foreigners often miss the emotional dimension in their cross-cultural transactions with Arabs. A British businessman once found that he and his wife were denied reservations on an airplane because the Arab ticketing official took offense at the manner in which he was addressed. The fact that seats were available was *not* an effective counter-argument. But when the Arab official noticed that the businessman's wife had begun to cry, he gave way and provided them with seats.

Arabs usually include human elements in their arguments. In arguing the Palestine issue, for instance, they have always placed emphasis on the suffering of individuals rather than on points of law or a recital of historical events.

Notes

1. Stewart, Desmond, *The Arab World,* pp. 9–10.
2. Dr. Levon H. Melikian (see bibliography) has studied the modal personality of some Arab students, searching for traits to define "national character."
The author administered a word-association test to a group of Lebanese university students in 1972. The most common responses associated with the word "Arabs" were "generous," "brave," "honorable," and "loyal." About half of the forty-three respondents added the word "misunderstood."
3. This subject is very thoroughly discussed by Abdel-Rahim Omran in his book, *Population in the Arab World,* in the chapter, "The Contribution of the Arabs to World Culture and Science," pp. 13–41.
4. Slade, Shelley, "The Image of the Arab in America: Analysis of a Poll of American Attitudes," *Middle East Journal,* p. 143. Many of the stereotypes about the Middle East which are taught in schools or depicted in American media are discussed in *The Middle East, The Image and Reality,* edited by Jonathan Friedlander (see bibliography).
5. Nasir, Sari J., *The Arabs and the English,* p. 171.
6. Atiyeh, George N., ed., *Arab and American Cultures,* p. 179.
7. Lawrence, T. E. *Seven Pillars of Wisdom,* p. 24.

Bibliography and References

Atiyeh, George N., ed., *Arab and American Cultures.* Washington, D.C.: American Enterprise Institute for Public Policy Research, 1977.
Friedlander, Jonathan, ed., *The Middle East: The Image and the Reality.* Los Angeles: University of California (Curriculum Inquiry Center) Press, 1981.
Lawrence, T. E., *Seven Pillars of Wisdom.* New York: Doubleday & Co., Inc., 1926.
Melikian, Levon H., *Jassim: A Study in the Psychological Development of a Young Man in Qatar.* London: Longman Group Ltd., 1981.
———"The Modal Personality of Saudi College Students: A Study in National Character," in *Psychological Dimensions of Near Eastern Studies,* edited by L. Carl Brown and Norman Itzkowitz. Princeton: The Darwin Press, 1977, pp. 166–209.
Nasir, Sari J., *The Arabs and the English,* Second edition. London: Longman Group Ltd., 1979.
Omran, Abdel-Rahim, *Population in the Arab World.* London: Croom Helm Ltd., 1980.
Stewart, Desmond, *The Arab World.* New York: Time-Life Books, 1972.
Slade, Shelley, "The Image of the Arab in America: Analysis of a Poll of American Attitudes," *Middle East Journal,* Vol. 35, No. 2, Spring 1981, pp. 143–162.

Tour of the City: Encounters between East and West

PICO IYER

To mention, however faintly, the West's cultural assault on the East 1
is, inevitably, to draw dangerously close to the fashionable belief
that the First World is corrupting the Third. And to accept that AIDS
and Rambo are the two great "Western" exports of 1985 is to encourage some all too easy conclusions: that the West's main contributions to the rest of the world are sex and violence, a cureless disease
and a killer cure; that America is exporting nothing but a literal kind
of infection and a bloody sort of indoctrination. In place of physical
imperialism, we often assert a kind of sentimental colonialism that
would replace Rambo myths with Sambo myths and conclude that
because the First World feels guilty, the Third World must be innocent—what Pascal Bruckner refers to as "compassion as contempt."

This, however, I find simplistic—both because corruption often 2
says most about those who detect it and because the developing
world may often have good reason to assent in its own transformation.

This is not to deny that the First World has indeed inflicted 3
much damage on the Third, especially through the inhuman calcula-
tions of geopolitics. If power corrupts, superpowers are super-
corrupting, and the past decade alone has seen each of the major
powers destroy a self-contained Asian culture by dragging it into the
cross fire of the Real World: Tibet was invaded for strategic reasons
by the Chinese, and now the dreamed-of Shangri-La is almost lost
forever; Afghanistan was overrun by Soviet tanks, and now the
Michauds' photographic record of its fugitive beauties must be subti-
tled, with appropriate melancholy, "Paradise Lost"; Cambodia, once
so gentle a land that cyclo drivers were said to tip their passengers,
fell into the sights of Washington and is now just a land of corpses.

On an individual level too, Western tourists invariably visit de- 4
struction on the places they visit, descending in droves on some

---

Pico Iyer (1957–   ), born in England of Indian parents and now
living in California, is a journalist and the author of *Video Night in
Kathmandu* (1988), about his travels across Asia. "Tour of the City:
Encounters between East and West" is from "Love Match," the
book's introductory chapter.

"authentic Eastern village" until only two things are certain: it is neither Eastern nor authentic. Each passing season (and each passing
tourist) brings new developments to the forgotten places of the
world—and in a never-never land, every development is a change
for the worse. In search of a lovely simplicity, Westerners saddle the
East with complexities; in search of peace, they bring agitation. As
soon as Arcadia is seen as a potential commodity, amenities spring
up on every side to meet outsiders' needs, and paradise is not so
much lost as remaindered. In Asia alone, Bali, Tahiti, Sri Lanka and
Nepal have already been so taken over by Paradise stores, Paradise
hotels and Paradise cafés that they sometimes seem less like utopias
than packaged imitations of utopia; Ladakh, Tibet and Ko Samui
may one day follow. No man, they say, is an island; in the age of international travel, not even an island can remain an island for long.

Like every tourist, moreover, I found myself spreading corrup-   5
tion even as I decried it. In northern Thailand, I joined a friend in
giving hill tribesmen tutorials in the songs of Sam Cooke until a
young Thai girl was breaking the silence of the jungle with a piercing refrain of "She was sixteen, too young to love, and I was too
young to know." In China, I gave a local boy eager for some English-language reading matter a copy of the only novel I had on
hand—Gore Vidal's strenuously perverse *Duluth*. And in a faraway
hill station in Burma, a group of cheery black marketeers treated me
to tea and I, in return, taught them the words "lesbian" and "skin
flicks," with which they seemed much pleased.

Yet that in itself betrays some of the paradoxes that haunt our   6
talk of corruption. For often, the denizens of the place we call paradise long for nothing so much as news of that "real paradise"
across the seas—the concrete metropolis of skyscrapers and burger
joints. And often what we call corruption, they might be inclined to
call progress or profit. As tourists, we have reason to hope that the
quaint anachronism we have discovered will always remain
"unspoiled," as fixed as a museum piece for our inspection. It is per-
ilous, however, to assume that its inhabitants will long for the same.
Indeed, a kind of imperial arrogance underlies the very assumption
that the people of the developing world should be happier without
the TVs and motorbikes that we find so indispensable ourselves. If
money does not buy happiness, neither does poverty.

In other ways too, our laments for lost paradises may really have   7
much more to do with our own state of mind than with the state of
the place whose decline we mourn. Whenever we recall the places
we have seen, we tend to observe them in the late afternoon glow of
nostalgia, after memory, the mind's great cosmetician, has softened
out rough edges, smoothed out imperfections and removed the

whole to a lovely abstract distance. Just as a good man, once dead, is remembered as a saint, so a pleasant place, once quit, is recalled as a utopia. Nothing is ever what it used to be.

If the First World is not invariably corrupting the Third, we are sometimes apt to leap to the opposite conclusion: that the Third World, in fact, is hustling the First. As tourists, moreover, we are so bombarded with importunities from a variety of locals—girls who live off their bodies and touts who live off their wits, merchants who use friendship to lure us into their stores and "students" who attach themselves to us in order to improve their English—that we begin to regard ourselves as beleaguered innocents and those we meet as shameless predators. 8

To do so, however, is to ignore the great asymmetry that governs every meeting between tourist and local: that we are there by choice and they largely by circumstance; that we are traveling in the spirit of pleasure, adventure and romance, while they are mired in the more urgent business of trying to survive; and that we, often courted by the government, enjoy a kind of unofficial diplomatic immunity, which gives us all the perks of authority and none of the perils of responsibility, while they must stake their hopes on every potential transaction. 9

Descending upon native lands quite literally from the heavens, *dei ex machinae*[1] from an alien world of affluence, we understandably strike many locals in much the same way that movie stars strike us. And just as some of us are wont to accost a celebrity glimpsed by chance at a restaurant, so many people in developing countries may be tempted to do anything and everything possible to come into contact with the free-moving visitors from abroad and their world of distant glamour. They have nothing to lose in approaching a foreigner—at worst, they will merely be insulted or pushed away. And they have everything to gain: a memory, a conversation, an old copy of *Paris Match*, perhaps even a friendship or a job opportunity. Every foreigner is a messenger from a world of dreams. 10

"Do you know Beverly Hills?" I was once asked by a young Burmese boy who had just spent nine months in jail for trying to escape his closed motherland. "Do you know Hollywood? Las Vegas? The Potomac, I think, is very famous. Am I right? Detroit, Michigan, is where they make cars. Ford. General Motors. Chevrolet. Do you 11

---

[1] "Gods from the machines," a reference to the technique of classical Greek theater in which gods literally descended on cranes to the stage. (Ed.)

know Howard Hughes? There are many Jewish people in New York. Am I right? And also at *Time* magazine? Am I right?" Tell us about life behind the scenes, we ask the star, and which is the best place in the whole wide world, and what is Liz Taylor really like.

The touts that accost us are nearly always, to be sure, worldly 12 pragmatists. But they are also, in many cases, wistful dreamers, whose hopes are not so different from the ones our culture encourages: to slough off straitened circumstances and set up a new life and a new self abroad, underwritten by hard work and dedication. American dreams are strongest in the hearts of those who have seen America only in their dreams.

I first met Maung-Maung as I stumbled off a sixteen-hour third- 13 class overnight train from Rangoon to Mandalay. He was standing outside the station, waiting to pick up tourists; a scrawny fellow in his late twenties, with a sailor's cap, a beard, a torn white shirt above his *longyi*[2] and an open, rough-hewn face—a typical tout, in short. Beside him stood his bicycle trishaw. On one side was painted the legend "My Life"; on the other, "B.Sc. (Maths)."

We haggled for a few minutes. Then Maung-Maung smilingly 14 persuaded me to part with a somewhat inflated fare—twenty cents—for the trip across town, and together we began cruising through the wide, sunny boulevards of the city of kings. As we set off, we began to exchange the usual questions—age, place of birth, marital status and education—and before long we found that our answers often jibed. Soon, indeed, the conversation was proceeding swimmingly. A little while into our talk, my driver, while carefully steering his trishaw with one hand, sank the other into his pocket and handed back to me a piece of jade. I admired it dutifully, then extended it back in his direction. "No," he said. "This is present."

Where, I instantly wondered, was the catch—was he framing 15 me, or bribing me, or cunningly putting me in his debt? What was the small print? What did he want?

"I want you," said Maung-Maung, "to have something so you 16 can always remember me. Also, so you can always have happy memories of Mandalay." I did not know how to respond. "You see," he went on, "if I love other people, they will love me. It is like Newton's law, or Archimedes."

This was not what I had expected. "I think," he added, "it is al- 17 ways good to apply physics to life."

---

[2] *longyi:* Traditional Burmese wrap-around skirt, usually worn with a short formal jacket. (Ed.)

That I did not doubt. But still I was somewhat taken aback. "Did 18 you study physics at school?"

"No, I study physics in college. You see, I am graduate from 19 University of Mandalay—B.Sc. Mathematics." He waved with pride at the inscription on the side of his trishaw.

"And you completed all your studies?"   20

"Yes. B.Sc. Mathematics."   21

"Then why are you working in this kind of job?"   22

"Other jobs are difficult. You see, here in Burma, a teacher earns 23 only two hundred fifty kyats [$30] in a month. Managing director has only one thousand kyats [$125]. Even President makes only four thousand kyats [$500]. For me, I do not make much money. But in this job, I can meet tourist and improve my English. Experience, I believe, is the best teacher."

"But surely you could earn much more just by driving a horse 24 cart?"

"I am Buddhist," Maung-Maung reminded me gently, as he 25 went pedaling calmly through the streets. "I do not want to inflict harm on any living creature. If I hit horse in this life, in next life I come back as horse."

"So"—I was still skeptical—"you live off tourists instead?" 26

"Yes," he said, turning around to give me a smile. My irony, it 27 seems, was wasted. "Until two years ago, in my village in Shan States, I had never seen a tourist."

"Never?"   28

"Only in movies." Again he smiled back at me.   29

I was still trying to puzzle out why a university graduate would 30 be content with such a humble job when Maung-Maung, as he pedaled, reached into the basket perched in front of his handlebars and pulled out a thick leather book. Looking ahead as he steered, he handed it back to me to read. Reluctantly, I opened it, bracing myself for porno postcards or other illicit souvenirs. Inside, however, was nothing but a series of black-and-white snapshots. Every one of them had been painstakingly annotated in English: "My Headmaster," "My Monk," "My Brothers and Sisters," "My Friend's Girlfriend." And his own girlfriend? "I had picture before. But after she broke my heart, and fall in love with other people, I tear it out."

At the very back of his book, in textbook English, Maung- 31 Maung had carefully inscribed the principles by which he lived.

1. Abstain from violence.

2. Abstain from illicit sexual intercourse.

3. Abstain from intoxicants of all kinds.

4. Always be helpful.

5. Always be kind.

"It must be hard," I said dryly, "to stick to all these rules." 32

"Yes. It is not always easy," he confessed. "But I must try. If 33
people ask me for food, my monk tell me, I must always give them
money. But if they want money for playing cards, I must give them
no help. My monk also explain I must always give forgiveness—
even to people who hurt me. If you put air into volleyball and throw
it against wall, it bounces back. But if you do not put in air, what
happens? It collapses against wall."

Faith, in short, was its own vindication. 34

I was now beginning to suspect that I would find no more en- 35
gaging guide to Mandalay than Maung-Maung, so I asked him if he
would agree to show me around. "Yes, thank you very much. But
first, please, I would like you to see my home."

Ah, I thought, here comes the setup. Once I'm in his house, far 36
from the center of a city I don't know, he will drop a drug in my tea
or pull out a knife or even bring in a few accomplices. I will find out
too late that his friendliness is only a means to an end.

Maung-Maung did nothing to dispel these suspicions as he ped- 37
aled the trishaw off the main street and we began to pass through
dirty alleyways, down narrow lanes of run-down shacks. At last we
pulled up before a hut, fronted with weeds. Smiling proudly, he got
off and asked me to enter.

There was not much to see inside his tiny room. There was a 38
cot, on which sat a young man, his head buried in his hands. There
was another cot, on which Maung-Maung invited me to sit as he introduced me to his roommate. The only other piece of furniture was
a blackboard in a corner on which my host had written out the statement reproduced in the epigraph to this book, expressing his
lifelong pledge to be of service to tourists.

I sat down, not sure what was meant to happen next. For a few 39
minutes, we made desultory conversation. His home, Maung-
Maung explained, cost 30 kyats ($4) a month. This other man was
also a university graduate, but he had no job: every night, he got
drunk. Then, after a few moments of reflection, my host reached
down to the floor next to his bed and picked up what I took to be his
two most valuable belongings.

Solemnly, he handed the first of them to me. It was a sociology 40
textbook from Australia. Its title was *Life in Modern America*. Then, as
gently as if it were his Bible, Maung-Maung passed across the other
volume, a dusty old English-Burmese dictionary, its yellowed pages

falling from their covers. "Every night," he explained, "after I am finished on trishaw, I come here and read this. Also, every word I do not know I look up." Inside the front cover, he had copied out a few specimen sentences. *If you do this, you may end up in jail. My heart is lacerated by what you said. What a lark.*

I was touched by his show of trust. But I also felt as uncertain as 41 an actor walking through a play he hasn't read. Perhaps, I said a little uneasily, we should go now, so we can be sure of seeing all the sights of Mandalay before sundown. "Do not worry," Maung-Maung assured me with a quiet smile, "we will see everything. I know how long the trip will take. But first, please, I would like you to see this."

Reaching under his bed, he pulled out what was clearly his most 42 precious treasure of all. With a mixture of shyness and pride, he handed over a thick black notebook. I looked at the cover for markings and, finding none, opened it up. Inside, placed in alphabetical order, was every single letter he had ever received from a foreign visitor. Every one was meticulously dated and annotated; many were accompanied by handwritten testimonials or reminiscences from the tourists Maung-Maung had met. On some pages, he had affixed wrinkled passport photos of his foreign visitors by which he could remember them.

Toward the end of the book, Maung-Maung had composed a 43 two-page essay, laboriously inscribed in neat and grammatical English, called "Guide to Jewelry." It was followed by two further monographs, "For You" and "For the Tourists." In them, Maung-Maung warned visitors against "twisty characters," explained something of the history and beauty of Mandalay and told his readers not to trust him until he had proved worthy of their trust.

Made quiet by this labor of love, I looked up. "This must have 44 taken you a long time to write."

"Yes," he replied with a bashful smile. "I have to look many 45 times at dictionary. But it is my pleasure to help tourists."

I went back to flipping through the book. At the very end of the 46 volume, carefully copied out, was a final four-page essay, entitled "My Life."

He had grown up, Maung-Maung wrote, in a small village, the 47 eldest of ten children. His mother had never learned to read, and feeling that her disability made her "blind," she was determined that her children go to school. It was not easy, because his father was a farmer and earned only 300 kyats a month. Still, Maung-Maung, as the eldest, was able to complete his education at the local school.

When he finished, he told his parents that he wanted to go to 48 university. Sorrowfully, they told him that they could not afford it—they had given him all they had for his schooling. He knew that was true, but still he was set on continuing his studies. "I have hand. I have head. I have legs," he told them. "I wish to stand on my own legs." With that, he left his village and went to Mandalay. Deeply wounded by his desertion, his parents did not speak to him for a year.

In Mandalay, Maung-Maung's narrative continued, he had be- 49
gun to finance his studies by digging holes—he got 4 kyats for every hole. Then he got a job cleaning clothes. Then he went to a monastery and washed dishes and clothes in exchange for board and lodging. Finally, he took a night job as a trishaw driver.

When they heard of that, his parents were shocked. "They think 50
I go with prostitutes. Everyone looks down on trishaw driver. Also other trishaw drivers hate me because I am a student. I do not want to quarrel with them. But I do not like it when they say dirty things or go with prostitutes." Nevertheless, after graduation Maung-Maung decided to pay 7 kyats a day to rent a trishaw full-time. Sometimes, he wrote, he made less than 1 kyat a day, and many nights he slept in his vehicle in the hope of catching the first tourists of the day. He was a poor man, he went on, but he made more money than his father. Most important, he made many friends. And through riding his trishaw he had begun to learn English.

His dream, Maung-Maung's essay concluded, was to buy his 51
own trishaw. But that cost four hundred dollars. And his greatest dream was, one day, to get a "Further Certificate" in mathematics. He had already planned the details of that far-off moment when he could invite his parents to his graduation. "I must hire taxi. I must buy English suit. I must pay for my parents to come to Mandalay. I know that it is expensive, but I want to express my gratitude to my parents. They are my lovers."

When I finished the essay, Maung-Maung smiled back his grati- 52
tude, and gave me a tour of the city as he had promised.

The American empire in the East: that was my grand theme as I set 53
forth. But as soon as I left the realm of abstract labels and generalized forces, and came down to individuals—to myself, Maung-Maung and many others like him—the easy contrasts began to grow confused. If cultures are only individuals writ large, as Salman Rushdie[3] and Gabriel García Márquez[4] have suggested, individuals

---

[3] See page 10. (Ed.)
[4] Colombian novelist (1928–   ). (Ed.)

are small cultures in themselves. Everyone is familiar with the slogan of Kipling's "Oh, East is East, and West is West, and never the twain shall meet." But few recall that the lines that conclude the refrain, just a few syllables later, exclaim, "But there is neither East nor West, border, nor breed, nor birth, / When two strong men stand face to face, though they come from the ends of the earth!"

On a grand collective level, the encounters between East and   54 West might well be interpreted as a battle; but on the human level, the meeting more closely resembled a mating dance (even Rambo, while waging war against the Vietnamese, had fallen in love with a Vietnamese girl). Whenever a Westerner meets an Easterner, each is to some extent confronted with the unknown. And the unknown is at once an enticement and a challenge; it awakens in us both the lover and the would-be conqueror. When Westerner meets Easterner, therefore, each finds himself often drawn to the other, yet mystified; each projects his romantic hopes on the stranger, as well as his designs; and each pursues both his illusions and his vested interests with a curious mix of innocence and calculation that shifts with every step.

Everywhere I went in Asia, I came upon variations on this same   55 uncertain pattern: in the streets of China, where locals half woo, half recoil from Westerners whose ways remain alien but whose goods are now irresistible; in the country-and-western bars of Manila, where former conqueror and former conquest slow-dance cheek to cheek with an affection, and a guilt, born of longtime familiarity; in the high places of the Himalayas, where affluent Westerners eager to slough off their riches in order to find religion meet local wise men so poor that they have made of riches a religion; and, most vividly of all, in the darkened bars of Bangkok, where a Western man and a Thai girl exchange shy questions and tentative glances, neither knowing whether either is after love or something else. Sometimes, the romance seemed like a blind date, sometimes like a passionate attachment; sometimes like a back-street coupling, sometimes like the rhyme of kindred spirits. Always, though, it made any talk of winners and losers irrelevant.

Usually, too, the cross-cultural affairs developed with all the   56 contradictory twists and turns of any romance in which opposites attract and then retract and then don't know exactly where they stand. The Westerner is drawn to the tradition of the Easterner, and almost covets his knowledge of suffering, but what attracts the Easterner to the West is exactly the opposite—his future, and his freedom from all hardship. After a while, each starts to become more like the other, and somewhat less like the person the other seeks. The New Yorker disappoints the locals by turning into a barefoot ascetic dressed in bangles and beads, while the Nepali peasant frustrates his foreign supplicants by turning out to be a traveling salesman in Levi's and Madonna T-shirt. Soon, neither is quite the person he was, or the one the other wanted. The upshot is confusion. "You cannot have pineapple for breakfast," a Thai waitress once admonished me. "Why?" I asked. "What do *you* have for breakfast?" "Hot dog."

It is never hard, in such skewed exchanges, to find silliness and 57 self-delusion. "Everybody thought that everybody else was ridiculously exotic," writes Gita Mehta of East-West relations in *Karma Cola*, "and everybody got it wrong." Yet Mehta's cold-eyed perspective does justice to only one aspect of this encounter. For the rest, I prefer to listen to her wise and very different compatriot, R. K. Narayan, whose typical tale "God and the Cobbler" describes a chance meeting in a crowded Indian street between a Western hippie and a village cobbler. Each, absurdly, takes the other to be a god. Yet the beauty of their folly is that each, lifted by the other's faith, surprises himself, and us, by somehow rising to the challenge and proving worthy of the trust he has mistakenly inspired: each, taken out of himself, becomes, not a god perhaps, but something better than a dupe or fraud. Faith becomes its own vindication. And at the story's end, each leaves the other with a kind of benediction, the more valuable because untypical.

Every trip we take deposits us at the same forking of the paths: 58 it can be a shortcut to alienation—removed from our home and distanced from our immediate surroundings, we can afford to be contemptuous of both; or it can be a voyage into renewal, as, leaving our selves and pasts at home and traveling light, we recover our innocence abroad. Abroad, we are all Titanias,[5] so bedazzled by strangeness that we comically mistake asses for beauties; but away from home, we can also be Mirandas,[6] so new to the world that our blind faith can become a kind of higher sight. "After living in Asia," John Krich[7] quotes an old hand as saying, "you trust nobody, but you believe everything." At the same time, as Edmond Taylor wrote, Asia is "the school of doubt in which one learns faith in man." If every journey makes us wiser about the world, it also returns us to a sort of childhood. In alien parts, we speak more simply, in our own or some other language, move more freely, unencumbered by the histories that we carry around at home, and look

[5] Titania is a character in Shakespeare's *A Midsummer Night's Dream* (c. 1594). (Ed.)
[6] Miranda is a character in Shakespeare's *The Tempest* (c. 1611). (Ed.)
[7] See page 18. (Ed.)

more excitedly, with eyes of wonder. And if every trip worth taking is both a tragedy and a comedy, rich with melodrama and farce, it is also, at its heart, a love story. The romance with the foreign must certainly be leavened with a spirit of keen and unillusioned realism; but it must also be observed with a measure of faith.

How to Compare Two Cultures

ROBERT LADO

"Culture," as we understand it here, is synonymous with the "ways 1
of a people." . . . More often than not the ways of a people are
praised by that same people while looked upon with suspicion or
disapproval by the others, and often in both cases with surprisingly
little understanding of what those ways really are and mean.

When a visitor is in the United States to study the American way 2
of life or American culture, almost everyone is glad to show him that
way and that culture, but what do we show him and what do we tell
him? How do we know what to show and tell him?

If we are near an automobile plant, we will show him of course 3
an assembly line and the tourist spots in the city. And perhaps we
will show him a farm and a school. And we will tell him the favorable generalities that we have been taught about ourselves, which
may happen to be the same favorable generalities he too has learned
about himself and his culture. Occasionally someone among us
wishing to pose as a detached intellectual may criticize a thing or
two, or everything. But we are really rather helpless to interpret
ourselves accurately and to describe what we do, because we have
grown up doing it and we do much of what we do through habit,
acquired almost unnoticed from our elders and our cultural environment.

Our inability to describe our cultural ways parallels our inability 4
to describe our language, unless we have made a special study of it.
The paradox is that we are able to use the complex structure that is
our language with astonishing ease and flexibility, but when someone asks us when to use *between* and *among,* for example, we will tell
him the most surprising fiction with the best intention of telling the
truth. Similarly, we may be able to tie a bow tie with speed and
ease, but the moment someone asks us to explain what we do, we

Robert Lado (1915–   ), born in Tampa, Florida, is former dean of
the Institute of Languages and Linguistics at Georgetown University and author, coauthor, or editor of textbooks and language
studies including *Language Teaching: A Scientific Approach* (1964) and
Contemporary Spanish (1967). "How to Compare Two Cultures" is
from *Linguistics across Cultures: Applied Linguistics for Language
Teachers* (1957).

become thoroughly confused and may give him completely false information. We describe ourselves as being free and at the same time may demand that our student visitors attend class regularly, a restriction that is considered an invasion of personal freedom in some countries.

We cannot hope to compare two cultures unless we have more accurate understanding of each of the cultures being compared. We must be able to eliminate the things we claim to do but actually don't do. We must be able to describe the things we do without being conscious of doing them, and we must make sure we are able to describe practices accurately, not haphazardly or ideally. And we must be able to describe the situations in which we do what we do.

I assume with others that cultures are structured systems of patterned behavior. Following is a good definition given by anthropologists.

> Cultural anthropologists, during the last twenty-five years, have gradually moved from an atomistic definition of culture, describing it as a more or less haphazard collection of traits, to one which emphasizes pattern and configuration. Kluckhohn and Kelly perhaps best express this modern concept of culture when they define it as "all those historically created designs for living, explicit and implicit, rational, irrational, and non-rational, which exist at any given time as potential guides for the behavior of men." Traits, elements, or better, patterns of culture in this definition are organized or structured into a system or set of systems, which, because it is historically created, is therefore open and subject to constant change.[1]

Compare also the statement by Edward Sapir that "All cultural behavior is patterned."[2]

The individual acts of behavior through which a culture manifests itself are never exactly alike. Each act is unique, and the very same act never occurs again. Even in performing a play many times, each act performed by the player is unique, and it can be shown to be different from the "same" act in the very next performance. Yet in every culture certain acts which in physical terms are thus different are nevertheless accepted as same. Having orange juice, coffee, fried eggs, and white toast one morning and grapefruit juice, coffee, scrambled eggs, and whole wheat toast the next morning would

---

[1] Harry Hoijer, "The Relation of Language to Culture," in *Anthropology Today*, ed. A. L. Kroeber (Chicago: Univ. Chi. Press, 1953), p. 554.

[2] "The Status of Linguistics as a Science," *Selected Writings of Edward Sapir*, ed. David G. Mandelbaum (Berkeley and Los Angeles: Univ. Calif. Press, 1949), p. 546.

usually be considered in the United States two occurrences of the same unit of behavior: eating breakfast. Yet they are different. The mold or design into which certain acts must fall to be considered breakfast in the United States constitutes a pattern of behavior, a functioning unit of behavior in that culture. These patterns are in turn made up of substitutible elements such as performer, act, objects, setting, time, manner, purpose, etc. These elements, though always unique and always different, are identified into "sames" and "differents" within certain molds which are cultural patterns also. These sames have characteristic features in each culture and they are usually of various classes. One such class in many cultures consists of items treated as static units, for example, men, women, children, doctor, nurse, teacher, barber, animals, horses, dogs, ghosts, witches, goblins, ideas, family, club, church, school, factory, store, farm, tree, building, museum, house, etc. Another class is constituted by items treated as processes, for example, to rest, to study, to fish, to run, to think, to sit, to die, etc. Still another includes items treated as qualities, as for example, fast, slow, good, bad, hot, cold, sleepy, sleepily, cruel, constructively, fishy, etc.

Such units of patterned behavior, which constitute the designs 8 that are each culture, have form, meaning, and distribution. . . .

The *forms* of these patterns of culture are identified functionally 9 on inspection by the members of that culture, although the same individuals may not be able accurately to define the very forms that they can identify. Even such a clear unit of behavior as eating breakfast, immediately identified by the performer if we ask him what he is doing, may be described by him as the morning meal or the meal when you eat cereal, bacon, eggs, and coffee, yet a man who works during the night might be eating his breakfast in the evening, and a meal of cereal, bacon, eggs, and coffee might be lunch or even supper.

What is breakfast then? Can we define it? Yes, but the point be- 10 ing made is that the very same individuals who can tell us without hesitation and with accuracy "I am eating breakfast" may not be able to define breakfast for us and may do it erroneously. We can describe breakfast by observing a representative number of occurrences of breakfast and by noting the contrasts with those occurrences which seem to resemble breakfast but are identified as lunch, dinner, a snack, or supper by natives.

Meanings, like forms, are culturally determined or modified. 11 They represent an analysis of the universe as grasped in a culture. Patterned forms have a complex of meanings, some representing features of a unit or process or quality, some grasped as primary, others as secondary, tertiary, etc. Eating breakfast, lunch, and dinner are engaged in usually to provide food and drink for the body. We say then that breakfast, lunch, and dinner usually have that primary meaning. In addition a particular form of breakfast at a particular time of day may have a meaning of good or bad on a moral or religious scale, on a health scale, on an economic scale, etc. A particular form of breakfast may carry as secondary meaning a social-class identification, a national origin identification, a religious identification. In short, any of the distinctions and groupings of a culture may be part of the meaning of a particular form unit.

All of these meaningful units of form are distributed in pat- 12 terned ways. Their distribution patterns are complexes involving various time cycles, space locations, and positions in relation to other units. Breakfast, for example, shows time distribution on a daily cycle, a weekly cycle, and a yearly cycle. Breakfast shows a space or location distribution. It is also distributed after some units of behavior and preceding others.

Form, meaning, and distribution probably do not exist indepen- 13 dent of each other in a culture, but they are spoken of operationally here as separate. Forms are relevant when they have meaning; meaning presupposes a form in order to be of relevance to us; and meaningful forms always occur in patterned distribution.

Within a culture we can assume that when an individual ob- 14 serves a significant patterned form in a patterned distribution spot, it will have a complex of culturally patterned meanings for him. Breakfast in the kitchen at 7 A.M., served by the same person who eats it, and including coffee, fruit juice, and cereal, will have a different complex of meanings than breakfast in bed at 11 A.M. served by a formally dressed waiter, and including caviar and other trimmings.

It may be worth pointing out at this time that the observation of 15 a form may occur directly, indirectly through still photography, motion pictures, television, etc., or indirectly again by means of a language report.

The patternings that make it possible for unique occurrences to 16 operate as sames among the members of a culture did not develop for operation across cultures. When they do occur in contact across cultures, many instances of predictable misinterpretation take place. We can assume that when the individual of culture A trying to learn culture B observes a form in culture B in a particular distribution spot, he grasps the same complex of meaning as in his own culture. And when he in turn engages actively in a unit of behavior in culture B he chooses the form which he would choose in his own culture to achieve that complex of meaning.

Comparison of Cultures

If the native culture habits are transferred when learning a foreign 17
culture, it is obvious that, by comparing the two culture systems, we
can predict what the trouble spots will be. Obviously, this is a huge
undertaking, and we will present a few examples that may facilitate
cultural analysis and comparison.

We will expect trouble when the same form has different 18
classification or meaning in two cultures.

A very interesting kind of trouble spot is seen when any element of 19
the form of a complex pattern has different classification or meaning
across cultures. The foreign observer gives to the entire pattern the
meaning of that different classification of one element.

Example. Bullfighting has always been in my observation a 20
source of cross-cultural misinformation. It is a particularly difficult
pattern of behavior to explain convincingly to an unsophisticated
United States observer. I therefore choose it as a test case.

Form. A bullfight has a very precise, complex form. A man, 21
armed with a sword and a red cape, challenges and kills a fighting
bull. The form is prescribed in great detail. There are specific vocabulary terms for seemingly minute variations. The bullfighter, the
bull, the picadors, the music, the dress, etc. are part of the form.

Meaning. The bullfight has a complex of meaning in Spanish cul- 22
ture. It is a sport. It symbolizes the triumph of art over the brute
force of a bull. It is entertainment. It is a display of bravery.

Distribution. The bullfight shows a complex distribution pattern. 23
There is a season for bullfights on a yearly cycle, there are favored
days on a weekly cycle, and there is a favored time on a daily cycle.
The bullfight occurs at a specific place, the bull ring, known to the
least person in the culture.

Form, meaning, and distribution to an alien observer. An American 24
observer seated next to a Spanish or Mexican spectator will see a
good deal of the form, though not all of it. He will see a man in a
special dress, armed with a sword and cape, challenging and killing
the bull. He will see the bull charging at the man and will notice
that the man deceives the bull with his cape. He will notice the music, the color, etc.

The meaning of the spectacle is quite different to him, however. 25
It is the slaughter of a "defenseless" animal by an armed man. It is
unfair because the bull always gets killed. It is unsportsmanlike—to
the bull. It is cruel to animals. The fighter is therefore cruel. The
public is cruel.

The distribution constitutes no particular problem to the American observer, since he has the experience of football, baseball, and other spectacles. 26

Misinformation. Is there an element of misinformation here, and if so, wherein is it? I believe there is misinformation. The secondary meaning "cruel" is found in Spanish culture, but it does not attach to the bullfight. The American observer ascribing the meaning cruel to the spectator and fighter is getting information that is not there. Why? 27

Since the cruelty is interpreted by the American observer as being perpetrated by the man on the bull, we can test to see if those parts of the complex form—the bull and the man—are the same in the two cultures. 28

Linguistic evidence. We find evidence in the language that seems interesting.[3] A number of vocabulary items that are applicable both to animals and to humans in English have separate words for animals and for humans in Spanish. In English both animals and persons have *legs.* In Spanish, animals have *patas,* "animal legs," and humans have *piernas,* "human legs." Similarly, in English, animals and humans have *backs* and *necks,* while in Spanish, animals have *lomo* and *pescuezo,* "animal back" and "animal neck," and humans have *espalda* and *cuello,* "human back" and "human neck." Furthermore, in English, both animals and humans *get nervous,* have *hospitals,* and have *cemeteries,* named by means of various metaphors. In Spanish, animals do not get nervous, or have hospitals or cemeteries. The linguistic evidence, though only suggestive, points to a differ- 29

---

[3] Cf. Edward Sapir, "Language is becoming increasingly valuable as a guide to the scientific study of a given culture. In a sense, the network of cultural patterns of a civilization is indexed in the language which expresses that civilization. It is an illusion to think that we can understand the significant outlines of a culture through sheer observation and without the guide of the linguistic symbolism which makes these outlines significant and intelligible to society. . . .

"Language is a guide to 'social reality.' Though language is not ordinarily thought of as of essential interest to the students of social science, it powerfully conditions all our thinking about social problems and processes. Human beings do not live in the objective world alone, nor alone in the world of social activity as ordinarily understood, but are very much at the mercy of the particular language which has become the medium of expression for their society. . . . The fact of the matter is that the 'real world' is to a large extent unconsciously built up on the language habits of the group. We see and hear and otherwise experience very largely as we do because the language habits of our community predispose certain choices of interpretation." *Op. cit.*, pp. 161–62.

Cf. also Harry Hoijer, "It is evident from these statements [quoted from Sapir and Whorf], if they are valid, that language plays a large and significant role in the totality of culture. Far from being simply a technique of communication, it is itself a way of directing the perceptions of its speakers and it provides for them habitual modes of analyzing experience into significant categories. And to the extent that languages differ markedly from each other, so should we expect to find significant and formidable barriers to cross-cultural communication and understanding." "The Sapir-Whorf Hypothesis," in *Language in Culture,* ed. Harry Hoijer (Chicago: Univ. Chi. Press, 1954), p. 94.

ence in the classification of *animal* in the two cultures.[4] In Hispanic culture the distinction between man and animal seems very great, certainly greater than that in American culture.

By further observation of what people say and do one finds ad- 30 ditional features of difference. In Spanish culture, man is not physically strong but is skillful and intelligent. A bull is strong but not skillful and not intelligent. In American culture a man is physically strong, and so is a bull. A bull is intelligent. A bull has feelings of pain, sorrow, pity, tenderness—at least in animal stories such as that of *Ferdinand the Bull*.[5] A bull deserves an even chance in a fight; he has that sportsman's right even against a man.

We can, then, hypothesize that the part of the complex form 31 represented by the bull has a different classification, a different meaning, in American culture, and that herein lies the source of the misinformation.

We should test this hypothesis by minimal contrast if possible. 32 We find something akin to a minimal contrast in American culture in tarpon fishing. In tarpon fishing we have a form: a fight to the exhaustion and death of the tarpon at the hands of a man with a line and camouflaged hooks. Much of the form is prescribed in detail. There is no large visible audience, but newspaper stories in a sense represent audience contact. In the complex of meaning, it is a sport, and it represents a triumph of skill over the brute fighting strength of the fish. The distribution seems somewhat different from that of a bullfight, but the difference does not seem relevant as an explanation of the difference we have hypothesized.

We now observe that the very same American who interpreted 33 the bullfight as cruel, and applied that meaning to the spectator and the bullfighter, will sit next to the same spectator on a fishing boat and never think of the fishing game as cruel. I conclude that the part of the complex form represented by the fish is quite distinct from "human being" in both American and Spanish cultures, while the

---

[4] Cf. Joseph H. Greenberg, "The existence of distinct E.M.U's [Elementary Meaning Units] makes us suspect a difference in response to the situations designated by the terms. It does not, in general, tell us the nature of this difference in response. For example, the existence of separate unanalyzable terms for *father's brother* and *mother's brother* makes us posit a difference in reaction to these relatives. It does not tell us wherein the difference consists, whether, for example, the first is treated with deference but the second with familiarity. To discover this, we must observe behavior, both verbal and nonverbal, that is, what things are habitually said and done with reference to the father's brother and the mother's brother." "Concerning Inferences from Linguistic to Nonlinguistic Data," in *Language in Culture*, ed., Harry Hoijer (Chicago: Univ. Chi. Press, 1954), pp. 9–10.

[5] Well-known motion picture prepared by Walt Disney Studies, from a children's story. [The movie was based on *The Story of Ferdinand*, written by Munro Leaf and illustrated by Robert Lawson (New York: Viking Press, 1936). Ed.]

part identified as the bull is much more like "human being" in American culture than in Spanish culture.

Marginal supporting evidence is the fact that in American cul- 34 ture there is a Society for the Prevention of Cruelty to Animals which concerns itself with the feelings of dogs, cats, horses, and other domestic animals. Recently there was a front-page story in the local papers reporting that the Humane Society of New York City had sent a Santa Claus to distribute gifts among the dogs in the New York City pounds. We would not conceive of a society for the prevention of cruelty to fish.

A form in culture B, identified by an observer from culture A as the 35 same form as one in his own culture, actually has a different meaning.

Example. A hiss, a sharp, voiceless sibilant sound, expresses dis- 36 approval in the United States. In Spanish-speaking countries it is the normal way to ask for silence in a group. Fries reports being taken aback the first time he faced a Spanish-speaking audience and heard the "hissing." He wondered if they were hissing at him. Later he learned that they were calling for silence.[6]

Example. Drinking milk at meals is a standard practice in the 37 United States. To us it has a primary meaning of food and drink, standard drink, at meal time. It does not have any special connotation of social class, national group, religious group, age group, or economic stratum. Wine, on the other hand, may be served on special occasions or by special groups of the population who have had special contacts with other cultures. Wine, thus, has the meanings special occasion, special group of people.

In France, milk at meals is not the standard drink. Some chil- 38 dren may drink milk, some adults may drink milk for special reasons, some individuals or families or groups may drink milk because of special cultural contacts. Drinking milk at meals in France has the secondary meanings of special drink, special occasion, or special group of people. Its primary meaning would be food and drink for the body.

The reader may recall the sensation that former Premier Pierre 39 Mendes-France caused in the United States when he began measures to extend the drinking of milk in France. Everybody recalls the favorable impression he made in the United States by drinking milk

---

[6] Charles C. Fries, "American Linguistics and the Teaching of English," *Language Learning* 6, nos. 1 and 2 (1955), p. 17.

in public. Now, discounting those who may be familiar with scientific studies on the relative food value of milk as against wine, I
take it that there was cross-cultural misinformation, and that there
will be trouble in understanding another culture in similar cases. To
the American public, Mendes-France was rescuing the French people from the special habit of drinking wine and teaching them the
standard, wholesome practice of drinking milk.

We can expect another kind of trouble spot when the same meaning   40
in two cultures is associated with different forms. The alien observer
seeking to act in the culture being learned will select his own form to
achieve the meaning, and he may miss altogether the fact that a different form is required.

   Example. A young man from Izfahan, Iran, gets off the train in a   41
small town of the United States. He claims his baggage and attempts
to hail a taxi. A likely car with a white license plate and black letters
goes by. The young man waves at it. The car does not stop. Another
car appears with the same type of license plate. The young man
waves again, without success. Frustrated because in the United
States taxis will not stop for him, he picks up his suitcases and walks
to his destination. He later finds out that taxis in the United States
are distinguished not by a white license plate, but by bright flashing
lights and loud colors. In Izfahan at that time the signal for a taxi
was a white license plate. This was an intelligent university-level
student stumbling over a predictable type of problem.

We can expect further trouble in the fact that the members of one   42
culture usually assume that their way of doing things, of understanding the world around them, their forms and their meanings,
are the correct ones. Hence, when another culture uses other forms
or other meanings it is wrong. Hence, when another culture adopts
a pattern of behavior from the first one, the imitated culture feels
that something good and correct is taking place.

   Example. When foreign visitors from areas where coffee is served   43
very black and very strong taste American coffee, they do not say
that it is different; they say that American coffee is bad. Likewise,
when Americans go abroad to countries where coffee is black and
strong, they taste the coffee and do not say that it is different; they,
too, say that it is bad.

   Example. When Americans go abroad during the cold season,   44
they complain that houses are cold. We often think that such cold
houses cannot be good for one's health. When foreign visitors spend
a winter in the colder areas of the United States, on the other hand,
they complain that our houses are kept too hot and that the changes

in temperature when going in and out of houses must be bad for one's health.

There is trouble in learning a foreign culture when a pattern that has 45 the same form and the same meaning shows different distribution. The observer of a foreign culture assumes that the distribution of a pattern in the observed culture is the same as in his native culture, and therefore on noticing more of, less of, or absence of a feature in a single variant he generalizes his observations as if it applied to all variants and therefore to the entire culture. Distribution is a source of a great many problems.

Example. For some time it was puzzling to me that on the one 46 hand Latin American students complained that North American meals abused the use of sugar, while on the other hand the dietitians complained that Latin Americans used too much sugar at meals. How could these seemingly contradictory opinions be true at the same time? We can observe that the average Latin American student takes more sugar in his coffee than do North Americans. He is not used to drinking milk at meals, but when milk is served he sometimes likes to put sugar in it. The dietitian notices this use of sugar in situations in which North Americans would use less or none at all. The dietitian notices also that the sugar bowls at tables where Latin Americans sit have to be filled more often than at other tables. She therefore feels quite confident in making her generalization.

The Latin American student for his part finds a salad made of 47 sweet gelatin, or half a canned pear on a lettuce leaf. Sweet salad? He may see beans for lunch—a treat! He sits at the table, all smiles (I have watched the process), he takes a good spoonful and, sweet beans! They are Boston baked beans. Turkey is served on Thanksgiving Day, but when the Latin American tastes the sauce, he finds that it is sweet—it is cranberry sauce. Sweet sauce for broiled turkey! That is the limit—these North Americans obviously use too much sugar in their food. And whatever secondary meanings are attached to too much sugar in a person's diet tend to be attached to the people of the country who prepare and eat such meals.

Another type of problem related to distribution differences, or rather 48 to assumed distribution differences, occurs when members of one culture, who normally recognize many subgroups in the population of their own culture, assume that another culture with which they come in contact is uniform. Hence, observations made about one individual of that other culture tend to be generalized to the entire population.

Example. Folk opinions abroad about the morals of American   49
women are partly connected with this assumed uniformity of population and partly, too, with the fact that the same form may have different meanings in the two cultures. Those who see American
movies or come in contact with American tourists often misinterpret
the forms of the behavior they observe, and often also they ascribe
to the whole culture, the whole population, what may well be restricted to a special group on a special distribution spot. We in turn
often ascribe to French and other Latin cultures normal behavior
that may be restricted to special samples coming in contact with special visitors.

The notions filtered through the above types of misinformation and   50
through others becomes part of the native culture as its "correct"
view of the reality of the foreign one, and as young members grow
up they receive these views as truth through verbal reports and all
the other vehicles of enculturation. These preconceived notions constitute very serious obstacles to the understanding of another culture.

Gathering Cultural Data for a Structural Description

Since good structural descriptions of the cultures that may require   51
our attention will usually not be found ready-made, we present below a checklist of possible patterns of behavior that in various cultures constitute functioning units. This checklist may be helpful in
calling attention to areas that might otherwise go unnoticed.

To prepare for a comparison of another culture with the native   52
one it may be valuable to use the informant approach coupled with
systematic observation of the culture in its normal undisturbed operation.

One can interview representative informants who are articulate   53
enough to talk about what they do. We can ask them what they do
each day of a typical week and on the various special days of the
month and year. We can ask them what is done on the special days
of the various turning points in the life cycle, that is, birth, growing
up, courtship and marriage, raising their young, retiring, dying.

What the informant reports may be classified for easier grasp   54
and later verification and comparison into things he does to meet
the needs of his body: sleep and rest, food and drink, shelter, clothing, exercise, healing, cleanliness, etc.; things he does to meet the
needs of his soul: religious activities. Other things may more conveniently be classified as tool activities: transportation, communication, work, training, organizations, government, etc. These groupings

do not imply valid cultural categories or units. Quite often a pattern of behavior, a structural unit such as marriage, will involve the body, the personality, the soul, and tool activities.

One must not make the mistake of generalizing on inadequate 55 sampling. The informants should represent at least the major significant groups of the population. In describing a culture as complex as that of the United States one should see that what a religious person does on Sunday is not generalized to all religious groups and much less to the nonreligious members of the culture.

Merely describing what any number of informants do in a cul- 56 ture does not constitute a structural description of the culture. Some of the things done will not be significant; that is, whether they are done or not or whether they are done one way or another will not change the unit of behavior. Other things, those we are interested in, will be significant: that is, doing something else will mean something else.

One must test variations to see if a change in meaning correlates 57 with them. For example, we would observe that people sleep in a given culture and that they sleep in all cultures. We might observe that, say, in culture A most of our informants slept from between nine and eleven at night to between six and eight in the morning. We would check to see what would be thought of a person who habitually slept from one in the morning to eleven. We might find that the person would be considered lazy, or rich and lazy, or sick. The time of sleep would therefore be considered structurally significant. If the reaction were that sleeping those hours was all right because the person liked those hours, we would consider the time of sleeping not structurally significant.

Still checking on the pattern of sleep, one might observe in cul- 58 ture B that most of the informants slept or rested after the midday meal. One can check to see if not sleeping or resting at that time would have any particular meaning. If we found that people who did not rest at that time would be considered reckless with their health, overly ambitious, or foreigners or foreign-influenced, we would consider the afternoon nap a significant type of rest pattern.

Similarly, if the informants in culture A do not sleep or rest after 59 the noon meal, we might check for the meaning to them of a member of their culture that sleeps afternoons. If he is considered lazy, or sick, or a weakling, we would take it that not sleeping after lunch was part of the rest structure in that culture.

In that same culture A if we found that one of the informants 60 slept regularly during the day and worked during the night, would it have any special meaning? It probably would. The meaning might be that the informant was a night watchman or had to work on a night shift at the factory.

We can illustrate this search for structure with eating patterns or any other patterns in the culture we seek to understand. If an informant in culture A eats fish on Friday, would he also eat meat? If he would not eat meat, it might be for a religious reason. 61

Systematic observation of the culture in operation will do much to eliminate the errors that the interviews will inevitably introduce in our data. Testing in various ways for significance will also help us eliminate useless information as well as errors. 62

Even though a total analysis and comparison of any two highly complex cultures may not be readily available for some time to come, the kind of model and sample comparison discussed in this chapter will be helpful in interpreting observations made in the actual contact of persons of one culture with another culture. 63

Kinesics and Cross-Cultural Understanding

GENELLE G. MORAIN

I grew up in Iowa and I knew what to do with butter: you put it on roastin' ears, pancakes, and popcorn. Then I went to France and saw a Frenchman put butter on radishes. I waited for the Cosmic Revenge—for the Eiffel Tower to topple, the Seine to sizzle, or the grape to wither on the vine. But that Frenchman put butter on his radishes, and the Gallic universe continued unperturbed. I realized then something I hadn't learned in five years of language study: not only was *speaking* in French different from speaking in English, but *buttering* in French was different from buttering in English. And that was the beginning of real cross-cultural understanding.[1]

Those who interact with members of a different culture know that a   1
knowledge of the sounds, the grammar, and the vocabulary of the foreign tongue is indispensable when it comes to sharing information. But being able to read and speak another language does not guarantee that *understanding* will take place. Words in themselves are too limited a dimension. The critical factor in understanding has to do with cultural aspects that exist beyond the lexical—aspects that include the many dimensions of nonverbal communication.

Students of human nature have always been aware of messages   2
sent by movement. Wily old Benjamin Franklin packed his new bifocals into his valise when he left for Paris and confided later to his diary how much they facilitated cross-cultural communication:

I wear my spectacles constantly. . . . When one's ears are not well accustomed to the sounds of the language, a sight of the movements in the features of him that speaks helps to explain: so that I understand better by the help of my spectacles.[2]

Genelle G. Morain (1928–   ), born in Indianola, Iowa, is professor of language education and romance languages at the University of Georgia and author of scholarly articles on culture and communication. "Kinesics and Cross-Cultural Understanding" is from the Center for Applied Linguistics series *Language in Education: Theory and Practice*, no. 7, 1978.

Today, 200 years later, Americans are becoming increasingly in-   3
terested in nonverbal communication. The current spurt of books on
movement and gesture finds an audience eager to speak "body language" and to "read a person like a book." To the student of communication, however, there is something disquieting about this popular approach to a sober subject. A book jacket whispers, "Read *body
language* so that you can penetrate the personal secrets, both of intimates and total strangers"—and one imagines a sort of kinesic peep-
ing Tom, eyeball to the keyhole, able to use his awful knowledge of
blinks, crossed legs, and puckers to some sinister end. In reality, the
need for gestural understanding goes far beyond power games or
parlor games. There is a critical need on the part of anyone who
works with people to be sensitive to the nonverbal aspects of human
interaction.

Dean Barnlund has developed a formula for measuring commu-   4
nicative success in person-to-person interaction. His "interpersonal
equation" holds that understanding between people is dependent
upon the degree of similarity of their belief systems, their perceptual
orientations, and their communicative styles.[3] With regard to belief
systems, Barnlund contends that people are likely to understand
and enjoy each other more when their beliefs coincide than when
their beliefs clash. Experience confirms that shared attitudes toward
fashion, sex, politics, and religion make for an agreeable luncheon
or golf game.

The second factor described by Barnlund—perceptual orienta-   5
tion—refers to the way people approach reality. There are those
who look at the world through a wide-angle lens—savoring new experiences, new ideas, new friends. Because they have a high tolerance for ambiguity, they can suspend judgment when confronted
with a new situation and postpone evaluation until further information is acquired. There are others who look at the world through a
narrower lens. They prefer familiar paths, predictable people, ideas
arranged in comfortable designs. Because the unknown unnerves
them, they do not go adventuring. They resolve ambiguities as
quickly as possible, using categories ("hippies," "Orientals," "good
old boys") to protect themselves from the pain of exploration. Those
who perceive the world through the same lens—be it wide-angle or
narrow—feel more comfortable with others who share the same perceptual orientation.

The third element of Barnlund's formula—similarity of commu-   6
nicative styles—presents the likelihood that congenial communi-
cants enjoy talking about the same topics, tune easily into the same
factual or emotional levels of meaning, share a preference for form
(argument, banter, self-disclosure, exposition), operate intelligibly

on the verbal band, and—most critical to the present discussion—understand each other at the nonverbal level.

Barnlund's formula underscores what Allport pointed out two decades ago in *The Nature of Prejudice:*[4] human beings are drawn to other human beings who share their own beliefs, customs, and values; they are repelled by those who disagree, who behave unpredictably, who speak—at every level of communication—an alien tongue. It follows that if language teachers are to help bridge gulfs in understanding between cultures, they must teach more than verbal language. They must help students develop a tolerance for belief systems at odds with their own and a sensitivity to differences in modes of perception and expression.

The Nonverbal Channel of Expression

Teachers in our highly literate society are oriented toward the verbal channel of expression. They tend to see the word as the central carrier of meaning. At an intuitive level they recognize the importance of prosodic elements (pitch, loudness, rhythm, stress, resonance, and pauses), because these add emotional dimension to the spoken word. They are less inclined, however, to accord importance to what Edward Hall terms "the silent language." Enmeshed in the warp and the woof of words, teachers find it hard to believe that the average American speaks for only 10 to 11 minutes a day and that more than 65 percent of the social meaning of a typical two-person exchange is carried by nonverbal cues.[5]

For simplicity, the nonverbal aspects of communication may be divided into three classes:

1. *Body language,* comprising movement, gesture, posture, facial expression, gaze, touch, and distancing.
2. *Object language,* including the use of signs, designs, realia, artifacts, clothing, and personal adornment to communicate with others.
3. *Environmental language,* made up of those aspects of color, lighting, architecture, space, direction, and natural surroundings which speak to man about his nature.

Although it is critical that students of other cultures be perceptive when it comes to understanding both object and environmental language,[6] the focus of this monograph is on body language. Ray L. Birdwhistell gave the name "kinesics" to the discipline concerned with the study of all bodily motions that are communicative.[7] An understanding of kinesics across cultures necessitates a close look at posture, movement, facial expression, eye management, gestures, and proxemics (distancing).

Posture and Movement

Because human bodies are jointed and hinged in the same fash-   11
ion, we tend to think of all people around the globe as sitting, standing, and lying in virtually identical postures. Actually, scholars have
found at least 1000 significantly different body attitudes capable of
being maintained steadily. The popularity of one posture over another and the emotion conveyed by a given posture seem to be
largely determined by culture.[8] Among those postures used to signal
humility, for example, Krout cites the following:

Sumatrans:	Bowing while putting joined hands be-tween those of other person and lifting them to one's forehead.
Chinese:	Joining hands over head and bowing (signifying: "I submit with tired hands").
Turks and Persians:	Bowing, extending right arm, moving arm down from horizontal position, raising it to the level of one's head, and lowering it again (meaning: "I lift the earth off the ground and place it on my head as a sign of submission to you").
Congo natives:	Stretching hands toward person and striking them together.
New Caledonians:	Crouching.
Dahomeans (now Benins):	Crawling and shuffling forward; walk-ing on all fours.
Batokas:	Throwing oneself on the back, rolling from side to side, slapping outside of thighs (meaning: "You need not sub-due me; I am subdued already").[9]

No matter how poetic the meaning, this gymnastic parade of   12
posture would either embarrass or disgust most Americans, who are
not readily inclined to show humility in any guise. A slight downward tilt of the head and lowering of the eyes are as much kinesic
signaling as they would be willing to accord that emotion. In fact,
Americans are conditioned to accept a relatively narrow band of postures. A few parental admonitions continue to ring in the ear long
after childhood and find their way to adult lips: "Stand tall!" "Sit up
straight!" "Keep your hands in your lap!" But because the postural

vocabulary of Americans is limited, they have difficulty accepting the wider range of postures found in other cultures. For example, the fact that one-fourth of the world's population prefers to squat rather than to sit in a chair leaves Americans uneasy. To most Americans, squatting is something savages do around campfires. They find it inconceivable that refined adults might sit on their heels in movie theater seats, as they sometimes do in Japan.[10]

The need to be aware of postural differences became dramati- 13 cally clear to an American student who was visited by a friend who had come home from a long stay in the Ivory Coast. She brought her little son along, and the student was enchanted when the child toddled over to him and climbed into his lap. Instead of cuddling there, however, the child squirmed under the student's arm, around his side, and crawled onto his back. The startled young man, suddenly ill at ease, expected the mother to instruct her son to get down. Instead, she explained that mothers in the Ivory Coast carry their infants on their backs. As a result, when a child seeks a warm and loving spot, it is not in a lap, but on a back. Unfortunately for cross-cultural understanding, Americans are conditioned to regard this position as onerous, an attitude reflected linguistically every time a harassed individual snarls, "Get off my back!"

Cross-cultural studies of posture and movement indicate that 14 macrokinesic systems may be determined by cultural norms. Sociologist Laurence Wylie, studying mime in Paris with students from 25 countries, found that national differences seemed to be accentuated by nonverbal techniques.[11] For example, when improvising trees, French students are "espaliered pear trees, and the Americans, unpruned apple trees." Differences in walking styles are so marked, Wylie maintains, that "in Paris one can recognize Americans two hundred yards away simply by the way they walk." To the French eye, the American walk is uncivilized. "You bounce when you walk" is their negative assessment. Wylie concludes that French child-rearing practices, which stress conformity to a disciplined social code, produce adults who reflect the tension and rigidity of French society. "They stand," he observes, "erect and square-shouldered, moving their arms when they walk as if the space around them were severely limited." Americans, on the other hand, seem to have a loose and easy gait. They walk with free-swinging arms, relaxed shoulders and pelvis, as though "moving through a broad space scarcely limited by human or physical obstacles."[12] Interestingly, this perception of American gait conflicts with the findings of an unpublished study reported by Hall, in which Spanish Americans perceive Anglo Americans as having an uptight, authoritarian walk whenever they aren't deliberately ambling; the

Anglo, conversely, perceives the Spanish American male walk as more of a swagger than a purposeful walk.[13]

The degree to which kinesic activity is culture-bound becomes [15] obvious when one watches a foreign movie where English has been dubbed in by the process of "lip synching." The audience watches the foreign actors but hears a specially taped version of the script read in English by native speakers. Although the English words are timed and even shaped to fit the lip movements, they do not accord with the total body gloss as represented by facial expression, gestures, and posture. French actors, for example, are seen gesturing in the tight, restricted French manner while seeming to say English words that require broad, loose gestures. Observers may feel amused or irritated, but the sense of imbalance is so subtle that they rarely pinpoint the source.[14]

Speeches given by New York's colorful mayor, Fiorello La [16] Guardia, who spoke fluent Italian, Yiddish, and American English, illustrate how closely kinesic activity is linked to culture. An observer familiar with the three cultures could watch LaGuardia on a newsreel film without a sound track and tell readily which of the three languages he was speaking. There seems to be a subtle shift of kinesic gears when a fluent speaker slips from one language to another.

Alan Lomax and associates analyzed folk dance styles with a [17] recording system called "choreometrics."[15] They found that the patterns of movement used by members of a culture in their work or recreation were reflected in the movements of their dances. Eskimo hunters, for example, assume a stocky, straddled stance and bring their weapon arm diagonally down across their body when harpooning a seal or spearing a salmon. When they dance, they assume the same stance, holding a drum in the left hand and bringing the drumstick held in the right hand diagonally down across the body.

Lomax's choreometric analysis revealed that people seem to fall [18] into two distinct groups: those who move the trunk as if it were a solid, one-unit block, and those who move the trunk as if it were two or more units—bending and swaying the upper and lower sections independently of each other. One-unit cultures—including, aboriginal Australians, American Indians, and most Eurasians—use rigid, energetic movements that contrast sharply with the undulating, sinuous motions of the multiunit cultures (Polynesian, African, and Indian). The choreometric contrast becomes clear when one pictures the fluid grace of the hula juxtaposed with the angular tension of an American Indian dance.

Recent studies of rhythm as it relates to body movement have [19] revealed astonishing new insights into human interaction.[16] William

Condon found that when individuals talk, their body keeps time to the rhythm of their own speech. We are aware of this synchrony when someone sings; the sight of people swinging and swaying (or tapping and twitching) to the beat of the song they sing is so familiar that we take it for granted. The same thing happens at a much subtler level when a person speaks. Movements of the fingers, eyelids and brows, head, and other body parts occur as a sort of rhythmic punctuation to the rise and fall of the voice and the flow of syllables. The whole body moves "in sync" with the words.

Not only are people in sync with themselves, but as they con- 20 verse with each other, their body movements gradually fall into rhythmic harmony with those of their conversation partner. Sometimes this interactional synchrony is on a microlevel and is not easy to observe. At other times, two people in synchrony will assume the same postural configurations, almost as if they were mirror images of one another. Condon found that when two people in conversation were wired to electroencephalographs, "the recording pens moved together as though driven by a single brain." When a third person entered the picture and called one of the speakers away, the recording pens no longer moved in unison. When synchrony does not occur between speakers, it is usually a signal that an unconscious tension is inhibiting the microdance.

It is probably unrealistic for foreign language students to expect 21 their textbooks to provide a model for behavior in this area ("Sync or Swim in Spanish"?). Nevertheless, as research uncovers significant information about differences in rhythms across cultures, it should be transmitted to language students to enhance their kinesic awareness.

Facial Expression

Poets and philosophers have always been aware of the role 22 played by the face in communication. "The features of our face are hardly more than gestures which have become permanent," wrote Marcel Proust in *Remembrance of Things Past*. And, according to Emerson, "A man finds room in the few square inches of his face for the traits of all his ancestors; for the expression of all his history, and his wants."[17] It takes a kinesicist like Birdwhistell, however, to analyze how man uses those few square inches of his face. According to his research, middle-class Americans display about 33 "kinemes" (single communicative movements) in the face area:[18]

Three head nod kinemes (single, double, and triple nod)
Two lateral head sweep kinemes (the single and double sweep)

One head cock kineme

One head tilt kineme

Three connective, whole head motion kinemes (head raise and hold, head lower and hold, and current head position hold)

Four eyebrow motion kinemes (lifted, lowered, knot, and single movement)

Four eyelid closure kinemes (over-open, slit, closed, and squeezed)

Four nose movement kinemes (wrinkled nose, compressed nostril, unilateral nostril flare, and bilateral nostril flare)

Seven mouth movement kinemes (compressed lips, protruded lips, retracted lips, apically withdrawn lips, snarl, lax open mouth, and mouth over-open)

Two chin thrust kinemes (anterior and lateral chin thrusts)

One puffed cheeks kineme

One sucked cheeks kineme

The implications of such complex kinesic behavior for language 23 learners who would master the nonverbal system of another culture are staggering. Even Americans cannot *consciously* produce the 33 subtle variations just listed without some instruction. To further complicate matters, kinesicists believe that in addition to the facial displays that are readily visible, there are others that are "micromomentary"—occurring so rapidly that they are invisible to the conscious eye. In one experiment, Ekman flashed pictures of facial expressions on a laboratory screen at speeds up to one-hundredth of a second. People staring at the screen insisted that they saw nothing but a blank screen. But when urged to guess what facial expression might be depicted by an image they perceived subliminally, they were astounded to discover that most of their "guesses" corresponded to the correct expressions on the "unseen" faces.[19] Ekman concluded that we all have the perceptual ability to decode facial messages at one-hundredth of a second but that we have been systematically taught in childhood not to pay attention to these fleeting expressions because they are too revealing.

A device that enables individuals to check their ability to judge 24 facial expressions is the Facial Meaning Sensitivity Test (FMST). Part I requires the taker to match 10 full-face photographs with "The ten basic classes of facial meaning": disgust, happiness, interest, sadness, bewilderment, contempt, surprise, anger, determination, and fear. In Parts II and III, the task involves 30 additional photos with more discriminating categories of facial expression. Dale Leathers contends that by working with the FMST, one can markedly improve both decoding and encoding skills—learning to be more sensitive to the expressions of others and to communicate one's own feelings more accurately through facial expression.[20]

Gaze and Eye Movement

Whether the eyes are "the windows of the soul" is debatable; [25] that they are intensely important in interpersonal communication is a fact. During the first two months of a baby's life, the stimulus that produces a smile is a pair of eyes.[21] The eyes need not be real: a mask with two dots will produce a smile. Significantly, a real human face with eyes covered will not motivate a smile, nor will the sight of only one eye when the face is presented in profile. This attraction to eyes as opposed to the nose or mouth continues as the baby matures. In one study, when American four-year-olds were asked to draw people, 75 percent of them drew people with mouths, but 99 percent of them drew people with eyes.[22] In Japan, however, where babies are carried on their mother's back, infants do not acquire as much attachment to eyes as they do in other cultures. As a result, Japanese adults make little use of the face either to encode or decode meaning. In fact, Argyle reveals that the "proper place to focus one's gaze during a conversation in Japan is on the neck of one's conversation partner."[23]

The role of eye contact in a conversational exchange between [26] two Americans is well defined: speakers make contact with the eyes of their listener for about one second, then glance away as they talk; in a few moments they reestablish eye contact with the listener to reassure themselves that their audience is still attentive, then shift their gaze away once more. Listeners, meanwhile, keep their eyes on the face of the speaker, allowing themselves to glance away only briefly. It is important that they be looking at the speaker at the precise moment when the speaker reestablishes eye contact; if they are not looking, the speaker assumes that they are disinterested and either will pause until eye contact is resumed or will terminate the conversation. Just how critical this eye maneuvering is to the maintenance of conversational flow becomes evident when two speakers are wearing dark glasses: there may be a sort of traffic jam of words caused by interruptions, false starts, and unpredictable pauses.[24]

There is evidence that eye management patterns differ among [27] American subgroups. In poor black families people look at one another less than in middle-class white families. It may even be that the pattern of "speaker looks away, listener looks at" is reversed to become "listener looks away, speakers looks at."[25] If so, this would account for the uneasy feelings that sometimes develop when even the best-intentioned members of the two races try to communicate. Similar differences in eye behavior have been noted between Puerto Rican children and their middle-class American teachers. And in Ohio, teachers of children moving from rural Appalachia to urban centers reported difficulties in adjusting to eye contact patterns in which the children looked down when talking to their teachers. Teachers had to learn that this was a culturally determined respect pattern, not a furtive avoidance signal.[26]

Erving Goffman discusses an American eye management tech- 28 nique that he calls "civil inattention."[27] An interpersonal ritual used in public places, it involves looking at other persons just long enough to catch their eye in recognition of the fact that they are other human beings, then looking away as if to say, "I trust that you will not harm me, and I recognize your right to privacy." When two people perform this ritual on the street, they may eye each other up to approximately eight feet, then cast their eyes down or away as the other passes—a kind of "dimming of lights," as Goffman puts it. Actually, the timing of this act requires considerable subtlety; the individual's gaze cannot be absent, or averted, or prolonged, or hostile, or invitational; it has to be *civilly inattentive*, and one acquires a feel for it without formal instruction.

Two strategies in contrast to the civil inattention courtesy are the 29 deliberate witholding of all eye contact—which has the effect of a dehumanizing, nonverbal snub—and the intense focusing of gaze known as "the hate stare." The author observed an example of the latter several years ago in a church. An obviously unhappy matron, perturbed to find a racially mixed couple seated in a pew near the front of "her" church, walked slowly down the aisle past the couple and fixed them with a baleful glare. So intent was she upon prolonging her hate stare that she maintained eye contact even after passing the couple, which necessitated considerable craning and twisting of her neck. Unable to watch where her steps were leading her, she smacked into a marble pillar with what was to most observers a satisfyingly painful thud.

In-depth studies of eye management in foreign cultures are not 30 readily available. A skimming of differences across cultures reveals that there is great variation in this aspect of communication.[28] British etiquette decrees that the speaker and listener focus attentively on each other. While an American listener nods and murmurs to signal that he is listening, the Englishman remains silent and merely blinks his eyes. Germans tend to maintain a steady gaze while talking. The American shift of gaze from eye to eye and away from the face entirely is not a pattern familiar to Germans. Peruvians, Bolivians, and Chileans consider insulting the absence of eye contact while talking.

Arabs, too, share a great deal of eye contact and regard too little gaze as rude and disrespectful. In North Africa, the Tuaregs stare unwaveringly at the eyes during a conversation, perhaps because the eyes are the only part of the body not hidden beneath a swirl of veils and robes. On the streets, Israelis stare at others without self-consciousness. The French are also likely to stare at strangers, as anyone who has ever walked past a sidewalk café can attest. Greeks actively enjoy staring and being stared at in public; when they travel in the West they feel slightly diminished because people do not look at them.

Just why one culture should evolve an eye contact pattern dia- 31 metrically opposed to that of another is not clear. Underlying some avoidance behaviors may be the primitive concept of "the evil eye." Believers feel that an actual substance—a malevolent ray—comes from the eye and influences the person or object it strikes. Witches endowed with the evil eye supposedly leave a thin film of poison on the surface of a mirror when their gaze strikes it. In Naples, even to-day, priests and monks are thought to possess the evil eye and passersby assiduously avoid their gaze.[29]

Research in kinesic communication has moved from the evil eye 32 to the revealing eye. Eckhard Hess has delineated a field of study that he calls "pupillometrics." His research shows that when people look at a sight that is pleasing to them, their pupils dilate measur-ably; conversely, when they regard something that is displeasing or repugnant, their pupils constrict. People interacting with others seem to respond to pupil size, albeit at an unconscious level. Hess showed a group of photographs to male subjects, including two os-tensibly identical photos of the same pretty girl. In one photo, how-ever, her pupils had been enlarged through a retouching process. The men's responses—measured by increases in the size of their own pupils—were more than twice as positive to the picture with the dilated pupils.[30] No cross-cultural studies on pupillometrics have been reported, but it seems likely that this is a physiological condi-tion that would be observable in all cultures. The differences among cultures would lie in the nature of the sight that was perceived as pleasing or displeasing.

Gestures

Members of the same culture share a common body idiom—that 33 is, they tend to read a given nonverbal signal in the same way. If two people read a signal in a different way, it is partial evidence that they belong to different cultures. In Colombia, an American Peace Corps worker relaxes with his feet up on the furniture; his shocked

Colombian hostess perceives the gesture as disgusting. Back in the United States, a university president poses for a photograph with his feet up on the desk; newspaper readers react with affection for "good old President Jones." While Americans use the feet-on-furniture gesture to signal "I'm relaxed and at home here," or "See how casual and folksy I am," neither message is received by a Colombian, who reads the signal as "boor!" An understanding of the role gestures play within a culture is critical to sensitive communication.

Hayes divides gestures into three categories that facilitate discussion: autistic gestures, technical gestures, and folk gestures.[31] Autistic—or nervous—gestures are made by individuals in response to their own inner turmoil and are thus not strictly conditioned by culture. They may take the form of biting the lips or fingernails, cracking the knuckles, jiggling a leg, or twitching a facial muscle. Occasionally, however, they become stereotyped signs for certain attitudes—toe tapping to indicate impatience, thumb twiddling to show boredom—and thus pass into the realm of tradition. 34

Other movements fall under the heading of technical gestures and include such complex systems of communication as the sign language of the deaf, the gestures of umpires and referees, military salutes, and the signals of music conductors, traffic directors, and radio performers. Technical gestures carry uniform meaning for members of a specialized group and are usually taught formally. 35

Folk gestures, on the other hand, are the property of an entire culture and are passed on by imitation. Something as simple as the act of pointing is a folk gesture. Residents of Europe and North America point with the forefinger, the other fingers curled under the palm. American Indians, certain Mongoloid peoples, and sub-Saharan Africans point with their lips.[32] Members of these cultures are not taught by their parents *how* to point (although they may be told when *not* to point). They learn by observation—the same way in which they acquire a complete repertoire of folk gestures. 36

Descriptive gestures include movements used to accompany such statements as "He wound up like this and threw that old ball"; "It swooped down and flew under the bridge"; "She was about this tall." It might seem that these gestures are culture-free, determined simply by the nature of the motion described. Analysis reveals, however, that many descriptive gestures are indeed culture-bound. Reid Scott discusses the gestural background in Mexico for the statement "She was about this tall." 37

> In parts of Mexico the gesture for indicating how tall something is has three definite cultemes (aspects of culture essential to under-

standing). The arm held vertically with the index finger extended and the rest of the fingers folded indicates the height of a person. The arm and hand held horizontally, thumb up and little finger down, indicates the height of an animal. The same position, except with palm down, indicates the height of an inanimate object. In most countries, there is only one culteme; it includes measuring humans, subhumans, and all other objects, and it has a single gesture, the last one described, to express it. We can imagine the laughter and even anger that one would cause if he were to measure your dear aunt with the gesture reserved for cows.[33]

A knowledge of the folk gestures of any group provides one way to share in the humor of that culture. A few examples from the American folk gestural system will illustrate the possibilities. The elaborate handshake that began with jazz musicians and spread to other in-groups is today practiced with a kind of gleeful exaggeration by young black males. Mock handshakes are also used to characterize certain professions: the "politicians' handshake," for instance, begins with a great show of false enthusiasm and ends with both parties reaching over each other's shoulders to pick each other's pockets.[34] In some jokes, the humor is carried entirely on the nonverbal band. To illustrate how a stupid person "looks for a land mine," the joke teller covers his eyes with his hand and advances slowly forward, stomping the ground ahead of him with an extended foot. To demonstrate a numskull "hitching in the rain," the jokester makes the usual American hitchhiking signal of the hand with extended thumb, then holds his other hand protectively above it to shelter the thumb from the rain. 38

Because folk gestures are in circulation, they tend to develop variations in meaning and execution. Nevertheless, they are the gestures that are most profitably learned by those who intend to interact with members of another culture. Whether "learned" means incorporated into students' active kinesic systems so that they can produce the gesture on demand, or merely learned in the sense that they can recognize the meaning of the gesture in its appropriate social context, is a matter of debate among language educators. Jerald R. Green, author of *Kinesics in the Foreign Language Classroom*,[35] believes that the use of gestures adds dimension to language production. "It is neither unrealistic nor unreasonable," he writes, "to expect the language instructor to insist that his pupils use authentic foreign culture gestures whenever appropriate in dialogue repetition." On the other hand, some native speakers—perhaps in a display of kinesic territoriality—feel that it is offensive to see members of a foreign culture using imperfectly the gestural system of a culture that is not their own. Birdwhistell warns that even though a 39 gesture may be produced authentically by a sufficiently skilled non-native, its performance does not guarantee that the performer is aware of the full range of communicative contexts in which its use is appropriate.[36]

One solution would be for the teacher to draw up a list of gestures in order of their communicative value and teach them in descending order of importance. Gestures associated with greeting and leave taking are critical, since it is difficult to function courteously within any culture without participating actively in these rituals. Gestures used for "yes" and "no," for showing approval and disapproval, and for making and refusing requests would also be useful. 40

Eisenberg and Smith discuss the variation across cultures in the simple act of attracting the attention of a waiter:[37] 41

> In America, the customer moves his forefinger toward himself, then away from himself, then toward himself again. A Latin American customer would make a downward arc with his right hand almost identical to the American jocular "away with you." The Shans of Burma accomplish the same purpose by holding the palm down, moving the fingers as if playing an arpeggio. . . . Waiters in India are summoned by a click of the fingers, which on the face of it, is an inconspicuous and efficient gesture. But such a gesture might elicit anger from an American waiter. For us, snapping fingers is the act of a superior asserting power over a menial. As such, finger snapping as a call for service is a violation of the democratic ethos.

Gestures that would be wise to know but not emulate are those considered vulgar or obscene by the foreign culture. Equally important for cross-cultural understanding is a knowledge of those gestures that are repugnant to Americans but regarded as acceptable in other cultures. A quick survey reveals the complexity of emotional response to kinesic interaction. In New Zealand and Australia, the hitchhiking signal used by Americans is tabu. The "O.K." gesture so familiar to North Americans is considered obscene in several Latin American cultures. In Paraguay, signs made with crossed fingers are offensive, but crossing the legs is permissible as long as the ankle does not touch the knee (the leg-cross position preferred by many American men). In Germany, people who enter a row of seats in a theater should face those already seated in the row as they pass in front of them; to turn the back is considered insulting. Korean etiquette decrees that loud smacking and sucking sounds made while eating are a compliment to the host. And although one should never blow one's nose at a Korean table, sniffling throughout the repast is acceptable behavior. 42

Even within national boundaries, differences in kinesic behav- 43
iors exist. Black Americans use the index finger a great deal in gesturing and also show the palm more frequently than do white Americans. Teenage blacks from working-class families move their
shoulders much more than their white counterparts.[38] An interesting account of "cut-eye" and "suck-teeth," two gestures known to
many black Americans but virtually unknown to whites, is found in
the *Journal of American Folklore.*[39] The authors trace the origin of
these kinesic signals to Africa. Cut-eye is a kind of visual snub that
communicates disapproval and general rejection of the person at
whom it is aimed. It involves directing a hostile glare at the other
person, then moving the eyeballs down in a sight line cutting across
the person's body, another glare, and finally turning the entire head
contemptuously away—often to the accompaniment of a satisfying
suck-teeth. Suck-teeth by itself is also capable of conveying anger,
exasperation, or annoyance. It is made with the lips either pouted or
spread out. Air is drawn through the teeth and into the mouth to
create a loud sucking sound.

Proxemics

Edward T. Hall, whose book *The Hidden Dimension* deals with 44
the perception and use of space (proxemics), demonstrates that individuals follow predictable patterns in establishing the distance between themselves and those with whom they interact. In each culture the amount of space varies depending upon the nature of the
social interaction, but all cultures seem to distinguish the four basic
categories delineated by Hall.[40]

Middle-class Americans, for example, have established the fol- 45
lowing interaction distances within the four categories:[41]

1. *Intimate distance.* From body contact to a separation space of 18
   inches. An emotionally charged zone used for love making,
   sharing, protecting, and comforting.
2. *Personal distance.* From $1\frac{1}{2}$ to 4 feet. Used for informal contact between friends. A "small protective sphere or bubble" that separates one person from another.
3. *Social distance.* From 4 to 12 feet. The casual interaction distance
   between acquaintances and strangers. Used in business meetings, classrooms, and impersonal social affairs.
4. *Public distance.* Between 12 and 25 feet. A cool interaction distance used for one-way communication from speaker to audience. Necessitates a louder voice, stylized gestures, and more
   distinct enunciation.

Proxemic distances preferred by Americans do not correspond to 46
those preferred by people of other cultures. Observance of interaction zones is critical to harmonious relations, but because these
zones exist at a subconscious level, they are often violated by non-
members of a culture. The amount and type of all physical contacts—including touching and the exchange of breath and body
odors—vary among cultures. One study dealt with the number of
times couples touched each other in cafés: in San Juan, Puerto Rico,
they touched 180 times per hour; in Paris, 110; and in London, 0.[42]
The London couples would be prime candidates for culture shock in
an African culture where two people engaged in casual conversation
intertwine their legs as they talk.[43]

In general, high-contact cultures (Arabs, Latin Americans, 47
Greeks, and Turks) usually stand close to each other. Low-contact
cultures (northern Europeans, Americans) stand farther apart. Barnlund's cross-cultural study of the public and private self in Japan
and in the United States points out the dramatic contrasts in proxemic relationships between the two peoples. As a channel of communication, touch appears to be twice as important within the
American culture as it is among the Japanese.[44] Although during infancy and early childhood the Japanese foster a closer tactile relationship than do Americans, the situation changes markedly as the
child nears adolescence. In one study, a considerable number of
Japanese teenagers reported no physical contact at all with either
parent or with a friend.[45] The adult Japanese extends the pattern by
restricting not only tactile communication but facial and gestural display as well.

The reasons why one culture will prefer a close interaction dis- 48
tance and another demand more space are not clear. Hall theorizes
that cultures have different perceptions of where the boundaries of
the self are located.[46] Americans and northern Europeans think of
themselves as being contained within their skin. The zone of privacy
is extended to include the clothes that cover the skin and even a
small space around the body. Any infringement of these areas is
looked upon as an invasion of privacy. But in the Arab culture, the
self is thought of as being located at a sort of central core. "Tucking
the ego down within the body shell," as Hall puts it, results in a totally different proxemic patterning. Arabs tolerate crowding, noise
levels, the touching of hands, the probing of eyes, the moisture of
exhaled breath, and a miasma of body odors that would overwhelm
a Westerner. The ultimate invasion of privacy to the Western
mind—rape—does not even have a lexical equivalent in Arabic.[47]

In the areas of France that belong to the Mediterranean culture, 49
there is a high level of sensory involvement and a degree of proxemic

crowding that would make members of northern European cultures uncomfortable. In sharp contrast, the German concept of self necessitates a privacy sphere with wide boundaries.

Kinesic Universals

In the midst of an overwhelming number of gestures whose mean- 50 ings differ across cultures, scholars are searching for examples of kinesic behavior whose meaning is universal. The so-called nature/ nurture controversy finds researchers divided as to whether some expressive behaviors might stem from phylogenetic origins (nature) and thus be common to all mankind, or whether kinesic behaviors are learned from social contacts (nurture) and thus differ from one culture to another.

Birdwhistell, a cultural relativist on the "nurture" side, wrote in 51 *Kinesics and Context* in 1970 (p. 81):

> Insofar as we know, there is no body motion or gesture that can be regarded as a universal symbol. That is, we have been unable to discover any single facial expression, stance, or body position which conveys an identical meaning in all societies.

Back in 1872, however, Charles Darwin, arguing from the 52 "nature" standpoint, hypothesized that the headshake to indicate "no" had its origins when the baby, satiated, turned its head away from the breast and emphasized refusal by rhythmic repetition of this sideways movement.[48] (It has since been pointed out, however, that in some cultures the use of the headshake signals "yes.")

A strong contemporary voice for the innate side of the contro- 53 versy is that of Eibl-Eibesfeldt, who has isolated the "eyebrow flash" as one expressive movement that occurs across many cultures. It is executed by raising the eyebrows with a rapid movement, keeping them maximally raised for about one-sixth of a second, and then lowering them. This maneuver, which signals readiness for social contact and is used mainly when greeting, has been recorded on film among the Europeans, Balinese, Papuans of New Guinea, Samoans, South American Indians, and the Bushmen. Certainly it plays an important role in the American kinesic system. It is suppressed in only a few cultures: in Japan, for instance, it is considered indecent.

Eibl-Eibesfeldt contends that kinesic similarities exist across cul- 54 tures not only in basic expressions but in whole syndromes of behavior.

Such patterns include greetings that involve embracing and kissing (Eibl-Eibesfeldt feels that these are apparently very old since they occur also in chimpanzees), the smiling response, and actions to indicate coyness, embarrassment, and flirting (hiding the entire face, or concealing the mouth behind one hand). Another example is the cluster of actions that express anger, including "opening the corners of the mouth in a particular way," scowling, stamping the foot, clenching the fist, and striking out to hit objects. The anger syndrome can be observed in the congenitally deaf-blind, who have had no opportunity to learn by watching others. In fact, Eibl-Eibesfeldt's studies of these children show that they portray the facial expressions regarded as "typical" when they laugh, smile, sulk, cry, and express fear or surprise, a fact that tends to support the "innate" viewpoint.

Researching facial expressions across cultures, Paul Ekman and associates concluded that "there are a set of facial components that are associated with emotional categories in the same way for all men, since the same faces were found to be judged as showing the same emotions in many cultures."[49] People in Borneo, Brazil, Japan, the United States, and New Guinea all identified the "primary emotions" (happiness, anger, sadness, fear, surprise, and disgust) with a high rate of agreement. Ekman points out, however, that each society has its own display rules that govern when it is appropriate to exhibit or to conceal these expressions.[50]

Ekman is also searching for gestures ("emblems") that carry consistent meaning across cultures. His research in such disparate cultures as the United States, New Guinea, Japan, and Argentina seems to support the hypothesis that there *are* pan-cultural gestures and that they relate primarily to bodily functions such as eating, sleeping, and love making.[51] For example, one widely distributed emblem is the "I've had enough to eat" motion in which gesturers put a hand on their stomach and either pat or rub it. Since food—be it an American hamburger or Japanese sukiyaki—goes predictably to the stomach when swallowed, the logic of the gesture accounts for its universality. On the other hand, more complex activities produce culture-specific gestures. As Davis points out in *Inside Intuition* (p. 77):

> Though the emblem for eating always involves a hand-to-mouth pantomime, in Japan one hand cups an imaginary bowl at about chin level, while the other scoops imaginary food into the mouth; but in New Guinea, where people eat sitting on the floor, the hand shoots out to arm's length, picks up an imaginary tidbit, and carries it to the mouth.

55

56

The Role of Kinesics

While it is clear that all cultures make use of kinesic behaviors in   57
communication, scholars do not agree on the precise nature of the
role they play. Scheflen points out that there are currently two
schools of thought in the behavioral sciences.[52] The "psychological
school" follows the view set forth by Charles Darwin that nonverbal
behavior expresses emotions. Most students of language and culture
are aware of the emotive role of gesture, posture, and facial expression: drooping shoulder indicates depression; a scowl registers dis-
pleasure, etc. The more recent "communication school," including
many ethologists and anthropologists, holds that nonverbal behaviors are used to regulate human interaction. Scheflen insists that the
two views are not incompatible—that the behaviors of human communication are both expressive and social.[53]

To understand the idea of kinesic behavior as social control,   58
however, one must become sensitive to the nonverbal behaviors that
regulate—or monitor—social interactions. Ordinarily they are performed so automatically and at such an unconscious level that even
those performing them are unaware of their own actions. Some of
these monitoring behaviors are probably universal in man and have
counterparts in the behavior of animals. Examples of this type of
monitoring include:[54]

1. Turning and looking at the source of a disruption (often quells
   the disturbance).
2. Looking "through" a person who is trying to join a gathering (a
   signal that he is not wanted).
3. Turning away from someone who is initiating an action (indicates that he will not receive support).
4. Recoiling or flinching from a sudden loud or aggressive display
   (warns the offender to step back or speak more softly).

Another group of monitors that are less automatic and seem to   59
have evolved from the reactions mentioned above include such facial expressions as those of disgust, boredom, and anger. These
monitors are used to provide a running commentary on another's
behavior. A monitoring signal of this type common in America is the
act of wiping the index finger laterally across the nostrils. It comes
into play when someone violates the norms of the group by such actions as lying, using profanity, or encroaching on personal space.
This was the kinesic signal used unconsciously by President Eisen-
hower when he chose to be less than candid during press interviews. He was reportedly warned of the revealing nature of this ac-

tion so that he could avoid its use thereafter. The anecdote points up the fact that most monitoring acts are carried out without the actor's awareness. It also illustrates a third type of monitoring—self-monitoring—in which those who transgress the social norms perform the monitoring act upon themselves.[55]

60   Kinesicists are in agreement that nonverbal signals can be more powerful than verbal ones. Verbal signals call for cognitive processing; nonverbal signals operate directly, bypassing conscious analysis and evoking immediate action.[56] Since information can be carried simultaneously on both verbal and nonverbal channels, one is able to negotiate social relationships and supply emotional feedback while exchanging information of a cognitive nature verbally. Emotions, feelings, and interpersonal attitudes are often more effectively expressed by the nonverbal than by the verbal. And while the spoken word does not always convey the truth, kinesic evidence tends to depict reality. As Charles Galloway puts it, "It is to the fidelity of human experience that nonverbal meanings have value."[57]

Kinesics and Perceptual Education

61   Sapir* spoke of nonverbal behavior as "an elaborate and secret code that is written nowhere, known by none, and understood by all." Unfortunately for cross-cultural understanding, the "all" refers only to members of the same culture. Bursack filmed Minneapolis men and women who deliberately tried to express "agreement" and "courtesy" nonverbally in an interview situation.[58] The filmed sequences were studied by citizens of Beirut, Tokyo, and Bogatá. The foreigners were unable to "read" with accuracy the Americans' nonverbal attempts to communicate the two feelings critical to establishing a warm social climate.

62   We have seen how inextricably movement is linked to meaning. Those who have "learned" a language without including the nonverbal component are seriously handicapped if they intend to interact with living members of the culture instead of with paper and print. Insights into posture, movement, facial expression, eye management, gestures, and distancing as they affect communication not only increase sensitivity to other human beings but deepen inevitably students' understanding of their own kinesic systems.

63   Research on nonverbal communication is patiently unraveling Sapir's "elaborate and secret code." We know now that in order to

---

*Edward Sapir (1884–1939), American linguist and anthropologist. See Amy Tan's essay in Chapter 1, "The Language of Discretion," for a discussion of Sapir's ideas. (Ed.)

really *understand,* we must be able to hear the silent message and read the invisible world. The study of kinesics across cultures must be a crucial part of our perceptual education.

Notes

1. Genelle Morain, speech at Foreign Language Association of Georgia, Macon, 1977.
2. Benjamin Franklin, *Diary,* quoted by Raymond J. Cromier in "A Legacy from the Founding Fathers," *Temple,* fall 1976, 16.
3. Dean C. Barnlund, *Public and Private Self in Japan and the United States,* pp. 12–16, Simul Press, Tokyo, 1975.
4. Gordon Allport, *The Nature of Prejudice,* Anchor Press/Doubleday, Garden City, N.Y., 1958.
5. Ray L. Birdwhistell, "The Language of the Body: The Natural Environment of Words," in *Human Communication: Theoretical Explorations,* p. 213, ed. Albert Silverstein, Lawrence Erlbaum Associates, Hillsdale, N.J., 1974.
6. Genelle Morain, "Visual Literacy: Reading Signs and Designs in the Foreign Culture," *Foreign Language Annals,* 9 (3), 210–216.
7. Birdwhistell, in *Human Communication,* p. 124.
8. Gordon W. Hewes, "World Distribution of Certain Postural Habits," *American Anthropologist,* 57 (1), 231.
9. M. H. Krout, *Introduction to Social Psychology,* Harper & Row, New York, 1942.
10. Gordon W. Hewes, "The Anthropology of Posture," *Scientific American,* 196 (February), 123–132.
11. Lawrence Wylie and Rick Stafford, *Beaux Gestes: A Guide to French Body Talk,* pp. x–xiii, The Undergraduate Press, Cambridge, Mass, 1977.
12. Ann Banks, "French without Language," *Harvard Today,* 18 (1), 4.
13. Edward T. Hall, *Beyond Culture,* p. 218, Anchor Press/Doubleday, Garden City, N.Y., 1976.
14. Abne M. Eisenberg and Ralph R. Smith, *Nonverbal Communication,* p. 83, Bobbs-Merrill, Indianapolis and New York, 1971.
15. Alan Lomax, *Folk Song Style and Culture,* pp. 235–247, American Association for the Advancement of Science, Washington, D.C., 1968.
16. For the following discussion on interactional synchrony, see Hall, *Beyond Culture,* pp. 61–73.
17. Ralph Waldo Emerson, "Behavior," *The Conduct of Life,* 1860.
18. Ray L. Birdwhistell, *Kinesics and Context,* University of Pennsylvania Press, Philadelphia, 1970.
19. Flora Davis, *Inside Intuition,* pp. 51–52, Signet, New York, 1975.
20. Dale G. Leathers, *Nonverbal Communication Systems,* pp. 26–32, Allyn and Bacon, Boston, 1976.
21. Michael Argyle and Mark Cook, *Gaze and Mutual Gaze,* p. 10, Cambridge University Press, Cambridge, 1976.
22. *Ibid.,* p. 14.
23. Michael Argyle, *Bodily Communication,* International Universities Press, New York, 1975.
24. Davis, *Inside Intuition,* p. 62.
25. *Ibid.,* p. 102.
26. Charles Galloway, lecture at Athens Academy, Athens, Ga, May 1977.
27. Erving Goffman, *Behavior in Public Places,* pp. 83–88, The Free Press, New York, 1963.
28. Examples gleaned from *Intercultural Experiential Learning Aids,* Language Research Center, Brigham Young University, Provo, Utah, 1976; also from David, *Inside Intuition.*
29. Argyle, *Bodily Communication,* p. 247.
30. *Ibid.,* pp. 233–234.

31. Frances C. Hayes, "Should We Have a Dictionary of Gestures?" *Southern Folklore Quarterly*, 4, 239–245.

32. Eisenberg and Smith, *Nonverbal Communication*, p. 76.

33. Reid Scott, *Cultural Understanding: Spanish Level I*, p. 9, Alameda County School Department, Hayward, Calif., 1969. ED 046 292.

34. Jan H. Brunvald, *The Study of American Folklore*, p. 247, W. W. Norton, New York.

35. Jerald R. Green, *Kinesics in the Foreign Language Classroom*, ERIC Focus Report on the Teaching of Foreign Languages, No. 24, MLA/ACTFL Materials Center, New York, 1971. ED 055 511.

36. Birdwhistell, *Kinesics and Context*, p. 154.

37. Eisenberg and Smith, *Nonverbal Communication*, pp. 76–77.

38. Albert E. Scheflen and Alice Scheflen, *Body Language and the Social Order. Communication as Behavioral Control*, p. 90, Prentice-Hall, Englewood Cliffs, N.J., 1972.

39. John R. Rickford and Angela E. Rickford, "Cut-eye and Suck-teeth: African Words and Gestures in New World Guise," *Journal of American Folklore*, 89 (353), 294–309.

40. Shirley Weitz, "Spatial Behavior," in *Nonverbal Communication, Readings with Commentary*, p. 200, ed. Shirley Weitz, Oxford University Press, New York, 1974.

41. Edward T. Hall, *The Hidden Dimension*, pp. 117–125, Doubleday, Garden City, N.Y., 1969.

42. Argyle, *Bodily Communication*, p. 290.

43. *Ibid.*

44. Barnlund, *Public and Private Self in Japan and the United States*, p. 105.

45. *Ibid.*, p. 106.

46. Hall, *Hidden Dimension*, p. 157.

47. *Ibid.*, p. 158.

48. For this discussion of Darwin and the following views of Eibl-Eibesfeldt, see I. Eibl-Eibesfeldt, "Similarities and Differences between Cultures in Expressive Movements," in *Nonverbal Communication*, ed. Shirley Weitz, pp. 22–27.

49. Paul Ekman, Wallance V. Friesen, and Silvan S. Tomkins, "Facial Affect Scoring Technique: A First Validity Study," in *Nonverbal Communication*, ed. Shirley Weitz, p. 36.

50. Paul Ekman, Wallace V. Friesen, and Phoebe Ellsworth, *Emotions in the Human Face*, p. 179, Pergamon Press, New York, 1972.

51. Paul Ekman and Wallace V. Friesen, "The Repertoire and Nonverbal Behavior: Categories, Origins, Usage and Coding," *Semiotica*, 1 (1), 66–67.

52. Scheflen and Scheflen, *Body Language and the Social Order*, p. xii.

53. *Ibid.*, p. xiii.

54. *Ibid.*, p. 105.

55. *Ibid.*, p. 112.

56. Argyle, *Bodily Communication*, p. 362.

57. Charles Galloway, "Nonverbal: The Language of Sensitivity," in *The Challenge of Nonverbal Awareness. Theory into Practice*, 10 (4), p. 230, ed. Jack R. Frymier, The Ohio State University Press, Columbus, Ohio.

58. Lois Bursack, "North American Nonverbal Behavior as Perceived in Three Overseas Urban Cultures," Ph.D. dissertation, University of Minnesota, 1970.

Culture and Truth: The Erosion of Classic Norms

RENATO ROSALDO

Anthropology invites us to expand our sense of human possibilities 1
through the study of other forms of life. Not unlike learning another
language, such inquiry requires time and patience. There are no
shortcuts. We cannot, for example, simply use our imaginations to
invent other cultural worlds. Even those so-called realms of pure
freedom, our fantasy and our "innermost thoughts," are produced
and limited by our own local culture. Human imaginations are as
culturally formed as distinctive ways of weaving, performing a ritual, raising children, grieving, or healing; they are specific to certain
forms of life, whether these be Balinese, Anglo-American, Nya-
kyusa, or Basque.

Culture lends significance to human experience by selecting 2
from and organizing it. It refers broadly to the forms through which
people make sense of their lives, rather than more narrowly to the
opera or art museums. It does not inhabit a set-aside domain, as
does, for example, that of politics or economics. From the pirouettes
of classical ballet to the most brute of brute facts, all human conduct
is culturally mediated. Culture encompasses the everyday and the
esoteric, the mundane and the elevated, the ridiculous and the sub-
lime. Neither high nor low, culture is all-pervasive.

The translation of cultures requires one to try to understand 3
other forms of life in their own terms. We should not impose our
categories on other people's lives because they probably do not apply, at least not without serious revision. We can learn about other
cultures only by reading, listening, or being there. Although they often appear outlandish, brutish, or worse to outsiders, the informal
practices of everyday life make sense in their own context and on
their own terms. Human beings cannot help but learn the culture or
cultures of the communities within which they grow up. A New

Renato Rosaldo (1941–   ), born in Champaign, Illinois, is an anthropologist, professor of interdisciplinary studies at Stanford University, and author of *Ilongot Headhunting, 1883–1974: A Study in Society and History* (1980). "Culture and Truth: The Erosion of Classic
Norms" is from *Culture and Truth: The Remaking of Social Analysis*
(1989).

Yorker transferred at birth to the Pacific island of Tikopia will become a Tikopian, and vice versa. Cultures are learned, not genetically encoded.

Cultural Patterns and Cultural Borderlands

Let me use a series of illustrative anecdotes about dogs and children 4 to discuss two contrasting conceptions of the task of cultural studies. To begin close to home, most Anglo-Americans regard dogs as household pets, animals to be fed, cared for, and treated with a certain affection. Most families with dogs have one or maybe two. Relations between Anglo-Americans and their dogs are not altogether unlike relations between them and their children. Pet dogs are treated with impatience, indulgence, and affection.

The Ilongots of northern Luzon, Philippines, also have dogs, but 5 an enormous amount would be lost in translation if we simply said that the Ilongot name for dog is *atu*, and left it at that. Most of what we would assume about dog-human relations would be mistaken. For example, Ilongots find it important to say that, unlike certain of their neighbors, they don't eat their dogs. The very thought of doing so disgusts them. In addition, from eight to fifteen dogs (not zero, one, or two) live alongside the people who reside in one-room, unpartitioned homes. Used in the hunt, Ilongot dogs are skinny but strong; unlike other domestic animals (except pigs), they are fed cooked food, usually sweet potatoes and greens. Ilongots regard dogs as useful animals, not pets. In a hunting accident, for example, an Ilongot man gashed his dog's head. The man returned home in tears of anger and frustration; he fumed about the difficulty of replacing his dog, but showed no affection toward the wounded animal. On another occasion, however, a baby pig's illness moved its caretaker to tears accompanied by cooing, cuddling, and tender baby talk. In this respect, our notion of pets more nearly applies to Ilongot relations with their baby pigs than with their dogs. Yet the Ilongot term *bilek* applies not only to pets (baby pigs, but not puppies), but also to houseplants and an infant's playthings.

My contrast between Anglo-American and Ilongot dogs has 6 been drawn in accord with the classic anthropological style of analysis most influentially exemplified by Ruth Benedict in *Patterns of Culture*.[1] In accord with the classic style, each cultural pattern appears as unique and self-contained as each design in a kaleidoscope. Because the range of human possibilities is so great, one cannot predict cultural patterns from one case to the next, except to say that they will not match. One culture's pet is another's means of production; one group indulges its puppies, another coddles its baby pigs.

Where one group sees sentimental value, another finds utilitarian worth.

Although the classic vision of unique cultural patterns has 7 proven merit, it also has serious limitations. It emphasizes shared patterns at the expense of processes of change and internal inconsistencies, conflicts, and contradictions.[2] By defining culture as a set of shared meanings, classic norms of analysis make it difficult to study zones of difference within and between cultures.[3] From the classic perspective, cultural borderlands appear to be annoying exceptions rather than central areas for inquiry.

Conditioned by a changing world, classic norms of social analy- 8 sis have been eroded since the late 1960s, leaving the field of anthropology in a creative crisis of reorientation and renewal. The shift in social thought has made questions of conflict, change, and inequality increasingly urgent. Analysts no longer seek out harmony and consensus to the exclusion of difference and inconsistency. For social analysis, cultural borderlands have moved from a marginal to a central place. In certain cases, such borders are literal. Cities throughout the world today increasingly include minorities defined by race, ethnicity, language, class, religion, and sexual orientation. Encounters with "difference" now pervade modern everyday life in urban settings.

In my own life, I grew up speaking Spanish to my father and 9 English to my mother. Consider the cultural pertinence of my father's response, during the late 1950s, to having taken our dog, Chico, to the veterinarian. Born and raised in Mexico, my father arrived home with Chico in a mood midway between pain and amusement. Tears of laughter streamed down his cheeks until, finally, he mumbled something like, "What will these North Americans think of next?" He explained that when he entered the veterinarian's office a nurse in white greeted him at the door, sat him down, pulled out a form, and asked, "What is the patient's name?" In my dad's view, no Mexican would ever come so close to confusing a dog with a person. To him, it was unthinkable that a clinic for dogs could ever resemble one for people with its nurses in white and its forms for the "patient." His encounter across cultures and social classes gave him an acute case of borderlands hysteria. Yet a classic concept of culture seeks out the "Mexican" or the "Anglo-American," and grants little space to the mundane disturbances that so often erupt during border crossings.

Borderlands surface not only at the boundaries of officially rec- 10 ognized cultural units, but also at less formal intersections, such as those of gender, age, status, and distinctive life experiences. After

Michelle Rosaldo's death, for example, I suddenly discovered "the invisible community of the bereaved" as opposed to those who had suffered no major losses. Similarly, my son, Manny, came up against an unmarked internal border when he left a playgroup where his daily activities were only loosely organized and entered a nursery school shortly after his third birthday. Crossing this barrier proved so traumatic that he came home day after day in tears. We puzzled over his distress until the evening that he told the story of his day as a succession of "times": group time, snack time, nap time, play time, and lunch time. In other words, he was suffering the consequences of moving across the line from days of relatively free play to a world disciplined far beyond anything he had known before. On yet another occasion, when he reached kindergarten, Manny was carefully instructed to avoid strangers, especially those offering candy, rides, or even friendliness. Shortly thereafter, at a movie theater, he surveyed the audience around him and said, "It's good luck. There are no strangers here." To him, strangers were visibly evil, like robbers with masks, rather than people who were neither friends nor acquaintances. The cultural concept "stranger" evidently undergoes certain changes as it crosses the invisible border separating teachers from their kindergarten students.

We all cross such social boundaries in our daily lives. Even the 11 unity of that so-called building block, the nuclear family, is cross-cut by differences of gender, generation, and age. Consider the disparate worlds one passes through in daily life, a round that includes home, eating out, working hours, adventures in consumerland, and a range of relationships, from intimacy to collegiality and friendship to enmity. Encounters with cultural and related differences belong to all of us in our most mundane experiences, not to a specialized domain of inquiry housed in an anthropology department. Yet the classic norms of anthropology have attended more to the unity of cultural wholes than to their myriad crossroads and borderlands.

What follows is a mythic tale about the birth of the anthropologi- 12 cal concept of culture and its embodiment in the classic ethnography. Caricature best makes my point because it characterizes in bold strokes with a view not to preserve but to transform the reality it depicts. This "instant history" depicts present-day perceptions of disciplinary norms that guided graduate training until the late 1960s (and, in certain sectors, continue to do so) more than the actual complexities of past research.[4] These perceptions constitute the point of departure against which current experimental efforts attempt to remake ethnography as a form of social analysis. Without further ado, listen to the story of the Lone Ethnographer.

The Rise of Classic Norms

Once upon a time, the Lone Ethnographer rode off into the sunset 13
in search of "his native." After undergoing a series of trials, he encountered the object of his quest in a distant land. There, he under-
went his rite of passage by enduring the ultimate ordeal of
"fieldwork." After collecting "the data," the Lone Ethnographer returned home and wrote a "true" account of "the culture."

Whether he hated, tolerated, respected, befriended, or fell in 14
love with "his native," the Lone Ethnographer was willy-nilly com-
plicit with the imperialist domination of his epoch. The Lone Ethnographer's mask of innocence (or, as he put it, his "detached im-
partiality") barely concealed his ideological role in perpetuating the
colonial control of "distant" peoples and places. His writings represented the human objects of the civilizing mission's global enterprise
as if they were ideal recipients of the white man's burden.

The Lone Ethnographer depicted the colonized as members of a 15
harmonious, internally homogeneous, unchanging culture. When so
described, the culture appeared to "need" progress, or economic
and moral uplifting. In addition, the "timeless traditional culture"
served as a self-congratulatory reference point against which Western civilization could measure its own progressive historical evolution. The civilizing journey was conceived more as a rise than a fall,
a process more of elevation than degradation (a long, arduous journey upward, culminating in "us").

In the mythic past, a strict division of labor separated the Lone 16
Ethnographer from "his native" sidekick. By definition, the Lone
Ethnographer was literate, and "his native" was not. In accord with
fieldwork norms, "his native" spoke and the Lone Ethnographer
recorded "utterances" in his "fieldnotes."[5] In accord with imperialist
norms, "his native" provided the raw material ("the data") for processing in the metropolis. After returning to the metropolitan center
where he was schooled, the Lone Ethnographer wrote his definitive
work.

The sacred bundle the Lone Ethnographer handed to his succes- 17
sors includes a complicity with imperialism, a commitment to objectivism, and a belief in monumentalism. The context of imperialism
and colonial rule shaped both the monumentalism of timeless accounts of homogeneous cultures and the objectivism of a strict division of labor between the "detached" ethnographer and "his native." The key practices so bequeathed can be subsumed under the
general rubric of *fieldwork*, which is often regarded as an initiation
into the mysteries of anthropological knowledge. The product of the
Lone Ethnographer's labors, the ethnography, appeared to be a

transparent medium. It portrayed a "culture" sufficiently frozen to be an object of "scientific" knowledge. This genre of social description made itself, and the culture so described, into an artifact worthy of being housed in the collection of a major museum.

The myth of the Lone Ethnographer thus depicts the birth of ethnography, a genre of social description. Drawing on models from natural history, such accounts usually moved upward from environment and subsistence through family and kinship to religion and spiritual life. Produced by and for specialists, ethnographies aspired to the holistic representation of other cultures; they portrayed other forms of life as totalities. Ethnographies were storehouses of purportedly incontrovertible information to be mined by armchair theorists engaged in comparative studies. This genre seemingly resembled a mirror that reflected other cultures as they "really" were. 18

Much as routinization follows charisma and codification comes on the heels of insight, the heroic epoch of the Lone Ethnographer gave way to the classic period (say, not altogether inaccurately, but with mock precision, 1921–1971). During that period, the discipline's dominant objectivist view held that social life was fixed and constraining. In her recent ethnography, for example, anthropologist Sally Falk Moore emphasizes the absolute clarity and certitude of the objectivist research program: "A generation ago society was a system. Culture had a pattern. The postulation of a coherent whole discoverable bit by bit served to expand the significance of each observed particularity."[6] Phenomena that could not be regarded as systems or patterns appeared to be unanalyzable; they were dubbed exceptions, ambiguities, or irregularities. They held no theoretical interest because they could not be subsumed under the ongoing research agenda. By assuming the answers to the questions that should have been asked, the discipline confidently asserted that so-called traditional societies do not change.[7] 19

Classic ethnographers, particularly in Great Britain, usually invoked the French sociologist Emile Durkheim as their "founding father." In this tradition, culture and society determined individual personalities and consciousness; they enjoyed the objective status of systems. Not unlike a grammar, they stood on their own, independent from the individuals who followed their rules. After all, we did not, as individuals, invent the tools we use or the institutions within which we work. Like the languages we speak, culture and social structure existed before, during, and after any particular individual's lifetime. Although Durkheim's views have undeniable merit, they pass altogether too lightly over processes of conflict and change. 20

Along with objectivism, the classic period codified a notion of monumentalism. Until quite recently, in fact, I accepted without 21 qualification the monumentalist dogma that the discipline rests on a solid foundation of "classic ethnographies." For example, I recall that on a foggy night a short number of years ago I found myself driving with a physicist along the mountainous stretch of Route 17 between Santa Cruz and San Jose. Both of us felt anxious about the weather and somewhat bored, so we began to discuss our respective fields. My companion opened by asking me, as only a physicist could, what anthropologists had discovered.

"Discovered?" I asked, pretending to be puzzled. I was stalling   22
for time. Perhaps something would come to me.

"Yes, you know, something like the properties or the laws of   23
other cultures."

"Do you mean something like $E = mc^2$?"   24

"Yes," he said.   25

Inspiration unexpectedly arrived and I heard myself saying,   26
"There's one thing that we know for sure. We all know a good description when we see one. We haven't discovered any laws of culture, but we do think there are classic ethnographies, really telling descriptions of other cultures."

Classic works long served as models for aspiring ethnographers.   27
At once maps of past investigations and programs for future research, the classics were regarded as exemplary cultural descriptions. They did, indeed, appear to be the one thing we knew for sure, especially when pressed by an inquisitive physicist. Leading anthropologists continue to voice the monumentalist credo that theories rise and fall, but fine ethnographic descriptions represent enduring achievements. T. O. Beidelman, for example, introduced his recent ethnography in this manner: "Theories may change, but ethnography remains at the heart of anthropology; it is the test and measure of all theory."[8] In fact, classic ethnographies have proven durable compared with the relatively short shelf life of such schools of thought as evolutionism, diffusionism, culture and personality, functionalism, ethnoscience, and structuralism.

To anticipate the discussion in subsequent pages, monumental-   28
ism conflates a loosely shared, ever-changing analytical project with a canonical list of classic ethnographies. Even if one were to grant that the discipline's core resides in its "classics," it does not follow that, like a solid foundation, these esteemed works remain the "same." Practitioners constantly reinterpret them in light of changing theoretical projects and reanalyze them against newly available evidence. From the point of view of their reception, the cultural artifacts we call ethnographies constantly change, despite the fact that, as verbal texts, they are fixed.

The exploration of theoretical issues that arise from and play 29
themselves out in concrete ethnographic studies is the burden of
this book. What follows argues that present-day experiments with
ethnographic writing both reflect and contribute to an ongoing interdisciplinary program that has been transforming social thought. This
remaking of social analysis derives from the political and intellectual
movements that arose during the newly postcolonial, yet intensely
imperialistic, period of the late 1960s. In this context, certain social
thinkers redirected the agenda of theory from discrete variables and
lawlike generalizations to the interplay of different factors as they
unfold within specific cases.

The Politics of Remaking Social Analysis

If the classic period more tightly wove together the Lone Ethnogra- 30
pher's legacy—the complicity with imperialism, the doctrine of objectivism, and the credo of monumentalism—the political turbulence
of the late 1960s and early 1970s began a process of unraveling and
reworking that continues into the present. Not unlike the reorienta-
tions in other fields and in other countries, the initial impetus for the
conceptual shift in anthropology was the potent historical conjunc-
ture of decolonization and the intensification of American imperialism. This development led to a series of movements from the civil
rights struggle to the mobilization against the war in Vietnam.
Teach-ins, sit-ins, demonstrations, and strikes set the political tone
for this period on American college and university campuses.

During this period, the annual business meetings of the Ameri- 31
can Anthropological Association became a verbal battleground,
where resolutions on certain major issues of the day were fiercely
debated. Anthropological research in Chile and Thailand was attacked from within the discipline because of its potential uses in
counterinsurgency efforts. Elsewhere, the so-called natives began to
charge anthropologists with conducting research in ways that failed
to aid local efforts to resist oppression and with writing in ways that
perpetuated stereotypes.

The New Left in the United States helped produce a spectrum of 32
political movements responsive to internally imperialized groups
that organized around forms of oppression based on gender, sexual
preference, and race. Women, for example, began to organize because, among other reasons, the New Left more often placed them
in secretarial rather than leadership roles. As emergent feminists immediately realized, sexism permeated the entire society, not simply
the New Left in its beginning phases. Racism and homophobia led

to similar realizations in other sectors of society. The call for a social analysis that made central the aspirations and demands of groups usually deemed marginal by the dominant national ideology came from the counterculture, environmentalism, feminism, gay and lesbian movements, the Native American movement, and the struggles of blacks, Chicanos, and Puerto Ricans.[9]

My own vision of anthropology's possibilities and failings has 33 been shaped through participation in the campus Chicano movement. Involvement in this struggle has clarified my understanding of the need to attend with care to the perceptions and aspirations of subordinate groups. My resulting concerns include historical change, cultural difference, and social inequality. Ethnographic history, the translation of cultures, and social criticism now seem intertwined as fields of study laden with ethical imperatives.

The transformation of anthropology showed that the received 34 notion of culture as unchanging and homogeneous was not only mistaken but irrelevant (to use a key word of the time).[10] Marxist and other discussion groups sprang up. Questions of political consciousness and ideology came to the foreground. How people make their own histories and the interplay of domination and resistance seemed more compelling than textbook discussions of system maintenance and equilibrium theory. Doing committed anthropology made more sense than trying to maintain the fiction of the analyst as a detached, impartial observer. What once appeared to be archaic questions of human emancipation now began to sound an urgent note.

The reorientation of anthropology was itself part of a series of 35 much broader social movements and intellectual reformulations. In *The Restructuring of Social and Political Theory,* for example, Richard Bernstein attributes the redirection of American social thought after the late 1960s in large part to the revival of once-rejected intellectual currents. Among these critical currents, he includes linguistic philosophy, the history and philosophy of science, phenomenology, hermeneutics, and Marxism.[11] Bernstein attributes these changes in the project of social analysis to critical perspectives developed by younger academics who, as former student leaders, found that their criticism of society also led them to mount forceful critiques of their disciplines. Although educated in the most advanced formal research methods of the day, the new generation of students made their criticisms from within, which proved as effective as they were distressing to already established professionals who could otherwise easily fend off assaults from beyond disciplinary boundaries by calling them ill-informed or biased.

From within anthropology, Clifford Geertz has spoken elo- 36 quently about the "refiguration of social thought" since the late 1960s. Social scientists, he says, have increasingly turned their attention from general explanatory laws to cases and their interpretation. To achieve their new aims, they have blurred the boundaries between the social sciences and the humanities. Their forms of social description even use key words drawn from the humanities, such as text, story, and social drama. After thus characterizing the current ferment in the human sciences, Geertz argues that objectivist assumptions about theory, language, and detachment no longer hold because of how social analysis has shifted its agenda:

> A challenge is being mounted to some of the central assumptions of mainstream social science. The strict separation of theory and data, the "brute fact" idea; the effort to create a formal vocabulary of analysis purged of all subjective reference, the "ideal language" idea; and the claim to moral neutrality and the Olympian view, the "God's truth" idea—none of these can prosper when explanation comes to be regarded as a matter of connecting action to its sense rather than behavior to its determinants. The refiguration of social theory represents, or will if it continues, a sea change in our notion not so much of what knowledge is but of what we want to know.[12]

According to Geertz, the social sciences have undergone deep changes in their conceptions of (a) the object of analysis, (b) the language of analysis, and (c) the position of the analyst. The once-dominant ideal of a detached observer using neutral language to explain "raw" data has been displaced by an alternative project that attempts to understand human conduct as it unfolds through time and in relation to its meanings for the actors.

The task ahead is daunting. Both the methods and the subject matter of cultural studies have undergone major changes as their analytical project has taken a new turn. Culture, politics, and history have become intertwined and brought to the foreground as they were not during the classic period. This new turn has transformed the task of theory, which now must attend to conceptual issues raised by the study of particular cases rather than restrict itself to the pursuit of generalizations.

The "refiguration of social thought" has coincided with a critique of classic norms and a period of experimentation in ethnographic writing. Speaking zestfully of an "experimental moment," a number of anthropologists have become self-consciously playful about literary form.[13] Their writings celebrate the creative possibilities released by loosening the strict codes that governed the production of ethnographies during the classic period. Yet, rather than a case of experimentation for experimentation's sake or a matter of being caught between research paradigms, the current "experimental moment" in ethnographic writing has been driven by enduring, not transitory, ethical and analytical issues.[14] Changes in global relations of domination have conditioned both social thought and the experimental ethnography.

Decolonization and the intensification of imperialism have led [39] social analysis since the late 1960s to shift its research program, and this shift has in turn produced a crisis in ethnographic writing. The difficulties of attempting to use classic ethnographic forms for new research programs raise conceptual issues, which in turn call for a widening of ethnography's modes of composition. The "experimental moment" in ethnographic writing and the remaking of social analysis are inextricably linked. Social analysis has sought new forms of writing because it has changed its central topics and what it has to say about them.

Remaking Ethnography as a Form of Social Analysis

Arguably, ethnography has been cultural anthropology's most [40] significant contribution to knowledge. Social description outside the field of anthropology has both drawn on and reshaped ethnographic technique in its forms of documentary representation. James Clifford, for example, has argued persuasively that ethnography has become central to "an emergent interdisciplinary phenomenon" of descriptive and critical cultural studies that includes fields from historical ethnography to cultural criticism and from the study of everyday life to the semiotics of the fantastic.[15] In my view, even Clifford's expansive list of cultural studies should be extended beyond the academy to areas informed by an ethnographic sensibility, such as documentary film and photo essays, the new journalism, television docudramas, and certain historical novels. As a form of cross-cultural understanding, ethnography now plays a significant role for an array of academics, artists, and media people.

Whether speaking about shopping in a supermarket, the after- [41] math of a nuclear war, Elizabethan self-fashioning, academic communities of physicists, tripping through Las Vegas, Algerian marriage practices, or ritual among the Ndembu of central Africa, work in cultural studies sees human worlds as constructed through historical and political processes, and not as brute timeless facts of nature. It is marvelously easy to confuse "our local culture" with "universal human nature." If ideology often makes cultural facts appear natural, social analysis attempts to reverse the process. It dismantles the ideological in order to reveal the cultural, a peculiar blend of objective arbitrariness (things human could be, and indeed elsewhere are, otherwise) and subjective taken-for-grantedness (it's only common sense—how could things be otherwise?).

In presenting culture as a subject for analysis and critique, the 42 ethnographic perspective develops an interplay between making the familiar strange and the strange familiar. Home cultures can appear so normal to their members that their common sense seems to be based in universal human nature. Social descriptions by, of, and for members of a particular culture require a relative emphasis on defamiliarization, so they will appear—as they in fact are—humanly made, and not given in nature. Alien cultures, however, can appear so exotic to outsiders that everyday life seems to be floating in a bizarre primitive mentality. Social descriptions about cultures distant from both the writer and the reader require a relative emphasis on familiarization, so they will appear—as they also in fact are—sharply distinct in their differences, yet recognizably human in their resemblances.

Paradoxically, ethnography's success as an informing perspec- 43 tive for a wide range of cultural studies coincides with a crisis in its home discipline. Readers of classic ethnographies have increasingly become afflicted with "emperor's new clothes syndrome." Works that once looked fully clothed, even regal, now appear naked, even laughable. Words that once read like the "real truth" now appear parodic, or as only one among a number of perspectives. The shift in social thought—its object, its language, and the moral position of its analysts—has been profound enough to make the tedium of once-revered forms of ethnographic writing breathtakingly apparent.

The literary theorist Mary Louise Pratt, for example, has ob- 44 served, "There are strong reasons why field ethnographers so often lament that their ethnographic writings leave out or hopelessly impoverish some of the most important knowledge they have achieved, including the self-knowledge. For the lay person, such as myself, the main evidence of a problem is the simple fact that ethnographic writing tends to be surprisingly boring. How, one asks constantly, could such interesting people doing such interesting things produce such dull books? What did they have to do to themselves?"[16] Although they never did make the blood run faster, ethnographies written for a captive professional audience once appeared so authoritative that few dared say out loud that they were boring. Nor did it occur to readers to wonder about the kind of knowledge being suppressed by the discipline's relatively narrow norms of composition.

Critique from the outside has been more than matched by insid- 45 ers. An eminent ethnographer, the late Victor Turner, for example, spoke forcefully against received ethnographic form, saying, "It is becoming increasingly recognized that the anthropological monograph is itself a rather rigid literary genre which grew out of the notion that in the human sciences reports must be modeled rather abjectly on those of the natural sciences."[17] For Turner, classic ethnographies have proven dreadfully poor vehicles for apprehending how reason, feeling, and will come together in people's daily lives. In a more political vein, he goes on to say that older-style ethnographies split subject from object and present other lives as visual spectacles for metropolitan consumption. "Cartesian dualism," he says, "has insisted on separating subject from object, us from them. It has, indeed, made voyeurs of Western man, exaggerating sight by macro- and micro-instrumentation, the better to learn the structures of the world with an 'eye' to its exploitation."[18] Turner thus connects the "eye" of ethnography with the "I" of imperialism.

Similarly, the psychologist Jerome Bruner has argued that the 46 social descriptions of certain respected ethnographies initially appear persuasive, but then, on closer examination, crumble into implausibility. He begins by musing, "Perhaps there have been societies, at least for certain periods of time, that were 'classically' traditional and in which one 'derived' one's actions from a set of more or less fixed rules."[19] He remembers how his pleasure at reading about the classic Chinese family reminded him of watching a formal ballet where rules and roles were meticulously followed. Later, however, he learned about how Chinese warlords used brute force to gain people's allegiance and alter their lives, as legitimate rule rapidly passed from one party to the next. "I found myself concluding," he says, "that 'equilibrium' accounts of cultures are useful principally to guide the writing of older style ethnographies or as political instruments for use by those in power to subjugate psychologically those who must be ruled."[20] Although depictions of traditional societies where people slavishly follow strict rules have a certain charming formality, alternative accounts of the same societies lead Bruner to a harsh conclusion, not unlike my own. He regards the once-dominant ethnographic portrait of the timeless traditional society as a fiction used to aid in composition and to legitimate the subjugation of human populations.

Classic norms of ethnographic composition had a significant role 47 in reinforcing the slippage from working hypotheses to self-fulfilling prophecies about unchanging social worlds where people are caught in a web of eternal recurrence. Anthropological theory of the day was dominated by the concepts of structure, codes, and norms; it correspondingly developed largely implicit descriptive practices that prescribed composition in the present tense. Anthropologists have in fact proudly used the phrase "the ethnographic present" to designate a distanced mode of writing that normalized life by describing social activities as if they were always repeated in the same manner by everyone in the group.

The societies so described appeared uncomfortably close to Edward Said's notion of "orientalism."[21] Said underscored the links between power and knowledge, between imperialism and orientalism, by showing how seemingly neutral, or innocent, forms of social description both reinforced and produced ideologies that justified the imperialist project. In Said's view, the orientalist records observations about a transaction in the corner of the marketplace, or child care under a thatched roof, or a rite of passage, in order to generalize to a larger cultural entity, the Orient, which by definition is homogeneous in space and unchanging through time. Under such descriptions, the Orient appears to be both a benchmark against which to measure Western European "progress" and an inert terrain on which to impose imperialist schemes of "development."

The classic notion that stability, orderliness, and equilibrium characterized so-called traditional societies thus derived in part from the illusion of timelessness created by the rhetoric of ethnography. The following passage, from E. E. Evans-Pritchard's classic ethnography on the Nuer, a pastoralist group from the Sudan, illustrates the tendencies just depicted: "Seasonal and lunar changes repeat themselves year after year, so that a Nuer standing at any point of time has conceptual knowledge of what lies before him and can predict and organize his life accordingly. A man's structural future is likewise already fixed and ordered into different periods, so that the total changes in status a boy will undergo in his ordained passage through the social system, if he lives long enough, can be foreseen."[22] The ethnographer speaks interchangeably of the Nuer or of a Nuer man because, differences of age aside (questions of gender barely enter Evans-Pritchard's androcentric work), the culture is conceived as uniform and static. Yet, at the very time the ethnographer was conducting his research, the Nuer were being subjected to enforced changes by the British colonial regime's efforts at so-called pacification.

The Museum and the Garage Sale

Consider the art museum as an image of classic ethnographies and the cultures they describe. Cultures stand as sacred images; they have an integrity and coherence that enables them to be studied, as they say, on their own terms, from within, from the "native" point of view. Not unlike the grand art of museums, each culture stands alone as an aesthetic object worthy of contemplation. Once canonized, all cultures appear to be equally great. Questions of relative merit will only wind up with imponderables, incomparables, and incommensurables. Just as the professional literary critic does not argue about whether Shakespeare is greater than Dante, the ethnographer does not debate the relative merits of the Kwakiutl of the northwest coast versus the Trobriand Islanders of the Pacific. Both cultures exist and both can sustain extensive cultural analysis.

Ethnographic monumentalism, however, should not be con- 51 fused with that of high-culture humanism. Despite its problems, the ethnographic impulse to regard cultures as so many great works of art has a deeply democratic and egalitarian side. All cultures are separate and equal. If one culture lords it over another, it is not because of its cultural superiority. The high-culture monumentalists, in contrast, envision a sacred heritage extending directly from Homer through Shakespeare to the present. They find nothing of comparable value either in so-called popular culture or outside the "West." Anthropologists of any political persuasion appear subversive (and indeed, during the 1980s, have received relatively little institutional support) simply because their work valorizes other cultural traditions.

In his pithy discussion of the current ferment in anthropology, 52 Louis A. Sass cites an eminent anthropologist who worried that recent experimentation with ethnographic form could subvert the discipline's authority, leading to its fragmentation and eventual disappearance: "At a conference in 1980 on the crisis in anthropology, Cora Du Bois, a retired Harvard professor, spoke of the distance she felt from the 'complexity and disarray of what I once found a justifiable and challenging discipline. . . . It has been like moving from a distinguished art museum into a garage sale.' "[23] The images of the museum, for the classic period, and the garage sale, for the present, strike me as being quite apt, but I evaluate them rather differently than Du Bois. She feels nostalgia for the distinguished art museum with everything in its place, and I see it as a relic from the colonial past. She detests the chaos of the garage sale, and I find it provides a precise image for the postcolonial situation where cultural artifacts flow between unlikely places, and nothing is sacred, permanent, or sealed off.

The image of anthropology as a garage sale depicts our present 53 global situation.[24] Analytical postures developed during the colonial era can no longer be sustained. Ours is definitively a postcolonial epoch. Despite the intensification of North American imperialism, the "Third World" has imploded into the metropolis. Even the conservative national politics of containment, designed to shield "us" from "them," betray the impossibility of maintaining hermetically sealed cultures. Consider a series of efforts: police fight cocaine dealers, border guards detain undocumented workers, tariffs try to keep out Japanese imports, and celestial canopies promise to fend off Soviet missiles. Such efforts to police and barricade reveal, more than anything else, how porous "our" borders have become.

The Lone Ethnographer's guiding fiction of cultural compart- 54 ments has crumbled. So-called natives do not "inhabit" a world fully separate from the one ethnographers "live in." Few people simply remain in their place these days. When people play "ethnographers and natives," it is ever more difficult to predict who will put on the loincloth and who will pick up the pencil and paper. More people are doing both, and more so-called natives are among the ethnographer's readers, at times appreciative and at times vocally critical. One increasingly finds that Native American Tewas, South Asian Sinhalese, and Chicanos are among those who read and write ethnographies.

If ethnography once imagined it could describe discrete cultures, 55 it now contends with boundaries that crisscross over a field at once fluid and saturated with power. In a world where "open borders" appear more salient than "closed communities," one wonders how to define a project for cultural studies. Neither "getting on with the job" and pretending nothing has changed nor "moaning about meaning" and producing more discourse on the impossibility of anthropology will result in the needed remaking of social analysis. Such at any rate is the position from which I develop a critique of classic norms for doing ethnography.

Notes

1. Ruth Benedict, *Patterns of Culture* (Boston: Houghton Mifflin, 1959 [orig. 1934]).

2. This generalization admits to exceptions, particularly during the 1920s and 1930s, when a "diffusionist" agenda in anthropology was giving way to a more "functionist" one. Diffusionists saw culture as a collection of "traits" that were borrowed and lent from one group to another; they asked about degrees of resistance and receptivity to borrowing, and about whether or not traits necessarily diffused in clusters ("necessary versus accidental adhesions"). The diffusionists saw that culture had porous boundaries, but downplayed questions of internal patterning. As functionalist theory took hold, inquiries into the degree of cultural patterning slipped into assumptions that were beyond question. For thoughtful historical critiques of the oversystematization of the concept of culture during the early classic period (1921–1945), see George W. Stocking, Jr., "Ideas and Institutions in American Anthropology: Thoughts toward a History of the Interwar Years," in *Selected Papers from the American Anthropologist, 1921–1945*, ed. George W. Stocking, Jr. (Washington, D.C.: American Anthropological Association, 1976), pp. 1–49; James Clifford, "On Ethnographic Surrealism," in *The Predicament of Culture: Twentieth-Century Ethnography, Literature, and Art* (Cambridge, Mass.: Harvard University Press, 1988), pp. 117–51.

3. The distinction between cultural patterns and cultural borderlands, of course, closely resembles that drawn in the introduction between ritual as microcosm and ritual as a busy intersection.

4. My account of classic norms should not be conflated with the classic ethnographies themselves. The texts require more complex readings. See, e.g., Clifford Geertz, *Works and Lives: The Anthropologist as Author* (Stanford, Calif.: Stanford University Press, 1988).

5. The mythic form of my account imitates the mystique fieldwork holds for anthropologists. For a first person account that manifests the mystique, see Claude Lévi-Strauss, *Tristes Tropiques* (New York: Athenaeum, 1975). For a series of historical essays on fieldwork, see George W. Stocking, Jr., ed., *Observers Observed: Essays on Ethnographic Fieldwork* (Madison: University of Wisconsin Press, 1983). For a comprehensive account of anthropology during the nineteenth century, see George W. Stocking, Jr., *Victorian Anthropology* (New York: Free Press, 1987).

6. Sally Falk Moore, *Social Facts and Fabrications: "Customary" Law on Kilimanjaro, 1880–1980* (New York: Cambridge University Press, 1986), p. 4.

7. Although classic ethnographies often talked about "diachronic analysis," they usually studied the unfolding of structures, rather than open-ended processes. Among others, Bronislaw Malinowski introduced the so-called biographical method only to invent the composite life-cycle; Meyer Fortes studied households through time only to produce the developmental cycle of domestic groups; Edmund Leach lengthened his perspective beyond the lifespan only to construct the moving equilibrium of a political system. For the most part, so-called diachronic methods were used to study "structures of the long run" that revealed themselves only in periods of time more extended than the one- or two-year span of most fieldwork. Enduring social forms thus remained the object of anthropological knowledge. See Bronislaw Malinowski, *The Sexual Life of Savages* (London: George Routledge, 1929); Jack Goody, ed., *The Developmental Cycle of Domestic Groups* (Cambridge: Cambridge University Press, 1958); Edmund Leach, *Political Systems of Highland Burma* (Boston: Beacon Press, 1965).

8. T. O. Beidelman, *Moral Imagination of Kaguru Modes of Thought* (Bloomington: Indiana University Press, 1986), p. xi.

9. The political movements of the late sixties and early seventies more widely reshaped the intellectual agenda of American anthropology through the work of such figures as Laura Nader, Sidney Mintz, Karen Sacks, Kathleen Gough, Sydel Silverman, Michelle Rosaldo, Gerald Berreman, Eric Wolf, Rayna Rapp, June Nash, Dell Hymes, Joseph Jorgenson, Louise Lamphere, and David Aberle. The tenor of the times can be discerned from Dell Hymes, ed., *Reinventing Anthropology* (New York: Random House, 1969); Rayna Rapp Reiter, ed., *Toward an Anthropology of Women* (New York: Monthly Review Press, 1975); Talal Asad, ed., *Anthropology and the Colonial Encounter* (London: Ithaca Press, 1973); Michelle Zimbalist Rosaldo and Louise Lamphere, eds., *Woman, Culture, and Society* (Stanford, Calif.: Stanford University Press, 1974). Ethnic minorities have thus far had less of an impact on mainstream anthropology than have women. French and British anthropology of the time also influenced American research programs. For example, Pierre Bourdieu developed a theory of practice and Talal Asad developed an analysis of colonial domination. The "reinvention of anthropology" was also influenced by broader trends in social thought, ranging from such writers as Antonio Gramsci and Michel Foucault, through Anthony Giddens and Richard Bernstein, to Raymond Williams and E. P. Thompson.

10. To be more precise, the dissatisfaction with objectivism's emphasis on pattern and structure reached epidemic proportions during the early 1970s. During the 1970s, "history" and "politics" were often invoked to describe what classic analysts had overlooked. Even during the classic period, however, certain critics voiced dissatisfaction with objectivism. Their articulate criticisms never became a dominant intellectual movement, and as a result could not become cogent programs of research. For relatively early critical works, see, e.g., Kenelm Burridge, *Encountering Aborigines* (New York: Pergamon Press, 1973); Roy Wagner, *The Invention of Culture* (Chicago: University of Chicago Press, 1975). For a historical assessment of such alternative views, see Dan Jorgenson, *Taro and Arrows* (Ph.D. dissertation: University of British Columbia, 1981).

11. Richard Bernstein, *The Restructuring of Social and Political Theory* (Philadelphia: University of Pennsylvania Press, 1978), p. xii.

12. Clifford Geertz, "Blurred Genres: The Refiguration of Social Thought," in *Local Knowledge: Further Essays in Interpretive Anthropology* (New York: Basic Books 1983), p. 34.

13. Within anthropology a number of works on "ethnographies as texts" have appeared during the 1980s. See George Marcus and Dick Cushman, "Ethnographies as Texts," in *Annual Review of Anthropology* 11 (1982): 25–69; James Boon, *Other Tribes, Other Scribes: Symbolic Anthropology in the Comparative Study of Cultures, Histories, Religions, and Texts* (New York: Cambridge University Press, 1982); James Clifford and George E. Marcus, eds., *Writing Culture: The Poetics and Politics of Ethnography* (Berkeley: University of California Press, 1986); George E. Marcus and Michael M. J. Fischer, *Anthropology as Cultural Critique: An Experimental Moment in the Human Sciences* (Chicago: University of Chicago Press, 1986); Clifford Geertz, *Works and Lives*; James Clifford, *The Predicament of Culture*. For related works from other disciplines, see, e.g., Hayden White, *Metahistory: The Historical Imagination in Nineteenth-Century Europe* (Baltimore: Johns Hopkins University Press, 1973); Richard H. Brown, *A Poetic for Sociology: Toward a Logic of Discovery for the Human Sciences* (New York: Cambridge University Press, 1977); Dominick LaCapra, *Rethinking Intellectual History: Texts, Contexts, Language* (Ithaca, N.Y.: Cornell University Press, 1983); John S. Nelson, Allan Megill, and Donald N. McCloskey, eds., *The Rhetoric of the Human Sciences: Language and Argument in Scholarship and Public Affairs* (Madison: University of Wisconsin Press, 1987).

14. George E. Marcus and Michael M. J. Fischer's *Anthropology as Cultural Critique* (Chicago: University of Chicago Press, 1986) at once celebrates anthropology's "experimental moment" and claims that it neither should nor will last very long. Although they favor experimentation, Marcus and Fischer concede that over the long run the excesses of eclecticism and the free play of ideas could well prove debilitating to the discipline. Their mechanical reading of Thomas Kuhn's *Structure of Scientific Revolutions* (Chicago: University of Chicago Press, 2d ed., 1970) leads them to assert that anthropology's current experimentation is destined to end when the advent of a new paradigm ushers in the discipline's next extended period of "normal science." Not unlike an unruly child, according to them, anthropology will soon outgrow its current phase, and order will win out over chaos. Their message appears designed to reassure the antiexperimentalists. Why bother to combat experimental writing when Kuhnian prophecy has promised a new reign of stable enthnographic forms? I do not think that the "experimental moment" is a flash in the pan because the discipline's new project demands a wider array of rhetorical forms than were used during the classic period.

15. To appreciate its range, Clifford's list should probably be cited in full: "This blurred purview includes, to name only a few developing perspectives, historical ethnography (Emmanual Le Roy Ladurie, Natalie Davis, Carlo Ginzburg), cultural poetics (Stephen Greenblatt), cultural criticism (Hayden White, Edward Said, Fredric Jameson), the analysis of implicit knowledge and everyday practices (Pierre Bourdieu, Michel de Certeau), the critique of hegemonic structures of feeling (Raymond Williams), the study of scientific communities (following Thomas Kuhn), the semiotics of exotic worlds and fantastic spaces (Tzvetan Todorov, Louis Marin), and all those studies that focus on meaning systems, disputed traditions, or cultural artifacts" (James Clifford, "Introduction: Partial Truths," in *Writing Culture*, ed. Clifford and Marcus, p. 3).

16. Mary Louise Pratt, "Fieldwork in Common Places," in *Writing Culture*, ed. Clifford and Marcus, p. 33.

17. Victor Turner, "Dramatic Ritual/Ritual Drama: Performative and Reflexive Anthropology," in *From Ritual to Theater: The Human Seriousness of Play* (New York: Performing Arts Journal Publications, 1982), p. 89.

18. *Ibid.*, p. 100.

19. Jerome Bruner, *Actual Minds, Possible Worlds* (Cambridge, Mass.: Harvard University Press, 1986), p. 123.

20. *Ibid.*

21. Edward Said, *Orientalism* (New York: Pantheon Books, 1978).

22. E. E. Evans-Pritchard, *The Nuer* (Oxford: Oxford University Press, 1940), pp. 94–95. Also see Renato Rosaldo, "From the Door of His Tent: The Fieldworker and the Inquisitor," in *Writing Culture*, ed. Clifford and Marcus, pp. 77–97.

23. Louis A. Sass, "Anthropology's Native Problems: Revisionism in the Field," *Harpers* (May 1986), p. 52.

24. The contrast between the museum and the garage sale, of course, resembles that drawn early in this chapter between cultural patterning and cultural borderlands. The former distinction articulates on a geopolitical level what the latter expresses on the plane of social analysis. My claim is that changes in the world have conditioned changes in theory, which in turn shape changes in ethnographic writing, which return to raise new theoretical issues.

READING AND WRITING ABOUT CULTURES ABROAD

1.   Which categories among those offered by Philip L. Pearce or Peter Adler best describe your own experiences (whether close to home or overseas) as a traveler or as a victim of culture shock? Compare your experiences with those of your classmates. If neither Pearce's nor Adler's scheme adequately reflects your experience, how might you modify it or what new categories would you suggest?

2.   Ethnocentrism is the "belief in the superiority of one's own ethnic group" (*American Heritage Dictionary*). What is ethnocentric about Isak Dinesen's view "of natives and history"? How might Chinua Achebe respond to the examples that Dinesen offers of the cultural achievements of Western European civilization?

3.   What does Lawrence Durrell mean by "national character"? Discuss perceptions of Indian, Japanese, Chinese, Canadian, or U.S. national characters revealed in the Brief Encounters by Gary Snyder, Jan Morris, and Margaret Atwood. Which perceptions do you share and which do you disagree with? What do you learn about the "national characters" of the observers themselves—Durrell, Snyder, Morris, and Atwood?

4.   To whom is Nancy Sakamoto addressing her analysis of Western-style and Japanese-style conversations? How accurately do you think her tennis analogy represents typical American conversations? If you are familiar with communication patterns in another cultural tradition, devise your own analogy—based on something other than sports—to compare them with Anglo-American patterns.

5.   Trace the web of causes that Stanley Meisler offers to explain why "outsiders look on the French as the coldest and least welcoming people of Europe" (paragraph 3). Which causes are the most immediate, and which are deeper or more remote? Which result from other causes? Which does Meisler seem to feel are the most important?

6.   How successfully do you think Alice Bloom answers, in the case of Greece, the "only interesting question on a trip . . . —what sustains life elsewhere?" Why does she feel that tourists are "potentially dangerous" (paragraph 7)? To what extent do you agree with Bloom that the Greek peasant woman is "richer" than the blond tourist?

7.   Is Paul Theroux's expatriate Tarzan a fairer or less fair representation of Westerners than Bloom's blond tourist? If you find neither

of these portraits of Westerners to be accurate, explain why and propose an alternative comparison of visitor and visited (like Bloom's) or a different analogy for an expatriate (like Theroux's).

8. In what ways does Michelle Cliff's essay differ—in style, form, and organization—from the kinds of essays you are used to reading and writing? How do these differences affect you? What kinds or levels of prejudice and oppression does Cliff address, and which seem most urgent to her?

9. How seriously do you take Calvin Trillin's comment that he finds his friend "Barton" to be "a pain" for always wanting "to understand everything in its cultural context" (paragraph 5)? To what extent is Trillin guilty of what Margaret Nydell warns about in her essay—portraying Arabs "as excessively wealthy, irrational, sensuous, and violent" (paragraph 8)?

10. To which subset of Westerners is Nydell primarily addressing her explanation of Arab culture—students, social scientists, women, tourists, or business people? How can you tell? Write a brief guide to an American cultural event with which you're familiar—such as a high school athletic competition, college party, musical concert, or baby shower—aimed at a particular subset of the general category "visitors from abroad." (Don't specify the group directly, but reveal its identity through your choice of tone, language, and examples.) Describe how people are expected to behave at this cultural event and explain, as Nydell does for Arab culture, some of the basic beliefs, values, and attitudes that underlie these behaviors.

11. How successfully does Pico Iyer solve the paradox posed by Claude Lévi-Strauss in his Brief Encounter? Is Iyer, like Lévi-Strauss, "the victim of a double infirmity"?

12. Apply Robert Lado's method for comparing cultures in terms of *forms, meanings,* and *distributions* to examples of cross-cultural misunderstanding from the essays by Sakamoto, Meisler, Bloom, Theroux, Cliff, Trillin, Nydell, or Iyer. Divide the essays that you've read from Chapter 5 among partners or groups and try to find examples of each type of misunderstanding Lado presents—"same form, different meanings," "same meaning, different forms," and "same form, same meaning, different distribution."

13. Choose a nonverbal pattern of communication described by Genelle Morain—for example, eye management during conversa-

tion, Giffman's "civil inattention," or Hall's proxemic distances—
and study this behavior in a public place such as a restaurant, Laundromat, or your student union. If possible, observe and compare
people from different ethnic or national groups. Report your
findings to the class.

14. Analyze some aspect of Cliff's experience in terms of what Renato Rosaldo calls "cultural borderlands." How would Rosaldo criticize Nydell's explanation of Arab culture? How would he criticize
Lado's method of comparing cultures?

15. Writing in the social sciences is often accused of being wordy,
vague, abstract, dull, incoherent, or even incomprehensible. To
what extent do you think Lado, Morain, and Rosaldo overcome this
stigma? Discuss how these authors use concrete examples,
metaphors or analogies, and personal anecdotes to stretch what
Rosaldo calls the "narrow norms of composition" (paragraph 44) in
their fields.

16. "Insofar as ignorance makes a space," writes Bloom about her
own stereotyping of the blond tourist and the Greek woman,
"romance rushes in to people it." Discussion of "national character"
doesn't end with the Brief Encounters (see Question 3)—stereotyping or generalizing about other cultures is an ongoing theme in this
chapter. What degree of stereotyping is necessary or inevitable, and
when is it useful or even desirable? At what point does stereotyping
become excessive or lead to prejudice? Address this theme, drawing
on several selections from Chapter 5 as well as your own experience.

MAKING FURTHER CONNECTIONS

1. In her Chapter 1 essay, Cliff discusses her struggles as a writer,
her writing style, and some of the background for her Chapter 5 essay. Compare her self-analysis in Chapter 1 with your own analysis
of her writing.

2. How important do you think the difference is between visiting
another place and actually living there, in terms of your larger understanding of cultural similarities and differences? In your answer
consider both Theroux's expatriate experience (in this chapter and in
his Chapter 3 Brief Encounter) and Gretel Ehrlich's experience (in
Chapter 2) as a kind of "domestic expatriate."

3. Does spending less money during your visit allow you to see
more of a culture, as Bloom suggests? Test Bloom's advice by

studying the relationship between ease of travel and depth of experience or insight in two or more essays from Chapter 2 or Chapter 3. Apply your own travel experience, foreign or domestic, if relevant.

4. Test Durrell's idea that "human beings are expressions of their landscape" in two or more essays from Chapter 2 or Chapter 3. Do the writers you chose detect such a thing as Durrell's "invisible constant" in the places they write about?

5. Follow Lado's directions as you compare a particular aspect of two cultures or subcultures discussed in any of the selections in Chapter 3 or Chapter 4, and then evaluate the results. For example, how would you translate specific features of the Venezuelan upper and lower classes, as described by John Updike in Chapter 3, into Lado's scheme? How useful is this? Or, to what extent does Alexandra Tantranon-Saur transcend Lado's scheme in her analysis of Asian/Pacific communication patterns (Chapter 4)?

6. How would you revise Adler's five-stage theory to apply specifically to "subculture shock" rather than to culture shock in general? You'll need a working definition of "subculture shock," which you might describe in (Adler's) terms of the perceptions, emotional range, and behavior exhibited by members of ethnic, racial, and other minority groups in their encounter with the majority culture. Base your response on one or more essays from Chapter 4, such as those by Joan Didion, Richard Rodriguez, Julia Gilden, James Baldwin, Shelby Steele, and Randall Majors.

7. What justification do you find in Chapter 5 for Edith Folb's identification of the United States "as a conqueror and controller of other people" (Chapter 4, paragraph 19)? What evidence do you find to the contrary?

8. Use Rosaldo's ideas about "border crossings" or "cultural borderlands" to help you analyze the domestic subcultures in one of the Chapter 6 short stories, such as "Thanksgiving Border Crossing" by Arturo Islas, "Railroad Standard Time" by Frank Chin, "Tamurlane" by Bharati Mukherjee, or "Two Deserts" by Valerie Matsumoto.

9. To what extent does the Professor in Paul Bowles's story "A Distant Episode" (Chapter 6) reflect the attitudes and values of Rosaldo's "Lone Ethnographer"? Alternatively, how closely does the narrator in George P. Elliott's story "Among the Dangs"—a fictional anthropologist—resemble Rosaldo's caricature of the classic anthropologist, and how does he differ?

EXPLORING NEW SOURCES

1. Based on Morain's essay in this chapter and Robin Lakoff's examination of gender differences in terms of verbal behavior (Chapter 1), consider ways in which men and women differ in nonverbal behavior. Observe people in different social situations to test your impressions. (You might, if possible, borrow a video camera from your college media center and film your class interacting in small gender-mixed groups.) Consider your observations in the context of sociological studies on the subject.

2. Test Theroux's generalizations about race relations in Africa by examining a specific African nation with a colonial history. Propose a reasonable solution to a current racial issue there.

3. Using Nydell and her sources or Peter Farb (Chapter 1) and his sources as a starting place, investigate how cross-cultural misunderstanding or problems of translation have contributed to some aspect of a recent or continuing conflict in the Middle East, such as the Iranian Revolution of 1979, the Persian Gulf War of 1991, or the Arab-Israeli conflict.

4. Study the harmful effects and the beneficial aspects of Western tourism in a particular country you're interested in or have visited.

5. Read two or more books by either Paul Theroux, Michelle Cliff, or Calvin Trillin, focusing on either nonfiction or fiction and poetry, then discuss a significant thematic, formal, or stylistic aspect of the author's work. Consult secondary sources, such as literary criticism and book reviews, to test your ideas.

6. Pursue Rosaldo's argument for a rethinking of social analysis by focusing on a current debate about methodology or writing in a particular field such as anthropology, linguistics, or psychology.

6

THE IMAGINARY TRAVELER: A STRANGER COMES TO TOWN

It's been said that there are only two plots in fiction: Someone takes a journey, or, a stranger comes to town. These are, of course, really the same plot from two different perspectives. Although most of us can think of exceptions from the books we've read or the movies we've seen, the generalization proves useful for revealing the close bond between fiction in general and cultural interaction. The stories in Chapter 6 all conform to this basic plot line.

The journey, whether seen from the viewpoint of the traveler or of the people whom the traveler meets, may be our most natural plot. For most of human history—the eons before the development of agriculture—people were nomadic, moving from place to place with the seasons and available food supplies. Identification with the group was not only important psychologically but also essential to survival; banishment from the group constituted the worst punishment for an individual. Strangers could be dangerous. "To guard against the baneful influence exerted voluntarily or involuntarily by strangers," writes Scottish anthropologist James George Frazer in *The Golden Bough,*

> is therefore an elementary dictate of savage prudence. Hence before strangers are allowed to enter a district, or at least before they are permitted to mingle freely with the inhabitants, certain ceremonies are often performed by the natives of the country for the purpose of disarming them of their magical powers, of counteracting the baneful influence which is believed to emanate from them, or of disinfecting . . . the tainted atmosphere by which they are supposed to be surrounded.[1]

---

[1] *The New Golden Bough,* ed. by Theodor H. Gaster (New York: Criterion Books, 1959), Part II, section 160. Frazer's unabridged *Golden Bough,* which eventually ran to twelve volumes, was first published in 1890.

Sometimes, according to Frazer, the fear is so overpowering that strangers are not received at all. And the fear is mutual, so that the traveler "entering a strange land . . . takes steps to guard against the demons that haunt it and the magical arts of its inhabitants."[2] In some cultures, continues Frazer, travelers must purify themselves from the evil influence of strangers when they return home.

We need not look far to see that, in many cultural traditions, strangers can also have a positive influence or bring good news. The best news of all for Buddhists, Christians, and Moslems—for a majority of the world's population—was brought by "strangers" named Buddha, Jesus, and Mohammed. In many of the oldest stories we know, preserved in myths and fairy tales, the heroes and heroines are travelers. The underground or "night journey" motif in Western literature—in which the protagonist symbolically encounters the darker side of human nature—goes back at least as far as the ancient Egyptians, who were influenced by the older civilizations of Africa and the Middle East. In Greek mythology, heroes such as Perseus and Odysseus must complete arduous journeys (often encountering strange cultures) to achieve greater glory or merit—a pattern repeated over the centuries in works ranging from Dante's *Divine Comedy* to Mark Twain's *Huckleberry Finn* to George Lucas' *Star Wars* movies.

Our modern interest in cultural studies and cross-cultural communication gives a special resonance to this vintage story plot. In Chapter 6, when someone takes a journey or a stranger comes to town, that person crosses cultural boundaries as well. In the Brief Encounters, Sandra Cisneros's Esperanza, the new kid in town, juggles two cultures in meditating upon her name, and Toni Morrison tells how the black section of another town got its name from "a nigger joke." Jack Kerouac's young cross-country travelers encounter the sights, sounds, and smells of Mississippi Gulf culture with infectious enthusiasm. Krishnan Varma's narrator and his wife argue over a unique traveling solution to Calcutta's housing shortage, and Chitra Divakaruni's visiting couple struggle to see beyond the usual tourist spots of Rome. Amira Nowaira offers a Third-World's-eye view of the stranger bearing gifts from the United States, and Italo Calvino describes an imaginary city where strangers meet to exchange the gifts of their memories.

As in previous chapters, the main selections are all by American authors or authors who have settled in the United States and, with the exception of one novel excerpt, are all complete short stories. They follow the same general movement as the Brief Encounters, from domestic to international to imaginary cultural encounters.

Many themes introduced in earlier chapters get their fullest expression in these short stories:

- In Arturo Islas's "Thanksgiving Border Crossing" (from the novel *Migrant Souls*), a Mexican American family makes a comical smuggling run across the border that reveals their struggle to adjust to two cultures.

- In Frank Chin's "Railroad Standard Time," the narrator drives down Interstate 5, reflecting in highway-speed prose on his youth and Chinatown heritage.

- In Bharati Mukherjee's "Tamurlane," illegal immigrants from India are working in a Toronto restaurant when the Mounties come to "get their man."

- In Louise Erdrich's "American Horse," a welfare worker and police officers come to "salvage" a Native American boy from his alcoholic mother and crazy uncle.

- In David Leavitt's "Territory," a young gay man brings his lover home to meet his mother.

- In Valerie Matsumoto's "Two Deserts," a Japanese American woman and her daughter must deal with an obnoxious, retired neighbor man who wants more than just casual conversation.

- In Grace Paley's "The Long-Distance Runner," a middle-aged Jewish woman decides to visit her childhood home, now inhabited by a black family, and ends up staying much longer than she expected.

- In Paul Bowles's "A Distant Episode," a French linguist comes to North Africa to study the local language but gets a good deal more than he bargained for when he meets up with nomads from the Sahara Desert.

- In George P. Elliott's "Among the Dangs," a black American anthropologist has trouble keeping his identity separate from the subjects of his fieldwork, members of a preindustrial South American tribe.

- In Joanna Russ's "When It Changed," men from Earth mount an expedition to the planet Whileaway, where a plague had wiped out the male population six hundred years before and an all-female culture has evolved.

- In Ursula K. Le Guin's "The Ones Who Walk Away from Omelas," residents live in a joyous utopia "like a city in a fairy tale," untroubled except by the one dark secret they harbor "in a basement under one of the beautiful public buildings."

If you read these stories in conjunction with the essays from previous chapters, you will have many authors' autobiographical experiences with which to compare them and numerous intellectual frameworks with which to analyze them. You can also ask yourself how the form of fiction itself—the telling of a story—shapes and changes the message you receive about cultural encounters. The most apparent difference between fiction and nonfiction lies in the degree of explicitness about what the author wishes to say: a story's "ideas" are dramatized—made concrete in the form of characters and action—not stated directly or abstractly. But be careful when you make such comparisons, because a fully developed work of fiction may contain complexities too rich to easily reduce to a simple thesis or argument. So also read these stories as themselves, as complete self-created worlds, as worlds that may move you or persuade you, enlighten you or enrage you, but mainly as worlds that take you somewhere you haven't been before.

BRIEF ENCOUNTERS

My Name

SANDRA CISNEROS

In English my name means hope. In Spanish it means too many letters. It means sadness, it means waiting. It is like the number nine. A muddy color. It is the Mexican records my father plays on Sunday mornings when he is shaving, songs like sobbing.

It was my great-grandmother's name and now it is mine. She was a horse woman too, born like me in the Chinese year of the horse—which is supposed to be bad luck if you're born female—but I think this is a Chinese lie because the Chinese, like the Mexicans, don't like their women strong.

My great-grandmother. I would've liked to have known her, a wild horse of a woman, so wild she wouldn't marry until my great-grandfather threw a sack over her head and carried her off. Just like that, as if she were a fancy chandelier. That's the way he did it.

And the story goes she never forgave him. She looked out the window all her life, the way so many women sit their sadness on an elbow. I wonder if she made the best with what she got or was she sorry because she couldn't be all the things she wanted to be. Esperanza. I have inherited her name, but I don't want to inherit her place by the window.

At school they say my name funny as if the syllables were made out of tin and hurt the roof of your mouth. But in Spanish my name is made out of a softer something, like silver, not quite as thick as sister's name Magdalena which is uglier than mine. Magdalena who at least can come home and become Nenny. But I am always Esperanza.

I would like to baptize myself under a new name, a name more like the real me, the one nobody sees. Esperanza as Lisandra or Maritza or Zeze the X. Yes. Something like Zeze the X will do.

—FROM *THE HOUSE ON MANGO STREET*, 1984

The Bottom

TONI MORRISON

A joke. A nigger joke. That was the way it got started. Not the town, of course, but that part of town where the Negroes lived, the part they called the Bottom in spite of the fact that it was up in the hills. Just a nigger joke. The kind white folks tell when the mill closes down and they're looking for a little comfort somewhere. The kind colored folks tell on themselves when the rain doesn't come, or comes for weeks, and they're looking for a little comfort somehow.

A good white farmer promised freedom and a piece of bottom land to his slave if he would perform some very difficult chores. When the slave completed the work, he asked the farmer to keep his end of the bargain. Freedom was easy—the farmer had no objection to that. But he didn't want to give up any land. So he told the slave that he was very sorry that he had to give him valley land. He had hoped to give him a piece of the Bottom. The slave blinked and said he thought valley land was bottom land. The master said, "Oh, no! See those hills? That's bottom land, rich and fertile."

"But it's high up in the hills," said the slave.

"High up from us," said the master, "but when God looks down, it's the bottom. That's why we call it so. It's the bottom of heaven—best land there is."

So the slave pressed his master to try to get him some. He preferred it to the valley. And it was done. The nigger got the hilly land, where planting was backbreaking, where the soil slid down and washed away the seeds, and where the wind lingered all through the winter.

Which accounted for the fact that white people lived on the rich valley floor in that little river town in Ohio, and the blacks populated the hills above it, taking small consolation in the fact that every day they could literally look down on the white folks.

—FROM *SULA*, 1973

Crossing the Mississippi

JACK KEROUAC

We were suddenly driving along the blue waters of the Gulf, and at the same time a momentous mad thing began on the radio; it was the Chicken Jazz'n Gumbo disk-jockey show from New Orleans, all mad jazz records, colored records, with the disk jockey saying,

"Don't wory 'bout *nothing!*" We saw New Orleans in the night ahead of us with joy. Dean rubbed his hands over the wheel. "Now we're going to get our kicks!" At dusk we were coming into the humming streets of New Orleans. "Oh, smell the people!" yelled Dean with his face out the window, sniffing. "Ah! God! Life!" He swung around a trolley. "Yes!" He darted the car and looked in every direction for girls. "Look at *her!*" The air was so sweet in New Orleans it seemed to come in soft bandannas; and you could smell the river and really smell the people, and mud, and molasses, and every kind of tropical exhalation with your nose suddenly removed from the dry ices of a Northern winter. We bounced in our seats. "And dig her!" yelled Dean, pointing at another woman. "Oh, I love, love, love women! I think women are wonderful! I love women!" He spat out the window; he groaned; he clutched his head. Great beads of sweat fell from his forehead from pure excitement and exhaustion.

We bounced the car up on the Algiers ferry and found ourselves crossing the Mississippi River by boat. "Now we must all get out and dig the river and the people and smell the world," said Dean, bustling with his sunglasses and cigarettes and leaping out of the car like a jack-in-the-box. We followed. On rails we leaned and looked at the great brown father of waters rolling down from mid-America like the torrent of broken souls—bearing Montana logs and Dakota muds and Iowa vales and things that had drowned in Three Forks, where the secret began in ice. Smoky New Orleans receded on one side; old, sleepy Algiers with its warped woodsides bumped us on the other. Negroes were working in the hot afternoon, stoking the ferry furnaces that burned red and made our tires smell. Dean dug them, hopping up and down in the heat. He rushed around the deck and upstairs with his baggy pants hanging halfway down his belly. Suddenly I saw him eagering on the flying bridge. I expected him to take off on wings. I heard his mad laugh all over the boat— "Hee-hee-hee-hee-hee!" Marylou was with him. He covered everything in a jiffy, came back with the full story, jumped in the car just as everybody was tooting to go, and we slipped off, passing two or three cars in a narrow space, and found ourselves darting through Algiers.

"Where? Where?" Dean was yelling.

—FROM *ON THE ROAD*, 1955

Calcutta Freight Wagon

KRISHNAN VARMA

Later in the day Swapna and I moved into an abandoned-looking freight wagon at the railway terminus. A whole wagon to ourselves—a place with doors which could be opened and shut—we did nothing but open and shut them for a full hour—all the privacy a man and wife could want—no fear of waking up with a complete stranger in your arms . . . it was heaven. I felt I was God.

Then one night we woke to find that the world was running away from us: we had been coupled to a freight train. There was nothing for it but to wait for the train to stop. When it did, miles from Calcutta, we got off, took a passenger train back, and occupied another unwanted-looking wagon. That was not the only time we went to bed in Calcutta and woke up in another place. I found it an intensely thrilling experience, but not Swapna.

She wanted a a stationary home; she insisted on it. But she would not say why. If I persisted in questioning her she snivelled. If I tried to persuade her to change her mind, pointing out all the advantages of living in a wagon—four walls, a roof and door absolutely free of charge, and complete freedom to make love day or night—she still snivelled. If I ignored her nagging, meals got delayed, the rice undercooked, the curry over-salted. In the end I gave in. We would move, I said, even if we had to occupy a house by force, but couldn't she tell me the reason, however irrelevant, why she did not like the wagon?

For the first time in weeks Swapna smiled, a very vague smile. Then, slowly, she drew the edge of her sari over her head, cast her eyes down, turned her face from me, and said in a tremulous, barely audible whisper that she (short pause) did (long pause) not want (very long pause) her (at jet speed) baby-to-be-born-in-a-running-train. And she buried her face in her hands. Our fourth child. One died of diphtheria back home (no longer our home) in Dacca; two, from fatigue, on our long trek on foot to Calcutta. Would the baby be a boy? I felt no doubt about it; it would be. Someone to look after us in our old age, to do our funeral rites when we died. I suddenly kissed Swapna, since her face was hidden in her hands, on her elbow, and was roundly chided. Kissing, she holds, is a western practice, unclean also, since it amounts to licking, and should be eschewed by all good Hindus.

—FROM "THE GRASS-EATERS," IN *WASCANA REVIEW*, 1985

Tourists

CHITRA DIVAKARUNI

The heat is like a fist between the eyes. The man and woman wander down a narrow street of flies and stray cats looking for the Caracalla Baths. The woman wears a cotton dress embroidered Mexican style with bright flowers. The man wears Rayban glasses and knee-length shorts. They wipe at the sweat with white handkerchiefs because they have used up all the Kleenex they brought.

The woman is afraid they are lost. She holds on tightly to the man's elbow and presses her purse into her body. The purse is red leather, very new, bought by him outside the Uffizi museum after a half-hour of earnest bargaining. She wonders what they are doing in this airless alley with the odor of stale urine rising all around them, what they are doing in Rome, what they are doing in Europe. The man tries to walk tall and confident, shoulders lifted, but she can tell he is nervous about the youths in tight levis lounging against the fountain, eyeing, he thinks, their Leica. In his halting guidebook Italian he asks the passers-by—there aren't many because of the heat—*Dov'e terme di Caracalla?*[1] and then, *Dov'e la stazione?*[2] But they stare at him and do not seem to understand.

The woman is tired. It distresses her to not know where she is, to have to trust herself to the truth of strangers, their indecipherable mouths, their quick eyes, their fingers each pointing in a different direction, *eccolo, il treno per Milano, la torre pendente, la cattedrale, il palazzo ducale.*[3] She wants to go to the bathroom, to get a drink, to find a taxi. She asks if it is O.K. to wash her face in the fountain, but he shakes his head. It's not hygienic, and besides, a man with a pock-marked face and black teeth has been watching them from a doorway, and he wants to get out of the alley as soon as he can.

The woman sighs, gets out a crumpled tour brochure from her purse and fans herself and then him with it. They are walking faster now, she stumbling a bit in her sandals. She wishes they were back in the hotel or better still in her own cool garden. She is sure that in her absence the Niles Lilies are dying in spite of the automatic sprinkler system, and the gophers have taken over the lawn. Is it worth it, even for the colors in the Sistine Chapel, the curve of Venus' throat as she rises from the sea? The green statue of the boy with the

---

[1] *Dov'e terme di Caracalla?*: Where are the Caracalla [Roman] Baths? (Ed.)
[2] *Dov'e la stazione?*: Where's the subway station? (Ed.)
[3] *Eccolo, il treno per Milano, la torre pendente, la cattedrale, il palazzo ducale:* Here it is, the train to Milan, the Leaning Tower, the cathedral, the duke's palace. (Ed.)

goose among the rosemary in a Pompeii courtyard? She makes a mental note to pick up some gopher poison on the way back from the airport.

They turn a corner onto a broader street. Surely this is the one that will lead them back to the Circo Massimo and the subway. The man lets out a deep breath, starts to smile. Then suddenly, footsteps, a quick clattering on the cobbles behind. They both stiffen, remembering. Yesterday one of the tourists in their hotel was mugged outside the Villa Borghesi. Maybe they should have taken the bus tour after all. He tightens his hands into fists, his face into a scowl. Turns. But it is only a dog, its pink tongue hanging, its ribs sticking out of its scabby coat. It stops and observes them, wary, ready for flight. Then the woman touches his hand. *Look, look.* From where they are standing they can see into someone's backyard. Sheets and pillowcases drying whitely in the sun, a palm scattering shade over blocks of marble from a broken column, a big bougainvillea that covers the crumbling wall. A breeze comes up, lifting their hair. Sudden smell of rain. They stand there, man and woman and dog, watching the bright purple flowers tumble over the broken bricks.

—FROM *THE HOUSE ON VIA GOMBITO: WRITING BY NORTH AMERICAN WOMEN ABROAD*, 1991

American Foreign Aid

AMIRA NOWAIRA

Mr. Rokowski, with clothes studiedly casual, gives me a Jimmy Carter smile especially packaged for export. "Please call me Bill. But before we go on to business I would like to explain why I am here and what I am hoping to achieve." He speaks in Special English, or maybe in E.M.R.—English for the Mentally Retarded—a variety of English which he must have had to master before being sent to exotic lands. "I am here as part of a team of experts on education to help the Ministry in conceptualizing a framework within which the educational task in Egypt may be facilitated and improved."

Hello, America.

"What we are hoping to achieve is to construct a conceptually unified system of education that would take into account the needs of students—educational, moral, aesthetic, etcetera—and would respond to the changes that have taken place over the past few years."

Villages with no fresh water but with bottles of Coca-Cola.

"We will be concentrating a good deal of our attention on rural areas since these have traditionally been deprived, I believe, of their rightful share of interest. And the answer we came up with is this:

MUSIC. Our preliminary investigation into the matter showed that a good deal of the failure of the educational system in Egyptian rural areas, and to a lesser extent in urban areas, is a direct result of the unbelievable neglect of such a field of human achievement as music. Music is not only capable of enhancing the quality of life but it is also capable of improving the sense of harmony and mathematical precision which are absolutely essential for the development of the new Egyptian village."

A vision of peasant pupils running barefoot near a stagnant canal to the tune of Beethoven thrills my heart.

"Of course we are conscious of the fact that Western music may be culturally alien to pupils, and we are far from trying to impose it on them. What we will teach them is Egyptian music. We will start off by giving them a good grounding in classical Egyptian music and then will go on to Romantic Egyptian music and from there to modern music, folklore, pop, etcetera. Pupils can then have the option of studying comparative music, which will give them a chance to see their own cultural heritage in relation to other cultures."

—FROM "LOST AND FOUND," IN *EGYPTIAN TALES AND SHORT STORIES OF THE 1970S AND 1980S*, 1987

Trading Cities 1

ITALO CALVINO

Proceeding eighty miles into the northwest wind, you reach the city of Euphemia, where the merchants of seven nations gather at every solstice and equinox. The boat that lands there with a cargo of ginger and cotton will set sail again, its hold filled with pistachio nuts and poppy seeds, and the caravan that has just unloaded sacks of nutmegs and raisins is already cramming its saddlebags with bolts of golden muslin for the return journey. But what drives men to travel up rivers and cross deserts to come here is not only the exchange of wares, which you could find, everywhere the same, in all the bazaars inside and outside the Great Khan's empire, scattered at your feet on the same yellow mats, in the shade of the same awnings protecting them from the flies, offered with the same lying reduction in prices. You do not come to Euphemia only to buy and sell, but also because at night, by the fires all around the market, seated on sacks or barrels or stretched out on piles of carpets, at each word that one man says—such as "wolf," "sister," "hidden treasure," "battle," "scabies," "lovers"—the others tell, each one, his tale of wolves, sisters, treasures, scabies, lovers, battles. And you know that in the long journey ahead of you, when to keep awake against the camel's swaying or the junk's rocking, you start summoning up your memories one by one, your wolf will have become another wolf, your sister a different sister, your battle other battles, on your return from Euphemia, the city where memory is traded at every solstice and at every equinox.

—FROM *INVISIBLE CITIES,* 1972; TRANS. 1974

Thanksgiving Border Crossing

ARTURO ISLAS

For Thanksgiving in 1947, Eduviges, in a fit of guilt, decided to bake 1
a turkey with all the trimmings. She had memorized the recipes in
the glossy American magazines while waiting her turn at the Safe-
way checkout counter.

Because the girls were in public school and learning about North 2
American holidays and customs, Eduviges thought her plan would
please them. It did and even Josie allowed her mother to embrace
her in that quick, embarrassed way she had of touching them. As
usual, Sancho had no idea why she was going to such lengths
preparing for a ritual that meant nothing to him.

"I don't see why we can't have the enchiladas you always 3
make," he said. "I don't even like turkey. Why don't you let me
bring you a nice, fat pheasant from the Chihuahua mountains? At
least it'll taste like something. Eating turkey is going to turn my girls
into little *gringas.* Is that what you want?"

"Oh, Daddy, please! Everybody else is going to have turkey." 4
The girls, wearing colored paper headdresses they had made in art
class, were acting out the Pocahontas story and reciting from
"Hiawatha" in a hodgepodge of Indian sentiment that forced Sancho
to agree in order to keep them quiet.

"All right, all right," he said. "Just stop all the racket, please. 5
And Serena, *querida,* don't wear that stuff outside the house or
they'll pick you up and send you to a reservation. That would be
okay with me, but your mother wouldn't like it."

Serena and Josie gave each other knowing glances. "They" were 6
the *migra,* who drove around in their green vans, sneaked up on innocent dark-skinned people, and deported them. Their neighbor
down the block—Benito Cruz, who was lighter-skinned than Serena
and did not look at all like an Indian—had been picked up three
times already, detained at the border for hours, and then released
with the warning that he was to carry his identification papers at all
times. That he was an American citizen did not seem to matter to
the immigration officers.

Arturo Islas (1938–1991), from El Paso, Texas, was professor of English at Stanford University and author of the novels *The Rain God*
(1984) and *Migrant Souls* (1990). "Thanksgiving Border Crossing" is
from *Migrant Souls.*

The Angel children were brought up on as many deportation 7
stories as fairy tales and family legends. The latest border incident
had been the discovery of twenty-one young Mexican males who
had been left to asphyxiate in an airtight boxcar on their way to pick
cotton in the lower Rio Grande Valley.

When they read the newspaper articles about how the men 8
died, both Josie and Serena thought of the fluttering noises made by
the pigeons their mother first strangled and then put under a heavy
cardboard box for minutes that seemed eternal to the girls. They
covered their ears to protect their souls from the thumping and
scratching noises of the doomed birds.

Even their mother had shown sympathy for the Mexican youths, 9
especially when it was learned that they were not from the poorest
class. "I feel very bad for their families," she said. "Their mothers
must be in agony."

What about their fathers? Josie felt like asking but did not. Be- 10
cause of the horror she imagined they went through, Josie did not
want to turn her own feelings for the young men into yet another
argument with her mother about "wetbacks" or about who did and
did not "deserve" to be in the United States.

In the first semester of seventh grade, Josie had begun to won- 11
der why being make-believe North American Indians seemed to be
all right with their mother. "Maybe it was because those Indians
spoke English," Josie said to Serena. Mexican Indians were too close
to home and the truth, and the way Eduviges looked at Serena in
her art class getup convinced Josie she was on the right track.

That year on the Saturday before Thanksgiving, their mother 12
and father took them across the river in search of the perfect turkey.
Sancho borrowed his friend Tacho Morales' pickup and they drove
down the valley to the Zaragoza crossing. It was closer to the ranch
where Eduviges had been told the turkeys were raised and sold for
practically nothing. Josie and Serena sat in the front seat of the
pickup with their father. Eduviges and Ofelia followed them in the
Chevy in case anything went wrong.

Sancho was a slower, more patient driver than their mother, 13
who turned into a speed demon with a sharp tongue behind the
wheel. More refined than her younger sisters, Ofelia was scandalized by every phrase that came out of Eduviges' mouth when some
sorry driver from Chihuahua or New Mexico got in her way.

"Why don't they teach those imbecilic cretins how to drive?" she 14
said loudly in Spanish, window down and honking. Or, "May all
your teeth fall out but one and may that ache until the day you die"
to the man who pulled out in front of her without a signal.

Grateful that her mother was being good for once and following 15 slowly and at a safe distance behind the pickup, Ofelia dozed, barely aware of the clear day so warm for November. Only the bright yellow leaves of the cottonwood trees reminded her that it was autumn. They clung to the branches and vibrated in the breeze, which smelled of burning mesquite and Mexican alders. As they followed her father away from the mountains and into the valley, Ofelia began to dream they were inside one of Mama Chona's Mexican blue clay bowls, suspended in midair while the sky revolved around them.

To Josie and Serena, it seemed their father was taking forever to 16 get to where they were going. "Are we there yet?" they asked him until he told them that if they asked again, he would leave them in the middle of nowhere and not let their mother rescue them. The threat only made them laugh more and they started asking him where the middle of nowhere was until he, too, laughed with them.

"The middle of nowhere, smart alecks, is at the bottom of the 17 sea and so deep not even the fish go there," Sancho said, getting serious about it.

"No, no," Serena said. "It's in the space between two stars and 18 no planets around."

"I already said the middle of nowhere is in Del Sapo, Texas," 19 Josie said, not wanting to get serious.

"I know, I know. It's in the Sahara Desert where not even the 20 tumbleweeds will grow," their father said.

"No, Daddy. It's at the top of Mount Everest." Serena was 21 proud of the B she had gotten for her report on the highest mountain in the world. They fell silent and waited for Josie to take her turn.

"It's here," Josie said quietly and pointed to her heart. 22

"Oh, for heaven's sake, Josie, don't be so dramatic. You don't 23 even know what you are saying," Serena said. Their father changed the subject.

When they arrived at the ranch, he told Eduviges and the girls 24 that the worst that could happen on their return was that the turkey would be taken away from them. But the girls, especially, must do and say exactly as he instructed them.

Their mother was not satisfied with Sancho's simple directions 25 and once again told them about the humiliating body search her friend from New Mexico, *la señora* Moulton, had been subjected to at the Santa Fe Street bridge. She had just treated her daughter Ethel and her granddaughters, Amy and Mary Ann, to lunch at the old Central Cafe in Juarez. When *la señora* had been asked her citizenship, she had replied in a jovial way, "Well, what do I look like, sir?"

They made her get out of the car, led her to a special examining 26 cell, ordered her to undress, and made her suffer unspeakable mortifications while her relatives waited at least four hours in terror, wondering if they would ever see her again or be allowed to return to the country of their birth. Then, right on cue, Josie and Serena said along with Eduviges, "And they were Anglos and blond!"

While their parents were bargaining for the bird, the girls looked 27 with awe upon the hundreds of adult turkeys kept inside four large corrals. As they walked by each enclosure, one of the birds gobbled and the rest echoed its call until the racket was unbearable. Serena was struck by an attack of giggles.

"They sure are stupid," Josie said in Spanish to their Mexican 28 guide.

"They really are," he said with a smile. "When it rains, we have 29 to cover the coops of the younger ones so they won't drown." He was a dark red color and very shy. Josie liked him instantly.

"How can they drown?" Serena asked him. "The river is 30 nowhere near here. Does it flood?"

"No," the young man said, looking away from them. "Not from 31 the Rio Bravo. From the rain itself. They stretch their necks, open their beaks wide, and let it pour in until they drown. They keel over all bloated. That's how stupid they are." He bent his head back and showed them as they walked by an enclosure. "Gobble, gobble," the guide called and the turkeys answered hysterically.

Josie and Serena laughed all the way back to the pickup. Ofelia 32 had not been allowed to join them because of the way their mother thought the guide was looking at her. She was dreaming away in the backseat of the Chevy while their father struggled to get the newly bought and nervous turkey into a slatted crate. Eduviges was criticizing every move he made. At last, the creature was in the box and eerily silent.

"Now remember, girls," Sancho said, wiping his face, "I'll do all 33 the talking at the bridge. You just say 'American' when the time comes. Not another word, you hear? Think about Mrs. Moulton, Josie." He gave her a wink.

The turkey remained frozen inside the crate. Sancho lifted it 34 onto the pickup, covered it with a yellow plastic tablecloth they used on picnics, and told Serena to sit on top of it with her back against the rear window.

"Serena," he said, "I'd hate to lose you because of this stupid 35 bird, but if you open your mouth except to say 'American,' I won't be responsible for what happens. Okay?" He kissed her on the cheek as if in farewell forever, Josie thought, looking at them from the front seat. She was beginning to wish they had not begged so successfully for a traditional North American ceremony. Nothing would happen to Ofelia, of course. She was protected in their mother's car and nowhere near the turkey. Josie felt that Serena was in great peril and made up her mind to do anything to keep her from harm.

On the way to the bridge, Josie made the mistake of asking her 36 father if they were aliens. Sancho put his foot on the brake so hard that Eduviges almost rear-ended the truck. He looked at Josie very hard and said, "I do not ever want to hear you use that word in my presence again. About anybody. We are not aliens. We are American citizens of Mexican heritage. We are proud of both countries and have never and will never be that word you just said to me."

"Well," Josie said. Sancho knew she was not afraid of him. He 37 pulled the truck away from the shoulder and signaled for his wife to continue following them. "That's what they call Mexican people in all the newspapers. And Kathy Jarvis at school told me real snotty at recess yesterday that we were nothing but a bunch of resident aliens."

After making sure Eduviges was right behind them, Sancho said 38 in a calmer, serious tone, "Josie, I'm warning you. I do not want to hear those words again. Do you understand me?"

"I'm only telling you what Kathy told me. What did she mean? 39 Is she right?"

"Kathy Jarvis is an ignorant little brat. The next time she tells 40 you that, you tell her that Mexican and Indian people were in this part of the country long before any *gringos*, Europeans (he said 'Yur-rupbeans') or anyone else decided it was theirs. That should shut her up. If it doesn't, tell her those words are used by people who think Mexicans are not human beings. That goes for the newspapers, too. They don't think anyone is human." She watched him look straight ahead, then in the rearview mirror, then at her as he spoke.

"Don't you see, Josie. When people call Mexicans those words, 41 it makes it easier for them to deport or kill them. Aliens come from outer space." He paused. "Sort of like your mother's family, the blessed Angels, who think they come from heaven. Don't tell her I said that."

Before he made that last comment, Josie was impressed by her 42 father's tone. Sancho seldom became that passionate in their presence about any issue. He laughed at the serious and the pompous and especially at religious fanatics.

During their aunt Jesus Maria's visits, the girls and their cousins 43 were sent out of the house in the summer or to the farthest room away from the kitchen in the winter so that they would not be able to hear her and Sancho arguing about God and the Church. Unnoticed, the children sneaked around the house and crouched in the honeysuckle under the kitchen window, wide open to the heat of July. In horror and amusement, they listened to Jesus Maria tell Sancho that he would burn in hell for all eternity because he did not believe in an afterlife and dared to criticize the infallibility of the Pope.

"It's because they're afraid of dying that people make up an afterlife to believe in," Sancho said. 44

"That's not true. God created Heaven, Hell, and Purgatory before He created man. And you are going to end up in Hell if you don't start believing what the Church teaches us." Jesus Maria was in her glory defending the teachings of Roman Catholicism purged by the fires of the Spanish Inquisition. 45

"Oh, Jessie—" he began. 46

"Don't call me that. My name is Jesus Maria and I am proud of it." She knew the children were listening. 47

"Excuse me, Jesus Maria," he said with a flourish. "I just want to point out to you that it's hotter here in Del Sapo right now than in hell." He saw her bristle but went on anyway. "Haven't you figured it out yet? This is hell and heaven and purgatory right here. How much worse, better, or boring can the afterlife be?" Sancho was laughing at his own insight. 48

"If you are going to start joking about life-and-death matters, I simply won't talk about anything serious with you again," their aunt said. They knew she meant it. "I, like the Pope, am fighting for your everlasting soul, Sancho. If I did not love you because you are my sister's husband, I would not be telling you these things." 49

"Thank you, Jessie. I appreciate your efforts and love. But the pope is only a man. He is not Christ. Don't you read history? All most popes have cared about is money and keeping the poor in rags so that they can mince about in gold lamé dresses." 50

"Apostate!" their aunt cried. 51

"What's that?" Serena whispered to Josie. 52

"I don't know but it sounds terrible. We'll look it up in the dictionary as soon as they stop." They knew the arguing was almost over when their aunt began calling their father names. Overwhelmed by the smell of the honeysuckle, the children ran off to play kick the can. Later, when Josie looked up the word "apostate," she kept its meaning to herself because she knew that Serena believed in an afterlife and would be afraid for her father. 53

That one word affected her father more than another was a mystery to Josie. She loved words and believed them to be more real 54 than whatever they described. In her mind, she, too, suspected that she was an apostate but, like her father, she did not want to be an alien.

"All right, Daddy. I promise I won't say that word again. And I 55 won't tell Mother what you said about the Angels."

They were now driving through the main streets of Juarez, and 56 Sancho was fighting to stay in his lane. "God, these Mexicans drive like your mother," he said with affection.

At every intersection, young Indian women with babies at their 57 breast stretched out their hands. Josie was filled with dread and pity. One of the women knocked on her window while they waited for the light to change. She held up her baby and said, "*Señorita, por favor. Dinero para el niño.*"[1] Her hair was black and shiny and her eyes as dark as Josie's. The words came through the glass in a muted, dreamlike way. Silent and unblinking, the infant stared at Josie. She had a quarter in her pocket.

"Don't roll down the window or your mother will have a fit," 58 Sancho said. He turned the corner and headed toward the river. The woman and child disappeared. Behind them, Eduviges kept honking almost all the way to the bridge.

"I think it was blind," Josie said. Her father did not answer and 59 looked straight ahead.

The traffic leading to the declaration points was backed up sev- 60 eral blocks, and the stop-and-go movement as they inched their way to the American side was more than Josie could bear. She kept looking back at Serena, who sat like a *Virgen de Guadalupe* statue on her yellow plastic-covered throne.

Knowing her sister, Josie was certain that Serena was going to 61 free the turkey, jump out of the truck with it, gather up the beggarly women and children, and disappear forever into the sidestreets and alleys of Juarez. They drove past an old Indian woman, her long braids silver gray in the sun, begging in front of Curley's Club. And that is how Josie imagined Serena years from that day—an ancient and withered creature, bare feet crusted with clay, too old to recognize her little sister. The vision made her believe that the middle of nowhere was exactly where she felt it was. She covered her chest with her arms.

"What's the matter? Don't tell me you're going to be sick," her 62 father said.

---

[1] *Señorita, por favor. Dinero para el niño:* Please, miss. Money for the child. (Ed.)

"No. I'm fine. Can't you hurry?"   63

Seeing the fear in her face, Sancho told her gently that he had   64
not yet figured out how to drive through cars without banging them
up. Josie smiled and kept her hands over her heart.

When they approached the border patrolman's station, the   65
turkey began gobbling away. "Oh, no," Josie cried and shut her
eyes in terror for her sister.

"Oh, shit," her father said. "I hate this goddamned bridge." At   66
that moment, the officer stuck his head into the pickup and asked
for their citizenship.

"American," said Sancho.   67

"American," said Josie.   68

"Anything to declare? Any liquor or food?" he asked in an ac-   69
cusing way. While Sancho was assuring him that there was nothing
to declare, the turkey gobbled again in a long stream of high-pitched
gurgles that sent shivers up and down Josie's spine. She vowed to
go into the cell with Serena when the search was ordered.

"What's that noise?" the patrolman wanted to know. Sancho   70
shrugged and gave Josie and then the officer a look filled with the
ignorance of the world.

Behind them, Serena began gobbling along with the bird and it   71
was hard for them to tell one gobble from another. Their mother
pressed down on the horn of the Chevy and made it stick. Eduviges
was ready to jump out of the car and save her daughter from a fate
worse than death. In the middle of the racket, the officer's frown
was turning into anger and he started yelling at Serena.

"American!" she yelled back and gobbled.   72

"What have you got there?" The officer pointed to the plastic-   73
covered crate.

"It's a turkey," Serena shouted. "It's American, too." She kept   74
gobbling along with the noise of the horn. Other drivers had begun
honking with impatience.

The patrolman looked at her and yelled, "Sure it is! Don't   75
move," he shouted toward Sancho.

Eduviges had opened the hood and was pretending not to know   76
what to do. Rushing toward the officer, she grabbed him by the
sleeve and pulled him away from the pickup. Confused by the din,
he made gestures that Sancho took as permission to drive away.
"Relax, señora. Please let go of my arm."

In the truck, Sancho was laughing like a maniac and wiping the   77
tears and his nose on his sleeve. "Look at that, Josie. The guy is
twice as big as your mother."

She was too scared to laugh and did not want to look. Several   78
blocks into South Del Sapo, she was still trembling. Serena kept on

gobbling in case they were being followed by the *migra* in unmarked cars.

Fifteen minutes later, Eduviges and Ofelia caught up with them 79 on Alameda Street. Sancho signaled his wife to follow him into the vacant lot next to Don Luis Leal's Famous Tex-Mex Diner. They left the turkey unattended and silent once more.

"Dumb bird," Sancho said. With great ceremony, he treated 80 them to *menudo* and *gorditas*[2] washed down with as much Coca-Cola as they could drink.

---

[2] *menudo:* hominy and tripe soup; *gordita:* a kind of thick corn tortilla, stuffed with beans, meat, or vegetables. (Ed.)

Railroad Standard Time

FRANK CHIN

"This was your grandfather's," Ma said. I was twelve, maybe four- 1
teen years old when Grandma died. Ma put it on the table. The big
railroad watch, Elgin. Nineteen-jewel movement. American made.
Lever set. Stem wound. Glass facecover. Railroad standard all the
way. It ticked on the table between stacks of dirty dishes and cold
food. She brought me in here to the kitchen, always to the kitchen
to loose her thrills and secrets, as if the sound of running water and
breathing the warm soggy ghosts of stale food, floating grease, old
spices, ever comforted her, as if the kitchen was a paradise for con-
spiracy, sanctuary for us *juk sing* Chinamen from the royalty of pure-
talking China-born Chinese, old, mourning, and belching in the
other rooms of my dead grandmother's last house. Here, private, to
say in Chinese, "This was your grandfather's," as if now that her
mother had died and she'd been up all night long, not weeping,
tough and lank, making coffee and tea and little foods for the bro-
kenhearted family in her mother's kitchen, Chinese would be easier
for me to understand. As if my mother would say all the important
things of the soul and blood to her son, me, only in Chinese from
now on. Very few people spoke the language at me the way she did.
She chanted a spell up over me that conjured the meaning of what
she was saying in the shape of old memories come to call. Words I'd
never heard before set me at play in familiar scenes new to me, and
ancient.

She lay the watch on the table, eased it slowly off her fingertips 2
down to the tabletop without a sound. She didn't touch me, but put
it down and held her hands in front of her like a bridesmaid holding
an invisible bouquet and stared at the watch. As if it were talking to
her, she looked hard at it, made faces at it, and did not move or answer the voices of the old, calling her from other rooms, until I
picked it up.

A two-driver, high stepping locomotive ahead of a coal tender 3
and baggage car, on double track between two semaphores showing
a stop signal, was engraved on the back.

Frank Chin (1940–   ), from San Francisco, is author of the plays
The Chickencoop Chinaman (first staged in 1972) and *The Year of the
Dragon* (1974), stories, and the novel *Donald Duk* (1991). "Railroad
Standard Time" first appeared in *City Lights Journal* (1978).

"Your grandfather collected railroad watches," Ma said. "This 4
one is the best." I held it in one hand and then the other, hefted it,
felt out the meaning of "the best," words that rang of meat and vegetables, oils, things we touched, smelled, squeezed, washed, and
ate, and I turned the big cased thing over several times. "Grandma
gives it to you now," she said. It was big in my hand. Gold. A little
greasy. Warm.

I asked her what her father's name had been, and the manic 5
heat of her all-night burnout seemed to go cold and congeal. "Oh,"
she finally said, "it's one of those Chinese names I . . ." in English,
faintly from another world, woozy and her throat and nostrils full of
bubbly sniffles, the solemnity of the moment gone, the watch in my
hand turned to cheap with the mumbling of a few awful English
words. She giggled herself down to nothing but breath and moving
lips. She shuffled backward, one step at a time, fox trotting dreamily
backwards, one hand dragging on the edge of the table, wobbling
the table, rattling the dishes, spilling cold soup. Back down one side
of the table, she dropped her butt a little with each step then muscled it back up. There were no chairs in the kitchen tonight. She
knew, but still she looked. So this dance and groggy mumbling
about the watch being no good, in strange English, like an Indian
medicine man in a movie.

I wouldn't give it back or trade it for another out of the collec- 6
tion. This one was mine. No other. It had belonged to my grandfather. I wore it braking on the Southern Pacific, though it was two
jewels short of new railroad standard and an outlaw watch that
could get me fired. I kept it on me, arrived at my day-off courthouse
wedding to its time, wore it as a railroad relic/family heirloom/grin-
bringing affectation when I was writing background news in Seattle,
reporting from the shadows of race riots, grabbing snaps for the
11:00 P.M., timing today's happenings with a nineteenth-century es-
capement. (Ride with me, Grandmother.) I was wearing it on my
twenty-seventh birthday, the Saturday I came home to see my son
asleep in the back of a strange station wagon, and Sarah inside,
waving, shouting through an open window, "Goodbye Daddy,"
over and over.

I stood it. Still and expressionless as some good Chink, I 7
watched Barbara drive off, leave me, like some blonde white goddess going home from the jungle with her leather patches and briar
pipe sweetheart writer and my kids. I'll learn to be a sore loser. I'll
learn to hit people in the face. I'll learn to cry when I'm hurt and go
for the throat instead of being polite and worrying about being obnoxious to people walking out of my house with my things, taking

my kids away. I'll be more than quiet, embarrassed. I won't be likable anymore.

I hate my novel about a Chinatown mother like mine dying, 8
now that Ma's dead. But I'll keep it. I hated after reading *Father and Glorious Descendant, Fifth Chinese Daughter, The House That Tai Ming Built.* [1] Books scribbled up by a sad legion of snobby autobiographical Chinatown saps all on their own. Christians who never heard of each other, hardworking people who sweat out the exact same Chinatown book, the same cunning "Confucius says" joke, just like me. I kept it then and I'll still keep it. Part cookbook, memories of Mother in the kitchen slicing meat paper-thin with a cleaver. Mumbo jumbo about spices and steaming. The secret of Chinatown rice. The hands come down toward the food. The food crawls with culture. The thousand-year-old living Chinese meat makes dinner a safari into the unknown, a blood ritual. Food pornography. Black magic. Between the lines, I read a madman's detailed description of the preparation of shrunken heads. I never wrote to mean anything more than word fun with the food Grandma cooked at home. Chinese food. I read a list of what I remembered eating at my grandmother's table and knew I'd always be known by what I ate, that we come from a hungry tradition. Slop eaters following the wars on all fours. Weed cuisine and mud gravy in the shadow of corpses. We plundered the dust for fungus. Buried things. Seeds plucked out of the wind to feed a race of lace-boned skinnys, in high-school English, become transcendental Oriental art to make the dyke-ish spinster teacher cry. We always come to fake art and write the Chinatown book like bugs come to fly in the light. I hate my book now that Ma's dead, but I'll keep it. I know she's not the woman I wrote up like my mother, and dead, in a book that was like everybody else's Chinatown book. Part word map of Chinatown San Francisco, shop to shop down Grant Avenue. Food again. The wind sucks the shops out and you breathe warm roast ducks dripping fat, hooks into the neck, through the head, out an eye. Stacks of iced fish, blue and fluorescent pink in the neon. The air is thin soup, sharp up the nostrils.

All mention escape from Chinatown into the movies. But we all 9
forgot to mention how stepping off the streets into a faceful of Charlie Chaplin or a Western on a ripped and stained screen that became

---

[1] Pardee Lowe, *Father and Glorious Descendant* (Boston: Little, Brown, 1943); Jade Snow Wong, *Fifth Chinese Daughter* (New York: Harper, 1950); Virginia Chin-lan Lee, *The House That Tai Ming Built* (New York: Macmillan, 1963). (Ed.)

caught in the grip of winos breathing in unison in their sleep and
billowed in and out, that shuddered when cars went by . . . we all
of us Chinamans watched our own MOVIE ABOUT ME! I learned how to
box watching movies shot by James Wong Howe. Cartoons were our
nursery rhymes. Summers inside those neon-and-stucco downtown
hole-in-the-wall Market Street Frisco movie houses blowing three
solid hours of full-color seven-minute cartoons was school, was
rows and rows of Chinamans learning English in a hurry from Daffy
Duck.

When we ate in the dark and recited the dialogue of cartoon   10
mice and cats out loud in various tones of voice with our mouths
full, we looked like people singing hymns in church. We learned to
talk like everybody in America. Learned to need to be afraid to stay
alive, keep moving. We learned to run, to be cheerful losers, to take
a sudden pie in the face, talk American with a lot of giggles. To us a
cartoon is a desperate situation. Of the movies, cartoons were the
high art of our claustrophobia. They understood us living too close
to each other. How, when you're living too close to too many people, you can't wait for one thing more without losing your mind.
Cartoons were a fine way out of waiting in Chinatown around the
rooms. Those of our Chinamans who every now and then break a
reverie with, "Thank you, Mighty Mouse," mean it. Other folks
thank Porky Pig, Snuffy Smith, Woody Woodpecker.

The day my mother told me I was to stay home from Chinese   11
school one day a week starting today, to read to my father and teach
him English while he was captured in total paralysis from a vertebra
in the neck on down, I stayed away from cartoons. I went to a
matinee in a white neighborhood looking for the MOVIE ABOUT ME and
was the only Chinaman in the house. I liked the way Peter Lorre ran
along non-stop routine hysterical. I came back home with Peter
Lorre. I turned out the lights in Pa's room. I put a candle on the
dresser and wheeled Pa around in his chair to see me in front of the
dresser mirror, reading Edgar Allan Poe out loud to him in the voice
of Peter Lorre by candlelight.

The old men in the Chinatown books are all fixtures for Chinese   12
ceremonies. All the same. Loyal filial children kowtow to the old
and whiff food laid out for the dead. The dead eat the same as the
living but without the sauces. White food. Steamed chicken. Rice we
all remember as children scrambling down to the ground, to all
fours and bonking our heads on the floor, kowtowing to a dead
chicken.

My mother and aunts said nothing about the men of the family   13
except they were weak. I like to think my grandfather was a good
man. Even the kiss-ass steward service, I like to think he was tough,

had a few laughs and ran off with his pockets full of engraved watches. Because I never knew him, not his name, nor anything about him, except a photograph of him as a young man with something of my mother's face in his face, and a watch chain across his vest. I kept his watch in good repair and told everyone it would pass to my son someday, until the day the boy was gone. Then I kept it like something of his he'd loved and had left behind, saving it for him maybe, to give to him when he was a man. But I haven't felt that in a long time.

The watch ticked against my heart and pounded my chest as I 14 went too fast over bumps in the night and the radio on, on an all-night run downcoast, down country, down old Highway 99, Interstate 5, I ran my grandfather's time down past road signs that caught a gleam in my headlights and came at me out of the night with the names of forgotten high school girlfriends, BELLEVUE KIRKLAND, ROBERTA GERBER, AURORA CANBY, and sang with the radio to Jonah and Sarah in Berkeley, my Chinatown in Oakland and Frisco, to raise the dead. Ride with me, Grandfather, this is your grandson the ragmouth, called Tampax, the burned scarred boy, called Barbecue, going to San Francisco to bury my mother, your daughter, and spend Chinese New Year's at home. When we were sitting down and into our dinner after Grandma's funeral, and ate in front of the table set with white food for the dead, Ma said she wanted no white food and money burning after her funeral. Her sisters were there. Her sisters took charge of her funeral and the dinner afterwards. The dinner would most likely be in a Chinese restaurant in Frisco. Nobody had these dinners at home anymore. I wouldn't mind people having dinner at my place after my funeral, but no white food.

The whiz goes out of the tires as their roll bites into the steel 15 grating of the Carquinez Bridge. The noise of the engine groans and echoes like a bomber in flight through the steel roadway. Light from the water far below shines through the grate, and I'm driving high, above a glow. The voice of the tires hums a shrill rubber screechy mosquito hum that vibrates through the chassis and frame of the car into my meatless butt, into my tender asshole, my pelvic bones, the roots of my teeth. Over the Carquinez Bridge to CROCKETT MARTINEZ closer to home, roll the tires of Ma's Chevy, my car now, carrying me up over the water southwest toward rolls of fog. The fat man's coming home on a sneaky breeze. Dusk comes a drooly mess of sunlight, a slobber of cheap pawnshop gold, a slow building heat across the water, all through the milky air through the glass of the window into the closed atmosphere of a driven car, into one side of my bomber's face. A bomber, flying my mother's car into the unknown charted by the stars and the radio, feels the coming of some old night song climbing hand over hand, bass notes plunking as steady and shady as reminiscence to get on my nerves one stupid beat after the other crossing the high rhythm six-step of the engine. I drive through the shadows of the bridge's steel structure all over the road. Fine day. I've been on the road for sixteen hours straight down the music of Seattle, Spokane, Salt Lake, Sacramento, Los Angeles, and Wolfman Jack lurking in odd hours of darkness, at peculiar altitudes of darkness, favoring the depths of certain Oregon valleys and heat and moonlight of my miles. And I'm still alive. Country 'n' western music for the night road. It's pure white music. Like "The Star-Spangled Banner," it was the first official American music out of school into my jingling earbones sung by sighing white big tits in front of the climbing promise of FACE and Every Good Boy Does Fine chalked on the blackboard.

She stood up singing, one hand cupped in the other as if to 16 catch drool slipping off her lower lip. Our eyes scouted through her blouse to elastic straps, lacy stuff, circular stitching, buckles, and in the distance, finally some skin. The color of her skin spread through the stuff of her blouse like melted butter through bread nicely to our tongues and was warm there. She sat flopping them on the keyboard as she breathed, singing "Home on the Range" over her shoulder, and pounded the tune out with her palms. The lonesome prairie was nothing but her voice, some hearsay country she stood up to sing *a capella* out of her. Simple music you can count. You can hear the words clear. The music's run through Clorox and Simonized, beating so insistently right and regular that you feel to sing it will deodorize you, make you clean. The hardhat hit parade. I listen to it a lot on the road. It's that get-outta-town beat and tune that makes me go.

Mrs. Morales was her name. Aurora Morales. The music teacher 17 us boys liked to con into singing for us. Come-on opera, we wanted from her, not them Shirley Temple tunes the girls wanted to learn, but big notes, high long ones up from the navel that drilled through plaster and steel and skin and meat for bone marrow and electric wires on one long titpopping breath.

This is how I come home, riding a mass of spasms and death 18 throes, warm and screechy inside, itchy, full of ghostpiss, as I drive right past what's left of Oakland's dark wooden Chinatown and dark streets full of dead lettuce and trampled carrot tops, parallel all the time in line with the tracks of the Western Pacific and Southern Pacific railroads.

Tamurlane

BHARATI MUKHERJEE

We sleep in shifts in my apartment, three illegals on guard playing 1
cards and three bedded down on mats on the floor. One man next
door broke his leg jumping out the window. I'd been whistling in
the bathroom and he'd mistaken it for our warning tune. The walls
are flimsy. Nights I hear collective misery.

Was this what I left Ludhiana for? 2

It was below freezing and icy outside but inside the Mumtaz Bar 3
B-Q it was hot and crackly with static. Mohan the busboy was gobbling the mints by the cash register. The cook was asleep on the
bar's counter in his undershirt and shorts. He's a little guy and he
can squeeze into the skinniest space, come three o'clock, or during a
raid. The door is locked and the drapes are pulled. We have a
"CLOSED" sign in English and Hindi on the door, courtesy of Cinema Sahni, next door. Mr Aziz doesn't mind our spreading out of
the kitchen and into the dining room as long as we spray air fresh-
ener before the dinner crowd comes in. These days Mr A. is dividing his time between the Mumtaz in Toronto and a 67-unit motel on
the Gulf coast of Florida. Canadians don't want us, it's like Uganda
all over again, says Mr A. He says he can feel it in his bones.

So there we were, the regulars. The new tandoor chef, Gupta, 4
was at a table with a huffing and puffing gentleman I didn't know.
He had the crafty eyes of a Sindhi, but his graying hair was dyed
reddish so he could have been a Muslim. I've been too long here;
there was a time when I could tell them all apart, not just Hindu and
Muslim, but where, what caste and what they were hiding. Now all
I care about is legal or illegal? This man has called himself Muslim, a
Ugandan, a victim of Idi Amin. These sad rehearsals, heaping indig-
nity on top of being poor. As if poverty and opportunity weren't
enough, like it was for the Italians and Greeks and Portuguese. How
did this vast country suddenly get so filled? But Mr A. and this chap

Bharati Mukherjee (1940–   ), born in Calcutta, is professor of
English at Queens College, City University of New York, and au-
thor of novels, short stories, and memoirs including *The Tiger's
Daughter* (1972), *Days and Nights in Calcutta* (1977), and *The Middle-
man and Other Stories* (1988). "Tamurlane," which first appeared in
The Canadian Forum, was included in the collection *Darkness* (1985).

probably have their British passports and their tales of mistreatment, and the rest of us have a life time debt to a shifty agent in Delhi who got us here, with no hint of how to keep us. The new chef and his friend made Mohan and me watchful.

He didn't have an old man's harassed face. His skin was oily 5 still, and supple. He didn't look old enough to need to dye his hair. Vanity we're all guilty of; even the cook dropped a hundred and fifty dollars this December on hand-tooled, baby blue antelope boots. This man didn't look vain. He just seemed troubled. He held his cigarette Indian-style, high up near the glowing tip and in between the thumb and index finger, like a pencil.

I hadn't made up my mind about the new chef. He was a good 6 chef, but an improviser. We didn't have an authentic tandoor oven because Mr A. thinks people get bored of watching their meat cooked in a clay oven in front of them and if you aren't going to do the tandoor in public you might as well go down to Buffalo and buy one of the small, sturdy brick things from Khanna & Sons. We don't have one of the brick things either, not yet, but the new chef was doing wonders with chicken breasts and lamb chops under the broiler of our old gas stove. He didn't complain when he saw the Mumtaz's kitchen. He didn't say anything about the stove. He just limped into the freezer and took out two trays of lamb and chicken. Then he asked me where the cleaver was. But he wasn't friendly. He didn't want to talk. He walked like a man on unbending but fragile stilts. His knees didn't bend and when he sat his legs fell straight out. When he worked in the kitchen, he propped his stomach against the sink in order to keep his balance. Severe damage like that is difficult to watch, you want to pull away, as from a beggar.

Now he was doing the listening, and the man with the dyed 7 hair was doing the talking.

The man said, "Maharaj, I don't know why you stay in Toronto, 8 I really don't. I can find you a place in Atlanta, no immigration problems. Have you seen Atlanta in January? It's like a hill station, my friend. Like Simla, healthy. Or Dallas, here, let me check—" he took out a long list of names written on the back of a supermarket stub. "Ft. Worth, you are knowing?"

"Hey, man," Mohan called from the cash register, "you got a 9 place for me on that list? I want New York City. Or Miami, hot-hot like Bombay."

"Pah, in Miami and New York they are finding thousands of 10 boys like you. Big mouth and no skill. Don't bother me, I am talking to an artist with fish and fowl. Such a man is worth gold."

The man put a hand on the new chef's hands which were folded 11 and still, and red with tandoori masala in the knuckles and under

the nails. The new chef didn't move. He looked dead, or very relaxed. I couldn't make up my mind about him. He was odd.

"If you stay here, trouble's going to find you. I can guarantee 12
you that, my friend. Aziz-*sahib* has the right idea. Get out while you
can. You're one of the lucky ones."

Mohan rang the cash register. The drawer shot open and he 13
took out a couple of quarters and fed them into the juke box. A
noisy little number by a British group, and a duet by Chitra and Ajit
Kumar.

The agent said nothing during the singles. When the music 14
stopped, he said in the same hectoring tone he had used before,
"You don't have to go looking, friend. Because trouble's coming. If
you stay in Toronto, it's coming to your door. You know what happened to me when I was coming to see you? Right here on Gerrard
Street, a block and a half from your fancy Bar B-Q?"

Mohan didn't like the man. I could tell that from the way he 15
kept trying to disrupt his story. He thought the man was giving the
chef a hard time when all he wanted was a rest and smoke before
his next shift. Mohan said, not loud but loud enough for me to hear
and I was farther from him than the man was, "This place isn't
fancy. Mr A. is a tightwad. Mr A. couldn't run a fancy place."

The recruiter didn't even look Mohan's way. He said, "I was 16
walking as fast as I could so we'd have time together before you had
to cook again. You know how fast I can walk. You remember the
time I was running to catch that train from Grand Central and I was
stopped by a cop? He thought I was Puerto Rican, remember, because he had never seen an Indian run before. Well, I wasn't walking that fast, but fast, after getting off the trolley at the wrong stop.
It was like that time we got off in the middle of Harlem—remember?
I could see all the Indian shops up ahead, but I was still two blocks
away. I started running, when out pop three young chaps from an
arcade . . ."

"That must be Sinbad's," Mohan said. "The other arcade's four 17
blocks the other side."

"One boy knocked me down. Actually he tripped me, so it 18
looked like an accident. Then the other two spat on me, called me
names you wouldn't believe. I'm a Gandhian of the old school. I just
lay there with my face against a parking meter, to protect my eyes,
you know. The eyes are delicate, the rest is reparable. And all the
time the hooligans were belaboring me, my friend, I was thinking of
you. Why did Gupta come back to Toronto, I kept asking. You were
out once—I can get you back. I would be proud to sponsor a hero
like you. I am proud to call you brother or cousin. You can pay me
back a little every month—you'll be free in a year. Why, after what

happened to you?" He turned now to Mohan, and there was scorn in his voice. "This man is a hero to us all. Six years ago when you were naked in Bombay, he was thrown on the subway tracks in this city. He would never walk, they said. Now look. Like a true Gandhian, he forgave them. Good men left Canada for less cause. Dr Choudhury, he left his seventy-thousand-dollar-plus practice. On a matter of principle, you remember, when the courts let go those boys who beat up the worshippers at the Durga Puja festival."

"Poor Dr Choudhury," Mohan said to me. Principles are easy to 19 have when you're rich and have a skill like Dr Choudhury and Dallas is waiting. The problem is for Mohan and me and the little cook asleep on the bar. Hooligans and everyone else can do what they want and they know we don't dare complain.

"Why, my friend?" The man put out his cigarette. "What kind of 20 a life is this if your dignity is on the line every time you step out the door?" Ah, dignity. *Dignity!* that beautiful word that has never fed an empty stomach.

The chef just shrugged, but Mohan wasn't finished. He 21 shouted, "It's worse in British Columbia, except that the Sikhs can look after themselves better than we can. They go head-to-head with everyone. Thick skulls can be very useful."

At four-thirty, the cook woke up and put away his pillow. The tan- 22 door chef said goodbye to his friend, and walked back to his pans of marinating breasts and chops. The man said he was going back to Buffalo that night. Mohan was busier than the rest of us at any given hour. As a waiter I had it easiest. But it was lonely when the others went about their chores in the kitchen and I'd already folded the napkins into fancy shapes and laid the blue overcloths on the wobbly tables. Mr A. had been gone so long to the Gulf coast that he didn't know the cook stole supplies and that I had become very bored. The Indian patrons came only on nights Sahni-*sahib* screened a Bombay blockbuster in the cinema next door. The white Canadians barely came at all. Maybe some old English types, or Indian boys with Canadian girlfriends, trying to show off. I don't know why our food never caught on with Canadians the way Chinese food did. We kept waiting for a notice in the papers, something like that. Mr A. has a bigger place than this in Ft. Meyers. Light of India or Star of India, something like that. He said he wanted to get into the take-out roti kabab business. "They'll be eating roti kababs the way they do hamburgers by the time I'm through," he used to brag. "I want to be the McDonald's of Indian food." Maybe he will, in Miami or the Gulf coast. He had a British passport and he could always claim mistreatment at the hands of crazy blacks. His heart wasn't in Toronto. Mohan is right; those who can run, do.

At five minutes after five came the call we always listened for. 23 Two rings, then nothing. We had a drill. The little cook dove under the sink and piled the biggest aluminum platters around him. I locked the door. Gupta looked unconcerned, and he couldn't move anyway. Right then I knew he must have his papers. He just flipped the lamb chops over, then slid the broiler pan back under the flames. Mohan and I headed for the basement and since I was taller, I unscrewed the lightbulb on the way down.

That wasn't the first time. We knew where to hide, Mohan and I. 24 We even had bedrooms on the shelves behind the sacks of rice. We could hear the Mounties up in the kitchen, and we didn't know how Gupta would handle himself. Sometimes they'll let one of us off, if he can turn in three or four.

I knew it was all over when they opened the door to the base- 25 ment. "Light?" one of them called out. They sounded like they were right on top of us. One carried a torch, brighter than a searchlight.

"What have we here, eh?" He was a big fellow, blond with a 26 rusty-colored mustache, and he knew exactly where to look. The other was in plain clothes, an immigration officer. They traveled in twos, acting on tips.

They took us up to the kitchen. "There's another one," said the 27 immigration man. *Aziz-sahib* has enemies, and jealous friends. Someone else bought a little time for himself. We are all pawns.

"You, too," said the Mountie, pointing to Gupta. "We're all go- 28 ing down to the station."

"This is a business establishment," said Gupta. "I am responsi- 29 ble here while the owner is away."

"We're closing you down. When the owner comes back we'll get 30 him too."

Mohan was crying. For all his Bombay smart-talk, I could see he 31 was very young, maybe only twenty. Gupta the chef was propped up in his strange way against the sink and the small cabinet underneath it where the assistant cook was hiding. I had a silly thought just then: if they find him, what will he do with his hundred-and-fifty-dollar boots?

"Get out of my kitchen," said Gupta. "Get out immediately." 32

"It's cold. Get your coats," said the Mountie. "That goes for you, 33 too." It had become a personal thing between them.

"He is a lame man, sir," I said, "he cannot move without his 34 crutches."

"I don't care if I have to sling him over my shoulder—he's com- 35
ing with us now."

The plainclothesman stepped between them. "It will only go 36
harder if you resist," he said.

"I am not resisting. I am ordering you away from here." His 37
voice was very quiet, but I could see the color rising in his neck.

"Very well," said the Mountie, and he was suddenly in motion, 38
two quick steps toward the chef, one arm out to grab his neck, the
other to club him if necessary. But the chef was quicker. All he had
to do was slide his hand along the rim of the sink. The Mountie saw
it the same time I did—the cleaver—but he didn't have time to react.
Gupta whirled, falling as he took a step, with the cleaver high over
his head. He brought it down in a wild, practiced chop on the
Mountie's outstretched arm, and I could tell from the way it stuck,
the way Gupta couldn't extract it easily for a second swing, that it
had sunk well below the overcoat and service jacket. The Mountie
and Gupta fell simultaneously, and now Gupta was reaching into
his back pocket while the screaming Mountie rolled on one side.

Gupta managed to sit straight. He held his Canadian passport in 39
front of his face. That way, he never saw the drawn gun, nor did he
try to dodge the single bullet.

American Horse

LOUISE ERDRICH

The woman sleeping on the cot in the woodshed was Albertine 1
American Horse. The name was left over from her mother's short
marriage. The boy was the son of the man she had loved and let go.
Buddy was on the cot too, sitting on the edge because he'd been
awake three hours watching out for his mother and besides, she
took up the whole cot. Her feet hung over the edge, limp and brown
as two trout. Her long arms reached out and slapped at things she
saw in her dreams.

Buddy had been knocked awake out of hiding in a washing ma- 2
chine while herds of policemen with dogs searched through a large
building with many tiny rooms. When the arm came down, Buddy
screamed because it had a blue cuff and sharp silver buttons. "Tss,"
his mother mumbled, half awake, "wasn't nothing." But Buddy sat
up after her breathing went deep again, and he watched.

There was something coming and he knew it. 3

It was coming from very far off but he had a picture of it in his 4
mind. It was a large thing made of metal with many barbed hooks,
points, and drag chains on it, something like a giant potato peeler
that rolled out of the sky, scraping clouds down with it and jabbing
or crushing everything that lay in its path on the ground.

Buddy watched his mother. If he woke her up, she would know 5
what to do about the thing, but he thought he'd wait until he saw it
for sure before he shook her. She was pretty, sleeping, and he liked
knowing he could look at her as long and close up as he wanted. He
took a strand of her hair and held it in his hands as if it was the rein
to a delicate beast. She was strong enough and could pull him along
like the horse their name was.

Buddy had his mother's and his grandmother's name because 6
his father had been a big mistake.

"They're all mistakes, even your father. But *you* are the best 7
thing that ever happened to me."

That was what she said when he asked. 8

Louise Erdrich (1954–   ), born in Little Falls, Minnesota, is the
author of poetry, stories, and novels including *Love Medicine* (1984),
Beet Queen (1986), and *Tracks* (1988). "American Horse" first appeared in *Earth Power Coming: Short Fiction in Native American Literature* (1983).

Even Kadie, the boyfriend crippled from being in a car wreck, 9
was not as good a thing that had happened to his mother as Buddy
was. "He was a medium-sized mistake," she said. "He's hurt and I
shouldn't even say that, but it's the truth." At the moment, Buddy
knew that being the best thing in his mother's life, he was also the
reason they were hiding from the cops.

He wanted to touch the satin roses sewed on her pink tee shirt, 10
but he knew he shouldn't do that even in her sleep. If she woke up
and found him touching the roses, she would say, "Quit that,
Buddy." Sometimes she told him to stop hugging her like a gorilla.
She never said that in the mean voice she used when he oppressed
her, but when she said that he loosened up anyway.

There were times he felt like hugging her so hard and in such a 11
special way that she would say to him, "Let's get married." There
were also times he closed his eyes and wished that she would die,
only a few times, but still it haunted him that his wish might come
true. He and Uncle Lawrence would be left alone. Buddy wasn't
worried, though, about his mother getting married to somebody
else. She had said to her friend, Madonna, "All men suck," when
she thought Buddy wasn't listening. He had made an uncertain
sound, and when they heard him they took him in their arms.

"Except for you, Buddy," his mother said. "All except for you 12
and maybe Uncle Lawrence, although he's pushing it."

"The cops suck the worst, though," Buddy whispered to his 13
mother's sleeping face, "because they're after us." He felt tired
again, slumped down, and put his legs beneath the blanket. He
closed his eyes and got the feeling that the cot was lifting up beneath him, that it was arching its canvas back and then traveling,
traveling very fast and in the wrong direction for when he looked up
he saw the three of them were advancing to meet the great metal
thing with hooks and barbs and all sorts of sharp equipment to catch
their bodies and draw their blood. He heard its insides as it rushed
toward them, purring softly like a powerful motor and then they
were right in its shadow. He pulled the reins as hard as he could
and the beast reared, lifting him. His mother clapped her hand
across his mouth.

"Okay," she said. "Lay low. They're outside and they're gonna 14
hunt."

She touched his shoulder and Buddy leaned over with her to 15
look through a crack in the boards.

They were out there all right, Albertine saw them. Two officers and 16
that social worker woman. Vicki Koob. There had been no whistle,
no dream, no voice to warn her that they were coming. There was

only the crunching sound of cinders in the yard, the engine purring, the dust sifting off their car in a fine light brownish cloud and settling around them.

The three people came to a halt in their husk of metal—the car 17 emblazoned with the North Dakota State Highway Patrol emblem which is the glowing profile of the Sioux policeman, Red Tomahawk, the one who killed Sitting Bull. Albertine gave Buddy the blanket and told him that he might have to wrap it around him and hide underneath the cot.

"We're gonna wait and see what they do." She took him in her 18 lap and hunched her arms around him. "Don't you worry," she whispered against his ear. "Lawrence knows how to fool them."

Buddy didn't want to look at the car and the people. He felt his 19 mother's heart beating beneath his ear so fast it seemed to push the satin roses in and out. He put his face to them carefully and breathed the deep, soft powdery woman smell of her. That smell was also in her little face cream bottles, in her brushes, and around the washbowl after she used it. The satin felt so unbearably smooth against his cheek that he had to press closer. She didn't push him away, like he expected, but hugged him still tighter until he felt as close as he had ever been to back inside her again where she said he came from. Within the smells of her things, her soft skin, and the satin of her roses, he closed his eyes then, and took his breaths softly and quickly with her heart.

They were out there, but they didn't dare get out of the car yet be- 20 cause of Lawrence's big, ragged dogs. Three of these dogs had loped up the dirt driveway with the car. They were rangy, alert, and bounced up and down on their cushioned paws like wolves. They didn't waste their energy barking, but positioned themselves quietly, one at either car door and the third in front of the bellied-out screen door to Uncle Lawrence's house. It was six in the morning but the wind was up already, blowing dust, ruffling their short moth-eaten coats. The big brown one on Vicki Koob's side had unusual black and white markings, stripes almost, like a hyena and he grinned at her, tongue out and teeth showing.

"Shoo!" Miss Koob opened her door with a quick jerk. 21

The brown dog sidestepped the door and jumped before her, 22 tiptoeing. Its dirty white muzzle curled and its eyes crossed suddenly as if it was zeroing its cross-hair sights in on the exact place it would bite her. She ducked back and slammed the door.

"It's mean," she told Officer Brackett. He was printing out some 23 type of form. The other officer, Harmony, a slow man, had not yet reacted to the car's halt. He had been sitting quietly in the back seat, but now he rolled down his window and with no change in expression unsnapped his holster and drew his pistol out and pointed it at the dog on his side. The dog smacked down on its belly, wiggled under the car and was out and around the back of the house before Harmony drew his gun back. The other dogs vanished with him. From wherever they had disappeared to they began to yap and howl, and the door to the low shoebox-style house fell open.

"Heya, what's going on?"   24

Uncle Lawrence put his head out the door and opened wide the 25
one eye he had in working order. The eye bulged impossibly wider in outrage when he saw the police car. But the eyes of the two officers and Miss Vicki Koob were wide open too because they had never seen Uncle Lawrence in his sleeping get up or, indeed, witnessed anything like it. For his ribs, which were cracked from a bad fall and still mending, Uncle Lawrence wore a thick white corset laced up the front with a striped sneakers' lace. His glass eye and his set of dentures were still out for the night so his face puckered here and there, around its absences and scars, like a damaged but fierce little cake. Although he had a few gray streaks now, Uncle Lawrence's hair was still thick, and because he wore a special contraption of elastic straps around his head every night, two oiled waves always crested on either side of his middle part. All of this would have been sufficient to astonish, even without the most striking part of his outfit—the smoking jacket. It was made of black satin and hung open around his corset, dragging a tasseled belt. Gold thread dragons struggled up the lapels and blasted their furry red breath around his neck. As Lawrence walked down the steps, he put his arms up in surrender and the gold tassels in the inner seams of his sleeves dropped into view.

"My heavens, what a sight." Vicki Koob was impressed.   26

"A character," apologized Officer Harmony.   27

As a tribal police officer who could be counted on to help out 28
the State Patrol, Harmony thought he always had to explain about Indians or get twice as tough to show he did not favor them. He was slow-moving and shy but two jumps ahead of other people all the same, and now, as he watched Uncle Lawrence's splendid approach, he gazed speculatively at the torn and bulging pocket of the smoking jacket. Harmony had been inside Uncle Lawrence's house before and knew that above his draped orange-crate shelf of war medals a blue-black German luger was hung carefully in a net of flat-headed nails and fishing line. Thinking of this deadly exhibition, he got out of the car and shambled toward Lawrence with a dreamy little smile of welcome on his face. But when he searched Lawrence, he found that the bulging pocket held only the lonesome-looking

dentures from Lawrence's empty jaw. They were still dripping denture polish.

"I had been cleaning them when you arrived," Uncle Lawrence 29 explained with acid dignity.

He took the toothbrush from his other pocket and aimed it like a 30 rifle.

"Quit that, you old idiot." Harmony tossed the toothbrush 31 away. "For once you ain't done nothing. We came for your nephew."

Lawrence looked at Harmony with a faint air of puzzlement. 32

"Ma Frere, listen," threatened Harmony amiably, "those two 33 white people in the car came to get him for the welfare. They got papers on your nephew that give them the right to take him."

"Papers?" Uncle Lawrence puffed out his deeply pitted cheeks. 34 "Let me see them papers."

The two of them walked over to Vicki's side of the car and she 35 pulled a copy of the court order from her purse. Lawrence put his teeth back in and adjusted them with busy workings of his jaw.

"Just a minute," he reached into his breast pocket as he bent 36 close to Miss Vicki Koob. "I can't read these without I have in my eye."

He took the eye from his breast pocket delicately, and as he 37 popped it into his face the social worker's mouth fell open in a consternated O.

"What is this," she cried in a little voice. 38

Uncle Lawrence looked at her mildly. The white glass of the eye 39 was cold as lard. The black iris was strangely charged and menacing.

"He's nuts," Brackett huffed along the side of Vicki's neck. 40 "Never mind him."

Vicki's hair had sweated down her nape in tiny corkscrews and 41 some of the hairs were so long and dangly now that they disappeared into the zippered back of her dress. Brackett noticed this as he spoke into her ear. His face grew red and the backs of his hands prickled. He slid under the steering wheel and got out of the car. He walked around the hood to stand with Leo Harmony.

"We could take you in too," said Brackett roughly. Lawrence 42 eyed the officers in what was taken as defiance. "If you don't cooperate, we'll get out the handcuffs," they warned.

One of Lawrence's arms was stiff and would not move until 43 he'd rubbed it with witch hazel in the morning. His other arm worked fine though, and he stuck it out in front of Brackett.

"Get them handcuffs," he urged them. "Put me in a welfare 44 home."

Bracket snapped one side of the handcuffs on Lawrence's good 45
arm and the other to the handle of the police car.

"That's to hold you," he said. "We're wasting our time. Har- 46
mony, you search that little shed over by the tall grass and Miss
Koob and myself will search the house."

"My rights is violated!" Lawrence shrieked suddenly. They ig- 47
nored him. He tugged at the handcuff and thought of the good
heavy file he kept in his tool box and the German luger oiled and
ready but never loaded, because of Buddy, over his shelf. He should
have used it on these bad ones, even Harmony in his big-time white
man job. He wouldn't last long in that job anyway before somebody
gave him what for.

"It's a damn scheme," said Uncle Lawrence, rattling his chains 48
against the car. He looked over at the shed and thought maybe Albertine and Buddy had sneaked away before the car pulled into the
yard. But he sagged, seeing Albertine move like a shadow within
the boards. "Oh, it's all a damn scheme," he muttered again.

"I want to find that boy and salvage him," Vicki Koob explained to 49
Officer Brackett as they walked into the house. "Look at his family
life—the old man crazy as a bedbug, the mother intoxicated somewhere."

Brackett nodded, energetic, eager. He was a short hopeful red- 50
head who failed consistently to win the hearts of women. Vicki
Koob intrigued him. Now, as he watched, she pulled a tiny pen out
of an ornamental clip on her blouse. It was attached to a retractable
line that would suck the pen back, like a child eating one strand of
spaghetti. Something about the pen on its line excited Brackett to
the point of discomfort. His hand shook as he opened the screen-
door and stepped in, beckoning Miss Koob to follow.

They could see the house was empty at first glance. It was only 51
one rectangular room with whitewashed walls and a little gas stove
in the middle. They had already come through the cooking lean-to
with the other stove and washstand and rusty old refrigerator. That
refrigerator had nothing in it but some wrinkled potatoes and a
package of turkey necks. Vicki Koob noted in her perfect-bound
notebook. The beds along the walls of the big room were covered
with quilts that Albertine's mother, Sophie, had made from bits of
old wool coats and pants that the Sisters sold in bundles at the mission. There was no one hiding beneath the beds. No one was under
the little aluminum dinette table covered with a green oilcloth, or
the soft brown wood chairs tucked up to it. One wall of the big
room was filled with neatly stacked crates of things—old tools and

springs and small half-dismantled appliances. Five or six television sets were stacked against the wall. Their control panels spewed colored wires and at least one was cracked all the way across. Only the topmost set, with coathanger antenna angled sensitively to catch the bounding signals around Little Shell, looked like it could possibly work.

Not one thing escaped Vicki Koob's trained and cataloguing 52 gaze. She made note of the cupboard that held only commodity flour and coffee. The unsanitary tin oil drum beneath the kitchen window, full of empty surplus pork cans and beer bottles, caught her eye as did Uncle Lawrence's physical and mental deteriorations. She quickly described these "benchmarks of alcoholic dependency within the extended family of Woodrow (Buddy) American Horse" as she walked around the room with the little notebook open, pushed against her belly to steady it. Although Vicki had been there before, Albertine's presence had always made it difficult for her to take notes.

"Twice the maximum allowable space between door and 53 threshold," she wrote now. "Probably no insulation. Two three-inch cracks in walls inadequately sealed with white-washed mud." She made a mental note but could see no point in describing Lawrence's stuffed reclining chair that only reclined, the shadeless lamp with its plastic orchid in the bubble glass base, or the three-dimensional picture of Jesus that Lawrence had once demonstrated to her. When plugged in, lights rolled behind the water the Lord stood on so that he seemed to be strolling although he never actually went forward, of course, but only pushed the glowing waves behind him forever like a poor tame rat in a treadmill.

Brackett cleared his throat with a nervous rasp and touched 54 Vicki's shoulder.

"What are you writing?"   55

She moved away and continued to scribble as if thoroughly ab- 56 sorbed in her work. "Officer Brackett displays an undue amount of interest in my person," she wrote. "Perhaps?"

He snatched playfully at the book, but she hugged it to her chest 57 and moved off smiling. More curls had fallen, wetted to the base of her neck. Looking out the window, she sighed long and loud.

"All night on brush rollers for this. What a joke."   58

Brackett shoved his hands in his pockets. His mouth opened 59 slightly, then shut with a small throttled cluck.

When Albertine saw Harmony ambling across the yard with his big 60 brown thumbs in his belt, his placid smile, and his tiny black eyes moving back and forth, she put Buddy under the cot. Harmony stopped at the shed and stood quietly. He spread his arms to show her he hadn't drawn his big police gun.

"Ma Cousin," he said in the Michif dialect that people used if they were relatives or sometimes if they needed gas or a couple of dollars, "why don't you come out here and stop this foolishness?" 61

"I ain't your cousin," Albertine said. Anger boiled up in her suddenly. "I ain't related to no pigs." 62

She bit her lip and watched him through the cracks, circling, a big tan punching dummy with his boots full of sand so he never stayed down once he fell. He was empty inside, all stale air. But he knew how to get to her so much better than a white cop could. And now he was circling because he wasn't sure she didn't have a weapon, maybe a knife or the German luger that was the only thing that her father, Albert American Horse, had left his wife and daughter besides his name. Harmony knew that Albertine was a tall strong woman who took two big men to subdue when she didn't want to go in the drunk tank. She had hard hips, broad shoulders, and stood tall like her Sioux father, the American Horse who was killed threshing in Belle Prairie. 63

"I feel bad to have to do this," Harmony said to Albertine. "But for godsakes, let's nobody get hurt. Come on out with the boy, why don't you? I know you got him in there." 64

Albertine did not give herself away this time. She let him wonder. Slowly and quietly she pulled her belt through its loops and wrapped it around and around her hand until only the big oval buckle with turquoise chunks shaped into a butterfly stuck out over her knuckles. Harmony was talking but she wasn't listening to what he said. She was listening to the pitch of his voice, the tone of it that would tighten or tremble at a certain moment when he decided to rush the shed. He kept talking slowly and reasonably, flexing the dialect from time to time, even mentioning her father. 65

"He was a damn good man. I don't care what they say, Albertine, I knew him." 66

Albertine looked at the stone butterfly that spread its wings across her fist. The wings looked light and cool, not heavy. It almost looked like it was ready to fly. Harmony wanted to get to Albertine through her father but she would not think about American Horse. She concentrated on the sky blue stone. 67

Yet the shape of the stone, the color, betrayed her. 68

She saw her father suddenly, bending at the grille of their old gray car. She was small then. The memory came from so long ago it seemed like a dream—narrowly focused, snapshot-clear. He was bending by the grille in the sun. It was hot summer. Wings of 69 sweat, dark blue, spread across the back of his work shirt. He always wore soft blue shirts, the color of shade cloudier than this stone. His stiff hair had grown out of its short haircut and flopped over his forehead. When he stood up and turned away from the car, Albertine saw that he had a butterfly.

"It's dead," he told her. "Broke its wings and died on the grille." 70

She must have been five, maybe six, wearing one of the boy's 71 tee shirts Mama bleached in Hilex-water. American Horse took the butterfly, a black and yellow one, and rubbed it on Albertine's collarbone and chest and arms until the color and the powder of it were blended into her skin.

"For grace," he said. 72

And Albertine had felt a strange lightening in her arms, in her 73 chest, when he did this and said, "For grace." The way he said it, grace meant everything the butterfly was. The sharp delicate wings. The way it floated over grass. The way its wings seemed to breathe fanning in the sun. The wisdom of the way it blended into flowers or changed into a leaf. In herself she felt the same kind of possibilities and closed her eyes almost in shock or pain, she felt so light and powerful at that moment.

Then her father had caught her and thrown her high into the 74 air. She could not remember landing in his arms or landing at all. She only remembered the sun filling her eyes and the world tipping crazily behind her, out of sight.

"He was a damn good man," Harmony said again. 75

Albertine heard his starched uniform gathering before his boots 76 hit the ground. Once, twice, three times. It took him four solid jumps to get right where she wanted him. She kicked the plank door open when he reached for the handle and the corner caught him on the jaw. He faltered, and Albertine hit him flat on the chin with the butterfly. She hit him so hard the shock of it went up her arm like a string pulled taut. Her fist opened, numb, and she let the belt unloop before she closed her hand on the tip end of it and sent the stone butterfly swooping out in a wide circle around her as if it was on the end of a leash. Harmony reeled backward as she walked toward him swinging the belt. She expected him to fall but he just stumbled. And then he took the gun from his hip.

Albertine let the belt go limp. She and Harmony stood within 77 feet of each other, breathing. Each heard the human sound of air going in and out of the other person's lungs. Each read the face of the other as if deciphering letters carved into softly eroding veins of stone. Albertine saw the pattern of tiny arteries that age, drink, and hard living had blown to the surface of the man's face. She saw the spoked wheels of his iris and the arteries like tangled threads that sewed him up. She saw the living net of springs and tissue that held him together, and trapped him. She saw the random, intimate plan of his person.

She took a quick shallow breath and her face went strange and 78 tight. She saw the black veins in the wings of the butterfly, roads burnt into a map, and then she was located somewhere in the net of veins and sinew that was the tragic complexity of the world so she did not see Officer Brackett and Vicki Koob rushing toward her, but felt them instead like flies caught in the same web, rocking it.

"Albertine!" Vicki Koob had stopped in the grass. Her voice was 79 shrill and tight. "It's better this way, Albertine. We're going to help you."

Albertine straightened, threw her shoulders back. Her father's 80 hand was on her chest and shoulders lightening her wonderfully. Then on wings of her father's hands, on dead butterfly wings, Albertine lifted into the air and flew toward the others. The light powerful feeling swept her up the way she had floated higher, seeing the grass below. It was her father throwing her up into the air and out of danger. Her arms opened for bullets but no bullets came. Harmony did not shoot. Instead, he raised his fist and brought it down hard on her head.

Albertine did not fall immediately, but stood in his arms a mo- 81 ment. Perhaps she gazed still farther back behind the covering of his face. Perhaps she was completely stunned and did not think as she sagged and fell. Her face rolled forward and hair covered her features, so it was impossible for Harmony to see with just what particular expression she gazed into the head-splitting wheel of light, or blackness, that overcame her.

Harmony turned the vehicle onto the gravel road that led back to 82 town. He had convinced the other two that Albertine was more trouble than she was worth, and so they left her behind, and Lawrence too. He stood swearing in his cinder driveway as the car rolled out of sight. Buddy sat between the social worker and Officer Brackett. Vicki tried to hold Buddy fast and keep her arm down at the same time, for the words she'd screamed at Albertine had broken the seal of antiperspirant beneath her arms. She was sweating now as though she'd stored an ocean up inside of her. Sweat rolled down her back in a shallow river and pooled at her waist and between her breasts. A thin sheen of water came out on her forearms, her face. Vicki gave an irritated moan but Brackett seemed not to take notice, or take offense at least. Air-conditioned breezes were sweeping over the seat anyway, and very soon they would be comfortable. She smiled at Brackett over Buddy's head. The man grinned back. Buddy stirred. Vicki remembered the emergency chocolate bar she kept in her purse, fished it out, and offered it to Buddy. He did not react, so she closed his fingers over the package and peeled the paper off one end.

The car accelerated. Buddy felt the road and wheels pummeling 83 each other and the rush of the heavy motor purring in high gear. Buddy knew that what he'd seen in his mind that morning, the thing coming out of the sky with barbs and chains, had hooked him. Somehow he was caught and held in the sour tin smell of the pale woman's armpit. Somehow he was pinned between their pounds of breathless flesh. He looked at the chocolate in his hand. He was squeezing the bar so hard that a thin brown trickle had melted down his arm. Automatically he put the bar in his mouth.

As he bit down he saw his mother very clearly, just as she had 84 been when she carried him from the shed. She was stretched flat on the ground, on her stomach, and her arms were curled around her head as if in sleep. One leg was drawn up and it looked for all the world like she was running full tilt into the ground, as though she had been trying to pass into the earth, to bury herself, but at the last moment something had stopped her.

There was no blood on Albertine, but Buddy tasted blood now 85 at the sight of her, for he bit down hard and cut his own lip. He ate the chocolate, every bit of it, tasting his mother's blood. And when he had the chocolate down inside him and all licked off his hands, he opened his mouth to say thank you to the woman, as his mother had taught him. But instead of a thank you coming out he was astonished to hear a great rattling scream, and then another, rip out of him like pieces of his own body and whirl onto the sharp things all around him.

Territory

DAVID LEAVITT

Neil's mother, Mrs. Campbell, sits on her lawn chair behind a card   1
table outside the food co-op. Every few minutes, as the sun shifts,
she moves the chair and table several inches back so as to remain in
the shade. It is a hundred degrees outside, and bright white. Each
time someone goes in or out of the co-op a gust of air-conditioning
flies out of the automatic doors, raising dust from the cement.

Neil stands just inside, poised over a water fountain, and   2
watches her. She has on a sun hat, and a sweatshirt over her tennis
dress; her legs are bare, and shiny with cocoa butter. In front of her,
propped against the table, a sign proclaims: MOTHERS, FIGHT FOR YOUR
CHILDREN'S RIGHTS—SUPPORT A NON-NUCLEAR FUTURE. Women dressed
exactly like her pass by, notice the sign, listen to her brief spiel,
finger pamphlets, sign petitions or don't sign petitions, never give
money. Her weary eyes are masked by dark glasses. In the age of
Reagan, she has declared, keeping up the causes of peace and justice is a futile, tiresome, and unrewarding effort; it is therefore an effort fit only for mothers to keep up. The sun bounces off the window glass through which Neil watches her. His own reflection lines
up with her profile.

Later that afternoon, Neil spreads himself out alongside the pool   3
and imagines he is being watched by the shirtless Chicano gardener.
But the gardener, concentrating on his pruning, is neither seductive
nor seducible. On the lawn, his mother's large Airedales—Abigail,
Lucille, Fern—amble, sniff, urinate. Occasionally, they accost the
gardener, who yells at them in Spanish.

After two years' absence, Neil reasons, he should feel nostalgia,   4
regret, gladness upon returning home. He closes his eyes and tries
to muster the proper background music for the cinematic scene of
return. His rhapsody, however, is interrupted by the noises of his
mother's trio—the scratchy cello, whining violin, stumbling piano—
as she and Lillian Havalard and Charlotte Feder plunge through

---

David Leavitt (1961–   ), born in Pittsburgh, Pennsylvania, is the
author of stories and novels including *Family Dancing* (1984), *The
Lost Language of Cranes* (1986), and *Equal Affections* (1989).
"Territory" first appeared in *The New Yorker* (1982).

Mozart. The tune is cheery, in a Germanic sort of way, and utterly inappropriate to what Neil is trying to feel. Yet it *is* the music of his adolescence; they have played it for years, bent over the notes, their heads bobbing in silent time to the metronome.

It is getting darker. Every few minutes, he must move his towel   5 so as to remain within the narrowing patch of sunlight. In four hours, Wayne, his lover of ten months and the only person he has ever imagined he could spend his life with, will be in this house, where no lover of his has ever set foot. The thought fills him with a sense of grand terror and curiosity. He stretches, tries to feel seductive, desirable. The gardener's shears whack at the ferns; the music above him rushes to a loud, premature conclusion. The women laugh and applaud themselves as they give up for the day. He hears Charlotte Feder's full nasal twang, the voice of a fat woman in a pink pants suit—odd, since she is a scrawny, arthritic old bird, rarely clad in anything other than tennis shorts and a blouse. Lillian is the fat woman in the pink pants suit; her voice is thin and warped by too much crying. Drink in hand, she calls out from the porch, "Hot enough!" and waves. He lifts himself up and nods to her.

The women sit on the porch and chatter; their voices blend with   6 the clink of ice in glasses. They belong to a small circle of ladies all of whom, with the exception of Neil's mother, are widows and divorcées. Lillian's husband left her twenty-two years ago, and sends her a check every month to live on; Charlotte has been divorced twice as long as she was married, and has a daughter serving a long sentence for terrorist acts committed when she was nineteen. Only Neil's mother has a husband, a distant sort of husband, away often on business. He is away on business now. All of them feel betrayed—by husbands, by children, by history.

Neil closes his eyes, tries to hear the words only as sounds.   7 Soon, a new noise accosts him: his mother arguing with the gardener in Spanish. He leans on his elbows and watches them; the syllables are loud, heated, and compressed, and seem on the verge of explosion. But the argument ends happily; they shake hands. The gardener collects his check and walks out the gate without so much as looking at Neil.

He does not know the gardener's name; as his mother has re-   8 minded him, he does not know most of what has gone on since he moved away. Her life has gone on, unaffected by his absence. He flinches at his own egoism, the egoism of sons.

"Neil! Did you call the airport to make sure the plane's coming   9 in on time?"

"Yes," he shouts to her. "It is."   10

"Good. Well, I'll have dinner ready when you get back."   11

"Mom—"   12

"What?" The word comes out in a weary wail that is more of an   13
answer than a question.

"What's wrong?" he says, forgetting his original question.   14

"Nothing's wrong," she declares in a tone that indicates that ev-   15
erything is wrong. "The dogs have to be fed, dinner has to be made,
and I've got people here. Nothing's wrong."

"I hope things will be as comfortable as possible when Wayne   16
gets here."

"Is that a request or a threat?"   17

"Mom—"   18

Behind her sunglasses, her eyes are inscrutable. "I'm tired," she   19
says. "It's been a long day. I . . . I'm anxious to meet Wayne. I'm
sure he'll be wonderful, and we'll all have a wonderful, wonderful
time. I'm sorry. I'm just tired."

She heads up the stairs. He suddenly feels an urge to cover him-   20
self; his body embarrasses him, as it has in her presence since the
day she saw him shirtless and said with delight, "Neil! You're growing hair under your arms!"

Before he can get up, the dogs gather round him and begin to   21
sniff and lick at him. He wriggles to get away from them, but Abigail, the largest and stupidest, straddles his stomach and nuzzles his
mouth. He splutters and, laughing, throws her off. "Get away from
me, you goddamn dogs," he shouts, and swats at them. They are
new dogs, not the dog of his childhood, not dogs he trusts.

He stands, and the dogs circle him, looking up at his face expec-   22
tantly. He feels renewed terror at the thought that Wayne will be
here so soon: Will they sleep in the same room? Will they make
love? He has never had sex in his parents' house. How can he be expected to be a lover here, in this place of his childhood, of his earliest shame, in this household of mothers and dogs?

"Dinnertime! Abbylucyferny, Abbylucyferny, dinnertime!" His   23
mother's litany disperses the dogs, and they run for the door.

"Do you realize," he shouts to her, "that no matter how much   24
those dogs love you they'd probably kill you for the leg of lamb in
the freezer?"

Neil was twelve the first time he recognized in himself something   25
like sexuality. He was lying outside, on the grass, when Rasputin—
the dog, long dead, of his childhood—began licking his face. He felt
a tingle he did not recognize, pulled off his shirt to give the dog access to more of him. Rasputin's tongue tickled coolly. A wet nose
started to sniff down his body, toward his bathing suit. What he felt

frightened him, but he couldn't bring himself to push the dog away. Then his mother called out, "Dinner," and Rasputin was gone, more interested in food than in him.

It was the day after Rasputin was put to sleep, years later, that Neil finally stood in the kitchen, his back turned to his parents, and said, with unexpected ease, "I'm a homosexual." The words seemed insufficient, reductive. For years, he had believed his sexuality to be detachable from the essential him, but now he realized that it was part of him. He had the sudden, despairing sensation that though the words had been easy to say, the fact of their having been aired was incurably damning. Only then, for the first time, did he admit that they were true, and he shook and wept in regret for what he would not be for his mother, for having failed her. His father hung back, silent; he was absent for that moment as he was mostly absent—a strong absence. Neil always thought of him sitting on the edge of the bed in his underwear, captivated by something on television. He said, "It's O.K., Neil." But his mother was resolute; her lower lip didn't quaver. She had enormous reserves of strength to which she only gained access at moments like this one. She hugged him from behind, wrapped him in the childhood smells of perfume and brownies, and whispered, "It's O.K., honey." For once, her words seemed as inadequate as his. Neil felt himself shrunk to an embarrassed adolescent, hating her sympathy, not wanting her to touch him. It was the way he would feel from then on whenever he was in her presence—even now, at twenty-three, bringing home his lover to meet her.

All through his childhood, she had packed only the most nutritious lunches, had served on the PTA, had volunteered at the children's library and at his school, had organized a successful campaign to ban a racist history textbook. The day after he told her, she located and got in touch with an organization called the Coalition of Parents of Lesbians and Gays. Within a year, she was president of it. On weekends, she and the other mothers drove their station wagons to San Francisco, set up their card tables in front of the Bulldog Baths, the Liberty Baths, passed out literature to men in leather and denim who were loath to admit they even had mothers. These men, who would habitually do violence to each other, were strangely cowed by the suburban ladies with their informational booklets, and bent their heads. Neil was a sophomore in college then, and lived in San Francisco. She brought him pamphlets detailing the dangers of bathhouses and back rooms, enemas and poppers, wordless sex in alleyways. His excursion into that world had been brief and lamentable, and was over. He winced at the thought that she knew all his sexual secrets, and vowed to move to the East Coast to escape her. It was not very different from the days when she had campaigned for a better playground, or tutored the Hispanic children in the audiovisual room. Those days, as well, he had run away from her concern. Even today, perched in front of the co-op, collecting signatures for nuclear disarmament, she was quintessentially a mother. And if the lot of mothers was to expect nothing in return, was the lot of sons to return nothing?

Driving across the Dumbarton Bridge on his way to the airport, Neil   28
thinks, I have returned nothing; I have simply returned. He wonders if she would have given birth to him had she known what he would grow up to be.

Then he berates himself: Why should he assume himself to be   29
the cause of her sorrow? She has told him that her life is full of secrets. She has changed since he left home—grown thinner, more rigid, harder to hug. She has given up baking, taken up tennis; her skin has browned and tightened. She is no longer the woman who hugged him and kissed him, who said, "As long as you're happy, that's all that's important to us."

The flats spread out around him; the bridge floats on purple and   30
green silt, and spongy bay fill, not water at all. Only ten miles north, a whole city has been built on gunk dredged up from the bay.

He arrives at the airport ten minutes early, to discover that the   31
plane has landed twenty minutes early. His first view of Wayne is from behind, by the baggage belt. Wayne looks as he always looks—slightly windblown—and is wearing the ratty leather jacket he was wearing the night they met. Neil sneaks up on him and puts his hands on his shoulders; when Wayne turns around, he looks relieved to see him.

They hug like brothers; only in the safety of Neil's mother's car   32
do they dare to kiss. They recognize each other's smells, and grow comfortable again. "I never imagined I'd actually see you out here," Neil says, "but you're exactly the same here as there."

"It's only been a week."   33

They kiss again. Neil wants to go to a motel, but Wayne insists   34
on being pragmatic. "We'll be there soon. Don't worry."

"We could go to one of the bathhouses in the city and take a   35
room for a couple of aeons," Neil says. "Christ, I'm hard up. I don't even know if we're going to be in the same bedroom."

"Well, if we're not," Wayne says, "we'll sneak around. It'll be   36
romantic."

They cling to each other for a few more minutes, until they realize that people are looking in the car window. Reluctantly, they pull   37 apart. Neil reminds himself that he loves this man, that there is a reason for him to bring this man home.

He takes the scenic route on the way back. The car careers over 38 foothills, through forests, along white four-lane highways high in the mountains. Wayne tells Neil that he sat next to a woman on the plane who was once Marilyn Monroe's psychiatrist's nurse. He slips his foot out of his shoe and nudges Neil's ankle, pulling Neil's sock down with his toe.

"I have to drive," Neil says. "I'm very glad you're here." 39

There is a comfort in the privacy of the car. They have a com- 40 mon fear of walking hand in hand, of publicly showing physical affection, even in the permissive West Seventies of New York—a fear that they have admitted only to one another. They slip through a pass between two hills, and are suddenly in residential Northern California, the land of expensive ranch-style houses.

As they pull into Neil's mother's driveway, the dogs run barking 41 toward the car. When Wayne opens the door, they jump and lap at him, and he tries to close it again. "Don't worry. Abbylucyferny! Get in the house, damn it!"

His mother descends from the porch. She has changed into a 42 blue flower-print dress, which Neil doesn't recognize. He gets out of the car and halfheartedly chastises the dogs. Crickets chirp in the trees. His mother looks radiant, even beautiful, illuminated by the headlights, surrounded by the now quiet dogs, like a Circe with her slaves. When she walks over to Wayne, offering her hand, and says, "Wayne, I'm Barbara," Neil forgets that she is his mother.

"Good to meet you, Barbara," Wayne says, and reaches out his 43 hand. Craftier than she, he whirls her around to kiss her cheek.

Barbara! He is calling his mother Barbara! Then he remembers 44 that Wayne is five years older than he is. They chat by the open car door, and Neil shrinks back—the embarrassed adolescent, uncomfortable, unwanted.

So the dreaded moment passes and he might as well not have 45 been there. At dinner, Wayne keeps the conversation smooth, like a captivated courtier seeking Neil's mother's hand. A faggot son's sodomist—such words spit into Neil's head. She has prepared tiny meatballs with fresh coriander, fettucine with pesto. Wayne talks about the street people in New York; El Salvador is a tragedy; if only Sadat had lived; Phyllis Schlafly—what can you do?

"It's a losing battle," she tells him. "Every day I'm out there 46 with my card table, me and the other mothers, but I tell you, Wayne, it's a losing battle. Sometimes I think us old ladies are the only ones with enough patience to fight."

Occasionally, Neil says something, but his comments seem 47

stupid and clumsy. Wayne continues to call her Barbara. No one under forty has ever called her Barbara as long as Neil can remember.
They drink wine; he does not.

Now is the time for drastic action. He contemplates taking   48
Wayne's hand, then checks himself. He has never done anything in
her presence to indicate that the sexuality he confessed to five years
ago was a reality and not an invention. Even now, he and Wayne
might as well be friends, college roommates. Then Wayne, his savior, with a single, sweeping gesture, reaches for his hand, and
clasps it, in the midst of a joke he is telling about Saudi Arabians. By
the time he is laughing, their hands are joined. Neil's throat contracts; his heart begins to beat violently. He notices his mother's
eyes flicker, glance downward; she never breaks the stride of her
sentence. The dinner goes on, and every taboo nurtured since childhood falls quietly away.

She removes the dishes. Their hands grow sticky; he cannot tell   49
which fingers are his and which Wayne's. She clears the rest of the
table and rounds up the dogs.

"Well, boys, I'm very tired, and I've got a long day ahead of me   50
tomorrow, so I think I'll hit the sack. There are extra towels for you
in Neil's bathroom, Wayne. Sleep well."

"Good night, Barbara," Wayne calls out. "It's been wonderful   51
meeting you."

They are alone. Now they can disentangle their hands.   52

"No problem about where we sleep, is there?"   53

"No," Neil says. "I just can't imagine sleeping with someone in   54
this house."

His leg shakes violently. Wayne takes Neil's hand in a firm   55
grasp and hauls him up.

Later that night, they lie outside, under redwood trees, listening to   56
the hysteria of the crickets, the hum of the pool cleaning itself. Redwood leaves prick their skin. They fell in love in bars and apartments, and this is the first time that they have made love outdoors.
Neil is not sure he has enjoyed the experience. He kept sensing
eyes, imagined that the neighborhood cats were staring at them
from behind a fence of brambles. He remembers he once hid in this
spot when he and some of the children from the neighborhood were
playing sardines, remembers the intoxication of small bodies packed
together, the warm breath of suppressed laughter on his neck. "The
loser had to go through the spanking machine," he tells Wayne.

"Did you lose often?"   57

"Most of the time. The spanking machine never really hurt—just   58 a whirl of hands. If you moved fast enough, no one could actually get you. Sometimes, though, late in the afternoon, we'd get naughty. We'd chase each other and pull each other's pants down. That was all. Boys and girls together!"

"Listen to the insects," Wayne says, and closes his eyes.   59

Neil turns to examine Wayne's face, notices a single, small pim-   60 ple. Their lovemaking usually begins in a wrestle, a struggle for dominance, and ends with a somewhat confusing loss of identity— as now, when Neil sees a foot on the grass, resting against his leg, and tries to determine if it is his own or Wayne's.

From inside the house, the dogs begin to bark. Their yelps grow   61 into alarmed falsettos. Neil lifts himself up. "I wonder if they smell something," he says.

"Probably just us," says Wayne.   62

"My mother will wake up. She hates getting waked up."   63

Lights go on in the house; the door to the porch opens.   64

"What's wrong, Abby? What's wrong?" his mother's voice calls   65 softly.

Wayne clamps his hand over Neil's mouth. "Don't say any-   66 thing," he whispers.

"I can't just—" Neil begins to say, but Wayne's hand closes over   67 his mouth again. He bites it, and Wayne starts laughing.

"What was that?" Her voice projects into the garden. "Hello?"   68 she says.

The dogs yelp louder. "Abbylucyferny, it's O.K., it's O.K." Her   69 voice is soft and panicked. "Is anyone there?" she asks loudly.

The brambles shake. She takes a flashlight, shines it around the   70 garden. Wayne and Neil duck down; the light lands on them and hovers for a few seconds. Then it clicks off and they are in the dark—a new dark, a darker dark, which their eyes must readjust to.

"Let's go to bed, Abbylucyferny," she says gently. Neil and   71 Wayne hear her pad into the house. The dogs whimper as they follow her, and the lights go off.

Once before, Neil and his mother had stared at each other in the   72 glare of bright lights. Four years ago, they stood in the arena created by the headlights of her car, waiting for the train. He was on his way back to San Francisco, where he was marching in a Gay Pride Parade the next day. The train station was next door to the food co-op and shared its parking lot. The co-op, familiar and boring by day, took on a certain mystery in the night. Neil recognized the spot where he had skidded on his bicycle and broken his leg. Through the glass doors, the brightly lit interior of the store glowed, its rows

and rows of cans and boxes forming their own horizon, each can illuminated so that even from outside Neil could read the labels. All
that was missing was the ladies in tennis dresses and sweatshirts
pushing their carts past bins of nuts and dried fruits.

"Your train is late," his mother said. Her hair fell loosely on her   73
shoulders, and her legs were tanned. Neil looked at her and tried to
imagine her in labor with him—bucking and struggling with his
birth. He felt then the strange, sexless love for women which
through his whole adolescence he had mistaken for heterosexual desire.

A single bright light approached them; it preceded the low,   74
haunting sound of the whistle. Neil kissed his mother, and waved
goodbye as he ran to meet the train. It was an old train, with windows tinted a sort of horrible lemon-lime. It stopped only long
enough for him to hoist himself on board, and then it was moving
again. He hurried to a window, hoping to see her drive off, but the
tint of the window made it possible for him to make out only vague
patches of light—street lamps, cars, the co-op.

He sank into the hard, green seat. The train was almost entirely   75
empty; the only other passenger was a dark-skinned man wearing
bluejeans and a leather jacket. He sat directly across the aisle from
Neil, next to the window. He had rough skin and a thick mustache.
Neil discovered that by pretending to look out the window he could
study the man's reflection in the lemon-lime glass. It was only
slightly hazy—the quality of a bad photograph. Neil felt his mouth
open, felt sleep closing in on him. Hazy red and gold flashes
through the glass pulsed in the face of the man in the window, giving the curious impression of muscle spasms. It took Neil a few minutes to realize that the man was staring at him, or, rather, staring at
the back of his head—staring at his staring. The man smiled as
though to say, I know exactly what you're staring at, and Neil felt
the sickening sensation of desire rise in his throat.

Right before they reached the city, the man stood up and sat   76
down in the seat next to Neil's. The man's thigh brushed deliberately against his own. Neil's eyes were watering; he felt sick to his
stomach. Taking Neil's hand, the man said, "Why so nervous,
honey? Relax."

Neil woke up the next morning with the taste of ashes in his   77
mouth. He was lying on the floor, without blankets or sheets or pillows. Instinctively, he reached for his pants, and as he pulled them
on came face to face with the man from the train. His name was
Luis; he turned out to be a dog groomer. His apartment smelled of
dog.

"Why such a hurry?" Luis said.   78

"The parade. The Gay Pride Parade. I'm meeting some friends   79
to march."

"I'll come with you," Luis said. "I think I'm too old for these   80
things, but why not?"

Neil did not want Luis to come with him, but he found it impos-   81
sible to say so. Luis looked older by day, more likely to carry diseases. He dressed again in a torn T-shirt, leather jacket, bluejeans.
"It's my everyday apparel," he said, and laughed. Neil buttoned his
pants, aware that they had been washed by his mother the day before. Luis possessed the peculiar combination of hypermasculinity
and effeminacy which exemplifies faggotry. Neil wanted to be rid of
him, but Luis's mark was on him, he could see that much. They
would become lovers whether Neil liked it or not.

They joined the parade midway. Neil hoped he wouldn't meet   82
anyone he knew; he did not want to have to explain Luis, who
clung to him. The parade was full of shirtless men with oiled, muscular shoulders. Neil's back ached. There were floats carrying gar-
ishly dressed prom queens and cheerleaders, some with beards,
some actually looking like women. Luis said, "It makes me proud,
makes me glad to be what I am." Neil supposed that by darting into
the crowd ahead of him he might be able to lose Luis forever, but he
found it difficult to let him go; the prospect of being alone seemed
unbearable.

Neil was startled to see his mother watching the parade, holding   83
up a sign. She was with the Coalition of Parents of Lesbians and
Gays; they had posted a huge banner on the wall behind them pro-
claiming: OUR SONS AND DAUGHTERS, WE ARE PROUD OF YOU. She spotted
him; she waved, and jumped up and down.

"Who's that woman?" Luis asked.   84

"My mother. I should go say hello to her."   85

"O.K.," Luis said. He followed Neil to the side of the parade.   86
Neil kissed his mother. Luis took off his shirt, wiped his face with it,
smiled.

"I'm glad you came," Neil said.   87

"I wouldn't have missed it, Neil. I wanted to show you I cared."   88

He smiled, and kissed her again. He showed no intention of in-   89
troducing Luis, so Luis introduced himself.

"Hello, Luis," Mrs. Campbell said. Neil looked away. Luis   90
shook her hand, and Neil wanted to warn his mother to wash it,
warned himself to check with a V.D. clinic first thing Monday.

"Neil, this is Carmen Bologna, another one of the mothers,"   91
Mrs. Campbell said. She introduced him to a fat Italian woman with
flushed cheeks, and hair arranged in the shape of a clamshell.

"Good to meet you, Neil, good to meet you," said Carmen   92

Bologna. "You know my son, Michael? I'm so proud of Michael! He's doing so well now. I'm proud of him, proud to be his mother I am, and your mother's proud, too!"

The woman smiled at him, and Neil could think of nothing to say but "Thank you." He looked uncomfortably toward his mother, who stood listening to Luis. It occurred to him that the worst period of his life was probably about to begin and he had no way to stop it. 93

A group of drag queens ambled over to where the mothers were standing. "Michael! Michael!" shouted Carmen Bologna, and embraced a sticklike man wrapped in green satin. Michael's eyes were heavily dosed with green eyeshadow, and his lips were painted pink. 94

Neil turned and saw his mother staring, her mouth open. He marched over to where Luis was standing, and they moved back into the parade. He turned and waved to her. She waved back; he saw pain in her face, and then, briefly, regret. That day, he felt she would have traded him for any other son. Later, she said to him, "Carmen Bologna really was proud, and, speaking as a mother, let me tell you, you have to be brave to feel such pride." 95

Neil was never proud. It took him a year to dump Luis, another year to leave California. The sick taste of ashes was still in his mouth. On the plane, he envisioned his mother sitting alone in the dark, smoking. She did not leave his mind until he was circling New York, staring down at the dawn rising over Queens. The song playing in his earphones would remain hovering on the edges of his memory, always associated with her absence. After collecting his baggage, he took a bus into the city. Boys were selling newspapers in the middle of highways, through the windows of stopped cars. It was seven in the morning when he reached Manhattan. He stood for ten minutes on East Thirty-fourth Street, breathed the cold air, and felt bubbles rising in his blood. 96

Neil got a job as a paralegal—a temporary job, he told himself. When he met Wayne a year later, the sensations of that first morning returned to him. They'd been up all night, and at six they walked across the park to Wayne's apartment with the nervous, deliberate gait of people aching to make love for the first time. Joggers ran by with their dogs. None of them knew what Wayne and he were about to do, and the secrecy excited him. His mother came to mind, and the song, and the whirling vision of Queens coming alive below him. His breath solidified into clouds, and he felt happier than he had ever felt before in his life. 97

The second day of Wayne's visit, he and Neil go with Mrs. Campbell to pick up the dogs at the dog parlor. The grooming establish- 98 ment is decorated with pink ribbons and photographs of the owner's champion pit bulls. A fat, middle-aged woman appears from the back, leading the newly trimmed and fluffed Abigail, Lucille, and Fern by three leashes. The dogs struggle frantically when they see Neil's mother, tangling the woman up in their leashes. "Ladies, behave!" Mrs. Campbell commands, and collects the dogs. She gives Fern to Neil and Abigail to Wayne. In the car on the way back, Abigail begins pawing to get on Wayne's lap.

"Just push her off," Mrs. Campbell says. "She knows she's not 99 supposed to do that."

"You never groomed Rasputin," Neil complains. 100

"Rasputin was a mutt." 101

"Rasputin was a beautiful dog, even if he did smell." 102

"Do you remember when you were a little kid, Neil, you used to 103 make Rasputin dance with you? Once you tried to dress him up in one of my blouses."

"I don't remember that," Neil says. 104

"Yes. I remember," says Mrs. Campbell. "Then you tried to or- 105 ganize a dog beauty contest in the neighborhood. You wanted to have runners-up—everything."

"A dog beauty contest?" Wayne says. 106

"Mother, do we have to—" 107

"I think it's a mother's privilege to embarrass her son," Mrs. 108 Campbell says, and smiles.

When they are about to pull into the driveway, Wayne starts 109 screaming, and pushes Abigail off his lap. "Oh, my God!" he says. "The dog just pissed all over me."

Neil turns around and sees a puddle seeping into Wayne's 110 slacks. He suppresses his laughter, and Mrs. Campbell hands him a rag.

"I'm sorry, Wayne," she says. "It goes with the territory." 111

"This is really disgusting," Wayne says, swatting at himself with 112 the rag.

Neil keeps his eyes on his own reflection in the rearview mirror 113 and smiles.

At home, while Wayne cleans himself in the bathroom, Neil 114 watches his mother cook lunch—Japanese noodles in soup. "When you went off to college," she says, "I went to the grocery store. I was going to buy you ramen noodles, and I suddenly realized you weren't going to be around to eat them. I started crying right then, blubbering like an idiot."

Neil clenches his fists inside his pockets. She has a way of telling 115 him little sad stories when he doesn't want to hear them—stories of dolls broken by her brothers, lunches stolen by neighborhood boys on the way to school. Now he has joined the ranks of male children who have made her cry.

"Mama, I'm sorry," he says. 116

She is bent over the noodles, which steam in her face. "I didn't 117 want to say anything in front of Wayne, but I wish you had answered me last night. I was very frightened—and worried."

"I'm sorry," he says, but it's not convincing. His fingers prickle. 118 He senses a great sorrow about to be born.

"I lead a quiet life," she says. "I don't want to be a disciplinar- 119 ian. I just don't have the energy for these—shenanigans. Please don't frighten me that way again."

"If you were so upset, why didn't you say something?" 120

"I'd rather not discuss it. I lead a quiet life. I'm not used to get- 121 ting woken up late at night. I'm not used—"

"To my having a lover?" 122

"No, I'm not used to having other people around, that's all. 123 Wayne is charming. A wonderful young man."

"He likes you, too." 124

"I'm sure we'll get along fine." 125

She scoops the steaming noodles into ceramic bowls. Wayne re- 126 turns, wearing shorts. His white, hairy legs are a shocking contrast to hers, which are brown and sleek.

"I'll wash those pants, Wayne," Mrs. Campbell says. "I have a 127 special detergent that'll take out the stain."

She gives Neil a look to indicate that the subject should be 128 dropped. He looks at Wayne, looks at his mother; his initial embarrassment gives way to a fierce pride—the arrogance of mastery. He is glad his mother knows that he is desired, glad it makes her flinch.

Later, he steps into the back yard; the gardener is back, whack- 129 ing at the bushes with his shears. Neil walks by him in his bathing suit, imagining he is on parade.

That afternoon, he finds his mother's daily list on the kitchen table: 130

Tuesday
7:00—breakfast
Take dogs to groomer
Groceries (?)

Campaign against Draft—4–7

Buy underwear
Trios—2:00
Spaghetti
Fruit
Asparagus if sale

Peanuts
Milk

Doctor's Appointment (make)
Write Cranston/Hayakawa
re disarmament

Handi-Wraps
Mozart
Abigail
Top Ramen
Pedro

Her desk and trash can are full of such lists; he remembers them
from the earliest days of his childhood. He had learned to read from
them. In his own life, too, there have been endless lists—covered
with check marks and arrows, at least one item always spilling over
onto the next day's agenda. From September to November, "Buy
plane ticket for Christmas" floated from list to list to list.

The last item puzzles him: Pedro. Pedro must be the gardener. 131
He observes the accretion of names, the arbitrary specifics that give
a sense of his mother's life. He could make a list of his own selves:
the child, the adolescent, the promiscuous faggot son, and finally
the good son, settled, relatively successful. But the divisions
wouldn't work; he is today and will always be the child being licked
by the dog, the boy on the floor with Luis; he will still be everything
he is ashamed of. The other lists—the lists of things done and undone—tell their own truth: that his life is measured more properly
in objects than in stages. He knows himself as "jump rope," "book,"
"sunglasses," "underwear."

"Tell me about your family, Wayne," Mrs. Campbell says that 132
night, as they drive toward town. They are going to see an Esther
Williams movie at the local revival house: an underwater musical,
populated by mermaids, underwear Rockettes.

"My father was a lawyer," Wayne says. "He had an office in 133
Queens, with a neon sign. I think he's probably the only lawyer in
the world who had a neon sign. Anyway, he died when I was ten.
My mother never remarried. She lives in Queens. Her great claim to
fame is that when she was twenty-two she went on 'The $64,000
Question.' Her category was mystery novels. She made it to sixteen
thousand before she got tripped up."

"When I was about ten, I wanted you to go on 'Jeopardy,'" Neil 134
says to his mother. "You really should have, you know. You would
have won."

"You certainly loved 'Jeopardy,'" Mrs. Campbell says. "You 135
used to watch it during dinner. Wayne, does your mother work?"

"No," he says. "She lives off investments." 136

"You're both only children," Mrs. Campbell says. Neil wonders 137 if she is ruminating on the possible connection between that coincidence and their "alternative life style."

The movie theater is nearly empty. Neil sits between Wayne and 138 his mother. There are pillows on the floor at the front of the theater, and a cat is prowling over them. It casts a monstrous shadow every now and then on the screen, disturbing the sedative effect of water ballet. Like a teen-ager, Neil cautiously reaches his arm around Wayne's shoulder. Wayne takes his hand immediately. Next to them, Neil's mother breathes in, out, in, out. Neil timorously moves his other arm and lifts it behind his mother's neck. He does not look at her, but he can tell from her breathing that she senses what he is doing. Slowly, carefully, he lets his hand drop on her shoulder; it twitches spasmodically, and he jumps, as if he had received an electric shock. His mother's quiet breathing is broken by a gasp; even Wayne notices. A sudden brightness on the screen illuminates the panic in her eyes, Neil's arm frozen above her, about to fall again. Slowly, he lowers his arm until his fingertips touch her skin, the fabric of her dress. He has gone too far to go back now; they are all too far.

Wayne and Mrs. Campbell sink into their seats, but Neil re- 139 mains stiff, holding up his arms, which rest on nothing. The movie ends, and they go on sitting just like that.

"I'm old," Mrs. Campbell says later, as they drive back home. "I 140 remember when those films were new. Your father and I went to one on our first date. I loved them, because I could pretend that those women underwater were flying—they were so graceful. They really took advantage of Technicolor in those days. Color was something to appreciate. You can't know what it was like to see a color movie for the first time, after years of black-and-white. It's like trying to explain the surprise of snow to an East Coaster. Very little is new anymore, I fear."

Neil would like to tell her about his own nostalgia, but how can 141 he explain that all of it revolves around her? The idea of her life before he was born pleases him. "Tell Wayne how you used to look like Esther Williams," he asks her.

She blushes. "I was told I looked like Esther Williams, but really 142 more like Gene Tierney," she says. "Not beautiful, but interesting. I like to think I had a certain magnetism."

"You still do," Wayne says, and instantly recognizes the wrong- 143 ness of his comment. Silence and a nervous laugh indicate that he has not yet mastered the family vocabulary.

When they get home, the night is once again full of the sound of 144
crickets. Mrs. Campbell picks up a flashlight and calls the dogs.
"Abbylucyferny, Abbylucyferny," she shouts, and the dogs amble
from their various corners. She pushes them out the door to the
back yard and follows them. Neil follows her. Wayne follows Neil,
but hovers on the porch. Neil walks behind her as she tramps
through the garden. She holds out her flashlight, and snails slide
from behind bushes, from under rocks, to where she stands. When
the snails become visible, she crushes them underfoot. They make a
wet, cracking noise, like eggs being broken.

"Nights like this," she says, "I think of children without pants 145
on, in hot South American countries. I have nightmares about tanks
rolling down our street."

"The weather's never like this in New York," Neil says. "When 146
it's hot, it's humid and sticky. You don't want to go outdoors."

"I could never live anywhere else but here. I think I'd die. I'm 147
too used to the climate."

"Don't be silly." 148

"No, I mean it," she says. "I have adjusted too well to the 149
weather."

The dogs bark and howl by the fence. "A cat, I suspect," she 150
says. She aims her flashlight at a rock, and more snails emerge—un-
countable numbers, too stupid to have learned not to trust light.

"I know what you were doing at the movie," she says. 151
"What?" 152
"I know what you were doing." 153
"What? I put my arm around you." 154
"I'm sorry, Neil," she says. "I can only take so much. Just so 155
much."

"What do you mean?" he says. "I was only trying to show affec- 156
tion."

"Oh, affection—I know about affection." 157

He looks up at the porch, sees Wayne moving toward the door, 158
trying not to listen.

"What do you mean?" Neil says to her. 159

She puts down the flashlight and wraps her arms around her- 160
self. "I remember when you were a little boy," she says. "I remember, and I have to stop remembering. I wanted you to grow up
happy. And I'm very tolerant, very understanding. But I can only
take so much."

His heart seems to have risen into his throat. "Mother," he says, 161
"I think you know my life isn't your fault. But for God's sake, don't
say that your life is my fault."

"It's not a question of fault," she says. She extracts a Kleenex 162
from her pocket and blows her nose. "I'm sorry, Neil. I guess I'm
just an old woman with too much on her mind and not enough to
do." She laughs halfheartedly. "Don't worry. Don't say anything,"
she says. "Abbylucyferny, Abbylucyferny, time for bed!"

He watches her as she walks toward the porch, silent and regal. 163
There is the pad of feet, the clinking of dog tags as the dogs run for
the house.

He was twelve the first time she saw him march in a parade. He 164
played the tuba, and as his elementary-school band lumbered down
the streets of their then small town she stood on the sidelines and
waved. Afterward, she had taken him out for ice cream. He spilled
some on his red uniform, and she swiped at it with a napkin. She
had been there for him that day, as well as years later, at that more
memorable parade; she had been there for him every day.

Somewhere over Iowa, a week later, Neil remembers this scene, 165
remembers other days, when he would find her sitting in the dark,
crying. She had to take time out of her own private sorrow to appease his anxiety. "It was part of it," she told him later. "Part of being a mother."

"The scariest thing in the world is the thought that you could 166
unknowingly ruin someone's life," Neil tells Wayne. "Or even
change someone's life. I hate the thought of having such control. I'd
make a rotten mother."

"You're crazy," Wayne says. "You have this great mother, and 167
all you do is complain. I know people whose mothers have dis-
owned them."

"Guilt goes with the territory," Neil says.   168

"Why?" Wayne asks, perfectly seriously.   169

Neil doesn't answer. He lies back in his seat, closes his eyes, 170
imagines he grew up in a house in the mountains of Colorado, surrounded by snow—endless white snow on hills. No flat places, and
no trees; just white hills. Every time he has flown away, she has
come into his mind, usually sitting alone in the dark, smoking. Today she is outside at dusk, skimming leaves from the pool.

"I want to get a dog," Neil says.   171

Wayne laughs. "In the city? It'd suffocate."   172

The hum of the airplane is druglike, dazing, "I want to stay with 173
you a long time," Neil says.

"I know." Imperceptibly, Wayne takes his hand.   174

"It's very hot there in the summer, too. You know, I'm not 175
thinking about my mother now."

"It's O.K."   176

For a moment, Neil wonders what the stewardess or the old 177
woman on the way to the bathroom will think, but then he laughs
and relaxes.

Later, the plane makes a slow circle over New York City, and on 178
it two men hold hands, eyes closed, and breathe in unison.

Two Deserts

VALERIE MATSUMOTO

Emiko Oyama thought the Imperial Valley of California was the 1
loneliest place she had ever seen. It was just like the Topaz Reloca-
tion Camp, she told her husband, Kiyo, but without the barbed wire
fence and crowded barracks. Miles of bleached desert, punctuated
sparsely by creosote bush and debris, faced her from almost every
window in their small house. Only the living room had a view of the
dirt road which ended in front of their home, and across it, a row of
squat, faded houses where other farmers' families lived. They
waved to her and Kiyo in passing, and Jenny played with the Garcia
children, but Emiko's Spanish and their English were too limited for
more than casual greetings.

Emiko felt a tug of anticipation on the day the moving van 2
pulled up to the Ishikawa's place across the road—the house which
in her mind had become inextricably linked with friendship. She
had felt its emptiness as her own when Sats, Yuki, and their three
children gave up farming and departed for a life which later came to
her in delicious fragments in Yuki's hastily scrawled letters. Yuki
made the best sushi rice in the world and had given her the recipe.
She could draw shy Kiyo into happy banter. And her loud warm
laugh made the desert seem less drab, less engulfing.

The morning of moving day Emiko had been thinking about 3
Yuki as she weeded the yard and vegetable plot in preparation for
planting. Sats and Yuki had advised her to plant marigolds around
the vegetables to keep away nematodes, and she liked the idea of a
bold orange border. Emiko liked bright colors, especially the flaming
scarlet of the bougainvillea which rose above the front door, where
Kiki their cat lay sunning himself. There was a proud look in those
amber eyes, for Kiki the hunter had slain three scorpions and laid
them in a row on the porch, their backs crushed and deadly stingers
limp, winning extravagant praise from Jenny and Emiko. The scorpions still lay there, at Jenny's insistence, awaiting Kiyo's return that

Valerie Matsumoto (1957–   ), who grew up in Nogales, Arizona,
is professor of history at the University of California, Los Angeles,
and author of *The Cortez Colony: Family, Farm, and Community among
Japanese Americans, 1919–1982*. "Two Deserts" is from *Making Waves:
An Anthology by and about Asian American Women*, edited by Asian
Women United of California (1989).

562

evening. Emiko shuddered every time she entered the house, glancing at the curved stingers and thinking of Jenny's sandaled feet.

Emiko had finished weeding the front border and was about to   4
go inside to escape the heat, when she saw the new neighbor woman plodding across the sand toward her. A cotton shift could not conceal her thinness, nor a straw hat her tousled gray curls. Her eyes were fragile lilac glass above a wide smile.

"Hello, I'm Mattie Barnes. I just thought I'd come over and in-   5
troduce myself while Roy is finishing up with the movers. Your bougainvillea caught my eye first thing, and I thought, 'Those are some folks who know what will grow in the desert.' I hope you'll give me some advice about what to plant in my yard once we get settled in."

They talked about adjusting to desert life and Emiko learned   6
that Mattie's husband Roy had recently retired. "We decided to move here because the doctor said it would be better for my lungs," Mattie explained, wiping her brow.

"Would you like a glass of lemonade?" Emiko offered. "Or   7
maybe later, after you've finished moving."

"Oh, I'd love something cold," Mattie said, adding vaguely,   8
"Roy will take care of everything—he's more particular about those things than I am."

Emiko led Mattie into the house, hoping that Jenny was not ly-   9
ing on the cool linoleum, stripped to her underwear. As she crossed the threshold, Mattie gave a shriek and stopped abruptly, eyeing the scorpions lined up neatly on the porch.

"What on earth are these things doing here?"   10

"Our cat killed them," Emiko said, feeling too foolish to admit   11
her pride in Kiki's prowess. "Jenny wants me to leave them to show her father when he comes home from the field."

"Awful creatures," Mattie shuddered. "Roy can't stand them,   12
but then he can't abide insects. He said to me this morning, 'Of all the places we could have moved to, we had to choose the buggiest.'"

There was no buggier place than the Imperial Valley, Emiko   13
agreed, especially in the summer when the evening air was thick with mosquitoes, gnats, and moths, and cicadas buzzed in deafening chorus from every tree. They danced in frenzied legions around the porch light and did kamikaze dives into the bath water, and all of them came in dusty gray hordes, as though the desert had sapped their color, but not their energy. And late at night, long after Kiyo had fallen into exhausted sleep, Emiko would lie awake, perspiring, listening to the tinny scrabble of insects trapped between the window glass and screen.

". . . but I like the desert," Mattie was saying, dreamily clinking   14 the ice cubes in her glass. "It's so open and peaceful. As long as I can have a garden, I'll be happy."

Within a few weeks after their arrival, the Barneses had settled 15 into a routine: Roy made daily trips to the local store and the Roadside Cafe; Mattie tended her garden and walked to church once a week with Emiko and Jenny. By the end of June, Mattie had been enlisted with Emiko to make crepe paper flowers for the church bazaar.

"My, your flowers turned our beautifully," Mattie exclaimed one 16 morning, looking wistfully at the cardboard box filled with pink, yellow, scarlet, and lavender blossoms set on wire stems. "They'll make lovely corsages." She sighed. "I seem to be all thumbs—my flowers hardly look like flowers. I don't know how you do it. You Japanese are just very artistic people."

Emiko smiled and shook her head, making a polite disclaimer. 17 But the bright blur of flowers suddenly dissolved into another mass of paper blooms, carrying her more than a decade into the past. She was a teenager in a flannel shirt and denim pants with rolled cuffs, seated on a cot in a cramped barrack room, helping her mother fashion flowers from paper. Her own hands had been clumsy at first, though she strived to imitate her mother's precise fingers which gave each fragile petal lifelike curves, the look of artless grace. The only flowers for elderly Mr. Wasaka, shot by a guard in Topaz, were those which bloomed from the fingertips of *issei* and *nisei* women, working late into the night to complete the exquisite wreaths for his funeral. Each flower was a silent voice crying with color, each flower a tear.

"I did a little flower making as a teenager," Emiko said. 18

"Will you come over and show me how?" Mattie asked. "I'm too 19 embarrassed to take these awful things, and I've still got lots of crepe paper spread all over the kitchen."

"Sure," Emiko nodded. "I'll help you get started and you'll be a 20 whiz in no time. It isn't too hard; it just takes patience."

Mattie smiled, a slight wheeze in her voice when she said, "I've 21 got plenty of that, too."

They were seated at the Barneses' small table, surrounded by 22 bright masses of petals like fallen butterflies, their fingers sticky from the florist tape, when Roy returned from shopping. When he saw Emiko, he straightened and pulled his belt up over his paunch.

"A sight for sore eyes!" he boomed, giving her a broad wink. 23 "What mischief are you ladies up to?"

"Emi's teaching me how to make flowers," Mattie explained, 24 holding up a wobbly rose.

"Always flowers! I tell you," he leaned over Emiko's chair and 25 said in a mock conspiratorial voice, "all my wife thinks about is flowers. I keep telling her there are other things in life. Gardening is for old folks."

"And what's wrong with that?" Mattie protested, waving her 26 flower at him. "We *are* old folks.

"Speak for yourself," he winked at Emiko again. "What's so 27 great about gardens, anyway?"

"I hold with the poem that says you're closest to God's heart in 28 a garden," said Mattie.

"Well, I'm not ready to get that close to God's heart, yet." There 29 was defiance in Roy's voice. "What do you think about that, Emi?"

"I like working in the yard before it gets too hot," she said care- 30 fully. Her words felt tight and deliberate, like the unfurled petals on the yellow rose in her hands. "I don't have Mattie's talent with real flowers, though—aside from the bougainvillea and Jenny's petunias, nothing ever seems to bloom. The soil is too dry and saline for the things I used to grow. Now I've got my hopes pinned on the vegetable garden."

"Vegetables—hmph!" Roy snorted, stomping off to read the pa- 31 per.

"Oh, that Roy is just like a boy sometimes," Mattie said. "I tell 32 you, don't ever let your husband retire or you'll find him underfoot all day long."

"Doesn't Roy have any hobbies?" Emiko thought of her father 33 and his books, his Japanese brush painting, his meetings.

"He used to play golf," Mattie said, "but there's no golf course 34 here. He says this town is one giant sand trap."

"There have been times when I felt that way, too," Emiko admit- 35 ted lightly.

"Well, don't let Roy hear you say that or you'll never get him off 36 the topic," Mattie chuckled. "The fact is, Roy doesn't much know how to be by himself. I've had forty years to learn, and I've gotten to like it. And I suppose maybe he will, too."

Her voice trailed off, and Emiko suddenly realized that Mattie 37 didn't much care whether he did or not.

One day while Emiko was engrossed in pinning a dress pattern 38 for Jenny, she suddenly heard a tapping on the screen, like the scrabbling of a large beetle. She half turned and felt a jolt of alarm at the sight of a grinning gargoyle hunched before the window. It was Roy, his nose pushed up against the glass, hands splayed open on either side of his face, the caricature of a boy peering covetously into a toystore.

"Hey there! I caught you daydreaming!" he chortled. "Looks to 39 me like you need some company to wake you up."

"I'm not daydreaming; I'm trying to figure out how to make a 40 two-and-a-half yard dress out of two yards," she said. "Jenny is growing so fast, I can hardly keep up with her."

Roy walked into the house unbidden, confident of a welcome, 41 and drew a chair up to the table. He fingered the bright cotton print spread over the table and gazed at Emiko, his head cocked to one side.

"You must get pretty lonesome here by yourself all day. No 42 wonder you're sitting here dreaming."

"No," she said, her fingers moving the pattern pieces. "There's 43 so much to do, I don't have time to be lonesome. Besides, Jenny is here, and Kiyo comes home for lunch."

"But still—cooped up with a kiddie all day." Roy shook his 44 head. He chose to disregard Kiyo, who had no place in his imagined scenarios, and was hard at work miles away.

Emiko delicately edged the cotton fabric away from Roy's damp, 45 restless fingers. "I'll be darned if I offer him something to drink," she thought, as he mopped his brow and cast an impatient glance at the kitchen. "I haven't seen Mattie outside this week. How is she feeling?"

"Oh, 'bout the same, 'bout the same," he said, his irritation sub- 46 siding into brave resignation. "She has her good days and her bad days. The doctor told her to stay in bed for awhile and take it easy."

"It must be hard on Mattie, having to stay indoors," Emiko said, 47 thinking of her peering out through the pale curtains at the wilting zinnias and the new weeds in the back yard.

"I suppose so—usually you can't tear Mattie away from her gar- 48 den." Roy shook his head. "Mattie and me are real different. Now, I like people—I've always been the sociable type—but Mattie! All she cares about are plants."

"Well, Kiyo and I have different interests," Emiko said, "but it 49 works out well that way. Maybe you could learn a few things from Mattie about plants."

Even as the suggestion passed her lips, she regretted saying it. 50 Roy viewed the garden as the site of onerous labor. To Mattie, it was the true world of the heart, with no room for ungentle or impatient hands. It was a place of deeply sown hopes, lovingly nurtured, and its colors were the colors of unspoken dreams.

"Plants!" Roy threw up his hands. "Give me people any time. I 51 always liked people and had a knack for working with them—that's how I moved up in the business."

"Why don't you look into some of the clubs here?" Emiko tried 52 again. "The Elks always need people with experience and time."

"Sweetheart, I'm going to spend my time the way I want. I'm 53
finished with work—it's time to enjoy life! Besides, how much fun
can I have with a bunch of old geezers? That's not for me, Emily, my
dear." She stiffened as he repeated the name, savoring the syllables.
"Emily . . . Emily . . . Yes, I like the sound of that—Emily."

"My name is Emiko," she said quietly, her eyes as hard as agate. 54
"I was named after my grandmother." That unfaltering voice had
spoken the same words in first, second, third, fourth, fifth, and
sixth grades. All the grammar school teachers had sought to change
her name, to make her into an Emily: "Emily is so much easier to
pronounce, dear, and it's a nice American name." She was such a
well-mannered child, the teachers were always amazed at her stubbornness on this one point. Sometimes she was tempted to relent, to
give in, but something inside her resisted. "My name is Emiko," she
would insist politely. I am an American named Emiko. I was named
for my grandmother who was beautiful and loved to swim. When
she emerged from the sea, her long black hair would glitter white
with salt. I never met her, but she was beautiful and she would
laugh when she rose from the waves. "My name is Emiko; Emi for
short."

"But Emily is such a pretty name," Roy protested. "It fits you." 55

"It's not my name," she said, swallowing a hard knot of anger. 56
"I don't like to be called Emily!"

"Temper, temper!" He shook his finger at her, gleeful at having 57
provoked her.

"Well, I guess I'll be in a better temper when I can get some 58
work done," she said, folding up the cloth with tense, deliberate
hands. She raised her voice. "Jenny! Let's go out and water the vegetable garden now."

If Jenny thought this a strange task in the heat of the afternoon, 59
it did not show in her face when she skipped out of her room,
swinging her straw hat. It still sported a flimsy, rainbow-hued scarf
which had been the subject of much pleading in an El Centro dime
store. At that moment, Emiko found it an oddly reassuring sight.
She smiled and felt her composure return.

"Tell Mattie to let me know if there's anything I can do to help," 60
she told Roy, as he unwillingly followed them out of the house and
trudged away across the sand. After they went back inside, Emiko,
for the first time, locked the door behind them. When Kiyo returned
home, his face taut with fatigue, she told him it was because of the
hoboes who came around.

Emiko went to see Mattie less and less frequently, preferring in- 61
stead to call her on the phone, even though they lived so close. Roy,

however, continued to drop by, despite Emiko's aloofness. His unseemly yearning tugged at her with undignified hands, but what he
craved most was beyond her power to give. She took to darning and
mending in the bedroom with the curtains drawn, ignoring his insistent knock; she tried to do her gardening in the evening after dinner
when her husband was home, but it was hard to weed in the dusk.
She was beginning to feel caged, pent up, restless. Jenny and Kiyo
trod quietly, puzzled by her edginess, but their solicitude only made
her feel worse.

Finally one morning Emiko decided to weed the vegetables,   62
sprouting new and tender. Surely the midmorning heat would discourage any interference. Although perspiration soon trickled down
her face, she began to enjoy the satisfying rhythm of the work. She
was so engrossed she did not notice when Roy Barnes unlatched the
gate and stepped into the yard, a determined twinkle in his faded
eye.

"Howdy, Emi! I saw you working away out here by your lone-   63
some and thought maybe you could use some help."

"Thanks, but I'm doing all right," she said, wrenching a clump   64
of puncture vine from the soil and laying it in the weed box, careful
to avoid scattering the sharp stickers. Jenny was close by, digging at
her petunias and marigolds, ignoring Mr. Barnes, who had no place
in the colorful jungle she was imagining.

"If I had a pretty little wife, I sure wouldn't let her burn up out   65
here, no sir." His voice nudged at her as she squatted on the border
of the vegetable plot. If Mattie looked out of the window, she would
see only a pleasant tableau: Roy nodding in neighborly fashion as
Emiko pointed out young rows of zucchini and yellow squash, watermelon, cantaloupe, eggplant, and tomatoes. Mattie would not see
the strain on Emiko's face, which she turned away when Roy leaned
over and mumbled, "Say, you know what I like best in this garden?"

Emiko grabbed the handle of the shovel and stood up before he   66
could tell her, moving away from him to pluck a weed. "I know
Mattie likes cantaloupe," she said. "So do I. Kiyo prefers Cren-
shaws, but I couldn't find any seeds this year. What do you and
Mattie have in your garden?"

"Just grass," he said, undeterred. "Mattie's always fussing over   67
her flowers—you know what she's like," he chuckled indulgently.
"But I'd rather spend my time doing other things than slaving in the
yard."

Emiko hacked away at the stubborn clumps of grass roots and   68
the persistent runners with myriad finer roots, thread-thin, but
tough as wire. She worked with desperate energy, flustered, her
gloved hands sweating on the shovel handle, forehead damp. She

was groping for the language to make him understand, to make him leave her in peace, but he was bent on not understanding, not seeing, not leaving until he got what he wanted.

"You know what, Emi?" He moistened his dry lips, beginning to grin reminiscently. "You remind me of somebody I met in Tokyo. Have you ever been to Tokyo?" 69

"No," she said, digging hard. "Never." 70

"You'd like it; it's a wonderful place, so clean and neat, and the people so friendly. When I was in Tokyo, I met up with the cutest geisha girl you ever saw—just like a little doll. She'd never seen anybody with blue eyes before, and couldn't get over it." He chuckled. "I couldn't think who you reminded me of at first, and then it just hit me that you are the spitting image of her." 71

"Did Mattie like Tokyo, too?" Emiko said, continuing to spade vigorously, as his eyes slid over her, imagining a doll in exotic robes. 72

"She didn't go—it was a business trip," he said impatiently. Then his voice relaxed into a drawl, heavy with insinuation. "After all, I like to do some things on my own." He was moving closer again. 73

Then she saw it. Emiko had just turned over a rock, and as she raised the shovel, it darted from its refuge, pincers up, the deadly tail curved menacingly over the carapaced back. It moved a little to the left and then the right, beginning the poison dance. Emiko glanced to see where Jenny was and saw Roy jump back hastily; the scorpion, startled by his movement, scuttled sideways toward Jenny, who lay on her stomach, still dreaming of her jungle. 74

The blood pounded in Emiko's head. She brought down the shovel hard with one quick breath, all her rage shooting down the thick handle into the heavy crushing iron. She wielded the shovel like a samurai in battle, swinging it down with all her force, battering her enemy to dust. Once had been enough, but she struck again and again, until her anger was spent, and she leaned on the rough handle, breathing hard. 75

"Mommy! What did you do?" Jenny had scrambled to Emiko's side. There was fear in her eyes as she gazed at the unrecognizable fragments in the dirt. 76

"I killed a scorpion," Emiko said. She scornfully tossed the remains into the weed box, and wiped her brow on her arm, like a farmer, or a warrior. "I don't like to kill anything," she said aloud, "but sometimes you have to." 77

Roy Barnes recoiled from the pitiless knowledge in her eyes. He saw her clearly now, but it was too late. His mouth opened and closed, but the gush of words had gone dry. He seemed to age 78 before her eyes, like Urashima-taro who opened the precious box of youth and was instantly wrinkled and broken by the unleashed tide of years.

"You'll have to leave now, Mr. Barnes. I'm going in to fix 79 lunch." Emiko's smile was quiet as unsheathed steel. "Tell Mattie I hope she's feeling better."

She watched him pick his way across the dirt, avoiding the 80 puncture vine and rusted tin cans, and looking as gray as the rags that bleached beneath the fierce sun. Jenny stared past him and the small houses of their neighborhood, to the desert sand beyond, glittering like an ocean with shards of mica.

"Do you think we might ever find gold?" she asked.   81

They gazed together over the desert, full of unknown perils and 82 ancient secrets, the dust of dreams and battles.

"Maybe." Emiko stood tall, shading her eyes from the deceptive 83 shimmer. "Maybe."

The Long-Distance Runner

GRACE PALEY

One day, before or after forty-two, I became a long-distance runner. 1
Though I was stout and in many ways inadequate to this desire, I
wanted to go far and fast, not as fast as bicycles and trains, not as
far as Taipei, Hingwen, places like that, islands of the slant-eyed
cunt, as sailors in bus stations say when speaking of travel, but
round and round the county from the sea side to the bridges, along
the old neighborhood streets a couple of times, before old age and
urban renewal ended them and me.

I tried the country first, Connecticut, which being wooded is al- 2
ways full of buds in spring. All creation is secret, isn't that true? So I
trained in the wide-zoned suburban hills where I wasn't known. I
ran all spring in and out of dogwood bloom, then laurel.

People sometimes stopped and asked me why I ran, a lady in 3
silk shorts halfway down over her fat thighs. In training, I replied
and rested only to answer if closely questioned. I wore a white
sleeveless undershirt as well, with excellent support, not to attract
the attention of old men and prudish children.

Then summer came, my legs seemed strong. I kissed the kids 4
goodbye. They were quite old by then. It was near the time for parting anyway. I told Mrs Raftery to look in now and then and give
them some of that rotten Celtic supper she makes.

I told them they could take off any time they wanted to. Go lead 5
your private life, I said. Only leave me out of it.

A word to the wise . . . said Richard. 6

You're depressed, Faith, Mrs Raftery said. Your boyfriend Jack, 7
the one you think's so hotsy-totsy, hasn't called and you're as
gloomy as a tick on Sunday.

Cut the folkshit with me, Raftery, I muttered. Her eyes filled 8
with tears because that's who she is: folkshit from bunion to top-
knot. That's how she got liked by me, loved, invented and endured.

When I walked out the door they were all reclining before the 9
television set, Richard, Tonto and Mrs Raftery, gazing at the news.

Grace Paley (1922–   ), from New York City, is the author of *The
Little Disturbances of Man: Stories of Women and Men at Love* (1959)
and *Later the Same Day* (1985). "The Long-Distance Runner" is from
her other story collection, *Enormous Changes at the Last Minute*
(1974).

Which proved with moving pictures that there *had* been a voyage to the moon and Africa and South America hid in a furious whorl of clouds.

I said, Goodbye. They said, Yeah, OK, sure.   10

If that's how it is, forget it, I hollered and took the Independent   11
subway to Brighton Beach.

At Brighton Beach I stopped at the Salty Breezes Locker Room to   12
change my clothes. Twenty-five years ago my father invested $500
in its future. In fact he still clears about $3.50 a year, which goes di-
rectly (by law) to the Children of Judea to cover their deficit.

No one paid too much attention when I started to run, easy and   13
light on my feet. I ran on the boardwalk first, past my mother's
leafleting station—between a soft-ice-cream stand and a degenerated
dune. There she had been assigned by her comrades to halt the tides
of cruel American enterprise with simple socialist sense.

I wanted to stop and admire the long beach. I wanted to stop in   14
order to think admiringly about New York. There aren't many rotting cities so tan and sandy and speckled with citizens at their salty
edges. But I had already spent a lot of life lying down or standing
and staring. I had decided to run.

After about a mile and a half I left the boardwalk and began to trot   15
into the old neighborhood. I was running well. My breath was long
and deep. I was thinking pridefully about my form.

Suddenly I was surrounded by about three hundred blacks.   16

Who you?   17

Who that?   18

Look at her! Just look! When you seen a fatter ass?   19

Poor thing. She ain't right. Leave her, you boys, you bad boys.   20

I used to live here, I said.   21

Oh yes, they said, in the white old days. That time too bad to   22
last.

But we loved it here. We never went to Flatbush Avenue or   23
Times Square. We loved our block.

Tough black titty.   24

I like your speech, I said. Metaphor and all.   25

Right on. We get that from talking.   26

Yes, my people also had a way of speech. And don't forget the   27
Irish. The gift of gab.

Who they? said a small boy.   28

Cops.   29

Nowadays, I suggested, there's more than Irish on the police   30
force.

You right, said two ladies. More more, much much more.   31

They's French Chinamen Russkies Congoleans. Oh missee, you too right.

I lived in that house, I said. That apartment house. All my life. 32
Till I got married.

Now that *is* nice. Live in one place. My mother live that way in 33
South Carolina. One place. Her daddy farmed. She said. They ate.
No matter winter war bad times. Roosevelt. Something! Ain't that
wonderful! And it weren't cold! Big trees!

That apartment. I looked up and pointed. There. The third floor. 34

They all looked up. So what! You blubrous devil! said a dark 35
young man. He wore horn-rimmed glasses and had that intelligent
look that City College boys used to have when I was eighteen and
first looked at them.

He seemed to lead them in contempt and anger, even the littlest 36
ones who moved toward me with dramatic stealth singing, Devil,
Oh Devil. I don't think the little kids had bad feeling because they
poked a finger into me, then laughed.

Still I thought it might be wise to keep my head. So I jumped 37
right in with some facts. I said, How many flowers' names do you
know? Wild flowers, I mean. My people only knew two. That's
what they say now anyway. Rich or poor, they only had two
flowers' names. Rose and violet.

Daisy, said one boy immediately. 38

Weed, said another. That *is* a flower, I thought. But everyone 39
else got the joke.

Saxifrage, lupine, said a lady. Viper's bugloss, said a small Girl 40
Scout in medium green with a dark green sash. She held up a *Hand-
book of Wild Flowers.*

How many you know, fat mama? a boy asked warmly. He 41
wasn't against my being a mother or fat. I turned all my attention to
him.

Oh sonny, I said, I'm way ahead of my people. I know in yel- 42
lows alone: common cinquefoil, trout lily, yellow adder's-tongue,
swamp buttercup and common buttercup, golden sorrel, yellow or
hop clover, devil's-paintbrush, evening primrose, black-eyed Susan,
golden aster, also the yellow pickerelweed growing down by the
water if not in the water, and dandelions of course. I've seen all
these myself. Seen them.

You could see China from the boardwalk, a boy said. When it's 43
nice.

I know more flowers than countries. Mostly young people these 44
days have traveled in many countries.

Not me. I ain't been nowhere. 45

Not me either, said about seventeen boys. 46

I'm not allowed, said a little girl. There's drunken junkies.   47

But *I! I!* cried out a tall black youth, very handsome and well   48
dressed. I am an African. My father came from the high stolen
plains. *I* have been everywhere. I was in Moscow six months, learning machinery. I was in France, learning French. I was in Italy, observing the peculiar Renaissance and the people's sweetness. I was
in England, where I studied the common law and the urban blight. I
was at the Conference of Dark Youth in Cuba to understand our
passion. I am now here. Here am I to become an engineer and return to my people, around the Cape of Good Hope in a Norwegian
sailing vessel. In this way I will learn the fine old art of sailing in
case the engines of the new society of my old inland country should
fail.

We had an extraordinary amount of silence after that. Then one   49
old lady in a black dress and high white lace collar said to another
old lady dressed exactly the same way, Glad tidings when someone
got brains in the head not fish juice. Amen, said a few.

Whyn't you go up to Mrs Luddy living in your house, you lady,   50
huh? The Girl Scout asked this.

Why she just groove to see you, said some sarcastic snickerer.   51

She got palpitations. Her man, he give it to her.   52

That ain't all, he a natural gift-giver.   53

I'll take you, said the Girl Scout. My name is Cynthia. I'm in   54
Troop 355, Brooklyn.

I'm not dressed, I said, looking at my lumpy knees.   55

You shouldn't wear no undershirt like that without no runnin   56
number or no team writ on it. It look like a undershirt.

Cynthia! Don't take her up there, said an important boy. Her   57
head strange. Don't you take her. Hear?

Lawrence, she said softly, you tell me once more what to do I'll   58
wrap you round that lamp-post.

Git! she said, powerfully addressing *me*.   59

In this way I was led into the hallway of the whole house of my   60
childhood.

The first door I saw was still marked in flaky gold, 1A. That's where   61
the janitor lived, I said. He was a Negro.

How come like that? Cynthia made an astonished face. How   62
come the janitor was a black man?

Oh Cynthia, I said. Then I turned to the opposite door, first   63
floor front, 1B. I remembered. Now, here, this was Mrs Goreditsky,
very very fat lady. All her children died at birth. Born, then one,
two, three. Dead. Five children, then Mr Goreditsky said, I'm bad

luck on you Tessie and he went away. He sent $15 a week for seven years. Then no one heard.

I know her, poor thing, said Cynthia. The city come for her 64 summer before last. The way they knew, it smelled. They wrapped her up in a canvas. They couldn't get through the front door. It scraped off a piece of her. My Uncle Ronald had to help them, but he got disgusted.

Only two years ago. She was still here! Wasn't she scared? 65

So we all, said Cynthia. White ain't everything. 66

Who lived up here, she asked, 2B? Right now, my best friend 67 Nancy Rosalind lives here. She got two brothers, and her sister married and got a baby. She very light-skinned. Not her mother. We got all colors amongst us.

Your best friend? That's funny. Because it was *my* best friend. 68 Right in that apartment. Joanna Rosen.

What become of her? Cynthia asked. She got a running shirt 69 too?

Come on Cynthia, if you really want to know, I'll tell you. She 70 married this man, Marvin Steirs.

Who's he? 71

I recollected his achievements. Well, he's the president of a big 72 corporation, JoMar Plastics. This corporation owns a steel company, a radio station, a new Xerox-type machine that lets you do twenty-five different pages at once. This corporation has a foundation, The JoMar Fund for Research in Conservation. Capitalism is like that, I added, in order to be politically useful.

How come you know? You go over their house a lot? 73

No. I happened to read all about them on the financial page, just 74 last week. It made me think: a different life. That's all.

Different spokes for different folks, said Cynthia. 75

I sat down on the cool marble steps and remembered Joanna's 76 cousin Ziggie. He was older than we were. He wrote a poem which told us we were lovely flowers and our legs were petals, which nature would force open no matter how many times we said no.

Then I had several other interior thoughts that I couldn't share 77 with a child, the kind that give your face a blank or melancholy look.

Now you're not interested, said Cynthia. Now you're not gonna 78 say a thing. Who lived here, 2A? Who? Two men lives here now. Women coming and women going. My mother says, Danger sign: Stay away, my darling, stay away.

I don't remember, Cynthia. I really don't. 79

You got to. What'd you come for, anyways? 80

Then I tried. 2A. 2A. Was it the twins? I felt a strong obligation 81
as though remembering was in charge of the *existence* of the past.
This is not so.

Cynthia, I said, I don't want to go any further. I don't even want 82
to remember.

Come on, she said, tugging at my shorts, don't you want to see 83
Mrs Luddy, the one lives in your old house? That be fun, no?

No. No, I don't want to see Mrs Luddy. 84

Now you shouldn't pay no attention to those boys downstairs. 85
She will like you. I mean, she is kind. She don't like most white people, but she might like you.

No Cynthia, it's not that, but I don't want to see my father and 86
mother's house now.

I didn't know what to say. I said, Because my mother's dead. 87
This was a lie, because my mother lives in her own room with my
father in the Children of Judea. With her hand over her socialist
heart, she reads the paper every morning after breakfast. Then she
says sadly to my father, Every day the same. Dying . . . dying, dying from killing.

My mother's dead, Cynthia. I can't go in there. 88

Oh . . . oh, the poor thing, she said, looking into my eyes. Oh, 89
if my mother died, I don't know what I'd do. Even if I was old as
you. I could kill myself. Tears filled her eyes and started down her
cheeks. If my mother died, what would I do? She is my protector,
she won't let the pushers get me. She hold me tight. She gonna hide
me in the cedar box if my Uncle Rudford comes try to get me back.
She *can't* die, my mother.

Cynthia—honey—she won't die. She's young. I put my arm out 90
to comfort her. You could come live with me, I said. I got two boys,
they're nearly grown up. I missed it, not having a girl.

What? What you mean now, live with you and boys. She pulled 91
away and ran for the stairs. Stay away from me, honky lady. I know
them white boys. They just gonna try and jostle my black woman-
hood. My mother told me about that, keep you white honky devil
boys to your devil self, you just leave me be you old bitch you.
Somebody help me, she started to scream, you hear. Somebody
help. She gonna take me away.

She flattened herself to the wall, trembling. I was too frightened 92
by her fear of me to say, honey, I wouldn't hurt you, it's me. I heard
her helpers, the voices of large boys crying, We coming, we coming,
hold your head up, we coming. I ran past her fear to the stairs and
up them two at a time. I came to my old own door. I knocked like
the landlord, loud and terrible.

Mama not home, a child's voice said. No, no I said. It's me! a   93
lady! Someone's chasing me, let me in. Mama not home, I ain't allowed to open up for nobody.

It's me! I cried out in terror. Mama! Mama! let me in!   94

The door opened. A slim woman whose age I couldn't invent   95
looked at me. She said, Get in and shut that door tight. She took a
hard pinching hold on my upper arm. Then she bolted the door herself. Them hustlers after you. They make me pink. Hide this white
lady now, Donald. Stick her under your bed, you got a high bed.

Oh that's OK. I'm fine now, I said. I felt safe and at home.   96

You in my house, she said. You do as I say. For two cents, I   97
throw you out.

I squatted under a small kid's pissy mattress. Then I heard the   98
knock. It was tentative and respectful. My mama don't allow me to
open. Donald! Someone called. Donald!

Oh no, he said. Can't do it. She gonna wear me out. You know   99
her. She already tore up my ass this morning once. Ain't *gonna* open
up.

I lived there for about three weeks with Mrs Luddy and Donald and   100
three little baby girls nearly the same age. I told her a joke about
Irish twins. Ain't Irish, she said.

Nearly every morning the babies woke us at about 6:45. We   101
gave them all a bottle and went back to sleep till 8:00. I made coffee
and she changed diapers. Then it really stank for a while. At this
time I usually said, Well listen, thanks really, but I've got to go I
guess. I guess I'm going. She'd usually say, Well, guess again. *I*
guess you ain't. Or if she was feeling disgusted she'd say, Go on
now! Get! You wanna go, I guess by now I have snorted enough
white lady stink to choke a horse. Go on!

I'd get to the door and then I'd hear voices. I'm ashamed to say   102
I'd become fearful. Despite my wide geographical love of mankind, I
would be attacked by local fears.

There was sentimental truth that lay beside all that going and   103
not going. It *was* my house where I'd lived long ago my family life.
There was a tile on the bathroom floor that I myself had broken,
dropping a hammer on the toe of my brother Charles as he stood
dreamily shaving, his prick halfway up his undershorts. Astonishment and knowledge first seized me right there. The kitchen was
the same. The table was the enameled table common to our class,
easy to clean, with wooden undercorners for indigent and old cockroaches that couldn't make it to the kitchen sink. (However, it was
not the same table, because I have inherited that one, chips and all.)

The living-room was something like ours, only we had less plas- 104
tic. There may have been less plastic in the world at that time. Also,
my mother had set beautiful cushions everywhere, on beds and
chairs. It was the way she expressed herself, artistically, to embroider at night or take strips of flowered cotton and sew them across
ordinary white or blue muslin in the most delicate designs, the way
women have always used materials that live and die in hunks and
tatters to say: This is my place.

Mrs Luddy said, Uh huh!   105

Of course, I said, men don't have that outlet. That's how come 106
they run around so much.

Till they drunk enough to lay down, she said.   107

Yes, I said, on a large scale you can see it in the world. First they 108
make something, then they murder it. Then they write a book about
how interesting it is.

You got something there, she said. Sometimes she said, Girl, 109
you don't know *nothing*.

We often sat at the window looking out and down. Little tufts of 110
breeze grew on that windowsill. The blazing afternoon was around
the corner and up the block.

You say men, she said. Is that men? she asked. What you call— 111
a Man?

Four flights below us, leaning on the stoop, were about a dozen 112
people and around them devastation. Just a minute, I said. I had
seen devastation on my way, running, gotten some of the pebbles of
it in my running shoe and the dust of it in my eyes. I had thought
with the indignant courtesy of a citizen, This is a disgrace to the City
of New York which I love and am running through.

But now, from the commanding heights of home, I saw it 113
clearly. The tenement in which Jack my old and present friend had
come to gloomy manhood had been destroyed, first by fire, then by
demolition (which is a swinging ball of steel that cracks bedrooms
and kitchens). Because of this work, we could see several blocks
wide and a block and a half long. Crazy Eddy's house still stood, famous 1510 gutted, with black window frames, no glass, open laths.
The stubbornness of the supporting beams! Some persons or
families still lived on the lowest floors. In the lots between, a couple
of old sofas lay on their fat faces, their springs sticking up into the
air. Just as in wartime a half-dozen ailanthus trees had already
found their first quarter inch of earth and begun a living attack on
the dead yards. At night, I knew animals roamed the place,
squalling and howling, furious New York dogs and street cats and
mighty rats. You would think you were in Bear Mountain Park, the
terror of venturing forth.

Someone ought to clean that up, I said. 114

Mrs Luddy said, Who you got in mind? Mrs Kennedy?— 115

Donald made a stern face. He said, That just what I gonna do 116
when I get big. Gonna get the Sanitary Man in and show it to him.
You see that, you big guinea you, you clean it up right now! Then
he stamped his feet and fierced his eyes.

Mrs Luddy said, Come here, you little nigger. She kissed the top 117
of his head and gave him a whack on the backside all at one time.

Well, said Donald, encouraged, look out there now you all! Go 118
on I say, look! Though we had already seen, to please him we
looked. On the stoop men and boys lounged, leaned, hopped about,
stood on one leg, then another, took their socks off, and scratched
their toes, talked, sat on their haunches, heads down, dozing.

Donald said, Look at them. They ain't got self-respect. They got 119
Afros *on* their heads, but they don't know they black *in* their heads.

I thought he ought to learn to be more sympathetic. I said, 120
There are reasons that people are that way.

Yes, ma'am, said Donald. 121

Anyway, how come you never go down and play with the other 122
kids, how come you're up here so much?

My mama don't like me do that. Some of them is bad. Bad. I 123
might become a dope addict. I got to stay clear.

You just a dope, that's a fact, said Mrs Luddy. 124

He ought to be with kids his age more, I think. 125

He see them in school, miss. Don't trouble your head about it if 126
you don't mind.

Actually, Mrs Luddy didn't go down into the street either. Don- 127
ald did all the shopping. She let the welfare investigator in, the me-
terman came into the kitchen to read the meter. I saw him from the
back room, where I hid. She did pick up her check. She cashed it.
She returned to wash the babies, change their diapers, wash clothes,
iron, feed people, and then in free half hours she sat by that window. She was waiting.

I believed she was watching and waiting for a particular man. I 128
wanted to discuss this with her, talk lovingly like sisters. But before
I could freely say, Forget about that son of a bitch, he's a pig, I did
have to offer a few solid facts about myself, my kids, about fathers,
husbands, passers-by, evening companions, and the life of my father and mother in this room by this exact afternoon window.

I told her, for instance, that in my worst times I had given my- 129
self one extremely simple physical pleasure. This was cream cheese
for breakfast. In fact, I insisted on it, sometimes depriving the children of very important articles and foods.

Girl, you don't know nothing, she said. 130

Then for a little while she talked gently as one does to a person 131
who is innocent and insane and incorruptible because of stupidity.
She had had two such special pleasures for hard times she said. The
first, men, but they turned rotten, white women had ruined the
best, give them the idea their dicks made of solid gold. The second
pleasure she had tried was wine. She said, I do like wine. You *has* to
have something just for yourself by yourself. Then she said, But you
can't raise a decent boy when you liquor-dazed every night.

White or black, I said, returning to men, they did think they 132
were bringing a rare gift, whereas it was just sex, which is common
like bread, though essential.

Oh, you can do without, she said. There's folks does without.   133

I told her Donald deserved the best. I loved him. If he had 134
flaws, I hardly noticed them. It's one of my beliefs that children do
not have flaws, even the worst do not.

Donald was brilliant—like my boys except that he had an easier 135
disposition. For this reason I decided, almost the second moment of
my residence in that household, to bring him up to reading level at
once. I told him we would work with books and newspapers. He
went immediately to his neighborhood library and brought some
hard books to amuse me. *Black Folktales* by Julius Lester and *The
Pushcart War,*[1] which is about another neighborhood but relevant.

Donald always agreed with me when we talked about reading 136
and writing. In fact, when I mentioned poetry, he told me he knew
all about it, that David Henderson, a known black poet, had visited
his second-grade class. So Donald was, as it turned out, well ahead
of my nosy tongue. He was usually very busy shopping. He also
had to spend a lot of time making faces to force the little serious
baby girls into laughter. But if the subject came up, he could take *the*
poem right out of the air into which language and event had just
gone.

An example: That morning, his mother had said, Whew, I just 137
got too much piss and diapers and wash. I wanna just sit down by
that window and rest my self. He wrote a poem:

> Just got too much pissy diapers
> and wash and wash
> just wanna sit down by that window
> and look out
>   ain't nothing there.

---

[1] Julius Lester, *Black Folktales* (R. W. Baron, 1969); Jean Merrill, *The Pushcart War* (Dell, 1987).
(Ed.)

Donald, I said, you are plain brilliant. I'm never going to forget   138
you. For God's sakes don't you forget me.

You fool with him too much, said Mrs Luddy. He already don't   139
even remember his grandma, you never gonna meet someone like
her, a curse never come past her lips.

I do remember, Mama, I remember. She lying in bed, right   140
there. A man standing in the door. She say, Esdras, I put a curse on
you head. You worsen tomorrow. How come she said like that?

Gomorrah, I believe Gomorrah, she said. She know the Bible in-   141
side out.

Did she live with you?   142

No. No, she visiting. She come up to see us all, her children,   143
how we doing. She come up to see sights. Then she lay down and
died. She was old.

I remained quiet because of the death of mothers. Mrs Luddy   144
looked at me thoughtfully, then she said:

My mama had stories to tell, she raised me on. *Her* mama was a   145
little thing, no sense. Stand in the door of the cabin all day, sucking
her thumb. It was slave times. One day a young field boy come
storming along. He knock on the door of the first cabin hollering,
Sister, come out, it's freedom. She come out. She say, Yeah? When?
He say, Now! It's freedom now! Then he knock at the next door and
say, Sister! It's freedom! Now! From one cabin he run to the next
cabin, crying out, Sister, it's freedom now!

Oh I remember that story, said Donald. Freedom now! Freedom   146
now! He jumped up and down.

You don't remember nothing boy. Go on, get Eloise, she want to   147
get into the good times.

Eloise was two but undersized. We got her like that, said Don-   148
ald. Mrs Luddy let me buy her ice cream and green vegetables. She
was waiting for kale and chard, but it was too early. The kale liked
cold. You not about to be here November, she said. No, no. I turned
away, lonesomeness touching me, and sang our Eloise song:

> Eloise loves the bees
> the bees they buzz
> like Eloise does.

Then Eloise crawled all over the splintery floor, buzzing wildly.   149
Oh you crazy baby, said Donald, buzz buzz buzz.   150
Mrs Luddy sat down by the window.   151
You all make a lot of noise, she said sadly. You just right on   152
noisy.

The next morning Mrs Luddy woke me up.   153
Time to go, she said.   154

What?   155

Home.   156

What? I said.   157

Well, don't you think your little spoiled boys crying for you?   158
Where's Mama? They standing in the window. Time to go lady. This
ain't Free Vacation Farm. Time we was by ourself a little.

Oh Ma, said Donald, she ain't a lot of trouble. Go on, get Eloise,   159
she hollering. And button up your lip.

She didn't offer me coffee. She looked at me strictly all the time.   160
I tried to look strictly back, but I failed because I loved the sight of
her.

Donald was teary, but I didn't dare turn my face to him, until   161
the parting minute at the door. Even then, I kissed the top of his
head a little too forcefully and said, Well, I'll see you.

On the front stoop there were about half a dozen mid-morning   162
family people and kids arguing about who had dumped garbage out
of which window. They were very disgusted with one another.

Two young men in handsome dashikis stood in counsel and   163
agreement at the street corner. They divided a comment. How come
white womens got rotten teeth? And look so old? A young woman
waiting at the light said, Hush . . .

I walked past them and didn't begin my run till the road opened   164
up somewhere along Ocean Parkway. I was a little stiff because my
way of life had used only small movements, an occasional stretch to
put a knife or teapot out of reach of the babies. I ran about ten,
fifteen blocks. Then my second wind came, which is classical, famous among runners, it's the beginning of flying.

In the three weeks I'd been off the street, jogging had become   165
popular. It seemed that I was only one person doing her thing,
which happened like most American eccentric acts to be the most
"in" thing I could have done. In fact, two young men ran alongside
of me for nearly a mile. They ran silently beside me and turned off
at Avenue H. A gentleman with a mustache, running poorly in the
opposite direction, waved. He called out, Hi, señora.

Near home I ran through our park, where I had aired my chil-   166
dren on weekends and late-summer afternoons. I stopped at the
northeast playground, where I met a dozen young mothers intelligently handling their little ones. In order to prepare them, meaning
no harm, I said, In fifteen years, you girls will be like me, wrong in
everything.

At home it was Saturday morning. Jack had returned looking as   167
grim as ever, but he'd brought cash and a vacuum cleaner. While

the coffee perked, he showed Richard how to use it. They were playing tick tack toe on the dusty wall.

Richard said, Well! Look who's here! Hi!   168

Any news? I asked.   169

Letter from Daddy, he said. From the lake and water country in 170
Chile. He says it's like Minnesota.

He's never been to Minnesota, I said. Where's Anthony?   171

Here I am, said Tonto, appearing. But I'm leaving.   172

Oh yes, I said. Of course. Every Saturday he hurries through 173
breakfast or misses it. He goes to visit his friends in institutions.
These are well-known places like Bellevue, Hillside, Rockland State,
Central Islip, Manhattan. These visits take him all day and sometimes half the night.

I found some chocolate-chip cookies in the pantry. Take them, 174
Tonto, I said. I remember nearly all his friends as little boys and girls
always hopping, skipping, jumping and cookie-eating. He was annoyed. He said, No! Chocolate cookies is what the commissaries are
full of. How about money?

Jack dropped the vacuum cleaner. He said, No! They have par- 175
ents for that.

I said, Here, five dollars for cigarettes, one dollar each. 176

Cigarettes! said Jack. Goddamnit! Black lungs and death! Cancer! 177
Emphysema! He stomped out of the kitchen, breathing. He took the
bike from the back room and started for Central Park, which has
been closed to cars but opened to bicycle riders. When he'd been
gone about ten minutes, Anthony said, It's really open only on Sundays.

Why didn't you say so? Why can't you be decent to him? I 178
asked. It's important to me.

Oh Faith, he said, patting me on the head because he'd grown 179
so tall, all that air. It's good for his lungs. And his muscles! He'll be
back soon.

You should ride too, I said. You don't want to get mushy in 180
your legs. You should go swimming once a week.

I'm too busy, he said. I have to see my friends.   181

Then Richard, who had been vacuuming under his bed, came 182
into the kitchen. You still here, Tonto?

Going going gone, said Anthony, don't bat your eye.   183

Now listen, Richard said, here's a note. It's for Judy, if you get 184
as far as Rockland. Don't forget it. Don't open it. Don't read it. I
know he'll read it.

Anthony smiled and slammed the door.   185

Did I lose weight? I asked. Yes, said Richard. You look OK. You 186 never look too bad. But where were you? I got sick of Raftery's boiled potatoes. Where were you, Faith?

Well! I said. Well! I stayed a few weeks in my old apartment,   187 where Grandpa and Grandma and me and Hope and Charlie lived, when we were little. I took you there long ago. Not so far from the ocean where Grandma made us very healthy with sun and air.

What are you talking about? said Richard. Cut the baby talk.   188

Anthony came home earlier than expected that evening because   189 some people were in shock therapy and someone else had run away. He listened to me for a while. Then he said, I don't know what she's talking about either.

Neither did Jack, despite the understanding often produced by   190 love after absence. He said, Tell me again. He was in a good mood. He said, You can even tell it to me twice.

I repeated the story. They all said, What?   191

Because it isn't usually so simple. Have you known it to happen   192 much nowadays? A woman inside the steamy energy of middle age runs and runs. She finds the houses and streets where her childhood happened. She lives in them. She learns as though she was still a child what in the world is coming next.

A Distant Episode

PAUL BOWLES

The September sunsets were at their reddest the week the Professor 1
decided to visit Aïn Tadouirt, which is in the warm country. He
came down out of the high, flat region in the evening by bus, with
two small overnight bags full of maps, sun lotions and medicines.
Ten years ago he had been in the village for three days; long
enough, however, to establish a fairly firm friendship with a café-
keeper, who had written him several times during the first year after
his visit, if never since. "Hassan Ramani," the Professor said over
and over, as the bus bumped downward through ever warmer layers of air. Now facing the flaming sky in the west, and now facing
the sharp mountains, the car followed the dusty trail down the
canyons into air which began to smell of other things besides the
endless ozone of the heights: orange blossoms, pepper, sun-baked
excrement, burning olive oil, rotten fruit. He closed his eyes happily
and lived for an instant in a purely olfactory world. The distant past
returned—what part of it, he could not decide.

The chauffeur, whose seat the Professor shared, spoke to him 2
without taking his eyes from the road. *"Vous êtes géologue?"*

"A geologist? Ah, no! I'm a linguist." 3

"There are no languages here. Only dialects." 4

"Exactly. I'm making a survey of variations on Moghrebi." 5

The chauffeur was scornful. "Keep on going south," he said. 6
"You'll find some languages you never heard of before."

As they drove through the town gate, the usual swarm of ur- 7
chins rose up out of the dust and ran screaming beside the bus. The
Professor folded his dark glasses, put them in his pocket; and as
soon as the vehicle had come to a standstill he jumped out, pushing
his way through the indignant boys who clutched at his luggage in
vain, and walked quickly into the Grand Hotel Saharien. Out of its
eight rooms there were two available—one facing the market and
the other, a smaller and cheaper one, giving onto a tiny yard full of

---

Paul Bowles (1910–   ), born in New York City but residing most
of his life in Tangiers, Morocco, is a composer and author of memoirs, translations, poetry, stories, and novels including *The Sheltering Sky* (1949), *A Hundred Camels in the Courtyard* (1962), *Collected
Stories 1939–1976* (1979), and *Points in Time* (1982). "A Distant
Episode" first appeared in *Partisan Review* (1947).

refuse and barrels, where two gazelles wandered about. He took the smaller room, and pouring the entire pitcher of water into the tin basin, began to wash the grit from his face and ears. The afterglow was nearly gone from the sky, and the pinkness in objects was disappearing, almost as he watched. He lit the carbide lamp and winced at its odor.

After dinner the Professor walked slowly through the streets to Hassan Ramani's café, whose back room hung hazardously out above the river. The entrance was very low, and he had to bend down slightly to get in. A man was tending the fire. There was one guest sipping tea. The *qaouaji*[1] tried to make him take a seat at the other table in the front room, but the Professor walked airily ahead into the back room and sat down. The moon was shining through the reed latticework and there was not a sound outside but the occasional distant bark of a dog. He changed tables so he could see the river. It was dry, but there was a pool here and there that reflected the bright night sky. The *qaouaji* came in and wiped off the table. 8

"Does this café still belong to Hassan Ramani?" he asked him in the Moghrebi he had taken four years to learn. 9

The man replied in bad French: "He is deceased." 10

"Deceased?" repeated the Professor, without noticing the absurdity of the word. "Really? When?" 11

"I don't know," said the *qaouaji*. "One tea?" 12

"Yes. But I don't understand . . ." 13

The man was already out of the room, fanning the fire. The Professor sat still, feeling lonely, and arguing with himself that to do so was ridiculous. Soon the *qaouaji* returned with the tea. He paid him and gave him an enormous tip, for which he received a grave bow. 14

"Tell me," he said, as the other started away. "Can one still get those little boxes made from camel udders?" 15

The man looked angry. "Sometimes the Reguibat bring in those things. We do not buy them here." Then insolently, in Arabic: "And why a camel-udder box?" 16

"Because I like them," retorted the Professor. And then because he was feeling a little exalted, he added, "I like them so much I want to make a collection of them, and I will pay you ten francs for every one you can get me." 17

"*Khamstache*," said the *qaouaji*, opening his left hand rapidly three times in succession. 18

"Never. Ten." 19

---

[1] *qaouaji:* café manager. (Ed.)

"Not possible. But wait until later and come with me. You can 20
give me what you like. And you will get camel-udder boxes if there
are any."

He went out into the front room, leaving the Professor to drink 21
his tea and listen to the growing chorus of dogs that barked and
howled as the moon rose higher into the sky. A group of customers
came into the front room and sat talking for an hour or so. When
they had left, the *qaouaji* put out the fire and stood in the doorway
putting on his burnous. "Come," he said.

Outside in the street there was very little movement. The booths 22
were all closed and the only light came from the moon. An occasional pedestrian passed, and grunted a brief greeting to the *qaouaji*.

"Everyone knows you," said the Professor, to cut the silence be- 23
tween them.

"Yes." 24

"I wish everyone knew me," said the Professor, before he real- 25
ized how infantile such a remark must sound.

"*No* one knows you," said his companion gruffly. 26

They had come to the other side of the town, on the promontory 27
above the desert, and through a great rift in the wall the Professor
saw the white endlessness, broken in the foreground by dark spots
of oasis. They walked through the opening and followed a winding
road between rocks, downward toward the nearest small forest of
palms. The Professor thought: "He may cut my throat. But his
café—he would surely be found out."

"Is it far?" he asked, casually. 28

"Are you tired?" countered the *qaouaji*. 29

"They are expecting me back at the Hotel Saharien," he lied. 30

"You can't be there and here," said the *qaouaji*. 31

The Professor laughed. He wondered if it sounded uneasy to the 32
other.

"Have you owned Ramani's café long?" 33

"I work there for a friend." The reply made the Professor more 34
unhappy than he had imagined it would.

"Oh. Will you work tomorrow?" 35

"That is impossible to say." 36

The Professor stumbled on a stone, and fell, scraping his hand. 37
The *qaouaji* said: "Be careful."

The sweet black odor of rotten meat hung in the air suddenly. 38

"Agh!" said the Professor, choking. "What is it?" 39

The *qaouaji* had covered his face with his burnous and did not 40
answer. Soon the stench had been left behind. They were on flat
ground. Ahead the path was bordered on each side by a high mud
wall. There was no breeze and the palms were quite still, but behind

the walls was the sound of running water. Also, the odor of human excrement was almost constant as they walked between the walls.

The Professor waited until he thought it seemed logical for him 41 to ask with a certain degree of annoyance: "But where are we going?"

"Soon," said the guide, pausing to gather some stones in the 42 ditch.

"Pick up some stones," he advised. "Here are bad dogs." 43

"Where?" asked the Professor, but he stooped and got three 44 large ones with pointed edges.

They continued very quietly. The walls came to an end and the 45 bright desert lay ahead. Nearby was a ruined marabout, with its tiny dome only half standing, and the front wall entirely destroyed. Behind it were clumps of stunted, useless palms. A dog came running crazily toward them on three legs. Not until it got quite close did the Professor hear its steady low growl. The *qaouaji* let fly a large stone at it, striking it square in the muzzle. There was a strange snapping of jaws and the dog ran sideways in another direction, falling blindly against rocks and scrambling haphazardly about like an injured insect.

Turning off the road, they walked across the earth strewn with 46 sharp stones, past the little ruin, through the trees, until they came to a place where the ground dropped abruptly away in front of them.

"It looks like a quarry," said the Professor, resorting to French 47 for the word "quarry," whose Arabic equivalent he could not call to mind at the moment. The *qaouaji* did not answer. Instead he stood still and turned his head, as if listening. And indeed, from somewhere down below, but very far below, came the faint sound of a low flute. The *qaouaji* nodded his head slowly several times. Then he said: "The path begins here. You can see it well all the way. The rock is white and the moon is strong. So you can see well. I am going back now and sleep. It is late. You can give me what you like."

Standing there at the edge of the abyss which at each moment 48 looked deeper, with the dark face of the *qaouaji* framed in its moonlit burnous close to his own face, the Professor asked himself exactly what he felt. Indignation, curiosity, fear, perhaps, but most of all relief and the hope that this was not a trick, the hope that the *qaouaji* would really leave him alone and turn back without him.

He stepped back a little from the edge, and fumbled in his 49 pocket for a loose note, because he did not want to show his wallet. Fortunately there was a fifty-franc bill there, which he took out and handed to the man. He knew the *qaouaji* was pleased, and so he

paid no attention when he heard him saying: "It is not enough. I
have to walk a long way home and there are dogs. . . ."

"Thank you and good night," said the Professor, sitting down   50
with his legs drawn up under him, and lighting a cigarette. He felt
almost happy.

"Give me only one cigarette," pleaded the man.   51

"Of course," he said, a bit curtly, and he held up the pack.   52

The *qaouaji* squatted close beside him. His face was not pleasant   53
to see. "What is it?" thought the Professor, terrified again, as he
held out his lighted cigarette toward him.

The man's eyes were almost closed. It was the most obvious reg-   54
istering of concentrated scheming the Professor had ever seen.
When the second cigarette was burning, he ventured to say to the
still-squatting Arab: "What are you thinking about?"

The other drew on his cigarette deliberately, and seemed about   55
to speak. Then his expression changed to one of satisfaction, but he
did not speak. A cool wind had risen in the air, and the Professor
shivered. The sound of the flute came up from the depths below at
intervals, sometimes mingled with the scraping of nearby palm
fronds one against the other. "These people are not primitives," the
Professor found himself saying in his mind.

"Good," said the *qaouaji*, rising slowly. "Keep your money. Fifty   56
francs is enough. It is an honor." Then he went back into French:
"Ti n'as qu'à discendre, to' droit." [2] He spat, chuckled (or was the Professor hysterical?), and strode away quickly.

The Professor was in a state of nerves. He lit another cigarette,   57
and found his lips moving automatically. They were saying: "Is this
a situation or a predicament? This is ridiculous." He sat very still for
several minutes, waiting for a sense of reality to come to him. He
stretched out on the hard, cold ground and looked up at the moon.
It was almost like looking straight at the sun. If he shifted his gaze a
little at a time, he could make a string of weaker moons across the
sky. "Incredible," he whispered. Then he sat up quickly and looked
about. There was no guarantee that the *qaouaji* really had gone back
to town. He got to his feet and looked over the edge of the
precipice. In the moonlight the bottom seemed miles away. And
there was nothing to give it scale; not a tree, not a house, not a person. . . . He listened for the flute, and heard only the wind going by
his ears. A sudden violent desire to run back to the road seized him,

---

[2] *Ti n'as qu'à discendre, to' droit:* You only have to go down. (Ed.)

and he turned and looked in the direction the *qaouaji* had taken. At the same time he felt softly of his wallet in his breast pocket. Then he spat over the edge of the cliff. Then he made water over it, and listened intently, like a child. This gave him the impetus to start down the path into the abyss. Curiously enough, he was not dizzy. But prudently he kept from peering to his right, over the edge. It was a steady and steep downward climb. The monotony of it put him into a frame of mind not unlike that which had been induced by the bus ride. He was murmuring "Hassan Ramani" again, repeatedly and in rhythm. He stopped, furious with himself for the sinister overtones the name now suggested to him. He decided he was exhausted from the trip. "And the walk," he added.

He was now well down the gigantic cliff, but the moon, being 58 directly overhead, gave as much light as ever. Only the wind was left behind, above, to wander among the trees, to blow through the dusty street of Aïn Tadouirt, into the hall of the Grand Hotel Saharien, and under the door of his little room.

It occurred to him that he ought to ask himself why he was do- 59 ing this irrational thing, but he was intelligent enough to know that since he was doing it, it was not so important to probe for explanations at that moment.

Suddenly the earth was flat beneath his feet. He had reached the 60 bottom sooner than he expected. He stepped ahead distrustfully still, as if he expected another treacherous drop. It was so hard to know in this uniform, dim brightness. Before he knew what had happened the dog was upon him, a heavy mass of fur trying to push him backwards, a sharp nail rubbing down his chest, a straining of muscles against him to get the teeth into his neck. The Professor thought: "I refuse to die this way." The dog fell back; it looked like an Eskimo dog. As it sprang again, he called out, very loud: "Ay!" It fell against him, there was a confusion of sensations and a pain somewhere. There was also the sound of voices very near to him, and he could not understand what they were saying. Something cold and metallic was pushed brutally against his spine as the dog still hung for a second by his teeth from a mass of clothing and perhaps flesh. The Professor knew it was a gun, and he raised his hands, shouting in Moghrebi: "Take away the dog!" But the gun merely pushed him forward, and since the dog, once it was back on the ground, did not leap again, he took a step ahead. The gun kept pushing; he kept taking steps. Again he heard voices, but the person directly behind him said nothing. People seemed to be running about; it sounded that way, at least. For his eyes, he discovered, were still shut tight against the dog's attack. He opened them. A group of men was advancing toward him. They were dressed in the black clothes of the Reguibat. "The Reguiba is a cloud across the face of the sun." "When the Reguiba appears the righteous man turns away." In how many shops and market-places he had heard these maxims uttered banteringly among friends. Never to a Reguiba, to be sure, for these men do not frequent towns. They send a representative in disguise, to arrange with shady elements there for the disposal of captured goods. "An opportunity," he thought quickly, "of testing the accuracy of such statements." He did not doubt for a moment that the adventure would prove to be a kind of warning against such foolishness on his part—a warning which in retrospect would be half sinister, half farcical.

Two snarling dogs came running from behind the oncoming 61 men and threw themselves at his legs. He was scandalized to note that no one paid any attention to this breach of etiquette. The gun pushed him harder as he tried to sidestep the animals' noisy assault. Again he cried: "The dogs! Take them away!" The gun shoved him forward with great force and he fell, almost at the feet of the crowd of men facing him. The dogs were wrenching at his hands and arms. A boot kicked them aside, yelping, and then with increased vigor it kicked the Professor in the hip. Then came a chorus of kicks from different sides, and he was rolled violently about on the earth for a while. During this time he was conscious of hands reaching into his pockets and removing everything from them. He tried to say: "You have all my money; stop kicking me!" But his bruised facial muscles would not work; he felt himself pouting, and that was all. Someone dealt him a terrific blow on the head, and he thought: "Now at least I shall lose consciousness, thank Heaven." Still he went on being aware of the guttural voices he could not understand, and of being bound tightly about the ankles and chest. Then there was black silence that opened like a wound from time to time, to let in the soft, deep notes of the flute playing the same succession of notes again and again. Suddenly he felt excruciating pain everywhere—pain and cold. "So I have been unconscious, after all," he thought. In spite of that, the present seemed only like a direct continuation of what had gone before.

It was growing faintly light. There were camels near where he 62 was lying; he could hear their gurgling and their heavy breathing. He could not bring himself to attempt opening his eyes, just in case it should turn out to be impossible. However, when he heard someone approaching, he found that he had no difficulty in seeing.

The man looked at him dispassionately in the gray morning 63 ⁻ht. With one hand he pinched together the Professor's nostrils. ⁻ Professor opened his mouth to breathe, the man swiftly ⁻e and pulled on it with all his might. The Professor was gagging and catching his breath; he did not see what was happening. He could not distinguish the pain of the brutal yanking from that of the sharp knife. Then there was an endless choking and spitting that went on automatically, as though he were scarcely a part of it. The word "operation" kept going through his mind; it calmed his terror somewhat as he sank back into darkness.

The caravan left sometime toward midmorning. The Professor, 64 not unconscious, but in a state of utter stupor, still gagging and drooling blood, was dumped doubled-up into a sack and tied at one side of a camel. The lower end of the enormous amphitheater contained a natural gate in the rocks. The camels, swift *mebara*, were lightly laden on this trip. They passed through single file, and slowly mounted the gentle slope that led up into the beginning of the desert. That night, at a stop behind some low hills, the men took him out, still in a state which permitted no thought, and over the dusty rags that remained of his clothing they fastened a series of curious belts made of the bottoms of tin cans strung together. One after another of these bright girdles was wired about his torso, his arms and legs, even across his face, until he was entirely within a suit of armor that covered him with its circular metal scales. There was a good deal of merriment during this decking-out of the Professor. One man brought out a flute and a younger one did a not ungraceful caricature of an Ouled Naïl executing a cane dance. The Professor was no longer conscious; to be exact, he existed in the middle of the movements made by these other men. When they had finished dressing him the way they wished him to look, they stuffed some food under the tin bangles hanging over his face. Even though he chewed mechanically, most of it eventually fell out onto the ground. They put him back into the sack and left him there.

Two days later they arrived at one of their own encampments. 65 There were women and children here in the tents, and the men had to drive away the snarling dogs they had left there to guard them. When they emptied the Professor out of his sack, there were screams of fright, and it took several hours to convince the last woman that he was harmless, although there had been no doubt from the start that he was a valuable possession. After a few days they began to move on again, taking everything with them, and traveling only at night as the terrain grew warmer.

Even when all his wounds had healed and he felt no more pain, 66 the Professor did not begin to think again; he ate and defecated, and he danced when he was bidden, a senseless hopping up and down that delighted the children, principally because of the wonderful jangling racket it made. And he generally slept through the heat of the day, in among the camels.

Wending its way southeast, the caravan avoided all stationary 67
civilization. In a few weeks they reached a new plateau, wholly wild
and with a sparse vegetation. Here they pitched camp and remained, while the *mebara* were turned loose to graze. Everyone was
happy here; the weather was cooler and there was a well only a few
hours away on a seldom-frequented trail. It was here they conceived
the idea of taking the Professor to Fogara and selling him to the
Touareg.

It was a full year before they carried out this project. By this time 68
the Professor was much better trained. He could do a handspring,
make a series of fearful growling noises which had, nevertheless, a
certain element of humor; and when the Reguibat removed the tin
from his face they discovered he could grimace admirably while he
danced. They also taught him a few basic obscene gestures which
never failed to elicit delighted shrieks from the women. He was now
brought forth only after especially abundant meals, when there was
music and festivity. He easily fell in with their sense of ritual, and
evolved an elementary sort of "program" to present when he was
called for: dancing, rolling on the ground, imitating certain animals,
and finally rushing toward the group in feigned anger, to see the resultant confusion and hilarity.

When three of the men set out for Fogara with him, they took 69
four *mebara* with them, and he rode astride his quite naturally. No
precautions were taken to guard him, save that he was kept among
them, one man always staying at the rear of the party. They came
within sight of the walls at dawn, and they waited among the rocks
all day. At dusk the youngest started out, and in three hours he returned with a friend who carried a stout cane. They tried to put the
Professor through his routine then and there, but the man from Fogara was in a hurry to get back to town, so they all set out on the
mebara.

In the town they went directly to the villager's home, where 70
they had coffee in the courtyard sitting among the camels. Here the
Professor went into his act again, and this time there was prolonged
merriment and much rubbing together of hands. An agreement was
reached, a sum of money paid, and the Reguibat withdrew, leaving
the Professor in the house of the man with the cane, who did not
delay in locking him into a tiny enclosure off the courtyard.

The next day was an important one in the Professor's life, for it 71
was then that pain began to stir again in his being. A group of men
came to the house, among whom was a venerable gentleman, better
clothed than those others who spent their time flattering him, setting
fervent kisses upon his hands and the edges of his garments. This
person made a point of going into classical Arabic from time to time,

to impress the others, who had not learned a word of the Koran. Thus his conversation would run more or less as follows: "Perhaps at In Salah. The French there are stupid. Celestial vengeance is approaching. Let us not hasten it. Praise the highest and cast thine anathema against idols. With paint on his face. In case the police wish to look close." The others listened and agreed, nodding their heads slowly and solemnly. And the Professor in his stall beside them listened, too. That is, he was *conscious* of the sound of the old man's Arabic. The words penetrated for the first time in many months. Noises, then: "Celestial vengeance is approaching." Then: "It is an honor. Fifty francs is enough. Keep your money. Good." And the *qaouaji* squatting near him at the edge of the precipice. Then "anathema against idols" and more gibberish. He turned over panting on the sand and forgot about it. But the pain had begun. It operated in a kind of delirium, because he had begun to enter into consciousness again. When the man opened the door and prodded him with his cane, he cried out in a rage, and everyone laughed.

They got him onto his feet, but he would not dance. He stood 72 before them, staring at the ground, stubbornly refusing to move. The owner was furious, and so annoyed by the laughter of the others that he felt obliged to send them away, saying that he would await a more propitious time for exhibiting his property, because he dared not show his anger before the elder. However, when they had left he dealt the Professor a violent blow on the shoulder with his cane, called him various obscene things, and went out into the street, slamming the gate behind him. He walked straight to the street of the Ouled Naïl, because he was sure of finding the Reguibat there among the girls, spending the money. And there in a tent he found one of them still abed, while an Ouled Naïl washed the tea glasses. He walked in and almost decapitated the man before the latter had even attempted to sit up. Then he threw his razor on the bed and ran out.

The Ouled Naïl saw the blood, screamed, ran out of her tent 73 into the next, and soon emerged from that with four girls who rushed together into the coffeehouse and told the *qaouaji* who had killed the Reguiba. It was only a matter of an hour before the French military police had caught him at a friend's house, and dragged him off to the barracks. That night the Professor had nothing to eat, and the next afternoon, in the slow sharpening of his consciousness caused by increasing hunger, he walked aimlessly about the courtyard and the rooms that gave onto it. There was no one. In one room a calendar hung on the wall. The Professor watched nervously, like a dog watching a fly in front of its nose. On the white paper were black objects that made sounds in his head. He heard them: *"Grande Epicerie du Sabel. Juin. Lundi, Mardi, Mercredi. . . ."*[3]

The tiny ink marks of which a symphony consists may have 74 been made long ago, but when they are fulfilled in sound they become imminent and mighty. So a kind of music of feeling began to play in the Professor's head, increasing in volume as he looked at the mud wall, and he had the feeling that he was performing what had been written for him long ago. He felt like weeping; he felt like roaring through the little house, upsetting and smashing the few breakable objects. His emotion got no further than this one overwhelming desire. So, bellowing as loud as he could, he attacked the house and its belongings. Then he attacked the door into the street, which resisted for a while and finally broke. He climbed through the opening made by the boards he had ripped apart, and still bellowing and shaking his arms in the air to make as loud a jangling as possible, he began to gallop along the quiet street toward the gateway of the town. A few people looked at him with great curiosity. As he passed the garage, the last building before the high mud archway that framed the desert beyond, a French soldier saw him. *"Tiens,"* he said to himself, "a holy maniac."

Again it was sunset time. The Professor ran beneath the arched 75 gate, turned his face toward the red sky, and began to trot along the Piste d'In Salah, straight into the setting sun. Behind him, from the garage, the soldier took a potshot at him for good luck. The bullet whistled dangerously near the Professor's head, and his yelling rose into an indignant lament as he waved his arms more wildly, and hopped high into the air at every few steps, in an access of terror.

The soldier watched a while, smiling, as the cavorting figure 76 grew smaller in the oncoming evening darkness, and the rattling of the tin became a part of the great silence out there beyond the gate. The wall of the garage as he leaned against it still gave forth heat, left there by the sun, but even then the lunar chill was growing in the air.

---

[3] *Grande Epicerie du Sabel. Juin. Lundi, Mardi, Mercredi:* Grand Grocery Store of Sabel. June. Monday, Tuesday, Wednesday. (Ed.)

Among the Dangs

GEORGE P. ELLIOTT

I graduated from Sansom University in 1937 with honors in history,   1
having intended to study law, but I had no money and nowhere to
get any; by good fortune the anthropology department, which had
just been given a grant for research, decided that I could do a job for
them. In idle curiosity I had taken a course in anthro, to see what I
would have been like had history not catapulted my people a couple
of centuries ago up into civilization, but I had not been inclined to
enlarge on the sketchy knowledge I got from that course; even yet,
when I think about it, I feel like a fraud teaching anthropology.
What chiefly recommended me to the department, aside from a
friend, was a combination of three attributes: I was a good mimic, a
long-distance runner, and black.

The Dangs live in a forested valley in the eastern foothills of the   2
Andes. The only white man to report on them (and, it was loosely
gossiped, the only one to return from them alive), Sir Bewley Morehead, owed his escape in 1910 to the consternation caused by Halley's comet. Otherwise, he reported, they would certainly have
sacrificed him as they were preparing to do; as it was they killed the
priest who was to have killed him and then burned the temple
down. However, Dr. Sorish, our most distinguished Sansom man,
in the early thirties developed an interest in the Dangs which led to
my research grant; he had introduced a tribe of Amazonian head-
shrinkers to the idea of planting grain instead of just harvesting it,
as a result of which they had fattened, taken to drinking brew by the
tubful, and elevated Sorish to the rank of new god. The last time he
had descended among them—it is Sansom policy to follow through
on any primitives we "do"—he had found his worshipers holding a
couple of young Dang men captive and preparing them for ceremonies which would end only with the processing of their heads;
his godhood gave him sufficient power to defer these ceremonies
while he made half-a-dozen transcriptions of the men's conversations and learned their language well enough to arouse the curiosity

---

George P. Elliott (1918–1980), born in Knightstown, Indiana, was
professor of English at Syracuse University and author of essays,
poetry, and novels including *Parktilden Village* (1958) and *In the
World* (1972). "Among the Dangs" is from *Among the Dangs: Ten
Short Stories* (1961).

of his colleagues. The Dangs were handy with blowpipes; no one knew what pleased them; Halley's comet wasn't due till 1986. But among the recordings Sorish brought back was a legend strangely chanted by one of these young men, whose very head perhaps you can buy today from a natural science company for $150 to $200, and the same youth had given Sorish a sufficient demonstration of the Dang prophetic trance, previously described by Morehead, to whet his appetite.

I was black, true; but as Sorish pointed out, I looked as though I   3
had been rolled in granite dust and the Dangs as though they had been rolled in brick dust; my hair was short and kinky, theirs long and straight; my lips were thick, theirs thin. It's like dressing a Greek up in reindeer skins, I said, and telling him to go pass himself off as a Lapp in Lapland. Maybe, they countered, but wouldn't he be more likely to get by than a naked Swahili with bones in his nose? I was a long-distance runner, true, but as I pointed out with a good deal of feeling I didn't know the principles of jungle escape and had no desire to learn them in, as they put it, the field. They would teach me to throw the javelin and wield a machete, they would teach me the elements of judo, and as for poisoned darts and sacrifices they would insure my life—that is, my return within three years—for five thousand dollars. I was a good mimic, true; I would be able to reproduce the Dang speech and especially the trance of the Dang prophets for the observation of science—"make a genuine contribution to learning." In the Sansom concept the researcher's experience is an inextricable part of anthropological study, and a good mimic provides the object for others' study as well as for his own. For doing this job I would be given round-trip transportation, an M.S. if I wrote a thesis on the material I gathered, the temporary insurance on my life, and one hundred dollars a month for the year I was expected to be gone. After I'd got them to throw in a fellowship of some sort for the following year I agreed. It would pay for filling the forty cavities in my brothers' and sisters' teeth.

Dr. Sorish and I had to wait at the nearest outstation for a thun-   4
derstorm; when it finally blew up I took off all my clothes, put on a breechcloth and leather apron, put a box of equipment on my head, and trotted after him; his people were holed in from the thunder and we were in their settlement before they saw us. They were taller than I, they no doubt found my white teeth as disagreeable as I found their stained, filed teeth, but when Sorish spoke to me in English (telling me to pretend indifference to them while they sniffed me over) and in the accents of American acquaintances rather than in the harsh tones of divinity their eyes filled with awe of me. Their taboo against touching Sorish extended itself to me; when a baby

ran up to me and I lifted him up to play with him, his mother crawled, beating her head on the ground till I freed him.

The next day was devoted chiefly to selecting the man to fulfill Sorish's formidable command to guide me to the edge of the Dang country. As for running—if those characters could be got to the next Olympics, Ecuador would take every long-distance medal on the board. I knew I had reached the brow of my valley only because I discovered that my guide, whom I had been lagging behind by fifty feet, at a turn in the path had disappeared into the brush.

Exhaustion allayed my terror; as I lay in the meager shade recuperating I remembered to execute the advice I had given myself before coming: to act always as though I were not afraid. What would a brave man do next? Pay no attention to his aching feet, reconnoiter, and cautiously proceed. I climbed a jutting of rock and peered about. It was a wide, scrubby valley; on the banks of the river running down the valley I thought I saw a dozen mounds too regular for stones. I touched the handle of the hunting knife sheathed at my side, and trotted down the trackless hill. 5

The village was deserted, but the huts, though miserable, were clean and in good repair. This meant, according to the movies I had seen, that hostile eyes were watching my every gesture. I had to keep moving in order to avoid trembling. The river was clear and not deep. The corpse of a man floated by. I felt like going downstream, but my hypothesized courage drove me up. 6

In half a mile I came upon a toothless old woman squatting by the track. She did not stop munching when I appeared, nor did she scream, or even stand up. I greeted her in Dang according to the formula I had learned, whereupon she cackled and smiled and nodded as gleefully as though I had just passed a test. She reminded me of my grandmother, rolled in brick dust, minus a corncob pipe between her gums. Presently I heard voices ahead of me. I saw five women carrying branches and walking very slowly. I lurked behind them until they came to a small village, and watched from a bush while they set to work. They stripped the leaves off, carefully did something to them with their fingers, and then dropped them in small-throated pots. Children scrabbled around, and once a couple of them ran up and suckled at one of the women. There remained about an hour till sunset. I prowled, undetected. The women stood, like fashion models, with pelvis abnormally rocked forward; they were wiry, without fat even on their breasts; not even their thighs and hips afforded clean sweeping lines undisturbed by bunched muscles. I saw no men. 7

Before I began to get into a lather about the right tack to take I stepped into the clearing and uttered their word of salutation. If a 8 strange man should walk in your wife's front door and say "How do you do" in an accent she did not recognize, simultaneously poking his middle finger at her, her consternation would be something like that of those Dang women, for unthinkingly I had nodded my head when speaking and turned my palm up as one does in the United States; to them this was a gesture of intimacy, signifying desire. They disappeared into huts, clutching children.

I went to the central clearing and sat with my back to a log, 9 knowing they would scrutinize me. I wondered where the men were. I could think of no excuse for having my knife in my hand except to clean my toenails. So astonishing an act was unknown to the Dangs; the women and children gradually approached in silence, watching; I cleaned my fingernails. I said the word for food; no one reacted, but presently a little girl ran up to me holding a fruit in both hands. I took it, snibbed her nose between my fingers, and with a pat on the bottom sent her back to her mother. Upon this there were hostile glances, audible intakes of breath, and a huddling about the baby who did not understand any more than I did why she was being consoled. While I ate the fruit I determined to leave the next move up to them. I sheathed my knife and squatted on my hunkers, waiting. To disguise my nervousness I fixed my eyes on the ground between my feet, and grasped my ankles from behind in such a way—right ankle with right hand, left with left—as to expose the inner sides of my forearms. Now this was, as I later learned, pretty close to the initial posture taken for the prophetic trance; also I had a blue flower tattooed on my inner right arm and a blue serpent on my left (from the summer I'd gone to sea), the like of which had never been seen in this place.

At sundown I heard the men approach; they were anything but 10 stealthy about it; I had the greatest difficulty in suppressing the shivers. In simple fear of showing my fear I did not look up when the men gathered around, I could understand just enough of what the women were telling the men to realize that they were afraid of me. Even though I was pelted with pebbles and twigs till I was angry I still did not respond, because I could not think what to do. Then something clammy was plopped onto my back from above and I leaped high, howling. Their spears were poised before I landed.

"Strangers!" I cried, my speech composed. "Far kinsmen! I come 11 from the mountains!" I had intended to say *from the river lands*, but the excitement tangled my tongue. Their faces remained expressionless but no spears drove at me, and then to be doing something I shoved the guts under the log with my feet.

And saved my life by doing so. That I seemed to have taken, 12 though awkwardly, the prophetic squat; that I bore visible marvels on my arm; that I was fearless and inwardly absorbed; that I came from the mountains (their enemies lived toward the river lands); that I wore their apron and spoke their language, albeit poorly, all these disposed them to wonder at this mysterious outlander. Even so they might very well have captured me, marvelous though I was, possibly useful to them, dangerous to antagonize, had I not been unblemished, which meant that I was supernaturally guarded. Finally, my scrutinizing the fish guts, daring to smile as I did so, could mean only that I was prophetic; my leap when they had been dropped onto my back was prodigious, "far higher than a man's head," and my howl had been vatic; and my deliberately kicking the guts aside, though an inscrutable act, demonstrated at least that I could touch the entrails of an eel and live.

So I was accepted to the Dangs. The trouble was that they had 13 no ceremony for naturalizing me. For them every act had a significance, and here they were faced with a reverse problem for which nothing had prepared them. They could not possibly just assimilate me without marking the event with an act (that is, a ceremony) signifying my entrance. For them nothing *just happened*, certainly nothing that men did. Meanwhile, I was kept in a sort of quarantine while they deliberated. I did not, to be sure, understand why I was being isolated in a hut by myself, never spoken to except efficiently, watched but not restrained. I swam, slept, scratched, watched, swatted, ate; I was not really alarmed because they had not restrained me forcibly and they gave me food. I began making friends with some of the small children, especially while swimming, and there were two girls of fifteen or so who found me terribly funny. I wished I had some magic, but I knew only card tricks. The sixth day, swimming, I thought I was being enticed around a point in the river by the two girls, but when I began to chase them they threw good-sized stones at me, missing me only because they were such poor shots. A corpse floated by; when they saw it they immediately placed the sole of their right foot on the side of their left knee and stood thus on one leg till the corpse floated out of sight; I followed the girls' example, teetering. I gathered from what they said that some illness was devastating their people; I hoped it was one of the diseases I had been inoculated against. The girls' mothers found them talking with me and cuffed them away.

I did not see them for two days, but the night of my eighth day 14 there the bolder of them hissed me awake at the door of my hut in a way that meant "no danger." I recognized her when she giggled. I was not sure what their customs were in these matters, but while I was deliberating what my course of wisdom should be she crawled into the hut and lay on the mat beside me. She liked me, she was ut-

terly devoid of reticence, I was twenty-one and far from home; even
a scabby little knotty-legged fashion model is hard to resist under
such circumstances. I learned before falling asleep that there was a
three-way debate among the men over what to do with me: initiate
me according to the prophet-initiation rites, invent a new ceremony,
or sacrifice me as propitiation to the disease among them as was
usually done with captives. Each had its advantages and drawbacks;
even the news that some of the Dangs wanted to sacrifice me did
not excite me as it would have done a week before; now, I half-
sympathized with their trouble. I was awakened at dawn by the outraged howl of a man at my door; he was the girl's father. The village
men gathered and the girl cowered behind me. They talked for
hours outside my hut, men arrived from other villages up and down
the valley, and finally they agreed upon a solution to all the problems: they proposed that I should be made one of the tribe by marriage on the same night that I should be initiated into the rites of
prophecy.

The new-rite men were satisfied by this arrangement because of 15
the novelty of having a man married and initiated on the same day,
but the sacrifice party was visibly unmollified. Noticing this and
reflecting that the proposed arrangement would permit me to do all
my trance research under optimum conditions and to accumulate a
great deal of sexual data as well I agreed to it. I would of course only
be going through the forms of marriage, not meaning them; as for
the girl, I took this vow to myself (meaning without ceremony): "So
long as I am a Dang I shall be formally a correct husband to her."
More's a pity.

Fortunately a youth from down the valley already had been cho- 16
sen as a novice (at least a third of the Dang men enter the novitiate
at one time or another, though few make the grade), so that I had
not only a companion during the four-month preparation for the
vatic rites but also a control upon whom I might check my experience of the stages of the novitiate. My mimetic powers stood me in
good stead; I was presumed to have a special prophetic gift and my
readiness at assuming the proper stances and properly performing
the ritual acts confirmed the Dangs' impressions of my gift; but also,
since I was required to proceed no faster than the ritual pace in my
learning, I had plenty of leisure in which to observe in the smallest
detail what I did and how I, and to some extent my fellow novice,
felt. If I had not had this self-observing to relieve the tedium I think
I should have been unable to get through that mindless holding of
the same position hour after hour, that mindless repeating of the
same act day after day. The Dangs *appear* to be bored much of the
time, and my early experience with them was certainly that of

ennui, though never again ennui so acute as during this novitiate. Yet I doubt that it would be accurate to say they actually are bored, and I am sure that the other novice was not, as a fisherman waiting hours for a strike cannot be said to be bored. The Dangs do not sate themselves on food; the experience which they consider most worth seeking, vision, is one which cannot glut either the prophet or his auditors; they cannot imagine an alternative to living as they live or, more instantly, to preparing a novice as I was being prepared. The people endure; the prophets, as I have learned, wait for the time to come again, and though they are bitten and stung by ten thousand fears, about this they have no anxiety—the time will surely come again. Boredom implies either satiety, and they were poor and not interested in enriching themselves, or the frustration of impulse, and they were without alternatives and diversions. The intense boredom which is really a controlled anxiety, they are protected from by never doubting the worth of their vision or their power to achieve it.

I was assisted through these difficult months during which I was 17 supposed to do nothing but train by Redadu, my betrothed. As a novice I was strictly to abstain from sexual intercourse, but as be-trothed we were supposed to make sure before marriage that we satisfied one another, for adultery by either husband or wife was punishable by maiming. Naturally the theologians were much exer-cised by this impasse, but while they were arguing Redadu and I took the obvious course—we met more or less surreptitiously. Since my vatic training could not take place between sunrise and sun-down I assumed that we could meet in the afternoon when I woke up, but when I began making plans to this effect I discovered that she did not know what I was talking about. It makes as much sense in Dang to say, "Let's blow poisoned darts at the loss of the moon," as to say, "Let's make love in broad daylight." Redadu dissolved in giggles at the absurdity. What to do? She found us a cave. Everyone must have known what I was up to, but we were respectable (the Dang term for it was harsher, *deed-liar*) so we were never disturbed. Redadu's friends would not believe her stories of my luxurious love ways, especially my biting with lips instead of teeth. At one time or another she sent four of them to the cave for me to demonstrate my prowess upon; I was glad that none of them pleased me as much as she did for I was beginning to be fond of her. My son has told me that lip-biting has become if not a customary at any rate a possible caress.

As the night of the double rite approached, a night of full moon, 18 a new conflict became evident: the marriage must be consummated exactly at sundown, but the initiation must begin at moonrise, less than two hours later. For some reason that was not clear to me preparing for the initiation would incapacitate me for the consummation. I refrained from pointing out that it was only technically that this marriage needed consummating and even from asking why I would not be able to do it. The solution, which displeased everyone, was to defer the rites for three nights, when the moon, though no longer perfectly round, would rise sufficiently late so that I would, by hurrying, be able to perform both of my functions. Redadu's father, who had been of the sacrifice party, waived ahead of time his claim against me; legally he was entitled to annul the marriage if I should leave the marriage hut during the bridal night. And although I in turn could legally annul it if she left the hut I waived my claim as well so that she might attend my initiation.

The wedding consisted chiefly of our being bound back to back 19 by the elbows and being sung to and danced about all day. At sunset we were bound face to face by the elbows (most awkward) and sent into our hut. Outside the two mothers waited—a high prophet's wife took the place of my mother (my Methodist mother!)—until our orgastic cries indicated that the marriage had been consummated, and then came in to sever our bonds and bring us the bridal foods of cold stewed eel and parched seeds. We fed each other bite for bite and gave the scraps to our mothers, who by the formula with which they thanked us pronounced themselves satisfied with us. Then a falsetto voice called to me to hurry to the altar. A man in the mask of a moon slave was standing outside my hut on his left leg with the right foot against his left knee, and he continued to shake his rattle so long as I was within earshot.

The men were masked. Their voices were all disguised. I won- 20 dered whether I was supposed to speak in an altered voice; I knew every stance and gesture I was to make, but nothing of what I was to say; yet surely a prophet must employ words. I had seen some of the masks before—being repaired, being carried from one place to another—but now, faced with them alive in the failing twilight, I was impressed by them in no scientific or aesthetic way—they terrified and exalted me. I wondered if I would be given a mask. I began trying to identify such men as I could by their scars and missing fingers and crooked arms, and noticed to my distress that they too were all standing one-legged in my presence. I had thought that was the stance to be assumed in the presence of the dead! We were at the entrance to The Cleft, a dead-end ravine in one of the cliffs along the valley; my fellow novice and I were each given a gourdful of some vile-tasting drink and were then taken up to the end of The Cleft, instructed to assume the first position, and left alone. We squatted as I had been squatting by the log on my first day, except that my head was cocked in a certain way and my hands clasped my ankles from the front. The excitements of the day seemed to have addled my wits, I could concentrate on nothing and lost my impulse to observe coolly what was going on; I kept humming *St. James Infirmary* to myself, and though at first I had been thinking the words, after awhile I realized that I had nothing but the tune left in my head. At moonrise we were brought another gourd of the liquor to drink, and were then taken to the mouth of The Cleft again. I did, easily, whatever I was told. The last thing I remember seeing before taking the second position was the semicircle of masked men facing us and chanting, and behind them the women and children—all standing on the left leg. I lay on my back with my left ankle on my right and my hands crossed over my navel, rolled my eyeballs up and held the lids open without blinking, and breathed in the necessary rhythm, each breath taking four heartbeats, with an interval of ten heartbeats between each exhalation and the next inspiration. Then the drug took over. At dawn when a called command awakened me, I found myself on an islet in the river dancing with my companion a leaping dance I had not known or even seen before, and brandishing over my head a magnificent red and blue, new-made mask of my own. The shores of the river were lined with the people chanting as we leaped, and all of them were either sitting or else standing on both feet. If we had been dead the night before we were alive now.

After I had slept and returned to myself, Redadu told me that 21 my vision was splendid, but of course she was no more permitted to tell me what I had said than I was able to remember it. The Dangs' sense of rhythm is as subtle as their ear for melody is monotonous, and for weeks I kept hearing rhythmic snatches of *St. James Infirmary* scratched on calabash drums and tapped on blocks.

Sorish honored me by rewriting my master's thesis and adding 22 my name as co-author of the resultant essay, which he published in *JAFA* (*The Journal of American Field Anthropology*): "Techniques of Vatic Hallucinosis among the Dangs." And the twenty-minute movie I made of a streamlined performance of the rites is still widely used as an audio-visual aid.

By 1939 when I had been cured of the skin disease I had brought 23 back with me and had finished the work for my M.S. I still had no money. I had been working as the assistant curator of the University's Pre-Columbian Museum and had developed a powerful aversion to devoting my life to cataloguing, displaying, restoring, warehousing. But my chances of getting a research job, slight enough with a Ph.D., were nil with only an M.S. The girl I was going with said (I had not told her about Redadu) that if we married she would work as a nurse to support me while I went through law school; I was tempted by the opportunity to fulfill my original ambition, and probably I would have done it had she not pressed too hard; she wanted me to leave anthropology, she wanted me to become a lawyer, she wanted to support me, but what she did not want was to make my intentions, whatever they might be, her own. So when a new grant gave me the chance to return to the Dangs I gladly seized it; not only would I be asserting myself against Velma, but also I would be paid for doing the research for my Ph.D. thesis; besides, I was curious to see the Congo-Maryland-Dang bastard I had left in Redadu's belly.

My assignment was to make a general cultural survey but especially to discover the *content* of the vatic experience—not just the technique, not even the hallucinations and stories, but the qualities of the experience itself. The former would get me a routine degree, but the latter would, if I did it, make me a name and get me a job. After much consultation I decided against taking with me any form of magic, including medicine; the antibiotics had not been invented yet, and even if there had been a simple way to eradicate the fever endemic among the Dangs, my advisers persuaded me that it would be an error to introduce it since the Dangs were able to procure barely enough food for themselves as it was and since they might worship me for doing it, thereby making it impossible for me to do my research with the proper empathy. I arrived the second time provided only with my knife (which had not seemed to impress these stone-agers), salve to soothe my sores, and the knowledge of how to preserve fish against a lean season, innovation enough but not one likely to divinize me. 24

I was only slightly worried how I would be received on my return, because of the circumstances under which I had disappeared. I had become a fairly decent hunter—the women gathered grain and fruit—and I had learned to respect the Dangs' tracking abilities enough to have been nervous about getting away safely. While hunting with a companion in the hills south of our valley I had run into a couple of hunters from an enemy tribe which seldom foraged so far north as this. They probably were as surprised as I and probably would have been glad to leave me unmolested; however, outnumbered and not knowing how many more were with them, I whooped for my companion; one of the hunters in turn, not knowing how many were with me, threw his spear at me. I side-stepped it and reached for my darts, and though I was not very accurate with a blowpipe I hit him in the thigh; within a minute he was writhing on the ground, for in my haste I had blown a venomous 25 dart at him, and my comrade took his comrade prisoner by surprise. As soon as the man I had hit was dead I withdrew my dart and cut off his ear for trophy, and we returned with our captive. He told our war chief in sign language that the young man I had killed was the son and heir of their king and that my having mutilated him meant their tribe surely would seek to avenge his death. The next morning a Dang search party was sent out to recover the body so that it might be destroyed and trouble averted, but it had disappeared; war threatened. The day after that I chose to vanish; they would not think of looking for me in the direction of Sorish's tribe, north, but would assume that I had been captured by the southern tribe in retribution for their prince's death. My concern now, two years later, was how to account for not having been maimed or executed; the least I could do was to cut a finger off, but when it came to the point I could not even bring myself to have a surgeon do it, much less do it myself; I had adequate lies prepared for their other questions, but about this I was a bit nervous.

I got there at sundown. Spying, I did not see Redadu about the 26 village. On the chance, I slipped into our hut when no one was looking; she was there, playing with our child. He was as cute a little preliterate as you ever saw suck a thumb, and it made me chuckle to think he would never be literate either. Redadu's screams when she saw me fetched the women, but when they heard a man's voice they could not intrude. In her joy she lacerated me with her fingernails (the furrows across my shoulder festered for a long time); I could do no less than bite her arm till she bled; the primal scene we treated our son to presumably scarred him for life—though I must say the scars haven't shown up yet. I can't deny I was glad to see her too, for, though I felt for her none of the tender, complex emotions I had been feeling for Velma, emotions which I more or less identified as being love, yet I was so secure with her sexually, knew so well what to do and what to expect from her in every important matter that it was an enormous, if cool, comfort to me to be with her. *Comfort* is a dangerous approximation to what I mean; being with her provided, as it were, the condition for doing; in Sansom I did not consider her my wife and here I did not recognize in myself the American emotions of love or marriage, yet it seemed to me right to be with her and our son was no bastard. *Cool*—I cannot guarantee that mine was the usual Dang emotion, for it is hard for the cool to gauge the warmth of others (in my reports I have denied any personal experience of love among the Dangs for this reason). When we emerged from the hut there was amazement and relief among the women: amazement that I had returned and relief that it had not been one of their husbands pleasuring the widow. But the men were more ambiguously pleased to see me. Redadu's scratches were not enough and they doubted my story that the enemy king had made me his personal slave who must be bodily perfect. They wanted to hear me prophesy.

Redadu told me afterward, hiding her face in my arms for fear of 27 being judged insolent, that I surpassed myself that night, that only the three high prophets had ever been so inspired. And it was true that even the men most hostile to me did not oppose my reëntry into the tribe after they had heard me prophesy; they could have swallowed the story I fed them about my two-year absence only because they believed in me the prophet. Dangs make no separation between fact and fantasy, apparent reality and visionary reality, truth and beauty. I once saw a young would-be prophet shudder away from a stick on the ground saying it was a snake, and none of the others except the impressionable was afraid of the stick; it was said of him that he was a beginner. Another time I saw a prophet scatter the whole congregation, myself included, when he screamed at the sight of a beast which he called a cougar; when sober dawn found the speared creature to be a cur it was said of the prophet that he was strong, and he was honored with an epithet, Cougar-Dog. My prophesying the first night of my return must have been of this caliber, though to my disappointment I was given no epithet, not even the nickname I'd sometimes heard before, Bush-Hair.

I knew there was a third kind of prophesying, the highest, per- 28 formed only on the most important occasions in the Cave-Temple where I had never been. No such occasion had presented itself during my stay before, and when I asked one of the other prophets about that ceremony he put me off with the term Wind-Haired Child of the Sun; from another I learned that the name of this sort of prophesying was Stone is Stone. Obviously I was going to have to stay until I could make sense of these mysteries.

There was a war party that wanted my support; my slavery was 29 presumed to have given me knowledge which would make a raid highly successful; because of this as well as because I had instigated the conflict by killing the king's son I would be made chief of the raiding party. I was uneasy about the fever, which had got rather worse among them during the previous two years, without risking my neck against savages who were said always to eat a portion of their slain enemy's liver raw and whose habitat I knew nothing of. I persuaded the Dangs, therefore, that they should not consider attacking before the rains came, because their enemies were now the stronger, having on their side their protector, the sun. They listened to me and waited. Fortunately it was a long dry season, during which I had time to find a salt deposit and to teach a few women the rudiments of drying and salting fish; and during the first week of the rains every night there were showers of falling stars to be seen in the sky; to defend against them absorbed all energies for weeks, including the warriors'. Even so, even though I was a prophet, a journeyman prophet as it were, I was never in on these rites in the Cave-Temple. I dared not ask many questions. Sir Bewley Morehead had described a temple surrounded by seventy-six poles, each topped by a human head; he could hardly have failed to mention that it was in a cave, yet he made no such mention, and I knew of no temple like the one he had described. At a time of rains and peace in the sky the war party would importune me. I did not know what to do but wait.

The rains became violent, swamping the villages in the lower 30 valley and destroying a number of huts, yet the rainy season ended abruptly two months before its usual time. Preparations for war had already begun, and day by day as the sun's strength increased and the earth dried the war party became more impatient. The preparations in themselves lulled my objections to the raid, even to my leading the raid, and stimulated my desire to make war. But the whole project was canceled a couple of days before we were to attack because of the sudden fever of one of the high prophets; the day after he came down five others of the tribe fell sick, among them Redadu. There was nothing I could do but sit by her, fanning her and sponging her till she died. Her next older sister took our son to rear. I would allow no one to prepare her body but myself, though her mother was supposed to help; I washed it with the proper infusions of herbs, and at dawn, in the presence of her clan, I laid her body on the river. Thank heaven it floated or I should have had to spend another night preparing it further. I felt like killing someone now; I recklessly called for war now, even though the high prophet had not yet died; I was restrained, not without admiration. I went up into the eastern hills by myself and returned after a week bearing the hide of a cougar; I had left the head and claws on my trophy in a way the Dangs had never seen; when I put the skin on in play by daylight and bounded and snarled only the bravest did not run in terror. They called me Cougar-Man. Redadu's younger sister came to sleep with me; I did not want her, but she so stubbornly refused to be expelled that I kept her for the night, for the next night, for the next; it was not improper.

The high prophet did not die, but lay comatose most of the time. 31 The Dangs have ten master prophets, of whom the specially gifted, whether one or all ten, usually two or three, are high prophets. Fifteen days after Redadu had died, well into the abnormal dry spell, nearly all the large fish seemed to disappear from the river. A sacrifice was necessary. It was only because the old man was so sick that a high prophet was used for this occasion, otherwise a captive or a woman would have served the purpose. A new master prophet must replace him, to keep the complement up to ten. I was chosen.

The exultation I felt when I learned that the master prophets had co-opted me among them was by no means cool and anthropological, for now that I had got what I had come to get I no longer wanted it for Sansom reasons. *If the conditions of my being elevated,* I said to myself, *are the suffering of the people, Redadu's death, and the sacrifice of an old man, then I must make myself worthy of the great price. Worthy*—a value word, not a scientific one. Of course, my emotions were not the simple pride and fear of a Dang. I can't say what sort they were, but they were fierce.

At sundown all the Dangs of all the clans were assembled about the entrance to The Cleft. All the prophets, masked, emerged from The Cleft and began the dance in a great wheel. Within this wheel, rotating against it, was the smaller wheel of the nine able-bodied master prophets. At the center, facing the point at which the full moon would rise, I hopped on one leg, then the other. I had been given none of the vatic liquor, that brew which the women, when I had first come among the Dangs, had been preparing in the small-throated pots, and I hoped I should be able to remain conscious throughout the rites. However, at moonrise a moon slave brought me a gourdful to drink without ceasing to dance. I managed to allow a good deal of it to spill unnoticed down with the sweat streaming off me, so that later I was able to remember what had happened, right up to the prophesying itself. The dance continued for at least two more hours, then the drums suddenly stopped and the prophets began to file up The Cleft with me last dancing after the high prophets. We danced into an opening in the cliff from which a disguising stone had been rolled away. The people were not allowed to follow us. We entered a great cavern illuminated by ten smoking torches and circled a palisade of stakes; the only sound was the shuffle of our feet and the snorts of our breathing. There were seventy-six stakes, as Morehead had seen, but only on twenty-eight of them were heads impaled, the last few with flesh on them still, not yet skulls cleaned of all but hair. In the center was a huge stone under the middle of which a now dry stream had tunneled a narrow passage; on one side of the stone, above the passage, were two breastlike protuberances, one of which had a recognizable nipple in the suitable place. Presently the dancing file reversed so that I was the leader. I had not been taught what to do; I wove the file through the round of stakes, and spiraled inward till we were three deep about The Stone; I straddled the channel, raised my hands till they were touching the breasts, and gave a great cry. I was, for reasons I do not understand, shuddering all over; though I was conscious and though I had not been instructed, I was not worried that I might do the wrong thing next. When I touched The Stone a dread shook me without affecting my exaltation. Two moon slaves seized my arms, took off my mask, and wrapped and bound me—arms at my side and legs pressed together in a deer hide—and then laid me on my back in the channel under The Stone with my head only half out, so that I was staring up the sheer side of rock. The dancers continued, though the master prophets had disappeared. My excitement, the new unused position, being mummied tightly, the weakness of the drug, my will to observe, all kept me conscious for a long time. Gradually, however, my eyes began to roll up into my head, I strained less powerfully against the thongs that bound me, and I felt my breathing approach the vatic rhythm. At this point I seemed to break out in a new sweat, on my forehead, my throat, in my hair; I could hear a splash, groggily I licked my chin—an odd taste—I wondered if I was bleeding. Of course, it was the blood of the sick old high prophet, who had just been sacrificed on The Stone above me; well, his blood would give me strength. Wondering remotely whether his fever could be transmitted by drinking his blood I entered the trance. At dawn I emerged into consciousness while I was still prophesying; I was on a ledge in the valley above all the people, in my mask again. I listened to myself finish the story I was telling. "He was afraid. A third time a man said to him: 'You are a friend of the most high prophet.' He answered: 'Not me. I do not know that man they are sacrificing.' Then he went into a dark corner, he put his hands over his face all day." When I came to the Resurrection a sigh blew across the people. It was the best story they had ever heard. Of course. But I was not really a Christian. For several weeks I fretted over my confusion, this new, unsuspected confusion.

I was miserable without Redadu; I let her sister substitute only 34 until I had been elevated, and then I cast her off, promising her however that she and only she might wear an anklet made of my teeth when I should die. Now that I was a master prophet I could not be a warrior; I had enough of hunting and fishing and tedious ceremonies. Hunger from the shortage of fish drove the hunters high into the foothills; there was not enough; they ate my preserved fish, suspiciously, but they ate them. When I left it was not famine that I was escaping but my confusion; I was fleeing to the class-rooms and the cool museums where I should be neither a leftover Christian nor a mimic of a Dang.

My academic peace lasted for just two years, during which time 35
I wrote five articles on my researches, publishing them this time under my name only, did some of the work for my doctorate, and married Velma. Then came World War II, in which my right hand was
severed above the wrist; I was provided with an artificial hand and
given enough money so that I could afford to finish my degree in
style. We had two daughters and I was given a job at Sansom. There
was no longer a question of my returning to the Dangs. I would become a settled anthropologist, teach, and quarrel with my colleagues
in the learned journals. But by the time the Korean War came along
and robbed us of a lot of our students, my situation at the university
had changed considerably. Few of my theoretical and disputatious
articles were printed in the journals, and I hated writing them; I was
not given tenure and there were some hints to the effect that I was
considered a one-shot man, a flash-in-the-pan; Velma nagged for
more money and higher rank. My only recourse was further research, and when I thought of starting all over again with some
other tribe—in northern Australia, along the Zambesi, on an African
island—my heart sank. The gossip was not far from the mark—I
was not a one hundred per cent scientist and never would be. I had
just enough reputation and influential recommendations to be
awarded a Guggenheim Fellowship; supplemented by a travel grant
from the university this made it possible for me to leave my family
comfortably provided for and to return to the Dangs.

A former student now in Standard Oil in Venezuela arranged to 36
have me parachuted among them from an SO plane. There was the
real danger that they would kill me before they recognized me, but
if I arrived in a less spectacular fashion I was pretty sure they would
sacrifice me for their safety's sake. This time, being middle-aged, I
left my hunting knife and brought instead at my belt a pouch filled
with penicillin and salves. I had a hard time identifying the valley
from the air; it took me so long that it was sunset before I jumped. I
knew how the Dangs were enraged by airplanes, especially by the
winking lights of night fliers, and I knew they would come for me if
they saw me billowing down. Fortunately I landed in the river, for
though I was nearly drowned before I disentangled my parachute
harness I was also out of range of the blowpipes. I finally identified
myself to the warriors brandishing their spears along the shore; they
had not quite dared to swim out after so prodigious a being; even after they knew who I said I was and allowed me to swim to shore
they saw me less as myself than as a supernatural being. I was recognized by newcomers who had not seen me so closely swinging
from the parachute (the cloud); on the spot my epithet became, and
remained, Sky-Cougar. Even so no one dared touch me till the high

prophet—there was only one now—had arrived and talked with me; my artificial hand seemed to him an extension of the snake tattooed onto my skin, he would not touch it; I suddenly struck him with it and pinched his arm. "Pinchers," I said using the word for a crayfish claw, and he laughed. He said there was no way of telling whether I was what I seemed to be until he had heard me prophesy; if I prophesied as I had done before I had disappeared I must be what I seemed to be; meanwhile, for the three weeks till full moon I was to be kept in the hut for captives.

At first I was furious at being imprisoned, and when mothers 37 brought children from miles about to peek through the stakes at the man with the snake hand I snarled or sulked like a caged wolf. But I became conscious that one youth, squatting in a quiet place, had been watching me for hours. I demanded of him who he was. He said, "I am your son," but he did not treat me as his father. To be sure, he could not have remembered what I looked like; my very identity was doubted; even if I were myself, I was legendary, a stranger who had become a Dang and had been held by an enemy as captive slave for two years and had then become a master prophet with the most wonderful vision anyone knew. Yet he came to me every day and answered all the questions I put to him. It was, I believe, my artificial hand that finally kept him aloof from me; no amount of acquaintance could accustom him to that. By the end of the first week it was clear to me that if I wanted to survive—not to be accepted as I once had been, just to survive—I would have to prophesy the Passion again. And how could I determine what I would say when under the vatic drug? I imagined a dozen schemes for substituting colored water for the drug, but I would need an accomplice for that and I knew that not even my own son would serve me in so forbidden an act.

I called for the high prophet. I announced to him in tones all the 38 more arrogant because of my trepidations that I would prophesy without the vatic liquor. His response to my announcement astonished me: he fell upon his knees, bowed his head, and rubbed dust into his hair. He was the most powerful man among the Dangs, except in time of war when the war chief took over, and furthermore he was an old man of personal dignity, yet here he was abasing himself before me and, worse, rubbing dust into his hair as was proper in the presence of the very sick to help them in their dying. He told me why: prophesying successfully from a voluntary trance was the test which I must pass to become a high prophet; normally a master prophet was forced to this, for the penalty for failing it was death. I dismissed him with a wave of my claw.

I had five days to wait until full moon. The thought of the risk I 39
was running was more than I could handle consciously; to avoid the
jitters I performed over and over all the techniques of preparing for
the trance, though I carefully avoided entering it. I was not sure I
would be able to enter it alone, but whether I could or not I knew I
wanted to conserve my forces for the great test. At first during those
five days I would remind myself once in a while of my scientific purpose in going into the trance consciously; at other times I would as-
sure myself that it was for the good of the Dangs that I was doing it,
since it was not wise or safe for them to have only one high prophet.
Both of these reasons were true enough, but not very important. As
scientist I should tell them some new myth, say the story of Abraham and Isaac or of Oedipus, so that I could compare its effect on
them with that of the Passion; as master prophet I should ennoble
my people if I could. However, thinking these matters over as I held
my vatic squat hour after hour, visited and poked at by prying eyes,
I could find no myth to satisfy me; either, as in the case of Abraham,
it involved a concept of God which the Dangs could not reach, or
else, as with Oedipus, it necessitated more drastic changes than I
trusted myself to keep straight while prophesying—that Oedipus
should mutilate himself was unthinkable to the Dangs and that the
gods should be represented as able to forgive him for it was impi-
ous. Furthermore, I did not think, basically, that any story I could
tell them would in fact ennoble them. I was out to save my own
skin.

The story of Christ I knew by heart; it had worked for me once, 40
perhaps more than once; it would work again. I rehearsed it over
and over, from the Immaculate Conception to the Ascension. But
such was the force of that story on me that by the fifth day my cynicism had disappeared along with my scientism, and I believed, not
that the myth itself was true, but that relating it to my people was
the best thing it was possible for me to do for them. I remember
telling myself that this story would help raise them toward
monotheism, a necessary stage in the evolution toward freedom. I
felt a certain satisfaction in the thought that some of the skulls on
the stakes in the Cave-Temple were very likely those of missionaries
who had failed to convert these heathen.

At sundown of the fifth day I was taken by moon slaves to a 41
cave near The Cleft, where I was left in peace. I fell into a troubled
sleep from which I awoke in a sweat. "Where am I? What am I about
to do?" It seemed to me dreadfully wrong that I should be telling
these, my people, a myth in whose power, but not in whose truth, I
believed. Why should I want to free them from superstition into

monotheism and then into my total freedom, when I myself was half-returning, voluntarily, down the layers again? The energy for these sweating questions came, no doubt, from my anxiety about how I was going to perform that night, but I did not recognize this fact at the time. Then I thought it was my conscience speaking, and that I had no right to open to the Dangs a freedom I myself was rejecting. It was too late to alter my course; honesty required me, and I resolved courageously, not to prophesy at all.

When I was fetched out the people were in assembly at The 42 Cleft and the wheel of master prophets was revolving against the greater wheel of dancers. I was given my cougar skin. Hung from a stake, in the center where I was to hop, was a huge, terrific mask I had never seen before. As the moon rose her slaves hung this mask on me; the thong cut into the back of my neck cruelly, and at the bottom the mask came to a point that pressed my belly; it was so wide my arms could only move laterally. It had no eye holes; I broke into a sweat wondering how I should be able to follow the prophets into the Cave-Temple. It turned out to be no problem; the two moon slaves, one on each side, guided me by prodding spears in my ribs. Once in the cave they guided me to the back side of The Stone and drove me to climb it, my feet groping for steps I could not see; once, when I lost my balance, the spears' pressure kept me from falling backward. By the time I reached the top of The Stone I was bleeding and dizzy. With one arm I kept the mask from gouging my belly while with the other I helped my aching neck support the mask. I did not know what to do next. Tears of pain and anger poured from my eyes. I began hopping. I should have been moving my arms in counterpoint to the rhythm of my hop, but I could not bear the thought of letting the mask cut into me more. I kept hopping in the same place for fear of falling off; I had not been noticing the sounds of the other prophets, but suddenly I was aware they were making no sounds at all. In my alarm I lurched to the side and cut my foot on a sharp break in the rock. Pain converted my panic to rage.

I lifted the mask and held it flat above my head. I threw my 43 head back and howled as I had never howled in my life, through a constricted, gradually opening throat, until at the end I was roaring; when I gasped in my breath I made a barking noise. I leaped and leaped, relieved of pain, confident. I punched my knee desecratingly through the brittle hide of the mask, and threw it behind me off The Stone. I tore off my cougar skin, and holding it with my claw by the tip of its tail I whirled it around my head. The prophets, massed below me, fell onto their knees. I felt their fear. Howling, I soared the skin out over them; one of those on whom it landed screamed hideously. A commotion started; I could not see very well what was happening. I barked and they turned toward me again. I leaped three times and then, howling, jumped wide-armed off The Stone. The twelve-foot drop hurt severely my already cut foot. I rolled exhausted into the channel in the cave floor.

Moon slaves with trembling hands mummied me in the deerskin 44 and shoved me under The Stone with only my head sticking out. They brought two spears with darts tied to the points; rolling my head to watch them do this I saw that the prophets were kneeling over and rubbing dirt into their hair. Then the slaves laid the spears alongside the base of the Stone with the poisoned pricks pointed at my temples; exactly how close they were I could not be sure, but close enough so that I dared not move my head. In all my preparations I had, as I had been trained to do, rocked and weaved at least my head; now, rigidity, live rigidity. A movement would scratch me and a scratch would kill me.

I pressed my hook into my thigh, curled my toes, and pressed 45 my tongue against my teeth till my throat ached. I did not dare relieve myself even with a howl, for I might toss my head fatally. I strained against my thongs to the verge of apoplexy. For a while I was unable to see, for sheer rage. Fatigue collapsed me. Yet I dared not relax my vigilance over my movements. My consciousness sealed me off. Those stone protuberances up between which I had to stare in the flickering light were merely chance processes on a boulder, similes to breasts. The one thing I might not become unconscious of was the pair of darts waiting for me to err. For a long time I thought of piercing my head against them, for relief, for spite. Hours passed. I was carefully watched.

I do not know what wild scheme I had had in mind when I had 46 earlier resolved not to prophesy, what confrontation or escape; it had had the pure magnificence of a fantasy resolution. But the reality, which I had not seriously tried to evade, was that I must prophesy or die. I kept lapsing from English into a delirium of Dang. By the greatest effort of will I looked about me rationally. I wondered whether the return of Halley's comet, at which time all the stakes should be mounted by skulls, would make the Dangs destroy the Cave-Temple and erect a new one. I observed the straight, indented seam of sandstone running slantwise up the boulder over me and wondered how many eons this rotting piece of granite had been tumbled about by water. I reflected that I was unworthy both as a Christian and as a Dang to prophesy the life of Jesus. But I convinced myself that it was a trivial matter, since to the Christians it was the telling more than the teller that counted and to the Dangs this myth would serve as a civilizing force they needed. Surely, I thought, my hypocrisy could be forgiven me, especially since I resolved to punish myself for it by leaving the Dangs forever as soon as I could. Having reached this rational solution I smiled and gestured to the high prophet with my eyes; he did not move a muscle. When I realized that nothing to do with hypocrisy would unbind me desperation swarmed in my guts and mounted toward my brain; with this question it took me over: *How can I make myself believe it is true?* I needed to catch hold of myself again. I dug my hook so hard into my leg—it was the only action I was able to take—that I gasped with pain; the pain I wanted. I did not speculate on the consequences of gouging my leg, tearing a furrow in my thigh muscle, hurting by the same act the stump of my arm to which the hook was attached; just as I knew that the prophets, the torches, the poisoned darts were there in the cave, so also I knew that far far back in my mind I had good enough reasons to be hurting myself, reasons which I could find out if I wanted to, but which it was not worth my trouble to discover; I even allowed the knowledge that I myself was causing the pain to drift back in my mind. The pain itself, only the pain, became my consciousness, purging all else. Then, as the pain subsided leaving me free and equipoised, awareness of the stone arched over me flooded my mind. Because it had been invested by the people with great mystery, it was an incarnation; the power of their faith made it the moon, who was female; at the same time it was only a boulder. I understood Stone is Stone, and that became my consciousness.

My muscles ceased straining against the bonds, nor did they 47 slump; they ceased aching, they were at ease, they were ready. I said nothing, I did not change the upward direction of my glance, I did not smile, yet at this moment the high prophet removed the spears and had the moon slaves unbind me. I did not feel stiff nor did my wounds bother me, and when I put on my cougar skin and leaped, pulled the head over my face and roared, all the prophets fell onto their faces before me. I began chanting and I knew I was doing it all the better for knowing what I was about; I led them back out to the waiting people, and until dawn I chanted the story of the birth, prophesying, betrayal, sacrifice, and victory of the most high prophet. I am a good mimic, I was thoroughly trained, the story is the best; what I gave them was, for them, as good as a vision. I did not know the difference myself.

But the next evening I knew the difference. While I performed 48 my ablutions and the routine ceremonies to the full moon I thought with increasing horror of my state of mind during my conscious trance. What my state of mind actually had been I cannot with confidence now represent, for what I know of it is colored by my reaction against it the next day. I had remained conscious, in that I could recall what happened, yet that observer and commentator in myself of whose existence I had scarcely been aware, but whom I had always taken for my consciousness, had vanished. I no longer had been thinking, but had lost control so that my consciousness had become what I was doing; almost worse, when I had told the story of Christ I had done it not because I had wanted to or believed in it but because, in some obscure sense, I had had to. Thinking about it afterward I did not understand or want to understand what I was drifting toward, but I knew it was something that I feared. And I got out of there as soon as I was physically able.

Here in Sansom what I have learned has provided me with material for an honorable contribution to knowledge, has given me a tenure to a professorship—thereby pleasing my wife—whereas if I had stayed there among the Dangs much longer I would have reverted until I had become one of them, might not have minded when the time came to die under the sacrificial knife, would have taken in all ways the risk of prophecy—as my Dang son intends to do—until I had lost myself utterly. 49

When It Changed

JOANNA RUSS

Katy drives like a maniac; we must have been doing over 120 kilo- 1
meters per hour on those turns. She's good, though, extremely
good, and I've seen her take the whole car apart and put it together
again in a day. My birthplace on Whileaway was largely given to
farm machinery and I refuse to wrestle with a five-gear shift at un-
holy speeds, not having been brought up to it, but even on those
turns in the middle of the night, on a country road as bad as only
our district can make them, Katy's driving didn't scare me. The
funny thing about my wife, though: she will not handle guns. She
has even gone hiking in the forests above the forty-eighth parallel
without firearms, for days at a time. And that *does* scare me.

Katy and I have three children between us, one of hers and two 2
of mine. Yuriko, my eldest, was asleep in the back seat, dreaming
twelve-year-old dreams of love and war: running away to sea, hunting in the North, dreams of strangely beautiful people in strangely
beautiful places, all the wonderful guff you think up when you're
turning twelve and the glands start going. Some day soon, like all of
them, she will disappear for weeks on end to come back grimy and
proud, having knifed her first cougar or shot her first bear, dragging
some abominably dangerous dead beastie behind her, which I will
never forgive for what it might have done to my daughter. Yuriko
says Katy's driving puts her to sleep.

For someone who has fought three duels, I am afraid of far, far 3
too much. I'm getting old. I told this to my wife.

"You're thirty-four," she said. Laconic to the point of silence, 4
that one. She flipped the lights on, on the dash—three kilometers to
go and the road getting worse all the time. Far out in the country.
Electric-green trees rushed into our headlights and around the car. I
reached down next to me where we bolt the carrier panel to the door
and eased my rifle into my lap. Yuriko stirred in the back. My height
but Katy's eyes, Katy's face. The car engine is so quiet, Katy says,

---

Joanna Russ (1937–   ), born in New York City, is the author of
science fiction, criticism, stories, and novels including *And Chaos
Died* (1970), *The Female Man* (1975), and *How to Suppress Women's
Writing* (1983). "When It Changed" first appeared in *Again, Dangerous Visions* (1972), edited by Harlan Ellison.

that you can hear breathing in the back seat. Yuki had been alone in the car when the message came, enthusiastically decoding her dot-dashes (silly to mount a wide-frequency transceiver near an I. C. engine, but most of Whileaway is on steam). She had thrown herself out of the car, my gangly and gaudy offspring, shouting at the top of her lungs, so of course she had had to come along. We've been intellectually prepared for this ever since the Colony was founded, ever since it was abandoned, but this is different. This is awful.

"Men!" Yuki had screamed, leaping over the car door. "They've 5 come back! Real Earth men!"

We met them in the kitchen of the farmhouse near the place 6 where they had landed; the windows were open, the night air very mild. We had passed all sorts of transportation when we parked outside—steam tractors, trucks, an I. C. flatbed, even a bicycle. Lydia, the district biologist, had come out of her Northern taciturnity long enough to take blood and urine samples and was sitting in a corner of the kitchen shaking her head in astonishment over the results; she even forced herself (very big, very fair, very shy, always painfully blushing) to dig up the old language manuals—though I can talk the old tongues in my sleep. And do. Lydia is uneasy with us; we're Southerners and too flamboyant. I counted twenty people in that kitchen, all the brains of North Continent. Phyllis Spet, I think, had come in by glider. Yuki was the only child there.

Then I saw the four of them. 7

They are bigger than we are. They are bigger and broader. Two 8 were taller than I, and I am extremely tall, one meter eighty centimeters in my bare feet. They are obviously of our species but *off*, indescribably off, and as my eyes could not and still cannot quite comprehend the lines of those alien bodies, I could not, then, bring myself to touch them, though the one who spoke Russian—what voices they have—wanted to "shake hands," a custom from the past, I imagine. I can only say they were apes with human faces. He seemed to mean well, but I found myself shuddering back almost the length of the kitchen—and then I laughed apologetically—and then to set a good example (*intersteller amity*, I thought) did "shake hands" finally. A hard, hard hand. They are heavy as draft horses. Blurred, deep voices. Yuriko had sneaked in between the adults and was gazing at *the men* with her mouth open.

He turned *his* head—those words have not been in our language 9 for six hundred years—and said, in bad Russian:

"Who's that?" 10

"My daughter," I said, and added (with that irrational attention 11 to good manners we sometimes employ in moments of insanity),

"My daughter, Yuriko Janetson. We use the patronymic. You would say matronymic."

He laughed, involuntarily. Yuki exclaimed, "I thought they would be *good-looking!*" greatly disappointed at this reception of herself. Phyllis Helgason Spet, whom someday I shall kill, gave me across the room a cold, level, venomous look, as if to say: *Watch what you say. You know what I can do.* It's true that I have little formal status, but Madam President will get herself in serious trouble with both me and her own staff if she continues to consider industrial espionage good clean fun. Wars and rumors of wars, as it says in one of our ancestor's books. I translated Yuki's words into *the man's* dog-Russian, once our *lingua franca,* and *the man* laughed again. 12

"Where are all your people?" he said conversationally. 13

I translated again and watched the faces around the room; Lydia embarrassed (as usual), Spet narrowing her eyes with some damned scheme, Katy very pale. 14

"This is Whileaway," I said. 15

He continued to look unenlightened. 16

"Whileaway," I said. "Do you remember? Do you have records? There was a plague on Whileaway." 17

He looked moderately interested. Heads turned in the back of the room, and I caught a glimpse of the local professions-parliament delegate; by morning every town meeting, every district caucus, would be in full session. 18

"Plague?" he said. "That's most unfortunate." 19

"Yes," I said. "Most unfortunate. We lost half our population in one generation." 20

He looked properly impressed. 21

"Whileaway was lucky," I said. "We had a big initial gene pool, we had been chosen for extreme intelligence, we had a high technology and a large remaining population in which every adult was two or three experts in one. The soil is good. The climate is blessedly easy. There are thirty millions of us now. Things are beginning to snowball in industry—do you understand?—give us seventy years and we'll have more than one real city, more than a few industrial centers, full-time professions, full-time radio operators, full-time machinists, give us seventy years and not everyone will have to spend three-quarters of a lifetime on the farm." And I tried to explain how hard it is when artists can practice full-time only in old age, when there are so few, so very few who can be free, like Katy and myself. I tried also to outline our government, the two houses, the one by professions and the geographic one; I told him the district caucuses handled problems too big for the individual towns. And that population control was not a political issue, not yet, though give us time 22

and it would be. This was a delicate point in our history; give us
time. There was no need to sacrifice the quality of life for an insane
rush into industrialization. Let us go our own pace. Give us time.

"Where are all the people?" said that monomaniac.   23

I realized then that he did not mean people, he meant *men*, and   24
he was giving the word the meaning it had not had on Whileaway
for six centuries.

"They died," I said. "Thirty generations ago."   25

I thought we had poleaxed him. He caught his breath. He made   26
as if to get out of the chair he was sitting in; he put his hand to his
chest; he looked around at us with the strangest blend of awe and
sentimental tenderness. Then he said, solemnly and earnestly:

"A great tragedy."   27

I waited, not quite understanding.   28

"Yes," he said, catching his breath again with the queer smile,   29
that adult-to-child smile that tells you something is being hidden
and will be presently produced with cries of encouragement and
joy, "a great tragedy. But it's over." And again he looked around at
all of us with the strangest deference. As if we were invalids.

"You've adapted amazingly," he said.   30

"To what?" I said. He looked embarrassed. He looked inane. Fi-   31
nally he said, "Where I come from, the women don't dress so
plainly."

"Like you?" I said. "Like a bride?" for the men were wearing sil-   32
ver from head to foot. I had never seen anything so gaudy. He made
as if to answer and then apparently thought better of it; he laughed
at me again. With an odd exhilaration—as if we were something
childish and something wonderful, as if he were doing us an enormous favor—he took one shaky breath and said, "Well, we're here."

I looked at Spet, Spet looked at Lydia, Lydia looked at Amalia,   33
who is the head of the local town meeting, Amalia looked at I don't
know whom. My throat was raw. I cannot stand local beer, which
the farmers swill as if their stomachs had iridium linings, but I took
it anyway, from Amalia (it was her bicycle we had seen outside as
we parked), and swallowed it all. This was going to take a long
time. I said, "Yes, here you are," and smiled (feeling like a fool), and
wondered seriously if male-Earth-people's minds worked so very
differently from female-Earth-people's minds, but that couldn't be
so or the race would have died out long ago. The radio network had
got the news around planet by now and we had another Russian
speaker, flown in from Varna; I decided to cut out when *the man*
passed around pictures of his wife, who looked like the priestess of
some arcane cult. He proposed to question Yuki, so I barreled her
into a back room in spite of her furious protests, and went out on

the front porch. As I left, Lydia was explaining the difference between parthenogenesis (which is so easy that anyone can practice it) and what we do, which is the merging of ova. That is why Katy's baby looks like me. Lydia went on to the Ansky Process and Katy Ansky, our one full-polymath genius and the great-great I don't know how many times great-grandmother of my own Katharina.

A dot-dash transmitter in one of the outbuildings chattered 34 faintly to itself: operators flirting and passing jokes down the line.

There was a man on the porch. The other tall man. I watched 35 him for a few minutes—I can move very quietly when I want to— and when I allowed him to see me, he stopped talking into the little machine hung around his neck. Then he said calmly, in excellent Russian, "Did you know that sexual equality has been reestablished on Earth?"

"You're the real one," I said, "aren't you? The other one's for 36 show." It was a great relief to get things cleared up. He nodded affably.

"As a people, we are not very bright," he said. "There's been 37 too much genetic damage in the last few centuries. Radiation. Drugs. We can use Whileaway's genes, Janet." Strangers do not call strangers by the first name.

"You can have cells enough to drown in," I said, "Breed your 38 own."

He smiled. "That's not the way we want to do it." Behind him I 39 saw Katy come into the square of light that was the screened-in door. He went on, low and urbane, not mocking me, I think, but with the self-confidence of someone who has always had money and strength to spare, who doesn't know what it is to be second-class or provincial. Which is very odd, because the day before, I would have said that was an exact description of me.

"I'm talking to you, Janet," he said, "because I suspect you have 40 more popular influence than anyone else here. You know as well as I do that parthenogenetic culture has all sorts of inherent defects, and we do not—if we can help it—mean to use you for anything of the sort. Pardon me; I should not have said 'use.' But surely you can see that this kind of society is unnatural."

"Humanity is unnatural," said Katy. She had my rifle under her 41 left arm. The top of that silky head does not quite come up to my collarbone, but she is as tough as steel; he began to move, again with that queer smiling deference (which his fellow had showed to me but he had not), and the gun slid into Katy's grip as if she had shot with it all her life.

"I agree," said the man. "Humanity is unnatural. I should 42 know. I have metal in my teeth and metal pins here." He touched his shoulder. "Seals are harem animals," he added, "and so are men; apes are promiscuous and so are men; doves are monogamous and so are men; there are even celibate men and homosexual men. There are homosexual cows, I believe. But Whileaway is still missing something." He gave a dry chuckle. I will give him the credit of believing that it had something to do with nerves.

"I miss nothing," said Katy, "except that life isn't endless."   43

"You are—?" said the man, nodding from me to her.   44

"Wives," said Katy. "We're married." Again the dry chuckle.   45

"A good economic arrangement," he said, "for working and tak-   46 ing care of the children. And as good an arrangement as any for randomizing heredity, if your reproduction is made to follow the same pattern. But think, Katharina Michaelason, if there isn't something better that you might secure for your daughters. I believe in instincts, even in Man, and I can't think that the two of you—a machinist, are you? and I gather you are some sort of chief of police—don't feel somehow what even you must miss. You know it intellectually, of course. There is only half a species here. Men must come back to Whileaway."

Katy said nothing.   47

"I should think, Katharina Michaelason," said the man gently,   48 "that you, of all people, would benefit most from such a change," and he walked past Katy's rifle into the square of light coming from the door. I think it was then that he noticed my scar, which really does not show unless the light is from the side: a fine line that runs from temple to chin. Most people don't even know about it.

"Where did you get that?" he said, and I answered with an in-   49 voluntary grin. "In my last duel." We stood there bristling at each other for several seconds (this is absurd but true) until he went inside and shut the screen door behind him. Katy said in a brittle voice, "You damned fool, don't you know when we've been insulted?" and swung up the rifle to shoot him through the screen, but I got to her before she could fire and knocked the rifle out of aim; it burned a hole through the porch floor. Katy was shaking. She kept whispering over and over, "That's why I never touched it, because I knew I'd kill someone. I knew I'd kill someone." The first man—the one I'd spoken with first—was still talking inside the house, something about the grand movement to recolonize and rediscover all the Earth had lost. He stressed the advantages to Whileaway: trade, exchange of ideas, education. He, too, said that sexual equality had been reestablished on Earth.

Katy was right, of course; we should have burned them down   50 where they stood. Men are coming to Whileaway. When one culture has the big guns and the other has none, there is a certain predictability about the outcome. Maybe men would have come eventually in any case. I like to think that a hundred years from now my great-grandchildren could have stood them off or fought them to a standstill, but even that's no odds; I will remember all my life those four people I first met who were muscled like bulls and who made me—if only for a moment—feel small. A neurotic reaction, Katy says. I remember everything that happened that night; I remember Yuki's excitement in the car, I remember Katy's sobbing when we got home as if her heart would break, I remember her lovemaking, a little peremptory as always, but wonderfully soothing and comforting. I remember prowling restlessly around the house after Katy fell asleep with one bare arm hung into a patch of light from the hall. The muscles of her forearms are like metal bars from all that driving and testing of her machines. Sometimes I dream about Katy's arms. I remember wandering into the nursery and picking up my wife's baby, dozing for a while with the poignant, amazing warmth of an infant in my lap, and finally returning to the kitchen to find Yuriko fixing herself a late snack. My daughter eats like a Great Dane.

"Yuki," I said, "do you think you could fall in love with a man?" 51 and she whooped derisively. "With a ten-foot toad!" said my tactful child.

But men are coming to Whileaway. Lately I sit up nights and 52 worry about the men who will come to this planet, about my two daughters and Betta Katharinason, about what will happen to Katy, to me, to my life. Our ancestors' journals are one long cry of pain and I suppose I ought to be glad now, but one can't throw away six centuries, or even (as I have lately discovered) thirty-four years. Sometimes I laugh at the question those four men hedged about all evening and never quite dared to ask, looking at the lot of us, hicks in overalls, farmers in canvas pants and plain shirts: *Which of you plays the role of the man?* As if we had to produce a carbon copy of their mistakes! I doubt very much that sexual equality has been reestablished on Earth. I do not like to think of myself mocked, of Katy deferred to as if she were weak, of Yuki made to feel unimportant or silly, of my other children cheated of their full humanity or turned into strangers. And I'm afraid that my own achievements will dwindle from what they were—or what I thought they were—to the not-very-interesting curiosa of the human race, the oddities you read about in the back of the book, things to laugh at sometimes because they are so exotic, quaint but not impressive, charming but not useful. I find this more painful than I can say. You will agree that for a woman who has fought three duels, all of them kills, indulging in such fears is ludicrous. But what's around the corner now is a duel so big that I don't think I have the guts for it; in Faust's words: *Verweile doch, du bist so schoen!* Keep it as it is. Don't change.

Sometimes at night I remember the original name of this planet,   53
changed by the first generation of our ancestors, those curious women for whom, I suppose, the real name was too painful a reminder after the men died. I find it amusing, in a grim way, to see it all so completely turned around. This, too, shall pass. All good things must come to an end.

Take my life but don't take away the meaning of my life.   54

For-A-While.   55

The Ones Who Walk Away from Omelas

Variations on a Theme by William James[1]

URSULA K. LE GUIN

With a clamor of bells that set the swallows soaring, the Festival of 1
Summer came to the city Omelas, bright-towered by the sea. The
rigging of the boats in harbor sparkled with flags. In the streets between houses with red roofs and painted walls, between old moss-
grown gardens and under avenues of trees, past great parks and
public buildings, processions moved. Some were decorous: old people in long stiff robes of mauve and grey, grave master workmen,
quiet, merry women carrying their babies and chatting as they
walked. In other streets the music beat faster, a shimmering of gong
and tambourine, and the people went dancing, the procession was a
dance. Children dodged in and out, their high calls rising like the
swallow's crossing flights over the music and the singing. All the
processions wound towards the north side of the city, where on the
great water-meadow called the Green Fields boys and girls, naked in
the bright air, with mud-stained feet and ankles and long, lithe
arms, exercised their restive horses before the race. The horses wore
no gear at all but a halter without bit. Their manes were braided
with streamers of silver, gold, and green. They flared their nostrils
and pranced and boasted to one another; they were vastly excited,
the horse being the only animal who has adopted our ceremonies as
his own. Far off to the north and west the mountains stood up half
encircling Omelas on her bay. The air of morning was so clear that
the snow still crowning the Eighteen Peaks burned with white-gold

---

[1] Le Guin's subtitle refers to the American philosopher and psychologist William James
(1842–1910), who speculated about the idea of the scapegoat in his essay "The Moral Philosopher
and the Moral Life."

Ursula K. Le Guin (1929–   ), from Portland, Oregon, is the author of essays, poems, stories, and novels including *A Wizard of
Earthsea* (1968), *The Lathe of Heaven* (1971), and *The Dispossessed: An
Ambiguous Utopia* (1974). "The Ones Who Walk Away from Omelas" first appeared in *New Dimensions* (1973).

fire across the miles of sunlit air, under the dark blue of the sky. There was just enough wind to make the banners that marked the racecourse snap and flutter now and then. In the silence of the broad green meadows one could hear the music winding through the city streets, farther and nearer and ever approaching, a cheerful faint sweetness of the air that from time to time trembled and gathered together and broke out into the great joyous clanging of the bells.

Joyous! How is one to tell about joy? How describe the citizens of Omelas?   2

They were not simple folk, you see, though they were happy.   3 But we do not say the words of cheer much any more. All smiles have become archaic. Given a description such as this one tends to make certain assumptions. Given a description such as this one tends to look next for the King, mounted on a splendid stallion and surrounded by his noble knights, or perhaps in a golden litter borne by great-muscled slaves. But there was no king. They did not use swords, or keep slaves. They were not barbarians. I do not know the rules and laws of their society, but I suspect that they were singularly few. As they did without monarchy and slavery, so they also got on without the stock exchange, the advertisement, the secret police, and the bomb. Yet I repeat that these were not simple folk, not dulcet shepherds, noble savages, bland utopians. They were not less complex than us. The trouble is that we have a bad habit, encouraged by pedants and sophisticates, of considering happiness as something rather stupid. Only pain is intellectual, only evil interesting. This is the treason of the artist: a refusal to admit the banality of evil and the terrible boredom of pain. If you can't lick 'em, join 'em. If it hurts, repeat it. But to praise despair is to condemn delight, to embrace violence is to lose hold of everything else. We have almost lost hold; we can no longer describe a happy man, nor make any celebration of joy. How can I tell you about the people of Omelas? They were not naive and happy children—though their children were, in fact, happy. They were mature, intelligent, passionate adults whose lives were not wretched. O miracle! but I wish I could describe it better. I wish I could convince you. Omelas sounds in my words like a city in a fairy tale, long ago and far away, once upon a time. Perhaps it would be best if you imagined it as your own fancy bids, assuming it will rise to the occasion, for certainly I cannot suit you all. For instance, how about technology? I think that there would be no cars or helicopters in and above the streets; this follows from the fact that the people of Omelas are happy people. Happiness is based on a just discrimination of what is necessary, what is neither necessary nor destructive, and what is destructive. In the

middle category, however—that of the unnecessary but undestruc-
tive, that of comfort, luxury, exuberance, etc.—they could perfectly
well have central heating, subway trains, washing machines, and all
kinds of marvelous devices not yet invented here, floating light-
sources, fuelless power, a cure for the common cold. Or they could
have none of that: it doesn't matter. As you like it. I incline to think
that people from towns up and down the coast have been coming in
to Omelas during the last days before the Festival on very fast little
trains and double-decked trams, and that the train station of Omelas
is actually the handsomest building in town, though plainer than
the magnificent Farmers' Market. But even granted trains, I fear that
Omelas so far strikes some of you as goody-goody. Smiles, bells, parades, horses, bleh. If so, please add an orgy. If an orgy would help,
don't hesitate. Let us not, however, have temples from which issue
beautiful nude priests and priestesses already half in ecstasy and
ready to copulate with any man or woman, lover or stranger, who
desires union with the deep godhead of the blood, although that
was my first idea. But really it would be better not to have any temples in Omelas—at least, not manned temples. Religion yes, clergy
no. Surely the beautiful nudes can just wander about, offering themselves like divine soufflés to the hunger of the needy and the rap-
ture of the flesh. Let them join the processions. Let tambourines be
struck above the copulations, and the glory of desire be proclaimed
upon the gongs, and (a not unimportant point) let the offspring of
these delightful rituals be beloved and looked after by all. One thing
I know there is none of in Omelas is guilt. But what else should
there be? I thought at first there were no drugs, but that is puritani-
cal. For those who like it, the faint insistent sweetness of *drooz* may
perfume the ways of the city, *drooz* which first brings a great lightness and brilliance to the mind and limbs, and then after some
hours a dreamy languor, and wonderful visions at last of the very
arcana and inmost secrets of the Universe, as well as exciting the
pleasure of sex beyond all belief; and it is not habit-forming. For
more modest tastes I think there ought to be beer. What else, what
else belongs in the joyous city? The sense of victory, surely, the celebration of courage. But as we did without clergy, let us do without
soldiers. The joy built upon successful slaughter is not the right kind
of joy; it will not do; it is fearful and it is trivial. A boundless and
generous contentment, a magnanimous triumph felt not against
some outer enemy but in communion with the finest and fairest in
the souls of all men everywhere and the splendor of the world's
summer: this is what swells the hearts of the people of Omelas, and
the victory they celebrate is that of life. I really don't think many of
them need to take *drooz*.

Most of the processions have reached the Green Fields by now.   4
A marvelous smell of cooking goes forth from the red and blue tents
of the provisioners. The faces of small children are amiably sticky; in
the benign grey beard of a man a couple of crumbs of rich pastry are
entangled. The youths and girls have mounted their horses and are
beginning to group around the starting line of the course. An old
woman, small, fat, and laughing, is passing out flowers from a basket, and tall young men wear her flowers in their shining hair. A
child of nine or ten sits at the edge of the crowd, alone, playing on a
wooden flute. People pause to listen, and they smile, but they do
not speak to him, for he never ceases playing and never sees them,
his dark eyes wholly rapt in the sweet, thin magic of the tune.

He finishes, and slowly lowers his hands holding the wooden   5
flute.

As if that little private silence were the signal, all at once a trum-   6
pet sounds from the pavilion near the starting line: imperious,
melancholy, piercing. The horses rear on their slender legs, and
some of them neigh in answer. Sober-faced, the young riders stroke
the horses' necks and soothe them, whispering, "Quiet, quiet, there
my beauty, my hope. . . ." They begin to form in rank along the
starting line. The crowds along the racecourse are like a field of
grass and flowers in the wind. The Festival of Summer has begun.

Do you believe? Do you accept the festival, the city, the joy? No?   7
Then let me describe one more thing.

In a basement under one of the beautiful public buildings of   8
Omelas, or perhaps in the cellar of one of its spacious private
homes, there is a room. It has one locked door, and no window. A
little light seeps in dustily between cracks in the boards, secondhand
from a cobwebbed window somewhere across the cellar. In one corner of the little room a couple of mops, with stiff, clotted, foul-
smelling heads, stand near a rusty bucket. The floor is dirt, a little
damp to the touch, as cellar dirt usually is. The room is about three
paces long and two wide: a mere broom closet or disused tool room.
In the room a child is sitting. It could be a boy or a girl. It looks
about six, but actually is nearly ten. It is feeble-minded. Perhaps it
was born defective, or perhaps it has become imbecile through fear,
malnutrition, and neglect. It picks its nose and occasionally fumbles
vaguely with its toes or genitals, as it sits hunched in the corner farthest from the bucket and the two mops. It is afraid of the mops. It
finds them horrible. It shuts its eyes, but it knows the mops are still
standing there; and the door is locked; and nobody will come. The
door is always locked; and nobody ever comes, except that sometimes—the child has no understanding of time or interval—sometimes the door rattles terribly and opens, and a person, or several

people, are there. One of them may come in and kick the child to make it stand up. The others never come close, but peer in at it with frightened, disgusted eyes. The food bowl and the water jug are hastily filled, the door is locked, the eyes disappear. The people at the door never say anything, but the child, who has not always lived in the tool room, and can remember sunlight and its mother's voice, sometimes speaks. "I will be good," it says. "Please let me out. I will be good!" They never answer. The child used to scream for help at night, and cry a good deal, but now it only makes a kind of whining, "eh-haa, eh-haa," and it speaks less and less often. It is so thin there are no calves to its legs; its belly protrudes; it lives on a half-bowl of corn meal and grease a day. It is naked. Its buttocks and thighs are a mass of festered sores, as it sits in its own excrement continually.

They all know it is there, all the people of Omelas. Some of them have come to see it, others are content merely to know it is there. They all know that it has to be there. Some of them understand why, and some do not, but they all understand that their happiness, the beauty of their city, the tenderness of their friendships, the health of their children, the wisdom of their scholars, the skill of their makers, even the abundance of their harvest and the kindly weathers of their skies, depend wholly on this child's abominable misery.

This is usually explained to children when they are between eight and twelve, whenever they seem capable of understanding; and most of those who come to see the child are young people, though often enough an adult comes, or comes back, to see the child. No matter how well the matter has been explained to them, these young spectators are always shocked and sickened at the sight. They feel disgust, which they had thought themselves superior to. They feel anger, outrage, impotence, despite all the explanations. They would like to do something for the child. But there is nothing they can do. If the child were brought up into the sunlight out of that vile place, if it were cleaned and fed and comforted, that would be a good thing, indeed; but if it were done, in that day and hour all the prosperity and beauty and delight of Omelas would wither and be destroyed. Those are the terms. To exchange all the goodness and grace of every life in Omelas for that single, small improvement: to throw away the happiness of thousands for the chance of the happiness of one: that would be to let guilt within the walls indeed.

The terms are strict and absolute; there may not even be a kind word spoken to the child.

Often the young people go home in tears, or in a tearless rage, 12
when they have seen the child and faced this terrible paradox. They
may brood over it for weeks or years. But as time goes on they begin
to realize that even if the child could be released, it would not get
much good of its freedom: a little vague pleasure of warmth and
food, no doubt, but little more. It is too degraded and imbecile to
know any real joy. It has been afraid too long ever to be free of fear.
Its habits are too uncouth for it to respond to humane treatment. Indeed, after so long it would probably be wretched without walls
about it to protect it, and darkness for its eyes, and its own excrement to sit in. Their tears at the bitter injustice dry when they begin
to perceive the terrible justice of reality, and to accept it. Yet it is
their tears and anger, the trying of their generosity and the acceptance of their helplessness, which are perhaps the true source of the
splendor of their lives. Theirs is no vapid, irresponsible happiness.
They know that they, like the child, are not free. They know compassion. It is the existence of the child, and their knowledge of its
existence, that makes possible the nobility of their architecture, the
poignancy of their music, the profundity of their science. It is because of the child that they are so gentle with children. They know
that if the wretched one were not there snivelling in the dark, the
other one, the flute-player, could make no joyful music as the young
riders line up in their beauty for the race in the sunlight of the first
morning of summer.

Now do you believe in them? Are they not more credible? But 13
there is one more thing to tell, and this is quite incredible.

At times one of the adolescent girls or boys who go to see the 14
child does not go home to weep or rage, does not, in fact, go home
at all. Sometimes also a man or woman much older falls silent for a
day or two, and then leaves home. These people go out into the
street, and walk down the street alone. They keep walking, and
walk straight out of the city of Omelas, through the beautiful gates.
They keep walking across the farmlands of Omelas. Each one goes
alone, youth or girl, man or woman. Night falls; the traveler must
pass down village streets, between the houses with yellow-lit windows, and on out into the darkness of the fields. Each alone, they
go west or north, towards the mountains. They go on. They leave
Omelas, they walk ahead into the darkness, and they do not come
back. The place they go towards is a place even less imaginable to
most of us than the city of happiness. I cannot describe it at all. It is
possible that it does not exist. But they seem to know where they
are going, the ones who walk away from Omelas.

READING AND WRITING ABOUT THE IMAGINARY TRAVELER

1. Describe Esperanza's personality in Cisneros's "My Name" and Dean's personality in Kerouac's "Crossing the Mississippi." How is personality revealed in each case? What do you learn about the narrator in Kerouac's piece?

2. What story or legend have you heard about how your hometown was named or originally settled? Write this story down—or create one yourself as Morrison does for "the Bottom."

3. Discuss the different ways Varma and Nowaira use exaggeration to create humorous or ironic effects in their Brief Encounters. What purpose do you think the humor or irony serves in each case?

4. What is the effect, in Divakaruni's story, of the tourists being known as only "the woman" and "the man"? Where are they from, and what can you tell about their relationship? What is significant about the ending, when they "see into someone's backyard"? Have you had a similar experience when visiting an unfamiliar place?

5. Based on his description of the fictional city of Euphemia, how would Calvino answer the question, What do people have to gain from contact with other cultures?

6. Describe the various relationships among the family members in the excerpt from Islas's novel. How do the children, Sancho, and Eduviges react in different ways to contact with the Anglo culture?

7. Chin's narrator in "Railroad Standard Time" makes several jumps in time as he recalls past events; trace how he uses his grandfather's watch as a transitional device for these time-shifts. What is happening in the present time of the story, the situation from which the narrator looks back? In what ways does the watch symbolize the narrator's internal conflicts?

8. Discuss the various conflicts and tensions within the Toronto immigrant community as portrayed in Mukherjee's "Tamurlane." To what extent are these tensions resolved by the appearance of a common enemy, the Mounties?

9. Objectively, from the information given in Erdrich's "American Horse," what do you think best serves the interests of Buddy—going with the social worker, or staying with his mother? How does Erdrich get the reader to sympathize with Buddy, his mother, and

Uncle Lawrence? The police officers in this story—Brackett and Harmony—are portrayed in much more detail than the Mounties in Mukherjee's "Tamurlane"; what kind of people are they?

10. Think about your own experience bringing a boyfriend or girlfriend home to visit, or simply introducing him or her to your family. In Leavitt's "Territory," to what extent are the problems that Neil faces in bringing his lover home independent of his homosexuality? Neil says to Wayne on their way back to New York that "guilt goes with the territory" (paragraph 168); if Neil has accepted and grown comfortable with his sexual orientation, then what does he feel guilty about?

11. In Matsumoto's "Two Deserts," how does Emiko express her dislike for Roy Barnes? Why doesn't she simply tell him what she thinks? Is Roy portrayed as more racist than sexist, or more sexist than racist?

12. Reread the first section (paragraphs 1–14) of Paley's "The Long-Distance Runner," then discuss Faith's reasons for leaving home. Do you find her motivation convincing? How much do Faith and Mrs Luddy turn out to have in common? From what you can gather about Faith's own family life—in the brief glimpses we get at the beginning and the end of the story—how does it differ from Mrs Luddy's?

13. Consider the ways in which the first paragraph of Bowles's "A Distant Episode" anticipates and helps us interpret the events that follow. What early hints are there about where the Professor is from and where the story takes place? Of what mistakes and misjudgments is the Professor guilty in his dealings with the local people? To what extent do you think that he is responsible for what the Reguibat do to him? To what extent does the Professor represent European civilization and culture in general?

14. Review, in Elliott's "Among the Dangs," the narrator's reasons for going on each of his three trips to study the Dang tribe. What evidence is there for the way he feels about his American home culture and the culture of academia? Why, other than for the convenience of the plot (the narrator's "blending in" with the Dangs "like dressing a Greek up in reindeer skins"—paragraph 3), is it important that the narrator is black?

15. Western academics come to study a Third World culture in both Bowles's and Elliott's stories, with dramatically different results.

What effects, positive and negative, does each professor have on the culture he comes to study? How much is each man changed by the experience? If you have traveled to another country, what effects do you think your visit had on the culture, and how much were you changed by the experience?

16. Why does Janet, the narrator of Russ's "When It Changed," "doubt very much that sexual equality has been reestablished on Earth"? Put together all the evidence for the way social relations and roles have evolved on Whileaway; how much do you think this all-female society has changed in the thirty generations since the men died?

17. Relations between the sexes is a major theme in Matsumoto's and Paley's stories as well as in Russ's. Explore what aspects of gender relations each author emphasizes by imagining a conversation about men among the characters Emiko, Faith or Mrs Luddy, and Janet.

18. What country or countries might Le Guin have in mind as a real-world model for her imaginary Omelas?

19. Le Guin writes that "the treason of the artist" (or writer) is "a refusal to admit the banality of evil and the terrible boredom of pain" (paragraph 3). Test this view in one of the stories in Chapter 6. For example, to what extent is evil portrayed as banal in Erdrich's "American Horse" or Matsumoto's "Two Deserts"? Or, to what extent is Bowles or Elliott guilty of this artistic "treason" in his portrayal of evil or suffering?

20. In any story in this chapter, take the viewpoint of another character—other than the narrator or the main character—and rewrite one of the action scenes from her or his perspective (or create a new scene of your own). Choose a character with a different view of events, with other things at stake, than the original protagonist—for example, the Indian policeman, Harmony, in "American Horse," Mrs. Campbell in "Territory," Roy Barnes in "Two Deserts," or the *qaouaji* in "A Distant Episode."

EXPLORING NEW SOURCES

1. Read additional works by a Chapter 6 author or authors and write a series of book reviews—or one longer book review—for a general audience (such as readers of your local or student newspaper). Study published reviews to help you make decisions about style and organization. It is common, for example, to summarize the situation or plot of a novel (but without giving away the ending), to comment on the writing itself (perhaps offering quoted examples), and to give your view of the book (do you recommend it, and why or why not?). If you review a newly published book, consider submitting your work for publication.

2. Read three or more works by one of this chapter's authors. Before consulting any critical sources, decide on a thematic or stylistic angle that interests you and a tentative thesis you want to explore. Then, in a literary research paper, refine and test your idea against critical essays about, or reviews of, the author's work.

3. Research a social, political, historical, economic, psychological, philosophical, or other issue raised in this chapter that you find compelling. General subjects from these stories—echoing issues raised in previous chapters—include: living conditions in Calcutta; American foreign aid programs in Egypt; the U.S.–Mexican border; Chinese coolie labor and the history of U.S. railroads; Asian Indian immigrants in Canada; welfare policy and Native American Indians; the detention of Japanese Americans during World War II; the culture of a North African desert tribe such as the Reguibat; the culture of a South American tribe similar to the fictional Dangs. (All of these subjects will need narrowing and refining to make a good research topic.)

4. Science fiction often involves galactic travel and contact between alien cultures. Read other works in this genre and discuss to what extent this obviously imaginary kind of travel frees or limits the writer in the way she or he addresses earthbound social issues.

5. Write a short story of your own in which someone takes a journey or a stranger comes to town, exploring an interaction across cultural borders.

Acknowledgments

Chinua Achebe, "What Marco Polo Failed to See" from "An Image of Africa" from *Hopes and Impediments*. Copyright © 1988 by Chinua Achebe. Reprinted by permission of Bantam, Doubleday, Dell Publishing Group, Inc.

Peter S. Adler, "Five Stages of Culture Shock" from The Journal of Humanistic Psychology, 15, 1975, Table 5.4. Copyright © 1975, by P. S. Adler. Reprinted by permission of Sage Publications, Inc.

Paula Gunn Allen, "American History and Native Americans" from *The Sacred Hoop* by Paula Gunn Allen. Copyright © 1986 by Paula Gunn Allen. Reprinted by permission of Beacon Press.

Siu Wai Anderson, "A Letter to My Daughter" from *Making Face Making Soul/Haciendo Caras*, ed. Gloria Anzaldua. © 1990. Reprinted by permission of Aunt Lute Books. (415) 558-8116.

Maya Angelou, "Revival Meeting in Stamps, Arkansas" from *I Know Why the Caged Bird Sings* by Maya Angelou. Copyright © 1969 by Maya Angelou. Reprinted by permission of Random House, Inc.

Gloria Anzaldua, "Writing Blocks and Cultural Shifts" from "Tlilli, Tlapalli: The Path of the Red and Black Ink" from *Borderlands/La Frontera* by Gloria Anzaldua. © 1987. Reprinted by permission of Aunt Lute Books. (415) 558-8116.

Margaret Atwood, "Over the Fence in Canada" from "Canada: Through the One-Way Mirror." First published in *The Nation*, March 22, 1986. Copyright © 1986 The Nation Co., Inc.

Ellyn Bache, "Vietnamese Refugees: Overcoming Culture Clash" from *Culture Clash*, second edition. Copyright © 1989. Yarmouth, ME: Intercultural Press, Inc. Used with permission.

Richard W. Bailey, "English in the Next Decade" from *State of the Language* by Leonard Michaels and Christopher Ricks. Copyright © 1980 The Regents of the University of California. Reprinted by permission.

James Baldwin, "Fifth Avenue, Uptown: A Letter from Harlem" from *Nobody Knows My Name* © 1961; copyright renewed 1989. First published in *Esquire*, July, 1960. Reprinted by permission of The James Baldwin Estate.

Charles F. Berlitz, "The Etymology of the International Insult." Reprinted by permission of the author. Mr. Berlitz has not been associated with the Berlitz Language School since 1967.

Alice Bloom, "On a Greek Holiday" from The Hudson Review. Reprinted by permission from The Hudson Review, Vol. XXXVI, No. 3 (Autumn 1983). Copyright © 1983 by Alice Bloom.

Haig A. Bosmajian, "The Language of Indian Derision" from *The Language of Oppression*. Copyright © 1973 by Haig A. Bosmajian. Reprinted by permission of University Press of America and the author. Parts of this chapter first appeared in *Speech Teacher*, March 1973, published by the Speech Communication Association.

Paul Bowles, "A Distant Episode" from *Collected Stories 1939–1976*. Copyright © 1950 by Paul Bowles. Reprinted from *Collected Stories 1939–1976* with the permission of Black Sparrow Press.

Juan Cadena, "It's My Country Too" from *Mexican Voices/American Dreams* by Marilyn P. Davis. Copyright © 1990 by Marilyn P. Davis. Reprinted by permission of Henry Holt and Company, Inc.

Italo Calvino, "Trading Cities 1" from *Invisible Cities* by Italo Calvino, translated by William Weaver, copyright © 1972 by Giulio Einaudi editore, s.p.a., translation copyright © 1974 by Harcourt Brace Jovanovich, Inc., reprinted by permission of Harcourt Brace Jovanovich, Inc.

Frank Chin, "Railroad Standard Time" first appeared in *Chinaman Pacific and Frisco R.R. Co.*, short stories by Frank Chin, Coffee House Press, 1988. Reprinted by permission of the publisher. Copyright © 1988 by Frank Chin.

Sandra Cisneros, "My Name" from *The House on Mango Street*. Copyright © by Sandra Cisneros, 1984, 1991. Published in *The House of Mango Street* by Vintage Books, a division of Random House, Inc., New York. Reprinted by permission of Susan Bergholz Literary Services, New York, NY.

Robert Claiborne, "The Wasp Stereotype" from *A Wasp Stings Back*. Copyright © 1974 by Robert Claiborne. All rights reserved. Reprinted by permission of the Estate of Robert Claiborne.

Michelle Cliff, "A Journey into Speech" and "If I Could Write This in Fire, I Would Write This in Fire" from *The Land of Look Behind*. Published by Firebrand Books, Ithaca, New York. Copyright © 1985.

Alexis de Tocqueville, "The Founding of New England" from *Democracy in America* by Alexis de Tocqueville. Edited by J. P. Mayer and Max Lerner, translated by George Lawrence. English translation copyright © 1965 by Harper & Row, Publishers, Inc. Reprinted by permission of HarperCollins Publishers.

Joan Didion, "Las Vegas" from "Marrying Absurd" from *Slouching Towards Bethlehem* by Joan Didion. Copyright © 1967, 1968 by Joan Didion. Reprinted by permission of Farrar, Straus and Giroux, Inc. "El Salvador: The Mechanism of Terror" from *Salvador*. Copyright © 1983 by Joan Didion. Reprinted by permission of Simon & Schuster, Inc. "Miami: The Cuban Presence" from *Miami*. Copyright © 1987 by Joan Didion. Reprinted by permission of Simon & Schuster, Inc.

Isak Dineson, "Kamante and Odysseus" and "Of Natives and History" from *Out of Africa*. Copyright 1937 by Random House, Inc. and renewed 1965 by Rungstedlundfonden. Reprinted by permission of Random House and The Rungstedlund Foundation.

636

Margaret K. Nydell, "Beliefs and Values, Emotions and Logic in the Arab World" from *Understanding Arabs: A Guide for Westerners.* Copyright © 1987. Yarmouth, ME: Intercultural Press, Inc. Used with permission.

Grace Paley, "The Long-Distance Runner" from *Enormous Changes at the Last Minute* by Grace Paley. Copyright © 1974 by Grace Paley. Reprinted by permission of Farrar, Straus and Giroux, Inc.

Philip L. Pearce, "Fifteen Types of Travellers" from *Social Psychology of Tourist Behavior.* Copyright © 1982 Pergamon Press, Ltd. Volume 3 from *International Series in Experimental Social Psychology,* Michael Argyle, editor. Permission held by Dr. Philip L. Pearce, Department of Behavioral Science, James Cook University, Queensland, Australia.

Kit Yuen Quan, "The Girl Who Wouldn't Sing" from *Making Face Making Soul/Haciendo Caras,* ed. Gloria Anazaldua. © 1990. Reprinted by permission of Aunt Lute Books. (415) 558-8116.

Ishmael Reed, "America: The Multinational Society" from *Writin' is Fightin'* by Ishmael Reed. Reprinted with permission of Atheneum Publishers, an imprint of Macmillan Publishing Co. Copyright © 1988 by Ishmael Reed.

Richard Rodriguez, "Going Home Again: The New American Scholarship Boy" from *American Scholar.* Reprinted by permission of George Borchardt, Inc. for the author. Copyright © 1974 by Richard Rodriguez.

Renato Rosaldo, "Culture and Truth: The Erosion of Classic Norms" from *Culture and Truth* by Renato Rosaldo. Copyright © 1989 by Renato Rosaldo. Reprinted by permission of Beacon Press.

Salman Rushdie, "*The Satanic Verses:* A Migrant's-Eye View" from *In Good Faith.* Copyright © 1990 Salman Rushdie.

Joanna Russ, "When It Changed" from *Again, Dangerous Visions.* Reprinted by permission of Joanna Russ. Copyright © 1972 by Harlan Ellison.

Nancy Masterson Sakamoto, "Conversational Ballgames" from *Polite Fictions: Why Japanese and Americans Seem Rude to Eachother* by Nancy Sakamoto and Reiko Naotsuka. Copyright © 1982 by Nancy Sakamoto and Reiko Naotsuka. Reprinted by permission of Nancy Sakamoto. Published by Kinseido Ltd., Publishers, Tokyo, Japan.

Kate Simon, "Workers' Utopia, the Bronx" from *A Wider World: Portraits in an Adolescence* by Kate Simon. Copyright © 1986 by Kate Simon. Reprinted by permission of HarperCollins Publishers.

Gary Snyder, "Comparing India with Japan." © 1983 by Gary Snyder. Reprinted by permission of Gary Snyder, University of California at Davis.

Shelby Steele, "On Being Black and Middle Class" from *The Content of Our Character.* Copyright © 1990 by Shelby Steele. Reprinted with permission from St. Martin's Press, Inc., New York, NY.

Amy Tan, "The Language of Discretion" Copyright © 1990 by Amy Tan. Reprinted by permission of Amy Tan and The Sandra Dijkstra Literary Agency.

Alexandra Tantranon-Saur, "What's Behind the Asian Mask?" from the journal Our Asian Inheritance (1986, Issue #6), Rational Island Publishers, P.O. Box 2081, Main Office Station, Seattle, WA 98111.

Studs Terkel, "Ann Banks, Army Brat" from *American Dreams: Lost and Found* by Studs Terkel. Copyright © 1980 by Studs Terkel. Reprinted by permission of Pantheon Books, a division of Random House, Inc.

Paul Theroux, "The Subway Is a Madhouse," "Living among Strangers," and "Tarzan Is an Expatriate" from *Sunrise with Seamonsters: Travels and Discoveries* by Paul Theroux. Copyright © 1985 by Cape Cod Scriveners Co. Reprinted by permission of Houghton Mifflin Co.

Colin Thubron, "Mushroom Hunting in the Soviet Union" from *Where Nights Are Longest* by Colin Thubron. Copyright © 1983, 1984 by Colin Thubron. Reprinted by permission of Random House, Inc.

Calvin Trillin, "Saudi Women Drivers Alert!" from "Gender Equality." Reprinted with special permission of King Features Syndicate, Inc.

John Updike, "Venezuela for Visitors" from *Hugging the Shore.* Copyright © 1983 by John Updike. Reprinted by permission of Alfred A. Knopf.

Krishnan Varma, "Calcutta Freight Wagon" from "The Grain Eaters." Copyright © 1985 Wascana Review. Reprinted by permission of the editor.

Michael Ventura, "Talkin' American 2." Copyright © 1990 by Michael Ventura. This article first appeared as one of Michael Ventura's "Letters at 3am" in the *L.A. Weekly,* November 16, 1990.

Kurt Vonnegut, "Sound like Yourself." Copyright 1980 Kurt Vonnegut, by permission of Donald C. Farber, attorney for Mr. Vonnegut.

Alice Walker, "Definition of Womanist" from In Search of Our Mothers' Gardens, copyright © 1983 by Alice Walker, reprinted by permission of Harcourt Brace Jovanovich, Inc.

Evelyn Waugh, "American Tourists in Egypt" from *When the Going Was Good.* Reprinted by permission of Sterling Lord Literistic, Inc. and Little, Brown and Company. Copyright © 1934, 1946, © 1962 by Evelyn Waugh.

Edith Wharton, "Merinid Court, Morocco" from *In Morocco.* Copyright © 1920 by Jonathan Cape Ltd., 1984 by Century Publishing Co. Ltd. Reprinted by permission of Watkins/Loomis Literary Agency, Inc.

RHETORICAL INDEX

Oral History/Transcript

Main Selections

Process Analysis

Brief Encounters

Main Selections

INDEX OF AUTHORS
AND TITLES